READINGS ON
THE DEVELOPMENT OF CHILDREN

READINGS ON
THE DEVELOPMENT OF CHILDREN

FOURTH EDITION

Edited by

Mary Gauvain
University of California, Riverside

Michael Cole
University of California, San Diego

WORTH PUBLISHERS

READINGS ON THE DEVELOPMENT OF CHILDREN, FOURTH EDITION

Sponsoring Editor: Jessica Bayne
Development Editor: Cecilia Gardner
Project Editor: Richard Rothschild/Print Matters, Inc.
Marketing Manager: Renée Altier
Art Director/Cover Design: Barbara Reingold
Interior Design: Paul Lacy
Project Management: Print Matters, Inc.
Production Manager: Barbara Anne Seixas
Composition: Compset, Inc.
Printing and Binding: Quebecor World Dubuque

Cover Art: *Claude Drawing, Francoise and Paloma*, Pablo Picasso, May 17, 1954. Valauris. Oil on Canvas. © 2004 Estate of Pablo Picasso / Artists Rights Society (ARS), New York.

ISBN: 0-7167-0961-9
EAN 9780716709619

First printing, 2004

Manufactured in the United States of America

Library of Congress Cataloging-in-Publication Number: 2003107775

Worth Publishers
41 Madison Avenue
New York, NY 10010
www.worthpublishers.com

Contents

Preface

Human development is a process of change that occurs over the entire life span. It involves the interaction of biological, social, and cultural factors that together define the course of human growth. Developmental psychologists strive to explain this process of change by observing children, conducting experiments, and devising theories.

Students approach the subject of human development with rich backgrounds based on their own experiences growing up as well as on their observations of people of all ages. This background is a valuable resource for students attempting to understand the scientific approaches to the study of human development that they encounter in textbooks. However, it has been our experience as instructors that textbooks alone, despite their great value as organized overviews of the field, often leave students puzzled about the process by which developmental psychologists construct their theories, collect their data, and draw conclusions. Textbooks, by their very nature, cannot devote sufficient space to the in-depth discussion of concepts or studies that form the basis of developmental theory.

The articles included in this book of readings have been selected with this issue in mind. Our intention has been to provide students with primary source material that introduces them to a broad range of scientific thinking about human development in all its diversity. We do not shy away from exposing students to classical contributions to the field simply because they do not carry an up-to-the-minute publication date; after all, physicists do not hesitate to teach about Newton's laws of motion although they were formulated several hundred years ago. Of course, the scientific study of human development is a rapidly growing discipline, so most of our selections—especially research reports—were first published in the past few years.

The theoretical articles provide students with direct access to important and provocative statements by acknowledged leaders in the field. For example, selections by Jean Piaget and Lev Vygotsky are included. Each theoretical article was chosen for its power in capturing the essence of the theorist's ideas in a brief, but compelling, way. The articles focusing on research were selected to stimulate thought and discussion about how researchers collect evidence on the process of development and how they interpret and draw conclusions from this evidence. We have taken special care to include articles about the development of children from many cultures to avoid the misrepresentation of middle-class European Americans as the criterion against which the development of all children is measured.

The inspiration for this reader came from *The Development of Children,* Fifth Edition, by Michael Cole, Sheila Cole, and Cynthia Lightfoot. Although typical of introductory texts in many ways, *The Development of Children* is unusual in its balanced analysis of the biological, social, and cultural factors that make up development. We have not, however, specifically keyed these readings to any one textbook. Instead we have selected articles that provide a representative sample of the wide range of approaches to the study of human development.

We have changed this reader significantly for this, its fourth edition. We have expanded the selection from 32 to 37 articles, 21 of which, or 57 percent, are new to this edition. This new collection is not substantially longer than its predecessor, although it provides students with an updated look at the field in several ways. First, recent empirical articles in some of the most rapidly changing areas in the field, such as brain development, early concepts, socioemotional development, and adolescent well-being, have been added. Second, we have added several articles that focus on some of the policy issues that are at the center of the field today. Finally, we have retained articles that we believe represent classic and central issues in the field. We hope you agree that this reader is a comprehensive and up-to-date presentation of the major topics and concerns in developmental psychology today.

All the articles were selected with the undergraduate reader in mind. Because most of them were originally written for a professional audience, they contain some concepts that at first may be difficult to grasp. To orient the reader to the article's main points, we have provided an introductory headnote for each article. To help students understand the important issues raised in the selections, we pose a series of ten questions after each article. These questions are designed to help students identify and summarize the key points of the article, as well as to provoke them to think critically about what they have read.

Over the years, this book has changed as the field has changed. Our efforts to select and update the readings have been aided by valuable comments from colleagues, students, and the following reviewers: Gregory Braswell, *Illinois State University;* Ellen Domm, *Capilano College;* Jennifer Henderlong, *Reed College;* Avidan Milevsky, *Kutztown University of Pennsylvania;* Cynthia O'Dell, *Indiana University Northwest;* Maureen Smith, *San Jose State University;* and Theodore Walls, *Pennsylvania State University.*

M.G.
M.C.

READINGS ON
THE DEVELOPMENT OF CHILDREN

Introduction

Most developmental theory and research today emphasizes the coordination of the biological, social, and cultural aspects of the human experience. At the heart of this research are assumptions about the nature of the human organism, which includes the idea that humans are social beings that strive to create meaning and understanding in their daily lives. These efforts to know and understand are supported and constrained by the type of biological organism we are and by the complex and highly structured social and cultural system in which we live.

The articles in this section describe, in various ways, how human development occurs. Each places a somewhat different emphasis on biological, social, and cultural contributions to growth. The first article, by Urie Bronfenbrenner, describes an ecological approach to development that includes the complex set of social and contextual factors that influence human psychological growth. It is important to remember that even though the social and cultural context plays a huge role in psychological development, context in and of itself does not define development. Research has shown quite clearly that even when children are raised in similar contexts, they have different experiences, and those experiences affect their development in different ways. This point is taken up in two other articles in this section. The article on attachment theory by Ross A. Thompson describes how early social relationships contribute to development both in childhood and throughout life. The article by Emmy E. Werner discusses longitudinal research showing that early experiences, even negative ones, do not have a predetermined effect on future development. Finally, two articles in this section examine the relation between learning and development. Their authors, Jean Piaget and Lev S. Vygotsky, proposed different theories about cognitive development, and their views are debated and used to guide research to this day.

These articles introduce several of the main theoretical issues that guide much contemporary research on psychological development: What is the human context, and how does it contribute to psychological growth? What is the significance of early social experience for later development? And how do the processes of learning and development work together to support intellectual change over the course of childhood?

1 Ecological Models of Human Development

Urie Bronfenbrenner

Human development occurs in the midst of a vibrant, complex environment. From a psychological perspective, the environment is largely defined by social and cultural practices and institutions that provide most of the experiences that people have. This perspective leads to an interesting question for developmental psychologists: How do social and cultural experiences interact with the child's biological or maturational capabilities to influence development? It is not easy to understand the contributions that society and culture make to psychological development and how these contributions coordinate with children's developing capabilities. An initial step in gaining this understanding is to describe the social and cultural context in relation to the psychological experiences of childhood.

Much of the psychological research of the mid-twentieth century, including developmental psychology, was conducted in laboratory settings. As a result, it provided few insights into the environmental aspects of psychological development. However, in the late 1970s an important contribution along these lines was made by the developmental psychologist Urie Bronfenbrenner. Bronfenbrenner introduced the ecological systems approach, which is discussed in the following article. Based on ecology, the branch of biology concerned with the interrelationship of organisms and their environments, the ecological systems approach describes the social and cultural aspects of the human environment.

Bronfenbrenner's framework concentrates on the subsystems, or components, of the human ecological niche as well as the ways that these subsystems interact with and influence each other. The subsystems are conceptualized as a series of layers, similar to the layers of an onion or to *matryoshka*, the nested dolls from Russia (Bronfenbrenner's native country). The subsystems range from the immediate, or proximal, processes of development (the microsystem), such as the family or school, to patterns of culture, such as the economy, customs, and bodies of knowledge (the macrosystem). The historical context of development is described in the chronosystem.

Bronfenbrenner's framework provided developmental psychologists with a new way of thinking about the many environmental influences that affect human development. This framework does not provide a simple story about psychological development; nor does it offer ready answers about specific issues or challenges that confront children as they grow. Rather, its contribution is in the types of questions, hypotheses, and designs for research that it inspires. This potential is illustrated in this article's description of research on the developmental challenges that control low-birthweight babies and on the effect that growing up during the Great Depression had on later development.

Ecological models encompass an evolving body of theory and research concerned with the processes and conditions that govern the lifelong course of human development in the actual environments in which human beings live. Although most of the systematic theory-building in this domain has been done by [Urie] Bronfenbrenner, his work is based on an analysis and integration of results from empirical investigations conducted over many decades by researchers from diverse disciplines, beginning with a study carried out in Berlin in 1870 on the effects of neighborhood on the development of children's concepts (Schwabe and Bartholomai 1870). This entry consists of an exposition of Bronfenbrenner's theoretical system, which is also used as a framework for illustrating representative research findings.

Reprinted from the *International Encyclopedia of Education*, Vol. 3, 2nd ed., 1643–1647. Copyright 1994 with permission from Elsevier.

1. THE EVOLUTION OF ECOLOGICAL MODELS

Bronfenbrenner's ecological paradigm, first introduced in the 1970s (Bronfenbrenner 1974, 1976, 1977, 1979), represented a reaction to the restricted scope of most research then being conducted by developmental psychologists. The nature of both the restriction and the reaction is conveyed by this oft-quoted description of the state of developmental science at that time: "It can be said that much of developmental psychology is the science of the strange behavior of children in strange situations with strange adults for the briefest possible periods of time" (Bronfenbrenner 1977, p. 513).

In the same article, Bronfenbrenner presented a conceptual and operational framework (supported by the comparatively small body of relevant research findings then available) that would usefully provide the basis and incentive for moving the field in the desired direction. During the same period, he also published two reports pointing to the challenging implications of an ecological approach for child and family policy (1974) and educational practice (1976).

Within a decade, investigations informed by an ecological perspective were no longer a rarity. By 1986, Bronfenbrenner was able to write:

> Studies of children and adults in real-life settings, with real-life implications, are now commonplace in the research literature on human development, both in the United States and, as this volume testifies, in Europe as well. This scientific development is taking place, I believe, not so much because of my writings, but rather because the notions I have been promulgating are ideas whose time has come. (1986b p. 287).

At the same time, Bronfenbrenner continued his work on the development of a theoretical paradigm. What follows is a synopsis of the general ecological model as delineated in its most recent reformulations (Bronfenbrenner 1989, 1990, Bronfenbrenner and Ceci 1993).

2. THE GENERAL ECOLOGICAL MODEL

Two propositions specifying the defining properties of the model are followed by research examples illustrating both.

Proposition 1 states that, especially in its early phases, and to a great extent throughout the life course, human development takes place through processes of progressively more complex reciprocal interaction between an active, evolving biopsychological human organism and the persons, objects, and sym-

bols in its immediate environment. To be effective, the interaction must occur on a fairly regular basis over extended periods of time. Such enduring forms of interaction in the immediate environment are referred to as *proximal processes*. Examples of enduring patterns of proximal process are found in parent-child and child-child activities, group or solitary play, reading, learning new skills, studying, athletic activities, and performing complex tasks.

A second defining property identifies the three-fold source of these dynamic forces. Proposition 2 states that the form, power, content, and direction of the proximal processes effecting development vary systematically as a joint function of the characteristics of the developing person; of the environment—both immediate and more remote—in which the processes are taking place; and the nature of the developmental outcomes under consideration.

Propositions 1 and 2 are theoretically interdependent and subject to empirical test. A research design that permits their simultaneous investigation is referred to as a process-person-context model. A first example illustrating the model is shown in Figure 1. The data are drawn from a classic longitudinal study by Drillien (1963) of factors affecting the development of children of low birth weight compared to those of normal weight. The figure depicts the impact of the quality of mother-infant interaction at age 4 on the number of observed problems at age 4 as a joint function of birth weight and social class. As can be seen, a proximal process, in this instance mother-infant interaction across time, emerges as the most powerful predictor of developmental outcome. In all instances, good maternal treatment appears to reduce substantially the degree of behavioral disturbance exhibited by the child. Furthermore, as stipulated in

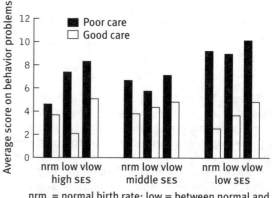

nrm = normal birth rate: low = between normal and
5.5 lbs: vlow = 5.5 lbs or less

FIGURE 1

Problem behavior at age 4 (by birth weight, mother's care, and social class).

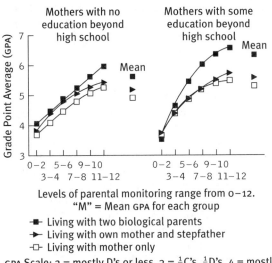

Levels of parental monitoring range from 0–12.
"M" = Mean GPA for each group

—■— Living with two biological parents
—▶— Living with own mother and stepfather
—□— Living with mother only

GPA Scale: 2 = mostly D's or less. 3 = $\frac{1}{2}$C's, $\frac{1}{2}$D's. 4 = mostly C's.
5 = $\frac{1}{2}$B's, $\frac{1}{2}$C's. 6 = mostly B's. 7 = $\frac{1}{2}$A's, $\frac{1}{2}$B's. 8 = mostly A's.

FIGURE 2
Effect of parental monitoring on grades in high school by family structure and mother's level of education.

Proposition 2, the power of the process varies systematically as a function of the environmental context (in this instance, social class) and of the characteristics of the person (in this case, weight at birth). Note also that the proximal process has the general effect of reducing or buffering against environmental differences in developmental outcome; specifically, under high levels of mother-child interaction, social class differences in problem behavior become much smaller.

Unfortunately, from the perspective of an ecological model the greater developmental impact of proximal processes in poorer environments is to be expected only for indices of developmental dysfunction, primarily during childhood. For outcomes reflecting developmental competence (e.g., mental ability, academic achievement, social skills) proximal processes are posited as having greater impact in more advantaged and stable environments throughout the life course. An example of this contrasting pattern is shown in Figure 2, which depicts the differential effects of parental monitoring on school achievement for high school students living in the three most common family structures found in the total sample of over 4,000 cases. The sample is further stratified by two levels of mother's education, with completion of high school as the dividing point. Parental monitoring refers to the effort by parents to keep informed about, and set limits on, their children's activities outside the home. In the present analysis, it was assessed by a series of items in a questionnaire administered to adolescents in their school classes.

Once again, the results reveal that the effects of proximal processes are more powerful than those of the environmental contexts in which they occur. In this instance, however, the impact of the proximal process is greatest in what emerges as the most advantaged ecological niche, that is, families with two biological parents in which the mother has had some education beyond high school. The typically declining slope of the curve reflects the fact that higher levels of outcome are more difficult to achieve so that at each successive step, the same degree of active effort yields a somewhat smaller result.

3. ENVIRONMENTS AS CONTEXTS OF DEVELOPMENT

The foregoing example provides an appropriate introduction to another distinctive feature of the ecological model, its highly differentiated reconceptualization of the environment from the perspective of the developing person. Based on Lewin's theory of psychological fields (Bronfenbrenner 1977; Lewin 1917, 1931, 1935), the ecological environment is conceived as a set of nested structures, each inside the other like a set of Russian dolls. Moving from the innermost level to the outside, these structures are defined as described below.

3.1 MICROSYSTEMS

A microsystem is a pattern of activities, social roles, and interpersonal relations experienced by the developing person in a given face-to-face setting with particular physical, social, and symbolic features that invite, permit, or inhibit engagement in sustained, progressively more complex interaction with, and activity in, the immediate environment. Examples include such settings as family, school, peer group, and workplace.

It is within the immediate environment of the microsystem that proximal processes operate to produce and sustain development, but as the above definition indicates, their power to do so depends on the content and structure of the microsystem. Specific hypotheses regarding the nature of this content and structure, and the as yet limited research evidence on which they are based are documented in the work of Bronfenbrenner (1986a, 1986b, 1988, 1989, 1993). Most of the relevant studies of proximal processes have focused on the family, with all too few dealing with other key developmental settings, such as classrooms and schools. A notable exception in this regard is the work of Stevenson and his colleagues (Stevenson and Stigler 1992, see also Ceci 1990).

3.2 MESOSYSTEMS

The mesosystem comprises the linkages and processes taking place between two or more settings containing the developing person (e.g., the relations between home and school, school and workplace, etc.). In other words, a mesosystem is a system of microsystems.

An example in this domain is the work of Epstein (1983a, 1983b) on the developmental impact of two-way communication and participation in decision-making by parents and teachers. Elementary school pupils from classrooms in which such joint involvement was high not only exhibited greater initiative and independence after entering high school, but also received higher grades. The effects of family and school processes were greater than those attributable to socioeconomic status or race.

3.3 EXOSYSTEMS

The exosystem comprises the linkages and processes taking place between two or more settings, at least one of which does not contain the developing person, but in which events occur that indirectly influence processes within the immediate setting in which the developing person lives (e.g., for a child, the relation between the home and the parent's workplace; for a parent, the relation between the school and the neighborhood peer group).

Especially since the early 1980s, research has focused on three exosystems that are especially likely to affect the development of children and youth indirectly through their influence on the family, the school, and the peer group. These are the parents' workplace (e.g., Eckenrode and Gore 1990), family social networks (e.g., Cochran et al. 1990), and neighborhood-community contexts (e.g., Pence 1988).

3.4 MACROSYSTEMS

The macrosystem consists of the overarching pattern of micro-, meso-, and exosystems characteristic of a given culture or subculture, with particular reference to the belief systems, bodies of knowledge, material resources, customs, life-styles, opportunity structures, hazards, and life course options that are embedded in each of these broader systems. The macrosystem may be thought of as a societal blueprint for a particular culture or subculture.

This formulation points to the necessity of going beyond the simple labels of class and culture to identify more specific social and psychological features at the macrosystem level that ultimately affect the particular conditions and processes occurring in the microsystem (see Bronfenbrenner 1986a, 1986b, 1988, 1989, 1993).

3.5 CHRONOSYSTEMS

A final systems parameter extends the environment into a third dimension. Traditionally in the study of human development, the passage of time was treated as synonymous with chronological age. Since the early 1970s, however, an increasing number of investigators have employed research designs in which time appears not merely as an attribute of the growing human being, but also as a property of the surrounding environment not only over the life course, but across historical time (Baltes and Schaie 1973, Clausen 1986, Elder 1974, Elder et al. 1993).

A chronosystem encompasses change or consistency over time not only in the characteristics of the person but also of the environment in which that person lives (e.g., changes over the life course in family structure, socioeconomic status, employment, place of residence, or the degree of hecticness and ability in everyday life).

An excellent example of a chronosystem design is found in Elder's classic study *Children of the Great Depression* (1974). The investigation involved a comparison of two otherwise comparable groups of families differentiated on the basis of whether the loss of income as a result of the Great Depression of the 1930s exceeded or fell short of 35 percent. The availability of longitudinal data made it possible to assess developmental outcomes through childhood, adolescence, and adulthood. Also, the fact that children in one sample were born eight years earlier than those in the other permitted a comparison of the effects of the Depression on youngsters who were adolescents when their families became economically deprived with the effects of those who were still young children at the time.

The results for the two groups presented a dramatic contrast. Paradoxically, for youngsters who were teenagers during the Depression years, the families' economic deprivation appeared to have a salutary effect on their subsequent development, especially in the middle class. As compared with the nondeprived who were matched on pre-Depression socioeconomic status, deprived boys displayed a greater desire to achieve and a firmer sense of career goals. Boys and girls from deprived homes attained greater satisfaction in life, both by their own and by societal standards. Though more pronounced for adolescents from middle-class backgrounds, these favorable outcomes were evident among their lower-class counterparts as well. Analysis of interview and observation protocols enabled Elder to identify what he regarded as a critical factor in investigating this favorable developmental trajectory: the loss of economic security forced the family to mobilize its own human resources, including its teenagers, who had to take on new roles and responsibilities both within and outside the home and to work together toward the common goal of getting and keeping the family on its feet. This experience provided effective training in initiative, responsibility, and cooperation.

4. GENETIC INHERITANCE IN ECOLOGICAL PERSPECTIVE

The most recent extension of the ecological paradigm involves a reconceptualization of the role of genetics in human development (Bronfenbrenner and Ceci 1993). The new formulation calls into question and replaces some of the key assumptions underlying the established "percentage-of-variance" model employed in behavior genetics. Specifically, in addition to incorporating explicit measures of the environment conceptualized in systems terms, and allowing for nonadditive, synergistic effects in genetics-environment interaction, the proposed "bioecological" model posits proximal processes as the empirically assessable mechanisms through which genotypes are transformed into phenotypes. It is further argued, both on theoretical and empirical grounds, that heritability, defined by behavioral geneticists as "the proportion of the total phenotypic variance that is due to additive genetic variation" (Cavalli-Storza and Bodmer 1971 p. 536), is in fact highly influenced by events and conditions in the environment. Specifically, it is proposed that heritability can be shown to vary substantially as a direct function of the magnitude of proximal processes and the quality of the environments in which they occur, potentially yielding values of heritability that, at their extremes, are both appreciably higher and lower than those hitherto reported in the research literature.

If this bioecological model sustains empirical testing, this would imply that many human beings may possess genetic potentials for development significantly beyond those that they are presently manifesting, and that such unrealized potentials might be actualized through social policies and programs that enhance exposure to proximal processes in environmental settings providing the stability and resources that enable such processes to be maximally effective.

Certainly, thus far it has by no means been demonstrated that this latest extension of the ecological paradigm has any validity. Nor is the validation of hypotheses the principal goal that ecological models are designed to achieve. Indeed, their purpose may be

better served if the hypotheses that they generate are found wanting, for the primary scientific aim of the ecological approach is not to claim answers, but to provide a theoretical framework that, through its application, will lead to further progress in discovering the processes and conditions that shape the course of human development.

However, beyond this scientific aim lies a broader human hope. That hope was expressed in the first systematic exposition of the ecological paradigm:

> Species *Homo sapiens* appears to be unique in its capacity to adapt to, tolerate, and especially to create the ecologies in which it lives and grows. Seen in different contexts, human nature, which I had once thought of as a singular noun, turns out to be plural and pluralistic; for different environments produce discernible differences, not only across but within societies, in talent, temperament, human relations, and particularly in the ways in which each culture and subculture brings up the next generation. The process and product of making human beings human clearly varies by place and time. Viewed in historical as well as cross-cultural perspective, this diversity suggests the possibility of ecologies as yet untried that hold a potential for human natures yet unseen, perhaps possessed of a wiser blend of power and compassion than has thus far been manifested. (Bronfenbrenner 1979 p. xiii)

REFERENCES

Baltes, P. B., Schaie, W. 1973. *Life-span Developmental Psychology: Personality and Socialization.* Academic Press, New York.

Bronfenbrenner, U. 1974. Developmental research, public policy, and the ecology of childhood. *Child Dev.* 45(1): 1–5.

Bronfenbrenner, U. 1976. The experimental ecology of education. *Teach. Coll. Rec.* 78(2): 157–204.

Bronfenbrenner, U. 1977. Toward an experimental ecology of human development. *Am. Psychol.* 32: 515–31.

Bronfenbrenner, U. 1979. *The Ecology of Human Development: Experiments by Nature and Design.* Harvard University Press, Cambridge, Massachusetts.

Bronfenbrenner, U. 1986a. Ecology of the family as a context for human development: Research perspectives. *Dev. Psychol.* 22(6): 723–42.

Bronfenbrenner, U. 1986b. Recent advances in the ecology of human development. In: Silbereisen, R. K., Eyferth, K., Rudinger, G. (eds.) 1986 *Development as Action in Context: Problem Behavior and Normal Youth Development.* Springer-Verlag, Berlin.

Bronfenbrenner, U. 1988. Interacting systems in human development: Research paradigms, present and future. In: Bolger, N., Caspi, A., Downey, G., Moorehouse, M. (eds.) 1988 *Persons in Context: Developmental Processes.* Cambridge University Press, Cambridge.

Bronfenbrenner, U. 1989. Ecological systems theory. In: Vasta, R. (ed.) 1989 *Six Theories of Child Development: Revised Formulations and Current Issues*. Vol. 6. JAI Press, Greenwich, Connecticut.

Bronfenbrenner, U. 1990. The ecology of cognitive development. *Zeitschrift für Sozialisationsforschung und Erziehungssoziologie (ZSE)*. 10(2): 101–14.

Bronfenbrenner, U. 1993. The ecology of cognitive development: Research models and fugitive findings. In: Wozniak, R. H., Fischer, K. (eds.) 1993 *Thinking in Context*. Erlbaum, Hillsdale, New Jersey.

Bronfenbrenner, U., Ceci, S. J. 1993. Heredity, environment, and the question "how?": A new theoretical perspective for the 1990s. In: Plomin, R., McClearn, G. E. (eds.) 1993 *Nature, Nurture, and Psychology*. APA Books, Washington, DC.

Cavalli-Storza, L. L., Bodmer, W. F. 1971. *The Genetics of Human Populations*. W. H. Freeman, San Francisco, California.

Ceci, S. J. 1990. *On Intelligence . . . More or Less: A Bioecological Treatise on Intellectual Development*. Prentice-Hall, Englewood Cliffs, New Jersey.

Clausen, J. A. 1986. *The Life Course: A Sociological Perspective*. Prentice-Hall, Englewood Cliffs, New Jersey.

Cochran, M., Larner, M., Riley, D., Gunnarsson, L., Henderson, C. R., Jr. 1990. *Extending Families: The Social Networks of Parents and their Children*. Cambridge University Press, New York.

Drillien, C. M. 1963. *The Growth and Development of the Prematurely Born Infant*. E. and S. Livingston Ltd., Edinburgh.

Eckenrode, J., Gore, S. (eds.) 1990. *Stress between Work and Family*. Plenum Press, New York.

Elder, G. H., Jr. 1974. *Children of the Great Depression: Social Change in the Life Experience*. University of Chicago Press, Chicago, Illinois.

Elder, G. H., Jr., Modell, J., Parke, R. D. 1993. *Children in Time and Place: Individual, Historical and Developmental Insights*. Cambridge University Press, New York.

Epstein, J. L. 1983a. *Effects on Parents of Teacher Practices of Parent Involvement*. Center for the Social Organization of Schools, Johns Hopkins University, Baltimore, Maryland.

Epstein, J. L. 1983b. Longitudinal effects of family-school-person interactions on student outcomes. *Research in Sociology of Education and Socialization* 4: 101–27.

Lewin, K. 1917. Kriegslandschaft. *Zeitschrift für Angewandte Psychologie* 12: 440–47.

Lewin, K. 1931. Environmental forces in child behavior and development. In: Murchison, C. (ed.) 1931 *A Handbook of Child Psychology*. Clark University Press, Worcester, Massachusetts.

Lewin, K. 1935. *A Dynamic Theory of Personality*. McGraw-Hill, New York.

Pence, A. R. (ed.) 1988. *Ecological Research with Children and Families: From Concepts to Methodology*. Teachers College, Columbia University, New York.

Schwabe, H., Bartholomai, F. 1870. Der Vorstellungskreis der Berliner Kinder beim Eintritt in die Schule. In: *Berlin und seine Entwicklung: Städtisches Jahrbuch für Volkswirthschaft und Statistik Vierter Jahrgang*. Guttentag, Berlin.

Stevenson, H. W., Stigler, J. W. 1992. *The Learning Gap: Why Our Schools are Failing and What We Can Learn from Japanese and Chinese Education*. Summit Books, New York.

QUESTIONS

1. Why did Bronfenbrenner adopt the ecological approach from biology to describe psychological development?
2. What do you think Bronfenbrenner meant when he wrote: "Much of developmental psychology is the science of the strange behavior of children in strange situations with strange adults for the briefest possible periods of time"?
3. Why must proximal processes, to be effective, occur regularly and over an extended period of time?
4. What are the subsystems of the ecological approach to psychological development? Think of a particular process of development, such as peer relations or language development, and describe it in relation to each of these subsystems.
5. What is the chronosystem, and why should it be included in an ecological approach to psychological development?
6. Why is Bronfenbrenner interested in the role that genetic inheritance may play in the ecology of psychological development?
7. What types of interventions could be provided for parents from disadvantaged backgrounds that would increase the likelihood that their children will have fewer behavior problems in childhood and succeed in high school?
8. How might the ecological systems framework contribute to research and social policy related to children's nutrition and the problem of child obesity?
9. What do you think will be the psychological consequences for a child if his or her experiences in two different microsystems are in conflict with one another—if, for example, the family emphasizes cooperation but the school rewards competition?
10. One implication of the ecological systems approach is that a change made in one element or subsystem will have little effect if the other subsystems remain the same. Does this mean that only large-scale interventions are worthwhile? In other words, can small changes in a child's life ever make a difference?

2 The Legacy of Early Attachments

Human beings are social animals. We cannot survive without social contact and support. Beyond ensuring our survival, other people enhance even our most mundane experiences by providing us with emotional solace, intellectual stimulation, and enjoyment. Psychologists who study human social interaction have shown that we do not just passively receive information and assistance from others. Rather, human social experience is an active process. From early in life babies elicit and respond to social contact; they also exhibit behaviors that help direct and sustain these contacts. Social contacts between infants and other people are strengthened by ties of affection—the "glue" of human relationships. Because of the great importance that sustained social contact has in psychological development, psychologists have conducted much research on how and when early relationships are formed, what role they play in development, and what happens when they don't work very well.

Sigmund Freud, writing in the early twentieth century, was the first psychological researcher to emphasize the importance of early social relationships for later development, especially the child's relationship with the mother. Interest in this topic increased substantially in the years following World War II. The writings of the British psychologist John Bowlby were especially influential. Bowlby introduced the idea of attachment, defining it as an enduring emotional bond between an infant and another person. Bowlby considered attachment essential to human survival. He was especially interested in how attachment provides emotional security for new members of the human species as well as a secure base for their exploration and learning.

In the 1960s, the American psychologist Mary Ainsworth extended Bowlby's basic formulation to the analysis of individual differences in attachment. Since that time, the study of early relationships, particularly attachment, has been at the center of research in socioemotional development. The early ties that infants form with caregivers are considered critical to adjustment in infancy and throughout childhood. Some psychologists have even extended this concept into adulthood by investigating how adult relationships reflect our original attachment to our primary caregivers.

In the following article, Ross Thompson, a developmental psychologist who has conducted research on early relationships, discusses the legacy of early attachments. The term *legacy*, which means something that is handed down from the past, is used in two ways in this article: (1) to describe the consequences of early relationships, especially attachment to caregivers, for the later development of an individual and (2) to refer to the influence that the concept of attachment has had on psychological research since the time it was introduced and studied by Bowlby and Ainsworth. Thompson describes many of the current avenues of research on early relationships and raises provocative questions regarding future study and the practical application of these ideas.

The impact of early close relationships on psychological development is one of the enduring questions of developmental psychology that is addressed by attachment theory and research. This essay evaluates what has been learned, and offers ideas for future research, by examining the origins of continuity and change in the security of attachment early in life, and its prediction of later behavior. The discussion evaluates research on the impact of changing family circumstances and quality of care on changes in attachment security, and offers new hypotheses for future study. Considering the representations (or internal working models) associated with

Reprinted with permission of Blackwell Publishers from Thompson, R. (2000). The legacy of early attachments. *Child Development, 71*, 145–152.

attachment security as developing representations, the discussion proposes that (1)attachment security may be developmentally most influential when the working models with which it is associated have sufficiently matured to influence other emerging features of psychosocial functioning; (2)changes in attachment security are more likely during periods of representational advance; and (3)parent–child discourse and other relational influences shape these developing representations after infancy. Finally, other features of early parent–child relationships that develop concurrently with attachment security, including negotiating conflict and establishing cooperation, also must be considered in understanding the legacy of early attachments.

INTRODUCTION

Attachment theory has become the dominant approach to understanding early socioemotional and personality development during the past quarter-century of research. It is easy to understand why. The questions studied by attachment researchers are some of the most compelling, longstanding issues of developmental psychology. How do early experiences, particularly in close relationships, affect social and personality development? What are the central features of parenting that have these influences? What internal and external factors mediate continuity and change in socio-personality functioning early in life? A large body of research generated by attachment theory offers developmental psychologists some of their best opportunities to empirically address these questions and to consider new empirical directions based on the answers of current research.

Assessing what has been learned from this research is especially important as attachment theory develops into a more mature and broadly applicable conceptual perspective within which issues of mental health, close relationships throughout life, and representations of self and others are considered. This is because central to many of these broader applications of attachment theory are basic questions concerning how early experiences of care are relevant to later socioemotional and personality growth. In this essay, I offer four conclusions/conjectures based on current research concerning the legacy of early attachment relationships, and discuss the directions they indicate for future inquiry. They are intended to summarize much of what has been learned about the broader impact of early attachment security, the questions this raises for future research, and some of the empirical dimensions of future study of these issues.

CHILDREN VARY SIGNIFICANTLY IN WHETHER EARLY ATTACHMENTS HAVE AN ENDURING IMPACT UPON THEM

Studies of continuity and change in attachment processes began with efforts to determine what was the typical consistency of attachment classifications over time. This was because earlier measures of parent-child interaction had such poor stability, and researchers needed to test theoretical predictions from an organizational view of early development (Masters & Wellman, 1974; Waters, 1978). The results of a large number of studies have now yielded the somewhat surprising conclusion that children vary considerably in the extent to which attachment security remains individually consistent over time. On one hand, research examining the stability of attachment classifications in the Strange Situation reports widely varying estimates of classification stability over periods of just a few months, with the most recent report indicating that approximately half the infants changed classification status over a 6- to 7-month period (Belsky, Campbell, Cohn, & Moore, 1996; see Thompson, 1998, Table 2.3, for a comprehensive review). On the other hand, some studies have found remarkable consistency between Strange Situation classifications and assessments of attachment conducted years later (e.g., Main & Cassidy, 1998; Wartner, Grossmann, Fremmer-Bombik, & Suess, 1994), although others have not (Zimmerman, Fremmer-Bombik, Spangler, & Grossmann, 1997).

From this research arises the conclusion that sometimes early attachment relationships remain consistent over time, and sometimes they change. This variability makes it impossible to identify a normative level of consistency in the security of attachment. Although unreliability of measurement is always an important consideration in interpreting stability coefficients (especially with a psychologically complex construct like attachment security), external correlates of discontinuity suggest that patterns of continuity and change are often real and meaningful. Based on these findings, attachment experiences are important, but they can be transformed by later experience (e.g., Sroufe, Carlson, Levy, & Egeland, 1999). In other words, both developmental history and current circumstances are influential, and it appears that their relative influence can vary for different children.

This conclusion also applies to research concerning attachment and its sequelae, which is another way of examining the legacy of attachment relationships. Studies using early attachment classifications to predict later features of sociopersonality development also reveal considerable variability in the prediction of later outcomes (see reviews by Belsky & Cassidy, 1994; Thompson, 1998). Although it is generally true that the effects of early experiences (including attachment security) tend to wane over time (Sroufe, Egeland, & Kreutzer, 1990), and attachment has different predictive power for different domains of later functioning (Belsky & Cassidy, 1994), it is nevertheless impressive how much variability exists in the strength of the relations between early attachment and later adaptation. On one hand, a recent report from the Minnesota Parent-Child Project found that attachment status in infancy predicted significant features of personality many years later, including risk for anxiety disorders in adolescence, even when taking into account other variables predictive of later difficulty (Warren, Huston, Egeland, & Sroufe, 1997). These findings are consistent with those of earlier reports from this study. On the other hand, many short-term longitudinal studies have failed to confirm expected relations between infant attachment security and later behavior (or associations are not replicated), leading some reviewers to conclude that the relation between attachment and later behavior is "modest, weak" (Belsky & Cassidy, 1994).

One additional conclusion of this literature is that attachment has much stronger *contemporaneous* associations with socioemotional adaptation than it does *predictive* relations (Thompson, 1999). This is hardly surprising considering the ways that intervening events can alter the developmental processes initiated by a secure or insecure attachment (or other early experiences). Although it is more difficult to denote causal influences when interpreting associations among concurrent variables, nevertheless, identifying the network of sociopersonality, emotional, and representational correlates concurrently associated with attachment security can help clarify the developmental significance of this construct, even though longitudinal predictive relations are weak or inconsistent.

Children vary considerably in the extent to which early attachment relationships have an enduring impact, but much less is known about the reasons for individual patterns of continuity or change. There are, however, several important hypotheses that merit greater exploration.

First, from the beginning, attachment researchers have hypothesized that changes in family stresses and living conditions can lead to changes in familiar patterns of interaction, and consequently in attachment security and its correlates (e.g., Vaughn, Egeland, Sroufe, & Waters, 1979). Continuity in attachment and its sequelae presumably derives from relatively greater stability in living conditions. No studies, however, have been designed to systematically examine the relations between stability in attachment and concurrent changes in family circumstances and, perhaps not surprisingly, the indirect evidence thus far is mixed. In the most recent study (Belsky et al., 1996), for example, there were no

relations between changes in the security of attachment and measures of parenting obtained between the two Strange Situation assessments (Belsky, personal communication). Furthermore, no research has examined the extent to which early attachment predicts later behavior better in samples characterized by stable living conditions than in samples featuring life changes between the two assessment sessions (but see Thompson & Lamb, 1983).

Second, a related hypothesis focuses primarily on continuity in the quality of care. Several studies have shown that early attachment does not predict later behavior when intervening changes occur in the quality of parental care. A secure attachment does not predict more positive psychosocial functioning when, for example, the mothers of initially secure infants are later observed to behave intrusively and insensitively (e.g., Erickson, Sroufe, & Egeland, 1985). A recent study by Teti, Sakin, Kucera, Corns, and Das Eiden (1996) is particularly informative. They found that attachment security in firstborn preschoolers decreased significantly following the birth of a new sibling, and that children whose security scores dropped most dramatically had mothers with significantly higher scores on depression, anxiety, and/or hostility compared with the mothers of children who maintained high security scores. Firstborns' security scores were also predicted by measures of the mothers' marital harmony and affective involvement with the firstborn.

It is, in short, not just changing family circumstances, but also their impact on the quality of parental care, that influences whether early attachments have an enduring impact. Broader family processes and the adult's adaptive capacities may either exacerbate or buffer the impact of family stresses on early child–parent attachment. The way an adult copes with family transitions (itself influenced by personality, relational schemas, and social support) can mediate the impact of these transitions on infant–parent attachment security.

It is possible to hypothesize more specifically about the nature of these broader family processes. Changes in family functioning that have comprehensive rather than delimited effects on family members—such as the birth of a new child, significant changes in marital harmony, or parental death or prolonged illness—are more likely to alter relational security because they force a renegotiation of familiar relational patterns. By contrast, changes in parental employment, family residence, or even child-care arrangements need not necessarily affect child–parent attachment quality because both parents and offspring can more readily adapt to them within the context of their established expectations for each other. Family changes relevant to attachment security are not only indirectly influential through their effects on parenting quality, however; they also may have direct influences on children by demanding emotion regulation and adaptive coping that can also influence attachment security, as suggested by Cummings and Davies' emotional security hypothesis (Cummings & Davies, 1994; Davies & Cummings, 1994). Stresses such as marital discord, for example, may not only indirectly influence attachment security through changes in the sensitivity of stressed parents; they also directly influence the security of attachment through the demands placed on young offspring who must cope with frightening parental conduct (Owen & Cox, 1997). In this regard, the child's temperamental vulnerability or adaptability may also be relevant to understanding the impact of family events on the security of attachment.

Finally, the ecology of early child development has changed significantly during the period that attachment researchers have been studying continuity and change in infant–parent attachment, and it is now important to take into greater consideration multiple attachment relationships experienced within the family (with fathers as well as mothers) and outside the family (e.g., in child-care settings; Berlin & Cassidy, 1999; Howes, 1999). Examining the constellation of relational influences that young children experience may provide significant insights into why attachment security is, for some children, highly vulnerable to family changes and stress, whereas for other children it seems to be buffered against the effects of these transitions. Other relational partners may help to protect the child from insecurity when the mother-child relationship is challenged, for example, or reinforce current or new internal working models of relationships during periods of family transition.

These new hypotheses concerning family processes are relevant also to new theoretical views of the dynamic processes of parenting and child development (Holden & Miller, 1999). In a recent meta-analysis, for example, Holden and Miller found evidence for both stability and variability in parental childrearing practices over time, and concluded that influences such as the child's changing developmental capabilities, normative changes in family structure (such as a sibling's birth), family processes (e.g., employment or child-care transitions), and changes in the parent (e.g., parenting satisfaction) can each contribute to variability in how a child is treated over time. Just as parental sensitivity initiates a secure attachment, the maintenance of age-appropriate sensitive responding is necessary to sustain that security as the child matures. The child's adaptive capacities and influences within the broader family ecology are also relevant to continuity and change in attachment.

CHILDREN'S INTERNAL REPRESENTATIONS OF EXPERIENCE SIGNIFICANTLY MEDIATE THE LEGACY OF EARLY ATTACHMENTS

Consistency and change in attachment can also be understood in terms of how they are mediated by children's representations—or "internal working models"—of themselves and their relationships with others. This is a compelling hypothesis because it focuses closely on the internal representations that mediate the impact of changing family circumstances, or changing caregiving quality, on attachment security and its correlates. Many attachment theorists argue, for example, that one source of continuity in socio-personality development is how children evoke responses from others that are consistent with their internal representations of self and others, construe relational experiences based on their working models, and make choices that reflect their prior representations of self (e.g., Bretherton & Munholland, 1999; Sroufe et al., 1999). Presumably, attachment does not predict later relational and psychosocial characteristics when the internal representations initially inspired by a secure or insecure attachment change over time.

Much less is known about how internal working models change over time, however. To learn more, we must understand these models as developing representations which evolve rapidly during the early years of life. Changes may occur as new modes of understanding alter earlier representations of experiences related to security or insecurity. Fortunately, understanding the development of internal working models is informed by the expanding research literature on many aspects of young children's thinking and reasoning, including the growth of event representation (scripts and event schemas), episodic memory, autobiographical understanding, theory of mind, developing social cognition, and other facets of early representations of self, others, and relationships that are incorporated into the internal working models construct (see Bretherton & Munholland, 1999; Thompson, 1998). Although there is considerable work to be done in connecting relational experience to these developing representations (see Harris, 1997), this literature has promise for elucidating how internal working models change over time. Research in theory of mind suggests, for example, that a young child's appreciation of another's feelings, thoughts, and motives, and of the reciprocal, complementary nature of relational transactions, expands significantly between the ages of three and five. Research on autobiographical memory suggests that young children are unlikely to begin creating a coherent, enduring self-narrative—integrating current and past events into developing self-understanding—before the age of three. As these studies inform an understanding of attachment-related representations and their development, the internal working models construct, which has been criticized as being unduly vague and generalized (e.g., Rutter, 1995), can be clarified.

Conceptualizing internal working models as developing representations has several implications for understanding the legacy of early attachment relationships. It suggests that changes in working models—and possibly, also, in the security of attachment—are more likely to occur during periods of significant representational advance. Such a view is consistent with the formulations of other attachment theorists (e.g., Ainsworth, 1989), and with the idea that advances in a child's capacities to represent experiences create new ways of conceptualizing and reconsidering prior experiences and the conclusions they have yielded. Thus, individual differences in the security of attachment and the internal working models with which they are associated may be less consistent and less predictive of other psychosocial achievements between representational transitions. Two transitions may be particularly important: when a young child begins to represent in more complex and memorially more sophisticated ways the experiences of care that were earlier interpreted using the simpler perceptual–affective schemas of infancy (see Nelson, 1996); and later, when an older child becomes capable of representing self and relationships with the abstract, hypothetical modes of formal operational thought (Ainsworth, 1989). During each of these transitions, and others, internal working models may be more prone to revision and reconceptualization, and this can account for changes in attachment security and in the sequelae of attachment.

A second implication of viewing internal working models as developing representations is that attachment may be developmentally most influential when the internal working models with which it is associated have sufficiently matured to influence other emerging features of psychosocial functioning. If an integrated, enduring sense of self-understanding begins to take shape after the age of three, for example, then a secure attachment may be most strongly associated with developing self-concept and self-esteem at or after this age rather than before (see, for example, Verschueren & Marcoen, 1999). Similarly, the associations between attachment and emotional understanding (Laible & Thompson, 1998) and emerging conscience (Kochanska, 1995) may be strongest when attachment is assessed in young preschoolers, when theory of mind is rapidly developing and when internal working models are likely to be most influential in the emergence of emotional and moral understanding.

Traditionally attachment researchers have used Strange Situation assessments in infancy as the basis for exploring how attachment predicts later psychosocial functioning. But internal representations of experience are very rudimentary in infants, and assessments at that time are unlikely to capture (except in general affective tone) the more complex conceptions of self, relationships, and other people that are encompassed within the working models construct, and which children begin to acquire in the years that follow. Depending on the outcome of interest, therefore, assessment of attachment security in the preschool period (or later) may reveal more profound influences on development than assessment in infancy because of the greater integrity and sophistication of the internal working models with which it is associated. Future studies of the predictive validity of attachment security may increasingly emphasize attachment during the preschool years, a period during which developing representations of self, relationships, and other people are more significantly influenced by a secure or insecure attachment than in infancy.

Finally, and most speculatively, children may vary individually in the extent to which a secure attachment has a lasting impact because of how the representations associated with secure or insecure working models interact harmoniously or discordantly with other developing systems of thought, including attitudes and attributional biases, personal beliefs related to ability and competence, and understanding of social processes. As young children develop more sophisticated understanding of self and others in close relationships, for example, they are also developing understanding of other features of their life experience, including conceptions of their relationships with teachers and peers in school, people in the neighborhood, their capabilities and vulnerabilities, and their place in the broader world. It is yet unclear, but important to learn, how these representations are related. For children from difficult backgrounds who are prone to hostility and distrust of others, for example, a secure attachment may buffer the development of negative attributional biases and this may be a source of psychosocial continuity for such children. These issues are important because they demonstrate the legacy of early attachments in the context of other influences on developing understanding, and can be explored by researchers who are informed by the conceptual and empirical tools of contemporary work in cognitive development to elucidate attachment theorists' concept of internal working models.

Parent–Child Discourse Is an Important Influence on How Young Children Represent Life Experience

How do the representations that constitute "internal working models" develop in the early years? The view of attachment theorists that the quality of parent–child interaction is important complements current theoretical views in the study of cognitive development. But according to Nelson (1996) and other cognitive theorists, it is the quality of shared discourse, enabled by the child's growing language competency, that significantly shapes representational development during the preschool years. Language permits the exchange of ideas and concepts that affords young children access to modes of thinking of the adult world and, in Nelson's phrase, the "collaborative construction of the mediated mind." The mind of the preschooler is linguistically mediated in ways that make thinking qualitatively different from what preceded it, reflecting a representational advance as earlier described. In particular, according to Nelson, parent–child discourse guides the emergence of many aspects of thought, including autobiographical memory (as parents establish an interpretive framework that defines the significance of personal events to a young child), theory of mind (as parents help clarify the thoughts, feelings, and motives of people, including themselves, to the child), cognitive models of the world (as parents impart, often implicitly, naive causal theories), and other cognitions related to what attachment theorists regard as internal working models of self, others, and relationships (see also Rogoff, 1990, and Tomasello, 1999, for similar views).

Empirical support for these formulations comes from studies reporting associations between features of parent–child discourse and early emotional understanding (e.g., Brown & Dunn, 1996; Fivush, 1993), autobiographical reference (e.g., Hudson, 1990; Miller, Fung, & Mintz, 1996), moral understanding (e.g., Dunn, Brown, & Maguire, 1995; Laible & Thompson, 2000), and theory of mind (Welch-Ross, 1997). Consistent with theoretical predictions, researchers have reported that conversations in which parents make more frequent reference to feelings and their causes, and who inquire frequently about and expand more elaboratively on the events a child describes, contribute to the growth of psychological understanding of others and the depth of the young child's autobiographical recollections. Moreover, in a recent study, the mothers of securely attached preschoolers responded more elaborately, and with more frequent reference to feelings and moral evaluatives, in their conversations with offspring—and both attachment and maternal discourse style predicted measures of children's conscience development (Laible & Thompson, 2000; see also Kochanska, 1995, for complementary findings).

These findings suggest that beyond early sensitive caregiving, parents contribute in other ways to the working models associated with secure and insecure attachment in preschoolers. With the growth of language in offspring, parents initiate conversations about the child's everyday experiences in which implicit as well as explicit understandings of self, emotion, morality, and relationships are co-constructed with the child. The manner in which the parent shares in these conversations—the parent's conversational style as well as content, the adult's implicit assumptions and attributions as well as explicit prompts and questions, the emotional tone of the adult's language as well as its semantic content—is related to how children represent central features of their experience and their representations of themselves and others. The working models associated with secure or insecure attachments likely have their origins, therefore, not only in the child's direct representations of the sensitivity of parental care, but in the secondary representations of their experience mediated through parent–child discourse. The latter may be especially important as these representations become part of broader networks of self-referential beliefs and social understanding during the preschool years.

Although considerable research remains to be done in exploring further the relations between parent–child discourse, children's representations of experience, and attachment-related relational processes, this theoretical and empirical work raises a number of important questions. Do early parent–child conversations provide a forum for young children to appropriate also the perceptual sets, emotional predispositions, or defensive styles thought to be elements of the working models associated with secure or insecure attachments (Bretherton & Munholland, 1999)? How do young children interpret marked dissonance that may occur between their primary representations of recent experiences and the secondary representations that occur in parent–child discourse (e.g., a child whose distressing trip to the dentist is represented much more positively by the adult; see Levine, Stein, & Liwag, 1999)? Finally, when significant changes in family life (such as the birth of a sibling) alter familiar relational patterns between children and parents, are there adaptations or changes in the style or content of parent–child conversations that may be related to continuity or change in the security of attachment? In general, understanding that internal working models are developing representations, and that parent–child discourse influences the nature of these representations, raises important new research questions concerning how parents contribute to security or insecurity for preschoolers whose representational systems of thought are maturing rapidly.

NEGOTIATING CONFLICT AND ESTABLISHING MUTUAL COOPERATION IS ANOTHER IMPORTANT ASPECT OF EARLY PARENT–CHILD RELATIONSHIPS

Attachment theory is the dominant approach to understanding early parent–child relationships, but from the beginning Bowlby (1969/1982) recognized that attachment encompasses only one dimension of this relationship. At the same time that a foundational sense of security is being established, infants and young children are learning about other facets of close relationships through parent–child interaction. One of these is how to cooperate in the context of conflict over differing goals and intentions.

Learning how to "repair" interactive disruptions is, along with interactive harmony, an early and enduring feature of parent–infant interaction (Tronick, 1989). But conflict heightens in scope and significance with the growth of self-produced locomotion toward the end of the first year (Biringen, Emde, Campos, & Appelbaum, 1995; Campos, Kermoian, & Zumbahlen, 1992). Toddlers become more assertive and goal-oriented as they become capable of independent mobility, while parents more actively monitor their toddlers' activity and increasingly use prohibitions and sanctions to protect children and control their wandering. Conflicts of will increase at the same time as positive affective exchanges, and both may be related to the growing autonomy consequent to the young child's independent locomotion. Moreover, the emotional communication between parents and children also changes to incorporate greater use of signals to convey approval or disapproval of the toddler's behavior (sometimes even before an act is committed), as well as to provide reassurance and emotional support.

The toddler's motoric advance thus inaugurates a change in the parent–child relationship at the same time that a secure or insecure attachment relationship is becoming consolidated. Toddlers are learning how to cope with the frustrations of complying with parental expectations at the same time that they are developing a secure (or insecure) relationship with the parent. Moreover, this change is the vanguard of a more extended developmental transition during the preschool years in which young children are increasingly striving to understand and comply with the behavior expectations of parents while also asserting independent judgment and self-will. Importantly, many of the predicted outcomes of a secure attachment, including the growth of an autonomous self,

the maintenance of a harmonious parent–child relationship, competence in other close relationships, and representations of self and others that are positive and balanced, are also likely to be influenced by the ease with which young children learn to successfully negotiate conflict and establish cooperative relations with others, a skill that develops initially in the parent–child relationship. Indeed (and consistent with Vygotskian theory), research on parent–child discourse indicates that experiences of conflict between children and their parents (and siblings) are significant catalysts for growth in understanding emotion, morality, self, and other constituents of the internal working models associated with attachment security (see, e.g., Dunn et al., 1995; Kochanska, 1995).

Although this final conclusion from research does not derive directly from attachment theory, it suggests that because the outcomes of secure or insecure attachments are influenced by many relational influences, developmental researchers will be wise to consider the multiple dimensions of early parent–child relationships that are emerging at the same time that attachment security is taking shape. With respect to parents, more than sensitivity is important in shaping the early psychosocial adaptation that begins in infancy and continues in the years that follow. With respect to offspring, the legacy of early attachments intersects with the legacy of other relational influences that have developmental origins concurrent with those of a secure or insecure attachment.

CONCLUSION

Understanding change as well as continuity in individual characteristics is essential to grasping the nature of psychological development. Although attachment theorists have contributed valuable conceptual models for describing "lawful discontinuity" in attachment processes, the emphasis of attachment theory and research has naturally been on identifying and understanding the continuities in individual characteristics that appear across developmental transitions.

Yet the attachment literature also offers insights into the nature of the "lawful discontinuities" that characterize attachment security and its outcomes. These include, especially in the early years, influences from the stability, quality, and stresses of the child's living conditions, the consistency of the quality of care provided by close relational partners, and influences of the multiple attachment relationships that sometimes overlap with and sometimes are independent from the mother–child relationship that has been the primary focus of attachment researchers. Influences on developmental discontinuity include also representational transitions that may effect change in the internal working models associated with attachment security. Moreover, viewing internal working models as developing representations means also that the legacy of a secure attachment may depend on the child's age and the maturity of the working models that attachment reflects, as well as other developing representational systems of thought. In some respects, attachment security in the preschool years may be more developmentally provocative than earlier attachment security.

Understanding "lawful discontinuity" also means appreciating the other influences, including those within the parent–child relationship, on the outcomes that attachment security is thought to affect, and recognizing that attachment security is forged in the context of the negotiation of conflict and cooperation in the same parent–child dyad. Further exploration of the legacy of attachment relationships promises to inform broader developmental theories concerning the importance of early experiences and the developmental processes that tend to maintain or revise initial influences.

References

Ainsworth, M. D. S. (1989). Attachments beyond infancy. *American Psychologist, 44,* 709–716.

Belsky, J., Campbell, S. B., Cohn, J. F., & Moore, G. (1996). Instability of infant–parent attachment security. *Developmental Psychology, 32,* 921–924.

Belsky, J., & Cassidy, J. (1994). Attachment: Theory and evidence. In M. Rutter & D. Hay (Eds.), *Development through life* (pp. 373–402). Oxford: Blackwell.

Berlin, L. J., & Cassidy, J. (1999). Relations among relationships: Contributions from attachment theory and research. In J. Cassidy & P. R. Shaver (Eds.), *Handbook of attachment* (pp. 688–712). New York: Guilford.

Biringen, Z., Emde, R. N., Campos, J. J., & Appelbaum, M. I. (1995). Affective reorganization in the infant, the mother, and the dyad: The role of upright locomotion and its timing. *Child Development, 66,* 499–514.

Bowlby, J. (1982). *Attachment and loss.* Vol. 1. *Attachment* (2nd Ed.). New York: Basic. (original work published 1969)

Bretherton, I., & Munholland, K. A. (1999). Internal working models in attachment relationships: A construct revisited. In J. Cassidy & P. R. Shaver (Eds.), *Handbook of attachment* (pp. 89–111). New York: Guilford.

Brown, J. R., & Dunn, J. (1996). Continuities in emotional understanding from 3 to 6 years. *Child Development, 67,* 789–802.

Campos, J. J., Kermoian, R., & Zumbahlen, M. R. (1992). Socioemotional transformations in the family system following infant crawling onset. In N. Eisenberg & R. A. Fabes (Eds.), *Emotion and its regulation in early development* (pp. 35–40). San Francisco: Jossey-Bass.

Cummings, E. M., & Davies, P. (1994). *Children and marital conflict.* New York: Guilford.

Davies, P. T., & Cummings, E. M. (1994). Marital conflict and child adjustment: An emotional security hypothesis. *Psychological Bulletin, 116,* 387–411.

Dunn, J., Brown, J., & Maguire, M. (1995). The development of children's moral sensibility: Individual differences and emotional understanding. *Developmental Psychology, 31,* 649–659.

Erickson, M. F., Sroufe, L. A., & Egeland, B. (1985). The relationship between quality of attachment and behavior problems in preschool in a high-risk sample. In I. Bretherton & E. Walters (Eds.), *Growing points of attachment theory and research. Monographs of the Society for Research in Child Development, 50*(1–2, Serial No. 209).

Fivush, R. (1993). Emotional content of parent–child conversations about the past. In C. A. Nelson (Ed.), *Minnesota Symposia on Child Psychology: Vol. 26. Memory and affect in development* (pp. 39–77). Hillsdale, NJ: Erlbaum.

Harris, P. L. (1997). Between strange situations and false beliefs: Working models and theories of mind. In W. Koops, J. Hoeksma, & D. Van den Boom (Eds.), *Early mother–child interaction and attachment: Old and new approaches* (pp. 187–199). Amsterdam: Royal Netherlands Academy of Arts and Sciences.

Holden, G. W., & Miller, P. C. (1999). Enduring and different: A meta-analysis of the similarity in parents' child rearing. *Psychological Bulletin, 125,* 223–254.

Howes, C. (1999). Attachment relationships in the context of multiple caregivers. In J. Cassidy & P. R. Shaver (Eds.), *Handbook of attachment* (pp. 671–687). New York: Guilford.

Hudson, J. A. (1990). The emergence of autobiographical memory in mother–child conversation. In R. Fivush & J. A. Hudson (Eds.), *Knowing and remembering in young children* (pp. 166–196). New York: Cambridge University Press.

Kochanska, G. (1995). Children's temperament, mothers' discipline, and security of attachment: Multiple pathways to emerging internalization. *Child Development, 66,* 597–615.

Laible, D. J., & Thompson, R. A. (1998). Attachment and emotional understanding in preschool children. *Developmental Psychology, 34,* 1038–1045.

Laible, D. J., & Thompson, R. A. (2000). Mother–child discourse, attachment security, shared positive affect, and early conscience development. *Child Development, 73,* 1424–1440.

Levine, L. J., Stein, N. L., & Liwag, M. D. (1999). Remembering children's emotions: Sources of concordant and discordant accounts between parents and children. *Developmental Psychology, 35,* 790–801.

Main, M., & Cassidy, J. (1988). Categories of response to reunion with the parent at age 6: Predictable from infant attachment classifications and stable over a 1-month period. *Developmental Psychology, 24,* 415–426.

Masters, J. C., & Wellman, H. M. (1974). The study of human infant attachment: A procedural critique. *Psychological Bulletin, 81,* 213–237.

Miller, P. J., Fung, H., & Mintz, J. (1996). Self-construction through narrative practices: A Chinese and American comparison of early socialization. *Ethos, 24,* 237–280.

Nelson, K. (1996). *Language in cognitive development: The emergence of the mediated mind.* New York: Cambridge University Press.

Owen, M. T., & Cox, M. J. (1997). Marital conflict and the development of infant–parent attachment relationships. *Journal of Family Psychology, 11,* 152–164.

Rogoff, B. (1990). *Apprenticeship in thinking.* New York: Oxford University Press.

Rutter, M. (1995). Clinical implications of attachment concepts: Retrospect and prospect. *Journal of Child Psychology and Psychiatry, 36,* 549–571.

Sroufe, L. A., Carlson, E. A., Levy, A. K., & Egeland, B. (1999). Implications of attachment theory for developmental psychopathology. *Development and Psychopathology, 11,* 1–13.

Sroufe, L. A., Egeland, B., & Kreutzer, T. (1990). The fate of early experience following developmental change: Longitudinal approaches to individual adaptation in childhood. *Child Development, 61,* 1363–1373.

Teti, D. M., Sakin, W. J., Kucera, E., Corns, K. M., & Das Eiden, R. (1996). And baby makes four: Predictors of attachment security among preschool-age firstborns during the transition to siblinghood. *Child Development, 67,* 579–596.

Thompson, R. A. (1998). Early sociopersonality development. In N. Eisenberg (Ed.), W. Damon (Series Ed.), *Handbook of child psychology: Vol. 3. Social, emotional, and personality development* (5th ed., pp. 25–104). New York: Wiley.

Thompson, R. A. (1999). Early attachment and later development. In J. Cassidy & P. R. Shaver (Eds.), *Handbook of attachment* (pp. 265–286). New York: Guilford.

Thompson, R. A., & Lamb, M. E. (1983). Security of attachment and stranger sociability in infancy. *Developmental Psychology, 19,* 184–191.

Tomasello, M. (in press). *The cultural origins of human cognition.* Cambridge, MA: Harvard University Press.

Tronick, E. Z. (1989). Emotions and emotional communication in infants. *American Psychologist, 44,* 112–119.

Vaughn, B. E., Egeland, B., Sroufe, L. A., & Waters, E. (1979). Individual differences in infant–mother attachment at twelve and eighteen months: Stability and change in families under stress. *Child Development, 50,* 971–975.

Verschueren, K., & Marcoen, A. (1999). Representation of self and socioemotional competence in kindergartners: Differential and combined effects of attachment to mother and to father. *Child Development, 70,* 183–201.

Warren, S. L., Huston, L., Egeland, B., & Sroufe, L. A. (1997). Child and adolescent anxiety disorders and early attachment. *Journal of the American Academy of Child and Adolescent Psychiatry, 36,* 637–641.

Wartner, U. G., Grossmann, K., Fremmer-Bombik, E., & Suess, G. (1994). Attachment patterns at age six in South Germany: Predictability from infancy and implications for preschool behavior. *Child Development, 65,* 1014–1027.

Waters, E. (1978). The reliability and stability of individual differences in infant–mother attachment. *Child Development, 49,* 483–494.

Welch-Ross, M. K. (1997). Mother–child participation in conversation about the past: Relationships to preschoolers' theory of mind. *Developmental Psychology, 33,* 618–629.

Zimmermann, P., Fremmer-Bombik, E., Spangler, G., & Grossmann, K. E. (1997). Attachment in adolescence: A longitudinal perspective. In W. Koops, J. B. Hoeksma, & D. C. van den Boom (Eds.), *Development of interaction and attachment* (pp. 281–292). Amsterdam: Elsevier.

QUESTIONS

1. What does research indicate about the type of attachment exhibited by an infant and caregiver: Is it stable over time, or does it change?
2. Are you surprised by Thompson's statement that attachment has been found to have much stronger contemporaneous associations with socioemotional adaptation (i.e., the two are measured at the same time) than predictive relations (i.e., attachment is studied over time)? Why or why not?
3. What are some of the family processes that explain why attachment security can change over time? Do these processes affect attachment security directly, or do they mainly work indirectly, through changes in the parent's behavior toward the child?
4. Why do you think the attachment security of firstborn children tends to decrease after the birth of a sibling? Is there anything a parent can or should do to prevent this decrease?
5. What is a child's internal working model of the attachment relationship?
6. How might changes in a child's cognitive abilities influence his or her internal working model of the attachment relationship?
7. What is parent–child shared discourse, and what role might it play in the development of a child's internal working model of attachment?
8. What types of talk are common in the conversations of mothers and securely attached preschoolers? Does this surprise you? Why or why not?
9. How might secure attachment contribute to the development of autonomy in adolescence?
10. What does Thompson mean by "lawful discontinuity," and why is this concept important for understanding the development of relationships over childhood?

3 Children of the Garden Island

EMMY E. WERNER

Does exposure to problematic and stressful experiences early in life lead to the development of an unhealthy personality? Are some individuals more resilient than others when confronted by developmental difficulties, such as birth complications or poverty? These are difficult but important questions to answer. After all, many children face hardships, and it is valuable to know if such children can be helped to overcome these early challenges and go on to lead happy, meaningful lives. The stories of individuals who have done so may teach us how to help others who confront barriers to healthy development early in life.

The best technique available in developmental psychology for determining how early experiences relate to later development is the longitudinal research design, in which the same individuals are observed over time. A classic longitudinal study of the long-term effects of early developmental difficulties was conducted on the Hawaiian island of Kauai. This study took place over a 30-year period and involved a group of approximately 700 individuals. Researcher Emmy E. Werner found that a number of "high risk" children were resistant to the stresses they had undergone and had developed into healthy adults. Resilient children such as these challenge the traditional assumption that there is a simple and direct link between early experiences and later development. Werner describes this research and its intriguing findings in the following article.

This study is regarded as one of the most important longitudinal studies in the field of developmental psychology. It stands as a model of how to conduct research that truly studies the process of development—that is, changes in the same individual over time. It also provides an explanation of psychological development that emphasizes the important contributions of the child's own behaviors and the social context. Finally, it attests to the adaptability of the human organism to various circumstances of growth.

In 1955, 698 infants on the Hawaiian island of Kauai became participants in a 30-year study that has shown how some individuals triumph over physical disadvantages and deprived childhoods.

Kauai, the Garden Island, lies at the northwest end of the Hawaiian chain, 100 miles and a half-hour flight from Honolulu. Its 555 square miles encompass mountains, cliffs, canyons, rain forests and sandy beaches washed by pounding surf. The first Polynesians who crossed the Pacific to settle there in the eighth century were charmed by its beauty, as were the generations of sojourners who visited there after Captain James Cook "discovered" the island in 1778.

The 45,000 inhabitants of Kauai are for the most part descendants of immigrants from Southeast Asia and Europe who came to the island to work on the sugar plantations with the hope of finding a better life for their children. Thanks to the islanders' unique spirit of cooperation, my colleagues Jessie M. Bierman and Fern E. French of the University of California at Berkeley, Ruth S. Smith, a clinical psychologist on Kauai, and I have been able to carry out a longitudinal study on Kauai that has lasted for more than three decades. The study has had two principal goals: to assess the long-term consequences of prenatal and perinatal stress and to document the effects of adverse early rearing conditions on children's physical, cognitive and psychosocial development.

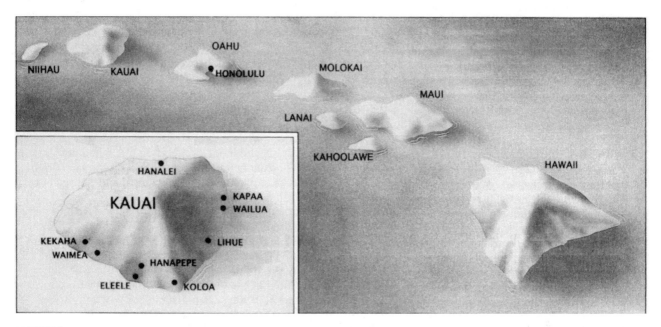

FIGURE 1

Kauai, the Garden Island, lies at the northwest end of the Hawaiian archipelago. The towns that participated in the Kauai Longitudinal Study are shown in the inset. Lihue is the county seat; it is about 100 miles from Honolulu, the capital of Hawaii.

The Kauai Longitudinal Study began at a time when the systematic examination of the development of children exposed to biological and psychosocial risk factors was still a bit of a rarity. Investigators attempted to reconstruct the events that led to physical or psychological problems by studying the history of individuals in whom such problems had already surfaced. This retrospective approach can create the impression that the outcome is inevitable, since it takes into account only the "casualties," not the "survivors." We hoped to avoid that impression by monitoring the development of all the children born in a given period in an entire community.

We began our study in 1954 with an assessment of the reproductive histories of all the women in the community. Altogether 2,203 pregnancies were reported by the women of Kauai in 1954, 1955 and 1956; there were 240 fetal deaths and 1,963 live births. We chose to study the cohort of 698 infants born on Kauai in 1955, and we followed the development of these individuals at one, two, 10, 18 and 31 or 32 years of age. The majority of the individuals in the birth cohort—422 in all—were born without complications, following uneventful pregnancies, and grew up in supportive environments.

But as our study progressed we began to take a special interest in certain "high risk" children who, in spite of exposure to reproductive stress, discordant and impoverished home lives and uneducated, alcoholic or mentally disturbed parents, went on to de-velop healthy personalities, stable careers and strong interpersonal relations. We decided to try to identify the protective factors that contributed to the resilience of these children.

Finding a community that is willing or able to cooperate in such an effort is not an easy task. We chose Kauai for a number of reasons, not the least of which was the receptivity of the island population to our endeavors. Coverage by medical, public-health, educational and social services on the island was comparable to what one would find in communities of similar size on the U.S. mainland at that time. Furthermore, our study would take into account a variety of cultural influences on childbearing and child rearing, since the population of Kauai includes individuals of Japanese, Philipino, Portuguese, Chinese, Korean and northern European as well as of Hawaiian descent.

We also thought the population's low mobility would make it easier to keep track of the study's participants and their families. The promise of a stable sample proved to be justified. At the time of the two-year follow-up, 96 percent of the living children were still on Kauai and available for study. We were able to find 90 percent of the children who were still alive for the 10-year follow-up, and for the 18-year follow-up we found 88 percent of the cohort.

In order to elicit the cooperation of the island's residents, we needed to get to know them and to introduce our study as well. In doing so we relied on the skills of a number of dedicated professionals from the University of California's Berkeley and Davis campuses, from the University of Hawaii and from the island of Kauai itself. At the beginning of the study five nurses and one social worker, all residents of Kauai, took a census of all households on the island, listing the occupants of each dwelling and recording demographic information, including a reproductive history of all women 12 years old or older. The interviewers asked the women if they were pregnant; if a woman was not, a card with a postage-free envelope was left with the request that she mail it to the Kauai Department of Health as soon as she thought she was pregnant.

Local physicians were asked to submit a monthly list of the women who were coming to them for prenatal care. Community organizers spoke to women's groups, church gatherings, the county medical society and community leaders. The visits by the census takers were backed up with letters, and milk cartons were delivered with a printed message urging mothers to cooperate. We advertised in newspapers, organized radio talks, gave slide shows and distributed posters.

Public-health nurses interviewed the pregnant women who joined our study in each trimester of pregnancy, noting any exposure to physical or emotional trauma. Physicians monitored any complications during the prenatal period, labor, delivery and the neonatal period. Nurses and social workers interviewed the mothers in the postpartum period and when the children were one and 10 years old; the interactions between parents and offspring in the home were also observed. Pediatricians and psychologists independently examined the children at two and 10 years of age, assessing their physical, intellectual and social development and noting any handicaps or behavior problems. Teachers evaluated the children's academic progress and their behavior in the classroom.

From the outset of the study we recorded information about the material, intellectual and emotional aspects of the family environment, including stressful life events that resulted in discord or disruption of the family unit. With the parents' permission we also were given access to the records of public-health, educational and social-service agencies and to the files of the local police and the family court. My collaborators and I also administered a wide range of aptitude, achievement and personality tests in the elementary grades and in high school. Last but not least, we gained the perspectives of the young people themselves by interviewing them at the age of 18 and then again when they were in their early 30's.

Of the 698 children in the 1955 cohort, 69 were exposed to moderate prenatal or perinatal stress, that is,

complications during pregnancy, labor or delivery. About 3 percent of the cohort—23 individuals in all—suffered severe prenatal or perinatal stress; only 14 infants in this group lived to the age of two. Indeed, nine of the 12 children in our study who died before reaching two years of age had suffered severe perinatal complications.

Some of the surviving children became "casualties" of a kind in the next two decades of life. One out of every six children (116 children in all) had physical or intellectual handicaps of perinatal or neonatal origin that were diagnosed between birth and the age of two and that required long-term specialized medical, educational or custodial care. About one out of every five children (142 in all) developed serious learning or behavior problems in the first decade of life that required more than six months of remedial work. By the time the children were 10 years old, twice as many children needed some form of mental-health service or remedial education (usually for problems associated with reading) as were in need of medical care.

By the age of 18, 15 percent of the young people had delinquency records and 10 percent had mental health problems requiring either in- or outpatient care. There was some overlap among these groups. By the time they were 10, all 25 of the children with long-term mental-health problems had learning problems as well. Of the 70 children who had mental health problems at 18, 15 also had a record of repeated delinquencies.

As we followed these children from birth to the age of 18 we noted two trends: the impact of reproductive stress diminished with time, and the developmental outcome of virtually every biological risk condition was dependent on the quality of the rearing environment. We did find some correlation between moderate to severe degrees of perinatal trauma and major physical handicaps of the central nervous system and of the musculo-skeletal and sensory systems; perinatal trauma was also correlated with mental retardation, serious learning disabilities and chronic mental-health problems such as schizophrenia that arose in late adolescence and young adulthood.

But overall rearing conditions were more powerful determinants of outcome than perinatal trauma. The better the quality of the home environment was, the more competence the children displayed. This could already be seen when the children were just two years old: toddlers who had experienced severe perinatal stress but lived in middle-class homes or in stable family settings did nearly as well on developmental tests of sensory-motor and verbal skills as toddlers who had experienced no such stress.

Prenatal and perinatal complications were consistently related to impairment of physical and psychological development at the ages of 10 and 18 only when they were combined with chronic poverty, fam-

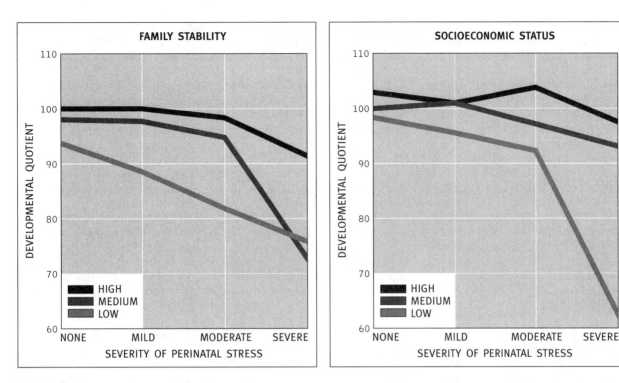

FIGURE 2

Influence of environmental factors such as family stability (left) *or socioeconomic status* (right) *appears in infancy. The "developmental quotients" derived from tests given at 20 months show that the rearing environment can buffer or* *worsen the stress of perinatal complications. Children who had suffered severe perinatal stress but lived in stable, middle-class families scored as well as or better than children in poor, unstable households who had not experienced such stress.*

ily discord, parental mental illness or other persistently poor rearing conditions. Children who were raised in middle-class homes, in a stable family environment and by a mother who had finished high school showed few if any lasting effects of reproductive stress later in their lives.

How many children could count on such a favorable environment? A sizable minority could not. We designated 201 individuals—30 percent of the surviving children in this study population—as being high-risk children because they had experienced moderate to severe perinatal stress, grew up in chronic poverty, were reared by parents with no more than eight grades of formal education or lived in a family environment troubled by discord, divorce, parental alcoholism or mental illness. We termed the children "vulnerable" if they encountered four or more such risk factors before their second birthday. And indeed, two-thirds of these children (129 in all) did develop serious learning or behavior problems by the age of 10 or had delinquency records, mental-health problems or pregnancies by the time they were 18.

Yet one out of three of these high-risk children— 72 individuals altogether—grew into competent young adults who loved well, worked well and played well. None developed serious learning or behavior problems in childhood or adolescence. As far as we could tell from interviews and from their record in the community, they succeeded in school, managed home and social life well and set realistic educational and vocational goals and expectations for themselves when they finished high school. By the end of their second decade of life they had developed into competent, confident and caring people who expressed a strong desire to take advantage of whatever opportunity came their way to improve themselves.

They were children such as Michael, a boy for whom the odds on paper did not seem very promising. The son of teen-age parents, Michael was born prematurely, weighing four pounds five ounces. He spent his first three weeks of life in a hospital, separated from his mother. Immediately after his birth his father was sent with the U.S. Army to Southeast Asia, where he remained for two years. By the time Michael was eight years old he had three siblings and his parents were divorced. His mother had deserted the family and had no further contact with her children. His father raised Michael and his siblings with the help of their aging grandparents.

Then there was Mary, born after 20 hours of labor to an overweight mother who had experienced several miscarriages before that pregnancy. Her father was an unskilled farm laborer with four years of formal education. Between Mary's fifth and 10th birthdays her mother was hospitalized several times for repeated bouts of mental illness, after having inflicted both physical and emotional abuse on her daughter.

Surprisingly, by the age of 18 both Michael and Mary were individuals with high self-esteem and sound values who cared about others and were liked by their peers. They were successful in school and looked forward to the future. We looked back at the lives of these two youngsters and the 70 other resilient individuals who had triumphed over their circumstances and compared their behavioral characteristics and the features of their environment with those of the other high-risk youths who developed serious and persistent problems in childhood and adolescence.

We identified a number of protective factors in the families, outside the family circle and within the resilient children themselves that enabled them to resist stress. Some sources of resilience seem to be constitutional: resilient children such as Mary and Michael tend to have characteristics of temperament that elicit positive responses from family members and strangers alike. We noted these same qualities in adulthood. They include a fairly high activity level, a low degree of excitability and distress and a high degree of sociability. Even as infants the resilient individuals were described by their parents as "active," "affectionate," "cuddly," "easygoing" and "even tempered." They had no eating or sleeping habits that were distressing to those who took care of them.

The pediatricians and psychologists who examined the resilient children at 20 months noted their alertness and responsiveness, their vigorous play and their tendency to seek out novel experiences and to ask for help when they needed it. When they entered elementary school, their classroom teachers observed their ability to concentrate on their assignments and noted their problem-solving and reading skills. Although they were not particularly gifted, these children used whatever talents they had effectively. Usually they had a special hobby they could share with a friend. These interests were not narrowly sex-typed; we found that girls and boys alike excelled at such activities as fishing, swimming, horseback riding and hula dancing.

We could also identify environmental factors that contributed to these children's ability to withstand stress. The resilient youngsters tended to come from families having four or fewer children, with a space of two years or more between themselves and the next sibling. In spite of poverty, family discord or parental mental illness, they had the opportunity to establish a close bond with at least one caretaker from whom they received positive attention during the first years of life.

The nurturing might come from substitute parents within the family (such as grandparents, older siblings, aunts or uncles) or from the ranks of regular baby-sitters. As the resilient children grew older they seemed to be particularly adept at recruiting such surrogate parents when a biological parent was unavailable (as in the case of an absent father) or incapacitated (as in the case of a mentally ill mother who was frequently hospitalized).

Maternal employment and the need to take care of younger siblings apparently contributed to the pronounced autonomy and sense of responsibility noted among the resilient girls, particularly in households where the father had died or was permanently absent because of desertion or divorce. Resilient boys, on the other hand, were often first-born sons who did not have to share their parents' attention with many additional children in the household. They also had some male in the family who could serve as a role model (if not the father, then a grandfather or an uncle). Structure and rules in the household and assigned chores were part of the daily routine for these boys during childhood and adolescence.

Resilient children also seemed to find a great deal of emotional support outside their immediate family. They tended to be well liked by their classmates and had at least one close friend, and usually several. They relied on an informal network of neighbors, peers and elders for counsel and support in times of crisis and transition. They seem to have made school a home away from home, a refuge from a disordered household. When we interviewed them at 18, many resilient youths mentioned a favorite teacher who had become a role model, friend and confidant and was particularly supportive at times when their own family was beset by discord or threatened with dissolution.

For others, emotional support came from a church group, a youth leader in the YMCA or YWCA or a favorite minister. Participation in extracurricular activities—such as 4-H, the school band or a cheerleading team which allowed them to be part of a cooperative enterprise—was also an important source of emotional support for those children who succeeded against the odds.

With the help of these support networks, the resilient children developed a sense of meaning in their lives and a belief that they could control their fate. Their experience in effectively coping with and mastering stressful life events built an attitude of hopefulness that contrasted starkly with the feelings of helplessness and futility that were expressed by their troubled peers.

In 1985, 12 years after the 1955 birth cohort had finished high school, we embarked on a search for the members of our study group. We managed to find 545 individuals—80 percent of the cohort—through parents or other relatives, friends, former classmates, local telephone books, city directories and circuit-court, voter-registration and motor-vehicle registration records and marriage certificates filed with the State Department of Health in Honolulu. Most of the young men and women still lived on Kauai, but 10 percent had moved to other islands and 10 percent lived on the mainland; 2 percent had gone abroad.

We found 62 of the 72 young people we had characterized as "resilient" at the age of 18. They had finished high school at the height of the energy crisis and joined the work force during the worst U.S. recession since the Great Depression. Yet these 30-year-old men and women seemed to be handling the demands of adulthood well. Three out of four (46 individuals) had received some college education and were satisfied with their performance in school. All but four worked full time, and three out of four said they were satisfied with their jobs.

Indeed, compared with their low-risk peers from the same cohort, a significantly higher proportion of high-risk resilient individuals described themselves as being happy with their current life circumstances (44 percent versus 10 percent). The resilient men and women did, however, report a significantly higher number of health problems than their peers in low-risk comparison groups (46 percent versus 15 percent). The men's problems seemed to be brought on by stress: back problems, dizziness and fainting spells, weight gain and ulcers. Women's health problems were largely related to pregnancy and childbirth. And although 82 percent of the women were married, only 48 percent of the men were. Those who were married had strong commitments to intimacy and sharing with their partners and children. Personal competence and determination, support from a spouse or mate, and a strong religious faith were the shared qualities that we found characterized resilient children as adults.

We were also pleasantly surprised to find that many high-risk children who had problems in their teens were able to rebound in their twenties and early thirties. We were able to contact 26 (90 percent) of the teen-age mothers, 56 (80 percent) of the individuals with mental-health problems and 74 (75 percent) of the former delinquents who were still alive at the age of 30.

Almost all the teen-age mothers we interviewed were better off in their early thirties than they had been at 18. About 60 percent (16 individuals) had gone on to additional schooling and about 90 percent (24 individuals) were employed. Of the delinquent youths, three-fourths (56 individuals) managed to avoid arrest on reaching adulthood. Only a minority (12 individuals) of the troubled youths were still in need of mental-health services in their early thirties. Among the critical turning points in the lives of these individuals were entry into military service, marriage, parenthood and active participation in a church group. In adulthood, as in their youth, most of these individuals relied on informal rather than formal sources of support: kith and kin rather than mental-health professionals and social-service agencies.

Our findings appear to provide a more hopeful perspective than can be had from reading the extensive literature on "problem" children that come to the attention of therapists, special educators and social-service agencies. Risk factors and stressful environments do not inevitably lead to poor adaptation. It seems clear that, at each stage in an individual's development from birth to maturity, there is a shifting balance between stressful events that heighten vulnerability and protective factors that enhance resilience.

As long as the balance between stressful life events and protective factors is favorable, successful adaptation is possible. When stressful events outweigh the protective factors, however, even the most resilient child can have problems. It may be possible to shift the balance from vulnerability to resilience through intervention, either by decreasing exposure to risk factors or stressful events or by increasing the number of protective factors and sources of support that are available.

It seems clear from our identification of risk and protective factors that some of the most critical determinants of outcome are present when a child is very young. And it is obvious that there are large individual differences among high-risk children in their responses to both negative and positive circumstances in their caregiving environment. The very fact of individual variation among children who live in adverse conditions suggests the need for greater assistance to some than to others.

If early intervention cannot be extended to every child at risk, priorities must be established for choosing who should receive help. Early-intervention programs need to focus on infants and young children who appear most vulnerable because they lack—permanently or temporarily—some of the essential social bonds that appear to buffer stress. Such children may be survivors of neonatal intensive care, hospitalized children who are separated from their families for extended periods of time, the young offspring of addicted or mentally ill parents, infants and toddlers whose mothers work full time and do not have access to stable child care, the babies of single or teen-age parents who have no other adult in the household and migrant and refugee children without permanent roots in a community.

Assessment and diagnosis, the initial steps in any early intervention, need to focus not only on the risk factors in the lives of the children but also on the protective factors. These include competencies and informal sources of support that already exist and that can be utilized to enlarge a young child's communication and problem-solving skills and to enhance his or her self-esteem. Our research on resilient children has shown that other people in a child's life—grandparents, older siblings, day-care providers or teachers—can play a supportive role if a parent is incapacitated or unavailable. In many situations it might make better sense and be less costly as well to strengthen such available informal ties to kin and community than it would to introduce additional layers of bureaucracy into delivery of services.

Finally, in order for any intervention program to be effective, a young child needs enough consistent nurturing to trust in its availability. The resilient children in our study had at least one person in their lives who accepted them unconditionally, regardless of temperamental idiosyncracies or physical or mental handicaps. All children can be helped to become more resilient if adults in their lives encourage their independence, teach them appropriate communication and self-help skills and model as well as reward acts of helpfulness and caring.

Thanks to the efforts of many people, several community-action and educational programs for high-risk children have been established on Kauai since our study began. Partly as a result of our findings, the legislature of the State of Hawaii has funded special mental-health teams to provide services for troubled children and youths. In addition the State Health Department established the Kauai Children's Services, a coordinated effort to provide services related to child development, disabilities, mental retardation and rehabilitation in a single facility.

The evaluation of such intervention programs can in turn illuminate the process by which a chain of protective factors is forged that affords vulnerable children an escape from adversity. The life stories of the resilient individuals on the Garden Island have taught us that competence, confidence and caring can flourish even under adverse circumstances if young children encounter people in their lives who provide them with a secure basis for the development of trust, autonomy and initiative.

FURTHER READING

Kauai's Children Come of Age. Emmy E. Werner and Ruth S. Smith. The University of Hawaii Press, 1977.

Vulnerable But Invincible: A Longitudinal Study of Resilient Children and Youth. Emmy E. Werner and Ruth S. Smith. McGraw-Hill Book Company, 1982.

Longitudinal Studies in Child Psychology and Psychiatry: Practical Lessons from Research Experience. Edited by A. R. Nichol. John Wiley & Sons, Inc., 1985.

High Risk Children in Young Adulthood: A Longitudinal Study from Birth to 32 Years. Emmy E. Werner in *American Journal of Orthopsychiatry*, Vol. 59, No. 1, pages 72–81; January, 1989.

QUESTIONS

1. What does it mean to say that children are at risk for unhealthy development?
2. Why is longitudinal research important for studying resilience in childhood?
3. What types of protective factors contribute to a favorable environment for child development?
4. How can one go about increasing a high-risk child's exposure to protective factors?
5. Does this article focus too much on the importance of nurture in development? Can the ill effects of early adverse events really be reversed?
6. In this research, did all the high-risk children who had problems in their teens end up with difficulties in adulthood? Why or why not?
7. What gender differences were found in this research, and how can they be explained?
8. What do these findings suggest about the long-term prognosis for children and adolescents who are identified as high risk?
9. Do you think that intervention programs for children or adolescents who are at risk are worthwhile? What ingredients should they have?
10. Could something about the culture on the island of Kauai have contributed to the results of this study, or do you think they would have been the same in any cultural setting?

4 Development and Learning

Jean Piaget

Jean Piaget was one of the twentieth century's most influential thinkers on the topic of child development. Although Piaget was not trained as a psychologist, his life's work was devoted to one important part of psychological development: the growth of intelligence, or cognitive development. A number of intellectual influences contributed to Piaget's theory of cognitive development; chief among them were biology and philosophy. From the field of biology, Piaget drew on ideas in evolutionary theory, such as organization and adaptation. From philosophy, Piaget relied mainly on the areas of logic, which is concerned with the formal principles of reasoning, and epistemology, which is concerned with the nature and grounds of knowledge. From these intellectual interests, Piaget carved out a new area of study called genetic epistemology, which focuses on the genesis, or origins, of logical thinking.

Piaget developed a theory of cognitive development in which he held that the child's thinking goes through four qualitatively distinct stages, beginning in infancy and concluding when biological maturity is reached in adolescence. For Piaget, cognitive development is the process by which the child's understanding of the world becomes increasingly adapted to the world. Like most psychologists who study cognitive development, Piaget considered learning a critical part of this process. However, for a child to learn, Piaget argued, he or she must be able to understand the information that is presented. In other words, the child needs to be at a stage of development that allows him or her to process this new information. Thus, Piaget believed that the child's current stage of development regulates the learning that can occur in a given situation.

In the following article, which is based on a lecture that he gave in the United States in 1961, Piaget describes his view of the relation between learning and development. Some of the concepts that Piaget discusses in this article you may find difficult. Be assured that many who read Piaget have difficulty understanding all his arguments. However, reading about his theory in his own words is worth the time and effort. Piaget's keen observational sense and creative examination of the developing mind are evident in his writings.

Before you read this article, several things are important to note. First, Piaget did not write like a modern psychologist. Recall that his intellectual influences were quite broad and included philosophy and biology in addition to psychology. Second, Piaget relied on forms of explanation that are rare in contemporary psychology, such as thought demonstrations. Third, Piaget introduced many complex terms, such as *operation* and *equilibration,* both of which are discussed in this article.

Piaget's thinking remains influential in developmental psychology today, although certain aspects of his theory have been challenged. He also proposed one of the few grand theories in the field of psychology in his attempt to explain the development of the human mind across domains of knowledge, historical periods, and cultural contexts.

In his opening remarks Piaget makes a distinction between development and learning—development being a spontaneous process tied to embryogenesis, learning being provoked by external situations. He proceeds to discuss the concept of an operation as an interiorized action linked to other operations in a structure. Four stages of development are enumerated—sensori-motor, pre-operational, concrete operations, and formal operations. Factors explaining the development of one structure of operations from another are discussed—

This article was reprinted with permission from R. E. Ripple (ed. with V.N. Rockcastle) from *Piaget Rediscovered,* 1964 and 1972, pp. 7–20.

*maturation, experience, social transmission, and equili-
bration. Equilibration is defended as the most fundamental factor. Commenting on the inadequacy of the
stimulus-response approach to understanding learning,
Piaget presents evidence negating the effectiveness of
external reinforcement in hastening the development of
operational structures. These operational structures can
be learned only if one bases the learning on simpler,
more elementary structures—only if there is a natural
relationship and development of structures. The learning of these structures is held to follow the same basic
laws as does their natural development, i.e., learning is
subordinated to development. Piaget concludes that the
fundamental relation involved in development and
learning is assimilation, not association.*

My dear colleagues, I am very concerned about what
to say to you, because I don't know if I shall accomplish the end that has been assigned to me. But I've
been told that the important thing is not what you
say, but the discussion which follows, and the answers to questions you are asked. So this morning I
shall simply give a general introduction of a few ideas
which seem to me to be important for the subject of
this conference.

First I would like to make clear the difference between two problems: the problem of *development* in
general, and the problem of *learning*. I think these
problems are very different, although some people do
not make this distinction.

The development of knowledge is a spontaneous
process, tied to the whole process of embryogenesis.
Embryogenesis concerns the development of the
body, but it concerns as well the development of the
nervous system, and the development of mental
functions. In the case of the development of knowledge in children, embryogenesis ends only in adulthood. It is a total developmental process which we
must resituate in its general biological and psychological context. In other words, development is a process which concerns the totality of the structures of
knowledge.

Learning presents the opposite case. In general,
learning is provoked by situations—provoked by a
psychological experimenter; or by a teacher, with respect to some didactic point; or by an external situation. It is provoked, in general, as opposed to
spontaneous. In addition, it is a limited process—
limited to a single problem, or to a single structure.

So I think that development explains learning,
and this opinion is contrary to the widely held opinion that development is a sum of discrete learning experiences. For some psychologists development is
reduced to a series of specific learned items, and development is thus the sum, the cumulation of this se-

ries of specific items. I think this is an atomistic view
which deforms the real state of things. In reality, development is the essential process and each element
of learning occurs as a function of total development,
rather than being an element which explains development. I shall begin, then, with a first part dealing
with development, and I shall talk about learning in
the second part.

To understand the development of knowledge, we
must start with an idea which seems central to me—
the idea of an *operation*. Knowledge is not a copy of
reality. To know an object, to know an event, is not
simply to look at it and make a mental copy, or image,
of it. To know an object is to act on it. To know is to
modify, to transform the object, and to understand
the process of this transformation, and as a consequence to understand the way the object is constructed. An operation is thus the essence of
knowledge; it is an interiorised action which modifies
the object of knowledge. For instance, an operation
would consist of joining objects in a class, to construct a classification. Or an operation would consist
of ordering, or putting things in a series. Or an operation would consist of counting, or of measuring. In
other words, it is a set of actions modifying the object, and enabling the knower to get at the structures
of the transformation.

An operation is an interiorised action. But in addition, it is a reversible action; that is, it can take place
in both directions, for instance, adding or subtracting,
joining or separating. So it is a particular type of action which makes up logical structures.

Above all, an operation is never isolated. It is always linked to other operations, and as a result it is
always a part of a total structure. For instance, a logical class does not exist in isolation; what exists is the
total structure of classification. An asymmetrical relation does not exist in isolation. Seriation is the natural, basic operational structure. A number does not
exist in isolation. What exists is the series of numbers,
which constitute a structure, an exceedingly rich
structure whose various properties have been revealed by mathematicians.

These operational structures are what seem to me
to constitute the basis of knowledge, the natural psychological reality, in terms of which we must understand the development of knowledge. And the central
problem of development is to understand the formation, elaboration, organization, and functioning of
these structures.

I should like to review the stages of development
of these structures, not in any detail, but simply as a
reminder. I shall distinguish four main stages. The
first is a sensory-motor, pre-verbal stage, lasting approximately the first 18 months of life. During this
stage is developed the practical knowledge which
constitutes the substructure of later representational

knowledge. An example is the construction of the schema of the permanent object. For an infant, during the first months, an object has no permanence. When it disappears from the perceptual field it no longer exists. No attempt is made to find it again. Later, the infant will try to find it, and he will find it by localizing it spatially. Consequently, along with the construction of the permanent object there comes the construction of practical, or sensory-motor, space. There is similarly the construction of temporal succession, and of elementary sensory-motor causality. In other words, there is a series of structures which are indispensable for the structures of later representational thought.

In a second stage, we have pre-operational representation—the beginnings of language, of the symbolic function, and therefore of thought, or representation. But at the level of representational thought, there must now be a reconstruction of all that was developed on the sensory-motor level. That is, the sensory-motor actions are not immediately translated into operations. In fact, during all this second period of pre-operational representations, there are as yet no operations as I defined this term a moment ago. Specifically, there is as yet no conservation which is the psychological criterion of the presence of reversible operations. For example, if we pour liquid from one glass to another of a different shape, the pre-operational child will think there is more in one than in the other. In the absence of operational reversibility, there is no conservation of quantity.

In a third stage the first operations appear, but I call these concrete operations because they operate on objects, and not yet on verbally expressed hypotheses. For example, there are the operations of classification, ordering, the construction of the idea of number, spatial and temporal operations, and all the fundamental operations of elementary logic of classes and relations, of elementary mathematics, of elementary geometry and even of elementary physics.

Finally, in the fourth stage, these operations are surpassed as the child reaches the level of what I call formal or hypothetic-deductive operations; that is, he can now reason on hypotheses, and not only on objects. He constructs new operations, operations of propositional logic, and not simply the operations of classes, relations, and numbers. He attains new structures which are on the one hand combinatorial, corresponding to what mathematicians call lattices; on the other hand, more complicated group structures. At the level of concrete operations, the operations apply within an immediate neighborhood: for instance, classification by successive inclusions. At the level of the combinatorial, however, the groups are much more mobile. These, then, are the four stages which we identify, whose formation we shall now attempt to explain.

What factors can be called upon to explain the development from one set of structures to another? It seems to me that there are four main factors: first of all, *maturation,* in the sense of Gesell, since this development is a continuation of the embryogenesis; second, the role of *experience* of the effects of the physical environment on the structures of intelligence; third, *social transmission* in the broad sense (linguistic transmission, education, etc.); and fourth, a factor which is too often neglected but one which seems to me fundamental and even the principal factor. I shall call this the factor of *equilibration* or if you prefer it, of self-regulation.

Let us start with the first factor, maturation. One might think that these stages are simply a reflection of an interior maturation of the nervous system, following the hypotheses of Gesell, for example. Well, maturation certainly does play an indispensable role and must not be ignored. It certainly takes part in every transformation that takes place during a child's development. However, this first factor is insufficient in itself. First of all, we know practically nothing about the maturation of the nervous system beyond the first months of the child's existence. We know a little bit about it during the first two years but we know very little following this time. But above all, maturation doesn't explain everything, because the average ages at which these stages appear (the average chronological ages) vary a great deal from one society to another. The ordering of these stages is constant and has been found in all the societies studied. It has been found in various countries where psychologists in universities have redone the experiments but it has also been found in African peoples for example, in the children of the Bushmen, and in Iran, both in the villages and in the cities. However, although the order of succession is constant, the chronological ages of these stages vary a great deal. For instance, the ages which we have found in Geneva are not necessarily the ages which you would find in the United States. In Iran, furthermore, in the city of Teheran, they found approximately the same ages as we found in Geneva, but there is a systematic delay of two years in the children in the country. Canadian psychologists who redid our experiments, Monique Laurendeau and Father Adrien Pinard, found once again about the same ages in Montreal. But when they redid the experiments in Martinique, they found a delay of four years in all the experiments and this in spite of the fact that the children in Martinique go to a school set up according to the French system and the French curriculum and attain at the end of this elementary school a certificate of higher primary education. There is then a delay of four years, that is, there are the same stages, but systematically delayed. So you see that these age variations show that maturation does not explain everything.

I shall go on now to the role played by experience. Experience of objects, of physical reality, is obviously a basic factor in the development of cognitive structures. But once again this factor does not explain everything. I can give two reasons for this. The first reason is that some of the concepts which appear at the beginning of the stage of concrete operations are such that I cannot see how they could be drawn from experience. As an example, let us take the conservation of the substance in the case of changing the shape of a ball of plasticene. We give this ball of plasticene to a child who changes its shape into a sausage form and we ask him if there is the same amount of matter, that is, the same amount of substance as there was before. We also ask him if it now has the same weight and thirdly if it now has the same volume. The volume is measured by the displacement of water when we put the ball or the sausage into a glass of water. The findings, which have been the same every time this experiment has been done, show us that first of all there is conservation of the amount of substance. At about eight years old a child will say, "There is the same amount of plasticene." Only later does the child assert that the weight is conserved and still later that the volume is conserved. So I would ask you where the idea of the conservation of substance can come from. What is a constant and invariant substance when it doesn't yet have a constant weight or a constant volume? Through perception you can get at the weight of the ball or the volume of the ball but perception cannot give you an idea of the amount of substance. No experiment, no experience, can show the child that there is the same amount of substance. He can weigh the ball and that would lead to the conservation of weight. He can immerse it in water and that would lead to the conservation of volume. But the notion of substance is attained before either weight or volume. This conservation of substance is simply a logical necessity. The child now understands that when there is a transformation something must be conserved because by reversing the transformation you can come back to the point of departure and once again have the ball. He knows that something is conserved but he doesn't know what. It is not yet the weight, it is not yet the volume; it is simply a logical form—a logical necessity. There, it seems to me, is an example of a progress in knowledge, a logical necessity for something to be conserved even though no experience can have led to this notion.

My second objection to the sufficiency of experience as an explanatory factor is that this notion of experience is a very equivocal one. There are, in fact, two kinds of experience which are psychologically very different and this difference is very important from the pedagogical point of view. It is because of the pedagocial that I emphasize this distinction. First of all, there is what I shall call physical experience, and secondly, what I shall call logical-mathematical experience.

Physical experience consists of acting upon objects and drawing some knowledge about the objects by abstraction from the objects. For example, to discover that this pipe is heavier than this watch, the child will weigh them both and find the difference in the objects themselves. This is experience in the usual sense of the term—in the sense used by empiricists. But there is a second type of experience which I shall call logical-mathematical experience where the knowledge is not drawn from the objects, but it is drawn by the actions effected upon the objects. This is not the same thing. When one acts upon objects, the objects are indeed there, but there is also the set of actions which modify the objects.

I shall give you an example of this type of experience. It is a nice example because we have verified it many times in small children under seven years of age, but it is also an example which one of my mathematician friends has related to me about his own childhood, and he dates his mathematical career from this experience. When he was four or five years old—I don't know exactly how old, but a small child—he was seated on the ground in his garden and he was counting pebbles. Now to count these pebbles he put them in a row and he counted them one, two, three, up to ten. Then he finished counting them and started to count them in the other direction. He began by the end and once again he found ten. He found this marvelous that there were ten in one direction and ten in the other direction. So he put them in a circle and counted them that way and found ten once again. Then he counted them in the other direction and found ten once more. So he put them in some other direction and found ten once more. So he put them in some other arrangement and kept counting them and kept finding ten. There was the discovery that he made.

Now what indeed did he discover? He did not discover a property of pebbles; he discovered a property of the action of ordering. The pebbles had no order. It was his action which introduced a linear order or a cyclical order, or any kind of an order. He discovered that the sum was independent of the order. The order was the action which he introduced among the pebbles. For the sum the same principle applied. The pebbles had no sum; they were simply in a pile. To make a sum, action was necessary—the operation of putting together and counting. He found that the sum was independent of the order, in other words, that the action of putting together is independent of the action of ordering. He discovered a property of actions and not a property of pebbles. You may say that it is in the nature of pebbles to let this be done to them and this is true. But it could have been drops of water, and drops of water would not have let this be done to them because two drops of water and two drops of water do not make four drops of water as you know very well. Drops of water then would not let this be done to them, we agree to that.

So it is not the physical property of pebbles which the experience uncovered. It is the properties of the actions carried out on the pebbles and this is quite another form of experience. It is the point of departure of mathematical deduction. The subsequent deduction will consist of interiorizing these actions and then of combining them without needing any pebbles. The mathematician no longer needs his pebbles. He can combine his operations simply with symbols and the point of departure of this mathematical deduction is logical-mathematical experience and this is not at all experience in the sense of the empiricists. It is the beginning of the coordination of actions, but this coordination of actions before the stage of operations needs to be supported by concrete material. Later, this coordination of actions leads to the logical-mathematical structures. I believe that logic is not a derivative of language. The source of logic is much more profound. It is the total coordination of actions, actions of joining things together, or ordering things, etc. This is what logical-mathematical experience is. It is an experience of the actions of the subject, and not an experience of objects themselves. It is an experience which is necessary before there can be operations. Once the operations have been attained this experience is no longer needed and the coordinations of actions can take place by themselves in the form of deduction and construction for abstract structures.

The third factor is social transmission—linguistic transmission or educational transmission. This factor, once again, is fundamental. I do not deny the role of any one of these factors; they all play a part. But this factor is insufficient because the child can receive valuable information via language or via education directed by an adult only if he is in a state where he can understand this information. That is, to receive the information he must have a structure which enables him to assimilate this information. This is why you cannot teach higher mathematics to a five-year-old. He does not yet have structures which enable him to understand.

I shall take a much simpler example, an example of linguistic transmission. As my very first work in the realm of child psychology, I spent a long time studying the relation between a part and a whole in concrete experience and in language. For example, I used Burt's test employing the sentence, "Some of my flowers are buttercups." The child knows that all buttercups are yellow, so there are three possible conclusions: the whole bouquet is yellow, or part of the bouquet is yellow, or none of the flowers in the bouquet is yellow. I found that up until nine years of age (and this was in Paris, so the children certainly did

understand the French language) they replied, "The whole bouquet is yellow or some of my flowers are yellow." Both of those mean the same thing. They did not understand the expression, "some *of* my flowers." They did not understand this *of* as a partitive genitive, as the inclusion of some flowers in my flowers. They understood some of my flowers to be my several flowers as if the several flowers and the flowers were confused as one and the same class. So there you have children who until nine years of age heard every day a linguistic structure which implied the inclusion of a sub-class in a class and yet did not understand this structure. It is only when they themselves are in firm possession of this logical structure, when they have constructed it for themselves according to the developmental laws which we shall discuss, that they succeed in understanding correctly the linguistic expression.

I come now to the fourth factor which is added to the three preceding ones but which seems to me to be the fundamental one. This is what I call the factor of equilibration. Since there are already three factors, they must somehow be equilibrated among themselves. That is one reason for bringing in the factor of equilibration. There is a second reason, however, which seems to me to be fundamental. It is that in the act of knowing, the subject is active, and consequently, faced with an external disturbance, he will react in order to compensate and consequently he will tend towards equilibrium. Equilibrium, defined by active compensation, leads to reversibility. Operational reversibility is a model of an equilibrated system where a transformation in one direction is compensated by a transformation in the other direction. Equilibration, as I understand it, is thus an active process. It's a process of self-regulation. I think that this self-regulation is a fundamental factor in development. I use this term in the sense in which it is used in cybernetics, that is, in the sense of processes with feedback and with feedforward, of processes which regulate themselves by a progressive compensation of systems. This process of equilibration takes the form of a succession of levels of equilibrium, of levels which have a certain probability which I shall call a sequential probability, that is, the probabilities are not established a priori. There is a sequence of levels. It is not possible to reach the second level unless equilibrium has been reached at the first level, and the equilibrium of the third level only becomes possible when the equilibrium of the second level has been reached, and so forth. That is, each level is determined as the most probable given that the preceding level has been reached. It is not the most probable at the beginning, but it is the most probable once the preceding level has been reached.

As an example, let us take the development of the idea of conservation in the transformation of the ball of plasticene into the sausage shape. Here you can discern four levels. The most probable at the beginning is for the child to think of only one dimension. Suppose that there is a probability of 0.8, for instance, that the child will focus on the length, and that the width has a probability of 0.2. This would mean that of ten children, eight will focus on the length alone without paying any attention to the width, and two will focus on the width without paying any attention to the length. They will focus only on one dimension or the other. Since the two dimensions are independent at this stage, focusing on both at once would have a probability of only 0.16. That is less than either one of the two. In other words, the most probable in the beginning is to focus only on one dimension and in fact the child will say, "It's longer, so there's more in the sausage." Once he has reached this first level, if you continue to elongate the sausage, there comes a moment when he will say, "No, now it's too thin, so there's less." Now he is thinking about the width, but he forgets the length, so you have come to a second level which becomes the most probable after the first level, but which is not the most probable at the point of departure. Once he has focused on the width, he will come back sooner or later to focus on the length. Here you will have a third level where he will oscillate between width and length and where he will discover that the two are related. When you elongate you make it more thin, and when you make it shorter, you make it thicker. He discovers that the two are solidly related and in discovering this relationship, he will start to think in terms of the transformation and not only in terms of the final configuration. Now he will say that when it gets longer it gets thinner, so it's the same thing. There is more of it in length but less of it in width. When you make it shorter it gets thicker; there's less in length and more in width, so there is compensation—compensation which defines equilibrium in the sense in which I defined it a moment ago. Consequently, you have operations and conservation. In other words, in the course of these developments you will always find a process of self-regulation which I call equilibration and which seems to me the fundamental factor in the acquisition of logical-mathematical knowledge.

I shall go on now to the second part of my lecture, that is, to deal with the topic of learning. Classically, learning is based on the stimulus-response schema. I think the stimulus-response schema, while I won't say it is false, is in any case entirely incapable of explaining cognitive learning. Why? Because when you think of a stimulus-response schema, you think usually that first of all there is a stimulus and then a response is set off by this stimulus. For my part, I am convinced that the response was there first, if I can express myself in this way. A stimulus is a stimulus only to the extent that it is significant and it becomes significant only to the extent that there is a structure which permits its assimilation, a structure which can integrate this stimulus but which at the same time sets off the response. In other words, I would propose that the stimulus-response schema be written in the circular form—in the form of a schema or of a structure which is not simply one way. I would propose that above all, between the stimulus and the response there is the organism, the organism and its structures. The stimulus is really a stimulus only when it is assimilated into a structure and it is this structure which sets off the response. Consequently, it is not an exaggeration to say that the response is there first, or if you wish at the beginning there is the structure. Of course we would want to understand how this structure comes to be. I tried to do this earlier by presenting a model of equilibration or self-regulation. Once there is a structure, the stimulus will set off a response, but only by the intermediary of this structure.

I should like to present some facts. We have facts in great number. I shall choose only one or two and I shall choose some facts which our colleague, Smedslund, has gathered. (Smedslund is currently at the Harvard Center for Cognitive Studies.) Smedslund arrived in Geneva a few years ago convinced (he had published this in one of his papers) that the development of the ideas of conservation could be indefinitely accelerated through learning of a stimulus-response type. I invited Smedslund to come to spend a year in Geneva to show us this, to show us that he could accelerate the development of operational conservation. I shall relate only one of his experiments.

During the year that he spent in Geneva he chose to work on the conservation of weight. The conservation of weight is, in fact, easy to study since there is a possible external reinforcement, that is, simply weighing the ball and the sausage on a balance. Then you can study the child's reactions to these external results. Smedslund studied the conservation of weight on the one hand, and on the other hand, he studied the transitivity of weights, that is, the transitivity of equalities if $A = B$ and $B = C$, then $A = C$, or the transitivity of the equalities if A is less than B, and B is less than C, then A is less than C.

As far as conservation is concerned, Smedslund succeeded very easily with five- and six-year-old children in getting them to generalize that weight is conserved when the ball is transformed into a different shape. The child sees the ball transformed into a sausage or into little pieces or into a pancake or into any other form, he weighs it, and he sees that it is always the same thing. He will affirm it will be the same thing, no matter what you do to it; it will come out to be the same weight. Thus Smedslund very easily achieved the conservation of weight by this sort of external reinforcement.

In contrast to this, however, the same method did not succeed in teaching transitivity. The children resisted the notion of transitivity. A child would predict correctly in certain cases but he would make his prediction as a possibility or a probability and not as a certainty. There was never this generalized certainty in the case of transitivity.

So there is the first example, which seems to me very instructive, because in this problem in the conservation of weight there are two aspects. There is the physical aspect and there is the logical-mathematical aspect. Note that Smedslund started his study by establishing that there was a correlation between conservation and transitivity. He began by making a statistical study on the relationships between the spontaneous responses to the questions about conservation and the spontaneous responses to the questions about transitivity, and he found a very significant correlation. But in the learning experiment, he obtained a learning of conservation and not of transitivity. Consequently, he was successful in obtaining learning of what I called earlier physical experience (this is not surprising; it is simply a question of noting facts about objects) but he was not successful in obtaining a learning in the construction of the logical structure. This doesn't surprise me either, since the logical structure is not the result of physical experience. It cannot be obtained by external reinforcement. The logical structure is reached only through internal equilibration, by self-regulation, and the external reinforcement of seeing the balance did not suffice to establish this logical structure of transitivity.

I could give many other comparable examples, but it seems to me useless to insist upon these negative examples. Now I should like to show that learning is possible in the case of these logical-mathematical structures, but on one condition—that is, that the structure which you want to teach to the subjects can be supported by simpler, more elementary, logical-mathematical structures. I shall give you an example. It is the example of the conservation of number in the case of one-to-one correspondence. If you give a child seven blue tokens and ask him to put down as many red tokens, there is a preoperational stage where he will put one red one opposite each blue one. But when you spread out the red ones, making them into a longer row, he will say to you, "Now, there are more red ones than there are blue ones."

Now how can we accelerate, if you want to accelerate, the acquisition of this conservation of number? Well, you can imagine an analogous structure but in a simpler, more elementary, situation. For example, with Mlle. Inhelder, we have been studying recently the notion of one-to-one correspondence by giving the child two glasses of the same shape and a big pile of beads. The child puts a bead into one glass with one hand and at the same time a bead into the other glass with the other hand. Time after time he repeats this action, a bead into one glass with one hand and at the same time a bead into the other glass with the other hand and he sees that there is always the same amount on each side. Then you hide one of the glasses. You cover it up. He no longer sees this glass but he continues to put one bead into it while putting at the same time one bead into the other glass which he can see. Then you ask him whether the equality has been conserved, whether there is still the same amount in one glass as in the other. Now you will find that very small children, about four years old, don't want to make a prediction. They will say, "So far, it has been the same amount, but now I don't know. I can't see anymore, so I don't know." They do not want to generalize. But the generalization is made from the age of about five and one-half years.

This is in contrast to the case of the red and blue tokens with one row spread out, where it isn't until seven or eight years of age that children will say there are the same number in the two rows. As one example of this generalization, I recall a little boy of five years and nine months who had been adding the beads to the glasses for a little while. Then we asked him whether, if he continued to do this all day and all night and all the next day, there would always be the same amount in the two glasses. The little boy gave this admirable reply, "Once you know, you know for always." In other words, this was recursive reasoning. So here the child does acquire the structure in this specific case. The number is a synthesis of class inclusion and ordering. This synthesis is being favored by the child's own actions. You have set up a situation where there is an iteration of one same action which continues and which is therefore ordered while at the same time being inclusive. You have, so to speak, a localized synthesis of inclusion and ordering which facilitates the construction of the idea of number in this specific case, and there you can find, in effect, an influence of this experience on the other experience. However, this influence is not immediate. We study the generalization from this recursive situation to the other situation where the tokens are laid on the table in rows, and it is not an immediate generalization but it is made possible through intermediaries. In other words, you can find some learning of this structure if you base the learning on simpler structures.

In this same area of the development of numerical structures, the psychologist Joachim Wohlwill, who spent a year at our Institute at Geneva, has also shown that this acquisition can be accelerated through introducing additive operations, which is what we introduced also in the experiment which I just described. Wohlwill introduced them in a different way but he too was able to obtain a certain learning effect. In other words, learning is possible if you base the more complex structure on simpler structures, that is, when there is a natural relationship and development of structures and not simply an external reinforcement.

Now I would like to take a few minutes to conclude what I was saying. My first conclusion is that learning of structures seems to obey the same laws as the natural development of these structures. In other words, learning is subordinated to development and not vice-versa as I said in the introduction. No doubt you will object that some investigators have succeeded in teaching operational structures. But, when I am faced with these facts, I always have three questions which I want to have answered before I am convinced.

The first question is, "Is this learning lasting? What remains two weeks or a month later?" If a structure develops spontaneously, once it has reached a state of equilibrium, it is lasting, it will continue throughout the child's entire life. When you achieve the learning by external reinforcement, is the result lasting or not and what are the conditions necessary for it to be lasting?

The second question is, "How much generalization is possible?" What makes learning interesting is the possibility of transfer of a generalization. When you have brought about some learning, you can always ask whether this is an isolated piece in the midst of the child's mental life, or if it is really a dynamic structure which can lead to generalizations.

Then there is the third question, "In the case of each learning experience what was the operational level of the subject before the experience and what more complex structures has this learning succeeded in achieving?" In other words, we must look at each specific learning experience from the point of view of the spontaneous operations which were present at the outset and the operational level which has been achieved after the learning experience.

My second conclusion is that the fundamental relation involved in all development and all learning is not the relation of association. In the stimulus-response schema, the relation between the response and the stimulus is understood to be one of association. In contrast to this, I think that the fundamental relation is one of assimilation. Assimilation is not the same as association. I shall define assimilation as the integration of any sort of reality into a structure, and it is this assimilation which seems to me fundamental in learning, and which seems to me the fundamental relation from the point of view of pedagogical or didactic applications. All of my remarks today represent the child and the learning subject as active. An operation is an activity. Learning is possible only when there is active assimilation. It is this activity on the part of the subject which seems to me underplayed in the stimulus-response schema. The presentation which I propose puts the emphasis on the idea of self-regulation, on assimilation. All the emphasis is placed on the activity of the subject himself, and I think that without this activity there is no possible didactic or pedagogy which significantly transforms the subject.

Finally, and this will be my last concluding remark, I would like to comment on an excellent publication by the psychologist Berlyne. Berlyne spent a year with us in Geneva during which he intended to translate our results on the development of operations into stimulus-response language, specifically into Hull's learning theory. Berlyne published in our series of studies of genetic epistemology a very good article on this comparison between the results of Geneva and Hull's theory. In the same volume, I published a commentary on Berlyne's results. Now the essence of Berlyne's results is this: our findings can very well be translated into Hullian language, but only on condition that two modifications are introduced. Berlyne himself found these modifications quite considerable, but they seemed to him to concern more the conceptualization than the Hullian theory itself. I'm not so sure about that. The two modifications are these. First of all, Berlyne wants to distinguish two sorts of responses in the S-R schema. First, responses in the ordinary, classical sense, which I shall call "copy responses," and secondly, what Berlyne called "transformation responses." Transformation responses consist of transforming one response of the first type into another response of the first type. These transformation responses are what I call operations, and you can see right away that this is a rather serious modification of Hull's conceptualization because here you are introducing an element of transformation and thus of assimilation and no longer the simple association of stimulus-response theory.

The second modification which Berlyne introduces into the stimulus-response language is the introduction of what he calls internal reinforcements. What are these internal reinforcements? They are what I call equilibration or self-regulation. The internal reinforcements are what enable the subject to eliminate contradictions, incompatibilities, and conflicts. All development is composed of momentary conflicts and incompatibilities which must be overcome to reach a higher level of equilibrium. Berlyne calls this elimination of incompatibilities internal reinforcements.

So you see that it is indeed a stimulus-response theory, if you will, but first you add operations and then you add equilibration. That's all we want!

Editor's note: A brief question and answer period followed Professor Piaget's presentation. The first question related to the fact that the eight-year-old child acquires conservation of substance prior to conservation of weight and volume. The question asked if this didn't contradict the order of emergence of the pre-operational and operational stages. Piaget's response follows:

The conservation of weight and the conservation of volume are not due only to experience. There is also involved a logical framework which is characterized by reversibility and the system of compensations. I am only saying that in the case of weight and volume, weight corresponds to a perception. There is an empirical contact. The same is true of volume. But in the case of substance, I don't see how there can be any perception of substance independent of weight or volume. The strange thing is that this notion of substance comes before the two other notions. Note that in the history of thought, we have the same thing. The first Greek physicists, the pre-Socratic philosophers, discovered conservation of substance independently of any experience. I do not believe this is contradictory with the theory of operations. This conservation of substance is simply the affirmation that something must be conserved. The children don't know specifically what is conserved. They know that since the sausage can become a ball again there must be something which is conserved, and saying "substance" is simply a way of translating this logical necessity for conservation. But this logical necessity results directly from the discovery of operations. I do not think that this is contradictory with the theory of development.

Editor's note: The second question was whether or not the development of stages in children's thinking could be accelerated by practice, training, and

exercise in perception and memory. Piaget's response follows:

I am not very sure that exercise of perception and memory would be sufficient. I think that we must distinguish within the cognitive function two very different aspects which I shall call the figurative aspect and the operative aspect. The figurative aspect deals with static configurations. In physical reality there are states, and in addition to these there are transformations which lead from one state to another. In cognitive functioning one has the figurative aspects—for example, perception, imitation, mental imagery, etc.

Secondly, there is the operative aspect, including operations and the actions which lead from one state to another. In children of the higher stages and in adults, the figurative aspects are subordinated to the operative aspects. Any given state is understood to be the result of some transformation and the point of departure for another transformation. But the pre-operational child does not understand transformations. He does not have the operations necessary to understand them so he puts all the emphasis on the static quality of the states. It is because of this, for example, that in the conservation experiments he simply compares the initial state and the final state without being concerned with the transformation.

In exercising perception and memory, I feel that you will reinforce the figurative aspect without touching the operative aspect. Consequently, I'm not sure that this will accelerate the development of cognitive structures. What needs to be reinforced is the operative aspect—not the analysis of states, but the understanding of transformations.

QUESTIONS

1. What does Piaget mean when he calls development a spontaneous process?
2. What is an operation, and why does Piaget claim that operations must exist in a structure, or ensemble, with other operations?
3. Piaget says that our knowledge of objects is not merely a mental copy of the object. What does he think our object knowledge is?
4. Does a child in the pre-operational stage use logical operations when he or she thinks?
5. What four factors explain development from one set of operational structures to another set?
6. Why is Piaget not concerned about age variations in the appearance of his stages across different cultures?
7. Piaget gives an example of a young child counting pebbles to explain logical-mathematical experience. Since the child was actually using pebbles during his learning, why did Piaget call this a logical-mathematical experience and not a physical experience?
8. What is equilibration, and what role does it play in cognitive development?
9. Piaget turns traditional learning theory on its head by stating that the response comes before the stimulus. What does he mean by this statement?
10. Piaget said he would be convinced that development results from learning if the answer to three questions proved to be yes. What were these three questions, and why was each important to Piaget in determining whether learning leads to development rather than vice versa?

5 Interaction Between Learning and Development

LEV S. VYGOTSKY

In the early part of the twentieth century, a new form of psychology developed in Russia. This psychology was different from that in the United States at the time because it emphasized (1) mental processes and (2) the contributions of society and culture to the development of mental processes. One of the main figures in this new theoretical approach was Lev S. Vygotsky. Although he died at the age of 37, Vygotsky was extremely creative and productive. His many and varied interests included the development of scientific reasoning, intellectual development in retarded children, and the role of language and culture in the development of thinking. He even studied how culture and social situations influence art and literature.

Underlying all these interests was a common question: How do social and cultural experiences become part of each individual's thinking? For Vygotsky, intelligence is a social product, and he strove to describe the development of intelligence from this vantage. He hypothesized that the development of thinking occurs in the everyday experiences that children have, particularly in their interactions with more experienced members of their cultural community. Through social interaction, adults pass on to children the practices, values, and goals of their culture. These interactions direct children's thinking toward the content and processes that are valued in their culture. In other words, social interaction helps organize the developing mind in ways that mesh with the needs and aspirations of the community at large.

The following article is reprinted from one of Vygotsky's books, *Mind in Society,* which was published in the United States posthumously. In it, Vygotsky describes one type of social interaction that he felt was the most likely to promote cognitive development—namely, interactions that occur within the child's zone of proximal (or potential) development. Vygotsky also discusses his views on the relation between learning and development. As you will see, Vygotsky's position on this topic is quite different from Piaget's: He argues that learning precedes development, not vice versa.

Vygotsky's theory and theories related to it, such as sociocultural approaches to development, are influential in research on cognitive development today. This influence stems largely from the fact that this approach is the first systematic attempt in modern psychological study to formalize a view of human development that takes into account the cultural and social experiences of intellectual growth. Given the powerful and pervasive effect that cultural and social experiences have on the development of the mind, many developmental psychologists think that this shift in emphasis is long overdue.

The problems encountered in the psychological analysis of teaching cannot be correctly resolved or even formulated without addressing the relation between learning and development in school-age children. Yet it is the most unclear of all the basic issues on which the application of child development theories to educational processes depends. Needless to say, the lack of theoretical clarity does not mean that the issue is removed altogether from current research efforts into learning; not one study can avoid this central theoretical issue. But the relation between learning and development remains methodologically

---

Reprinted by permission of the publisher from *Mind in Society: The development of higher psychological processes* by L. S. Vygotsky, edited by Michael Cole, Vera John-Steiner, Sylvia Scribner, and Ellen Souberman, pp. 71–91, Cambridge, MA: Harvard University Press. Copyright 1978 by the President and Fellows of Harvard College.

unclear because concrete research studies have embodied theoretically vague, critically unevaluated, and sometimes internally contradictory postulates, premises, and peculiar solutions to the problem of this fundamental relationship; and these, of course, result in a variety of errors.

Essentially, all current conceptions of the relation between development and learning in children can be reduced to three major theoretical positions.

The first centers on the assumption that processes of child development are independent of learning. Learning is considered a purely external process that is not actively involved in development. It merely utilizes the achievements of development rather than providing an impetus for modifying its course.

In experimental investigations of the development of thinking in school children, it has been assumed that processes such as deduction and understanding, evolution of notions about the world, interpretation of physical causality, and mastery of logical forms of thought and abstract logic all occur by themselves, without any influence from school learning. An example of such a theory is Piaget's extremely complex and interesting theoretical principles, which also shape the experimental methodology he employs. The questions Piaget uses in the course of his "clinical conversations" with children clearly illustrate his approach. When a five-year-old is asked "why doesn't the sun fall?" it is assumed that the child has neither a ready answer for such a question nor the general capabilities for generating one. The point of asking questions that are so far beyond the reach of the child's intellectual skills is to eliminate the influence of previous experience and knowledge. The experimenter seeks to obtain the tendencies of children's thinking in "pure" form entirely independent of learning.[1]

Similarly, the classics of psychological literature, such as the works by Binet and others, assume that development is always a prerequisite for learning and that if a child's mental functions (intellectual operations) have not matured to the extent that he is capable of learning a particular subject, then no instruction will prove useful. They especially feared premature instruction, the teaching of a subject before the child was ready for it. All effort was concentrated on finding the lower threshold of learning ability, the age at which a particular kind of learning first becomes possible.

Because this approach is based on the premise that learning trails behind development, that development always outruns learning, it precludes the notion that learning may play a role in the course of the development or maturation of those functions activated in the course of learning. Development or maturation is viewed as a precondition of learning but never the result of it. To summarize this position:

learning forms a superstructure over development, leaving the latter essentially unaltered.

The second major theoretical position is that learning is development. This identity is the essence of a group of theories that are quite diverse in origin.

One such theory is based on the concept of reflex, an essentially old notion that has been extensively revived recently. Whether reading, writing, or arithmetic is being considered, development is viewed as the mastery of conditioned reflexes; that is, the process of learning is completely and inseparably blended with the process of development. This notion was elaborated by James, who reduced the learning process to habit formation and identified the learning process with development.

Reflex theories have at least one thing in common with theories such as Piaget's: in both, development is conceived of as the elaboration and substitution of innate responses. As James expressed it, "Education, in short, cannot be better described than by calling it the organization of acquired habits of conduct and tendencies to behavior."[2] Development itself is reduced primarily to the accumulation of all possible responses. Any acquired response is considered either a more complex form of or a substitute for the innate response.

But despite the similarity between the first and second theoretical positions, there is a major difference in their assumptions about the temporal relationship between learning and developmental processes. Theorists who hold the first view assert that developmental cycles precede learning cycles; maturation precedes learning and instruction must lag behind mental growth. For the second group of theorists, both processes occur simultaneously; learning and development coincide at all points in the same way that two identical geometrical figures coincide when superimposed.

The third theoretical position on the relation between learning and development attempts to overcome the extremes of the other two by simply combining them. A clear example of this approach is Koffka's theory, in which development is based on two inherently different but related processes, each of which influences the other.[3] On the one hand is maturation, which depends directly on the development of the nervous system; on the other hand is learning, which itself is also a developmental process.

Three aspects of this theory are new. First, as we already noted, is the combination of two seemingly opposite viewpoints, each of which has been encountered separately in the history of science. The very fact that these two viewpoints can be combined into one theory indicates that they are not opposing and mutually exclusive but have something essential in common. Also new is the idea that the two processes that make up development are mutually dependent and interactive. Of course, the nature of the inter-action is left virtually unexplored in Koffka's work, which is limited solely to very general remarks regarding the relation between these two processes. It is clear that for Koffka the process of maturation prepares and makes possible a specific process of learning. The learning process then stimulates and pushes forward the maturation process. The third and most important new aspect of this theory is the expanded role it ascribes to learning in child development. This emphasis leads us directly to an old pedagogical problem, that of formal discipline and the problem of transfer.

Pedagogical movements that have emphasized formal discipline and urged the teaching of classical languages, ancient civilizations, and mathematics have assumed that regardless of the irrelevance of these particular subjects for daily living, they were of the greatest value for the pupil's mental development. A variety of studies have called into question the soundness of this idea. It has been shown that learning in one area has very little influence on overall development. For example, reflex theorists Woodworth and Thorndike found that adults who, after special exercises, had achieved considerable success in determining the length of short lines, had made virtually no progress in their ability to determine the length of long lines. These same adults were successfully trained to estimate the size of a given two-dimensional figure, but this training did not make them successful in estimating the size of a series of other two-dimensional figures of various sizes and shapes.

According to Thorndike, theoreticians in psychology and education believe that every particular response acquisition directly enhances overall ability in equal measure.[4] Teachers believed and acted on the basis of the theory that the mind is a complex of abilities—powers of observation, attention, memory, thinking, and so forth—and that any improvement in any specific ability results in a general improvement in all abilities. According to this theory, if the student increased the attention he paid to Latin grammar, he would increase his abilities to focus attention on any task. The words "accuracy," "quick-wittedness," "ability to reason," "memory," "power of observation," "attention," "concentration," and so forth are said to denote actual fundamental capabilities that vary in accordance with the material with which they operate; these basic abilities are substantially modified by studying particular subjects, and they retain these modifications when they turn to other areas. Therefore, if someone learns to do any single thing well, he will also be able to do other entirely unrelated things well as a result of some secret connection. It is assumed that mental capabilities function independently of the material with which they operate, and that the development of one ability entails the development of others.

Thorndike himself opposed this point of view. Through a variety of studies he showed that particular forms of activity, such as spelling, are dependent on the mastery of specific skills and material necessary for the performance of that particular task. The development of one particular capability seldom means the development of others. Thorndike argued that specialization of abilities is even greater than superficial observation may indicate. For example, if, out of a hundred individuals we choose ten who display the ability to detect spelling errors or to measure lengths, it is unlikely that these ten will display better abilities regarding, for example, the estimation of the weight of objects. In the same way, speed and accuracy in adding numbers are entirely unrelated to speed and accuracy in being able to think up antonyms.

This research shows that the mind is not a complex network of general capabilities such as observation, attention, memory, judgment, and so forth, but a set of specific capabilities, each of which is, to some extent, independent of the others and is developed independently. Learning is more than the acquisition of the ability to think; it is the acquisition of many specialized abilities for thinking about a variety of things. Learning does not alter our overall ability to focus attention but rather develops various abilities to focus attention on a variety of things. According to this view, special training affects overall development only when its elements, material, and processes are similar across specific domains; habit governs us. This leads to the conclusion that because each activity depends on the material with which it operates, the development of consciousness is the development of a set of particular, independent capabilities or of a set of particular habits. Improvement of one function of consciousness or one aspect of its activity can affect the development of another only to the extent that there are elements common to both functions or activities.

Developmental theorists such as Koffka and the Gestalt School—who hold to the third theoretical position outlined earlier—oppose Thorndike's point of view. They assert that the influence of learning is never specific. From their study of structural principles, they argue that the learning process can never be reduced simply to the formation of skills but embodies an intellectual order that makes it possible to transfer general principles discovered in solving one task to a variety of other tasks. From this point of view, the child, while learning a particular operation, acquires the ability to create structures of a certain type, regardless of the diverse materials with which she is working and regardless of the particular elements involved. Thus, Koffka does not conceive of learning as limited to a process of habit and skill acquisition. The relationship he posits between learning and development is not that of an identity but of a more complex relationship. According to Thorndike, learning and development coincide at all points, but for Koffka, development is always a larger set than learning. Schematically, the relationship between the two processes could be depicted by two concentric circles, the smaller symbolizing the learning process and the larger the developmental process evoked by learning.

Once a child has learned to perform an operation, he thus assimilates some structural principle whose sphere of application is other than just the operations of the type on whose basis the principle was assimilated. Consequently, in making one step in learning, a child makes two steps in development, that is, learning and development do not coincide. This concept is the essential aspect of the third group of theories we have discussed.

ZONE OF PROXIMAL DEVELOPMENT: A NEW APPROACH

Although we reject all three theoretical positions discussed above, analyzing them leads us to a more adequate view of the relation between learning and development. The question to be framed in arriving at a solution to this problem is complex. It consists of two separate issues: first, the general relation between learning and development; and second, the specific features of this relationship when children reach school age.

That children's learning begins long before they attend school is the starting point of this discussion. Any learning a child encounters in school always has a previous history. For example, children begin to study arithmetic in school, but long beforehand they have had some experience with quantity—they have had to deal with operations of division, addition, subtraction, and determination of size. Consequently, children have their own preschool arithmetic, which only myopic psychologists could ignore.

It goes without saying that learning as it occurs in the preschool years differs markedly from school learning, which is concerned with the assimilation of the fundamentals of scientific knowledge. But even when, in the period of her first questions, a child assimilates the names of objects in her environment, she is learning. Indeed, can it be doubted that children learn speech from adults; or that, through asking questions and giving answers, children acquire a variety of information; or that, through imitating adults and through being instructed about how to act, children develop an entire repository of skills? Learning and development are interrelated from the child's very first day of life.

Koffka, attempting to clarify the laws of child learning and their relation to mental development, concentrates his attention on the simplest learning processes, those that occur in the preschool years. His error is that, while seeing a similarity between preschool and school learning, he fails to discern the difference—he does not see the specifically new elements that school learning introduces. He and others assume that the difference between preschool and school learning consists of non-systematic learning in one case and systematic learning in the other. But "systematicness" is not the only issue; there is also the fact that school learning introduces something fundamentally new into the child's development. In order to elaborate the dimensions of school learning, we will describe a new and exceptionally important concept without which the issue cannot be resolved: the zone of proximal development.

A well known and empirically established fact is that learning should be matched in some manner with the child's developmental level. For example, it has been established that the teaching of reading, writing, and arithmetic should be initiated at a specific age level. Only recently, however, has attention been directed to the fact that we cannot limit ourselves merely to determining developmental levels if we wish to discover the actual relations of the developmental process to learning capabilities. We must determine at least two developmental levels.

The first level can be called the *actual developmental level*, that is, the level of development of a child's mental functions that has been established as a result of certain already completed developmental cycles. When we determine a child's mental age by using tests, we are almost always dealing with the actual developmental level. In studies of children's mental development it is generally assumed that only those things that children can do on their own are indicative of mental abilities. We give children a battery of tests or a variety of tasks of varying degrees of difficulty, and we judge the extent of their mental development on the basis of how they solve them and at what level of difficulty. On the other hand, if we offer leading questions or show how the problem is to be solved and the child then solves it, or if the teacher initiates the solution and the child completes it or solves it in collaboration with other children—in short, if the child barely misses an independent solution of the problem—the solution is not regarded as indicative of his mental development. This "truth" was familiar and reinforced by common sense. Over a decade even the profoundest thinkers never questioned the assumption; they never entertained the notion that what children can do with the assistance of others might be in some sense even more indicative of their mental development than what they can do alone.

Let us take a simple example. Suppose I investigate two children upon entrance into school, both of whom are ten years old chronologically and eight years old in terms of mental development. Can I say that they are the same age mentally? Of course. What does this mean? It means that they can independently deal with tasks up to the degree of difficulty that has been standardized for the eight-year-old level. If I stop at this point, people would imagine that the subsequent course of mental development and of school learning for these children will be the same, because it depends on their intellect. Of course, there may be other factors, for example, if one child was sick for half a year while the other was never absent from school; but generally speaking, the fate of these children should be the same. Now imagine that I do not terminate my study at this point, but only begin it. These children seem to be capable of handling problems up to an eight-year-old's level, but not beyond that. Suppose that I show them various ways of dealing with the problem. Different experimenters might employ different modes of demonstration in different cases: some might run through an entire demonstration and ask the children to repeat it, others might initiate the solution and ask the child to finish it, or offer leading questions. In short, in some way or another I propose that the children solve the problem with my assistance. Under these circumstances it turns out that the first child can deal with problems up to a twelve-year-old's level, the second up to a nine-year-old's. Now, are these children mentally the same?

When it was first shown that the capability of children with equal levels of mental development to learn under a teacher's guidance varied to a high degree, it became apparent that those children were not mentally the same age and that the subsequent course of their learning would obviously be different. This difference between twelve and eight, or between nine and eight, is what we call *the zone of proximal development. It is the distance between the actual developmental level as determined by independent problem solving and the level of potential development as determined through problem solving under adult guidance or in collaboration with more capable peers.*

If we naively ask what the actual developmental level is, or, to put it more simply, what more independent problem solving reveals, the most common answer would be that a child's actual developmental level defines functions that have already matured, that is, the end products of development. If a child can do such-and-such independently, it means that the functions for such-and-such have matured in her. What, then, is defined by the zone of proximal development, as determined through problems that children cannot solve independently but only with assistance? The zone of proximal development defines those functions that have not yet matured but are in the process of maturation, functions that will mature tomorrow but are currently in an embryonic state. These functions could be termed the "buds" or "flowers" of development rather than the "fruits" of development. The actual developmental level characterizes mental development retrospectively, while the zone of proximal development characterizes mental development prospectively.

The zone of proximal development furnishes psychologists and educators with a tool through which the internal course of development can be understood. By using this method we can take account of not only the cycles and maturation processes that have already been completed but also those processes that are currently in a state of formation, that are just beginning to mature and develop. Thus, the zone of proximal development permits us to delineate the child's immediate future and his dynamic developmental state, allowing not only for what already has been achieved developmentally but also for what is in the course of maturing. The two children in our example displayed the same mental age from the viewpoint of developmental cycles already completed, but the developmental dynamics of the two were entirely different. The state of a child's mental development can be determined only by clarifying its two levels: the actual developmental level and the zone of proximal development.

I will discuss one study of preschool children to demonstrate that what is in the zone of proximal development today will be the actual developmental level tomorrow—that is, what a child can do with assistance today she will be able to do by herself tomorrow.

The American researcher Dorothea McCarthy showed that among children between the ages of three and five there are two groups of functions: those the children already possess, and those they can perform under guidance, in groups, and in collaboration with one another but which they have not mastered independently. McCarthy's study demonstrated that this second group of functions is at the actual developmental level of five-to-seven-year-olds. What her subjects could do only under guidance, in collaboration, and in groups at the age of three-to-five years they could do independently when they reached the age of five-to-seven years.[5] Thus, if we were to determine only mental age—that is, only functions that have matured—we would have but a summary of completed development while if we determine the maturing functions, we can predict what will happen to these children between five and seven, provided the same developmental conditions are maintained. The zone of proximal development can become a powerful concept in developmental research, one that can markedly enhance the effectiveness and utility of the application of diagnostics of mental development to educational problems.

A full understanding of the concept of the zone of proximal development must result in reevaluation of the role of imitation in learning. An unshakable tenet of classical psychology is that only the independent activity of children, not their imitative activity, indicates their level of mental development. This view is expressed in all current testing systems. In evaluating mental development, consideration is given to only those solutions to test problems which the child reaches without the assistance of others, without demonstrations, and without leading questions. Imitation and learning are thought of as purely mechanical processes. But recently psychologists have shown that a person can imitate only that which is within her developmental level. For example, if a child is having difficulty with a problem in arithmetic and the teacher solves it on the blackboard, the child may grasp the solution in an instant. But if the teacher were to solve a problem in higher mathematics, the child would not be able to understand the solution no matter how many times she imitated it.

Animal psychologists, and in particular Köhler, have dealt with this question of imitation quite well.[6] Köhler's experiments sought to determine whether primates are capable of graphic thought. The principal question was whether primates solved problems independently or whether they merely imitated solutions they had seen performed earlier, for example, watching other animals or humans use sticks and other tools and then imitating them. Köhler's special experiments, designed to determine what primates could imitate, reveal that primates can use imitation to solve only those problems that are of the same degree of difficulty as those they can solve alone. However, Köhler failed to take account of an important fact, namely, that primates cannot be taught (in the human sense of the word) through imitation, nor can their intellect be developed, because they have no zone of proximal development. A primate can learn a great deal through training by using its mechanical and mental skills, but it cannot be made more intelligent, that is, it cannot be taught to solve a variety of more advanced problems independently. For this reason animals are incapable of learning in the human sense of the term; *human learning presupposes a specific social nature and a process by which children grow into the intellectual life of those around them.*

Children can imitate a variety of actions that go well beyond the limits of their own capabilities. Using imitation, children are capable of doing much more in collective activity or under the guidance of adults. This fact, which seems to be of little significance in itself, is of fundamental importance in that it demands a radical alteration of the entire doctrine concerning the relation between learning and development in children. One direct consequence is a change in conclusions that may be drawn from diagnostic tests of development.

Formerly, it was believed that by using tests, we determine the mental development level with which education should reckon and whose limits it should not exceed. This procedure oriented learning toward yesterday's development, toward developmental stages already completed. The error of this view was discovered earlier in practice than in theory. It is demonstrated most clearly in the teaching of mentally retarded children. Studies have established that mentally retarded children are not very capable of abstract thinking. From this the pedagogy of the special school drew the seemingly correct conclusion that all teaching of such children should be based on the use of concrete, look-and-do methods. And yet a considerable amount of experience with this method resulted in profound disillusionment. It turned out that a teaching system based solely on concreteness—one that eliminated from teaching everything associated with abstract thinking—not only failed to help retarded children overcome their innate handicaps but also reinforced their handicaps by accustoming children exclusively to concrete thinking and thus suppressing the rudiments of any abstract thought that such children still have. Precisely because retarded children, when left to themselves, will never achieve well-elaborated forms of abstract thought, the school should make every effort to push them in that direction and to develop in them what is intrinsically lacking in their own development. In the current practices of special schools for retarded children, we can observe a beneficial shift away from this concept of concreteness, one that restores look-and-do methods to their proper role. Concreteness is now seen as necessary and unavoidable only as a stepping stone for developing abstract thinking—as a means, not as an end in itself.

Similarly, in normal children, learning which is oriented toward developmental levels that have already been reached is ineffective from the viewpoint of a child's overall development. It does not aim for a new stage of the developmental process but rather lags behind this process. Thus, the notion of a zone of proximal development enables us to propound a new formula, namely that the only "good learning" is that which is in advance of development.

The acquisition of language can provide a paradigm for the entire problem of the relation between learning and development. Language arises initially as a means of communication between the child and the people in his environment. Only subsequently, upon conversion to internal speech, does it come to organize the child's thought, that is, become an internal mental function. Piaget and others have shown that reasoning occurs in a children's group as an argument intended to prove one's own point of view before it occurs as an internal activity whose distinctive feature is that the child begins to perceive and check the basis of his thoughts. Such observations prompted Piaget to conclude that communication produces the need for checking and confirming thoughts, a process that is characteristic of adult thought.[7] In the same way that internal speech and reflective thought arise from the interactions between the child and persons in her environment, these interactions provide the source of development of a child's voluntary behavior. Piaget has shown that cooperation provides the basis for the development of a child's moral judgment. Earlier research established that a child first becomes able to subordinate her behavior to rules in group play and only later does voluntary self-regulation of behavior arise as an internal function.

These individual examples illustrate a general developmental law for the higher mental functions that we feel can be applied in its entirety to children's learning processes. We propose that an essential feature of learning is that it creates the zone of proximal development; that is, learning awakens a variety of internal developmental processes that are able to operate only when the child is interacting with people in his environment and in cooperation with his peers. Once these processes are internalized, they become part of the child's independent developmental achievement.

From this point of view, learning is not development; however, properly organized learning results in mental development and sets in motion a variety of developmental processes that would be impossible apart from learning. Thus, learning is a necessary and universal aspect of the process of developing culturally organized, specifically human, psychological functions.

To summarize, the most essential feature of our hypothesis is the notion that developmental processes do not coincide with learning processes. Rather, the developmental process lags behind the learning process; this sequence then results in zones of proximal development. Our analysis alters the traditional view that at the moment a child assimilates the meaning of a word, or masters an operation such as addition or written language, her developmental processes are basically completed. In fact, they have only just begun at that moment. The major consequence of analyzing the educational process in this manner is to show that the initial mastery of, for example, the four arithmetic operations provides the basis for the subsequent development of a variety of highly complex internal processes in children's thinking.

Our hypothesis establishes the unity but not the identity of learning processes and internal developmental processes. It presupposes that the one is converted into the other. Therefore, it becomes an important concern of psychological research to show how external knowledge and abilities in children become internalized.

Any investigation explores some sphere of reality. An aim of the psychological analysis of development is to describe the internal relations of the intellectual processes awakened by school learning. In this respect, such analysis will be directed inward and is analogous to the use of x-rays. If successful, it should reveal to the teacher how developmental processes stimulated by the course of school learning are carried through inside the head of each individual child. The revelation of this internal, subterranean developmental network of school subjects is a task of primary importance for psychological and educational analysis.

A second essential feature of our hypothesis is the notion that, although learning is directly related to the course of child development, the two are never accomplished in equal measure or in parallel. Development in children never follows school learning the way a shadow follows the object that casts it. In actuality, there are highly complex dynamic relations between developmental and learning processes that cannot be encompassed by an unchanging hypothetical formulation.

Each school subject has its own specific relation to the course of child development, a relation that varies as the child goes from one stage to another. This leads us directly to a reexamination of the problem of formal discipline, that is, to the significance of each particular subject from the viewpoint of overall mental development. Clearly, the problem cannot be solved by using any one formula; extensive and highly diverse concrete research based on the concept of the zone of proximal development is necessary to resolve the issue.

NOTES

1. J. Piaget, *The Language and Thought of the Child* (New York: Meridian Books, 1955).

2. William James, *Talks to Teachers* (New York: Norton, 1958), pp. 36–37.

3. Koffka, *The Growth of the Mind* (London: Routledge and Kegan Paul, 1924).

4. E. L. Thorndike, *The Psychology of Learning* (New York: Teachers College Press, 1914).

5. Dorothea McCarthy, *The Language Development of the Pre-school Child* (Minneapolis: University of Minnesota Press, 1930).

6. W. Köhler, *The Mentality of Apes* (New York: Harcourt, Brace, 1925).

7. Piaget, *Language and Thought.*

QUESTIONS

1. According to Vygotsky, are learning and development the same thing? How are they alike? How are they different?
2. Why was Vygotsky dissatisfied with Piaget's view of cognitive development?
3. What is the zone of proximal development?
4. What does interaction in the zone of proximal development contribute to cognitive development?
5. According to Vygotsky, can children imitate any action they observe, or are they limited in what they can imitate? Why did this question interest Vygotsky?
6. If you were to design a new IQ test based on Vygotsky's idea of the zone of proximal development, what would it be like? How might a child's score on this test be interpreted?
7. How do social and cultural experiences become part of each individual's way of thinking?
8. Vygotsky worked as a psychologist during the Russian Revolution of the early 1900s, when socialism took hold in that country. Do you think that this circumstance had any influence on his ideas about the development of intellectual functioning?
9. Think of a skill you have today that you learned as a child, and then think about how you learned it. Did other people help you in this learning? Was the way you learned this skill similar to the process described in Vygotsky's discussion of the zone of proximal development? Explain.
10. If Vygotsky's ideas were incorporated into public school curricula, how would current educational practices change?

PART I

In the Beginning

The articles in this section concentrate on early development, with particular attention to biological contributions and the dynamic interplay of biology and experience in the perinatal period.

Over the last few decades there has been dramatic change in our understanding of biological contributions to psychological development. Much of this change has been based on progress in two areas of research, neuroscience and genetics. Neuroscience has contributed to developmental study by producing a better understanding of early brain development, which is discussed in the article by Neal Halfon, Ericka Shulman, and Miles Hochstein. The second biological article in this section, by Bernard Brown, discusses research on the human genome. This research has redefined the way that developmental psychologists conceptualize the fundamental issue of nature versus nurture.

In addition to progress in these two biologically based areas of developmental research, there has been significant change in our understanding of the competencies and character of the newborn. The article by Anthony J. DeCasper and William P. Fifer, which describes research on the auditory competence of newborns that was conducted in the 1970s, is a classic in this area of study. Finally, the article by Barry S. Hewlett and his colleagues, on the social and cultural organization of experience in infancy, and the article by Jerome Kagan, on temperament and early behavioral development, describe how, very early in childhood, the rich biological template of the human organism combines with social experiences to steer the individual's development.

Together, these articles underscore the importance of taking an interactional view of the study of human development. That is, the contributions of the biological and the social aspects of growth should be considered as mutually defining and inseparable.

6 Brain Development in Early Childhood

NEAL HALFON • ERICKA SHULMAN • MILES HOCHSTEIN

The human brain goes through enormous changes over the course of childhood. These changes are primarily due to two characteristics of the brain at the time of birth: its immaturity and its responsiveness to experiential input. The brain's immaturity at birth means that there is much room for growth. Its responsiveness means that much of its development will reflect the experiences that occur as it grows. Thus, brain development results from the interaction of the maturing neural system and the unique experiences of an individual's childhood.

Scientists who study brain development are interested in how experiences that modify the brain early in life affect a person's functioning later in childhood and into adulthood. Recent research in neuroscience, a relatively new scientific discipline that combines biology and psychology and focuses on brain development and functioning, has revealed a number of important, sometimes even amazing, aspects of this process. Neuroscientists have also discovered that describing how experience relates to brain development is more complex than anyone ever realized.

In the following article, a team of researchers, consisting of a physician, a policy analyst, and a developmental psychologist, describes four general findings from studies of brain development. These findings pertain to the rapid pace of brain development, the responsiveness of the brain to experience, the fact that the timing of experiences is more important for some regions of the brain than for others, and the effects that relationships with other people, especially emotionally significant ones, have on brain development. Taken individually, each of these findings raises interesting questions and ideas about early brain development. Taken together, they convey the profound impact that experience has on this development. Half a century ago, when the eminent psychologist Donald Hebb was asked how much nature and how much nurture contribute to human behavior, he answered that human behavior is 100 percent due to nature and 100 percent due to nurture. This article will help you understand what he meant.

Beyond describing scientific wonders, the article offers a brief but pertinent discussion about their implications. As scientists discover how the developing brain coordinates with experience, they also learn about the consequences of this interactional process for children's health and well-being. Specifically, they learn which experiences (or protective factors) promote healthy outcomes and which experiences (or risk factors) jeopardize them. Armed with this information, practitioners, educators, and parents may be better able to prevent problems in children's brain development.

Parents and policymakers have become increasingly interested in the role of early childhood experiences in promoting emotional and intellectual well-being. Much of this interest has been sparked by popular-press articles claiming that recent advances in brain research give guidance on everything from buying toys to choosing a preschool–sometimes spreading inaccurate information about the practical conclusions that can be drawn. The report summarized here addresses many questions regarding the science of brain development; we conclude that, used cautiously, this science can begin to inform the decisions that policymakers, service providers, and parents make for young children. The emerging picture of

Reprinted from the UCLA Center for Healthier Children, Families and Communities, California Policy Research Center, University of California. Halfon, N., Shulman, E., and Hochstein, M. (2001). Brain development in early childhood. *Policy Brief, No. 13*, 1–4.

the human brain suggests that Americans may have underestimated how critical the earliest years are to health and functioning throughout childhood and adulthood.

A KEY BODY OF FINDINGS

Scientists have learned that human brain development results from a complex interaction between nature and nurture. Much of what we know is derived from experiments on rats, monkeys, and other animals that are based on reasonable assumptions about the extent to which animal and human brain development and psychological behaviors are similar. These experiments enable researchers to directly observe brain development by measuring and comparing physiological processes from the brains of animals reared under various conditions. Four general findings, elaborated below, may have important implications for both parenting and public-policy efforts to support optimal brain development during early childhood.

A CHILD'S BRAIN IS NOT MATURE AT BIRTH

Most of the brain's functional capacity doesn't develop until after birth, since the synapses connecting the neurons (brain cells) haven't yet fully formed. But nearly all the neurons develop prenatally, so that most of the "scaffolding" for synaptic connections is in place at birth. If a fetus is exposed to malnutrition, viral infections, drugs, environmental toxins, and other harmful substances that inhibit or alter brain-cell formation, this scaffolding may fail to develop normally and may result in negative outcomes such as schizophrenia, mental retardation, or more minor deficits, depending on when the exposure occurs.

A newborn has about the same number of neurons as an adult, but only 25% of its brain volume has developed. Infants' brain cells are connected by some 50 trillion synapses. By age 3, the synapses number about 1,000 trillion, many more than will ultimately be present in the adult brain. Beginning at age 3, synapses are selectively eliminated; by age 15, they number about 500 trillion, a number that remains relatively stable thereafter. The selective elimination of synapses is an indication of just how much the brain is shaped by experience.

A CHILD'S BRAIN IS CHANGED BY EXPERIENCE

The relative influence of genetic versus experiential influences can differ by type of function. For example, the regions of the brain that control breathing and heart rate are relatively hard-wired at birth, whereas higher functions related to learning and memory are sculpted and modified by experience. This yields a picture of the human brain as a plastic and self-organizing organ in which the development and maintenance of nerve connections are based on experiential demands and aren't strictly predetermined.

Experiences that stimulate activity in particular brain regions facilitate the growth of connections in those regions, so that synapses can be said to form in a "use-dependent" manner. The brain's response to external stimuli (e.g., the taste of warm milk, the feeling of a mother's caress, the sound of a father's voice) is known as sensory-driven neural activity. Synaptic firing under the influence of new, external stimuli leads neurons to form connections to other neurons that have also been activated by sensory stimuli and experiences. Sensory-driven neural activity steers a young child's brain circuitry toward increasing organization.

Besides influencing synaptic growth and formation, experiences determine which synapses will survive the selective elimination noted above. Again, the use-dependent principle applies: Experiences that utilize the connections in particular regions of the brain help those connections to continue, while unused connections may be lost. Hence, extreme deprivation can have serious consequences for human brain development and functioning.

This use-dependent growth and formation of synapses indicate the human brain is fundamentally an adaptive organ whose physical organization is shaped by the environment. In this sense, learning is the process by which the brain responds adaptively to the environment in which a young child is reared. Moreover, the learning process starts long before children enter school and consists of much more than the verbal and cognitive skills that K–12 classroom education focuses on.

THE TIMING OF EXPERIENCE CAN BE IMPORTANT

Different brain regions, each associated with a particular set of abilities or behaviors, become connected to other regions at different times in a hierarchical fashion, enabling increasingly complex behavior. Because the regions develop, organize, and become fully functional at different times, specific kinds of experiences facilitate these changes during each region's developmental period. These periods range from short, well-defined "critical periods" to longer "sensitive periods," in which a particular area may begin to develop abruptly, continue to develop over many years, then gradually cease developing. Critical periods are far less common than sensitive periods.

During critical and sensitive periods, the brain seems relatively more plastic, and therefore both amenable and vulnerable to the influence of experience. Synapses in particular regions are thought to stabilize at some point in time, suggesting that it may become more difficult to create new connections in those regions. Therefore, neuroscientists believe that the critical or sensitive period for each developing region represents a window of opportunity during which specific experiences and stimuli are required in order to promote use-dependent synaptic growth and formation. It is also during these windows of opportunity that efforts to optimize brain development are likely to have the greatest impact, suggesting that such efforts must be timed appropriately in order to be effective and efficient.

The brain plasticity that occurs during critical periods—enabling the development of abilities such as vision, hearing, and the capacity for language—has been called "experience-expectant" development, because the brain is responding to stimuli that are practically guaranteed to be available in daily life. The critical timing issues associated with experience-expectant development of the brain are one of the most important reasons that children require early, prompt, and timely access to health services, so that developmental problems can be detected.

For other abilities (e.g., to learn a new language or a musical instrument) the window of opportunity would be more accurately described as a sensitive period in that it appears to remain open longer, perhaps a whole lifetime. This type of brain plasticity has been called "experience-dependent"—responsive to experiences that aren't necessarily present in everyday life.

From a policy perspective, many of the most important brain-based capacities of children are experience-dependent. Literacy is a complex set of skills that can be encouraged by being read to daily or being enrolled in early childhood education (which may not be available to everyone). The goal of policy and practice should therefore be to ensure not only that all children develop functional sensory and motor skills, but that they are exposed to the experiences and social interactions thought to encourage the experience-dependent neural foundation on which literacy and other abilities can be built.

RELATIONSHIPS INFLUENCE SOCIAL AND EMOTIONAL FUNCTIONING

For young children, relationships have a particularly strong influence on their social and emotional functioning. They learn to regulate emotional responses to individuals and events through perception of their caregiver's behavior. If the relationship is secure, a child learns to rely on the caregiver to help regulate her response to stressful situations and, over time, begins to regulate her own behavior. If the caregiver's behavior is habitually inappropriate, inconsistent, or ineffective, the child can experience prolonged episodes of unregulated stress and, in extreme cases, fail to develop self-regulating abilities.

One group of parents whose children may be at risk for insecure attachment and prolonged stress is depressed mothers. In the immediate postpartum period about 40% of mothers experience mild depression, and about 10%, moderate or severe depression. But depression doesn't affect only new mothers. National surveys show that clinical depression affects 16% of mothers with infants and toddlers, and as many as 25% of mothers of 17-month-olds and 17% of mothers of 35-month-olds reported experiencing elevated depressive symptoms.

Studies suggest that depressed mothers are either more intrusive and controlling or less attentive and engaged than mothers who aren't. Their children tend to be more irritable, display sadness and anger more frequently, and have higher and more persistently elevated levels of the stress hormone cortisol. In animal studies, high and persistent cortisol levels are associated with atrophy of the hippocampus, a brain region involved in memory and learning. One conclusion is that maternal depression may have a permanent effect not only on a child's sense of security, but on the ability to retain memories and therefore learn. For example, some studies show diminished cognitive performance in preschoolers whose mothers were depressed during their infancy.

RISK FACTORS AND PROTECTIVE FACTORS

Researchers are only beginning to learn what conditions threaten or protect cognitive and social/emotional development. A single risk factor doesn't appear to be enough to result in psychopathology or school failure. But the combined effect of multiple risk factors on a child presents a risk for negative social/emotional and cognitive outcomes. One study found that children whose mothers were depressed *or* had low educational attainment *or* lacked social support were more likely to develop normally than children whose mothers were depressed *and* had low educational attainment *and* lacked social support.

Certain parental behaviors and activities are thought to optimize their children's cognitive and social/emotional development. Children should be encouraged to explore their surroundings and be made to feel safe doing so. They require assistance in learning the basic skills they will need during the transition to school and throughout their lives and have to engage in guided rehearsal and extension of each skill as they attain it. Children should be rewarded for developmental advances and shielded from inappropriate disapproval, teasing, or punishment if they haven't reached them. And children need a rich and responsive language environment if they are to develop the early literacy skills that will prepare them for school. Parents and other caregivers, including family members and professional child care workers, should strive to provide children with an environment conducive to these experiences.

Policymakers and the laws and programs they create have a significant role in empowering families to rear their children in a manner conducive to what we know spurs optimal cognitive and social/emotional development. Policymakers may want to look to examples of successful programs developed over the last 40 years: the Chicago Parent–Child Center, the High/Scope Perry Preschool Project, the Carolina Abecedarian Project, the Infant Health and Development Program, the Prenatal/Early Infancy Project, Reach Out and Read, and Healthy Steps.

CONCLUSIONS AND DIRECTIONS

The four findings emerging from our growing understanding of neurobiology and psychology help explain why early childhood is so important and carry strong implications for parenting and public policy. A safe, stimulating environment and access to nurturing, supportive caregiving positively affect child development. Programs and policies that support families—especially those at risk for depression, poverty, and substance abuse—can help parents promote optimal brain development and cognitive, social, and emotional well-being in their children. The implications of the brain research are fairly straightforward:

The early years of life are no less important for the child's physical, social, and emotional development than the school years. Profoundly important forms of learning occur long before the child enters school; they depend on the earliest infant–caregiver interactions, the emotional context of these early relationships, and the nature of the experiences. These early learning experiences do more than simply shape the cognitive content of knowledge: they shape emotional and self-regulatory behaviors, as well as the very brain architecture enabling children to seek and absorb knowledge when they enter school.

The first years of life may set the course for future development. While neural and behavioral plasticity are present throughout life, the brain's flexibility in the first years of life, and its adaptive capacity to lay the groundwork for cognitive and emotional capacities in later life, is probably unmatched at any other time. It is quite possible that the developing human brain can be more efficiently and more profoundly supported and enriched in the first years of life than at any other stage. This possibility is too important to be ignored by parents, policymakers, and the community at large.

Early childhood is an investment opportunity for each family, each community, and our society as a whole. At present there are fewer educational, health, and social-service systems available to families with very young children than are needed, suggesting that investments in young children are out of sync with what we know about when and how brain development occurs. California's First 5 and its emphasis on early childhood can inspire policymakers to correct this imbalance.

Early childhood offers us the chance to ensure that no child experiences severe or even mild deprivation that may impair brain development and impose significant fiscal costs on school and health systems later. To realize the human potential represented by infancy and early childhood, it will be increasingly important to understand the long-term costs and benefits associated with various approaches to addressing the needs of families with young children. It takes a well-functioning family, supported by a community, to promote optimal brain development.

QUESTIONS

1. What does it mean to say that synapses form in a "use-dependent" manner?
2. Why does extreme deprivation have such serious consequences for brain development?
3. What is "experience-expectant" development? Give an example from your own childhood.
4. What is "experience-dependent" development? Give an example from your own childhood.
5. Would the timing of an intervention be more critical for a developmental process that is experience-expectant or for one that is experience-dependent?

6. How might being reared by a depressed mother affect a child's brain development?

7. We know that having one risk factor presents challenges to healthy development, but why does having more than one risk factor substantially elevate the likelihood that a child will have developmental difficulties?

8. What parental behaviors contribute to healthy brain development? Why do you think these behaviors are effective?

9. What does research on early brain development tell us about how experiences in the preschool years can affect a child's success in school?

10. If you had the chance to enact one social policy to enhance children's well-being, what, on the basis of the information in this article, would it be?

7 Optimizing Expression of the Common Human Genome for Child Development

BERNARD BROWN

The age of biology is upon us, and no field of study has done more to redefine our understanding of human biology than genetics. In fact, the effort to chart the structure of the human genome has been granted vast amounts of federal funds and put on an accelerated research track as the Human Genome Project. Progress in the field of genetics has been stunning, and treatments that were merely a dream just a decade ago are now commonplace. The explosion in our knowledge of human genes has brought the realization that gene expression is complex and indeterminate. The vast array of possible expressions of genetic information is due, in large part, to one remarkable capability of the human gene: its responsiveness to environmental input. The down side of this complexity is that a complete understanding of genetic expression will require substantial research, if it is attainable at all. However, the up side is that there appears to be more potential than was previously thought for changing how genes are expressed in a human being. For individuals with a genetic inheritance that includes potentially deleterious outcomes, this news is extremely welcome.

In the following article, Bernard Brown describes what genes are and how they get expressed in human behavior. His goal is to provide enough background information to enable someone with little expertise in this area to appreciate how critical the environment is to the operation and expression of the human potential that is contained in genes. Brown concludes that genes are not destiny. That is, there are many ways in which the environment influences genetic expression: It can activate, modify, and even suppress or inhibit genes. He illustrates this point with intriguing examples of a range of environmental influences, including nutrition, the physical setting, and psychological experience. He uses this information to show that a systems approach to studying genes—an approach that includes a broad range of biological and environmental information—is necessary to advance our understanding of child development.

This article conveys much of the excitement and promise of this area of research and raises many questions about its eventual consequences. Most of us would agree that altering the environment to enhance opportunities for healthy child development is highly desirable. However, the worry persists that this research may become overly prescriptive and promote too narrow a definition of the optimal environment for children's growth.

Molecular biology has moved the gene-environment issue in behavior genetics to how and when expression of the human genome is triggered and maintained. How does environment influence gene expression? How many genes are expressed in producing a given behavior? The genome is a data bank and does not automatically create a working brain. The body and brain grow well when (a) endocrine hormones initiate and promote the expression of genes, (b) nutrition is sufficient to sustain the production of proteins, and (c) stress does not suppress gene expression. The growth of brain synapses also requires appropriate neural stimulation. To study gene expression, it is essential to view the complex biology of the cell from a system context that includes the

Reprinted with permission of Blackwell Publishers from Brown, B. (1999). Optimizing expression of the common human genome for child development. *Current Directions in Psychological Science, 8,* 37–41. Copyright 1999 American Psychological Society.

entire genome plus the biological and psychological environments. Optimizing gene expression for child growth can be achieved by a balance of medicine, nutrition, and appropriate physical, educational, and psychological environments.

The nature-versus-nurture debate is now informed by current research on molecular biology that moves the question from which factor is more important to how and when expression of the human genome is triggered and maintained. The basic behavior genetics issue has become how environment influences gene expression. How do human physiology and biochemistry, which react to the external environment, affect gene expression? Can facilitated gene expression enhance children's development, physical and mental health, and cognitive ability or rehabilitate brain injury and inadequate nurture?

WHAT IS A GENE?

The human cell can be viewed as a protein factory in which genes transmit molecular messages to ribosomes to produce protein from amino acids. A gene is a small unit of the DNA molecule that contains information for building a single protein. The genome is the equivalent of a database in a computer ROM memory. Located in the DNA molecule, a long string of genes shaped like a double helix, the genome contains codes that prescribe the structure and function of the cell. A gene is activated when the external environment asks the genome to supply information. The information from the activated gene is then processed by the body's basic operating system, the DNA-ribosome protein factory. The ROM's information is essential for the operation of the protein factory, but it is only information, a blueprint, and not otherwise part of the control system that regulates the factory's production of protein. A vast array of biological structures is built from the information in the human genome's 50,000 to 100,000 genes (Lewin, Siciliano, & Klotz, 1997).

In a critical number of cells affecting human growth, the genetic machinery of the cell does not by itself issue instructions to assemble proteins from the genetic blueprint. Rather, gene expression is triggered by hormones, messenger proteins secreted by endocrine glands. Hormone levels are influenced by biological and psychological environments. Many structural genes that code for proteins remain quiescent until the environment gives rise to hormones and chains of molecules created by hormones, such as steroids, that signal cells to activate genes. An activated gene's structure is copied (transcribed) to produce a new molecule, a messenger RNA molecule, which is then sent to tell a ribosome to produce a protein. To get the messages across the bridge from gene to ribosome, the cell requires biochemical promoters and inhibitors, as well as certain biochemical and physiological conditions within the cell, such as sufficient levels of energy and nutrients (Lewin et al., 1997).

GROWTH AND DIFFERENTIATION

Stress, nutrition, health, endocrine hormones, and the psychological environment all affect the rate and magnitude of brain growth, information processing and storage, and competition among neural networks. The rate at which the brain absorbs, processes, and consolidates information depends on the neural stimulation it receives and on its biochemical resources for processing and absorbing information.

Homeostasis is an organism's tendency to preserve its state. The body is a multiply redundant fail-safe system controlled by multiple feedback loops in which genes play a protective role, ensuring function under adverse conditions and survivability across generations. Genes conserve the organism's form, sequence of development, and function, supplying mechanisms for adapting to the environment. Even when severe stress, malnutrition, or lack of stimulation slows the growth of brain structures, the order of gene expression is conserved. Each stage of brain growth follows its predecessor, and the genetic plan still unfolds, albeit more slowly and less perfectly.

After an early period of exponential growth, human children grow in stages of differentiation; simple cells and tissues specialize into more complex forms and functions. The genome specifies the order in which genes are expressed and provides sets of contingency plans for the different conditions the organism may encounter. Hundreds of genes that eventually affect behavior are expressed in each of hundreds of differentiation waves. A child's development reflects a series of genetically programmed steps that start at different ages. As the steps progress, old and newly expressed genes interact with successive environments. In brain growth, neurons (nerve cells) increase in the early stages and connecting tissues (axons and dendrites) increase and organize in later stages. Brain plasticity, the capacity of the brain to change as a result of experience, concerns changes in the number and size of synapses and synaptic networks. When sufficient electrical signals are sent from a neuron through an axon to a synapse (a small attachment point on the dendrite of a second neuron) and the biological environment of the synapse is supportive, the synapse will grow. The brain grows in cycles of synaptic growth and pruning (elimination). If a door opens on a favorable microenvironment, synapses tend to form and neural networks grow. But if the door opens on an unfavorable microenvironment, synapses are more likely to be pruned.

TRIGGERING AND MAINTAINING GENETIC ACTION

Hormones secreted by the endocrine glands are the primary source of genetic action. Stress has a major impact on which hormones are secreted and hence on how children grow. The influence of hormones and neural stimulation on brain growth also depends on nutrition at the cellular level.

THE ENDOCRINE SYSTEM

As a child grows, the endocrine system—under the influence of its biochemical, biophysical, and psychological environments—generates many hormones, chemicals that signal body cells to change the rates of chemical reactions. Levels of hormones change with nutrition, stress, illness, medication, and mood (Wilson & Foster, 1985). The hormones, in turn, trigger the expression of tens of thousands of genes. Hormonal levels influence the growth and function of the brain at many levels (Kuhn & Shanberg, 1984).

Thyroid hormones trigger gene transcription and accelerate the functional maturation of the brain. Too much thyroid hormone produces adverse effects, such as over-rapid growth. When thyroid hormone levels are insufficient, brain growth slows and cell division persists past the normal time of termination. There are reductions in cell size, synaptic density, and density of brain cell connections, and delayed functional development. Gene expression is slowed, impairing production of proteins and decreasing RNA content and T3 thyroid hormone receptors (Kuhn & Shanberg, 1984).

Steroids, the molecular end products of the thyroid hormone chemical chain, which is activated by stress, profoundly suppress growth in all tissues. Large doses of steroids suppress brain growth. Stress, medication, and some illnesses raise levels of cortisol, the thyroid chain's final end product, delaying development and suppressing DNA synthesis. Steroids affect nervous system plasticity (McEwen, 1992).

Growth hormone directly affects the rate at which genes transcribe their messages to produce proteins. Growth hormone is necessary for normal body and brain development.

STRESS

Stress is universal, and children must learn to cope with normal stressful events; however, continuing, uncontrolled stress slows mental growth (Brown & Rosenbaum, 1985). Stress has strong effects on endocrine function (Chrousos & Gold, 1992). High stress-related cortisol levels damage the brain's hippocampus (Sapolsky, 1996) and slow body growth (Wilson & Foster, 1985). Meerson (1984) found that stressed rats increased cellular weight and had higher levels of DNA, RNA, and protein synthesis. The diversion of energy and cellular resources toward the buildup of large stress-resisting cellular structures clearly competes with growth.

NUTRITION

The role of nutrition in physical growth and brain growth is well established (Brown, 1972). For example, Bogin (1988) found Guatemalan children raised in the United States gain greater stature than their fathers and children in Guatemala. For optimum gene expression, it is essential to provide nutrients that maintain cellular energy and sufficient cellular concentrations of amino acids (basic protein components; Chan & Hargrove, 1993).

ASPECTS OF GENETIC ACTION

The 19th century saw tremendous scientific progress as physics and biology moved beyond global analysis and examined small subsystems. Developmental biology, influenced by Mendel, adapted a mechanistic model that separated the inside of the body from the outside environment. In Mendelian genetics, the gene was conceptualized as unitary, independent, and the determinant of the final state of the developing organism (Lewontin, 1994). However, molecular biology now shows that gene expression is more complex.

Gene expression has often been measured in terms of the number of gene copies found in a chromosome, a section of the DNA helix. Although relating the number of copies of a gene in a chromosome to the color of peas worked well in Mendel's context, inherited traits are not a simple function of the number of gene copies. Within the various chromosomes of DNA, there are many copies and reverse copies of genes, as well as pseudo-genes, all of which may look like true copies but will not be expressed. The alternative to measuring the number of gene copies, and the only sure way to study the likelihood that a given gene has been expressed, is to test for the presence of a specific messenger RNA.

Often, gene expression is measured inadequately in terms of copies of receptor genes. Receptors are molecules, created from receptor genes, that sit on membranes (e.g., the surfaces of cells) and act as entry portals. When a receptor recognizes an incoming molecule and binds to it, a chain of chemical reactions that leads to gene expression (production of a protein) begins. A receptor gene is not the same as the gene of the molecule that binds to it. Both the receptor and the molecule that binds to it are needed to create a chemical pathway leading to the creation of a protein. Moreover, the number of receptors will change with tissue needs. Hormonal changes can increase the density of receptors at a site by a factor of 10.

The D4DR dopamine receptor gene is an important and well-known gene that has been associated with sensation seeking, risk taking, substance abuse, attention deficit hyperactivity disorder (ADHD), dyslexia, delinquency, and antisocial behavior (Hamer & Copeland, 1998). Practitioners treat these conditions with nutritional regimes, biofeedback, behavior modification, cognitive therapy, and various medications such as ritalin.

The D4DR receptor is part of a larger system that regulates behavior. Many neurons produce the neurotransmitter dopamine. Dopamine is transmitted from a neuron to a synapse on a second neuron and then binds to the second neuron's receptor, delivering the first neuron's message. But the D4DR receptor is only one of many dopamine receptors that sit on the surface of some neurons. Once the dopamine is delivered to the receptor, dopamine transporters return the dopamine across the synapse to the first neuron, to be used again. Mutations in transporter genes can cause the dopamine secreted by the synapse to be returned before it binds to the dopamine receptor and delivers its message. Behavior problems attributed to D4DR may instead result from the level of dopamine; from different kinds of neurons, synapses, receptors, or molecular agents; or from their various combinations. In the brain, synaptic growth and function depend on complex biochemical systems that regulate many different kinds of molecules that act as neurotransmitters, receptors, release agents, and promotors, inhibitors, modulators, and integrators of the chemical reactions that lead to gene transcription and protein production.

Although Mendel viewed both parents as the source of inheritance, molecular pathways are more complex. Lamond and Earnshaw (1998) showed that the cell nucleus (in which DNA resides) has a dynamic structure. Genes are generally kept in inactive nuclear regions, but the most recently activated genes are located at nuclear processing sites in the best position to be processed again if there is an environmental trigger. Human female XX chromosomes, for example, have been observed with one X chromosome (from one parent) in an active region and the other (from the other parent) in an inactive region, potentially increasing the influence of one parent over the other. The elevated reaction probability of genes in activated nuclear regions may explain many aspects of learning. Mitochondria, the cellular energy sources, are inherited only from the mother. The tiny mitochondrion has a small DNA-like strand with genes for 37 energy-generating molecules. There are about 100 mitochondria per cell. Genetic disorders stemming from mitochondria may be involved in many energy-related behavior problems, especially in the aged (Wallace, 1997). Stressed or malnourished mothers may develop low mitochondrial density and pass the environmental condition on to their children through their ova.

OPTIMIZING GENETIC EXPRESSION

Genes are not destiny. There are many places along the gene–behavior pathway where genetic expression can be regulated. Environmental factors such as temperature; nutrition; light level; the timing, pace, and intensity of stimuli; and effective coping skills can promote or inhibit the expression of specific genes and proteins that lead to specific behaviors. Treatment of a single factor may be too weak to effect change. It is important to use system thinking as treatments for behavior problems are combined and optimized.

MEDICINE

Physicians use thousands of drugs that alter biochemical pathways to reduce or remove genetically related illness and dysfunction. Some drugs modify physiological pathways through which genes are expressed; many target gene products, proteins. The use of drugs to promote learning in schools has become commonplace. New generations of psychoactive drugs regulate receptor function. Some regulate neurotransmitters in synapses, such as serotonin and dopamine. More than 20 antidepressant drugs, such as Prozac, are regularly prescribed to increase serotonin concentrations in synapses. Benzodiazipines are now used to treat anxiety, insomnia, and seizures. The enormous progress in molecular biology may lead to drugs that improve cognitive ability and cure schizophrenia.

NUTRITION

Alternative medicine is developing wellness models, as opposed to deficit models, to meet growth-retarded and ADHD children's nutritional needs. One current approach is a learning-nutrition discipline that adjusts diets to optimize energy and levels of amino acids, vitamins, gene-promoting enzymes, and minerals.

PHYSICAL ENVIRONMENT

Physical environment involves factors such as light, temperature, noise, humidity, wind, space, and air pressure. Genes determine the eye's iris color and retinal pigmentation. Children with dark eyes may need more light for optimum visual performance than other children. They would have no problem if school lighting met prescribed standards and teachers did not draw the shades and turn off the lights at 2:00, as children taking ritalin become less tractable because their medicine wears off. This real genetic problem has a simple practical solution. Another example of the relationship between light and behavior concerns the use of high light levels. Intense light is used to treat depression by changing levels of the neurotransmitter serotonin and to regulate daily body rhythms by changing levels of melatonin.

Regulation of home and school temperatures is important. High temperature, which can cause sleepiness in hot classrooms, shunts blood away from the brain into the peripheral vascular system, reducing the energy and nutrient supply needed for gene expression.

PSYCHOLOGICAL ENVIRONMENT

In child development, gene expression responds to love; security; effective role models; stimulating language and cognitive environments; a positive family environment including support, discipline, values, and positive directions; education; and appropriate management of stress and anxiety. These psychological factors modulate genetic expression through the endocrine system and the brain, and when deficient can be improved through psychotherapy.

Providing stress-coping skills and controlling the intensity, frequency, and duration of stress are essential for optimizing gene expression. Mind–body therapies such as biofeedback and progressive relaxation promote relaxation, improving health and performance.

Adverse psychological environment can slow gene expression, leading to slower mental growth, especially when a child is subject to malnutrition, stress, illness, or suboptimal physical environments. Psychological environment also plays a role in the origins and outcomes of known brain disorders with genetic components, including stress-induced dysfunction of the amygdala and hippocampus, substance abuse, and some disorders of sleep, metabolism, vision, hearing, and speech. In addition to psychotherapy and pharmacology, education has played a vital role in the treatment of these disorders.

GENETIC DIFFERENCES BETWEEN THE SEXES

Sex, the most obvious genetic difference, has received too little study. When scaled tests are used to measure cognitive differences, the selection of test items to ensure equal responses by males and females obscures male–female differences. Hanlon (1996) found dramatic sex differences in brain growth and in the areas at which brain activity occurs. Young girls are more verbal than young boys, who show better spatial and gross motor ability. Are boys taught to read before genes for reading are expressed? Would the Swedish approach to education, which delays reading instruction, reduce boys' reading disabilities in the United States? Someday genetic testing may help determine when a child is ready for a given educational program.

CONCLUSION

The gene is as a framed canvas, an invariant plane on which the organic environment molds a variegated hormonal surface, upon which the psychological environment paints a person.

The genome gives rise to an enormous, complex array of balanced chemical subsystems highly resistant to change. Regulatory pathways often overlap. Exciting or inhibiting one pathway can affect a series of pathways, sometimes leading to side effects. A single gene by itself may not be sufficiently strong to affect the system. A gene may be present, but there may not be a trigger to express the gene. A gene may lead to dysfunction in one environment yet produce exceptional function in another environment.

To optimize gene expression, it is essential to adopt a multidisciplinary system approach that takes into account the entire genome plus the biological and psychological environments. Even if a gene is the direct source of a behavior problem, there may be ways to alter its expression or to bypass it by promoting alternative genetic pathways. Treatment needs to balance medicine, nutrition, and physical, educational, and psychological environments and must be sensitive to gender differences. A narrow focus on a given gene, a given condition, or a single treatment is not likely to change the system. From the viewpoint of molecular biology, growth involves very complex and continuing interaction of genes and environment. But within the complexity lies a vast number of possibilities for improving children's growth.

RECOMMENDED READING

Bogin, B. (1988). (See References)

Diamond, M.C. (1988). *The impact of the environment on the anatomy of the brain.* New York: Free Press.

Hamer, D.H., & Copeland, P. (1998). (See References)

REFERENCES

Bogin, B. (1988). *Patterns of human growth.* Cambridge, England: Cambridge University Press.

Brown, B. (1972). *Growth retardation: A systems study of the educational problems of the disadvantaged child.* Unpublished doctoral dissertation, American Univerity, Washington, DC.

Brown, B., & Rosenbaum, L. (1985). Stress and competence. In J.H. Humphrey (Ed.), *Stress in childhood* (pp. 127–154). New York: AMS Press.

Chan, D.K.-C., & Hargrove, J.L. (1993). Effects of dietary protein on gene expression. In C.D. Berdanier & J.L. Hargrove (Eds.), *Nutrition and gene expression* (pp. 353–375). Boca Raton, Fl: CRC.

Chrousos, G.P., & Gold, P.W. (1992). The concepts of stress and stress system disorders: Overview of physical and behavioral homeostasis. *Journal of the American Medical Association, 267,* 1244–1252.

Hamer, D.H., & Copeland, P. (1998). *Living with our genes.* New York: Doubleday.

Hanlon, H. (1996). Topographically different regional networks impose structural limitations on both sexes in early post-natal development. In K.H. Pribram & J. King (Eds.), *Learning as self-organization* (pp. 311–376). Hillsdale, NJ: Erlbaum.

Kuhn, C., & Shanberg, S. (1984). Hormones and brain development. In C.B. Nemeroff & A.D. Dunn (Eds.), *Peptides, hormones and behavior* (pp. 775–821). New York: SP Medical and Scientific Books.

Lamond, A.I., & Earnshaw, W.C. (1998). Structure and function in the nucleus. *Science, 280,* 547–553.

Lewin, B., Siliciano, P., & Klotz, M. (1997). *Genes VI.* Oxford, England: Oxford University.

Lewontin, R.C. (1994). *Inside and outside: Gene, environment and organism.* Worcester, MA: Clark University.

McEwen, B.S. (1992). Effects of the steroid/thyroid hormone family on neural and behavioral plasticity. In C.B. Nemeroff (Ed.), *Neuroendocrinology* (pp. 333–351). Boca Raton, Fl: CRC.

Meerson, F.Z. (1984). *Adaptation, stress and prophylaxis.* New York: Springer-Verlag.

Saplosky, R.M. (1996). Why stress is bad for your brain. *Science, 273,* 749–750.

Wallace, D.C. (1997). Mitochondrial DNA in aging and disease. *Scientific American, 277,* 40–47.

Wilson, J.D., & Foster, D.W. (1985). *Williams textbook of endocrinology* (7th ed.). Philadelphia: Saunders.

QUESTIONS

1. What is the human genome?
2. What biological system activates gene expression?
3. What is homeostasis, and why it is important to the functioning of genes?
4. What are steroids, and what risks are associated with the use of steroids by athletes?
5. How does stress affect biological growth?
6. What are receptor genes, and what role do they play in gene expression?
7. What kind of gene is D4DR dopamine, and with what type of behaviors is this gene associated?
8. In general, how might stress in malnourished mothers affect their offspring, especially with regard to energy-related behaviors?
9. How might aspects of the environment, such as nutrition, ambient light, and the family environment, be manipulated to optimize gene expression?
10. Do our genes determine our destiny? Why or why not?

8 Of Human Bonding: Newborns Prefer Their Mothers' Voices

ANTHONY J. DeCASPER • WILLIAM P. FIFER

The last two decades have seen technical innovations that have made possible a huge increase in developmental research describing such infant capabilities as attention, emotional regulation, and social behavior. The following article describes one of these early human capabilities: the ability to discriminate the sounds of particular human voices. Authors Anthony DeCasper and William Fifer devised an ingenious method of study that allowed them to probe the capabilities of babies less than 3 days of age. What is particularly remarkable about their method is that it used the very limited behavioral abilities of neonates as a way of showing what they are able to understand.

The ability to discriminate human voices early in life has immense consequences for human adaptation and attests to the complex biological preparedness of the human infant—a preparedness that helps even newborn babies play an active role in their own development. The research described here, along with many other studies that demonstrate the amazing capabilities of newborns, has redefined our understanding of human development. No longer considered helpless, reactive beings, infants are now seen as active, information-seeking organisms that are ready to learn about and interact with the world. This research also indicates that infants are biased toward, or prefer, information from other people. We do not yet know whether a preference for the mother's voice early in an infant's life is a result of familiarity acquired while the baby was in utero or of some other complex process, such as emotional arousal immediately after birth. But it is certain that a preference for the sound and sight of other human beings helps infants become integrated with their surroundings, especially the social world in which they live. Moreover, this integration sets the stage for further development. After all, caregivers not only protect infants but are also a fount of information about the world and how it works. One cannot imagine a preference that is better suited to helping the developing infant face the many tasks that lie ahead.

By sucking on a nonnutritive nipple in different ways, a newborn human could produce either its mother's voice or the voice of another female. Infants learned how to produce the mother's voice and produced it more often than the other voice. The neonate's preference for the maternal voice suggests that the period shortly after birth may be important for initiating infant bonding to the mother.

Human responsiveness to sound begins in the third trimester of life and by birth reaches sophisticated levels (1), especially with respect to speech (2). Early auditory competency probably subserves a variety of developmental functions such as language acquisition (1, 3) and mother-infant bonding (4, 5). Mother-infant bonding would best be served by (and may

even require) the ability of a newborn to discriminate its mother's voice from that of other females. However, evidence for differential sensitivity to or discrimination of the maternal voice is available only for older infants for whom the bonding process is well advanced (6). Therefore, the role of maternal voice discrimination in formation of the mother-infant bond is unclear. If the newborn's sensitivities to speech subserves bonding, discrimination of and preference for the maternal voice should be evident near birth. We now report that a newborn infant younger than 3 days of age can not only discriminate its mother's voice but also will work to produce her voice in preference to the voice of another female.

The subjects were ten Caucasian neonates (five male and five female) (7). Shortly after delivery we tape-recorded the voices of mothers of infants se-

Reprinted with permission from the authors and *Science, 208*, 1980, pp. 1174–1176. Copyright 1980 by the American Association for the Advancement of Science.

lected for testing as they read Dr. Seuss's *To Think That I Saw It On Mulberry Street*. Recordings were edited to provide 25 minutes of uninterrupted prose, and testing of whether infants would differentially produce their mothers' voices began within 24 hours of recording. Sessions began by coaxing the infant to a state of quiet alertness (*8*). The infant was then placed supine in its basinette, earphones were secured over its ears, and a nonnutritive nipple was placed in its mouth. An assistant held the nipple loosely in place; she was unaware of the experimental condition of the individual infant and could neither hear the tapes nor be seen by the infant. The nipple was connected, by way of a pressure transducer, to the solid-state programming and recording equipment. The infants were then allowed 2 minutes to adjust to the situation. Sucking activity was recorded during the next 5 minutes, but voices were never presented. This baseline period was used to determine the median interburst interval (IBI) or time elapsing between the end of one burst of sucking and the beginning of the next (*9*). A burst was defined as a series of individual sucks separated from one another by less than 2 seconds. Testing with the voices began after the baseline had been established.

For five randomly selected infants, sucking burst terminating IBI's equal to or greater than the baseline median (*t*) produced only his or her mother's voice (IBI ≥ *t*), and bursts terminating intervals less than the median produced only the voice of another infant's mother (*10*). Thus, only one of the voices was presented, stereophonically, with the first suck of a burst and remained on until the burst ended, that is, until 2 seconds elapsed without a suck. For the other five infants, the conditions were reversed. Testing lasted 20 minutes.

A preference for the maternal voice was indicated if the infant produced it more often than the nonmaternal voice. However, unequal frequencies not indicative of preference for the maternal voice per se could result either because short (or long) IBI's were easier to produce or because the acoustic qualities of a particular voice, such as pitch or intensity, rendered it a more effective form of feedback. The effects of response requirements and voice characteristics were controlled (i) by requiring half the infants to respond after short IBI's to produce the mother's voice and half to respond after long ones and (ii) by having each maternal voice also serve as the nonmaternal voice for another infant.

Preference for the mother's voice was shown by the increase in the proportion of IBI's capable of producing her voice; the median IBI's shifted from their baseline values in a direction that produced the maternal voice more than half the time. Eight of the ten medians were shifted in a direction of the maternal voice (mean = 1.90 seconds, a 34 percent increase)

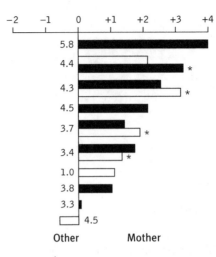

FIGURE 1

For each subject, signed difference scores between the median IBI's without vocal feedback (baseline) and with differential vocal feedback (session1). Differences of the four reversal sessions (*) are based on medians with differential feedback in sessions 1 and 2. Positive values indicate a preference for the maternal voice and negative values a preference for the nonmaternal voice. Filled bars indicate that the mother's voice followed IBI's of less than the baseline median; open bars indicate that her voice followed intervals equal to or greater than the median. Median IBI's of the baseline (in seconds) are shown opposite the bars.

(sign test, $P = .02$), one shifted in the direction that produced the nonmaternal voice more often, and one median did not change from its baseline value (Figure 1).

If these infants were working to gain access to their mother's voice, reversing the response requirements should result in a reversal of their IBI's. Four infants, two from each condition, who produced their mother's voice more often in session 1 were able to complete a second session 24 hours later, in which the response requirements were reversed (*11*). Differential feedback in session 2 began immediately after the 2-minute adjustment period. The criterion time remained equal to the baseline median of the first session. For all four infants, the median IBI's shifted toward the new criterion values and away from those which previously produced the maternal voice. The average magnitude of the difference between the medians of the first and reversal sessions was 1.95 seconds.

Apparently the infant learned to gain access to the mother's voice. Since specific temporal properties of sucking were required to produce the maternal voice, we sought evidence for the acquisition of temporally

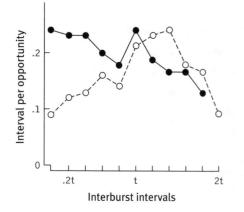

FIGURE 2

Interburst interval per opportunity when the maternal voice followed intervals less than the baseline median (solid line) and intervals equal to or greater than the median (dashed line). The IBI's are represented on the abscissa by the lower bound of interval classes equal to one-fifth the baseline median (t).

TABLE 1   MEAN $\bar{X}$ AND STANDARD DEVIATION (S.D.) OF THE RELATIVE FREQUENCY OF SUCKING DURING A STIMULUS ASSOCIATED WITH THE MATERNAL VOICE DIVIDED BY THE RELATIVE FREQUENCY OF SUCKING DURING A STIMULUS ASSOCIATED WITH THE NONMATERNAL VOICE

Stimulus associated with maternal voice	First third		Last third	
	$\bar{X}$	S.D.	$\bar{X}$	S.D.
Tone	0.97	.33	1.26	.33
No tone	1.04	.31	1.22	.19
Last: Combined	1.00[a]	.32	1.24	.27

[a]A ratio of 1.0 indicates no preference.

differentiated responding. Temporal discrimination within each condition was ascertained by constructing the function for IBI per opportunity: IBI's were collected into classes equal to one-fifth the baseline median, and the frequency of each class was divided by the total frequency of classes having equal and larger values (*12*). When IBI's less than the baseline median were required, the likelihood of terminating interburst intervals was highest for classes less than the median (Figure 2), whereas when longer intervals were required, the probability of terminating an IBI was maximal for intervals slightly longer than the median. Feedback from the maternal voice effectively differentiated the temporal character of responding that produced it: the probability of terminating IBI's was highest when termination resulted in the maternal voice.

Repeating the experiment with 16 female neonates and a different discrimination procedure confirmed their preference for the maternal voice (*13*). The discriminative stimuli were a 400-Hz tone of 4 seconds duration (tone) and a 4-second period of silence (no tone). Each IBI contained an alternating sequence of tone-no-tone periods, and each stimulus was equally likely to begin a sequence. For eight infants, a sucking burst initiated during a tone period turned off the tone and produced the Dr. Seuss story read by the infant's mother, whereas sucking bursts during a no-tone period produced the nonmaternal voice. The elicited voice remained until the sucking burst ended, at which time the tone-no-tone alterna-

tion began anew. The discriminative stimuli were reversed for the other eight neonates. Testing with the voices began immediately after the 2-minute adjustment period and lasted 20 minutes. Each maternal voice also served as a nonmaternal voice.

During the first third of the testing session, the infants were as likely to suck during a stimulus period correlated with the maternal voice as during one correlated with the nonmaternal voice (Table 1). However, in the last third of the session the infants sucked during stimulus periods associated with their mother's voice approximately 24 percent more often than during those associated with the nonmaternal voice, a significant increase [$F(1, 14) = 8.97, P < .01$]. Thus, at the beginning of testing there was no indication of stimulus discrimination or voice preference. By the end of the 20-minute session, feedback from the maternal voice produced clear evidence of an auditory discrimination; the probability of sucking during tone and no-tone periods was greater when sucking produced the maternal voice.

The infants in these studies lived in a group nursery; their general care and night feedings were handled by a number of female nursery personnel. They were fed in their mothers' rooms by their mothers at 9:30 A.M. and at 1:30, 5:00, and 8:30 P.M. At most, they had 12 hours of postnatal contact with their mothers before testing. Similarly reared infants prefer the human voice to other acoustically complex stimuli (*14*). But, as our data show, newborns reared in group nurseries that allow minimal maternal contact can also discriminate between their mothers and other speakers and, moreover, will work to produce their mothers' voices in preference to those of other females. Thus, within the first 3 days of postnatal development, newborns prefer the human voice, discriminate between speakers, and demonstrate a preference for their mothers' voices with only limited maternal exposure.

The neonate's capacity to rapidly acquire a stimulus discrimination that controls behavior (15) could provide the means by which limited postnatal experience with the mother results in preference for her voice. The early preference demonstrated here is possible because newborns have auditory competencies adequate for discriminating individual speakers: they are sensitive to rhythmicity (16), intonation (17), frequency variation (1, 13), and phonetic components of speech (18). Their general sensory competency may enable other maternal cues, such as her odor (19) and the manner in which she handles her infant (20), to serve as supporting bases for discrimination and vocal preference. Prenatal (intrauterine) auditory experience may also be a factor. Although the significance and nature of intrauterine auditory experience in humans is not known, perceptual preferences and proximity-seeking responses of some infrahuman infants are profoundly affected by auditory experience before birth (21).

REFERENCES AND NOTES

1. R. B. Eisenberg, *Auditory Competence in Early Life: The Roots of Communicative Behavior* (University Park Press, Baltimore, 1976.)

2. P. D. Eimas, in *Infant Perception: From Sensation to Cognition*, L. B. Cohen and P. Salapatek, Eds. (Academic Press, New York, 1975), vol. 2., p. 193.

3. B. Friedlander, *Merrill-Palmer Q., 16*, 7 (1970).

4. R. Bell, in *The Effect of the Infant on Its Caregiver*, M. Lewis and L. A. Rosenblum, Eds. (Wiley, New York, 1974), p. 1; T. B. Brazelton, E. Tronick, L. Abramson, H. Als, S. Wise, *Ciba Found. Symp., 33*, 137 (1975).

5. M. H. Klaus and J. H. Kennel, *Maternal Infant Bonding* (Mosby, St. Louis, 1976); P. DeChateau, *Birth Family J., 41*, 10 (1977).

6. M. Miles and E. Melvish, *Nature (London) 252*, 123 (1974); J. Mehler, J. Bertoncini, M. Baurière, D. Jassik-Gershenfeld, *Perception, 7*, 491 (1978).

7. The infants were randomly selected from those meeting the following criteria: (i) gestation, full term; (ii) delivery, uncomplicated; (iii) birth weight, between 2500 and 3850 grams; and (iv) APGAR score, at least eight at 1 and 5 minutes after birth. If circumsized, males were not observed until at least 12 hours afterward. Informed written consent was obtained from the mother, and she was invited to observe the testing procedure. Testing sessions began between 2.5 and 3.5 hours after the 6 A.M. or 12 P.M. feeding. All infants were bottle-fed.

8. P. H. Wolff, *Psychol. Issues, 5*, 1 (1966). The infants were held in front of the experimenter's face, spoken to, and then presented with the nonnutritive nipple. Infants failing to fixate visually on the experimenter's face or to suck on the nipple were returned to the nursery. Once begun, a session was terminated only if the infant cried or stopped sucking for two consecutive minutes. The initial sessions of two infants were terminated because they cried for 2 minutes. Their data are not reported. Thus, the results are based on 10 of 12 infants meeting the behavioral criteria for entering and remaining in the study.

9. With quiet and alert newborns, nonnutritive sucking typically occurs as bursts of individual sucks, each separated by a second or so, while the bursts themselves are separated by several seconds or more. Interburst intervals tend to be unimodally distributed with modal values differing among infants. [K. Kaye, in *Studies in Mother-Infant Interaction*, H. R. Schaffer, Ed. (Academic Press, New York, 1977)]. A suck was said to occur when the negative pressure exerted on the nipple reached 20 mm-Hg. This value is almost always exceeded during nonnutritive sucking by healthy infants, but is virtually never produced by nonsucking mouth movement.

10. The tape reels revolved continuously, and one or the other of the voices was electronically switched to the earphones when the response threshold was met. Because the thresholds were detected electronically, voice onset occurred at the moment the negative pressure reached 20 mm-Hg.

11. Two infants were not tested a second time, because we could not gain access to the testing room, which served as an auxiliary nursery and as an isolation room. The sessions of two infants who cried were terminated. Two other infants were tested a second time, but in their first session one had shown no preference and the other had shown only a slight preference for the nonmaternal voice. Their performance may have been affected by inconsistent feedback. Because their peak sucking pressures were near the threshold of the apparatus, very similar sucks would sometimes produce feedback and sometimes not, and sometimes feedback would be terminated in the midst of a sucking burst. Consequently, second session performances of these two infants, which were much like their initial performances, were uninterpretable.

12. D. Anger, *J. Exp. Psychol., 52*, 145 (1956).

13. Three other infants began testing with the voices, but their sessions were terminated because they cried. Their data are not included. This study is part of a doctoral thesis submitted by W.P.F.

14. E. Butterfield and G. Siperstein, in *Oral Sensation and Perception: The Mouth of the Infant*, J. Bosma, Ed. (Thomas, Springfield, Ill., 1972).

15. E. R. Siqueland and L. P. Lipsitt, *J. Exp. Child. Psychol. 3*, 356 (1966); R. E. Kron, in *Recent Advances in Biological Psychiatry*, J. Wortis, Ed. (Plenum, New York, 1967), p. 295.

16. W. S. Condon and L. W. Sander, *Science, 183*, 99 (1974).

17. R. B. Eisenberg, D. B. Cousins, N. Rupp, *J. Aud. Res., 7*, 245 (1966); P. A. Morse, *J. Exp. Child. Psychol., 14*, 477 (1972).

18. E. C. Butterfield and G. F. Cairns, in *Language Perspectives: Acquisition, Retardation and Intervention*, R. L. Schiefelbusch and L. L. Lloyd, Eds. (University Park

Press, Baltimore, 1974), p. 75; A. J. DeCasper, E. C. Butterfield, G. F. Cairns, paper presented at the fourth biennial conference on Human Development, Nashville. April 1976.

19. A. MacFarlane, *Ciba Found. Symp., 33*, 103 (1975).
20. P. Burns, L. W. Sander, G. Stechler, H. Julia. *J. Am. Acad. Child Psychiatry, 11*, 427 (1972), E. B. Thoman, A. F. Korner, L. Bearon-Williams, *Child Dev., 48*, 563 (1977).
21. G. Gottlieb, *Development of Species Identification in Birds: An Inquiry into the Prenatal Determinants of Perception* (Univ. of Chicago Press, Chicago, 1971); E. H. Hess. *Imprinting* (Van Nostrand-Reinhold, New York, 1973).
22. Supported by Research Council grant 920. We thank the infants, their mothers, and the staff of Moses Cane Hospital, where this work was performed, and A. Carstens for helping conduct the research.

QUESTIONS

1. Briefly describe the method that DeCasper and Fifer used to test an infant's preference for the mother's voice. Are you surprised that infants are capable of doing this task? Why?
2. Why was the study designed so that, to hear the mother's voice, half of the infants needed to increase their sucking rate to hear the mother's voice and the other half needed to decrease their sucking rate?
3. Do you think that prenatal exposure to the mother's voice may play a role in the preferences shown in this study?
4. What function does such early auditory discrimination serve for infants?
5. What types of perceptual information about mothers do you think deaf infants might rely on in the early days of life?
6. What other early sensory capabilities help prepare infants to interact socially?
7. What do these findings suggest about the nature of human development, especially the role that social experiences play in it?
8. Do you think that, like normal babies, infants with autism—a dysfunction in which children are not interested in social interaction—exhibit a preference for the human voice in early infancy? Why or why not?
9. How might the ability to discriminate sounds contribute to the development of language?
10. Research with children in the years beyond infancy indicates that girls show more social responsiveness than boys do. Do you think that innate gender differences may influence these early capabilities—perhaps not differences in preferences per se but in some other aspects of this behavior, such as how quickly infants respond or how aroused they get when they hear their mother's voice?

9 Culture and Early Infancy Among Central African Foragers and Farmers

BARRY S. HEWLETT • MICHAEL E. LAMB • DONALD SHANNON
BIRGIT LEYENDECKER • AXEL SCHÖLMERICH

One technique used by psychologists to study the contributions of experience to human development involves comparing the behaviors and abilities of children reared in different cultural settings. Behavioral observations are the main method of data collection in this type of research. To conduct the research described in the following article, a team of developmental psychologists went to two communities in central Africa and studied how adults care for infants. These neighboring communities, the Aka and the Ngandu, were of interest to the researchers because they are both small in scale, have little consumerism, and are socioeconomically similar to each other. However, they differ in some interesting ways, primarily in their subsistence practices—that is, the means by which they obtain the necessities of life. The Aka are hunter-gatherers, or foragers, and the Ngandu are settled, or sedentary, people who farm.

Barry Hewlett and his colleagues observed adults' caregiving of two age groups of infants, 3- to 4-month-olds and 9- to 10-month-olds, as families went about their daily activities. Using an observational technique called time sampling the researchers observed and recorded adult caregiving behaviors (such as physical affection and vocalizing), the dyadic behaviors of adults and infants (such as holding and face-to-face contact), and the independent behaviors of the infants (such as fussing and smiling). The main differences observed were that Aku infants were more likely to be in close proximity to their care providers, to sleep more, and to fuss less than the Ngandu infants. Did differences in the behaviors of the caregivers correlate in any systematic way with these infant behaviors? As you read the article, you will discover differences in caregiver behavior that may explain why babies behaved differently in these two communities.

This study illustrates the utility of investigating child development as it occurs in different cultural circumstances. Such research can advance understanding of how cultural context, social experience, and individual behavior fit together. Finding different patterns of child rearing and infant behaviors in different communities does not explain why these patterns exist, however. This article concludes with an interesting discussion of some of the possible explanations for the differences that were observed in these two communities. As you will see, potential explanations are many, ranging from differences in subsistence patterns to maternal workloads to environmental hazards to cultural ideologies. Perhaps future research will reveal which of these explanations is the most useful for understanding variations in child-rearing practices and infant development across cultural communities.

Everyday infant experiences among the Aka hunter-gathers and the neighboring Ngandu farmers were observed and compared. Twenty Aka and 21 Ngandu 3- to 4-month-olds and 20 Aka and 20 Ngandu 9- to 10-month-olds were observed for 3 hr on each of 4 days so that all 12 daylight hr were covered. The Aka infants were more likely to be held, fed, and asleep or drowsy, whereas Ngandu infants were more likely to be alone and to fuss or cry, smile, vocalize, or play. The amount of crying, soothing, feeding, and sleeping declined over

Reprinted from Hewlett, B.S., Lamb, M.E., Shannon, D., Leyendecker, B., & Schölmerich, A. (1998). Culture and early infancy among Central African foragers and farmers. *Developmental Psychology, 34,* 653–661. Article in the Public Domain.

time in both groups. Distal social interaction increased over time among the Ngandu but not among the Aka. Despite striking cultural differences on many variables, however, functional context systematically affected the relative prominence of the infants' behavior in both cultural groups.

In this article, we examine infant care among two culturally distinct peoples in central Africa—Aka foragers and Ngandu farmers. Both cultures could be described as "traditional," small scale, preindustrial, or non-Western because industrial production and wage labor are minimal and no socioeconomic class structure (beyond age and sex) exists. Infancy in small-scale traditional cultures is frequently contrasted with infancy in European American cultures, which are typically referred to as global scale, industrial, or Western (Dixon, Tronick, Keefer, & Brazelton, 1981; Konner, 1977; LeVine, 1994; Super & Harkness, 1981; Tronick, Morelli, & Winn, 1987). Although comparative studies of these types of cultures have contributed substantially to the understanding of infant development, they often give the impression that infant care practices vary little across traditional non-Western societies or that the variability between Western and small-scale traditional cultures is greater than the variability within either one of these groups. LeVine (1974, 1989, 1994), for instance, described two parenting strategies—the agrarian (or pediatric) and the urban-industrial (or pedagogical)—following his work among the Gusii of East Africa. In his view, agrarian parents focus on the survival, health, and physical development of their infants because infant mortality levels are high, with half of the children not surviving to reproductive maturity. To monitor and respond to indicators of health and survival, agrarian parents hold or keep their infants in close proximity, quickly respond to fusses or cries, and feed their infants on demand. By contrast, urban-industrial parents focus on active engagement, social exchange, stimulation, and proto-conversation with their infants because these parents are concerned with the acquisition of cognitive skills essential to success in an environment in which infant mortality is low, children cost more and contribute less, and a competitive labor market builds on an academically graded occupational hierarchy.

Several researchers have confirmed that European Americans emphasize verbal and distal interaction, whereas mothers in traditional small-scale societies stress proximal interaction (Bakeman, Adamson, Konner, & Barr, 1990; Barr, 1990; Goldberg, 1977; Keller, Schölmerich, & Eibl-Eibesfeldt, 1988; Konner, 1976, 1977; Richman et al., 1988; Richman, Miller, & LeVine, 1992; Super & Harkness, 1981). Unfortunately, these comparative studies tended to sample from only one traditional non-Western group (e.g., Gusii in the Richman studies, Kipsigis in the Super and Harkness study, and !Kung in the Konner and Barr studies) compared with one or more European American groups, implicitly suggesting that traditional small-scale cultures have similar patterns of parenting. Some researchers have compared European Americans with more than one non-Western group (e.g., Bornstein et al., 1992; Roopnarine, Talukder, Jain, Joshi, & Srivastav, 1990), but the non-Western samples in these studies tend to be drawn from urban-industrial cultures (e.g., Japan and China). In this study, we focused on variability in infant care in small-scale or traditional non-Western cultures—cultures with minimal consumerism and social-economic stratification.

Researchers have also relied on brief observations (usually 1–2 hr of observation at each age), and this has precluded examination of the ways in which context might influence parent–infant interactions in different cultures. In addition, the differences between the Western and traditional small-scale cultures sampled have been so pronounced that the focus on these differences precluded analysis of within-group variability. High levels of parent–child proximity in traditional cultures are often attributed to high infant mortality and a resultant concern with survival, for example. In this article, our goal is to explore differences between two small-scale non-Western groups, on the assumption that a focus on both within- and between-culture variability promotes better understanding of the forces that shape infant development.

The comparison between Aka and Ngandu is interesting because these neighboring societies make a living in the same tropical forest, have similar mortality and fertility levels (infant mortality is 15–20%, juvenile [<15 years] mortality is 40–50%, total fertility rate is about six live births per woman); have frequent social, economic, and religious interactions; and are exposed to one another's practices on a regular basis, yet have distinct modes of production, male–female relations, and patterns of child care (see Hewlett, 1991b, for a detailed description of the cultures). The Aka are foragers (also known as hunter-gatherers), move their camps several times a year, have minimal political hierarchy, and have relatively high gender and intergenerational egalitarianism, whereas the Ngandu are sedentary "slash-and-burn" farmers with stronger chiefs and marked gender and intergenerational inequality. As a result, Aka–Ngandu comparisons may provide insights into several issues, including the role of natural selection (i.e., differential reproduction) in shaping infant care.

Noting that in comparison with Western cultures, non-Western foragers and farmers hold their infants extensively, breastfeed frequently, and respond promptly to fusses and cries, developmentalists have described these practices as part of a hazard-prevention strategy that serves to buffer vulnerable infants from health risks in contexts of high infant mortality (Blurton Jones, 1993; Kaplan & Dove, 1987; LeVine, 1994; Tronick, Morelli, & Ivey, 1992). By studying the Aka and Ngandu, we can evaluate this hypothesis because they both experience high infant mortality rates, have lived in association with each other for generations, and observe one another frequently. As a result, holding, responsiveness to fussing or crying, and the frequency of breastfeeding should be similarly high in the two cultures if they enhance infant survival. Moreover, parents in both cultures have had the opportunity both to evaluate the costs and benefits of different infant practices and to modify their own.

Studying these two cultures further allows researchers to explore the impact of different socioeconomic lifestyles on infant care. With the exception of Konner's (1977) research on the !Kung hunter-gathers and Tronick et al.'s (1987, 1992) research on the Efe hunter-gatherer-traders, most of the traditional non-Western societies studied have comprised agriculturists. Like LeVine (1974, 1989, 1994), the Whitings (Whiting & Edwards, 1988; Whiting & Whiting, 1975) have suggested that parenting practices are determined by the modes of production, which they called *maintenance systems,* because the subsistence demands, especially the workloads of women, lead to different patterns of child care. The Aka–Ngandu comparison may thus elucidate the differential effects of foraging and agricultural lifestyles on infant care.

Several cross-cultural theorists (such as Keller, 1997; Kornadt & Trommsdorff, 1990; Tronick et al., 1987) have hypothesized that differences between Western and traditional small-scale cultures with respect to infant–adult proximity are linked to distinct cultural goals: Western parents engage in frequent verbal and face-to-face interaction to promote independence and autonomy, whereas parents in small-scale and other non-Western cultures use close body contact and affective tuning to promote more social sensitivity and group-oriented tendencies. Structural aspects of a culture may also be significant in this regard. In cultures such as India, Japan, and China that are highly patriarchal, women can exert political and economic power and control primarily through their children (Keller, 1997). For example, Wolf (1972) has hypothesized that Chinese mothers hold, indulge, and limit access to their infants to develop more dependent and loyal children who will give support and status as the mothers grow older. As a result, both patriarchy and a strong cultural emphasis on social unity or conformity should be associated with more infant–adult proximity.

Both of the cultures we studied share more and are in many ways more egalitarian than European American cultures, but Aka sharing and egalitarianism are substantially greater than among the Ngandu. Ngandu households that accumulate more than others and do not share with neighboring families are prime targets of sorcery. This promotes some sharing between households, but there is marked inequality within Ngandu households, with men and elderly individuals receiving more than others. The Aka, by contrast, share with many people in many households on a daily basis, and there is greater gender and age egalitarianism. To foster egalitarianism, Aka also avoid drawing attention to themselves and eschew evaluative rankings, while also respecting individuality and autonomy. By contrast, the Ngandu promote social unity and conformity.

The Ngandu live alongside roads in sedentary communities of about 100 to 400 people. The Ngandu in this study lived in Bagandu, where two or three vehicles pass each day. Bagandu has a Catholic church, local market, health clinic, and several small shops, run mostly by Tchadians. Ngandu men build the 40-ft by 20-ft (12.19 m $\times$ 6.10 m), one- to three-roomed mud-and-thatch houses. Polygyny is common among the Ngandu (35% of the men have more than one wife), and each wife has her own room or house. Houses are about 40 ft (12.19 m) from each other, but there are no walls or fences between houses and other villagers frequently walk by. By contrast, the Aka live in camps of 25 to 35 blood or marriage relatives and move camp several times a year for various reasons (e.g., better hunting, death in camp). The dome-shaped Aka houses are made by women and have just enough room for a narrow 4-ft-long (1.22 m) log bed and a fire. Camps consist of four to six houses that are very close to each other (1–2 ft, .30 m–1.22 m) so all camp members live in an area (around 200 ft^2, 18.58 m^2) about the size of a large living and dining room in the United States. Cooperative net hunting involves men, women, and children, who connect their nets to form a circle. The men go to the center of the circle and try to chase game into the net, while the women stay close to the net, tackling the animals once they are trapped.

Whereas Aka men and women contribute equally to subsistence, Ngandu women are the primary providers. Ngandu men clear and burn plantations, whereas women plant, weed, harvest, and prepare all subsistence food items (manioc, corn, peanuts, plantains, etc.). Unlike the Aka, the Ngandu are actively engaged in a local cash economy, and many women are small-scale merchants, selling plantains, peanuts, nuts, mushrooms, and alcohol. Men are completely responsible for coffee production, hunting with trap lines or guns, and searching for gold or diamonds in the local streams. Ngandu women are responsible for home maintenance, laundry, and collecting water and firewood. Ngandu subsistence involves "delayed returns" (Woodburn, 1982, p. 435), in that the Ngandu have to delay the rewards of investment until harvest time. By contrast, the Aka subsistence system involves "immediate returns" (Woodburn, 1982, p. 435) in that the Aka consume everything within a day or two after capture or collection. The Aka may thus share more frequently in part because relatively little has been invested. The workload of Ngandu mothers also appears to be greater than that of the Aka, especially given the extensive sharing and cooperation among the Aka. Meanwhile, Aka infants are socialized in a denser social context than are Ngandu infants. Like the !Kung, Aka infants are carried in slings on the left-hand side of the adults' bodies (Konner, 1976, 1977). This leaves the head, arms, and legs free and allows the infant to nurse on demand. By contrast, Ngandu infants are tied rather snugly on the adults' backs. When the adults are sitting, both Aka and Ngandu care providers place infants on their laps or between their legs facing outwards. When infants are laid down, they are always placed on their backs. Aka infants sleep with their parents and siblings, whereas Ngandu infants often sleep with their mothers (or in separate cots, when husbands come to visit).

The Ngandu have more caregiving devices than Aka; some parents make small chairs, beds or mats for the infants to lie on. Ngandu infants also have more clothes, are often dressed more warmly than adults even in the middle of a hot day, and are washed once or twice a day. By comparison, Aka infants seldom have more than a protective forest cord around their waists and are infrequently given a complete bath. Both Aka and Ngandu caregivers carefully keep insects and debris off their infants.

METHOD

PARTICIPANTS

Twenty Aka and 21 Ngandu 3- to 4-month-olds and 20 Aka and 20 Ngandu 9- to 10-month-olds were observed for 3 hr on each of 4 different days so that all 12 daylight hours were covered (roughly, 6 a.m. to 6 p.m.). Thirteen of the Aka 3-month-olds, 12 of the Ngandu 3-month-olds, 9 of the Aka 9-month-olds, and 12 of the Ngandu 9-month-olds were boys. Six (3 Aka, 3 Ngandu) of the Aka and Ngandu 3- to 4-month-olds and 14 (6 Aka) of the 9- to 10-month-olds were firstborns, and 20% of the Aka and Ngandu fathers in both age cohorts had more than one wife. None of the Aka had received a formal education nor were they engaged in the cash economy, and all Aka parents engaged in subsistence activities during the observations. Most of the Ngandu men and several of

the Ngandu women had received some elementary education. Men and women engaged in subsistence and market activities, but none were employed outside the households.

PROCEDURE

Families were asked to follow their everyday activities and to ignore the observer, although, as always, it is difficult to know precisely how much the caregivers changed their daily activities to accommodate the observations. Ngandu mothers, in particular, seldom left their homes to participate in public activities (e.g., going to the market or standing in line for hours at the health clinic), in part, we believe, because the observer's presence elicited such curiosity. Aka generally do not accommodate others very much, and they pursued a great variety of activities outside their houses or camps. Observations took place in both rainy and dry seasons, but the majority of the 3- to 4-month-old observations took place in the dry season, whereas the majority of the observations of the 9- to 10-month-olds took place in the rainy season. Both Aka and Ngandu are more likely to stay home during the rainy season.

Using a 20-s observe–10-s record time sampling procedure for 45 min, observers noted on a checklist the occurrence of 11 adult and 9 infant behaviors, 5 dyadic behaviors, as well as the location, position, and identity of the adult near, holding, or caring for the infant. Observers then took a 15-min break before starting the next 45 min of observation. The beginning and end of each time sampling unit were signaled through an earphone from a small tape recorder.

The codes, which were also used and defined by Belsky, Gilstrap, and Rovine (1984) and by Fracasso, Lamb, Schölmerich, and Leyendecker (1997), are listed in Table 1. Observers were trained until they were reliable using videotaped interactions, but interobserver reliability was checked during the data gathering by having two different coders independently observe infants at the same time. Interobserver reliability coefficients were computed by correlating the two observers' scores on each variable. Mean reliability of codes was .82 (range = .65–.96), and the interobserver reliability of each code is provided in Table 1. Most (75%) of the observations were conducted by one observer. Interobserver reliability was checked twice—before observations began with each age group. Warm-up observations were used to acclimate Ngandu but not Aka parents and children. Because the observers were living with the Aka, Aka houses are open, and the camp is a public sphere (in contrast to the United States, where houses are considered pri-

TABLE 1   CODES USED FOR THE OBSERVATION OF CARE PROVIDER–INFANT INTERACTION

Behavior	Interobserver reliability
Dyadic behavior	
Face-to-face	.75
Mutual visual	.67
C holds	.96
C proximal (within arm's length)	.82
C grooms, dresses, cleans, etc.	.91
C feeds or nurses	.96
Care provider behavior	
C attention is focused on infant (watches)	.78
C checks on infant (brief glances)	.84
C stimulates or arouses infant	.83
C physical affect towards infant	.79
C nonphysical affect towards infant	.72
C physically soothes infant	.87
C nonphysically soothes infant	.82
C vocalizes to infant	.76
M leisure (no subsistence activity)	.73
M works	.70
C talks to others	.83
Infant behavior	
I fussing	.78
I crying	.95
I sleeps	.87
I drowses	.65
I looks at C	.83
I smiles	.73
I vocalizes	.81
I plays alone (distracts self with objects, including own body)	.81
I plays with objects	.86
I responds to care provider stimulation	.77
Other behavior	
Location (lap, bed, arms, sling)	.92
Room (in house, outside house, forest, plantation)	.89

Note. C = care provider; M = mother; I = infant.

vate spheres), there was no apparent need to acclimate Aka parents and children to the observers. The Aka adults and children appeared unaffected by the observers' activities.

In addition to assessing the number of intervals in which certain behaviors were observed, we also defined five mutually exclusive and exhaustive contexts (feeding, caretaking, object play, social interaction, and no interaction) to describe the overall activity of the dyad as suggested and previously demonstrated by Leyendecker, Lamb, Schölmerich, and Miranda Fricke (1997). As in Leyendecker et al.'s study, the feeding and caretaking contexts were identified as such by the coders, and even when other activities such as social play and object play occurred in one of these two contexts, the functional context was still labeled as *feeding* or *caretaking*, respectively, because feeding or care-providing were the adults' primary goals at the time. Dyadic *object play* was coded when both infant and adult were involved in object play outside of feeding and caretaking, and *social interaction* was coded when the dyads were engaged in visual-verbal interactions, physical and nonphysical affect, and soothing outside of the other contexts. Whereas feeding, caretaking, object play, and social interaction describe dyadic states, all monadic states were coded as *no interaction* (e.g., infant looks at mother while mother does not look at the infant and vice versa; infant plays with object while mother is at leisure, etc.) as were all other units not included in the other four contexts.

RESULTS

Because preliminary multi- and univariate analyses revealed no reliable effects of gender, the data concerning boys and girls were combined for the purposes of further analysis. A series of 2 (ethnic group: Aka or Ngandu) $\times$ 2 (age: 3–4 months or 9–10 months) multivariate analyses of variance (MANOVAs) were first used to assess the effects of ethnic group and age on the three groups of dependent variables—care provider behaviors, infant behaviors, and dyadic behaviors—and are displayed in Table 2. These analyses yielded significant effects for ethnic group on the care provider, $F(10, 68) = 3.56$, $p < .001$; infant, $F(11, 67) = 7.34$, $p < .0001$; and dyadic behaviors, $F(6, 72) = 26.38$, $p < .0001$, and significant effects for age on all three groups of dependent variables as well, $F(10, 68) = 6.76$, $p < .0001$; $F(11, 67) = 18.28$, $p < .0001$; $F(6, 72) = 4.57$, $p < .001$, respectively. Univariate analyses were used to explore these effects further, and the result of these analyses are provided in Table 2, along with the relevant means. Inspection of the table shows that, as expected, older infants slept and drowsed less, fussed

TABLE 2 AGE COHORT AND ETHNIC GROUP DIFFERENCES IN THE BEHAVIOR OF ADULTS AND INFANTS

| Variable | 3–4 Months | | | | 9–10 Months | | | | Effect | |
| | Aka | | Ngandu | | Aka | | Ngandu | | | |
	$\underline{M}^a$	SD	$\underline{M}^a$	SD	$\underline{M}^a$	SD	$\underline{M}^a$	SD	Ethnic	Age
Dyadic behavior										
Face-to-face	2.57	3.32	2.17	2.37	0.14	0.13	0.99	1.13	0.19	14.85***
Mutual visual	2.35	3.62	1.10	0.82	0.05	0.07	2.72	4.36	1.26	0.29
C holds I	95.91	6.57	54.21	19.99	86.71	10.98	54.46	16.17	132.55**	1.93
C proximal (within arm's length)	97.29	4.03	65.31	16.19	86.57	15.63	63.42	17.06	75.34***	3.94
C grooms, dresses, cleans, etc.	5.03	1.74	6.50	3.32	2.74	1.29	6.10	3.86	15.35***	4.75*
C nurses or feeds	15.23	5.53	12.63	5.02	13.30	4.50	10.13	4.20	7.19**	4.34*
Care provider behavior										
C watches or checks on I	30.14	8.87	23.50	12.62	22.35	6.95	31.72	10.59	0.37	0.01
C stimulates or arouses I	0.63	0.75	1.73	1.52	0.06	0.09	2.57	3.85	14.97***	0.07
C physical affect toward I	4.18	2.18	3.08	2.86	1.38	1.01	1.72	1.26	0.76	22.14***
C nonphysical affect toward I	0.90	1.67	2.14	3.03	1.31	1.37	1.29	1.51	1.88	0.23
C physically soothes I	3.39	2.30	4.22	4.11	0.75	0.60	1.56	1.02	2.25	23.60***
C nonphysically soothes I	2.28	1.93	4.04	4.33	0.86	0.82	1.22	1.03	3.67	14.59***
C vocalizes to I	3.91	3.45	2.84	2.22	2.31	1.59	5.23	5.21	1.52	0.27
Mother leisure: no subsistence activity	67.45	23.63	50.34	22.68	70.71	15.04	65.75	11.58	6.84**	4.89*
Mother works	28.29	20.46	39.13	20.40	28.34	15.15	29.81	11.88	2.53	1.44
C talks to others	40.19	12.66	30.95	13.57	43.13	10.37	41.23	15.16	3.68	5.18*
Infant behaviors										
I fusses or cries	4.67	3.26	12.38	7.03	2.42	1.39	6.81	5.67	81.07**	12.96***
I alone, asleep	0.47	0.94	10.56	9.72	1.09	1.67	9.81	8.63	40.82***	0.00
I alone, awake	0.06	0.19	4.81	7.12	0.43	0.82	6.09	8.42	17.79***	0.45
I sleeps	41.34	14.99	31.40	10.30	19.77	9.13	18.41	9.80	5.11**	47.81***
I drowses	19.30	14.48	11.38	10.30	11.72	7.83	6.90	5.36	8.09**	7.24**
I looks at C	4.16	4.23	2.62	2.03	0.95	1.12	3.64	6.38	0.73	2.65
I smiles	0.51	0.56	1.25	1.57	0.26	0.25	3.56	4.11	9.55**	1.16
I vocalizes	2.37	3.14	9.32	7.85	3.53	3.23	11.88	11.13	22.98***	1.36
I plays alone (distracts self with objects, fingers, etc.)	1.11	1.67	2.79	3.14	1.95	1.39	14.86	22.74	8.2**	6.42**
I plays with objects	1.69	2.93	2.15	2.83	12.41	7.45	28.62	17.11	15.58***	77.65***
I responds to C stimulation	0.16	0.28	0.81	1.05	0.08	0.17	1.78	2.71	13.14***	1.92

Note. C = care provider; I = infant. Watch or check, fuss or cry, infant alone (nobody present in room) and infant alone and awake are combined behaviors from Table 1.
Only significant *F* values are reported in the two right-hand columns; in each case (*dfs* = 1, 77).
[a]Represents the mean percentage of the total number of intervals (1,080) during which the behavior was observed.
*$p < .05$. **$p < .01$. ***$p < .001$.

or cried less, and consequently received less physical or nonphysical soothing than did the younger infants. The frequency of feeding, face-to-face interaction, and caregiving also declined over time, but the amount of adult leisure increased, presumably because observations of the young infants took place in the dry season, when the workload for Ngandu women is especially high, whereas observations of older infants took place in the rainy season, when maternal workloads are lower. The unavoidable confounds between age and season are unlikely to have accounted for any other effects reported here.

The Aka infants were substantially more likely than Ngandu infants to sleep, drowse, to be held or fed, or to be within proximity of their care providers, whereas Ngandu infants were more likely than Aka infants to be alone, fuss, cry, smile, vocalize to care providers, play alone, or play with objects. Ngandu infants were stimulated and aroused more by their care providers than Aka infants were. There were no differences between ethnic groups in the frequency of care provider soothing, affect, watching or checking the infant, and face-to-face or mutual visual interactions.

Significant multivariate interactions between age and ethnic group were also evident for care provider, $F(10, 68) = 2.62$, $p < .009$; infant, $F(11, 67) = 3.73$, $p < .0001$; and dyadic, $F(6, 72) = 2.44$, $p < .034$, behaviors. Subsequent analyses using Tukey honestly significant difference tests revealed no group differences in adult vocalizations to infants at 3 months, although the Ngandu engaged in more mutual visual interactions at 9 ($p < .02$) but not at 3 months, and en-face interactions increased over time among the Aka ($p < .003$) but not among the Ngandu. The frequency of looking at care providers decreased over time among the Aka ($p < .007$) but did not change among the Ngandu. There were no group differences in the frequencies of object play and playing alone at 3 months, but the Ngandu engaged in significantly more play than the Aka ($p < .0001$ and $p < .003$, respectively) at 9 months. The frequency of watching and checking by the adults did not change over time among the Aka but increased among the Ngandu ($p < .05$).

Although there were striking Aka–Ngandu differences on a number of variables, it is instructive to examine these differences across functional contexts. For illustrative purposes, we focus here only on the observations of the 3- to 4-month-olds; the same points could be made using the data for the 9- to 10-month-olds. Figures 1 to 4 graphically display variations across context on four variables in which there were significant differences between ethnic groups (fuss, cry, smile, and infant vocalization). In general, the figures indicate that, although ethnic differences were consistent across contexts (i.e., Ngandu infants fussed and cried more than Aka infants in all contexts), context systematically affected the relative prominence of the infants' behavior (i.e., both Aka and Ngandu fussed and cried more in social interaction). One implication is that both similarities and differences between Aka and Ngandu groups can be magnified or minimized unless steps are taken to ensure that observations take place in comparable contexts.

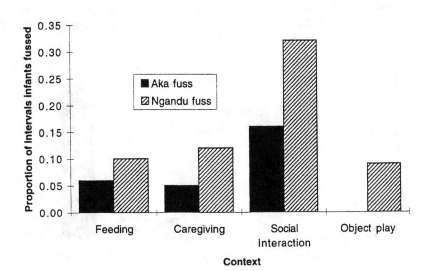

FIGURE 1

Aka and Ngandu infant fussing in various contexts.

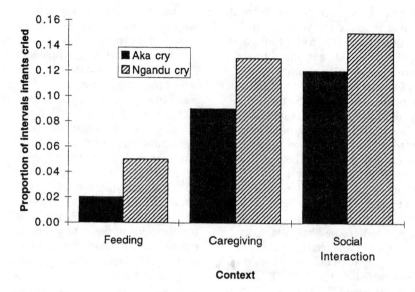

FIGURE 2
Aka and Ngandu infant crying in various contexts (there was no crying during object play).

DISCUSSION

Overall, the statistical analyses reported here revealed that Aka infant–adult interactions are more proximal, whereas Ngandu adult–infant interactions are more distal and that these differences become especially pronounced in late infancy. Aka care providers—usually mothers, fathers, or other adults—hold their infants, keep them close, feed them more frequently (2.2 vs. 4.0 times per hour) and longer, and soothe them just as long as Ngandu care providers do, even though Aka infants fuss or cry half as much as

Ngandu infants. Aka respond to each fuss or cry, often by soothing, whereas Ngandu care providers are more likely to let the infant fuss or cry (Hewlett, Lamb, Leyendecker, & Schölmerich, 1998). The differences are especially remarkable in light of the fact that Aka holding is energetically more costly to Aka mothers than to Ngandu mothers because, as pygmies, the Aka are considerably shorter and lighter than Ngandu women, whereas the Aka and Ngandu infants are of comparable weight. On the other hand, Ngandu stimulate their infants more by using distal behaviors; they are more likely to arouse and to vo-

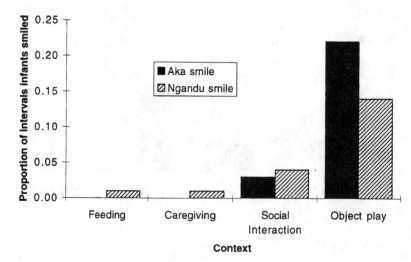

FIGURE 3
Aka and Ngandu infant smiling in various contexts.

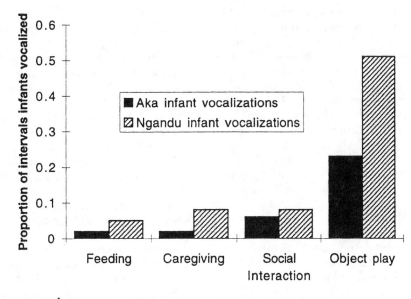

FIGURE 4

Aka and Ngandu infant vocalizations in various contexts.

calize to infants who are, in turn, more likely to respond by smiling and by vocalizing. The differentiation between these two non-Western populations is greater than the differences between and among those Western groups that have been studied at similar ages with comparable methods (e.g., Fracasso et al., 1997; Leyendecker et al., 1997).

The fact that the Aka infants are held almost all the time may explain why these infants sleep or drowse more than Ngandu infants do and may also increase the potential for nonverbal communication, like that documented by McKenna, Mosko, Dungy, and McAninch (1990). When infants are held, the body movements, heartbeats, sounds, and smells of infants and adults provide the basis for a subtle "dance" that is obviously not captured when gross observational methods are used, so we cannot conclude that Aka adults and infants interact rarely. Meanwhile, because Ngandu infants are held about half as frequently as Aka infants, their interactions tend to depend on more distal forms of communication: Ngandu infants thus fuss, cry, smile, and vocalize to maintain or attract their parents' attention, and Ngandu adults vocalize and stimulate their infants in return.

Although this may explain why distal interaction is more common in Ngandu than in Aka infant–adult dyads, it does not explain why the Aka hold their infants so much or why the Ngandu tend not to do so. Are these differences explained by considerations of infant survival (more hazards in Aka environment), mode of production (lower workload by Aka women), or cultural ideologies (social unity, communalism), as suggested by cross-cultural theorists (Bornstein et al., 1992; Keller, 1997; LeVine, 1994; Tronick et al., 1987; Whiting & Whiting,1975)?

Infant mortality is similarly high among both Aka and Ngandu, as it is in other contemporary forager and farmer environments (Bailey & Peacock, 1989; Bentley, Goldberg, & Jasienska, 1993; Cohen, 1989; Hewlett, 1991a), so this cannot explain the substantial cultural differences in the frequencies of proximal behaviors, although it might be argued that worries about survival are greater among Aka parents than among Ngandu parents, perhaps because the Aka environment is more dangerous (i.e., exposure to more hazards such as snakes, predators, or falling trees). Kaplan and Dove (1987) have suggested that Aché foragers in Paraguay hold their infants all the time because the forest is potentially hazardous, and Blurton Jones (1993) has developed a simulation model influenced, in part, by his observation that Hadza and !Kung foragers always hold their infants; the model predicts greater reproductive fitness from constant holding even when hazards are rare. The differential infant mortality hypothesis is also not supported by Barry S. Hewlett's observations during 25 years of fieldwork (1973–1997) that there are as many poisonous snakes, spiders, and scorpions in the Ngandu villages and fields as in the forest and that Ngandu fields attract large and dangerous game animals, including elephants. Nor is it clear how holding an infant as opposed to laying it down nearby would affect survival differentially or why survival-focused Aka mothers would have primary responsibility for tackling trapped animals, a task that requires them to put their infants down and run after game animals. And if holding, frequency of breastfeeding, and responsiveness to crying dramatically affect survival, why would the Ngandu not alter their behavior to match that of the neighbors they observe so frequently?

Nutritional factors or infant morbidity might also explain why Aka are more proximal; Wachs, Sigman, Bishry, and Moussa (1992) have shown that caregiver behaviors are influenced by infant nutritional status. The hypothesis would be that Aka infants, in general, have lower nutritional status than Ngandu infants and are therefore more proximal. Although we did not directly measure the nutritional status of these infants, previous studies of infant and child health among the Aka and Ngandu (Cordes & Hewlett, 1990) indicated that infants and children in both groups were healthier than most infants in the developing world (measures included weight for height, head circumference, and hemoglobin levels). Both Aka and Ngandu are more proximal with ill infants, but sick infants were excluded from the study. Overall, it appears that the observed differences between Aka and Ngandu caregiver–infant interactions cannot be explained by differential health or survival rates.

What about the workloads of Ngandu and Aka mothers? The Whitings' (1975) hypotheses suggest that Ngandu infant–adult dyads might involve more distal-verbal interactions because Ngandu women's workloads are greater or because Ngandu subsistence tasks are incompatible with holding infants. In fact, Ngandu women usually put infants down when they fall asleep rather than switching activities, and none of their subsistence tasks are incompatible with infant care. Meanwhile, Aka parents have plenty of opportunities (in camp and on the hunt) to put their infants down but do not do so. Further, one deficiency of the maternal work hypothesis is the implication that infants are a burden, constraining their mothers' activities; many parents may feel this way in European American cultures, but such complaints are rare among the Aka and Ngandu. In addition, the Ngandu and Aka women we studied devoted equivalent amounts of time to subsistence and household work, although the Aka mothers had slightly more leisure time than the Ngandu mothers, especially when the infants were younger. These differences are likely to be artifacts of seasonal variations, however; the observations of the 3-month-olds were conducted in the dry season, when Ngandu women are unusually busy preparing the fields before the rains, whereas the observations of the 9-month-olds were conducted in the rainy season, when both Ngandu and Aka women have more leisure time. Aka mothers also "work" much more than Ngandu women when child care is included because they hold their infants so often. On the other hand, Aka mothers' other work

may be less intense because they are not primary providers and they can count on extensive within-group sharing.

Cultural ideologies, such as the social unity hypothesis, do not explain the differences between the Aka and Ngandu either. Social unity, conformity, and patriarchy are central constructs in Ngandu culture, whereas autonomy in the context of the community and egalitarianism is the cultural script among the Aka. These cultural patterns predicted greater proximal behaviors among the Ngandu than among the Aka (Keller, 1997; Tronick et al., 1987), whereas the reverse was actually observed.

In sum, extant hypotheses, most of which were developed to explain Western versus non-Western differences rather than variation among Western or non-Western cultures (the Whitings' [1975] hypotheses being the exception) do not help explain the observed differences between the Aka and Ngandu.

Several features of the Aka and Ngandu cultures may be of explanatory value, however. First, the Aka move much more frequently than do the Ngandu: The whole camp moves from 4 to 18 times a year, camp composition changes daily as families arrive or leave temporarily to visit relatives and friends, and families travel several kilometers every day through open forest to hunt and gather. The Ngandu, on the other hand, stay in the same house for about 10 years and farm the same fields for 2 to 4 years. Absences are not as frequent or as long because the women have to maintain and protect their fields. As a result, the mobile Aka may perceive more risk than do the sedentary Ngandu because they are less familiar with their "home" and hold their infants more to accommodate potential hazards associated with the changing environment.

Second, differences between the social contexts may be pertinent. Aka camps comprise 25 to 35 people—many related to one another—who live together in an area about the size of a large living and dining room in the United States and engage in frequent cooperative activities like hunting. Ngandu households, by comparison, are much farther apart, and daily cooperation is limited to that between mothers and their children. Among nonhuman primates, interestingly, mothers in group-living pairs nurse and spend more time in contact with their infants than do mothers in isolated pairs (Konner, 1977). Isolated mothers distance themselves from, avoid, and punish their infants more. Similarly, Aka parents may be more willing to hold and nurse infants if their denser social contexts provide substantial alternative stimulation for both mothers and infants. Of course, by European American standards, the Ngandu are not socially isolated but by comparison with the Aka, their social contacts with other adults are fewer and shorter in duration.

Third, cooperative hunting and food sharing practices may ensure that the Aka are less concerned about having adequate supplies of food, and this may make them more willing (or able) to invest in energetically costly infant care.

Fourth, the Aka focus on immediate returns rather than on delayed gratification, and this may make them more willing to accommodate their infants' demands for gratification.

Whatever the reason for the observed differences between the Aka and the Ngandu, the data presented in this article suggest that there may be a forager pattern of infant care. When describing farming (agrarian) and urban-industrial parental goals and infant care patterns, LeVine (1989, p. 6) suggested a decade ago that foraging would generate unique parenting patterns, but he never described the distinguishing features. These data help describe the parenting style and some of the forces that shape it. Specifically, the Aka niche is marked by integration into small, dense groups of related individuals who have intimate relationships dominated by extensive sharing and cooperation in many activities, including hunting and gathering in the forest they inhabit and exploit on foot. Perhaps as a result, their infant care practices are characterized by almost continuous holding, frequent nursing, and prompt responsiveness, especially to signs of distress.

REFERENCES

Bailey, R. C., & Peacock, N. (1989, November). *The demography of foragers and farmers in the Ituri forest.* Paper presented at the meeting of the American Anthropological Association, Washington, DC.

Bakeman, R., Adamson, L. B., Konner, M., & Barr, R. G. (1990). !Kung infancy: The social context of object manipulations. *Child Development, 6,* 794–809.

Barr, R. G. (1990). The early crying paradox. *Human Nature, 1,* 355–389.

Belsky, J., Gilstrap, B., & Rovine, M. (1984). The Pennsylvania Infant and Family Development Project, I: Stability and change in mother–infant and father–infant interactions in a family setting at one, three and nine months. *Child Development, 55,* 692–705.

Bentley, G. R., Goldberg, T., & Jasienska, G. (1993). The fertility of agricultural and non-agricultural traditional societies. *Population Studies, 47,* 269–281.

Blurton Jones, N. (1993). The lives of hunter-gatherer children: Effects of parental behavior and parental reproductive strategy. In M. E. Pereira & L. A. Fairbanks (Eds.), *Juvenile primates* (pp. 309–326). New York: Oxford University Press.

Bornstein, M. H., Tamis-LeMonda, C., Tal, J., Ludemann, P., Toda, S., Rahn, C. W., Pecheux, M. G., Azuma, H., & Vardi, D. (1992). Maternal responsiveness to infants in three societies: The United States, France, and Japan. *Child Development, 63,* 808–821.

Cohen, M. N. (1989). *Health and the rise of civilization.* New Haven, CT: Yale University Press.

Cordes, L., & Hewlett, B. S. (1990, May). *Health and nutrition among Aka pygmies.* Paper presented at the International Conference on Hunting and Gathering Societies, Fairbanks, AK.

Dixon, S. D., Tronick, E. Z., Keefer, C., & Brazelton, T. B. (1981). Mother–infant interaction among the Gusii of Kenya. In T. M. Field, A. M. Sostek, P. Vietze, & P. H. Leiderman (Eds.), *Culture and early interactions* (pp. 149–170). Hillsdale, NJ: Erlbaum.

Fracasso, M. P., Lamb, M. E., Schölmerich, A., & Leyendecker, B. (1997). The ecology of mother–infant interaction in Euro-American and immigrant Central American families living in the United States. *International Journal of Behavioral Development, 20,* 207–217.

Goldberg, S. (1977). Infant development and mother–infant interaction in urban Zambia. In P. H. Leiderman, S. R. Tulkin, & A. Rosenfeld (Eds.), *Culture and infancy* (pp. 211–243). New York: Academic Press.

Hewlett, B. S. (1991a). Demography and childcare in preindustrial societies. *Journal of Anthropological Research, 47,* 1–37.

Hewlett, B. S. (1991b). *Intimate fathers.* Ann Arbor: University of Michigan Press.

Hewlett, B. S., Lamb, M. E., Leyendecker, B., & Schölmerich, A. (1998). *Internal working models, trust, and sharing among hunter-gatherers.* Unpublished manuscript, Washington State University, Pullman.

Kaplan, H., & Dove, H. (1987). Infant development among the Aché of Eastern Paraguay. *Development Psychology, 23,* 190–198.

Keller, H. (1997). Evolutionary approaches. In J. W. Berry, Y. H. Poortinga, & J. Pandey (Eds.), *Handbook of cross-cultural psychology. Vol. 1: Theory and method* (2nd ed., pp. 215–255). Boston: Allyn & Bacon.

Keller, H., Schölmerich, A., & Eibl-Eibesfeldt, I. (1988). Communication patterns in adult–infant interactions in Western and non-Western cultures. *Journal of Cross-Cultural Psychology, 19,* 427–445.

Konner, M. J. (1976). Maternal care, infant behavior and development among the !Kung. In R. B. Lee & I. DeVore (Eds.), *Kalahari hunter-gatherers* (pp. 218–245). Cambridge, MA: Harvard University Press.

Konner, M. (1977). Infancy among Kalahari Desert San. In P. H. Leiderman, S. T. Tulkin, & A. Rosenfeld (Eds.), *Culture and infancy: Variations in the human experience* (pp. 287–328). New York: Academic Press.

Kornadt, H. J., & Trommsdorff, G. (1990). Naive erziehungstheorien japanischer Mutter-deutsch-japanischer Kulturergleich [Naive theories of development: A cultural comparison between Japanese and German mother–infant interaction]. *Zeitschrift fur Sozialisations-forschung und Erziehungssoziologie, 2,* 357–376.

LeVine, R. A. (1974). Parental goals: A cross-cultural view. *Teachers College Record, 76,* 226–239.

LeVine, R. A. (1989). Human parental care: Universal goals, cultural strategies, individual behavior. In R. A. LeVine, P. M.

Miller, & M. M. West (Eds.), *Parental behavior in diverse societies* (pp. 3–12). San Francisco: Jossey-Bass.

LeVine, R. A. (1994). *Child care and culture: Lessons from Africa.* Cambridge, England: Cambridge University Press.

Leyendecker, B., Lamb, M. E., Schölmerich, A., & Miranda Fricke, D. (1997). Contexts as moderators of observed interaction: A study of Costa Rican mothers and infants from differing socio-economic backgrounds. *International Journal of Behavioral Development, 21,* 15–34.

McKenna, J. J., Mosko, S., Dungy, C., & McAninch, J. (1990). Sleep and arousal patterns of co-sleeping human mother/infant pairs: A preliminary physiological study with implications for the study of Sudden Infant Death Syndrome (SIDS). *American Journal of Physical Anthropology, 83,* 331–347.

Richman, A. L., LeVine, R. A., New, R., Howrigan, G. A., Welles-Nystrom, B., & LeVine, S. E. (1988). Maternal behavior to infants in five cultures. In R. A. LeVine, P. M. Miller, & M. West (Eds.), *Parental behavior in diverse societies* (pp. 81–98). San Francisco: Jossey-Bass.

Richman, A. L., Miller, P. M., & LeVine, R. A. (1992). Cultural and educational variations in maternal responsiveness. *Developmental Psychology, 28,* 614–621.

Roopnarine, J. L., Talukder, E., Jain, D., Joshi, P., & Srivastav, P. (1990). Characteristics of holding, patterns of play, and social behaviors between parents and infants in New Delhi, India. *Developmental Psychology, 26,* 667–673.

Super, C. M., & Harkness, S. (1981). The infant's niche in rural Kenya and metropolitan America. In L. L. Adler (Ed.), *Cross-cultural research at issue* (pp. 47–55). New York: Academic Press.

Tronick, E., Morelli, G. A., & Ivey, P. K. (1992). The Efe forager infant and toddler's pattern of social relationships: Multiple and simultaneous. *Developmental Psychology, 28,* 568–577.

Tronick, E., Morelli, G. A., & Winn, S. (1987). Multiple caretaking of Efe (Pygmy) infants. *American Anthropologist, 89,* 96–106.

Wachs, T. D., Sigman, M., Bishry, Z., & Moussa, W. (1992). Caregiver–child interaction patterns in two cultures in relation to nutritional intake. *International Journal of Behavioral Development, 15,* 1–18.

Whiting, B. B., & Edwards, C. P. (1988). *Children of different worlds: The formation of social behavior.* Cambridge, MA: Harvard University Press.

Whiting, B. B., & Whiting, J. W. M. (1975). *Children of six cultures.* Cambridge, MA: Harvard University Press.

Wolf, M. (1972). *Women and the family in rural Taiwan.* Stanford, CA: Stanford University Press.

Woodburn, J. (1982). Egalitarian societies. *Man* (New Series), *17,* 431–451.

QUESTIONS

1. What were some of the limitations of earlier cross-cultural research on parenting that Hewlett and his colleagues tried to overcome in this study?
2. Which two cultural communities were the focus of this research? What similarities and differences in the lifestyles of these two groups make their child-rearing practices interesting to compare?
3. How do the workloads of mothers differ in these two communities?
4. How are infants carried in these two communities? How might these different ways of carrying babies influence psychological development?
5. What were the main differences observed in Aku and Ngandu infant caregiving behaviors?
6. Using the histograms shown in Figures 1 and 2, what conclusions can you reach about how infants in these two communities behave? Do observations from different contexts, depicted in the histograms, support your conclusions? If so, how?
7. Can the different caregiving patterns of the Aku and Ngandu be explained by infant health or survival rates? Use evidence from the article to support your answer.
8. What do the researchers conclude about the explanations for differences in caregiving offered by previous cross-cultural research that compared Western and non-Western communities?
9. What explanations do Hewlett and colleagues offer for the caregiving differences they observed?
10. How might these observations of two cultures influence a more general understanding of the correlation between parenting practices and early infant development?

10 Temperament and the Reactions to Unfamiliarity

Jerome Kagan

Temperament is defined as the way an individual behaves. It includes stylistic aspects of behavior, such as the emotional vigor, tempo, and regularity of an infant's responsiveness to caregivers. Temperament is of interest to developmental psychologists because it is evident early in life, it relates to behavior across a wide range of situations, and it appears to be relatively stable over time. There is also evidence that some aspects of temperament may be inherited; for example, emotionality, activity, and sociability have been found to be more similar in identical than in fraternal twins. For these reasons, many psychologists consider temperament to be the seed of what becomes an individual's unique personality.

One way in which researchers measure temperament in infancy is by observing babies' reactions to unfamiliar events. Some babies react in a heightened fashion, with much movement and distress, while other babies remain relaxed and calm. In the following article, Jerome Kagan, a leading researcher in the area of infant temperament, discusses longitudinal research that examined how children reacted to unfamiliar events when they were infants, toddlers, and 5-year-olds. The types of reactions included motor activity, fearfulness, and friendliness. The data revealed some stability in these styles of reaction over this time period—and change in some aspects of temperament. In addition to describing behaviors associated with high and low reactivity and how these behaviors varied over time, Kagan discusses the biological bases of these behaviors and the possible connections between these behavioral tendencies and later psychopathology.

This research illustrates several important points about development. First, even when characteristics are developmentally stable, they may assume different forms at different ages. Second, maturation of the organism can sometimes modify even extreme behaviors. Third, the development of temperament involves the coordination of biologically based tendencies with the emotional, cognitive, and social aspects of psychological growth.

The behavioral reactions to unfamiliar events are basic phenomena in all vertebrates. Four-month-old infants who show a low threshold to become distressed and motorically aroused to unfamiliar stimuli are more likely than others to become fearful and subdued during early childhood, whereas infants who show a high arousal threshold are more likely to become bold and sociable. After presenting some developmental correlates and trajectories of these 2 temperamental biases, I consider their implications for psychopathology and the relation between propositions containing psychological and biological concepts.

INTRODUCTION

A readiness to react to events that differ from those encountered in the recent or distant past is one of the distinguishing characteristics of all mammalian species. Thus, the events with the greatest power to produce both an initial orienting and sustained attention in infants older than 3 to 4 months are variations on what is familiar, often called discrepant events (Fagan, 1981; Kagan, Kearsley, & Zelazo, 1980). By 8 months of age, discrepant events can produce a vigilant posture of quiet staring and, occasionally, a wary face and a cry of distress if the event cannot be assim-

Reprinted with permission of Blackwell Publishers from Kagan, J. (1997). Temperament and the reactions to unfamiliarity. *Child Development, 68,* 139–143.

ilated easily (Bronson, 1970). That is why Hebb (1946) made discrepancy a major basis for fear reactions in animals, why a fear reaction to strangers occurs in the middle of the first year in children growing up in a variety of cultural settings, and, perhaps, why variation in the initial behavioral reaction to novelty exists in almost every vertebrate species studied (Wilson, Coleman, Clark, & Biederman, 1993).

Recent discoveries by neuroscientists enrich these psychological facts. The hippocampus plays an important role in the detection of discrepant events (Squire & Knowlton, 1995). Projections from the hippocampus provoke activity in the amygdala and lead to changes in autonomic function and posture and, in older children, to reflection and anticipation (Shimamura, 1995). Because these neural structures and their projections are influenced by a large number of neurotransmitters and neuromodulators, it is reasonable to expect inherited differences in the neurochemistry of these structures and circuits and, therefore, in their excitability. Variation in the levels of, or receptors for, corticotropin releasing hormone, norepinephrine, cortisol, dopamine, glutamate, GABA, opioids, acetylcholine, and other molecules might be accompanied by differences in the intensity and form of responsivity to unfamiliarity (Cooper, Bloom, & Roth, 1991). This speculation is supported by research with infants and children (Kagan, 1994). This article summarizes what has been learned about two temperamental types of children who react in different ways to unfamiliarity, considers the implications of these two temperamental categories for psychopathology, and comments briefly on the relation between psychological and biological constructs.

INFANT REACTIVITY AND FEARFUL BEHAVIOR

About 20% of a large sample of 462 healthy, Caucasian, middle-class, 16-week-old infants became both motorically active and distressed to presentations of brightly colored toys moved back and forth in front of their faces, tape recordings of voices speaking brief sentences, and cotton swabs dipped in dilute butyl alcohol applied to the nose. These infants are called high reactive. By contrast, about 40% of infants with the same family and ethnic background remained motorically relaxed and did not fret or cry to the same set of unfamiliar events. These infants are called low reactive. The differences between high and low reactives can be interpreted as reflecting variation in the excitability of the amygdala and its projections to the ventral striatum, hypothalamus, cingulate, central gray, and medulla (Amaral, Price, Pitkanen, & Carmichael, 1992; Davis, 1992).

When these high and low reactive infants were observed in a variety of unfamiliar laboratory situations at 14 and 21 months, about one-third of the 73 high reactives were highly fearful (4 or more fears), and only 3% showed minimal fear (0 or 1 fear) at both ages. By contrast, one-third of the 147 low reactives were minimally fearful at both ages (0 or 1 fear), and only 4% displayed high levels of fear (Kagan, 1994).

The profiles of high and low fear to unfamiliar events, called inhibited and uninhibited, are heritable, to a modest degree, in 1- to 2-year-old middle-class children (DiLalla, Kagan, & Reznick, 1994; Robinson, Kagan, Reznick, & Corley, 1992). Further, high reactives show greater sympathetic reactivity in the cardiovascular system than low reactives during the first 2 years (Kagan, 1994; Snidman, Kagan, Riordan, & Shannon, 1995).

As children approach the fourth and fifth years, they gain control of crying to and reflex retreat from unfamiliar events and will only show these responses to very dangerous events or to situations that are not easily or ethically created in the laboratory. Hence, it is important to ask how high and low reactive infants might respond to unfamiliar laboratory situations when they are 4–5 years old. Each species has a biologically preferred reaction to novelty. Rabbits freeze, monkeys display a distinct facial grimace, and cats arch their backs. In humans, restraint on speech seems to be an analogue of the immobility that animals display in novel situations (Panksepp, Sacks, Crepeau, & Abbott, 1991), for children often become quiet as an initial reaction to unfamiliar situations (Asendorpf, 1990; Kagan, Reznick, & Gibbons, 1989; Kagan, Reznick, & Snidman, 1988; Murray, 1971). It is also reasonable to expect that the activity in limbic sites provoked by an unfamiliar social situation might interfere with the brain states that mediate the relaxed emotional state that is indexed by smiling and laughter (Adamec, 1991; Amaral et al., 1992).

When the children who had been classified as high and low reactive were interviewed at 4½ years of age by an unfamiliar female examiner who was blind to their prior behavior, the 62 high reactives talked and smiled significantly less often (means of 41 comments and 17 smiles) than did the 94 low reactives (means of 57 comments and 28 smiles) during a 1 hour test battery: $F(1, 152) = 4.51$, $p < .05$ for spontaneous comments; $F(1, 152) \neq 15.01$, $p < .01$ for spontaneous smiles. Although spontaneous comments and smiles were positively correlated ($r = 0.4$), the low reactives displayed significantly more smiles than would have been predicted from a regression of number of smiles on number of spontaneous comments. The high reactives displayed significantly fewer smiles than expected. Every one of the nine children who smiled more than 50 times had been a low reactive infant.

However, only a modest proportion of children maintained an extreme form of their theoretically expected profile over the period from 4 months to 4½ years, presumably because of the influence of intervening family experiences (Arcus, 1991). Only 19% of the high reactives displayed a high level of fear at both 14 and 21 months (> 4 fears), together with low values (below the mean) for both spontaneous comments and smiles at 4½ years. But not one low reactive infant actualized such a consistently fearful and emotionally subdued profile. By contrast, 18% of low reactive infants showed the opposite profile of low fear (0 or 1 fear) at both 14 and 21 months together with high values for both spontaneous smiles and spontaneous comments at 4½ years. Only one high reactive infant actualized that prototypic, uninhibited profile. Thus, it is uncommon for either temperamental type to develop and to maintain the seminal features of the other type, but quite common for each type to develop a profile that is characteristic of the less extreme child who is neither very timid nor very bold.

The 4½-year-old boys who had been high reactive infants had significantly higher resting heart rates than did low reactives, but the differences between high and low reactive girls at this older age took a different form. The high reactive girls did not show the expected high negative correlation (-0.6 to -0.8) between heart rate and heart rate variability. It is possible that the greater sympathetic reactivity of high reactive girls interfered with the usual, vagally induced inverse relation between heart rate and heart rate variability (Porges, Arnold, & Forbes, 1973; Richards, 1985).

Honest disagreement surrounds the conceptualization of infant reactivity as a continuum of arousal or as two distinct categories. The raw motor activity score at 4 months formed a continuum, but the distribution of distress cries did not. Some infants never fretted or cried; others cried a great deal. A more important defense of the decision to treat high and low reactivity as two distinct categories is the fact that within each of the two categories variation in motor activity and crying was unrelated to later fearfulness or sympathetic reactivity. If reactivity were a continuous trait, then a low reactive infant with extremely low motor and distress scores should be less fearful than one who showed slightly more arousal. But that prediction was not affirmed. Second, infants who showed high motor arousal but no crying or minimal motor arousal with frequent crying showed developmental profiles that were different from those who were categorized as low or high reactive. Finally, high and low reactives differed in physical and physiological features that imply qualitatively different genetic constitutions. For example, high reactives have narrower faces than low reactives in the second year of

life (Arcus & Kagan, 1995). Unpublished data from our laboratory reveal that the prevalence of atopic allergies among both children and their parents is significantly greater among high than low reactive infants. Studies of monozygotic and dizygotic same-sex twin pairs reveal significant heritability for inhibited and uninhibited behavior in the second year of life (Robinson et al., 1992). These facts imply that the two temperamental groups represent qualitatively different types and do not lie on a continuum of arousal or reactivity to stimulation.

The decision to regard individuals with very different values on a construct as members of the discrete categories or as falling on a continuum will depend on the scientists' purpose. Scientists who are interested in the relation, across families and genera, between brain size and body mass treat the two measurements as continuous. However, biologists interested in the maternal behavior of mice and chimpanzees regard these two mammals as members of qualitatively different groups. Similarly, if psychologists are interested in the physiological foundations of high and low reactives, it will be more useful to regard the two groups as categories. But those who are giving advice to mothers who complain about the ease of arousal and irritability of their infants may treat the arousal as a continuum.

IMPLICATIONS

The differences between high reactive–inhibited and low reactive–uninhibited children provoke speculation on many issues; I deal briefly with implications for psychopathology and the relation between psychological and biological propositions.

ANXIETY DISORDER

The high reactive infants who became very inhibited 4-year-olds—about 20% of all high reactives—have a low threshold for developing a state of fear to unfamiliar events, situations, and people. It is reasonable to expect that these children will be at a higher risk than most for developing one of the anxiety disorders when they become adolescents or adults. The childhood data do not provide a clue as to which particular anxiety profile will be most prevalent. However, an extensive clinical interview with early adolescents (13–14 years old), who had been classified 11 years earlier (at 21 or 31 months) as inhibited or uninhibited (Kagan et al., 1988), revealed that social phobia was more frequent among inhibited than among uninhibited adolescents, whereas specific phobias, separation anxiety, or compulsive symptoms did not differentiate the two groups (Schwartz, personal communication). This intriguing result, which requires replication, has interesting theoretical ramifications.

Research with animals, usually rats, suggests that acquisition of a fear reaction (e.g., freezing or potentiated startle) to a conditioned stimulus (light or tone) that had been paired with electric shock is mediated by a circuitry that is different from the one that mediates the conditioned response to the context in which the conditioning had occurred (LeDoux, 1995).

Davis (personal communication) has found that a potentiated startle reaction in the rat to the context in which light had been paired with shock involves a circuit from the amygdala to the bed nucleus of the stria terminalis and the septum. The potentiated startle reaction to the conditioned stimulus does not require that circuit. A phobia of spiders or bridges resembles an animal's reaction of freezing to a conditioned stimulus, but a quiet, avoidant posture at a party resembles a fearful reaction to a context. That is, the person who is extremely shy at a party of strangers is not afraid of any particular person or of the setting. Rather, the source of the uncertainty is a situation in which the shy person had experienced anxiety with other strangers. Thus, social phobia may rest on a neurophysiology that is different from that of specific phobia.

CONDUCT DISORDER

The correlation between social class and the prevalence of conduct disorder or delinquency is so high it is likely that the vast majority of children with these profiles acquired their risk status as a result of life conditions, without the mediation of a particular temperamental vulnerability. However, a small proportion—probably no more than 10%—who began their delinquent careers before age 10, and who often committed violent crimes as adolescents, might inherit a physiology that raises their threshold for the conscious experience of anticipatory anxiety and/or guilt over violating community standards for civil behavior (Tremblay, Pihl, Vitaro, & Dubkin, 1994). Damasio (1994) and Mountcastle (1995) have suggested that the surface of the ventromedial prefrontal cortex receives sensory information (from the amygdala) that originates in the peripheral targets, like heart, skin, gut, and muscles. Most children and adults who think about committing a crime experience a subtle feeling that accompanies anticipation of the consequences of an antisocial act. That feeling, which might be called anticipatory anxiety, shame, or guilt, provides an effective restraint on the action. However, if a small proportion of children possessed a less excitable amygdala, or a ventromedial surface that was less responsive, they would be deprived of the typical intensity of this feeling and, as a result, might be less

restrained than the majority (Kochanska, Murray, Jacques, Koenig, & Vandegeest, 1996; Zahn-Waxler, Cole, Welsh, & Fox, 1995). If these children are reared in homes and play in neighborhoods in which antisocial behavior is socialized, they are unlikely to become delinquents; perhaps they will become group leaders. However, if these children live in families that do not socialize aggression consistently and play in neighborhoods that provide temptations for antisocial behavior, they might be candidates for a delinquent career.

BIOLOGY AND PSYCHOLOGY

The renewed interest in temperament has brought some psychologists in closer intellectual contact with neuroscientists. Although this interaction will be beneficial to both disciplines, there is a tension between traditional social scientists who describe and explain behavioral and emotional events using only psychological terms and a smaller group who believe that an acknowledgment of biological events is theoretically helpful. The recent, dramatic advances in the neurosciences have led some scholars to go further and to imply that, in the future, robust generalizations about psychological processes might not be possible without study of the underlying biology (LeDoux, 1995).

Although some neuroscientists recognize that the psychological phenomena of thought, planning, and emotion are emergent—as a blizzard is emergent from the physics of air masses—the media suggest, on occasion, that the biological descriptions are sufficient to explain the psychological events. This publicity creates a misperception that the biological and psychological are competing explanations when, of course, they are not. Vernon Mountcastle notes that although "every mental process is a brain process, . . . not every mentalistic sentence is identical to some neurophysiological sentence. Mind and brain are not identical, no more than lung and respiration are identical" (Mountcastle, 1995, p. 294).

Some neuroscientists, sensing correctly the community resistance to a strong form of biological determinism, are emphasizing the malleability of the neuron's genome to environmental events. A few neurobiologists have come close to declaring that the human genome, like Locke's image of the child's mind, is a tabula rasa that is subject to continual change. This position tempts citizens unfamiliar with neuroscience to conclude that there may be a linear cascade that links external events (e.g., loss of a loved one) directly to changes in genes, physiology, and, finally, behavior, with the psychological layer (e.g., a mood of sadness) between brain physiology and apathetic behavior being relatively unimportant. This error is as serious as the one made by the behaviorists 60 years ago when they assumed a direct connection between a stimulus and an overt response and ignored what was happening in the brain. Both corpora of evidence are necessary if we are to understand the emergence of psychological qualities and their inevitable variation. "The phenomena of human existence and experience are always simultaneously biological and social, and an adequate explanation must involve both" (Rose, 1995, p. 380).

ACKNOWLEDGMENTS

This paper represents portions of the G. Stanley Hall Lecture delivered at the annual meeting of the American Psychological Association, New York City, August 1995. Preparation of this paper was supported, in part, by grants from the John D. and Catherine T. MacArthur Foundation, William T. Grant Foundation, and NIMH grant 47077. The author thanks Nancy Snidman and Doreen Arcus for their collaboration in the research summarized.

REFERENCES

Adamec, R. E. (1991). Anxious personality and the cat. In B. J. Carroll & J. E. Barett (Eds.), *Psychopathology in the brain* (pp. 153–168). New York: Raven.

Amaral, D. J., Price, L., Pitkanen, A., & Carmichael, S. T. (1992). Anatomical organization of the primate amygdaloid complex. In J. P. Aggleton (Ed.), *The amygdala* (pp. 1–66). New York: Wiley.

Arcus, D. M., (1991). *Experiential modification of temperamental bias in inhibited and uninhibited children*. Unpublished doctoral dissertation, Harvard University.

Arcus, D. M., & Kagan, J. (1995). Temperament and craniofacial variation in the first two years. *Child Development, 66,* 1529–1540.

Asendorpf, J. B. (1990). Development of inhibition during childhood. *Developmental Psychology, 26,* 721–730.

Bronson, G. W. (1970). Fear of visual novelty. *Developmental Psychology, 2,* 33–40.

Cooper, J. R., Bloom, F. E., & Roth, R. H. (1991). *Biochemical basis of neuropharmacology*. New York: Oxford University Press.

Damasio, A. (1994). *Descartes' error*. New York: Putnam.

Davis, M. (1992). The role of the amygdala in conditioned fear. In J. P. Aggleton (Ed.), *The amygdala* (pp. 256–305). New York: Wiley.

DiLalla, L. F., Kagan, J., & Reznick, J. S. (1994). Genetic etiology of behavioral inhibition among two year olds. *Infant Behavior and Development, 17,* 401–408.

Fagan, J. F. (1981). Infant intelligence. *Intelligence, 5,* 239–243.

Hebb, D. O. (1946). The nature of fear. *Psychological Review, 53,* 259–276.

Kagan, J. (1994). *Galen's prophecy*. New York: Basic.

Kagan, J., Kearsley, R. B., & Zelazo, P. R. (1980). *Infancy*. Cambridge, MA: Harvard University Press.

Kagan, J., Reznick, J. S., & Gibbons, J. (1989). Inhibited and uninhibited types of children. *Child Development, 60,* 838–845.

Kagan, J., Reznick, J. S., & Snidman, N. (1988). Biological bases of childhood shyness. *Science, 240,* 167–171.

Kochanska, G., Murray, K., Jacques, T. Y., Koenig, A. L., & Vandegeest, K. A. (1996). Inhibitory control in young children and its role in emerging internalization. *Child Development, 67,* 490–507.

LeDoux, J. E. (1995). In search of an emotional system in the brain. In M. S. Gazzinaga (Ed.), *The cognitive neurosciences* (pp. 1049–1062). Cambridge, MA: MIT Press.

Mountcastle, V. (1995). The evolution of ideas concerning the function of the neocortex. *Cerebral Cortex, 5,* 289–295.

Murray, D. C. (1971). Talk, silence, and anxiety. *Psychological Bulletin, 75,* 244–260.

Panksepp, J., Sacks, D. S., Crepeau, L. J., & Abbott, B. B. (1991). The psycho and neurobiology of fear systems in the brain. In M. R. Denny (Ed.), *Fear, avoidance, and phobias* (pp. 17–59). Hillsdale, NJ: Erlbaum.

Porges, S. W., Arnold, W. R., & Forbes, E. J. (1973). Heart rate variability: An index of attention responsivity in human newborns. *Developmental Psychology, 8,* 85–92.

Richards, J. E. (1985). Respiratory sinus arrhythmia predicts heart rate and visual responses during visual attention in 14 to 20 week old infants. *Psychophysiology, 22,* 101–109.

Robinson, J. L., Kagan, J., Reznick, J. S., & Corley, R. (1992). The heritability of inhibited and uninhibited behavior: A twin study. *Developmental Psychology, 28,* 1030–1037.

Rose, R. J. (1995). Genes and human behavior. In J. T. Spence, J. M. Darley, & D. P. Foss (Eds.), *Annual review of psychology* (pp. 625–654). Palo Alto, CA: Annual Reviews.

Shimamura, A. P. (1995). Memory and frontal lobe function. In M. S. Gazzinaga (Ed.), *The cognitive neurosciences* (pp. 803–814). Cambridge, MA: MIT Press.

Snidman, N., Kagan, J., Riordan, L., & Shannon, D. (1995). Cardiac function and behavioral reactivity in infancy. *Psychophysiology, 31,* 199–207.

Squire, L. R., & Knowlton, B. J. (1995). Memory, hippocampus, and brain systems. In M. S. Gazzinaga (Ed.), *The cognitive neurosciences* (pp. 825–838). Cambridge, MA: MIT Press.

Tremblay, R. E., Pihl, R. O., Vitaro, F., & Dubkin, P. L. (1994). Predicting early onset of male antisocial behavior from preschool behavior. *Archives of General Psychiatry, 51,* 732–739.

Wilson, D. S., Coleman, K., Clark, A. B., & Biederman, L. (1993). Shy-bold continuum in pumpkinseed sunfish (*Lepomis gibbosus*): An ecological study of a psychological trait. *Journal of Comparative Psychology, 107,* 250–260.

Zahn-Waxler, C., Cole, P., Welsh, J. D., & Fox, N. A. (1995). Psychophysiological correlates of empathy and prosocial behavior in preschool children with behavioral problems. *Development and Psychopathology, 7,* 27–48.

QUESTIONS

1. Why are reactions to unfamiliar events used to assess infant temperament?
2. What are the behavioral characteristics of inhibited and uninhibited children?
3. How was infant reactivity measured when the children in this study were 16 weeks old? How did high- and low-reactive infants react to this stimulus?
4. How did high-reactive children respond to the interview when they were 5 years of age? How did low-reactive children respond?
5. What do the longitudinal findings indicate about the stability of reactivity over the first 5 years of life?
6. Are shy children likely to be high-reactive or low-reactive children? Why?
7. Are boys or girls more likely to be classified as high-reactive? What are some implications of this gender difference for later development?
8. Are high-reactive children more likely than low-reactive children to have anxiety disorders when they grow up? Explain.
9. Does temperamental inhibition play a role in antisocial behavior in adolescence? If so, what proportion of antisocial behavior might it explain and why?
10. What implications might the long-term patterns of temperament described in this article have for parents, teachers, and others who work with young children?

PART II
Infancy

Infancy is a time of remarkable development. In fact, the rapid pace of change in the first two years of life makes infancy the fastest period of growth that humans experience after birth. Changes during infancy occur across the entire spectrum of human behavior, including physical growth, perceptual and cognitive skills, language, and social and emotional competence. Most research on infants concentrates on development in one of these areas. In part, this is because infant research is difficult to design and conduct. One reason for this difficulty is that infants have only brief periods every day during which their behavioral state is suited to research observation. Another is that infants' social and language skills are just emerging, so many of the usual data-gathering techniques that involve social interaction or conversation cannot be used.

Despite these challenges, two important points stand out in the research described in this section. First, infants are extremely competent in a number of ways. The articles that follow reveal infants' competence in social coordination (Jerome S. Bruner and V. Sherwood); locomotion (Sarah E. Berger and Karen Adolph); language and pattern recognition (Janet F. Werker; Olivier Pascalis, Michelle de Haan, and Charles A. Nelson); concept formation (Renee Baillargeon and Su-hua Wang); emotion (Joseph J. Campos, Bennett I. Bertenthal, and Rosanne Kermoian); and psychological adjustment following institutional deprivation (Michael L. Rutter, Jana M. Kreppner, and Thomas G. O'Connor). Considered together, these articles paint a portrait of the infant as an extremely complex organism that is on a rapid and directed course of growth.

Second, the articles in this section demonstrate several creative techniques that researchers have devised for observing infants. These techniques have allowed psychologists to begin to understand infants "on their own terms." That is, researchers can use these procedures to build on the capabilities and interests of infants to determine what is developing early in life.

11 Early Rule Structure: The Case of "Peekaboo"

JEROME S. BRUNER • V. SHERWOOD

From the beginning of life, infants participate in many social activities that are structured by adults. For these activities to be successful, they must be coordinated with the emerging skills and capabilities of the infants involved. A common activity involving adults and young children is the game of peekaboo. This game draws on the infant's emerging skills of responsiveness, anticipation, and object knowledge. The adult makes a major contribution to the play by coordinating the infant's skills with the rule structure of the game. But infants cannot simply be told the rules, as older children are, and then be expected to follow them. So how do they learn the rules of a game?

To answer this question, Bruner and Sherwood observed infants and mothers as they played peekaboo. These investigators were interested in when and how the babies' participation in this game changed. In particular, they wanted to see if changes in a baby's play behavior revealed an increased understanding and acceptance of the rules of the game, such as what counts as an opening move, who plays which role in the game, and which substitutions of moves are permissible.

In the following article, Bruner and Sherwood describe their research. One especially interesting feature of this study is that the same mother–child dyads were observed playing peekaboo over 10 months, beginning when the infants were about 7 months of age. The partners maintained interest in this game over the entire observation period, but in many ways the nature of the game changed. In large part, this change resulted from changes in the behaviors of the infants. The infants assumed more responsibility for their role in the game, and they showed increasing awareness of the conventions or rules of play. Even more remarkably, by the end of the observation period, children not only played the game well but even began to invent new ways to play it.

This research demonstrates that the flow of ordinary interactions involving infants and their caregivers provides opportunities for development. However, this research also shows that this flow, and therefore what can be learned from it, does not occur automatically. As you will see, not all dyads were successful at peekaboo. Variation in this type of mother–infant play exists, and different forms appear to have different consequences for development. The authors conclude that the social synchronization that emerges during games like peekaboo has the potential to contribute to social, cognitive, and emotional development in infancy.

Peekaboo surely must rank as one of the most universal forms of play between adults and infants. It is rich indeed in the mechanisms it exhibits. For in point of fact, the game depends upon the infant's capacity to integrate a surprisingly wide range of phenomena. For one, the very playing of the game depends upon the child having some degree of mastery of object permanence, the capacity to recognize the continued existence of an object when it is out of sight (e.g. Piaget, 1954). Charlesworth (1966) has shown, moreover, that the successful playing of the game is dependent in some measure on the child being able to keep track of the location in which a face has disappeared, the child showing more persistent effects when the reappearance of a face varied unexpectedly with respect to its prior position. Greenfield (1970) has also indicated that the initial effect of the game depends upon the presence not only of the reappearing face, but also of an accompanying vocalization by the mother, although with repetition the role of vocalization declined. She also found that the voice was increasingly important the less familiar the setting in which the game was played. It is quite plain, then, that complex expectancies are built up in the infant in the course of playing the game, and that these expectancies are characterized by considerable spatio-temporal structuring.

Another way of saying the same thing is to note that the child very soon becomes sensitive to the 'rules of the game' as he plays it. That is to say, he expects disappearance and reappearance to be in a certain place, at a certain time, accompanied by certain vocalizations, in certain general settings. The bulk of the studies reported in the literature suggest that these 'conventions', though they may rest upon certain preadapted readinesses to respond to disappearance and reappearance, are soon converted into rules for defining the pattern of play. If this were the case, one would expect that not only would the child have learned procedures, but would have learned them in a way that is characteristic of rule learning—i.e. in a general form, with assignable roles, with permissible substitutions of moves, etc.

The present study is concerned specifically with the conversion of peekaboo procedures into rule structures and, without intending to minimize the importance of preadapted patterns of response in making the game possible, we shall concentrate upon this aspect of the matter.

The study is based upon an intensive investigation of six infants over a period of 10 months, from seven to 17 months of age. The infants and their mothers were seen once a fortnight at our laboratory for an hour, and among the instructions given to the mothers was one asking them to show us the games that they and their infants most enjoyed playing. Our observations of peekaboo are all based upon behaviour spontaneously produced by the mothers in play, all but one of them including peekaboo in the play they exhibited. All sessions were videotaped and analysis was carried out on the video records. Partly for convenience of reporting and partly because each pair developed somewhat different procedures, we shall concentrate on a single mother-infant dyad over the 10-month period. The corpus of such play for this dyad consisted of 22 episodes of peekaboo, the first at 10 months, the last at 15 months. Peekaboo starts earlier than our initial age and goes on later, but the sample of games over the five-month period suffices to illustrate the points we wish to make. Though the other infant-mother dyads show some differences from the one we are reporting, they are in no sense different in pattern.

OBSERVATIONS

The first thing to be noted in the one mother–daughter (Diane) dyad on which we shall concentrate is that all instances of the game are quite notably constrained with respect to their limits. That is to say, the game always starts after the two players have made an explicit contact. This is the opening move, but it should be noted immediately that here, as in other features of the game, variation prevails. In most instances, initial contact is by face-to-face mutual looking. Where this does not occur, the mother may use either vocalization to contact the child or make the hiding 'instrument' conspicuous. The following table gives the frequencies of opening moves.

Face-to-face contact	16 (of 21 episodes in which orientation could be ascertained)
Vocalization	9 (of 22)
Highlighting of instrument	3 (of 22)

Typically, vocalization and face-to-face contact go together, with seven out of nine episodes of vocalization being accompanied by face-to-face contact. Interestingly enough, the mother will sometimes use a chance event as a 'starter' as when, inadvertently, her smock hides the child's face and the mother uses this as a start for a round of peekaboo. Also, there is what might best be called the 'opportunistic start', in which the mother when drying the child's hair after a bath 'lightens' the occasion by turning the drying with towel into an episode of peekaboo—a pattern also used by mothers to divert a fretting baby.

As Garvey (1974) has put it, social games can be described in terms of (a) the nature of the format, (b) the turns of each player and (c) the rounds in which the turns are sequenced. In the peekaboo situation, the initial round is a mutual attention-focusing episode that seems invariant although its form, as we have seen, may vary from one instance of the peekaboo format to the next.

The second round of peekaboo is the actual act of hiding and its accompaniments. Note first that there are four alternatives possible: mother can be hidden, or child, and the act of hiding can be initiated by the mother or the infant. The four alternatives and their frequencies are as follows.

M initiated, M hidden	8
C initiated, C hidden	2
M initiated, C hidden	11
C initiated, M hidden	0
[Ambiguous	1]

We may note that whilst there are at most three instances of the child initiating the hiding act, and all of these came at 15 months, they indicate that the child is by no means always a passive participant. We shall have more to say of this later in discussing role reversal. One of the striking features of what is hidden is that it is about equally distributed between the mother's face being masked and the child's—one of the forms of variation that the mother uses in order to keep uncertainty operative within the game. The child seems readily to accept this variation in the format and, indeed, seems to take a certain delight in it.

What is very notable is that there is virtually complete openness with regard to the instrument and mode used for hiding. The game when first observed was carried out exclusively with a nappy and hiding was controlled by the mother, and this occurred six times, hiding herself four times and the child twice. Thereafter, the distribution of the remaining episodes was five times nappy, five times clothing, three times a towel, two times a chair, and once with the child averting her head. In short, the nature of the hiding instrument and the masking act might almost be called optional in constrast to certain obligatory features, such as the requirement of initial contact.

During the period of hiding, and we shall discuss the limits on its length below, there is a further ancillary feature of the game—a mode of sustaining contact during hiding. This occurs both on the mother's side and on the child's. In 16 of the 22 episodes, mother uses either the rising intonation pattern of the typical Where question ('Where's Diane?' or 'Where's baby?' or 'Where's mummy?') or employs an extended 'Ahhhh', sometimes with a rising intonation pattern. In one sense, this act on the part of the mother can be thought of as helping the child sustain attention and bridging any uncertainty concerning the mother's 'conservation' behind the hiding instrument. The child's responses during hiding seem, on the other hand, to be expressions of excitement or anticipation, though they help the mother control her own output of bridging vocalizations to keep the child at an appropriate activation level. There are 13 in 19 episodes involving a hiding cloth where the child actively seeks to remove the hiding mask from the mother's or her own face. It is to these initiatives that the mother often responds with vocalization as if to control the child's activation. This part of the game is characteristically 'non-rule bound' and seems to be an instance, rather, of the mother providing a scaffold for the child.

We come now to a crucial round in the game: uncovering and reappearance. Note first a point already made—hiding time is very constrained: 19 of the 22 episodes range between two and seven seconds, with only one being above seven (at 10 months) and two

at one second. It is only at 15 months, when the child consistently controls reappearance, that there is a fairly homogeneous and rapid hiding time: five episodes in a row ranging from one to two seconds. But note that at this age the child has virtually given up 'static' peekaboo for an ambulatory version, so that variation is now in format rather than in timing. The five uniformly fast episodes were all with a nappy—an old and familiar game that is much less exciting for the child than the ambulatory game we shall describe below. One of these episodes, a one-second instance, was completely controlled by the child, and between two was an instance where the child demanded the game vocatively after she had failed to cover her own face successfully. We believe that the constraint on time of hiding is a reflection of the appreciation of the child's limited attention span by both members of the pair—the mother reacting to signs of the child's impatience, the child responding directly to his own.

The actual act of uncovering is open to considerable variation. We find instances where it is controlled by the child, others where the mother controls uncovering. Occasionally, the mother, by drawing near and vocalizing, provokes the child into removing the mask from her face, as if to stimulate more control from the infant. Indeed, one even encounters partial, 'tempting' uncovering by the mother to provoke the child into completion, where the mother exposes a corner of her eye. In terms of control of unmasking, we note that before 12 months, nine of 12 of the episodes of unmasking are controlled by the mother. From 12 on, none are, and six in 10 are controlled by the child alone—a phenomenon seen only once before this age.

Following uncovering, there is again a rather standard ritual: remaking contact. In the 19 episodes where we were able to determine it 14 uncoverings were accompanied by face-to-face contact immediately or shortly after. In all instances of uncovering but one, mother sought to establish such conduct, though in four she failed to do so. Moreover, in 16 of 22 episodes, mother vocalized upon uncovering, usually with a 'Boo' or a 'Hello' or an 'Ahhh'. Obviously, there is considerable release of tension at this point, since laughter accompanies the above 15 times for the child (and indeed 12 for the mother, always in accompaniment with the child).

At 15 months, the child invents and controls a new variation of the game, as already noted. It consists of her moving behind a chair, out of sight of her mother, then reappearing and saying 'Boo'. She has now become the agent in the play, mother being recipient of her action. The format has been revised by the child and the prior role of agent and recipient reversed. This variation in agency has, of course, appeared before in the more static form of the game involving a hiding instrument. But it is important to note that the child has now extended the rules under her own control to a new, but formally identical format–again involving initial face-to-face contact, hiding and reappearing by self-initiated movement, and reestablishing contact. From there on out, peekaboo is a game embedded in self-directed movement by the child that produces disappearance and reappearance. The child has not only learned to conform to the rules of the static game as initiated by mother and by child, but also to use the rules for the initiation of a variant of the old format. At this point, the range of possible games incorporating the basic rules of peekaboo becomes almost limitless, and what provides unity is the agreement of mother and infant to maintain a skeleton rule structure with new instruments for hiding and new settings in which to play. We can say that at this point the child is no longer performance-bound, but rather has achieved a proper 'competence' for generating new versions of an old game.

But we must turn now to the question of what brought the child to a full realization of the 'syntax' of the game of peekaboo so that he can henceforth be fully 'generative' in his disappearance-reappearance play. Before we do so, however, we must examine briefly three of the other children on whom we have sufficient data for analysis.

In the case of Lynn and her mother, the pattern is much the same as described, save for the fact that she begins to take over the active role of initiator of the game and controller of the mask as early as 10 months. She too, at 10 months, begins to use a stationary object, a chair, as a hiding mask behind which she moves, looking through the legs to effect reappearance. But she is still quite confused about it, and when mother says 'Boo' to herald her reappearance hides again rather than remaking contact. But she is on the way towards mastering the ambulatory variant.

Where Nan is concerned, the game is rather more sophisticated in an important respect. She and her mother share control. For example, at 11 months Nan lifts her petticoat over her face and leaves it in place until her mother says 'Boo' and then lowers it. This joint feature is a very consistent aspect of their games, but it must be regarded as a variant, for instances occur without joint control as well. Their turn-taking is also much more precisely segmented. For example, Nan raises her petticoat over her face, then lowers it after a few seconds, and waits for mother to say 'Boo' before showing any reaction herself–then usually responding to the mother's vocalizations with laughter. There is, in this instance, a separation between unmasking and vocalization, with a further timing element between the two.

Sandy and his mother are instances of a failure to develop workable rules because of excessive variation and some misreading by the mother. But the failure is instructive. Too often, the mother starts the game without having enlisted Sandy's attention. In other instances, when Sandy is having difficulty in hiding his own face behind a cloth, the mother takes the cloth (and the initiative) away from him and tries to do the masking herself. Interestingly, the game does not develop, and in its place there emerges a game in which Sandy crawls away from mother, she in pursuit, with excitement being exhibited by both when she catches him. He never serves as agent in this game. They are an instructive failure, and the disappearance of the game is reminiscent of the failures reported by Nelson (1973) that occur when mother attempts to correct the child's linguistic usage or insists upon an interpretation of the child's utterance that does not accord with his own. Under the circumstances, the lexical items in question disappear from the child's lexicon, just as peekaboo disappears from the game repertory of this pair.

DISCUSSION

When peekaboo first appears, our mothers often report, it is an extension or variation of a looming game in which the mother approaches the child from a distance of a meter or so, looms towards him almost to face-to-face contact, accompanying the close approach with a 'Boo' or a rising intonation. We know from the work of Bower (1971), Ball and Tronick (1971) and White (1963) that such looming produces considerable excitement and, indeed, when the loom is directly towards the face, a real or incipient avoidance response. The play may start by substituting disappearance of the face at a close point at which excitement has already been aroused. But this is not necessary. The only point one would wish to make is that, at the start, peekaboo involves an arousal of responses that are either innate or fairly close to innate. For even without the link to the looming game, disappearance and reappearance are 'manipulations' of object permanence, which is itself either innate or maturing through very early experience along the lines indicated by Piaget (1954). At least one can say unambiguously that, at the outset, peekaboo is not a game in the sense of it being governed by rules and conventions that are, in any respect, arbitrary. It is, rather, an exploitation by the mother of very strong, preadapted response tendencies in the infant, an exploitation that is rewarded by the child's responsiveness and pleasure.

William James (1890) comments in the *Principles* that an instinct is a response that only occurs once, thereafter being modified by experience. And surely one could say the same for the interaction involved in peekaboo. For once it has occurred, there rapidly develops a set of reciprocal anticipations in mother and child that begin to modify it and, more importantly, to conventionalize it. At the outset, this conventionalization is fostered by a quite standard or routine set of capers on the part of the mother—as we have noted, the early version involves a very limited range of hiding instruments, masking acts, vocalizations and time variations. At the outset, it is also very important for mother to keep the child's activation level at an appropriate intensity, and one is struck by the skill of mothers in knowing how to keep the child in an anticipatory mood, neither too sure of outcome nor too upset by a wide range of possibilities.

But what is most striking thereafter is precisely the systematic introduction of variations constrained by set rules. The basic rules are:

> Initial contact
>
> Disappearance
>
> Reappearance
>
> Reestablished contact

Within this rule context, there can be variations in degree and kind of vocalization for initial contact, in kind of mask, in who controls the mask, in whose face is masked, in who uncovers, in the form of vocalization upon uncovering, in the relation between uncovering and vocalization, and in the timing of the constituent elements (though this last is strikingly constrained by a capacity variable). What the child appears to be learning is not only the basic rules of the game, but the range of variation that is possible within the rule set. It is this emphasis upon patterned variation within a constraining rule set that seems crucial to the mastery of competence and generativeness. The process appears much as in concept attainment, in which the child learns the regularity of a concept by learning the variants in terms of which it expresses itself. What is different in peekaboo is that the child is not only learning such variants, but obviously getting great pleasure from the process and seeking it out.

It is hard to imagine any function for peekaboo aside from practice in the learning of rules in converting 'gut play' into play with conventions. But there may be one additional function. As Garvey (1974) has noted, one of the objectives of play in general is to give the child opportunity to explore the boundary between the 'real' and the 'make-believe'. We have never in our sample of peekaboo games seen a child exhibit the sort of separation pattern noted by

Ainsworth (1964) when mother *really* leaves the scene. Mothers often report, moreover, that they frequently start their career of playing peekaboo by hiding their own faces rather than the infant's for fear of his being upset. Eight of the nine mothers asked about this point reported behaving in this way (Scaife, 1974). This suggests a sensitivity on the part of mothers to where the line may be between 'real' and 'make-believe' for the child. This function doubtless dwindles in time. Yet the game continues in its formal pattern, sustained in its attractiveness by being incorporated into new formats involving newly emergent behaviours (such as crawling or walking). An old pattern seems, then, to provide a framework for the pleasurable expression of new behaviour and allows the new behaviour to be quickly incorporated into a highly skilled, rule-governed pattern.

REFERENCES

Ainsworth, M. D. S. (1964). Patterns of attachment behaviour shown by the infant in interaction with his mother. *Merrill-Palmer Quarterly, 10*, 51.

Ball, W., and Tronick, E. (1971). 'Infant responses to impending collision: optical and real', *Science, 171*, 818.

Bower, T. G. R. (1971). 'The object in the world of the infant', *Scientific American, 225*, 30.

Charlesworth, W. R. (1966). 'Persistence of orienting, and attending behaviour in infants as a function of stimulus-locus uncertainty', *Child Development, 37*, 473.

Garvey, C. (1974). 'Some properties of social play', *Merrill-Palmer Quarterly, 20,* 163–180.

Greenfield, P. M. (1970). 'Playing peekaboo with a four-month-old: a study of the role of speech and nonspeech sounds in the formation of a visual schema', Unpublished manuscript.

James, W. (1890). *The Principles of Psychology*, New York, Henry Holt.

Nelson, K. (1973). 'Structure and strategy in learning to talk', *Monographs of The Society for Research in Child Development, 38*, 1.

Piaget, J. (1954). *The Construction of Reality in the Child*, New York, Basic Books.

Scaife, M. (1974). Personal communication, Department of Experimental Psychology, Oxford University, Oxford.

White, B. L. (1963). 'Plasticity in perceptual development during the first six months of life', Paper presented to the American Association for the Advancement of Science, Cleveland, Ohio, 30 December.

QUESTIONS

1. What skills does an infant need in order to play peekaboo?
2. What behaviors need to be coordinated in order for the infant and mother to be successful at peekaboo?

3. How did the ways in which the mother and infant played peekaboo change over the 10-month observation period?

4. According to Garvey, what are the three components of social games? Does peekaboo have all these components? Explain.

5. What is an "opportunistic start" for the game of peekaboo, and what kinds of opportunistic starts were used by the mothers in the study? Do you think this type of initiation of the game might be especially enticing to infants? Why or why not?

6. About how old is an infant when he or she first initiates the hiding act of the game of peekaboo? Are you surprised by the age at which this ability appears? Why or why not?

7. How do a mother and child sustain contact with each other during hiding? Is this an important element of the game? Why?

8. What does playing games like peekaboo have to do with the development of a more general understanding of rule structures? What evidence do Bruner and Sherwood provide to support this claim?

9. What roles do emotional arousal and regulation of emotion play in infants' ability to sustain their part in this game?

10. What type of learning do you think results from interactions of dyads like Sandy and his mother, who were unsuccessful in following the rules of the game?

12 Infants Use Handrails as Tools in a Locomotor Task

SARAH E. BERGER · KAREN E. ADOLPH

After infants take their first step at about 1 year of age, they enter an amazing phase of childhood: They are now capable of traveling their world on their own. Developmental psychologists have long been interested in early locomotion. Gesell's research in the 1920s focused on the timing of the major milestones of locomotor development, such as crawling, standing, and walking. Since then, much of the research on infant locomotion has emphasized its perceptual and motor aspects. Some psychologists, mainly those who take a dynamic systems approach, have recently expanded this focus by emphasizing how the locomotor achievements of infancy involve the complex coordination of several actions or processes. However, what has been largely overlooked over the years is what locomotion enables an infant to do other than simply move his or her body around. One critical contribution of locomotion is that it helps infants reach their goals. That is, locomotion becomes part of a set of abilities available to infants as they try to solve problems in their everyday lives. Thus, locomotion is not merely an end in itself. It also functions as a means by which infants can carry out their own activities and achieve many of their own goals.

In the following article, Sarah Berger and Karen Adolph describe research in which they observed 16-month-old infants as they tried to reach a goal that entailed coordinating their skills at locomotion with the challenges and resources in the environment. These investigators devised an ingenious experimental apparatus; it involved bridges of different sizes spanning a gap that was 76 cm (about 2½ feet) deep. The infants were observed as they tried to walk across these bridges (beneath which was substantial foam padding). Handrails sometimes were and sometimes were not available for the infants to use in crossing the bridge. What the infants did in these situations will surprise you. In the main, they were remarkably inventive and showed amazing insight about what they needed to do to solve the problems presented by the different bridges.

The article concludes with an interesting discussion about how prior research on the development of infant locomotion may have overlooked a critical contribution of this process. Although locomotor skills are impressive in terms of the perceptual and motor competencies they reveal, they may also play an extremely valuable role in the development of complex cognitive abilities during infancy.

In 2 experiments the authors demonstrated that adaptive locomotion can involve means–ends problem solving. Sixteen-month-old toddlers crossed bridges of varying widths in the presence or absence of a handrail. Babies attempted wider bridges more often than narrow ones, and attempts on narrow bridges depended on handrail presence. Toddlers had longer latencies, examined the bridge and handrail more closely, and modified their gait when bridges were narrow and/or the handrail was unavailable. Infants who explored the bridge and handrail before stepping onto the bridge and devised alternative bridge-crossing strategies were more likely to cross successfully. Results challenge traditional conceptualizations of tools: Babies used the handrail as a means for augmenting balance and for carrying out an otherwise impossible goal-directed task.

Although independent locomotion is heralded as a setting event for important cognitive developments in object search, spatial skill, and causal and social

Copyright 2003 by the American Psychological Association. Reprinted by permission of the authors and the American Psychological Association from *Developmental Psychology, Vol. 39* (2003), pp. 594–605.

This article is based in part on a dissertation submitted to New York University by Sarah E. Berger in partial fulfillment of the PhD requirements. This research was supported by a 2001–2002 postdoctoral research fellowship from the American Association of University Women to Sarah E. Berger and by National Institute of Child Health and Human Development Grant HD33486 to Karen E. Adolph.

relationships (e.g., Bertenthal, Campos, & Barrett, 1984; Bremner, 1993; Campos et al., 2000; Campos, Hiatt, Ramsay, Henderson, & Svejda, 1978), researchers typically treat locomotion itself as a low-level perceptual-motor activity. For example, researchers in the biomechanical tradition have focused on infants' postural adjustments, changes in their crawling and walking patterns, interlimb coordination, and muscle actions (e.g., Adolph, Vereijken, & Denny, 1998; Bril & Breniere, 1993; Clark & Phillips, 1987; Thelen, Ulrich, & Niles, 1987). Researchers in the perception-action tradition have focused on infants' use of perceptual information via visual and haptic exploration to inform their motor decisions (e.g., Adolph, 1997; Adolph, Eppler, Marin, Weise & Clearfield, 2000; Gibson et al., 1987; Schmuckler, 1996). Gibson, for example, described infants' everyday activity on the playground as a "revelation of attention to affordances" (from K. Adolph's notes on a presentation given by Gibson, 1992), meaning that everyday playground encounters involve gathering perceptual information so as to determine new possibilities and constraints on action.

MEANS–ENDS PROBLEM SOLVING IN MANUAL AND LOCOMOTOR TASKS

In this article, we argue that locomotion can involve more than low-level perceptual-motor skills. Infants' everyday, goal-directed locomotor activities can involve higher level cognitive processes such as means–ends problem solving, strategy selection, inhibition, and sequencing a series of actions into a complex motor plan as they cope with obstacles in their path, coordinate the components of a plan to navigate the jungle gym or bouncing bridge, and inhibit compelling behaviors as they wait their turn on the slide. Moreover, we argue that problem solving that involves using environmental means to extend locomotor abilities may even represent a hallmark of human intelligence: tool use.

Since Piaget's (1954) descriptions of his children's sensorimotor behaviors, researchers of cognitive development have been comfortable using manual motor tasks as indices from which to infer infants' cognitive skill. For example, infant' abilities to manually search for a hidden object provide evidence about their understanding of object permanence (e.g., Butterworth, 1977; Wellman, Cross, & Bartsch, 1986), their spatial and temporal concepts (e.g., Bremner & Bryant, 1977), and their understanding of number (Feigenson & Carey, 2003). Using one object to retrieve another, such as retrieving a toy by pulling a blanket on which it rests, provides evidence for means–ends problem solving and a primitive sort of tool use (e.g., Chen, Sanchez, & Campbell, 1997; Willatts, 1984).

Despite the prevalence of manual means–ends tasks in the literature, there is a precedent for locomotor problem solving involving more of the body than the hands and arms. For example, Köhler's (1931) chimpanzees performed locomotor tasks, such as pole vaulting or building platforms, to obtain food that was out of reach. To pole vault, chimps had to recognize that the lure was beyond the reach of their jumps, notice the pole on the other side of the room, and seize on the pole as a means for vaulting their bodies to the appropriate height to grab the bananas. To build platforms, the chimps had to similarly recognize that boxes were available and potentially useful, seriate them to stack them appropriately, and then climb up to get the bananas. Both tasks are clever cognitive accomplishments that demonstrate sophisticated means–ends problem solving via the coordination of several substeps into a plan. Replicating Köhler's (1931) observations, McGraw (1935) trained twin toddlers, Jimmy and Johnny, to climb on furniture, stack boxes, or use sticks to reach a goal that was out of reach. Recent research indicates that even without several months of practice in a special training regimen, toddlers may be capable of using environmental support to solve gross locomotor problems as successfully as they use them in fine motor tasks. Adolph (1995, 1997) observed newly walking infants spontaneously grasp onto support posts prior to descending steep slopes, suggesting that they recognized the function of the posts as aids for maintaining balance while placing a foot out to explore the sloping surface. To use the poles in this way, infants had to recognize that they were in a potentially risky location, realize that a pole was available and could be used to augment balance, and then implement use of the pole. However, because the poles were out of reach once infants stepped onto the slope, infants' ability to use them as a means for completing a locomotor task could not be tested systematically.

MEANS–ENDS PROBLEM SOLVING AND TOOL USE

A pinnacle achievement for means–ends problem solving is tool use (Connolly & Dalgleish, 1989). Culling from several descriptions of infant and primate tool use, researchers seem to agree that tool use is a multistep process requiring users to (a) recognize a gap between their own abilities and their typical means for achieving the goal, (b) notice that a tool is available that can supply the missing means to fill the gap, and (c) modify their typical means to incorporate the role of the tool in obtaining the goal (e.g., Bushnell & Boudreau, 1998; McCarty, Clifton, & Collard, 1999, 2001; Tomasello & Call, 1997). Meeting these criteria may demand spatial skills because it requires coordination of the locations of the goal and the tool (Lockman, 2000). Indeed, infants frequently fail to make the connection between implements and their uses when the tools are not directly touching the target object, though they may lie next to each other on a table, and even 5-year-olds sometimes have difficulty when the tool and goal are on opposite sides of a room (Bates, Carlson-Luden, & Bretherton, 1980; Shapiro & Gerke, 1930/1991; van Leeuwen, Smitsman, & van Leeuwen, 1994). However, the tool use problem may not be about coordinating two points of spatial reference per se, but about coordinating multiple pieces of information simultaneously. For example, tool use requires mentally linking the tool to a goal if the relationship is not direct, or envisioning the desired outcome plus knowing how to use the tool as an aid to achieve it. This mental jump implies that the tool user can mentally coordinate the steps en route to the complete event (van Leeuwen et al., 1994). Prospective tool use involves inhibiting behaviors that would be unsuccessful without the aid of a tool, thereby eliminating inefficient trial and error.

Based on Köhler's (1931) famous chimpanzees piecing sticks together to rake in a banana through the bars of their cages (and perhaps our everyday use of the word *tool* to refer to those hand-held objects in a toolbox), our classic vision of infant tool use involves hand-held implements. Consequently, the literature on tool use has focused on manual tasks. For example, by 10 months, infants use sticks, hooks, rakes, and rings to drag over an object that is out of reach, and they adapt their behavior according to the implement provided (Bates et al., 1980; Brown, 1990; Chen & Seigler, 2000; van Leeuwen et al., 1994). By the time they are 2 years old, infants can use tools that are self-directed (eating with a spoon, brushing their hair) and can adjust their strategies to continue using tools that have been altered structurally, such as changing the way they grasp a spoon with a bent handle to continue scooping food from a bowl (Connolly & Dalgleish, 1989; McCarty et al., 2001; Steenbergen, van der Kamp, Smitsman, & Carson, 1997).

The locomotor problem-solving tasks described above (Adolph, 1995, 1997; Köhler, 1931; McGraw, 1935) are akin to these manual tool-use tasks where an implement found in the environment is used as an aid for achieving a goal. To date, however, no clear criteria have been established for what should and should not be considered a tool. For example, Parker and Gibson (1997) would likely have classified the pole vaults and stackable boxes only as *prototools*. In prototool use, only the object of change is freely mobile, such as when primates (agents of change) bang nuts in their shell (objects of change) to break them open. On their definition, Köhler's (1931) vaulting chimps did not engage in tool use to move themselves

in reach of the bananas, because an object (the chimp) was moved by means of a fixed implement (the vault) rather than by a detached one. In contrast, other definitions suggest that the pole vault, for example, may indeed count as a tool because it made an otherwise impossible action possible—it changed the relationship between the environment and the vaulter so that the reward became reachable (e.g., Connolly & Dalgleish, 1989; Steenbergen et al., 1997; van Leeuwen et al., 1994; Wagman & Carello, 2001). This discrepancy creates an ambiguous distinction between piecing together sticks to rake in food versus piecing together sticks to vault oneself to food hanging from the ceiling. Indeed, previous tool use discussions have typically not included examples in which the agent of change was also the object of change, that is, when infants or nonhuman primates use environmental support to make their way from one location to another.

GOALS OF THE CURRENT STUDY

This research had three primary goals. Our first goal was to extend the classic conceptualization of tool use into a new locomotor task domain. To determine whether infants could demonstrate the hallmarks of tool use, we designed a locomotor task that challenged infants' developing balance control—walking over wide and narrow bridges spanning a deep precipice. On the basis of previous research showing that toddlers respond adaptively to variations in ground surface (e.g., Adolph, 2000; Adolph & Avolio, 2000; Campos, Bertenthal, & Kermoian, 1992; Gibson & Walk, 1960; Richards & Rader, 1981, 1983; Schmuckler, 1996), we expected infants to scale their locomotor responses to bridge width. On narrow bridges they should recognize the discrepancy between their own limited abilities to keep balance and the possibility of walking to the goal.

We included environmental support that could serve as a means to achieve the goal—a handrail was present on some trials for infants to use as means to navigate the bridges. We reasoned that if infants could recognize the handrail as a means for augmenting balance control, they should ignore the handrail when walking over wide bridges but should notice and use it more frequently to walk over narrow bridges. In addition, we assessed whether means–ends analysis extends to the motor plan itself by observing whether infants update their motor plan by switching from one bridge-crossing strategy to another as they walk over the bridges. By placing a task with such strong cognitive demands in a locomotor context, this work highlights the integrated nature of different developmental domains. Although these domains are traditionally studied separately, success at this kind of task requires the coordination of both cognitive skills and lower level perceptual-motor skills into a plan of action.

Our second goal was to use infants' observable behaviors as a window onto underlying cognitive processes. Previous problem-solving research has been criticized for its inability to demarcate "the activity of planning from the activity of execution of the plan" (Bauer, Schwade, Wewerka, & Delaney, 1999, p. 1336). To address this concern, we examined how infants obtained information for making motor decisions via their exploratory behaviors and collected descriptions of infants' various handrail and bridge-crossing strategies to document how infants figured out how to use the handrail as a tool. We expected that infants would explore more and expend more effort figuring out how to use the handrail on the narrower bridges, where it was more difficult to walk.

Our third goal was to examine sources of individual differences. We kept age constant as a crude control for maturational factors and measured likely sources of individual differences in infants' means-ends problem solving on the basis of locomotor experience (e.g., Adolph, 1997, 2000; Bertenthal et al., 1984; Kingsnorth & Schmuckler, 2000; Schmuckler, 1996), body dimensions (e.g., Adolph & Avolio, 2000), or walking skill (e.g., Adolph, 1995). We also predicted that infants who did not spend time planning their locomotor decision before executing it or take the time to update their motor plan in the face of new information would be less accurate than those who explored the bridge and handrail to make informed decisions.

EXPERIMENT 1: BRIDGES AND HANDRAILS

METHOD

Participants. Twenty-four 16-month-old (± 1 week; M = 16.03 months) toddlers participated (12 girls and 12 boys). All could walk 10 feet (3.05 m) across a room without falling. Most infants were White and of middle-class socioeconomic status. All were healthy and born at term. A highly trained experimenter interviewed parents about infants' cruising and walking experience, prior handrail experience (on stairs and playground equipment), and serious falls. Interviewers followed a strict protocol used in previous studies (e.g., Adolph & Avolio, 2000), which involved a series of probing questions regarding dates of events. Parents used "baby books" or calendars to help provide milestone dates. Prior to walking onset, infants' cruising (i.e., walking sideways holding onto furniture) experience ranged from 0 to 5.65 months (M = 2.76 months). Infants' walking experience ranged from 0.76 to 6.89 months (M = 3.89 months). Eighteen infants had experience using a handrail on the playground or on stairs.

Bridges and handrails. The experimental apparatus was composed of wooden starting (76 cm wide × 106 cm long) and finishing platforms (76 cm wide × 157 cm long) connected by 74-cm-long wooden bridges of various widths (18 cm, 36 cm, 48 cm, and 72 cm). The bridges spanned a 76-cm-deep crevice between the two platforms padded with 13.5 cm of foam. They fit between the two platforms via a tongue-and-groove system and locked into place. When unlocked, they could be pulled out and quickly changed between trials. Lines down the length of the bridges' surface marked 2-cm increments. A 302-cm-long × 13.5-cm-wide × 4-cm-thick handrail could be installed on a permanent support structure on the starting and finishing platforms, creating a continuous handrail spanning the platforms along one side of the bridge (top panel, Figure 1), or the handrail could be removed to create a gap extending the length of the bridge plus 23.5 cm on each end (bottom panel, Figure 1).

Procedure. Each infant was presented with each bridge width three times with a handrail and three times without for a total of 24 trials. Trial order was counterbalanced across six combinations of bridge width and handrail presence (2 boys and 2 girls per order). Trials were blocked into six groups of four. Each block began with the widest (72-cm) bridge to maintain infants' motivation, and the next three trials included each of the other three bridge widths. Two trials in each block were handrail trials, and two were no-handrail trials. Parents called to their babies from the far side of the landing platform but did not tell children how to cross or caution them to be careful. An experimenter followed alongside infants to ensure their safety if they began to fall. The experimenter ended a trial if the infant did not start onto the bridge within 45 s. The session was videotaped with one camera that panned to provide a view of the baby on the starting platform, bridge, and finishing platform and one ceiling-mounted camera providing an overhead view of the bridge/handrail section of the walkway. Both views were mixed in real time onto a single videotape.

RESULTS AND DISCUSSION

Data coding. A primary coder scored outcome measures from video. Based on coding criteria used in earlier studies (e.g., Adolph, 1997), the coder scored trials as *attempts to walk* if infants stepped off the starting platform with both feet on the bridge and as *refusals to walk* if they remained on the starting platform, crawled over the bridge, stepped onto the bridge holding the experimenter's arm, or slid off the starting platform into the crevice. She scored attempted trials as *successful* if infants reached the finishing platform without assistance or as *failures* if they tried to walk but fell or grabbed the experimenter's arm midbridge.

(A)

(B)

FIGURE 1

Walkway with adjustable bridge widths and removable handrail. Infants began on the starting platform. Parents (not shown) stood at the far end of the finishing platform, offering encouragement. An experimenter (shown) followed alongside infants to ensure their safety, and the area underneath the bridge was lined with padding. An assistant (not shown) adjusted the bridge in 18-cm (Experiment 1) or 12-cm (Experiment 2) increments. (A) On handrail trials, a handrail spanned the length of the bridge and rested on permanent support posts. (B) On no-handrail trials, the permanent support posts remained on the starting and finishing platforms.

She counted *handrail use* on the basis of whether infants touched the handrail after stepping onto the bridge. The coder also scored details of infants' bridge and handrail strategies after embarking onto the bridge to document the components of infants' motor plans (*hand and body positions, duration of handrail use, walk time,* and *step number*). She scored infants' exploratory behaviors on the starting platform to determine how they decided whether bridges were safe for walking and when to use the handrail (*latency* to begin traversal, *touching* the bridge and handrail support posts, and *shifts* in body position).

A second coder independently scored 25% of trials from each infant. Interrater agreement for categorical measures ranged from 97% to 100%. Correlation coefficients for durations ranged from .98 to 1.00. Discrepancies between coders were resolved through discussion.

Attempts to walk and handrail use. Infants appeared to recognize both the discrepancy between their own ability and the likelihood of reaching the goal and that the handrail could augment their physical ability. All infants attempted to walk over the three wider bridges regardless of handrail presence, but they were more likely to walk over the narrow 18-cm bridge when a handrail was available and more likely to avoid it when a handrail was not available (see Table 1, Row 1, and Figure 2A, Experiment 1). A 4 (bridge width) × 2 (handrail presence) repeated measures analysis of variance (ANOVA) on attempts to walk revealed main effects for bridge width, $F(3, 69) = 33.59$, $p < .01$, and handrail presence, $F(1, 23) = 13.32$, $p < .01$, and an interaction between the two factors, $F(3, 69) = 9.47$, $p < 01$. Planned comparisons between handrail and no-handrail trials at each bridge width showed significant differences in attempts only on the 18-cm bridge, with more attempts in the handrail condition, $t(23) = 3.50$, $p < .01$.

Infants' handrail use increased on narrower bridges, suggesting that they were aware of the handrail and that they recognized it as a means for augmenting balance control (see Table 1, Row 5, and Figure 2B, Experiment 1). On narrower bridges, infants were more likely to hold on with both hands than with only one hand, and they were more likely to hold onto the handrail for longer periods of time before they moved forward along the bridge (see Table 1, Rows 6 and 7). Repeated measures ANOVAs on the proportion of trials on which infants used the handrail, on the number of hands with which infants held the handrail, and on the duration of their first handrail touch at each of the four bridge widths showed main effects for bridge width: $F(3, 69) = 55.79$, $p < .01$; $F(3, 69) = 57.39$, $p < .01$; and $F(3, 69) = 10.69$, $p < .01$, respectively. Infants who used the handrail were more successful at walking over the 18-cm bridge ($r = .56$, $p < .01$).

Overall, infants were very accurate in judging their abilities to walk over bridges. Only 6% of trials were failures, most of which occurred on the narrowest (18-cm) bridge (see Table 1, Row 2). Although 16 children failed at least once, there was no evidence of within-session learning; failures were split equally between first and second halves of the session ($p > .10$). Furthermore, there was no evidence that infants were more hesitant to cross on trials immediately following one on which they failed: They refused to walk on 8% of trials following trials on which they fell and on

TABLE 1   EXPERIMENT 1: MEAN VALUES OF TODDLERS' BEHAVIORS ON BRIDGES WITH AND WITHOUT HANDRAILS

| | With Handrail | | | | | | | |
| | 18 cm | | 36 cm | | 54 cm | | 72 cm | |
Behavior	M	SD	M	SD	M	SD	M	SD
Walking								
1. Attempts to walk (prop. of trials)[a,*,**,†]	.71	.40	1.00		1.00		1.00	
2. Failed attempts (prop. of trials)[b,*]	.29	.37	.01	.07	0		0	
3. Walk time (s)[b,*]	9.07	6.42	2.54	1.38	1.59	0.77	1.30	0.33
4. Mean number of steps taken[b,*]	12.09	4.83	7.11	2.18	5.60	1.08	5.25	0.61
Handrail								
5. Handrail use (prop. of trials)[c,*]	.86	.31	.72	.34	.25	.32	.07	.17
6. Mean number of hands on rail[c,*]	1.57	0.43	1.06	0.22	1.00		1.00	
7. Duration of first touch (s)[d,*]	5.03	3.69	1.63	1.35	0.96	0.86	0.58	0.51
Exploration								
8. Latency (s)[a,*,**,†]	20.51	14.67	4.03	1.79	2.59	0.87	2.30	0.78
9. Bridge exploration (prop. of trials)[a,*,**,†]	.51	.35	.10	.18	.01	.07	0	
10. Rail/post exploration (prop. of trials)[a,*,**,†]	.74	.33	.44	.38	.15	.22	.04	.11
11. Mean number of position shifts[a,*,**,†]	1.01	0.86	0.04	0.15	0		0	

Note. prop. = proportion.
[a]Calculated for all trials.   [b]Calculated for all attempted trials.   [c]Calculated for all handrail available trials.   [d]Calculated for all handrail used trials.
*Significant main effect for bridge width, all p values $< .01$.   **Significant main effect for handrail presence, all p values $< .01$.
†Significant interaction between bridge width and handrail presence, all p values $< .04$.

11.5% of trials following trials on which they crossed successfully.

On wide bridges, infants walked normally, but on narrow ones, they modified their gait to walk successfully. On some walk trials, infants took more than 25 baby steps and longer than 30 s to reach the finishing platform (see Table 1, Rows 3 and 4). Repeated measures ANOVAs testing the effect of bridge width on step number and time to cross the bridge could not be performed because some infants contributed no gait data at the narrowest bridges. Planned comparisons at each bridge width, comparing infants' walk time with a handrail and without, revealed no statistically significant differences. That is, the time infants took to walk across the bridges depended on the width of the bridge but not on the presence of the handrail.

In addition to modifying step length and step number, infants devised other ingenious strategies to navigate the narrowest (18-cm) bridge. Sometimes they turned sideways (33% of trials; number of children = 18), took a giant step when they neared the end of the bridge (22% of trials; $n = 17$), crawled over the bridge (3% of trials; $n = 3$), or grabbed the experimenter's arm or shoulder (5% of trials; $n = 7$). They used the handrail by facing forward and holding the rail with one hand (51% of handrail trials; $n = 20$), facing the rail and holding it with two hands (45% of handrail trials; $n = 14$), and—most surprising—one child turned her back to the rail and held on with her hands behind her back (3% of handrail trials; $n = 1$).

On 15% of all trials, 23 infants began traversing the bridge using one method, then updated their plan by switching to another method midbridge. On 74% of trials in which infants switched locomotor methods, they went from a more difficult strategy to a more effective one for walking over narrow bridges. For example, they started out walking forward, but then crawled or walked sideways the rest of the way

			Without Handrail				
18 cm		**36 cm**		**54 cm**		**72 cm**	
M	**SD**	**M**	**SD**	**M**	**SD**	**M**	**SD**
.43	.41	.94	.16	.99	.07	1.00	
.42	.44	.08	.18	0		0	
6.59	4.48	2.92	2.50	1.53	0.64	1.32	0.37
11.50	5.11	7.56	2.66	5.57	1.18	5.32	0.73
29.49	15.88	7.77	7.60	3.48	3.08	2.37	0.75
.51	.35	.24	.35	.04	.11	0	
.54	.34	.25	.34	.11	.23	.01	.07
1.07	1.06	0.19	0.42	0.07	0.34	0	

across, or they started out holding onto the rail with one hand before grabbing on with both hands. If infants had only been trying out different possible strategies without attempting to make their progress more effective, then the order in which strategies were performed would have been random. However, because they generally started out with their typical strategies and then refined them, it appears that infants updated their locomotor plans as they realized that their current method would decrease their chances of crossing safely.

Exploratory behaviors. We considered behaviors to be exploratory only while infants were still on the starting platform before they stepped onto the bridge. Infants' latency to leave the starting platform increased sharply on the 18-cm bridge, especially on trials with no handrail (see Table 1, Row 8, and Figure 2C, Experiment 1). A 4 (bridge width) × 2 (handrail presence) repeated measures ANOVA showed main effects for bridge width, $F(3, 69) = 61.72$, $p < .01$, and handrail presence, $F(1, 23) = 11.03$, $p < .01$, and an interaction between the two, $F(3, 69) = 6.40$, $p = .01$. Planned comparisons between handrail and no-handrail trials at each bridge width showed significant differences in latency between the handrail and the no-handrail conditions only on the 18- and 36-cm bridges, $t(23) = 3.01$, $p < .01$, and $t(23) = 2.32$, $p < .03$, respectively. Latency was longer when the handrail was not available, suggesting that infants required more time to figure out how to reach their goal when walking was most difficult.

During the time that infants hesitated, they were not simply standing still and avoiding the bridge. Rather, they actively gathered information by touching the bridges and/or the section of the handrail or supporting post that spanned the starting platform (see Table 1, Rows 9 and 10). Infants touched bridges by probing the surface with one foot or by bending

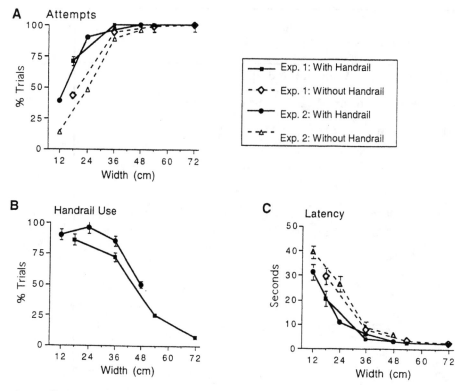

FIGURE 2

Experiments 1 (Exp. 1) and 2 (Exp. 2): effects of bridge width and handrail presence on infants'
locomotor decisions. A: infants' attempts to walk over bridges. B: the proportion of trials when
the handrail was used on each bridge width (calculated only for trials in which a handrail was
available). C: latency to embark onto the bridge.

down and pressing it with their hands. A 4 (bridge width) × 2 (handrail presence) repeated measures ANOVA on the proportion of trials in which infants touched the bridge revealed only a main effect for bridge width, $F(3, 69) = 47.44$, $p < .01$. A post hoc Scheffé test with a significance level of .05 revealed that infants explored the 18-cm bridge width on a significantly greater proportion of trials than they explored all other bridge widths. Furthermore, infants explored significantly more often on the 36-cm bridge than on the 72-cm bridge.

Infants touched the handrail or supporting post by gripping or patting it. Because exploratory behaviors were coded only while infants were on the starting platform, it was possible to code handrail exploration even when the handrail was not spanning the bridge. Permanent posts built into the walkway to support the handrail allowed infants to test whether they needed support to keep balance as they stepped onto the bridge, even on no-handrail trials (see Figure 1B). For example, when only the supporting post was available, they sometimes held it while stretching one foot out as far as they could onto the bridge to test

whether they could hold on and embark. Thus, we were able to code handrail/post exploration for all trials, regardless of handrail presence. A repeated measures ANOVA on touching the handrail/support post before stepping onto the bridge revealed main effects for bridge width, $F(3, 69) = 51.75$, $p < .01$, and handrail presence, $F(1, 23) = 11.50$, $p < .01$, and an interaction between the two variables, $F(3, 69) = 2.64$, $p = .05$. Planned comparisons between handrail and no-handrail trials showed increased touching of the supporting posts in the handrail condition on the 18-cm bridge, $t(23) = 2.70$, $p < .02$. A post hoc Scheffé test at the .05 significance level revealed that babies explored the handrail significantly more often on the 18-cm bridge than on all other bridge widths. Additionally, babies explored significantly more often on the 36-cm bridge than on the 72-cm and 54-cm widths. If babies had only reached for the handrail after they were already on the bridge, we might infer that they were simply reacting to being stuck in a precarious situation. However, the fact that they touched the handrail or supporting post before stepping onto the narrow bridges suggests that they recognized the environmental support as a tool to augment their balance.

Before stepping onto narrow bridges, infants frequently shifted their body positions to determine the best way to embark or to gather additional information (see Table 1, Row 11). They sometimes turned sideways to use the handrail, bent down to touch the bridges with their hands, or shifted from upright to other positions to test alternative methods of traversal. A 4 (bridge width) × 2 (handrail presence) repeated measures ANOVA on number of shifts in body position revealed only a main effect for bridge width, $F(3, 69) = 38.98$, $p < .01$. A post hoc Scheffé test at the .05 significance level revealed that babies shifted their body positions significantly more often on the 18-cm bridge than on any of the other bridge widths.

Individual differences. What distinguished the infants who displayed accurate judgments from those whose decisions were inaccurate? Because nearly all failures occurred on the 18-cm bridge, we analyzed potential sources of individual differences in infants' failure rate (the proportion of each infant's trials that were coded as failures) on the narrowest bridge. Previous studies have found that infants' locomotor experience (e.g., Adolph, 1997, 2000; Bertenthal et al., 1984; Kingsnorth & Schmuckler, 2000; Schmuckler, 1996), locomotor skill (e.g., Adolph, 1995), and body dimensions (e.g., Adolph & Avolio, 2000) predicted the adaptiveness of their responses in novel locomotor tasks. For the current study, parents' reports of infants' walking experience, prior handrail experience, and serious falls were not related to any of the behaviors that we coded on the narrowest (18-cm) bridge (i.e., attempts, successes, exploration). Possibly, walking experience was unrelated to bridge performance because infants were not pushed to their physical limits; even on the narrowest (18-cm) bridge, infants were proficient enough to cross successfully on more than half of the trials. Infants' body dimensions (height, weight, head circumference, shoulder width, and arm and leg lengths) and walking skill on solid ground (step velocity and step length) were also not related to their failure rate on the narrowest bridge, suggesting that the problem was not having a body too clumsy or too large to fit on the bridge.

The cause of failure appeared to depend in part on infants' ability to integrate information into an effective plan of action and to update their locomotor plans in accordance with new information. Lower levels of exploration were associated with higher failure rates in bridge crossing, suggesting that infants who neglected to gather information before deciding to cross were more likely to fail. Longer latencies and frequent shifts in body position predicted higher rates of success ($r = -.68$, $p < .01$, and $r = -.48$, $p < .02$, respectively). Moreover, of the 82 trials on which

infants attempted to cross the 18-cm bridge, the failure rate was lower (23%) on trials where infants updated their locomotor plans (switched strategies midbridge) than on trials where infants never switched strategies (60%). There was no correlation between failure rate and the average number of times infants switched strategies on the bridge ($r = .10$, *ns*), suggesting that falling off the bridge did not preclude infants from switching. Rather, not knowing to update their strategies for crossing the bridge prevented infants from crossing successfully.

Infants' handrail use on attempted handrail trials was also related to their exploratory behaviors. When stepwise multiple regression was used, bridge width significantly predicted handrail use when it was entered into the equation first ($R^2 = .65$), $F(1, 90) = 170.08$, $p < .01$. On the next step, the proportion of trials on which infants explored the handrail before stepping onto the bridge explained significant additional variance ($R^2 = .73$), $F(2, 89) = 119.91$, $p < .01$. Therefore, infants who knew to explore the handrail before stepping onto the walkway were more likely to use it for assistance. Experience with handrails prior to visiting the laboratory was not associated with handrail use ($r = .17$, *ns*).

SUMMARY

In sum, infants showed sophisticated means–ends problem solving behavior. They recognized the limits of their own abilities (i.e., they scaled walking attempts to bridge width), they noticed the availability of the handrail to augment their abilities (as shown by exploratory touching of the handrail while on the starting platform), and they perceived the relationship between themselves and the rail (as demonstrated by the interaction between bridge width and handrail condition). Infants' use of the handrail was toollike in these experiments because infants recognized that when their ability to walk across narrow bridges was limited, the handrail could assist them by extending their motor skill. Infants used the handrail to achieve goals that would have been impossible otherwise. Infants' recognition of the handrail as a tool appeared to result from direct, concerted exploration, both within and across trials. When bridge widths were wide enough that a handrail was unnecessary for successful crossing, prolonged exploration was infrequent. However, in more precarious situations, when infants needed to use the handrail for success, they appeared to figure out the role of the handrail in real time using information they obtained through active exploration. Infants explored the bridge and handrail before stepping onto bridges, constructed various strategies for using the handrail to cross the bridges, and modified handrail and crossing strategies midbridge. Higher levels of exploration predicted infants' success at walking over the narrowest bridge.

In the next experiment, we tested infants with narrower bridge widths, ranging from 12 cm to 48 cm. Our aim was to examine whether more infants would show differential use of the handrail to walk over narrower bridges and whether they could recognize that some bridges are too narrow for walking even with the help of a handrail.

EXPERIMENT 2: NARROWER BRIDGES AND HANDRAILS

METHOD

Twenty-four healthy, term 16-month-olds (± 1 week; $M = 16.08$ months) participated (12 girls and 12 boys). All could walk 10 feet across a room without

falling. Most infants were White and of middle-class socioeconomic status. Parents were interviewed about the same information and using the same protocol described in Experiment 1. Prior to walking onset, infants' cruising experience ranged from 0 to 6.71 months ($M = 2.70$ months). Walking experience ranged from 0.89 to 7.10 months ($M = 4.30$ months). Twenty-one infants had experience using a handrail on the playground or on stairs. We tested babies on the same walkway apparatus as in Experiment 1 with four bridge widths (12 cm, 24 cm, 36 cm, and 48 cm wide). The 36-cm width replicated an increment from the first experiment, allowing direct comparisons between the studies.

RESULTS AND DISCUSSION

Data coding. A primary coder scored all outcome measures from video as in Experiment 1. A second

---

TABLE 2 EXPERIMENT 2: MEAN VALUES OF TODDLERS' BEHAVIORS ON BRIDGES WITH AND WITHOUT HANDRAILS

	With Handrail							
	12 cm		24 cm		36 cm		48 cm	
Behavior	**M**	**SD**	**M**	**SD**	**M**	**SD**	**M**	**SD**
Walking								
1. Attempts to walk (prop. of trials)[a,*,**,†]	.39	.41	.90	.18	.96	.11	1.00	
2. Failed attempts (prop. of trials)[b,*]	.46	.48	.09	.19	.01	.07	0	
3. Walk time (s)[b,*]	31.23	19.90	8.24	9.09	2.94	1.57	2.08	1.16
4. Mean number of steps taken[b,*]	21.56	4.53	12.73	6.36	7.41	1.93	6.40	1.86
Handrail								
5. Handrail use (prop. of trials)[c,*]	.93	.17	.96	.11	.85	.23	.50	.41
6. Mean number of hands on rail[c,*]	1.67	0.40	1.47	0.41	1.13	0.25	1.06	0.30
7. Duration of first touch (s)[d,*]	5.23	3.70	2.47	1.53	1.36	1.21	0.90	0.60
Exploration								
8. Latency (s)[a,*,**,†]	31.19	15.51	10.63	8.20	6.10	6.15	3.15	1.65
9. Bridge exploration (prop. of trials)[a,*,**,†]	.57	.39	.33	.35	.15	.24	.04	.15
10. Rail/post exploration (prop. of trials)[a,*,**]	.86	.22	.67	.42	.58	.38	.24	.29
11. Mean number of position shifts[a,*,**,†]	1.96	1.04	0.73	0.65	0.28	0.45	0.07	0.34

Note. prop. = proportion.
[a]Calculated for all trials. [b]Calculated for all attempted trials. [c]Calculated for all handrail available trials. [d]Calculated for all handrail used trials.
*Significant main effect for bridge width, all p values < .01. **Significant main effect for handrail presence, all p values < .01.
†Significant interaction between bridge width and handrail presence, all p values < .04.

coder independently scored 25% of the trials from each infant. Interrater agreement for categorical measures ranged from 96% to 100%. Correlation coefficients for measures of duration ranged from .99 to 1.00. Discrepancies between coders were resolved through discussion.

Attempts to walk and handrail use. As predicted, narrower bridge widths elicited fewer attempts to walk and more frequent handrail use. As in Experiment 1, infants attempted to walk over wider bridges regardless of handrail presence but attempted the narrower bridges more often when the handrail was present (see Table 2, Row 1, and Figure 2A, Experiment 2). Without a handrail, 19 infants refused to walk over the 12-cm bridge on every trial, 8 refused all 24-cm bridge trials, and 2 refused all 36-cm bridge trials. A 4 (bridge width) × 2 (handrail presence) repeated measures ANOVA revealed main ef-

fects for bridge width, $F(3, 69) = 84.13$, $p < .01$, and handrail presence, $F(1, 23) = 21.97$, $p < .01$, and an interaction between the two factors, $F(3, 69) = 8.90$, $p < .01$. Planned comparisons at each bridge width showed significant differences between handrail and no-handrail trials, with more attempts in the handrail condition only on the 12-cm and 24-cm bridges, $t(23) = 3.00$, $p < .01$, and $t(23) = 4.81$, $p < .01$, respectively.

Infants used the handrail more often, held the rail with two hands, and held the rail for longer periods of time on narrower bridges (see Table 2, Rows 5, 6, and 7, and Figure 2B, Experiment 2). Repeated measures ANOVAs on proportion of trials on which the handrail was used, number of hands used to hold on, and duration of first touch of the handrail at each of the four bridge widths revealed main effects for bridge width, $F(3, 69) = 20.66$, $p < .01$; $F(3, 69) = 41.99$, $p < .01$; and

Without Handrail							
12 cm		24 cm		36 cm		48 cm	
M	**SD**	**M**	**SD**	**M**	**SD**	**M**	**SD**
.14	.29	.48	.40	.89	.29	.96	.11
1.00		.17	.29	.02	.07	.02	.10
		5.22	5.37	3.33	2.78	2.37	1.83
		10.68	4.66	7.95	2.77	6.95	2.17
39.27	12.37	26.47	15.70	8.70	12.60	5.77	5.56
.47	.38	.60	.37	.26	.34	.11	.25
.82	.29	.61	.36	.31	.39	.17	.32
2.64	1.52	1.27	1.09	0.33	0.61	0.08	0.28

$F(3, 48) = 20.26$, $p < .01$, respectively.[1] A post hoc Scheffé test at the .05 significance level revealed significant differences between handrail use at the 48-cm bridge and all other bridge widths, with infants using the handrail less often on the wide bridge.

As in the previous study, infants accurately judged their abilities to walk over bridges. Failures occurred on only 6% of trials and were relegated primarily to the narrowest (12-cm) bridge (see Table 2, Row 2). As in Experiment 1, failures were split evenly between infants' first 12 and second 12 trials, and infants showed no wariness on trials immediately following trials on which they failed. On successful trials, infants modified their gait on narrower bridges by increasing walk time and step number (see Table 2, Rows 3 and 4). Again, planned comparisons revealed no significant differences between the time it took infants to walk at each bridge width with a handrail and without a handrail.

Exploratory behaviors.   As in Experiment 1, infants hesitated longer on the narrower bridges, especially in the no-handrail condition (see Table 2, Row 8, and Figure 2C, Experiment 2). A 4 (bridge width) × 2 (handrail presence) repeated measures ANOVA on latency to embark showed main effects for bridge width, $F(3, 69) = 98.67$, $p < .01$, and handrail presence, $F(1, 23) = 24.36$, $p < .01$, and an interaction between the two, $F(3, 69) = 8.80$, $p < .01$. Planned comparisons at each bridge width between handrail and no-handrail trials showed longer latencies in the no-handrail condition only at 12-cm and 24-cm widths: $t(23) = 3.03$, $p < .01$, and $t(23) = 5.01$, $p < .01$, respectively.

Before stepping onto bridges, infants gathered information by touching the bridge with their hands or feet (see Table 2, Row 9). A 4 (bridge width) × 2 handrail presence) repeated measures ANOVA revealed main effects for bridge width, $F(3, 69) = 14.66$, $p < .01$, and handrail presence, $F(1, 23) = 5.04$, $p < .04$, and an interaction between the two, $F(3, 69) = 6.78$, $p < .01$. Unlike in Experiment 1, however, planned comparisons between handrail and no-handrail conditions showed more bridge touching when the handrail was unavailable at 24 cm, as if to figure out how to cross the bridge without assistance: $t(23) = 2.87$, $p < .01$. Exploration of the 12-cm bridge did not depend on handrail availability. A post hoc Scheffé test at the .05 significance level revealed that infants touched the two narrower bridges (12 cm and 24 cm) significantly more often than they touched the two wider bridges (36 cm and 48 cm). Infants also touched he handrail prior to stepping onto the bridges (see Table 2, Row 10). A 4 (bridge width) × 2 (handrail presence) repeated measures ANOVA revealed only main effects for bridge width, $F(3, 69) = 54.60$, $p < .01$, and

handrail presence, $F(1, 23) = 5.15$, $p < .04$. A post hoc Scheffé test at the .05 significance level revealed that infants explored the handrail significantly less often on the 48-cm bridge than on each of the three narrower bridges. In addition, infants explored the handrail significantly more often on the 12-cm bridge than they did on the 36-cm bridge.

Infants executed more shifts in body position (2–3, on average) in this experiment compared with the last one (1–2) (see Table 2, Row 11). A 4 (bridge width) × 2 (handrail presence) repeated measures ANOVA on the number of times infants shifted body position before embarking revealed main effects for bridge width, $F(3, 69) = 64.22$, $p < .01$, and handrail, $F(1, 23) = 10.41$, $p < .01$, and an interaction between the two factors, $F(3, 69) = 3.53$, $p < .02$. Planned comparisons at each bridge width between handrail and no-handrail trials showed more body shifts in the no-handrail condition only for the 12-cm and 24-cm bridges, $t(23) = 2.55$, $p < .02$, and $t(23) = 2.34$, $p < .03$, respectively. A post hoc Scheffé test at the .05 significance level revealed that the number of times infants shifted their position was significantly greater on the 12-cm bridge than on all others. Furthermore, infants shifted their body position significantly more often on the 24-cm bridge than they did on the 48-cm or 36-cm bridges.

Individual differences.   We analyzed potential sources of individual differences in infants' rate of failing on the 12-cm and 24-cm bridges. As in Experiment 1, locomotor experience, handrail experience, and body dimensions were not related to failures on the narrow bridges. However, in contrast to Experiment 1, locomotor skill was predictive of infants' attempts to walk. Infants who walked faster and took longer steps on solid ground were more likely to attempt to walk over the narrowest bridges than poorer walkers ($r = .59$, $p < .01$, and $r = .78$, $p < .01$, respectively). Furthermore, failure was correlated with poor walking skill ($r = -.43$, $p < .04$, and $r = -.51$, $p < 02$, for step time and step length respectively). The discrepancy between correlates of infants' performance in the two experiments is likely due to the greater sensitivity of Experiment 2. Walking over narrower bridges was physically more difficult, so that smaller differences in motor proficiency between subjects may not have been captured until the bridge widths were made more narrow. Apparently, infants took their own level of skill into account when planning a course of action that involved some risk and when determining whether to augment their abilities via alternative means (i.e., the handrail).

As in Experiment 1, lower levels of exploration were associated with increased rates of failure on the

---

[1]Degrees of freedom in the analysis for duration of first handrail touch reflect only the subset of handrail trials in which the handrail was actually used. The other analyses of handrail use were based on proportions of behaviors of all handrail trials.

12-cm and 24-cm bridges, suggesting that infants who did not gather information about environmental supports for action made less accurate decisions than children who spent time exploring. Failures on the 12-cm bridge were associated with shorter latencies ($r = -.84$, $p < .01$), less frequent shifts in body position ($r = -.47$, $p < .02$), and less exploratory touching of the handrail ($r = -.49$, $p < .02$). Failures on the 24-cm bridge were associated only with shorter latencies ($r = -.44$, $p < .04$). As in Experiment 1, the ability to update a locomotor plan predicted a lower failure rate on narrow bridges. On trials when infants attempted to cross the 12-cm (number of trials = 38; strategy data missing for 2 trials) and 24-cm (number of trials = 99; strategy data missing for 1 trial) bridges, there was a lower failure rate when infants updated their locomotor plans. One hundred percent of the 12-cm bridge trials on which infants did not update their crossing or handrail strategies resulted in failures. In contrast, only 32% of trials on which infants changed their strategies resulted in failed attempts. Similarly, on the 24-cm bridge, trials on which infants did not update their strategies resulted in failures more often (22%) than trials on which infants did update (5%).

When stepwise multiple regression was used, exploratory behaviors again predicted handrail use on attempted handrail trials. When bridge width was entered into the equation first, it accounted for a significant proportion of the variance of handrail use ($R^2 = .34$), $F(1, 83) = 43.15$, $p < .01$. On the next step, the proportion of trials on which infants explored the handrail before stepping onto the bridge was entered. Exploring the handrail before attempting to cross the bridge explained significant additional variance ($R^2 = .44$), $F(2, 82) = 32.76$, $p < .01$. Experience with handrails prior to visiting the laboratory was not associated with handrail use ($r = .28$, ns).

Overlaying the data figures from the two experiments (see Figure 2) illustrates that infants' responses were scaled neatly across experiments. On every primary outcome measure, infants treated the 36-cm bridge width common to both studies similarly. In both studies, infants were less likely to walk and more likely to use the handrail on narrower bridges.

GENERAL DISCUSSION

Adaptive locomotion is not simply a matter of muscles, biomechanics, and lower level perceptual-motor skills. In two experiments we demonstrated that adaptive locomotion can involve higher level cognitive abilities—namely a sophisticated form of means–ends problem solving. We encouraged 16-month-old infants to walk over wide and narrow bridges in the presence or absence of a handrail. On the wide bridges, infants always attempted to walk regardless

of whether the handrail was available, they rarely touched the handrail while crossing when it was available, they did not modify their gait to walk over the bridges, and exploratory activity on the starting platform was minimal. In contrast, on the narrow bridges, infants attempted to walk more often when the handrail was available than when it was absent, they used the handrail more often while crossing when it was available, they modified their gait by taking smaller, slower steps, and they spent more time on the starting platform exploring the handrail/posts and the bridges. These findings suggest that infants recognized the handrail as a means for augmenting their balance control in a precarious situation. That is, they viewed the handrail as a structure in the environment, separate from themselves, and separate from the bridges, which could be used as an intervening step to achieve the goal of crossing to the landing platform. Moreover, infants adopted multiple strategies for using the handrail successfully and updated their motor plan as they walked over the bridges by switching from less to more efficient strategies (e.g., from walking frontward to facing sideways while holding the rail), suggesting that their means–ends analysis extends to the motor plan itself. Thus, infants' handrail use was not simply a result of finding themselves stranded on a bridge but rather a central component of a planful attempt to reach a goal.

A primary aim of this research was to extend the classic conceptualization of tool use into a new locomotor task domain. By doing so, we attempted to clarify our understanding of the literature's central constructs, specifically, the constraints placed on the types of implements that are typically classified as tools and the types of behaviors that are considered tool use. To what extent is the means–ends problem solving demonstrated by infants in the bridges/handrails studies an example of tool use? Or put more broadly, is using a handrail to walk over bridges, down stairs, or along icy pavement an example of bona fide tool use, the pinnacle of means–ends problem solving? Is a crutch a tool? What about a blind person's cane or an elderly person's wheeled walker?

Traditionally, tool use has connoted an actor's manipulation of one object upon another, such as a hammer hitting a nail, or a hook pulling an out-of-reach object closer (e.g., Bates et al., 1980; Brown, 1990; McCarty et al., 2001). Tradition, however, does not provide a satisfactory rubric for understanding what should and should not count as a tool. On Parker and Gibson's (1977) more restrictive definition, intentionally augmenting one's abilities via a handrail, crutch, cane, walker, or pole vault would likely not be considered an example of tool use because the means are not freely mobile extensions of the actor's body. On others' less restrictive definitions (e.g., Connolly & Dalgleish, 1989; van Leeuwen et al.,

1994; Wagman & Carello, 2001), handrails and other objects used to augment balance and locomotion might be considered examples of tool use because they restructure the relationship between the actor and the environment to facilitate the completion of an action.

Like scientific traditions, definitions and criteria are useful only when they include and exclude the appropriate phenomena. On the one hand, the data from the current studies suggest that Parker and Gibson's (1977) definition may be overly narrow. Infants' elaborate, systematic, and prospective exploration of the bridges and handrail and their discovery of appropriate strategies for using the handrail suggest that their cognitive understanding surpasses that of monkeys who throw nuts at the hard ground to crack them open. On the other hand, the data from the current studies suggest that the less restrictive definitions might be overly inclusive. For example, on the less restrictive definitions, the bridges spanning the precipice and the experimenter spotting the infants—and similarly in other contexts, wheelchairs, wheelchair ramps, ladders, stairs, step stools, cleats, and so on—might be considered examples of tools because they augment actors' bodily abilities by enabling new affordances for action.

Like earlier investigators, we propose that the critical essence of tool use concerns its function and the underlying cognitive mechanisms. At its most fundamental level, the function of a tool is to enable the completion of a task that could not be accomplished otherwise. The heart of tool use is the cognitive understanding that an object external to oneself can serve as a means for connecting oneself to an otherwise unattainable goal, not simply the behavioral incorporation of an external object into a sequence of actions (McCarty et al., 2001). We suggest that the current studies offer a fresh approach to the problem of evaluating means–ends problem solving in terms of tool use: to observe participants in nontraditional tasks, gather rich descriptions of participants' exploratory behaviors and action strategies, and then assess the behavioral evidence on a case-by-case basis for the functional and cognitive hallmarks of tool use (Adolph & Lockman, 2002).

The second goal of this research was to examine individual differences in infants' performance as a way of identifying developmental and behavioral correlates of means–ends problem solving. With our age-held-constant design, we could examine walking experience, prior exposure to handrails on stairs and playground equipment, walking skill on flat ground, body dimensions, and real-time exploratory behaviors as predictors of success in the bridges/handrails task. In contrast to previous work (e.g., Adolph, 1997; Adolph & Avolio, 2000; Kingsnorth & Schmuckler, 2000), infants' locomotor experience and body dimensions were not predictive of performance. As in previous studies (e.g., Adolph, 1995), when the task pushed the limits of toddlers' physical abilities, their motor skill predicted their performance (i.e., walking skill on flat ground predicted success at crossing the narrowest 12-cm bridges). Consistent with previous studies (e.g., Adolph, 1995; Gibson et al., 1987), the most important predictor of success on this task was infants' real-time exploratory behaviors, selection of locomotor strategies, and updating of strategies midbridge. Exploration of the handrail significantly predicted its use, lack of exploration was significantly associated with failing, and choosing an effective locomotor strategy was related to successful bridge crossing. Apparently, the gathering of crucial information, the ability to understand and integrate the information into an effective plan of action, and the adoption of appropriate strategies were the most critical factors for means–ends problem solving. Thus, cognitive and perceptual-motor factors together determine the difficulty of a task, which in turn fluctuates according to continuously developing cognitive and locomotor systems.

The third goal of this research was to examine the processes underlying infants' invention, coordination, and execution of their locomotor plans. Whereas manual means–ends tasks have often lacked behavioral evidence for the underlying cognitive processes that they purport to measure, the current locomotor task provided a rich source of evidence concerning the processes underlying means–ends problem solving in infancy. For example, the sight of the narrow bridges elicited concerted visual and haptic exploration as infants assessed the likelihood of crossing the bridge successfully. On trials in which they did eventually walk, infants took the narrower bridge width into account by modifying their gait patterns. On trials in which they did not eventually walk, infants searched for alternative means of crossing by exploring the handrail and testing various locomotor positions. After discovering viable alternatives, infants reassessed the likelihood of crossing successfully by holding onto the handrail and stepping partway onto the bridge prior to leaving the starting platform or by executing a long first touch prior to beginning movement along the bridge. While crossing, infants continued to consider the effectiveness of their strategy, as evidenced by changes in strategy midbridge.

All of infants' observed behaviors—their exploratory behaviors, gait modifications, crossing strategies, and handrail use—helped to delineate the planning and execution components of general problem solving. After initially evaluating a goal as being unattainable (i.e., crossing the overly narrow bridge), infants subsequently reevaluate the goal as being attainable via the discovered means (i.e., the handrail). The search for and discovery of new means is prompted by the impasse between a desire to reach the goal and an inability to do so using typical methods. Adaptive locomotion may require infants to decide at each new locomotor situation whether walking is possible, but after deciding that a goal is currently unattainable, they should be able to fall back on an alternative strategy or tool that they have used in previous trials or similar contexts (Adolph, 1997). Indeed, the pattern of infants' behaviors in the current study–systematic, organized, intentional, and flexible with respect to bridge width and handrail presence–suggests true strategy use as defined in classic instances of children's problem solving such as reading, mathematics, memory, and so forth (Bjorklund, 1990).

Thus, the development of adaptive locomotion may involve higher level cognitive changes that improve infants' ability to assess possibilities for locomotion and to discover new means and incorporate them into a plan of action, as well as concurrent lower level perceptual-motor changes that introduce new possibilities for locomotion and more finely honed exploratory movements. As Campos and colleagues (2000) so aptly pointed out, infants' travels may help to broaden their minds; reciprocally, we have tried to show that infants' minds may enrich their travels.

REFERENCES

Adolph, K. E. (1995). A psychophysical assessment of toddlers' ability to cope with slopes. *Journal of Experimental Psychology: Human Perception and Performance, 21,* 734–750.

Adolph, K. E. (1997). Learning in the development of infant locomotion. *Monographs of the Society for Research in Child Development, 62*(3, Serial No. 251).

Adolph, K. E. (2000). Specificity of learning: Why infants fall over a veritable cliff. *Psychological Science, 2,* 290–295.

Adolph, K. E., & Avolio, A. (2000). Walking infants adapt locomotion to changing body dimensions. *Journal of Experimental Psychology: Human Perception and Performance, 26,* 1148–1166.

Adolph, K. E., Eppler, M. A., Marin, L., Weise, I. B., & Clearfield, M. W. (2000). Exploration in the service of prospective control. *Infant Behavior and Development: Special Issue on Perception-Action Coupling, 23,* 441–460.

Adolph, K. E., & Lockman, J. J. (2002, April). *How tools expand the potential for action: Hands, handles and handrails.* Symposium conducted at the International Conference on Infant Studies, Toronto, Ontario, Canada.

Adolph, K. E., Vereijken, B., & Denny, M. A.(1998). Learning to crawl. *Child Development, 69,* 1299–1312.

Bates, E., Carlson-Luden, V., & Bretherton, I. (1980). Perceptual aspects of tool using in infancy. *Infant Behavior and Development, 3,* 127–140.

Bauer, P. J., Schwade, J. A., Wewerka, S. S., & Delaney, K. (1999). Planning ahead: Goal-directed problem solving by 2-year-olds. *Developmental Psychology, 35,* 1321–1337.

Bertenthal, B. I., Campos, J. J., & Barrett, K. C. (1984). Self-produced locomotion: An organizer of emotional, cognitive, and social development in infancy. In R. Emde & R. Harmon (Eds.), *Continuities and discontinuities in development* (pp 175–210). New York: Plenum.

Bjorklund, D. F. (Ed.). (1990). *Children's strategies: Contemporary views of cognitive development.* Hillsdale, NJ: Erlbaum.

Bremner, J. G. (1993). Motor abilities as causal agents in infant cognitive development. In G. J. P. Savelsbergh (Ed.), *The development of coordination in infancy* (pp. 47–77). Amsterdam: North-Holland/Elsevier Science.

Bremner, J. G., & Bryant, P.E. (1977). Place versus response as the basis of spatial errors made by young infants. *Journal of Experimental Child Psychology, 23,* 162–171.

Bril, B., & Breniere, Y. (1993). Posture and independent locomotion in early childhood: Learning to walk or learning dynamic postural control? In G. J. P. Savelsbergh (Ed.), *The development of coordination in infancy* (pp. 337–358). Amsterdan: North-Holland/Elsevier Science.

Brown, A. (1990). Domain specific principles affect learning and transfer in children. *Cognitive Science, 14,* 107–133.

Bushnell, E. W., & Boudreau, J. P. (1998). Exploring and exploiting objects with the hands during infancy. In K. J. Connolly (Ed.), *The psychobiology of the hand* (pp. 144–161). London: Mac Keith Press.

Butterworth, G. (1977). Object disappearance and error in Piaget's Stage IV task, *Journal of Experimental Child Psychology, 23,* 391–401.

Campos, J. J., Anderson, D. I., Barbu-Roth, M. A., Hubbard, E. M., Hertenstein, M. J., & Witherington, D. (2000). Travel broadens the mind. *Infancy, 1,* 149–219.

Campos, J. J., Bertenthal, B. I., & Kermoian, R. (1992). Early experience and emotional development: The emergence of wariness of heights. *Psychological Science, 3*(1), 61–64.

Campos, J., Hiatt, S., Ramsay, D., Henderson, C., & Svejda, M. (1978). The emergence of fear on the visual cliff. In M. Lewis & L. Rosenblum (Eds.), *The development of affect* (pp. 149–182). New York: Plenum.

Chen, Z., Sanchez, R. P., & Campbell, T. (1997). From beyond to within their grasp: The rudiments of analogical problem solving in 10- and 13-month-olds. *Developmental Psychology, 33,* 790–801.

Chen, Z., & Seigler, R. S. (2000). Across the great divide: Bridging the gap between understanding of toddlers' and older children's thinking. *Monographs of the Society for Research in Child Development, 65*(2, Serial No. 261).

Clark, J. E., & Phillips, S. J. (1987). The step cycle organization of infant walkers. *Journal of Motor Behavior, 19,* 421–433.

Connolly, K., & Dalgleish, M. (1989). The emergence of a tool-using skill in infancy. *Developmental Psychology, 25,* 894–912.

Feigenson, L., & Carey, S. (2003). Tracking individuals via object-files: Evidence from infants' manual search. *Developmental Science, 6,* 568–584.

Gibson, E. J. (1992). *Perceptual learning and development.* Presentation to the Indiana University Psychology Department Colloquium, Bloomington, IN.

Gibson, E. J., Riccio, G., Schmuckler, M. A., Stoffregen, T. A., Rosenberg, D., & Taormina, J. (1987). Detection of the traversability of surfaces by crawling and walking infants. *Journal of Experimental Psychology: Human Perception and Performance, 13,* 533–544.

Gibson, E. J., & Walk, R. D. (1960). The "visual cliff." *Scientific American, 202,* 64–71.

Kingsnorth, S., & Schmuckler, M. A. (2000). Walking skill versus walking experience as a predictor of barrier crossing in toddlers. *Infant Behavior and Development, 23,* 331–350.

Köhler, W. (1931). *The mentality of apes.* London: Percy Lund, Humphries & Co.

Lockman, J. J. (2000). A perception-action perspective on tool use development. *Child Development, 71,* 137–144.

McCarty, M. E., Clifton, R. K., & Collard, R. R. (1999). Problem solving in infancy: The emergence of an action plan. *Developmental Psychology, 35,* 1091–1101.

McCarty, M. E., Clifton, R. K., & Collard, R. R. (2001). The beginnings of tool use by infants and toddlers. *Infancy, 2,* 233–256.

McGraw, M. B. (1935). *Growth: A study of Johnny and Jimmy.* New York: Appleton-Century.

Parker, S. T., & Gibson, K. R. (1977). Object manipulation, tool use and sensorimotor intelligence as feeding adaptations in cebus monkeys and great apes. *Journal of Human Evolution, 6,* 623–641.

Piaget, J. (1954). *The construction of reality in the child.* New York: Free Press.

Richards, J. E., & Rader, N. (1981). Crawling-onset age predicts visual cliff avoidance in infants. *Journal of Experimental Psychology: Human Perception and Performance, 7,* 382–387.

Richards, J. E., & Rader, N. (1983). Affective, behavioral, and avoidance responses on the visual cliff: Effects of crawling onset age, crawling experience, and testing age. *Psychophysiology, 20,* 633–642.

Schmuckler, M. A. (1996). The development of visually-guided locomotion: Barrier crossing by toddlers. *Ecological Psychology, 8,* 209–236.

Shapiro, S. A., & Gerke, E. D. (1991). The process of adaptation to environmental conditions in a child's behavior. *Soviet Psychology, 29*(6), 44–90. (Original work published in Russian in 1930)

Steenbergen, B., van der Kamp, J., Smitsman, A. W., & Carson, R. G. (1997). Spoon-handling in two- to four-year-old children. *Ecological Psychology, 9,* 113–129.

Thelen, E., Ulrich, B. D., & Niles, D. (1987). Bilateral coordination in human infants stepping on a split-belt treadmill. *Journal of Experimental Psychology: Human Perception and Performance, 13,* 405–410.

Tomasello, M., & Call, J. (1997). *Primate cognition.* New York: Oxford University Press.

van Leeuwen, L., Smitsman, A., & van Leeuwen, C. (1994). Affordances, perceptual complexity, and the development of tool use. *Journal of Experimental Psychology: Human Perception and Performance, 20,* 174–191.

Wagman, J. B., & Carello, C. (2001). Affordances and inertial constraints on tool use. *Ecological Psychology, 13,* 173–195.

Wellman, H. M., Cross, D., & Bartsch, K. (1986). Infant search and object permanence: A meta-analysis of the A-not-B error. *Monographs of the Society for Research in Child Development, 51*(3, Serial No. 214).

Willatts, P. (1984). The Stage IV infant's solution of problems requiring the use of supports. *Infant Behavior and Development, 7,* 125–134.

QUESTIONS

1. What types of higher-level cognitive processes do Berger and Adolph claim are involved in the manual and locomotor tasks of young children?
2. According to the authors, what role does planning play in the infant's ability to explore the bridge and handrail?
3. In Experiment 1, why were two conditions studied—one in which the bridges had a handrail and one in which they did not? Which bridges were the infants expected to have the most difficulty with when no handrails were present?
4. Do you think the infants in this study were accurate in judging their abilities for walking over the different types of bridges? Use evidence to support your answer.
5. What factor(s) regulated the time it took for an infant to cross a bridge? What does this suggest to you about the infant's judgment in crossing these bridges?
6. What were some of the strategies that the infants used to navigate the narrowest bridge?
7. The infants touched the handrail or supporting post before they stepped onto the narrow bridges. What do the authors say this behavior suggests about what the infants understood about the handrail and supporting post? Do you agree with them?
8. Why did the researchers conduct the second experiment and what did they find out?
9. What factors explained individual differences in children in Experiment 2? What do these differences suggest about how infants approach this task? In other words, what information do infants seem to consider as they embark on crossing narrow bridges?
10. What is means–ends problem solving, and what role do tools—like the handrails in this study—play in it?

13 Becoming a Native Listener

JANET F. WERKER

For many researchers, the development of language is humanity's most impressive accomplishment. In fact, some researchers argue that language is the distinguishing characteristic of the human species. But when does language development begin? A quick reply would most likely be "when someone begins to speak." However, this is not so. Long before children utter their first word at about 12 months of age, much has happened to mark the development of language. One important skill that develops before children produce speech is the ability to distinguish the speech sounds produced by others. Human speech is composed of a vast range of sounds, which are called *phones,* but only a subset of these sounds is used in any single language. Adults are quite adept at recognizing the phones in their own language, and this ability is what enables adults to process language so quickly and effectively. Learning to distinguish phones occurs in childhood, but when?

In the following article, Janet F. Werker describes her research on the development of this ability. The article reports the results of several studies in which Werker tried to home in on the timing and nature of early phonetic sensitivity. Her research focuses on changes in speech perception over the first year of life. Results indicate that children learn to discriminate the sounds of their own language even before they begin to speak. This ability provides a foundation for language learning in that it helps infants attend to the sounds of their own language, the very sounds that they will eventually learn to produce.

This research is important for several reasons. It describes achievements in the first year of life that are critical to later language learning. It also provides interesting information about how maturation, or biological change, and experience influence the perceptual abilities related to early language learning. Finally, it demonstrates the amazing capability of even very young members of our species to develop skills uniquely adapted to the circumstances in which growth occurs.

The syllables, words, and sentences used in all human languages are formed from a set of speech sounds called phones. Only a subset of the phones is used in any particular language. Adults can easily perceive the differences among the phones used to contrast meaning in their own language, but young infants go much farther: they are able to discriminate nearly every phonetic contrast on which they have been tested, including those they have never before heard. Our research has shown that this broad-based sensitivity declines by the time a baby is one year old. This phenomenon provides a way to describe basic abilities in the young infant and explore the effects of experience on human speech perception.

To put infants' abilities in perspective, adult speech perception must be understood. The phones that distinguish meaning in a particular language are called phonemes. There is considerable acoustic variability in the way each individual phoneme is realized in speech. For example, the phoneme /b/ is very

Reprinted with permission of Sigma Xi Scientific Research Society from *American Scientist,* 77(1989), pp. 54–59. Janet F. Werker is an assistant professor of developmental psychology at the University of British Columbia. She received a B.A. from Harvard University and a Ph.D. in psychology from the University of British Columbia in 1982. She was an assistant professor of psychology at Dalhousie University from 1982 to 1986, and joined the faculty at the University of British Columbia in 1986. The research reported here was supported by the Natural Sciences and Engineering Research Council of Canada and the Social Science and Humanities Research Council. In addition, portions of this work were made possible by an NICHD grant to Haskins Laboratories. Address: Department of Psychology, University of British Columbia, Vancouver, British Columbia, V6T 1Y7, Canada.

different before the vowel /ee/ in "beet" from the way it is before the vowel /oo/ in "boot." How do adults handle this variability? As first demonstrated in a classic study by Liberman and his colleagues (1967), they treat these acoustically distinct instances of a single phoneme as equivalent. This equivalency is demonstrated in the laboratory by presenting listeners with a series of pairs of computer-synthesized speech stimuli that differ by only one acoustic step along a physical continuum and asking them first to label and then to try to discriminate between the stimuli. Adult listeners are able to discriminate reliably only stimuli that they have labeled as different— that is, they cannot easily discriminate between two acoustically different stimuli that they labeled /pa/, but they can discriminate between two similar stimuli if one is from their /ba/ category and one from their /pa/ category.

The phenomenon by which labeling limits discrimination is referred to as categorical perception. This has obvious advantages for language processing. It allows a listener to segment the words he hears immediately according to the phonemic categories of his language and to ignore unessential variations within a category.

Given that adults perceive speech categorically, when do such perceptual capabilities appear? To find out, Eimas and his colleagues (1971) adapted the so-called high-amplitude sucking procedure for use in a speech discrimination task. This procedure involves teaching infants to suck on a pacifier attached to a pressure transducer in order to receive a visual or auditory stimulus. After repeated presentations of the same sight or sound, the sucking rate declines, indicating that the infants are becoming bored. The infants are then presented with a new stimulus. Presumably, if they can discriminate the new sight or sound from the old, they will increase their sucking rate.

In Eimas's experiment, infants one and four months old heard speech sounds that varied in equal steps from /ba/ to /pa/. Like adults, they discriminated between differences in the vicinity of the /ba/-/pa/ boundary but were unable to discriminate equal acoustic changes from within the /ba/ category. Rather than having to learn about phonemic categories, then, infants seem capable of grouping speech stimuli soon after birth.

Experiments in the 17 years since Eimas's original study have shown that infants can discriminate nearly every phonetic contrast on which they are tested but are generally unable to discriminate differences within a single phonemic category (for a review, see Kuhl 1987). That is, like adults, infants perceive acoustically distinct instances of a single phoneme as equivalent but easily discriminate speech sounds from two different categories that are not more acoustically distinct.

Of special interest are demonstrations that young infants are even able to discriminate phonetic contrasts not used in their native language. In an early study, Streeter (1976) used the high-amplitude sucking procedure to test Kikuyu infants on their ability to discriminate the English /ba/-/pa/ distinction, which is not used in Kikuyu. She found that the infants could discriminate these two syllable types. Similar results have been obtained from a variety of laboratories using other nonnative phonetic contrasts (Lasky et al. 1975; Trehub 1976; Aslin et al. 1981; Eilers et al. 1982). This pattern of results indicates that the ability to discriminate phones from the universal phonetic inventory may be present at birth.

DEVELOPMENTAL CHANGES

Given these broad-based infant abilities, one might expect that adults would also be able to discriminate nearly all phonetic contrasts. However, research suggests that adults often have difficulty discriminating phones that do not contrast meaning in their own language. An English-speaking adult, for example, has difficulty perceiving the difference between the two /p/ phones that are used in Thai (Lisker and Abramson 1970). So too, a Japanese-speaking adult initially cannot distinguish between the English /ra/ and /la/, because Japanese uses a single phoneme intermediate between the two English phonemes (Miyawaki et al. 1975; MacKain et al. 1981). This pattern of extensive infant capabilities and more limited capabilities in the adult led to the suggestion that infants may have a biological predisposition to perceive all possible phonetic contrasts and that there is a decline in this universal phonetic sensitivity by adulthood as a function of acquiring a particular language (Eimas 1975; Trehub 1976).

My work has been designed to explore this intriguing possibility. In particular, I wanted to trace how speech perception changes during development. Are infants actually able to discriminate some pairs of speech sounds better than adults, or have they simply been tested with more sensitive procedures? If infants do have greater discriminative capacities than adults, when does the decline occur and why?

The first problem that my colleagues and I faced was to find a testing procedure which could be used with infants, children of all ages, and adults. We could then begin a program of studies comparing their relative abilities to perceive the differences between phonetic contrasts of both native and nonnative languages.

The testing routine we chose is a variation of the so-called infant head turn procedure (for a complete description, see Kuhl 1987). Subjects are presented with several slightly different versions of the same

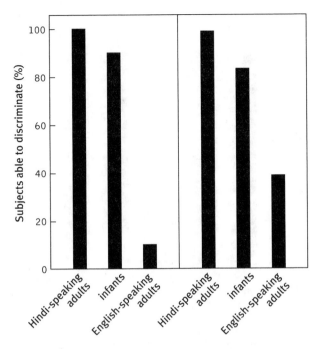

FIGURE 1

When tested on their ability to discriminate two Hindi syllables that are not used in English, six-to-eight-month-old infants from English-speaking families do nearly as well as Hindi-speaking adults. English-speaking adults, however, have great difficulty with this discrimination task, depending on the degree of difference from English sounds. The graph on the left shows a contrast involving two "t" sounds, one dental (i.e., made with the tip of the tongue touching the upper front teeth) and the other retroflex (made with the tongue curled back under the palate). This contrast is rare in the world's languages. The contrast in the graph on the right involves two kinds of voicing, a phenomenon that is less unusual and thus somewhat more recognizable to English-speaking adults. (After Werker et al. 1981.)

In the first series of experiments, we compared English-speaking adults, infants from English-speaking families, and Hindi-speaking adults on their ability to discriminate the /ba/-/da/ distinction, which is used in both Hindi and English, as well as two pairs of syllables that are used in Hindi but not in English (Werker et al. 1981). The two pairs of Hindi syllables were chosen on the basis of their relative difficulty. The first pair contrasts two "t" sounds that are not used in English. In English, we articulate "t" sounds by placing the tongue a bit behind the teeth at the alveolar ridge. In Hindi, there are two different "t" phonemes. One is produced by placing the tongue on the teeth (a dental t—written /t/). The other is produced by curling the tip of the tongue back and placing it against the roof of the mouth (a retroflex t—written /T/). This contrast is not used in English, and is in fact very rare among the world's languages.

The second pair of Hindi syllables involves different categories of voicing—the timing of the release of a consonant and the amount of air released with the consonant. Although these phonemes, called /tʰ/ and /dʰ/, are not used in English, we had reason to believe that they might be easier for English-speaking adults to discriminate than the /t/-/T/ distinction. The timing difference between /tʰ/ and /dʰ/ spans the English /t/-/d/ boundary. Moreover, this contrast is more common among the world's languages.

The results of this study, which are presented in Figure 1, were consistent with the hypothesis of universal phonetic sensitivity in the young infant and a decline by adulthood. As expected, all subjects could discriminate /ba/ from /da/. Of more interest, the infants aged six to eight months performed like the Hindi adults and were able to discriminate both pairs of Hindi speech contrasts. The English-speaking adults, on the other hand, were considerably less able to make the Hindi distinctions, especially the difficult dental-retroflex one.

TIMING OF DEVELOPMENTAL CHANGES

The next series of experiments was aimed at determining when the decline in nonnative sensitivity occurs. It was originally believed that this decline would coincide with puberty, when, as Lenneberg (1967) claims, language flexibility decreases. However, our work showed that twelve-year-old English-speaking children were no more able to discriminate non-English syllables than were English-speaking adults (Werker and Tees 1983). We then tested eight- and four-year-old English-speaking children, and, to our surprise, even the four-year-olds could not discriminate the Hindi contrasts. Hindi-speaking four-year-olds, of course, showed no trouble with this discrimination.

phoneme (e.g., /ba/) repeated continuously at 2-sec intervals. On a random basis every four to twenty repetitions, a new phoneme is introduced. For example, a subject will hear "ba," "ba," "ba," "ba," "ba," "da," "da." Babies are conditioned to turn their heads toward the source of the sound when they detect the change from one phoneme to another (e.g., from "ba" to "da"). Correct head turns are reinforced with the activation of a little toy animal and with clapping and praise from the experimental assistant. Adults and children are tested the same way, except that they press a button instead of turning their heads when they detect a change in the phoneme, and the reinforcement is age-appropriate.

Before testing children even younger than age four, we felt it was necessary to determine that the phenomenon of developmental loss extended to other languages. To this end, we chose a phonemic contrast from a North American Indian language of the Interior Salish family, called Nthlakapmx by native speakers in British Columbia but also referred to as Thompson.

North American Indian languages include many consonants produced in the back of the vocal tract, behind our English /k/ and /g/. The pair of sounds we chose contrasts a "k" sound produced at the velum with another "k" sound (written /q/) produced by raising the back of the tongue against the uvula. Both are glottalized—that is, there is an ejective portion (similar to a click) at the beginning of the release of the consonants.

Again, we compared English-speaking adults, infants from English-speaking families, and Nthlakapmx-speaking adults in their abilities to discriminate this pair of sounds (Werker and Tees 1984a). As was the case with the Hindi syllables, both the Nthlakapmx-speaking adults and the infants could discriminate the non-English phonemes, but the English-speaking adults could not.

We were now satisfied that there is at least some generality to the notion that young infants can discriminate across the whole phonetic inventory but that there is a developmental decline in this universal sensitivity. Our next series of experiments involved testing children between eight months and four years of age to try to determine just when the decline in sensitivity might start. It quickly became apparent that something important was happening within the first year of life. We accordingly compared three groups of infants aged six to eight, eight to ten, and ten to twelve months. Half of each group were tested with the Hindi (/ta/-Ta/) and half with the Nthlakapmx (/k̓/-/q̓i/) contrast.

As shown in Figure 2, the majority of the six-to-eight-month-old infants from English-speaking families could discriminate the two non-English contrasts, whereas only about one-half of the eight-to-ten-month-olds could do so. Only two out of ten ten-to-twelve-months-olds could discriminate the Hindi contrast, and only one out of ten the Nthlakapmx. This provided strong evidence that the decline in universal phonetic sensitivity was occurring between six and twelve months of age. As a further test to see if this developmental change would be apparent within the same individuals, six infants from English-speaking families were tested at two-month intervals beginning when they were about six to eight months old. All six infants could discriminate both the Hindi and Nthlakapmx contrasts at the first testing, but by the third testing session, when they were ten to

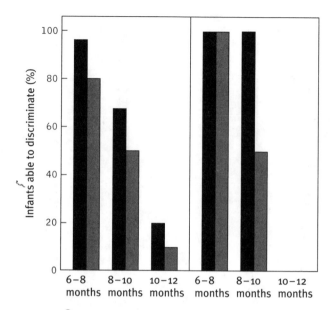

FIGURE 2

Infants show a decline in the universal phonetic sensitivity demonstrated in Figure 1 during the second half of their first year, as shown here in the results of experiments performed with babies from English-speaking families and involving non-English syllables from Hindi (dark gray bars) and Nthlakapmx, a language spoken by some native Indians in British Columbia (light gray bars). The graph on the left gives results from experiments with three groups of infants aged six to eight months, eight to ten months, and ten to twelve months. The graph on the right gives results from testing one group of infants three times at the appropriate ages. None of the latter group were able to discriminate either of the non-English contrasts when they were ten to twelve months old. (After Werker and Tees 1984a.)

twelve months old, they were not able to discriminate either contrast.

To verify that the decline in nonnative sensitivity around ten to twelve months was a function of language experience, we tested a few infants from Hindi- and Nthlakapmx-speaking families when they reached eleven to twelve months old. As predicted, these infants were still able to discriminate their native contrasts, showing quite clearly that the decline observed in the infants from English-speaking families was a function of specific language experience. Since doing these studies, we have charted the decline between six and twelve months old using a computer-generated set of synthetic syllables which model another pair of Hindi sounds not used in English (Werker and Lalonde 1988).

HOW DOES EXPERIENCE AFFECT DEVELOPMENT?

A theoretical model for considering the possible effects of experience on perceptual development was suggested by Gottlieb in 1976. As expanded by both Gottlieb (1981) and Aslin (1981), the model includes several roles experience might—or might not—play, as shown in Figure 3.

Induction refers to cases in which the emergence and form of a perceptual capability depend entirely on environmental input. In this case, an infant would not show categorical perception of speech sounds without prior experience. Attunement refers to a situation in which experience influences the full development of a capability, enhancing the level of performance; for example, categorical boundaries between phonetic contrasts might be sharper with experience than without. In facilitation, experience affects the rate of development of a capability, but it does not affect the end point. If this role were valid, speech perception would improve even without listening experience, but hearing specific sounds would accelerate the rate of improvement. Maintenance loss refers to the case in which a perceptual ability is fully developed prior to the onset of specific experience, which is required to maintain that capability. Without adequate exposure an initial capability is lost. Finally, maturation refers to the unfolding of a perceptual capability independent of environmental exposure. According to this hypothetical possibility, the ability to discriminate speech sounds would mature regardless of amount or timing of exposure.

Our work is often interpreted as an illustration of maintenance/loss, since it suggests that young infants can discriminate phonetic contrasts before they have gained experience listening but that experience hearing the phones used in their own language is necessary to maintain the ability to discriminate at least some pairs of phones.

Support for this view was provided by another study in which we tested English-speaking adults who had been exposed to Hindi during the first couple of years of life and had learned their first words in Hindi but had little or no subsequent exposure. These subjects could discriminate the Hindi syllables much more easily than other English-speaking adults, and performed virtually as well as native Hindi speakers on the discrimination task (Tees and Werker 1984). This is consistent with the view that early ex-

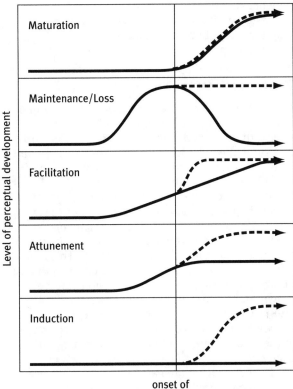

onset of
experience

FIGURE 3

Researchers have suggested several roles that experience might—or might not—play in the development of particular perceptual capabilities. These possibilities are shown graphically here: ――― *curves represent development after the onset of experience, and* ―――― *curves represent development in the absence of experience. Induction refers to cases in which a capability depends entirely on experience. Attunement refers to a situation in which experience makes possible the full development of a capability. In facilitation, experience affects only the rate of development of a capability. Maintenance/loss refers to the case in which a capability is fully developed before the onset of experience, but experience is necessary to maintain the capability. Maturation refers to the development of a capability independent of experience. The phenomenon of universal phonetic sensitivity followed by a narrowing of sensitivity to native language sounds appears to illustrate maintenance/loss, since it suggests that young infants can discriminate phonetic contrasts before they have gained experience listening but that experience with language is necessary to maintain the full ability. (After Aslin 1981; Gottlieb 1981.)*

perience functions to maintain perceptual abilities, suggesting that no further experience is necessary to maintain them into adulthood.

RECOVERY OF SENSITIVITY

Our early work led us to believe that the loss of non-native sensitivity is difficult to reverse in adults. In one study, we tested English-speaking adults who had studied Hindi for various lengths of time. Adults who had studied Hindi for five years or more were able to discriminate the non-English Hindi syllables, but those who had studied Hindi for one year at the university level could not do so. In fact, even several hundred trials were insufficient to teach English-speaking adults to discriminate the more difficult Hindi contrasts (Tees and Werker 1984). This implies that while the ability is recoverable, considerable experience is required. Similar conclusions can be drawn from a study by MacKain and her colleagues (1981), who tested Japanese speakers learning English. Only after one year of intensive English training in the United States could they discriminate /ra/ from /la/.

The question still remained whether recovery of nonnative sensitivity results from new learning in adulthood or from a latent sensitivity. To explore this question, we asked English-speaking adults to discriminate both the full syllables of the difficult Hindi and Nthlakapmx phonemes and shortened portions of the syllables which do not sound like speech at all but contain the critical acoustic information specifying the difference between the phonemes (Werker and Tees 1984b). Subjects were first tested on the shortened stimuli and then on the full syllables. To our surprise, they were able to discriminate the shortened stimuli easily but were still not able to discriminate the full syllables, even immediately after hearing the relevant acoustic information in shortened form. This finding reveals that the auditory capacity for discriminating the acoustic components of these stimuli has not been lost but that it is difficult to apply when processing language-like sounds.

In a further set of experiments, we attempted to make English-speaking adults discriminate the full-syllable nonnative stimuli (Werker and Logan 1985). One task involved presenting adults with pairs of stimuli and asking them to decide simply if the stimuli were the same or different, a test that proved to be much more sensitive than the head turn procedure. In this "same/different" task, listeners have to compare only two stimuli at a time. Moreover, if the interval between the two stimuli is short enough, listeners can hold the first stimulus in auditory memory while comparing it to the second. In the head turn task, on the other hand, listeners have to compare each stim-

ulus to a whole set of variable stimuli and judge whether it is a member of the same category.

We found that English-speaking adults could discriminate the Hindi syllables when tested in the same/different procedure, particularly after practice. Thus there was evidence that adults can discriminate nonnative contrasts if tested in a more sensitive procedure. Similar results have been reported by other researchers (Pisoni et al. 1982). This suggests that the developmental changes between infancy and adulthood should be considered a language-based reorganization of the categories of communicative sounds rather than an absolute loss of auditory sensitivity. The increasing reliance on language-specific categories accounts for the age-related decline, implying that maintenance has its effect at the level of linguistic categories rather than simple peripheral auditory sensitivity (see Best et al. 1988).

PARALLELS IN SPEECH PRODUCTION

It is interesting to compare our findings of developmental changes in speech perception to recent work on speech production. Although it is impossible to survey this substantial literature here, there appear to be systematic regularities in the repertoire of sounds produced at different stages of babbling. These regularities may reflect vocal tract and neuromuscular maturation, with phones appearing as a child develops the ability to articulate them (Locke 1983). In contrast to early work suggesting that the sounds produced during babbling gradually narrow to those that are used in the language-learning environment, recent research shows very little influence from the native language on vocal development during the babbling stage. This conclusion is particularly strong for consonants. However, it is clear that after the acquisition of the first word children's vocal productions start becoming differentiated on the basis of language experience. That is, once a child begins to talk, the sounds produced conform more and more closely to the subset of phones used in his native language. The stage at which these changes occur is consistent with our work showing universal sensitivity in early infancy followed by only language-specific sensitivity beginning around ten to twelve months.

This leads us to believe that just as a reorganization of language production is related to the emergence of the first spoken word, so too may the reorganization of perceptual abilities be related to the emergence of the ability to understand words. By the time he is one year old, a child understands a fair amount of spoken language, even though he may produce only a few words. We are currently conducting experiments to see if the reorganization of speech perception is related to the emerging ability to understand words. This work will add another piece to the solution of the puzzle of how early sensitivity to all language sounds becomes limited to the functional categories that are necessary for communicating in one's own language.

REFERENCES

Aslin, R. N. 1981. Experiential influences and sensitive periods in perceptual development: A unified model. In *Development of Perception*, ed. R. N. Aslin, J. R. Alberts, and M. R. Petersen, vol. 2, pp. 45–94. Academic Press.

Aslin, R. N., D. B. Pisoni, B. L. Hennessy, and A. J. Perey. 1981. Discrimination of voice onset time by human infants: New findings and implications for the effect of early experience. *Child Devel.* 52:1135–45.

Best, C. T., G. W. McRoberts, and N. N. Sithole. 1988. The phonological basis of perceptual loss for non-native contrasts: Maintenance of discrimination among Zulu clicks by English-speaking adults and infants. *J. Exper. Psychol.: Human Percept. Perform.* 14:345–60.

Eilers, R. E., W. I. Gavin, and D. K. Oller. 1982. Cross-linguistic perception in infancy: Early effects of linguistic experience. *J. Child Lang.* 9:289–302.

Eimas, P. D. 1975. Developmental studies in speech perception. In *Infant Perception: From Sensation to Cognition*, ed. L. B. Cohen and P. Salapatek, vol. 2, pp. 193–231. Academic Press.

Eimas, P. D., E. R. Siqueland, P. W. Jusczyk, and J. Vigorito. 1971. Speech perception in infants. *Science*, 171:303–06.

Gottlieb, G. 1976. The roles of experience in the development of behavior and the nervous system. In *Studies on the Development of Behavior and the Nervous System*, ed. G. Gottlieb, vol. 3, pp. 1–35. Academic Press.

_____ 1981. Roles of early experience in species-specific perceptual development. In *Development of Perception*. ed. R. N. Aslin, J. R. Alberts, and M. R. Petersen, vol. 1, pp. 5–44. Academic Press.

Kuhl, P. K. 1987. Perception of speech and sound in early infancy. In *Handbook of Infant Perception*, ed. P. Salapatek and L. Cohen, vol. 2., pp. 275–382. Academic Press.

Lasky, R. E., A. Syrdal-Lasky, and R. E. Klein. 1975. VOT discrimination by four to six and a half month old infants from Spanish environments. *J. Exper. Child Psychol.* 20:215–25.

Lenneberg, E. H. 1967. *Biological Foundations of Language.* Wiley.

Liberman, A. M., F. S. Cooper, D. P. Shankweiler, and M. Studdert-Kennedy. 1967. Perception of the speech code. *Psychol. Rev.* 74:431–61.

Lisker, L., and A. S. Abramson. 1970. The voicing dimension: Some experiments in comparative phonetics. In *Proceedings of the 6th International Congress of Phonetic Sciences*, pp. 563–67. Prague: Academia.

Locke, J. L. 1983. *Phonological Acquisition and Change.* Academic Press.

MacKain, K. S., C. T. Best, and W. Strange. 1981. Categorical perception of English /r/ and /l/ by Japanese bilinguals. *Appl. Psycholing.* 2:269–90.

Miyawaki, K., et al. 1975. An effect of linguistic experience: The discrimination of [r] and [l] by native speakers of Japanese and English. *Percept. Psychophy.* 18:331–40.

Pisoni, D. B., R. N. Aslin, A. J. Perey, and B. L. Hennessy. 1982. Some effects of laboratory training on identification and discrimination of voicing contrasts in stop consonants. *J. Exper. Psychol.: Human Percept. Perform.* 8:297–314.

Streeter, L. A. 1976. Language perception of two-month old infants shows effects of both innate mechanisms and experience. *Nature* 259:39–41.

Tees, R. C., and J. F. Werker. 1984. Perceptual flexibility: Maintenance or recovery of the ability to discriminate non-native speech sounds. *Can. J. Psychol.* 34:579–90.

Trehub, S. 1976. The discrimination of foreign speech contrasts by infants and adults. *Child Devel.* 47:466–72.

Werker, J. F., J. H. V. Gilbert, K. Humphrey, and R. C. Tees. 1981. Developmental aspects of cross-language speech perception. *Child Devel.* 52:349–53.

Werker, J. F., and C. E. Lalonde. 1988. The development of speech perception: Initial capabilities and the emergence of phonemic categories. *Devel. Psychol.* 24:672–83.

Werker, J. F., and J. S. Logan. 1985. Cross-language evidence for three factors in speech perception. *Percept. Psychophys.* 37:35–44.

Werker, J. F., and R. C. Tees. 1983. Developmental changes across childhood in the perception of non-active speech sounds. *Can. J. Psychol.* 37:278–86.

_____ 1984a. Cross-language speech perception: Evidence for perceptual reorganization during the first year of life. *Infant Behav. Devel.* 7:49–63.

_____ 1984b. Phonemic and phonetic factors in adult cross-language speech perception. *J. Acoustical Soc. Am.* 75:1866–78.

QUESTIONS

1. What are phones, and how are they related to phonemes?
2. What is categorical perception, and what role does it play in the development of language?
3. What laboratory procedure did Werker use to study infants' perception of phonetic contrasts?
4. Why were Hindi-speaking adults, English-speaking adults, and infants compared in the study involving two "t" sounds? Why was it interesting to use this same sample in a second study to compare the participants' perception of different types of voicing?

5. Early theories of language development suggested that the major changes in linguistic sensitivity occurred at puberty. On the basis of Werker's evidence, would you say that these theories were correct? Use Figure 2 to support your answer.

6. To study developmental change in sensitivity to nonnative languages, Werker studied infants in English-speaking communities. Why do you think she did follow-up research in which she also tested a few infants from Hindi-speaking and Nthlakapmx-speaking families?

7. Of the five types of explanations for the role that experience plays in development, represented in Figure 3, which one best explains the evidence Werker provides about the development of the ability to perceive phonetic contrasts in infancy?

8. Is the ability to discriminate sounds that do not appear in a person's native language completely lost in infancy? Use evidence to support your answer.

9. Werker's results suggest that one important development in the first year is a reorganization of speech-related functions in the brain. How do you think this process develops for children raised in bilingual homes?

10. What do you think this research suggests about the importance of language to human functioning?

14 Is Face Processing Species-Specific During the First Year of Life?

OLIVIER PASCALIS · MICHELLE DE HAAN · CHARLES A. NELSON

Research in language development, some of which is reported by Janet Werker in the preceding article, indicates that over the first year of life infants develop sensitivity to the sounds of their own language. By the end of the first year, infants attend to the sounds of their own language more than to sounds that are not part of their language. The rapid pace of this learning, along with the high degree of phonetic sensitivity that appears so early in life, has intrigued researchers. Because many researchers believe that language is a special characteristic of the species, it has also been assumed that the learning that is associated with language development must also be special. However, this assumption may not be correct. Although language surely relies on one type of perceptual discrimination, other perceptual distinctions also have great importance for human survival and development; these too may be learned early in life and at a rapid pace. Consider face perception.

The ability to perceive faces in infancy has garnered much research attention. As a result, we know that infants prefer visual information that has features like those of the human face. We also know that this preference appears early in life and that over the first year infants show increasing sensitivity to and preference for specific faces, especially the faces of their primary caregivers. By and large, this research has concentrated on infant perception of the human face relative to other visual information. It has not, until recently, addressed a more basic question of perceptual discrimination regarding faces: Do human infants develop sensitivity to human faces as compared to the faces of individual members of other species?

Sensitivity for the details of human faces certainly seems important, clearly as important as sensitivity to human sounds. In fact, sensitivity to human sounds and human faces may be informative to each other; after all, human sounds come out of human faces. When one considers that some other species, especially other primates, have faces that have many human-like qualities, the question becomes interesting indeed. Do infants have more sensitivity to the details of human faces than they do to the details of the faces of other primates, such as monkeys? And, if so, when do infants learn to distinguish these visual details? The following article answers these questions and, in so doing, raises fascinating questions about early learning. The article is also interesting because it includes a set of sample stimuli that may intrigue you. Try to see if you have lost your ability to perceive the individual uniqueness that is present in the faces of monkeys.

Between 6 and 10 months of age, the infant's ability to discriminate among native speech sounds improves, whereas the same ability to discriminate among foreign speech sounds decreases. Our study aimed to determine whether this perceptual narrowing is unique to language or might also apply to face processing. We tested discrimination of human and monkey faces by 6-month-olds, 9-month-olds, and adults, using the visual paired-comparison procedure. Only the youngest group showed discrimination between individuals of both species; older infants and adults only showed evidence of discrimination of their own species. These results suggest that the "perceptual narrowing" phenomenon may represent a more general change in neural networks involved in early cognition.

At first glance the development of the ability to recognize faces appears to follow a typical trajectory: rapid change during infancy, followed by more gradual improvement into adolescence (1). This pattern contrasts with some aspects of language development. For example, speech perception is characterized by a loss of ability with age, such that 4- to 6-month-olds can discriminate phonetic differences that distinguish syllables in both their native and unfamiliar languages, whereas 10- to 12-month-olds can only discriminate the phonetic variations used in their native language (2, 3). Here we describe a similar phenomenon for face recognition: Specifically, we demonstrate that 6-month-old infants are equally good at recognizing facial identity in both human and nonhuman primates, whereas 9-month-old infants and adults show a marked advantage for recognizing only human faces.

Nelson (4) has proposed that the ability to perceive faces narrows with development, due in large measure to the cortical specialization that occurs with experience viewing faces. In this view, the sensitivity of the face recognition system to differences in identity among the faces of one's own species will increase with age and with experience in processing those faces. By adulthood the extensive experience with human faces can be mentally represented as a prototype that is "tuned" to the face inputs most frequently observed (human faces), with individual faces encoded in terms of how they deviate from the prototype (5). Because infants begin to show evidence of forming face prototypes by 3 months of age (6), their face recognition should become more "human face specific" some time after this. This leads to the prediction that younger infants, who possess less experience with faces than older infants and adults, should be better than older infants or adults at discriminating between individual faces of other species.

This hypothesis is indirectly supported by several lines of research. For example, human adults are far more accurate in recognizing individual human than monkey faces; the opposite is true for monkeys (7). Such species-specificity may be due to the differential expertise in the two groups: monkeys are more familiar with monkey than human faces, whereas humans are more familiar with human than monkey faces. Human infants, of course, likely have no experience with monkey faces and relatively little experience with human faces. This may confer upon them a more broadly tuned face recognition system and, in turn, an advantage in recognizing facial identity in general (i.e., regardless of species). This prediction is supported by a preliminary study (8) in which it was demonstrated using event-related potentials (ERPs) that young infants, but not adults, could discriminate monkey face identity across changes in facial orientation. A second ERP study examined the influence of stimulus inversion, a manipulation that in behavioral studies impairs adults' recognition of identity of human faces more than objects (9). In adults, inversion affected only the processing of human faces and

not monkey faces, whereas in 6-month-olds, inversion affected the ERPs similarly for human and monkey faces (10). This suggests that infants were processing facial identity in the two species comparably. It is noteworthy that this was not because they failed to detect the difference between the two species, as the early-latency sensory components of the ERP differed for human and monkey faces for both ages. None of these studies directly tested the discrimination abilities of older and younger infants and adults in the same experimental procedure. We compared the ability of 6- and 9-month-old infants and adults to process human and monkey faces with the same visual paired-comparison procedure. We hypothesized that if face recognition follows the same developmental pattern as language, the ability to process other species' faces will be present only in the youngest age group studied. A similar development (tuning period) for face recognition and for language may indicate a more general sensitive or tuning period for various cognitive functions. A visual paired-comparison procedure (VPC) was used to assess recognition in both infants and adults. VPC indexes the relative interest in the members of a pair of visual stimuli made of one novel item and one item already seen in a prior familiarization period. Recognition is inferred from the participant's tendency to fixate the novel stimulus significantly longer. The stimuli were colored pictures (Fig. 1) of human Caucasian (male and female faces from our collection) and monkey faces (*Macaca fascicularis*) [details of materials and methods (11)].

Eleven adult participants with no special expertise in monkey face recognition were tested (11). For human face stimuli, the average looking time toward the novel stimulus during the 5-s recognition tests was significantly longer (2.79 s) than that toward the familiar stimulus (1.63 s) (paired two-tailed t test, $t = 3.93$, df = 10; $P < 0.01$). By contrast, for monkey face stimuli, participants looked as long at the novel stimulus (2.42 s) as at the familiar stimulus (2.31 s) (paired two-tailed t test, $t = 0.30$, df = 10; $P > 0.05$).

Infant participants were 30 healthy, full-term 6-month-old infants and 30 healthy, full-term 9-month-old infants. No differences were found in the amount of time required to reach the familiarization time between age groups nor between species of face (11). In 6-month-olds, for human face stimuli, the average looking time toward the novel stimulus during the 10-s recognition test for human face stimuli was significantly longer (4.55 s) than that toward the familiar face (3.57 s) (paired two-tailed t test, $t = 2.67$, df = 14; $P < 0.05$). During the parallel test for monkey face stimuli, 6-month-olds looked at the novel face significantly longer (4.04 s) than at the familiar face (2.31 s) (paired two-tailed t test, $t = 3.78$, df = 14; $P < 0.05$). During the 10-s test for human face stimuli, 9-month-

FIGURE 1
Examples of stimuli used (11).

old infants looked significantly longer toward the novel stimulus (4.50 s) than toward the familiar stimulus (3.63 s) (paired two-tailed *t* test, *t* = 3.44, df = 14; *P* < 0.05). In contrast, for monkey face stimuli, 9-month-olds looked as long at the novel stimulus (3.86 s) as at the familiar stimulus (3.74 s) (paired two-tailed *t* test, *t* = 0.35, df = 14; *P* < 0.05).

Our results with adults support our prediction and are consistent with prior findings (*7*). It is important to note that this failure to recognize monkey face identity is not due to the lack of explicit instruction to do so. Our previous work shows that even in a classic forced-choice task, human adults are worse at recognizing monkey faces (55%) than human faces (73%) (*12*).

The infants' results support our predictions: 9-month-olds showed a pattern similar to that of adults, whereas 6-month-olds showed a preference for the novel facial identity both when tested with human faces and with monkey faces. The results of 6-month-olds and adults are also consistent with previous elec-

trophysiological studies showing a difference in the specificity of face processing between these ages (*8, 10*). Our experiments support the hypothesis that the perceptual window narrows with age and that during the first year of life the face processing system is tuned to a human template (*4*). This early adjustment does not rule out the possibility that later in life individuals can learn how to discriminate a new class of stimuli on a perceptual basis (*13*). As is the case for speech perception, our evidence with face processing indicates the existence of an early tuning period that is likely dependent on experience. Although it is difficult to compare directly the tuning of speech perception with the tuning of face perception, there may be overlap between these systems. By 3 months of age infants are already relating these two types of information, as they are able to associate faces with voices (*14*). Systems for processing faces and for processing speech may thus develop in parallel, with a similar timing and a mutual influence. One possibility is that there is a general perceptuo-cognitive tuning apparatus that is not specific to a single modality and that can be described as an experience-expectant system [for discussion see (*15*)]. Alternatively, the concordance in age may simply be a developmental coincidence, thus reflecting a modality-specific, experience-dependent process. Distinguishing between these views will be facilitated by further developmental and comparative studies.

REFERENCES AND NOTES

1. M. de Haan, in *Handbook of Developmental Cognitive Neuroscience*, M. Luciana, C. A. Nelson, Eds. (MIT Press, Cambridge, MA, 2001), pp. 381–398.
2. M. Cheour et al., *Nature Neurosci.* 1, 351 (1998).
3. P. K. Kuhl, K. A. Williams, F. Lacerda, K. N. Stevens, *Science 255*, 606 (1992).
4. C. A. Nelson, *Infant Child Dev.* 10, 3 (2001).
5. T. Valentine, *Q. J. Exp. Psychol. A Hum. Exp. Psychol.* 43, 161 (1991).
6. M. de Haan, M. H. Johnson, D. Maurer, D. I. Perrett, *Cogn. Dev.* 16, 659 (2001).
7. O. Pascalis, J. Bachevalier, *Behav. Process.* 43, 87 (1998).
8. C. A. Nelson, in *Developmental Neurocognition: Speech and Face Processing in the First Year of Life*, B. de Boysson-Bardies, S. de Schonen, P. Jusczyk, P. MacNeilage, J. Morton, Eds. (Kluwer Academic Publishers, Dordrecht, Netherlands, 1993), pp. 165–178.
9. R. K. Yin, *J. Exp. Psychol.* 81, 141 (1969).
10. M. de Haan, O. Pascalis, M. H. Johnson, *J. Cogn. Neurosci. 14,* 199 (2002).
11. Materials and methods are available as supporting material on *Science* Online.
12. O. Pascalis, M. Coleman, R. Campbell, *Cognitive Neuroscience Abstract Book*, Seventh Annual Meeting of the Cognitive Neuroscience Society, San Francisco, CA, 10 April 2000 (Cognitive Neuroscience Society, MIT Press, Cambridge, MA, 2000), p. 76.
13. I. Gauthier, M. J. Tarr, A. W. Anderson, P. Skudlarski, J. C. Gore, *Nature Neurosci.* 2, 568 (1999).
14. H. Brookes *et al., Infant Child Dev.* 10, 75 (2001).
15. W. T. Greenough, J. E. Black, in *Developmental Behavioral Neuroscience: The Minnesota Symposia on Child Psychology*, M.R. Gunnar, C. A. Nelson, Eds. (Lawrence Erlbaum, Hillsdale, NJ, 1992), pp. 155–200.

QUESTIONS

1. Why does the ability to perceive faces narrow with development, and what underlying biological change may account for this narrowing?
2. What is a face prototype, and when do infants begin to form face prototypes? Does the pace of this development surprise you? Why or why not?
3. Which do human adults recognize better, individual human faces or individual monkey faces? Why?
4. Why did Pascalis and colleagues want to compare the ability of 6- and 9-month-old infants and adults to process human and monkey faces?
5. Describe the visual paired-comparison procedure (VPC). Why did these investigators use this procedure? In other words, what information does this procedure yield that may help answer the research question posed here?
6. Who was better at recognizing individual monkey faces: adults, 6-month-olds, or 9-month-olds? What evidence supports your conclusion?
7. How did you do on the two sets of stimuli? Can you discriminate human and monkey faces with equal ease?
8. How might the results of this study fit together with results from research on early phonetic sensitivity? In other words, do phonetic sensitivity and face sensitivity have anything to do with each other?
9. Do you think different results from those reported in this article would emerge for a child, such as Jane Goodall's son, who had much experience early in life with nonhuman primates?
10. Are you surprised by the findings of this study? Why or why not?

15 Event Categorization in Infancy

Renée Baillargeon · Su-hua Wang

Much of the psychological research on cognitive development early in life has concentrated on infants' understanding of physical features of the world. Even Jean Piaget, in describing cognitive development during the sensorimotor stage, focused on the emergence and development of infants' understanding of objects, which he referred to as the object concept. For many years, Piaget and his followers argued that infants' physical knowledge is limited and that it takes the entire first two years of life for children to develop a basic understanding of the physical properties of the world, including objects. Recently, as researchers have devised new methods for studying infant cognition, this view has changed. The consensus now is that infants have a far better understanding of physical properties than Piaget and other researchers once thought.

In the following article, Renée Baillargeon and Su-hua Wang describe their research on early infant cognition. They are particularly interested in the ability of infants to sort physical information into distinct categories, described in this article as events. Event knowledge of the physical world basically includes information about things that can happen to objects; for example, an object can be put inside another object, which is a containment event, or an object can be hidden behind another object, which is an occlusion event. Much of what we know about the physical world consists of such event-based information.

The research described in this article relied primarily on the violation-of-expectation method, which is quite effective at revealing what infants understand about the physical world. The results of several studies using this method are reviewed; in addition, graphic illustrations are provided that will help you follow the behavior of the experimenters and the infants in these studies. Baillargeon and Wang use this research to argue that (1) over the first year of life, infants develop a rather complex set of understandings about physical events; and (2) this body of knowledge allows infants to categorize events and create expectations or predictions about the likely outcomes of these events. In other words, this knowledge helps form the foundation of the comforting realization that the physical world is an ordered and predictable place in which to live.

Recent research suggests that one of the mechanisms that contribute to infants' acquisition of their physical knowledge is the formation of event categories, such as occlusion and containment. Some of this research compared infants' identification of similar variables in different event categories. Marked developmental lags were found, suggesting that infants acquire event-specific rather than event-general expectations. Other research on variable priming, perseveration, and object individuation presented infants with successive events from the same or from different event categories. To understand the world as it unfolds, infants must not only represent each separate event, but also link successive events; this research begins to explore how infants respond to multiple events over time.

Over the past 15 years, a dramatic change has taken place in the field of infant cognition: researchers have come to realize that, contrary to traditional claims [1, 2], infants possess sophisticated expectations

Reprinted from Baillargeon, R., & Wang, S-H. (2002). Event categorization in infancy, *Trends in Cognitive Science*, 6, 85–93. Copyright 2002, with permission from Elsevier.

The preparation of this article was supported by a grant from the National Institute of Child Health and Human Development (HD-21104) to the first author. We would like to thank Jerry DeJong, Cindy Fisher, and Kris Onishi for helpful comments and discussions, and the Assistant Editor of *TICS* for help in preparing the article for publication.

about physical events [3–12]. Of main concern today is the issue of how infants acquire their physical knowledge. In particular, what specialized mechanisms contribute to this acquisition process [13–17]? In this article, we review evidence that one such mechanism involves the formation of *event categories*: Infants appear to 'sort' physical events into distinct categories, and to learn and reason in terms of these categories.

The article is organized into two main sections. In the first, we summarize experiments that compared infants' knowledge of similar expectations in different event categories. This research has brought to light striking developmental lags (or décalages, to use a Piagetian term [18]) in infants' acquisition of their physical knowledge, with several months separating similar acquisitions across categories. In the second section of the article, we review experiments on variable priming, perseveration, and object individuation, all of which presented infants with successive events from the same or from different event categories. Depending on the task, the change in event category either improved or impaired infants' performance.

LEARNING ABOUT EVENT CATEGORIES

Research conducted during the 1990s revealed a clear overall pattern in the development of infants' physical knowledge (for reviews, see Refs [13,19–21]). When learning about occlusion, support, and other physical events, infants first form an initial concept centered on a primitive, all-or-none distinction. With further experience, infants identify discrete and continuous variables that elaborate this initial concept, resulting in increasingly accurate predictions over time.

One limitation of this research was that it left unclear how general or specific were infants' expectations. Because the events examined—such as occlusion and support—were physically very different, the variables identified for each event were naturally also very different. To ascertain whether infants acquire general or specific expectations about events, it was necessary to compare their knowledge of the same variable in different events. Evidence that infants considered a given variable when reasoning about all relevant events would suggest that their expectations were 'event-general'. On the other hand, evidence that infants took into account a given variable when reasoning about one but not other, equally relevant events, would suggest that their expectations were 'event-specific'.

To date, three series of experiments have compared infants' reasoning about similar variables in different events. All of these experiments used the violation-of-expectation method [21]. In a typical experiment conducted with this method, infants see two test events: one (expected event) is consistent with the expectation being examined in the experiment; the other (unex-

pected event) violates this expectation. With appropriate controls, evidence that infants look reliably longer at the unexpected than at the expected event indicates that they: (1) possess the expectation under examination; (2) detect the violation in the unexpected event; and (3) are interested or surprised by this violation.

HEIGHT IN OCCLUSION AND CONTAINMENT EVENTS

In a recent experiment, Hespos and Baillargeon [22] compared 4.5-month-old infants' ability to reason about the variable height in occlusion and in containment events. The infants watched test events in which an object was lowered either behind an occluder (occlusion condition; Fig. 1a) or inside a container (containment condition; Fig. 1b). The object consisted of a tall cylinder with a knob affixed to its top; in all of the events, the object was lowered until only the knob remained visible. In the expected events, the occluder or container was as tall as the cylindrical portion of the object; in the unexpected events, the occluder or container was only half as tall, so that it should have been impossible for the cylindrical portion of the object to become fully hidden (see Fig. 1). The tall and short occluders were identical to the tall and short containers with their back halves and bottoms removed.

The infants in the occlusion condition looked reliably longer at the unexpected than at the expected event, but those in the containment condition did not. These and control results indicated that, at 4.5 months of age, infants realize that the height of an object relative to that of an occluder determines whether the object can be fully or only partly hidden behind the occluder, but they do not yet realize that the height of an object relative to that of a container determines whether the object can be fully or only partly hidden inside the container.

The positive results obtained in the occlusion condition were confirmed in a second experiment in which the tall object was lowered behind, rather than inside, the tall and short containers. In this experiment, the containers served merely as occluders, and the infants again detected the violation in the unexpected event (see also Refs [23,24]).

In a third experiment, 5.5-, 6.5-, and 7.5-month-old infants were shown the containment condition test events. Only the 7.5-month-old infants looked reliably longer at the unexpected than at the expected event. These and control results indicated that it is not until infants are about 7.5 months of age that they begin to consider height information when predicting the outcomes of containment events.

Together, the results of these experiments suggested three conclusions. First, infants view occlusion

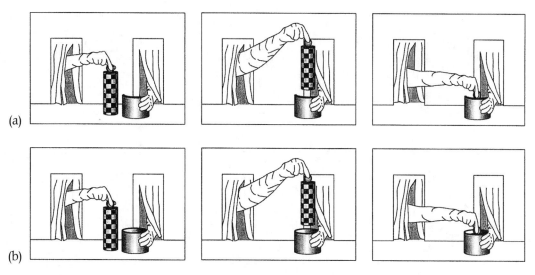

FIGURE 1

Schematic drawing of the unexpected test events in the experiment of Hespos and Baillargeon [22]. (a) Occlusion condition. (b) Containment condition. (See text for discussion.)

and containment as distinct event categories. Second, infants do not generalize the variable height from occlusion to containment, even though it is relevant to both categories and invokes in each case the same general physical principles. Third, several months typically separate infants' acquisition of the variable height in occlusion and in containment events, resulting in a marked décalage in their responses to these events.

HEIGHT IN CONTAINMENT AND COVERING EVENTS

Building on the results of Hespos and Baillargeon [22], Wang *et al.* (unpublished data, reviewed in Ref. [25]) compared 9-month-old infants' ability to reason about the variable height in containment and in covering events. The infants saw either test events in which a tall object was lowered inside a container (containment condition; Fig. 2a), or test events in which a cover was lowered over the same tall object (covering condition; Fig. 2b). In all of the events, the object became fully hidden. In the expected events, the container or cover was slightly taller than the object; in the unexpected events, the container or cover was only half as tall, so that it should have been impossible for the object to become fully hidden (see Fig. 2). The tall and short covers were identical to the containers turned upside-down.

The infants in the containment condition looked reliably longer at the unexpected than at the expected event, but those in the covering condition did not. In a subsequent experiment, 11- and 12-month-

old infants were tested with the covering condition events. Only the 12-month-old infants detected the violation in the unexpected event. These results, together with those discussed in the last section, indicated that, although infants recognize at about 7.5 months of age that the height of an object relative to that of a container determines whether the object can be fully or only partly hidden inside the container, it is not until infants are about 12 months of age that they realize that the height of an object relative to that of a cover determines whether the object can be fully or only partly hidden under the cover.

TRANSPARENCY IN OCCLUSION AND CONTAINMENT EVENTS

All of the experiments described in the preceding sections examined infants' reasoning about height information in various events. A recent series of experiments focused on a different variable, that of transparency. Luo and Baillargeon (unpublished data, reviewed in Ref. [25]) compared 8.5-month-old infants' reasoning about transparency information in occlusion and in containment events.

At the beginning of each test event, the infants saw either a transparent occluder (occlusion condition; Fig. 3a) or a transparent container (containment condition; Fig. 3b); to the right of the occluder or container was a slightly shorter object. First, an opaque screen was raised to hide the occluder or container. Next, the object was lifted above the screen and then lowered behind the transparent occluder or inside the transparent container. Finally, the opaque

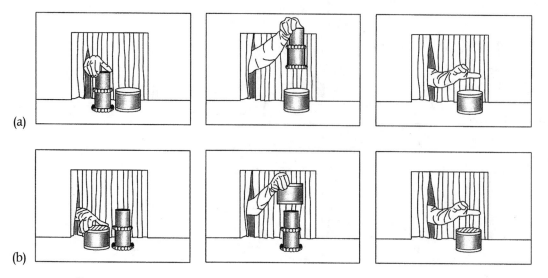

FIGURE 2

Schematic drawing of the unexpected test events in the experiment of Wang et al. (unpublished data). (a) Containment condition. (b) Covering condition.

screen was removed to reveal the occluder or container once more. In the expected events, the object was visible through the front of the occluder or container. In the unexpected events, the object was absent (Fig. 3). The container was made of Plexiglas, and its edges were outlined with red tape; the occluder was identical to the front of the container.

The infants in the occlusion condition looked reliably longer at the unexpected than at the expected event, but those in the containment condition did

not. In subsequent experiments, it was found that older, 10-month-old infants tested with the containment condition events succeeded in detecting the violation in the unexpected event; and that 7.5-month-old (but not 7-month-old) infants tested with the occlusion condition events were similarly successful. These and control results thus revealed another décalage in infants' reasoning about occlusion and containment events: infants realize at about 7.5 months of age that an object placed behind a trans-

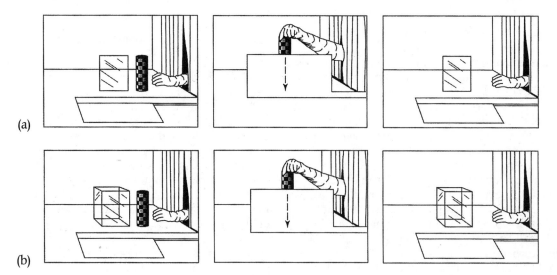

FIGURE 3

Schematic drawing of the unexpected test events in the experiment of Luo and Baillargeon (unpublished data). (a) Occlusion condition. (b) Containment condition.

parent occluder should remain visible, but do not realize until about 10 months of age that an object placed inside a transparent container should also remain visible.

CONCLUSIONS

The experiments reported in the preceding sections suggest three general conclusions. First, infants appear to sort physical events into distinct categories, such as occlusion, containment, and covering events. Second, infants learn separately how each category operates. A variable identified in one category is not generalized to other relevant categories; rather, it is kept tied to the individual category where it was first acquired. Third, when weeks or months separate the acquisition of the same variable in two or more categories, striking décalages arise in infants' responses to events from the different categories. Thus, infants are surprised when a tall object becomes hidden behind but not inside a short container; when a tall object becomes hidden inside a short container but not under a short cover; and when an object becomes hidden behind a transparent occluder but not inside a transparent container.

REASONING ACROSS EVENT CATEGORIES

If infants do form distinct event categories, one might expect them to respond differently, in some situations at least, when exposed to successive events from the same or from different event categories. How infants reason about an event from one category might affect—for better or for worse—their reasoning about a subsequent event from the same or from another category. To date, such category effects have been observed in three areas of infancy research: variable priming, perseveration, and object individuation.

VARIABLE PRIMING

Spelke has proposed that from birth core principles of continuity (objects exist continuously in time and space) and solidity (two objects cannot exist at the same time in the same space) guide infants' interpretation of physical events [11, 17, 26]. This proposal might be taken to suggest that infants, at all ages, should detect all salient violations of the continuity and solidity principles. As we saw in the previous sections, however, infants often fail to detect such core violations. Recall, for example, that 8.5-month-olds are not surprised when an object is placed inside a transparent container which is then revealed to be empty, and that 11-month-olds are not surprised

when a short cover is lowered over a tall object until it becomes fully hidden.

Over the past few years, we have been developing an account of infants' physical reasoning that attempts to reconcile these and other similar failures with the proposal that infants possess core continuity and solidity principles [6,25,27,28]. This account assumes that, when watching a physical event, infants build a *physical representation* that includes basic spatial, temporal, and mechanical [15] information. This information is used, early in the representation process, to categorize the event. Infants then access their knowledge of the event category selected; this knowledge specifies the variables that have been identified as relevant to the event category and hence that should be encoded when representing the event. Both the basic and the variable information in the physical representation are interpreted in accord with infants' core principles.

To illustrate this account, consider once again the finding that infants aged 11 months and younger are not surprised when a short cover is lowered over a tall object until it becomes fully hidden. Upon seeing the cover being lowered over the object, infants would categorize the event as a covering event and would then access their knowledge of this category. Because this knowledge does not yet include the variable height—which is typically not identified until about 12 months—infants would include no information in their physical representation about the relative heights of the cover and object. As a result, infants would be unable to detect the core violation in the event.

The preceding account makes an intriguing prediction. If infants could be 'primed' to include information about a key variable in their physical representation of an event, this information would then be interpreted in terms of their core principles, allowing them to detect core violations involving this key variable.

To test this prediction, we recently conducted a priming experiment with 8-month-old infants focusing on the variable height in covering events (Wang and Baillargeon, unpublished data, reviewed in Ref. [25]). The infants saw the same expected and unexpected covering events as in the experiment by Wang *et al.* (unpublished data) that was described earlier, with one exception. Prior to each test trial, the infants watched a pre-trial intended to prime them to attend to the relative heights of the cover and object (see Fig. 4a). In designing these pre-trials, we took advantage of the fact that heights is identified as an occlusion variable very early, at about 3.5 months of age [23]. In each pre-trial, the cover was first slid in front of the object, to create an occlusion event; after 5s, the cover was slid back to its original position, and then the trial proceeded as in Wang *et al.*'s

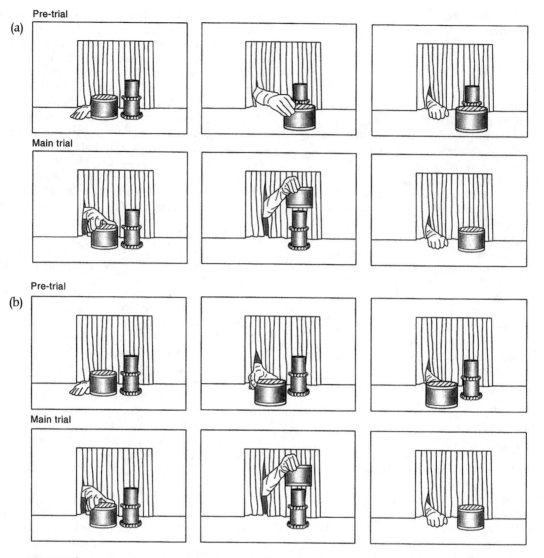

FIGURE 4

Schematic drawing of the unexpected test events in the experiment of Wang and Baillargeon (unpublished data). (a) Occlusion priming condition. (b) Display priming condition.

experiment, with the cover being lowered over the object. We reasoned that the infants would categorize the event as an occlusion event and would then access their knowledge of this category; because this knowledge at 8 months includes the variable height, the infants would include information about the relative heights of the cover and object in their physical representation of the event. We speculated that this information might still be available (or might once again be included) when the infants next represented the covering event.

The results supported our prediction: the infants looked reliably longer at the unexpected than at the

expected event, suggesting that the occlusion priming pre-trials led them to include the key height information in their representation of the covering event. This conclusion was supported by the results of a control condition with different pre-trials. In this condition, the cover was simply slid forward, next to the object, so that the infants saw a display rather than an occlusion event (Fig. 4b). These infants failed to detect the violation in the unexpected event, suggesting that they did not include information about the heights of the cover and object in their representation of either the display or the covering event.

PERSEVERATION

When watching physical events, do infants always engage in the careful monitoring process described in the last section, attending to all of the variables they have identified as relevant to the events? Recent findings by Aguiar and Baillargeon [29] suggest that the answer to this question is negative. When infants are shown the same event repeatedly for several trials, they determine in a *preliminary analysis* at the start of each trial whether the event before them is similar or different from that on preceding trials. If they judge the event to be similar, infants do not engage in any careful monitoring of the event, but simply retrieve their previous prediction about its likely outcome. If they judge the event to be different, infants monitor it carefully and compute a new prediction about its likely outcome. This response pattern makes for efficient problem solving—as long as infants are accurate in their preliminary analyses. If infants fail to notice a crucial change and as a result mistakenly judge an event to be similar to that on preceding trials, they will retrieve their previous prediction instead of computing a new one, thus committing a perseverative error.

To explore infants' perseverative tendencies in a violation-of-expectation task, Aguiar and Baillargeon [29] conducted experiments focusing on 6.5-month-old infants' reasoning about the variable width in containment events; infants this age were known to be able to reason about this variable [30]. In one condition (same-category condition), the infants watched containment events during both familiarization and test (Fig. 5a). In the familiarization event, a ball attached to the end of a rod was lowered into a wide, shallow container. In the test events, the same ball was lowered into a tall container that was either slightly wider (expected event) or much narrower (unexpected event) than the ball; in either case, only the rod protruded from the rim of the container. In another condition (different-categories condition), the infants saw containment events during test but not familiarization: the bottom and back of the wide, shallow container were removed to create a rounded occluder (Fig. 5b).

The infants in the different-categories condition looked reliably longer at the unexpected than at the expected event, but those in the same-category condition did not. Aguiar and Baillargeon [29] speculated that the infants in the same-category condition did not notice the change in the width of the container in their preliminary analyses of the test events. As a result, the infants judged the events to be similar to the familiarization event, and they retrieved the prediction they had formed for this event ('the ball will fit into the container'). Because this prediction was correct for the expected but not the unexpected event, the infants failed to detect the violation in the latter event. By contrast, the infants in the different-

categories condition noticed in their preliminary analyses of the test events that these were from a different category than the familiarization event, namely, containment rather than occlusion. The infants thus judged the test events to be novel, computed appropriate predictions for their outcomes, and detected the violation in the unexpected event.

Additional experiments by Aguiar and Scott (unpublished data) confirmed and extended these initial results. First, 5.5-month-old infants tested in the same-category condition also responded perseveratively. Second, 5.5- and 6.5-month-old infants did not perseverate when tested with a novel version of the different categories condition. This new version was similar to the last with one exception: during familiarization, the occluder was removed and the infants saw a simple display event in which the ball was lowered to the apparatus floor. Finally, further evidence of perseveration was obtained in new experiments focusing on the variable height in containment events (recall that this variable is identified at about 7.5 months of age [22]). After watching a tall object being repeatedly hidden in a very tall container, 9-month-old infants were not surprised to see the same object being hidden in a very short container (same-category condition); however, they did show surprise at this event when no container was present during familiarization and the tall object was simply lowered to the apparatus floor (different-categories condition).

OBJECT INDIVIDUATION

The field of object individuation focuses on infants' ability to determine, when faced with an event, how many distinct objects are involved in the event. Current research suggests that, although infants typically succeed at individuating objects when given spatio-temporal information [27,31–33], the same is not true of featural information.

This last point was first uncovered by Xu and Carey [33]. In one experiment, 12- and 10-month-old infants received expected and unexpected test trials. During the initial phase of each trial, the infants repeatedly watched an occlusion event: an object (e.g., a ball) emerged from behind one edge of a screen and then returned behind it; next, a different object (e.g., a bottle) emerged from behind the other edge of the screen and again returned behind it. During the final phase, the screen was removed to reveal either one (unexpected trials) or both (expected trials) of the objects resting on the apparatus floor. Only the 12-month-old infants showed surprise during the unexpected trials. Xu and Carey concluded that the younger infants did not realize that two distinct objects were involved in the occlusion event. They speculated that 10-month-old infants still lack specific

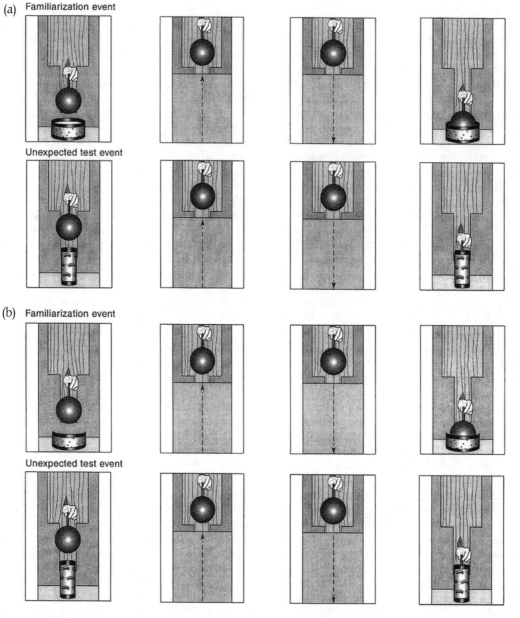

FIGURE 5

Schematic drawing of the familiarization and unexpected test events in the experiment of Aguiar and Baillargeon [29]. (a) Same-category condition. (b) Different-categories condition.

object concepts such as ball and bottle, and that these concepts are not acquired until word learning begins, at the end of the first year.

Although the negative finding Xu and Carey [33] obtained with the 10-month-old infants has been confirmed in additional experiments [32–36], their interpretation of this finding has been questioned. First, rhesus macaques succeed at similar tasks, despite their lack of language [37, 38]. Second, prelinguistic infants also succeed at similar tasks when processing

demands are reduced [32, 35, 36, 39–41]. For example, Wilcox and Schweinle [41] found that even 5.5-month-old infants show surprise during unexpected trials when the occlusion event is made very brief (e.g., the first object disappears behind one edge of the screen, the second object emerges from behind the other edge, and the screen is immediately lowered).

Wilox and Baillargeon [32, 40] have proposed a novel intepretation of the negative results obtained by Xu and Carey [33], which rests on the distinction

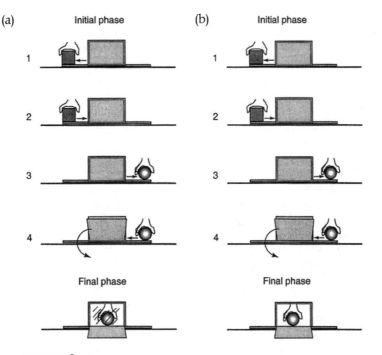

FIGURE 6

Schematic drawing of the unexpected test trials in the experiment of Wilcox and Chapa [35] (a) Event-monitoring condition. (b) Event-mapping condition. (Redrawn with permission from the description in Wilcox et al. [36].)

between event-mapping and event-monitoring tasks. In an event-mapping task, infants see events from *two* different event categories and judge whether the two events are consistent. In an event-monitoring task, infant see an event from *one* event category and judge whether the successive portions of the event are consistent. According to this scheme, the task devised by Xu and Carey is an event-mapping task: each test trial involves first an occlusion event (during the initial phase, when the objects emerge successively from behind the screen) and then a display event (during the final phase, when one or both objects rest on the apparatus floor). To succeed, infants must (1) retrieve their representation of the occlusion event and (2) map the objects in this representation onto those in the display event. The negative results obtained by Xu and Carey and others suggest that, under some conditions, young infants have difficulty completing this retrieval and mapping process.

The preceding analysis makes a number of interesting predictions, several of which have already been experimentally confirmed (for reviews, see Refs [36, 42]). For example, in one experiment by Wilcox and Chapa, 9.5-month-old-infants were assigned to an event-monitoring or an event-mapping condition, and again received expected or unexpected test trials

composed of an initial and a final phase [35] (see Fig. 6). During the initial phase, a ball (expected trials) or a box (unexpected trials) emerged from behind the left edge of a screen and then returned behind it; next, the ball emerged from behind the right edge of the screen and again returned behind it. During the final phase, the central portion of the screen was lowered, leaving a thin rectangular frame; through this frame, the infants could see the ball resting alone on the apparatus floor. For the infants in the event-monitoring condition (Fig. 6a), the frame was filled with a clear plastic, to create a transparent screen; for the infants in the event-mapping condition (Fig. 6b), the frame was empty.

The infants in the event-monitoring condition looked reliably longer during the unexpected than the expected trials, but those in the event-mapping condition did not. According to Wilcox and Chapa [35], the infants tested with the empty frame faced an event-mapping task: they saw first an occlusion and then a display event, as in Xu and Carey's experiment [33], and they experienced the usual difficulty mapping the objects from one event onto the other. By contrast, the infants tested with the filled frame faced an event-monitoring task: they saw a singular, ongoing occlusion event involving first an opaque and then a transparent occluder, and they easily kept track of the objects as the event unfolded.

CONCLUSIONS

The research reviewed in this final section suggests several conclusions about infants' representations of physical events. When watching an event, infants first categorize it and then access their knowledge of the category selected; this knowledge specifies the variables that have been identified as relevant to the category and should be included in the event representation. Under special priming conditions, however, infants can be induced to include a novel variable in their representation of an event, leading to more accurate predictions about the event's outcome. When presented with similar events repeatedly, infants judge in a preliminary analysis at the start of each event whether it is familiar (in which case they retrieve their prior prediction) or novel (in which case they compute a new prediction). Events from different event categories are consistently judged to be novel, suggesting that category information is a salient part of the preliminary analysis.

Finally, when presented with an occlusion event followed by a display or other event, infants sometimes have difficulty mapping the objects from the first to the second event. This result suggests that an event representation is maintained until a category change occurs, at which point a new event representation is set up; and that establishing links between successive representations can be challenging for young infants.

REFERENCES

1. Piaget, J. (1952) *The Origins of Intelligence in Children,* International University Press.
2. Piaget, J. (1954) *The Construction of Reality in the Child,* Basic Books.
3. Aguiar, A. and Baillargeon, R. (1999) 2.5-month-old infants' reasoning about when objects should and should not be occluded. *Cogn. Psychol. 39,* 116–157.
4. Baillargeon, R. *et al.* (1985) Object permanence in 5-month-old infants. *Cognition 20,* 191–208.
5. Goubet, N. and Clifton, R. K. (1998) Object and event representation in 6.5-month-old-infants. *Dev. Psychol. 34,* 63–76.
6. Hespos, S. J. and Baillargeon, R. (2001) Knowledge about containment events in very young infants. *Cognition 78,* 204–245.
7. Hood, B. and Willatts, P. (1986) Reaching in the dark to an object's remembered position: evidence of object permanence in 5-month-old infants. *Br. J. Dev. Psychol. 4,* 57–65.
8. Kotovsky, L. and Baillargeon, R. (1998) The development of calibration-based reasoning about collision events in young infants. *Cognition 67,* 311–351.
9. Leslie, A.M. and Keeble, S. (1987) Do six-month-old infants perceive causality? *Cognition 25,* 265–288.
10. Needham, A. and Baillargeon, R. (1993) Intuitions about support in 4.5-month-old infants. *Cognition 47,* 121–148.
11. Spelke, E.S. *et al.* (1992) Origins of knowledge. *Psychol. Rev. 99,* 605–632.
12. Wilcox, T. *et al.* (1996) Location memory in healthy preterm and full-term infants. *Infant Behav. Dev. 19,* 309–323.
13. Baillargeon, R. (1994) How do infants learn about the physical world? *Curr. Dir. Psychol. Sci. 3,* 133–140.
14. Karmiloff-Smith, A. (1992) *Beyond Modularity: A Developmental Perspective on Cognitive Science,* MIT Press.
15. Leslie, A.M. (1995) A theory of agency. In *Causal Cognition: A Multidisciplinary Debate* (Sperber, D. *et al.,* eds), pp. 121–141, Clarendon Press.
16. Mandler, J.M. (1992) How to build a baby: II. Conceptual primitives. *Psychol. Rev. 99,* 587–604.
17. Spelke, E.S. (1994) Initial knowledge: six suggestions. *Cognition 50,* 431–445.
18. Flavell, J.H. (1963) *The Developmental Psychology of Jean Piaget,* Nostrand.
19. Baillargeon, R. (1995) A model of physical reasoning in infancy. In *Advances in Infancy Research* (Rovee-Collier, C. and Lipsitt, L.P., eds), pp. 305–371, Ablex.
20. Baillargeon, R. *et al.* (1995) The acquisition of physical knowledge in infancy. In *Causal Cognition: A Multidisciplinary Debate* (Sperber, D. *et al.,* eds), pp. 79–116, Clarendon Press.
21. Baillargeon, R. (1998) Infants' understanding of the physical world. In *Advances in Psychological Science* (Sabourin, M. *et al.,* eds), pp. 503–529, Psychology Press.
22. Hespos, S.J. and Baillargeon, R. (2001) Infants' knowledge about occlusion and containment events: a surprising discrepancy. *Psychol. Sci. 12,* 140–147.
23. Baillargeon, R. and DeVos, J. (1991) Object permanence in 3.5- and 4.5-month-old infants: further evidence. *Child Dev. 62,* 1227–1246.
24. Baillargeon, R. and Graber, M. (1987) Where's the rabbit? 5.5-month-old infants' representation of the height of a hidden object. *Cogn. Dev. 2,* 375–392.
25. Baillargeon, R. (2002) The acquisition of physical knowledge in infancy: A summary in eight lessons. In *Handbook of Childhood Cognitive Development* (Goswami, U., ed.), pp. 47–83, Blackwell.
26. Spelke, E.S. *et al.* (1995) Infants' knowledge of object motion and human action. In *Causal Cognition: A Multidisciplinary Debate* (Sperber, D. *et al.,* eds), pp. 44–78, Clarendon Press.
27. Aguiar, A. and Baillargeon, R. (2002) Developments in young infants' reasoning about occluded objects. *Cogn. Psychol. 45,* 267–336.
28. Baillargeon, R. Infants' physical knowledge: of acquired expectations and core principles. In *Language, Brain, and Cognitive Development: Essays in Honor of Jacques Mehler* (Dupoux, E., ed.), MIT Press (in press).
29. Aguiar, A. and Baillargeon, R. (2000) Perseveration and problem solving in infancy. In *Advances in Child Development and Behavior* (Reese, H.W., ed.), pp. 135–180, Academic Press.

30. Sitskoorn, S.M. and Smitsman, A.W. (1995) Infants' perception of dynamic relations between objects: passing through or support? *Dev. Psychol. 31,* 437–447.

31. Spelke, E.S. *et al.* (1995) Spatio-temporal continuity, smoothness of motion, and object identity in infancy. *Br. J. Dev. Psychol.* 13, 113–142.

32. Wilcox, T. and Baillargeon, R. (1998) Object individuation in infancy: the use of featural information in reasoning about occlusion events. *Cogn. Psychol.* 17, 97–155.

33. Xu, F. and Carey, S. (1996) Infants' metaphysics: the case of numerical identity. *Cogn. Psychol.* 30, 111–153.

34. Van de Walle, G. *et al.* (2001) Bases for object individuation in infancy: evidence from manual search. *J. Cogn. Dev.* 1, 249–280.

35. Wilcox, T. and Chapa, C. (2002) Infants' reasoning about opaque and transparent occluders in an individuation task. *Cognition 85*, B1–B10.

36. Wilcox T. *et al.* Object individuation in infancy. In *Progress in Infancy Research* (Fagan, F. and Hayne, H., eds), Erlbaum (in press).

37. Santos, L.R. *et al.* (2002) Object individuation using property/kind information in rhesus macaques (macaca mulatta). *Cognition 83*, 241–264.

38. Uller, C. *et al.* (1997) Is language needed for constructing sortal concepts? A study with nonhuman primates. In *Proceedings of the 21st Annual Boston University Conference on Language Development* (Hughes, E., ed.), pp. 665–677, Oxford University Press.

39. Wilcox, T. (1999) Object individuation: infants' use of shape, size, pattern, and color. *Cognition* 72, 125–166.

40. Wilcox, T. and Baillargeon, R. (1998) Object individuation in young infants: further evidence with an event-monitoring task. *Dev. Sci.* 1, 127–142.

41. Wilcox, T. and Schweinle, A. (2002) Object individuation and event mapping: developmental changes in infants' use of featural information. *Dev. Sci. 5*, 132–150.

42. Needham, A. and Baillargeon, R. (2000) Infants' use of featural and experiential information in segregating and individuating objects: a reply to Xu, Carey, and Welch. *Cognition* 74, 255–284.

43. Baldwin, D.A. *et al.* (1993) Infants' ability to draw inferences about non-obvious object properties: evidence from exploratory play. *Child Dev.* 64, 711–728.

44. Mandler, J.M. (2000) Perceptual and conceptual processes in infancy. *J. Cogn. Dev.* 1, 3–36.

45. Needham, A. and Modi, A. (2000) Infants' use of prior experiences with objects in object segregation: Implications for object recognition in early infancy. In *Advances in Child Development and Behavior* (Reese, H.W., ed.), pp. 99–133. Academic Press.

46. Quinn, P.C. and Eimas, P.D. (1996) Perceptual organization and categorization in young infants. In *Advances in Infancy Research* (Rovee-Collier, C. and Lipsitt, L.P., eds), pp. 1–36, Ablex.

QUESTIONS

1. In research conducted in the 1990s on infants' physical knowledge, such as occlusion and support, what general conclusion was reached about the development of this understanding?

2. What is the violation-of-expectation method, and why is it useful for studying infants' physical knowledge?

3. At what age are infants able to consider height information when they predict the outcomes of containment events and covering events? Does transparency of the screening material matter in infants' assessments of such events?

4. What does the infants' behavior on tasks involving occlusion, containment, and covering events suggest about their understanding of the physical world?

5. What does Elizabeth Spelke claim about infants' knowledge of continuity and solidity, and what does her claim imply about the development of this understanding?

6. What does it mean to say that infants were "primed" in an experiment? Can you give an example of priming from the research described in this article?

7. Do infants act differently when they are shown the same event repeatedly and when they are shown a new event? How?

8. What is the difference between event-mapping and event-monitoring tasks? Is one more difficult than the other for infants to do?

9. What, according to Baillargeon and Wang, explains the development of event categorization in infants?

10. Try to think of an alternative explanation for the infant behavior observed in one of the studies described in this article. Do you prefer the researchers' interpretation or your own? Explain.

16 Early Experience and Emotional Development: The Emergence of Wariness of Heights

Joseph J. Campos · Bennett I. Bertenthal · Rosanne Kermoian

Many people are afraid of heights–specifically, of falling from a height. Falls are dangerous and can be fatal, so it is not surprising that many people have strong emotional responses to heights. If you are afraid of heights or know someone who is, you may have wondered if this fear was always there or if it was learned. One way that psychologists have tried to answer this question is by studying infants to determine if and when they exhibit fear or wariness of heights. One might hypothesize that such wariness appears as soon as infants are able to move around on their own, but this is not the case. Infants show little avoidance of heights after learning to crawl; they may crawl right over the edge of a bed or stairway if caregivers do not stop them.

Infants who have just learned to crawl show no avoidance of heights because they have not yet developed a fear of heights. However, once children do become fearful of heights, this wariness stays with them throughout life. What explains this pattern of development? In the early years of psychology, it was believed that humans have many instincts, including fear of heights. Following from this belief, if fear of heights is built into human physiology in the form of an instinct, developmental changes in this emotional response would not occur. This longstanding assumption was challenged by the research described in the following article.

Joseph J. Campos and his colleagues examined the relation between early locomotor experience and the development of fear. They demonstrated that fear of heights is a learned, not an instinctual, emotional response. Their results also identify a direct link between early perceptual and motor experience and emotional development. In order to study this link, the researchers needed to (1) adapt a method that is used for studying infants who can crawl for infants who have not yet learned to crawl; (2) devise an ecologically valid way of testing fear in infants; and (3) identify experiences of prelocomotive children that are similar to the experience of locomotion.

Because of its biological adaptive value, wariness of heights is widely believed to be innate or under maturational control. In this report, we present evidence contrary to this hypothesis, and show the importance of locomotor experience for emotional development. Four studies bearing on this conclusion have shown that (1) when age is held constant, locomotor experience accounts for wariness of heights; (2) "artificial" experience locomoting in a walker generates evidence of wariness of heights; (3) an orthopedically handicapped infant tested longitudinally did not show wariness of heights so long as he had no locomotor experience; and (4) regardless of the age when infants begin to crawl, it is the duration of locomotor experience and not age that predicts avoidance of heights. These findings suggest that when infants begin to crawl, experiences generated by locomotion make possible the development of wariness of heights.

Between 6 and 10 months of age, major changes occur in fearfulness in the human infant. During this period, some fears are shown for the first time, and many others show a step-function increase in prevalence (Bridges, 1932; Scarr & Salapatek, 1970; Sroufe,

Reprinted with permission of Blackwell Publishers from Campos, J. J., Bertenthal, B. I. & Kermoian, R. (1992). Early experience and emotional development: The emergence of wariness of heights. *Psychological Science, 3,* 61–64.
This research was supported by grants from the National Institutes of Health (HD-16195, HD-00695, and HD-25066) and from the John D. and Catherine T. MacArthur Foundation.

1979). These changes in fearfulness occur so abruptly, involve so many different elicitors, and have such biologically adaptive value that many investigators propose maturational explanations for this developmental shift (Emde, Gaensbauer, & Harmon, 1976; Kagan, Kearsley, & Zelazo, 1978). For such theorists, the development of neurophysiological structures (e.g., the frontal lobes) precedes and accounts for changes in affect.

In contrast to predominantly maturational explanations of developmental changes, Gottlieb (1983, 1991) proposed a model in which different types of experiences play an important role in developmental shifts. He emphasized that new developmental acquisitions, such as crawling, generate experiences that, in turn, create the conditions for further developmental changes. Gottlieb called such "bootstrapping" processes probabilistic epigenesis. In contrast to most current models of developmental transition, Gottlieb's approach stresses the possibility that, under some circumstances, psychological function may precede and account for development of neurophysiological structures.

There is evidence in the animal literature that a probabilistic epigenetic process plays a role in the development of wariness of heights. Held and Hein (1963), for instance, showed that dark-reared kittens given experience with active self-produced locomotion in an illuminated environment showed avoidance of heights, whereas dark-reared littermates given passive experience moving in the same environment manifested no such avoidance. In these studies, despite equivalent maturational states in the two groups of kittens, the experiences made possible by correlated visuomotor responses during active locomotion proved necessary to elicit wariness of heights.

So long as they are prelocomotor, human infants, despite their visual competence and absence of visual deprivation, may be functionally equivalent to Held and Hein's passively moved kittens. Crawling may generate or refine skills sufficient for the onset of wariness of heights. These skills may include improved calibration of distances, heightened sensitivity to visually specified self-motion, more consistent coordination of visual and vestibular stimulation, and increased awareness of emotional signals from significant others (Bertenthal & Campos, 1990; Campos, Hiatt, Ramsay, Henderson, & Svejda, 1978).

There is anecdotal evidence supporting a link between locomotor experience and development of wariness of heights in human infants. Parents commonly report that there is a phase following the acquisition of locomotion when infants show no avoidance of heights, and will go over the edge of a bed or other precipice if the caretaker is not vigilant.

Parents also report that this phase of apparent fearlessness is followed by one in which wariness of heights becomes quite intense (Campos et al., 1978).

In sum, both the kitten research and the anecdotal human evidence suggest that wariness of heights is not simply a maturational phenomenon, to be expected even in the absence of experience. From the perspective of probabilistic epigenesis, locomotor experience may operate as an organizer of emotional development, serving either to induce wariness of heights (i.e., to produce a potent emotional state that would never emerge without such experience) or to facilitate its emergence (i.e., to bring it about earlier than it otherwise would appear). The research reported here represents an attempt to determine whether locomotor experience is indeed an organizer of the emergence of wariness of heights.

Pinpointing the role of locomotion in the emergence of wariness of heights in human infants requires solution of a number of methodological problems. One is the selection of an ecologically valid paradigm for testing wariness of heights. Another is the determination of an outcome measure that can be used with both prelocomotor and locomotor infants. A third is a means of determining whether locomotion is playing a role as a correlate, an antecedent, an inducer, or a facilitator of the onset of wariness of heights.

The ecologically valid paradigm we selected for testing was the visual cliff (Walk, 1966; Walk & Gibson, 1961)—a large, safety-glass-covered table with a solid textured surface placed immediately underneath the glass on one side (the "shallow" side) and a similar surface placed some 43 in. underneath the glass on the floor below on the other side (the "deep" side).

To equate task demands for prelocomotor and locomotor infants, we measured the infants' wariness reactions while they were slowly lowered toward either the deep or the shallow side of the cliff. This descent procedure not only allowed us to assess differences in wariness reactions as a function of locomotor experience in both prelocomotor and locomotor infants but also permitted us to assess an index of depth perception, that is, a visual placing response (the extension of the arms and hands in anticipation of contact with the shallow, but not the deep, surface of the cliff [Walters, 1981]).

To assess fearfulness with an index appropriate to both pre- and postlocomoting infants, we measured heart rate (HR) responses during the 3-s period of descent onto the surface of the cliff. Prior work had shown consistently that heart rate decelerates in infants who are in a state of nonfearful attentiveness, but accelerates when infants are showing either a defensive response (Graham & Clifton, 1966) or a precry state (Campos, Emde, Gaensbauer, & Henderson, 1975).

To relate self-produced locomotion to fearfulness, we used a number of converging research operations. One was an *age-held-constant design*, contrasting the performance of infants who were locomoting with those of the same age who were not yet locomoting; the second was an analog of an experiential *enrichment* manipulation, in which infants who were otherwise incapable of crawling or creeping were tested after they had a number of hours of experience moving about voluntarily in walker devices; the third was an analog of an experiential *deprivation* manipulation, in which an infant who was orthopedically handicapped, but otherwise normal, was tested longitudinally past the usual age of onset of crawling and again after the delayed acquisition of crawling; and the fourth was a *cross-sequential lag design* aimed at teasing apart the effects of age of onset of locomotion and of duration of locomotor experience on the infant's avoidance of crossing the deep or the shallow side of the cliff to the mother.

EXPERIMENT 1: HR RESPONSES OF PRELOCOMOTOR AND LOCOMOTOR INFANTS

In the first study, a total of 92 infants, half locomoting for an average of 5 weeks, were tested at 7.3 months of age. Telemetered HR, facial expressions (taped from a camera under the deep side of the cliff), and the visual placing response were recorded. Each infant was lowered to each side of the cliff by a female experimenter, with the mother in another room.

As predicted from the work of Held and Hein (1963), locomotor infants showed evidence of wariness of heights, and prelocomotor infants did not. Only on deep trials did the HR of locomotor infants accelerate significantly from baselevels (by 5 beats/min), and differ significantly from the HR responses of prelocomotor infants. The HR responses of prelocomotor infants did not differ from baselevels on either the deep or shallow sides. Surprisingly, facial expressions did not differentiate testing conditions, perhaps because the descent minimized the opportunity to target these expressions to social figures.

In addition, every infant tested, regardless of locomotor status, showed visual placing responses on the shallow side, and no infant showed placing responses on the deep side of the cliff. Thus, all infants showed evidence for depth perception on the deep side, but only locomotor infants showed evidence of fear-related cardiac acceleration in response to heights.

EXPERIMENT 2: ACCELERATION OF LOCOMOTOR EXPERIENCE

Although correlated, the development of locomotion and the emergence of wariness of heights may be jointly determined by a third factor that brings about both changes. Disambiguation of this possibility required a means of providing "artificial" locomotor experience to infants who were not yet able to crawl. This manipulation was achieved by providing wheeled walkers to infants and testing them after their mothers had reported at least 32 hr of voluntary forward movement in the device.

Infants who received walkers were divided into two groups: prelocomotor walkers ($N = 9M$, 9F, Mean Age = 224 days, Walker Experience = 47 hr of voluntary forward movement) and locomotor walkers ($N = 9M$, 7F, Mean Age = 222 days, Walker Experience = 32 hr). The performance of infants in these two groups was compared with the performance of age-matched subjects, also divided into two groups: prelocomotor controls ($N = 9M$, 9F, Mean Age = 222 days) and locomotor controls ($N = 9M$, 7F, Mean Age = 222 days). The average duration of crawling experience was only 5 days in the locomotor walker and the locomotor control groups. All infants were tested using the same procedure as in the prior study. No shallow trials were administered in order to minimize subject loss due to the additional testing time required for such trials.

As revealed in Figure 1, the three groups of infants with any type of locomotor experience showed evidence of cardiac acceleration, whereas the prelocomotor control infants did not. It is noteworthy that all 16 infants in the locomotor walker group (who had a "double dosage" of locomotor experience consisting of walker training and some crawling) showed HR accelerations upon descent to the cliff. Planned comparisons revealed significant differences between (1) all walker infants and all controls, (2) all spontaneously locomoting infants and prelocomotor controls, and (3) prelocomotor walkers and prelocomotor controls. These findings show that the provision of "artificial" locomotor experience may facilitate or induce wariness of heights, even for infants who otherwise have little or no crawling experience. Locomotor experience thus appears to be an antecedent of the emergence of wariness.

EXPERIMENT 3: DEPRIVATION OF LOCOMOTOR EXPERIENCE

Although Experiment 2 showed that training in locomotion accelerates the onset of wariness of heights, it is possible that this response would eventually develop even in the absence of locomotor experience. To deter-

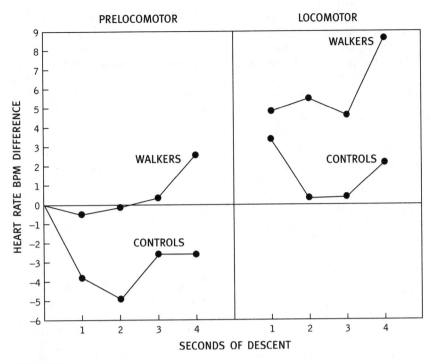

FIGURE 1

Heart rate response while the infant is lowered toward the deep side of the visual cliff as a function of locomotor experience. The left panel contrasts the performance of prelocomotor infants with and without "artificial" walker experience. The right panel contrasts the performance of crawling infants with and without "artificial" walker experience. Heart rate is expressed as difference from baseline in beats/min.

mine whether the delayed acquisition of crawling precedes the delayed emergence of wariness of heights, we longitudinally tested an infant with a peripheral handicap to locomotion. This infant was neurologically normal and had a Bayley Developmental Quotient of 126, but was born with two congenitally dislocated hips. After an early operation, he was placed in a full body cast. The infant was tested on the visual cliff monthly between 6 and 10 months of age using the procedures described above. While the infant was in the cast, he showed no evidence of crawling. At 8.5 months of age (i.e., 1.5 months after the normative age of onset of locomotion), the cast was removed, and the infant began crawling soon afterward.

This infant showed no evidence of differential cardiac responsiveness on the deep versus shallow side of the cliff until 10 months of age, at which time his HR accelerated markedly on the deep side, and decelerated on the shallow. Although we cannot generalize from a single case study, these data provide further support for the role of self-produced locomotion as a facilitator or inducer of wariness of heights.

EXPERIMENT 4: AGE OF ONSET OF LOCOMOTION VERSUS LOCOMOTOR EXPERIENCE

In the studies described so far, HR was used as an imperfect index of wariness. However, we felt that a study using behavioral avoidance was needed to confirm the link between locomotor experience and wariness of heights. We thus used the locomotor crossing test on the visual cliff, in which the infant is placed on the center of the cliff, and the mother is instructed to encourage the infant to cross to her over either the deep or the shallow side. In this study, we also assessed separately the effects of age of onset of crawling (early, normative, or late) and of duration of locomotor experience (11 or 41 days), as well as their interaction, using a longitudinal design.

The results of this study demonstrated a clear effect of locomotor experience independent of the age when self-produced locomotion first appeared. This effect of experience was evident with both nominal data (the proportion of infants who avoided descending onto the deep side of the cliff on the first test trial) and interval data (the latency to descend from the center board of the visual cliff onto the deep side on deep trials minus the latency to descend onto the shallow side on shallow trials). At whatever age the infant had begun to crawl, only 30% to 50% of infants avoided the deep side after 11 days of locomotor experience. However, after 41 days of locomotor experience, avoidance increased to 60% to 80% of infants. The latency data revealed a significant interaction of side of cliff with locomotor experience, but not a main effect of age, nor of the interaction of age with experience. The results of this study further suggest that locomotor experience paces the onset of wariness of heights.

PROCESSES UNDERLYING THE DEVELOPMENT OF WARINESS OF HEIGHTS

The pattern of findings obtained in these four studies, taken together with the animal studies by Held and Hein (1963), demonstrates a consistent relation between locomotor experience and wariness of heights. We propose the following interpretations for our findings.

We believe that crawling initially is a goal in itself, with affect solely linked to the success or failure of implementing the act of moving. Locomotion is initially not context dependent, and infants show no wariness of heights because the goal of moving is not coordinated with other goals, including the avoidance of threats. However, as a result of locomotor experience, infants acquire a sense of both the efficacy and the limitations of their own actions. Locomotion stops being an end in itself, and begins to be goal corrected and coordinated with the environmental surround. As a result, infants begin to show wariness of heights once locomotion becomes context dependent (cf. Bertenthal & Campos, 1990).

The context-dependency of the infants' actions may come about from falling and near-falling experiences that locomotion generates. Near-falls are particularly important because they are frequent, they elicit powerful emotional signals from the parent, and they set the stage for long-term retention of negative affect in such contexts.

There is still another means by which the infant can acquire a sense of wariness of depth with locomotion. While the infant moves about voluntarily, visual information specifying self-movement becomes more highly correlated with vestibular information specifying the same amount of self-movement (Bertenthal & Campos, 1990). Once expectancies re-

lated to the correlation of visual and vestibular information are formed, being lowered toward the deep side of the cliff creates a violation of the expected correlation. This violation results from the absence of visible texture near the infant when lowered toward the deep side of the cliff, relative to the shallow side. As a consequence, angular acceleration is not detected by the visual system, whereas it is detected by the vestibular system. This violation of expectation results in distress proportional to the magnitude of the violation. A test of this interpretation requires assessment of the establishment of visual-vestibular coordination as a function of locomotor experience and confirmation that wariness occurs in contexts that violate visual-vestibular coordination.

LOCOMOTOR EXPERIENCE AND OTHER EMOTIONAL CHANGES

The consequences of the development of self-produced locomotion for emotional development extend far beyond the domain of wariness of heights. Indeed, the onset of locomotion generates an entirely different emotional climate in the family. For instance, as psychoanalytic theories predict (e.g., Mahler, Pine, & Bergman, 1975), the onset of locomotion brings about a burgeoning of both positive and negative affect—positive affect because of the child's new levels of self-efficacy; negative affect because of the increases in frustration resulting from thwarting of the child's goals and because of the affective resonance that comes from increased parental expressions of prohibition (Campos, Kermoian, & Zumbahlen, in press). Locomotion is also crucial for the development of attachment (Ainsworth, Blehar, Waters, & Wall, 1978; Bowlby, 1973), because it makes physical proximity to the caregiver possible. With the formation of specific attachments, locomotion increases in significance as the child becomes better able to move independently toward novel and potentially frightening environments. Infants are also more sensitive to the location of the parent, more likely to show distress upon separation, and more likely to look to the parent in ambiguous situations.

Locomotion also brings about emotional changes in the parents. These changes include the increased pride (and sometimes sorrow) that the parents experience in their child's new mobility and independence and the new levels of anger parents direct at the baby when the baby begins to encounter forbidden objects. It seems clear from the findings obtained in this line of research that new levels of functioning in one behavioral domain can generate experiences that profoundly affect other developmental domains, including affective, social, cognitive, and sensorimotor ones (Kermoian & Campos, 1988). We thus propose that theoretical orientations like probabilistic epigenesis provide a novel, heuristic, and timely perspective for the study of emotional development.

REFERENCES

Ainsworth, M. D. S., Blehar, M., Waters, E., & Wall, S. (1978). *Patterns of attachment.* Hillsdale, NJ: Erlbaum.

Bertenthal, B., & Campos, J. J. (1990). A systems approach to the organizing effects of self-produced locomotion during infancy. In C. Rovee-Collier & L. P. Lipsitt (Eds.), *Advances in infancy research* (Vol. 6, pp. 1–60). Norwood, NJ: Ablex.

Bowlby, J. (1973). *Attachment and loss: Vol. 2. Separation.* New York: Basic Books.

Bridges, K. M. (1932). Emotional development in early infancy. *Child Development, 3,* 324–341.

Campos, J. J., Emde, R. N., Gaensbauer, T. J., & Henderson, C. (1975). Cardiac and behavioral interrelationships in the reactions of infants to strangers. *Developmental Psychology, 11,* 589–601.

Campos, J. J., Hiatt, S., Ramsay, D., Henderson, C., & Svejda, M. (1978). The emergence of fear of heights. In M. Lewis & L. Rosenblum (Eds.), *The development of affect* (pp. 149–182). New York: Plenum Press.

Campos, J. J., Kermoian, R., & Zumbahlen, R. M. (In press). In N. Eisenberg (Ed.), *New directions for child development.* San Francisco: Jossey-Bass.

Emde, R. N., Gaensbauer, T. J., & Harmon, R. J. (1976). Emotional expression in infancy: A biobehavioral study. *Psychological Issues* (Vol. 10, No. 37). New York: International Universities Press.

Gottlieb, G. (1983). The psychobiological approach to developmental issues. In P. Mussen (Ed.), *Handbook of child psychology: Vol. II. Infancy and developmental psychobiology* (4th ed.) (pp. 1–26). New York: Wiley.

Gottlieb, G. (1991). Experiential canalization of behavioral development: Theory. *Developmental Psychology, 27,* 4–13.

Graham, F. K., & Clifton, R. K. (1966). Heartrate change as a component of the orienting response. *Psychological Bulletin, 65,* 305–320.

Held, R. & Hein, A. (1963). Movement-produced stimulation in the development of visually guided behavior. *Journal of Comparative and Physiological Psychology, 56,* 872–876.

Kagan, J., Kearsley, R., & Zelazo, P. R. (1978). *Infancy: Its place in human development.* Cambridge, MA: Harvard University Press.

Kermoian, R., & Campos, J. J. (1988). Locomotor experience: A facilitator of spatial cognitive development. *Child Development, 59,* 908–917.

Mahler, M., Pine, F., & Bergman, A. (1975). *The psychological birth of the human infant.* New York: Basic Books.

Scarr, S., & Salapatek, P. (1970). Patterns of fear development during infancy. *Merrill-Palmer Quarterly, 16,* 53–90.

Sroufe, L. A. (1979). Socioemotional development. In J. Osofsky (Ed.), *Handbook of infant development* (pp. 462–516). New York: Wiley.

Walk, R. (1966). The development of depth perception in animals and human infants. *Monographs of the Society for Research in Child Development, 31* (Whole No. 5).

Walk, R., & Gibson, E. (1961). A comparative and analytical study of visual depth perception. *Psychological Monographs, 75* (15, Whole No. 5).

Walters, C. (1981). Development of the visual placing response in the human infant. *Journal of Experimental Child Psychology, 32,* 313–329.

QUESTIONS

1. Why did psychologists initially propose maturational explanations for fearfulness in human infants?
2. How do developmental acquisitions, like crawling, serve to "bootstrap" further development?
3. How is the development of wariness of heights in human infants like the development of wariness of heights that was observed in kittens who were reared in the dark?
4. What is the visual cliff, and how is it used to study the development of depth perception and fear of heights in infants?
5. How did the heart rates of locomotor and prelocomotor infants differ when they were lowered onto the two sides of the visual cliff?
6. Why was it important that Campos and his colleagues use a research design in which the age of the infants was held constant?
7. Which was a better predictor of wariness of heights in infants, age of onset of locomotion or locomotor experience? What does this result indicate about the development of wariness of heights?
8. What was it important that Campos and his colleagues distinguish the development of *awareness* of heights from the development of *wariness* of heights?
9. If you were caring for two 6-month-olds, one who had been using a walker for a month or more and one who had no experience with walkers, would you have different concerns about keeping an eye on them?
10. If an infant was deprived of the ability to crawl or squirm from one place to another, do you think he or she would development wariness of heights?

17 Specificity and Heterogeneity in Children's Responses to Profound Institutional Privation

MICHAEL L. RUTTER • JANA M. KREPPNER • THOMAS G. O'CONNOR

A universal characteristic of the human species is that children have a lengthy period of dependence on adults. During early development, other people, especially primary caregivers, provide children with the social and emotional support that children need for psychological growth. In fact, many theories of social and emotional development, most notably attachment theory, consider a child's early relationships to be fundamental to healthy development. Children reared in institutional settings in which they experience extreme privation, receiving little or no social and emotional support, may be especially vulnerable to long-term psychological dysfunction as a result of their institutionalization.

The following article describes how a team of researchers examined the development of Romanian children who had spent their early years in institutions in which their physical and psychological needs were barely met. These children were adopted by parents in the United Kingdom (UK) before they were 42 months of age. The researchers compared them on a variety of measures at age 4 and age 6 with children who had been born in the UK and adopted before they were 6 months of age. The researchers measured the children's socioemotional functioning (including their difficulties with attachment and peer relationships, attentional needs, and activity levels) and cognitive impairments. The results indicate more dysfunction on several of these measures among children who had been reared in institutions than among children who had not. There were also some areas of functioning in which these two groups of children were similar.

This research tells us that, while extreme early deprivation can interfere with psychological development, these problems are not inevitable and these experiences may not be directly linked with later psychopathology. In addition, the problems that result from severe privation are likely to involve some areas of psychological functioning more than others. These results hold out hope for children who experience extreme privation early in life and offer encouragement to individuals who care for such children.

Background *The sequelae of profound early privation are varied.*

Aims *To delineate the behavioural patterns that are specifically associated with institutional privation.*

Method *A group of 165 children adopted from Romania before the age of 42 months were compared at 4 years and 6 years with 52 non-deprived UK children adopted in infancy. Dysfunction was assessed for seven domains of functioning. The groups were compared on which, and how many, domains were impaired.*

Results *Attachment problems, inattention/overactivity, quasi-autistic features and cognitive impairment were associated with institutional privation, but emotional difficulties, poor peer relationships and conduct problems were not. Nevertheless, one-fifth of children who spent the longest time in institutions showed normal functioning.*

Reproduced with permission from Rutter, M. L., Kreppner, J. M., & O'Connor, T. G. (2001). Specificity and heterogeneity in children's responses to profound institutional privation, from the *British Journal of Psychiatry, 179*, 97–103. (c) 2001 The Royal College of Psychiatrists.

The research was supported by funds from the Department of Health, the Medical Research Council and the Helmut Horten Foundation.

Conclusions *Attachment disorder behaviours, inattention/overactivity and quasi-autistic behaviour constitute institutional privation patterns.*

Studies of children suffering profound institutional privation in infancy and early childhood have shown that it results in major developmental impairment, that there is considerable developmental catch-up following adoption into well-functioning families, and that there are clinically significant sequelae in some of the children (Chisholm *et al*, 1995; Ames, 1997; Fisher *et al*, 1997; Chisholm, 1998; Rutter *et al*, 1998, 2001; O'Connor *et al*, 2000). However, the studies also show that, at least in relation to specific outcomes, there is considerable heterogeneity in response. Thus, in our own study, for children who experienced at least 2 years of institutional privation in infancy, the measured IQ scores at 6 years ranged from the severely retarded range to high superior (O'Connor *et al*, 2000). Because the published reports all consider outcomes in relation to specific impairments, it is not known whether the children who fare well on one type of outcome also fare well on others. It is necessary to determine the extent to which impairments tend to be pervasive across domains and to ask what proportion of profoundly deprived children achieves generally normal psychological functioning. Equally, it is not known whether profound institutional privation results in a general increase in all forms of psychopathology or whether there are certain behavioural patterns or syndromes that are particularly strongly associated with early privation. The aim of this investigation was to use findings from a follow-up study (to age 6 years) of institution-reared Romanian children who were adopted into UK families to answer these questions on specificity and heterogeneity in children's responses to profound institutional privation.

METHOD

SUBJECTS

The sample comprised 165 children adopted from Romania before the age of 42 months, selected at random from within bands stratified according to age of entry to the UK, and a comparison group of 52 non-deprived within-UK adoptees placed before the age of 6 months (for details see Rutter *et al*, 1998). Of these, 156 children from Romania and 50 within-UK adoptees had complete data-sets and were used for analyses where these were required. Four-fifths of the Romanian adoptees had been reared in institutions for most of their life and nearly all had been admitted to institutions in the neonatal period (mean age of admission was 0.34 months). The conditions in the Ro-

manian institutions were generally extremely bad (see Kaler & Freeman, 1994; Castle *et al*, 1999; Johnson, 2001); and the condition of most of the children on arrival in the UK was also very poor. Their mean weight was 2.4 standard deviations below the mean (with over half below the third percentile) and the (retrospectively administered) Denver scale produced a mean quotient of 63, with three-fifths functioning in the severely retarded range. By the time the children reached the age of 4 years substantial catch-up had occurred, with the mean weight and Denver quotient both being near normal for UK children (Rutter *et al*, 1998). Eighty-one per cent of the adoptive parents of Romanian children who were approached to participate in the study agreed to do so.

MEASURES

The assessments at age 6 years comprised a standardised investigator-based interview that included (among other things) systematic questions on attachment disorder behaviours (O'Conner *et al*, 1999, 2001), completion of parent and teacher versions of the Rutter behavioural scales (Elander & Rutter, 1996; Hogg *et al*, 1997) and individually administered McCarthy Scales of Children's Abilities (McCarthy, 1972). In order to assess possible autistic features, the parents completed the Autism Screening Questionnaire (ASQ; Berument *et al*, 1999). In addition, the Autism Diagnostic Interview–Revised (ADI–R; Le Couteur *et al*, 1989; Lord *et al*, 1994) was given by a researcher experienced in its use (M.L.R.) when parental interview reports suggested the possibility of autistic features (see Rutter *et al*, 1999).

In order to obtain a categorical measure of probable dysfunction in each of seven specific domains of functioning, the data were dealt with as follows.

Attachment problems Three items from the parental interview–definite lack of differentiation between adults; clear indication that the child would readily go off with a stranger; and definite lack of checking back with the parent in anxiety-provoking situations–were scored as 0 for 'no abnormality', 1 for 'probable problem' and 2 for 'definite problem'. These were summated to produce a composite score ranging from 0 to 6, and a cut-off of 4 or more was used to indicate dysfunction.

Inattention/overactivity The Rutter scales completed by mothers and fathers were standardised and then averaged to produce a single parent score (see Kreppner *et al*, 2001). The teachers' scale was similarly standardised. The inattention/overactivity items on the parents' scale were: very restless, has difficulty staying seated for long; squirmy, fidgety child; cannot settle to anything for more than a few moments and inattentive; and easily distracted. The teachers' scale included all the preceding items plus: excessive demands for teacher's attention; and fails to finish things started–short attention span. Using the distribution of scores in the within-UK adoptees sample, three categories were created for the parents' and teachers' scales separately with a score of 0 for a score below the median, 1 for a score between the median and the top 10% cut-off, and 2 for a score in the top 10% of the range. Pervasive inattention/overactivity required a score of 2 on either the parents' or teachers' scale and a score of 1 or 2 on the other scale. Children with a missing score on one scale were not included in the 'pervasive' category.

Emotional difficulties   The scores on the Rutter parents' and teachers' scales were standardised in the same way as for hyperactivity. The emotional difficulties items were: has had tears on arrival at school or has refused to go into the building in the past 12 months; gives up easily; often worried, worries about many things; often appears miserable, unhappy, tearful or distressed; cries easily; tends to be fearful or afraid of new things or new situations; stares into space and often complains of aches and pains (see Hogg *et al*, 1997). These were dealt with according to the distribution of scores in the within-UK adoptees sample. Children with scores in the top 5% on either or both of the parents' and teachers' scales were treated as having emotional difficulties.

Autistic features   Using the ASQ and the ADI–R, 20 children were diagnosed as showing quasi-autistic features (Rutter *et al*, 1999). As this provided the combination of total screening coverage of both groups and individual diagnoses, this categorisation was used.

Cognitive impairment   The general cognitive index (GCI) of the McCarthy Scales was used as the measure. Children who scored at least 2 standard deviations below the UK sample's mean were treated as showing cognitive impairment. The UK sample mean was 117, with a standard deviation of 18. Twice the standard deviation (36) subtracted from 117 equated to a score of 81; accordingly all children with an IQ of 81 or less were included in this domain of dysfunction.

Peer difficulties   Peer difficulties were assessed through a combination of the Rutter parents' and teachers' scales, together with nine items from the parental interview. The three items in the parents' scale were 'not much liked by other children', 'tends to be solitary' and 'does not get on well with other children'. The mother and father scales were combined into a parental composite, using the approach described for inattention/overactivity. The three items in the teachers' scale were 'not much liked by other children', 'tends to be on own' and 'cannot work in a small peer group'. The nine parental interview items were: group play; differentiation between children (i.e. clear preferences, with one or more special friends); popu-

larity; age preference of peers; harmony of peer interaction; teased by other children; teases others; picked on/bullied; and picks on/bullies others. Peer group difficulties were regarded as present if the score on any of the three measures was in the top (most deviant) 5% of the distribution for the UK sample.

Conduct problems   The scores on the Rutter parents' and teachers' scales were standardised as for hyperactivity and emotional difficulties. The conduct items were: often destroys own or others' property; frequently fights or is extremely quarrelsome with other children; is often disobedient; often tells lies; has stolen things on one or more occasions in the past 12 months; disturbs other children; bullies other children; blames others for things; is inconsiderate of others; kicks, bites other children (see Hogg *et al*, 1997). Children who scored in the top 5% of scores in the UK sample distribution on either scale were categorised as showing conduct problems.

STATISTICAL ANALYSIS

Between-group differences in the proportion of children showing dysfunction on each of the seven domains were examined using Fisher's two-tailed exact test and one degree of freedom. Within-group differences according to age of entry to the UK were examined for a linear trend on a chi square comparing entry at under 6 months, 6–24 months, and over 24 months ($n = 58$, 59 and 48 respectively). Polychoric correlations were used to examine the association among the binary domains of dysfunction variables.

Cluster analysis was used to examine the ways in which children in the Romanian adoptees sample showed similarities in their patterns of dysfunction. The technique is valuable for grouping individuals according to shared patterns of psychopathology. The

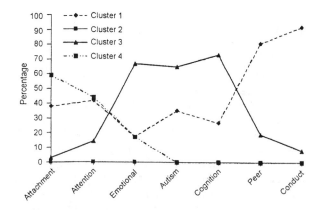

FIGURE 1

Percentage extreme score across seven outcomes according to cluster membership.

seven dichotomous variables were cluster analysed using Ward's method of agglomeration based on squared Euclidean distance (Aldenderfer & Blashfield, 1988). A four-cluster solution was chosen based on coefficient of linkage, practical considerations (such as sample size) and interpretability. The cluster analyses were then rerun using alternative indices of similarity in order to determine the consistency of the cluster profiles. All approaches gave patterns closely similar to those displayed in Fig. 1. As an additional check, cluster analyses were repeated using continuously distributed dimensions, rather than binary categories, again with similar findings (further details available from the authors upon request).

RESULTS

Of the seven domains of dysfunction when the children were aged 6 years, three (emotional problems, peer difficulties and conduct problems) showed no difference in rate between the adoptees from Romania and the within-UK adoptees (Table 1). For each of these three domains, there was no association, within the Romanian adoptees sample, with the children's age at the time of entry to the UK. In sharp contrast, the other four domains (attachment problems, inattention/overactivity, quasi-autistic problems and cognitive impairment) were all much more common in the Romanian sample and, in each case, there was a significant association with age at entry, the rate of problems being much higher in those who left Romania when they were older. The implication is that the former three domains are not particularly associated with institutional privation, whereas the latter four seem to be.

Table 2 summarises the findings on the number of domains showing dysfunction in the two groups, together with the association with age at entry within the Romanian sample. As would be expected in any general population sample, a substantial minority of the UK adoptees showed dysfunction in at least one domain. Less than four-fifths were free of dysfunction on any domain. Nevertheless, dysfunction was substantially more likely to be present in the Romanian adoptees, and the proportion without dysfunction on at least one domain was significantly lower in those who came to the UK when they were older. Of those leaving Romania after their second birthday, between a fifth and a quarter were free of any measurable dysfunction at 6 years of age. The trend for more dysfunction, and more pervasive dysfunction, in Romanian adoptees and for an association with age at entry was apparent at all levels of frequency of dysfunction. The main difference between the groups, however, was evident in the presence or absence of any dysfunction, rather than in the pervasiveness of dysfunction across domains.

What characterised the Romanian adoptees sample were the particular domains involved in the pervasive dysfunction pattern. Almost always, this involved some admixture of attachment problems, inattention/overactivity and quasi-autistic problems. In contrast, in the UK sample pervasive impairment usually involved either conduct or emotional disturbance plus another problem, but not one of the patterns that was distinctive of the institutional privation children.

Of the 40 children in the Romanian adoptees group who showed impairment on just one domain, 13 did so on attachment problems, 11 on inattention/overactivity, 7 on peer difficulties and 6 on cog-

---

TABLE 1 SEVEN DOMAINS OF DYSFUNCTION AT 6 YEARS OF AGE IN ROMANIAN AND WITHIN-UK ADOPTED CHILDREN

Domains	Rate in Romanian Adoptees		Rate in Within-UK Adoptees		Between-Group Differences	Association with Age at Entry to UK	
					Fisher's Exact P (Two-tailed)		
	%	n	%	n		χ² Trends	P
Attachment problems	20.7	164	3.8	52	0.003	11.13	0.001
Inattention/overactivity	25.3	162	9.6	52	0.019	9.04	0.003
Emotional difficulties	3.7	162	9.6	52	NS	0.03	NS
Quasi-autistic features	12.1	165	0.0	52	0.005	4.61	0.032
Cognitive impairment	14.0	157	2.0	50	0.018	14.61	0.001
Peer difficulties	18.9	164	9.6	52	NS	0.45	NS
Conduct problems	8.0	162	9.6	52	NS	0.97	NS

TABLE 2   ROMANIAN AND WITHIN-UK ADOPTED CHILDREN: PERCENTAGES OF CHILDREN WITH IMPAIRMENT IN 0, 1, 2, OR 3 OR MORE DOMAINS

Number of Domains in Which There Is Impairment	Within-UK Adoptees (n=50)	Romanian Adoptees, Age at Entry into UK			χ^2 Trends	P
		<6 Months (n=56)	6–24 Months (n=35)	24–42 Months (n=45)		
0 (n=112) (%)	78.0	69.6	43.6	23.9	34.81	0.001
1 (n=46) (%)	12.0	17.9	23.6	37.0	19.79	0.002
2 (n=20) (%)	2.0	7.1	12.7	17.4	9.75	0.002
3 or more (n=28) (%)	8.0	5.4	20.0	21.7	6.73	0.009

nitive impairment (with only an additional 3 on other domains). Of the 6 children in the within-UK adoptees group with impairment on just one domain, 2 showed it on emotional difficulties, 2 on inattention/overactivity, 1 on conduct problems and 1 on attachment problems.

Table 3 presents the polychoric correlations among domains of dysfunction within the Romanian adoptees sample. The intercorrelations are no more than moderate in most instances but there was a stronger correlation (0.66) between autistic features and cognitive impairment and between autistic features and peer difficulties (0.59). Cognitive impairment showed a near-zero correlation with emotional difficulties and with conduct problems. Attachment problems had their strongest correlation with inattention/overactivity (0.47). There were only 6 children in the Romanian sample with emotional difficulties but 5 of these showed a quasi-autistic pattern, giving rise to a high polychoric correlation.

Figure 1 shows the cluster analysis for Romanian adoptees. The largest cluster (n=74) was cluster 2, in which there was no dysfunction on any of the seven domains (Table 4). Cluster 1 was the one with the greatest pervasiveness of dysfunction, with about half of the children (or more) showing difficulties in attachment, inattention/overactivity, peer relationships and conduct. A few also showed quasi-autistic features or cognitive impairment. Cluster 3 is largely defined by the presence of both quasi-autistic features and cognitive impairment. Cluster 4 comprised children who showed only attachment problems and inattention/overactivity (apart from one child who also showed an emotional difficulty). The mean age at entry was 10.3 months for cluster 2, 18.4 months for cluster 1, 22.3 months for cluster 3 and 20.0 months for cluster 4. The only significant contrast was that between cluster 2 and the other three clusters. The effect of age at entry was similarly shown in the trend across the three age-at-entry groups. Thus, the pro-

TABLE 3   POLYCHORIC CORRELATION AMONG DOMAINS OF DYSFUNCTION IN ROMANIAN ADOPTEE SAMPLE

	Attachment Problems	Inattention/ Overactivity	Emotional Difficulties	Autistic Features	Cognitive Impairment	Peer Difficulties
Attachment problems						
Inattention/overactivity	0.47					
Emotional difficulties	0.16	0.29				
Autistic features	0.25	0.24	0.81			
Cognitive impairment	0.20	0.26	0.05	0.66		
Peer difficulties	0.30	0.48	0.39	0.59	0.47	
Conduct problems	0.38	0.49	0.46	0.36	0.03	0.68

Correlations based on dichotomous variables; n = 157.

Cluster	Domains							Mean No. of Domains Impaired per Child
	Attachment Problems	Inattention/ Overactivity	Emotional Difficulties	Autistic Features	Cognitive Impairment	Peer Difficulties	Conduct Problems	
2 (*n*=74)	0	0	0	0	0	0	0	0.0
1 (*n*=29)	13	17	1	7	6	25	12	2.79
3 (*n*=23)	1	6	4	13	16	6	1	2.04
4 (*n*=31)	20	18	1	0	0	0	0	1.25

TABLE 4 ASSOCIATIONS BETWEEN CLUSTERS AND DOMAINS IMPAIRED

portion in the late-placed group (over 2 years) was 15% in cluster 2, compared with 38% in cluster 1, with 52% in cluster 3 and with 39% in cluster 4.

There were no gender differences among the seven domains or among the four clusters.

DISCUSSION

ESCAPE FROM DYSFUNCTION

In order to determine whether children who experience prolonged early institutional privation could nevertheless show normal psychological function at age 6 years, several years after leaving the depriving environment and after being adopted into generally well-functioning adoptive homes, we assessed dysfunction across seven different domains that were relevant at that age, occurred with a reasonable frequency and could be assessed with reasonable reliability. Normal functioning was defined according to the stringent criterion of no abnormality on any of the seven domains. As would be expected, over a fifth of the children in the non-deprived within-UK adoptee sample failed to show normal functioning on this very strict criterion.

Two findings stand out with respect to the Romanian sample. First, the proportion with normal functioning among those who left Romania before the age of 6 months was nearly as high (70%) as in the within-UK adopted sample. Second, even among the children who were over the age of 2 years when they left Romania, between a fifth and a quarter showed normal functioning on all seven domains. It is sometimes supposed that lasting damage is inevitable after prolonged early institutional privation, but our results run counter to that view. The chances of normal social functioning were substantially less the older the child was at the time of leaving the institution, but some of the children who had the most long-lasting privation appeared to be

functioning entirely normally by the age of 6 years. Of course, it would be wrong to suppose that there are no scars and it is possible that there may be sequelae that become evident only at a later age. Nevertheless, the degree of resilience shown was remarkable. Because our sample extended only up to an age of entry of 42 months, we can draw no conclusions on whether or not there is an age at which recovery becomes extremely unlikely. Extrapolation from the linear trends found on all analyses suggests that the chance of normal functioning diminishes progressively the older the child at the time when profound privation comes to an end, but it is not known whether—or when—that chance eventually ceases to exist.

The findings on pervasiveness of dysfunction make the additional point that, of the children showing some form of impairment, nearly half showed impairment on only one domain, and only just over a quarter showed impairment on at least three domains. Even within the group of children who were over the age of 2 years when they arrived in the UK, only just over a fifth showed pervasive dysfunction of that extent.

SPECIFICITY OF SEQUELAE OF INSTITUTIONAL PRIVATION

Across a large number of studies, the relative non-specificity of the patterns of psychopathology associated with psychosocial stresses and adversity has been the general finding (Rutter, 2001). Thus, negative life events carrying long-term threat have been associated with a wide range of psychiatric disorders (Brown & Harris, 1989; Goodyer, 1990), and the same applies to the experience of physical and sexual abuse (Kendall-Tackett *et al*, 1993; Trickett & McBridge-Chang, 1995). Accordingly, it might have been expected that prolonged institutional privation would be associated with a general increase in all forms of psychopathology. However, that is not what we found. Strikingly, there was no increase in either emotional or conduct problems, and although the rate of peer difficulties was twice as high in the Romanian adoptees, the difference between groups fell short of statistical significance. The finding that none of these three domains of dysfunction showed any association with the children's age at entry to the UK also indicates that it is unlikely that these particular areas of problem at 6 years of age were consequences of the children's early institutional experiences. The children are too young for any firm conclusions with respect to late sequelae but, at least up to the age of 6 years, these do not seem to be a particular consequence of the depriving institutional upbringing. Accordingly, if such problems occur in young institution-reared children, they may arise for reasons that have little to do with their early adverse upbringing. However, this might change in later childhood and adolescence, when the situations with respect to both emotional disturbance and peer relationships are different.

Although there was no single pattern that characterised children who experienced institutional privation, three main features stood out, occurring both on their own and in varying combinations. First, there were attachment disturbances of various kinds (O'Connor *et al*, 1999, 2001). These were particularly characterised by a relatively undiscriminating social approach, a seeming lack of awareness of social boundaries and a difficulty in picking up social cues on what is socially appropriate or acceptable to other people. This is a pattern also identified in a parallel Canadian study of adoptees from Romania (Chisholm *et al*, 1995; Chisholm, 1998). Second, there was the pattern of inattention/overactivity. Of the 41 children in the Romanian sample who showed this behaviour, nearly half (16) showed it in association with attachment problems, but 11 children showed only inattention/overactivity and 8 showed it in association with quasi-autistic behaviour (in 4 of the 8 cases also with attachment problems). Attention-deficit and hyperkinetic disorders have usually been thought of as psychiatric conditions that are strongly influenced by genetic factors, with psychosocial influences playing only a subsidiary role in aetiology (Taylor, 1994, 1999). It is striking, therefore, that this has emerged as one of the patterns most strongly associated with prolonged institutional privation. It could be, of course, that the key causal influence derived from nutritional privation rather than psychological privation in the institutions. On the other hand, more detailed analyses suggest that nutritional privation was not the key risk factor (further details available from the authors upon request). The finding that inattention/overactivity is also common in children reared in group homes within the UK, where nutritional priva-

tion is not an issue, suggests that it may well be the psychological features of the institutional environment that are more important (Roy *et al*, 2000). It remains to be determined whether the clinical picture of inattention/overactivity in these children is the same as in more 'ordinary' varieties of attention-deficit or hyperkinetic disorders, and a follow-up study that is now in progress should throw light on this point. Meanwhile, the evidence suggests that the problems may lie more in dealing with social group situations than with overactivity as such.

The third pattern particularly associated with a background of institutional privation was that of quasi-autistic features. Again, this appears surprising at first sight because of the evidence that autism as diagnosed in children from more ordinary backgrounds involves a strong genetic influence, with little evidence of psychosocial features playing a part in the causal process (Rutter, 2000). The clinical picture in the sample of Romanian adoptees was, however, somewhat different from that characteristic of 'ordinary' autism with respect to the tendency to improve between the ages of 4 and 6 years and the extent of social approach (Rutter *et al*, 1999).

Institutional privation was quite strongly associated with cognitive impairment (Rutter *et al*, 1998, 2000; O'Connor *et al*, 2000). In 6 of the 22 children showing cognitive impairment, this occurred without dysfunction on any of the other domains. It was, however, much more common for it to be accompanied by either quasi-autistic patterns (present in 10 out of the 20 children and in some cases with dysfunction in other domains as well) or with attachment disturbances (7 children). At the age of 6 years, there was nothing particularly distinctive about the patterns of impairment but distinctive features may be more evident at age 11 years, when the children are to be seen again. With the Romanian adoptee sample, it is also noteworthy that inattention/overactivity was more strongly associated with attachment problems (17/41 cases) than with cognitive impairment (7/41). Moreover, of these 7 children characterised by inattention/overactivity and cognitive impairment, 5 also showed attachment disturbance.

In summary, profound institutional privation was particularly associated with patterns involving attachment disturbance, inattention/overactivity, quasi-autistic features and cognitive impairment in varying combinations, but it was not associated with any marked general increase in other forms of psychopathology. There is a need for more detailed study of these psychopathological patterns; in the meantime, clinicians need to be alert to their occurrence and to the possibility that these patterns derive from early institutional privation. It is important, too, that effective methods of intervention should be developed for these privation-related problems (Rutter *et al*, 2000).

CLINICAL IMPLICATIONS

- Profound early institutional privation tends to be particularly associated with attachment disorder behaviours, inattention/overactivity (especially when associated with attachment disturbances) and quasi-autistic behaviour.
- Such privation is not followed by a significant increase in conduct problems, emotional disturbance or peer relationship difficulties other than in the context of institutional privation patterns (see first implication), at least by age 6 years.
- Profound institutional privation from infancy to age 3 years is still compatible with normal psychological functioning provided that the child has experienced several years in a good adoptive family.

LIMITATIONS

- So far, the children have been followed only up to the age of 6 years.
- Only some of the children have received detailed individual clinical assessments.
- Because the children could not be studied while in the Romanian institutions, it was not possible to determine which aspect of privation was most influential.

REFERENCES

Aldenderfer, M. & Blashfield, R. (1988) *Cluster Analysis.* San Francisco, CA: Jossey-Bass.

Ames, E. W. (1997) *The Development of Romanian Orphanage Children Adopted to Canada.* Final report to Human Resources Development, Canada. Available upon request from the Adoptive Families Association of British Columbia, Ste. #205, 15463–104th Avenue, Surrey, BC, V3R IN0, Canada.

Berument, S. K., Rutter, M., Lord, C., *et al* (1999) Autism screening questionnaire: diagnostic validity. *British Journal of Psychiatry, 175,* 444–451.

Brown, G. W. & Harris, T. O. (1989) *Life Events and Illness,* London: Unwin & Hyman.

Castle, J., Groothues, C., Bredenkamp, D., *et al* (1999) Effects of qualities of early institutional care on cognitive attainment. *American Journal of Orthopsychiatry, 40,* 424–437.

Chisholm, K. (1998) A three year follow-up of attachment and indiscriminate friendliness in children adopted from Romanian orphanages. *Child Development, 69,* 1092–1106.

——, Carter, M. C., Ames, E. W., *et al* (1995) Attachment security and indiscriminately friendly behavior in children adopted from Romanian orphanages. *Development and Psychopathology. 7,* 283–294.

Elander, J. & Rutter, M. (1996) Use and development of the Rutter parents' and teachers' scales. *International Journal of Methods in Psychiatric Research, 6,* 63–78.

Fisher, L., Ames, E. W., Chisholm, K., *et al* (1997) Problems reported by parents of Romanian orphans adopted to British Columbia. *International Journal of Behavioural Development, 20,* 67–82.

Goodyer, I. M. (1990) *Life Experiences, Development and Child Psychopathology.* Chichester: John Wiley & Sons.

Hogg, C., Rutter, M. & Richman, N. (1997) Emotional and behavioural problems in children. In *Child Psychology Portfolio* (ed. I. Sclare), pp. 1–34. Windsor: NFER–Nelson.

Johnson, D. E. (2001) Medical and developmental sequelae of early childhood institutionalization in international adoptees from Romania and the Russian Federation. In *The Effects of Early Adversity on Neurobehavioral Development* (ed. C. Nelson). Mahwah, NJ: Lawrence Erlbaum.

Kaler, S. R. & Freeman, B. J. (1994) Analysis of environmental deprivation: cognitive and social development in Romanian orphans. *Journal of Child Psychology and Psychiatry, 35,* 769–781.

Kendall-Tackett, K. A., Meyer Williams, L. & Finkelhor, D. (1993) Impact of sexual abuse on children: a review and synthesis of recent empirical studies. *Psychological Bulletin, 113,* 164–180.

Kreppner, J. M., O'Connor, T. G., Rutter, M., *et al.* (2001) Can inattention/hyperactivity be an institutional deprivation syndrome? *Journal of Abnormal Child Psychology, 29,* 513–528.

Le Couteur, A., Rutter, M., Lord, C., *et al* (1989) Autism Diagnostic Interview: a standardized investigator-based instrument. *Journal of Autism and Developmental Disorders, 19,* 363–387.

Lord, C., Rutter, M. & Le Couteur, A. (1994) Autism Diagnostic Interview–Revised: a revised version of a diagnostic interview for caregivers of individuals with possible pervasive developmental disorders. *Journal of Autism and Developmental Disorders, 24,* 659–685.

McCarthy, D. (1972) *The McCarthy Scales of Children's Abilities.* New York: Psychological Corporation/Harcourt Brace.

O'Connor, T. G., Bredenkamp, D., Rutter, M., *et al* (1999) Attachment disturbances and disorders in children exposed to early severe deprivation. *Infant Mental Health Journal, 20,* 10–29.

——, Rutter, M., Beckett, C., *et al* (2000) The effects of global severe privation on cognitive competence: extension and longitudinal follow-up. *Child Development, 72,* 376–390.

——, —— & the English and Romanian Adoptees Study Team (2001) Attachment disorder behavior following early severe deprivation: extension and longitudinal follow-up. *Journal of the American Academy of Child and Adolescent Psychiatry, 39,* 703–712.

Roy, P., Rutter, M. & Pickles, A. (2000) Institutional care: risk from family background or pattern of rearing? *Journal of Child Psychology and Psychiatry, 41,* 139–149.

Rutter, M. (2000) Genetic studies of autism: from the 1970s into the millennium. *Journal of Abnormal Child Psychology, 28,* 3–14.

—— (2001) Psychological influences: critiques, findings and research needs. *Development and Psychopathology,* in press.

—— & the English and Romanian Adoptees (ERA) Study Team (1998) Developmental catch-up, and deficit, following adoption after severe early privation. *Journal of Child Psychology and Psychiatry, 39,* 465–476.

——, Andersen-Wood, L., Beckett, C., *et al* (1999) Quasi-autistic patterns following severe early global privation. *Journal of Child Psychology and Psychiatry 40,* 537–549.

——, O'Connor, T. G., Beckett, C., *et al* (2000) Recovery and deficit following profound early deprivation. In *Inter-country Adoption: Developments, Trends and Perspectives* (ed. P. Selman), pp. 107–125. London: BAAF.

Taylor, E. (1994) Syndromes of attention deficit and overactivity. In *Child and Adolescent Psychiatry: Modern Approaches* (3rd edn) (eds M. Rutter, E. Taylor & L. Hersov), pp. 285–307. Oxford: Blackwell.

—— (1999) Developmental neuropsychopathology of attention deficit and impulsiveness. *Development and Psychopathology, II,* 607–629.

Trickett, P. K. & McBridge-Chang, C. (1995) The developmental impact of different forms of child abuse and neglect. *Developmental Review, 15,* 311–337.

QUESTIONS

1. What conclusions did earlier studies reach about children who had suffered extreme institutional privation?
2. Why did Rutter and his colleagues think it was necessary to determine whether the impairments of children who had experienced extreme privation were evident across domains of functioning or were limited to one type of outcome?
3. Which areas of functioning were assessed in this research, and why were these particular areas chosen for study?
4. In which types of dysfunction were no differences found between the Romanian adoptees and the children who had been adopted from within the UK?
5. Which types of dysfunction were more common among the Romanian adoptees than among the children who had been adopted from within the UK?
6. Did the age at which children from Romania had been adopted relate to the severity of the difficulties they showed at age 6?
7. What behavioral patterns were exhibited by Romanian adoptees who had attachment difficulties?
8. Do these results make you think that extreme institutional deprivation early in life necessarily has negative lifelong consequence? Why or why not?
9. This study followed the children until they were 6 years of age. What patterns do you predict for these two groups of children when they enter puberty? Are there any specific areas of dysfunction that may present difficulties at this later point in development?
10. Do this study's findings suggest any types of interventions that would help children who experienced extreme privation early in life?

PART III
Early Childhood

In much of the early research on child development, the age period from 2 to 5 years was largely ignored. One reason for this neglect was that many of the issues that captivated researchers, such as logical reasoning and peer relations, flourish later, in middle childhood. Another reason was that psychologists were more interested in studying the behaviors and abilities of older, school-age children, because their findings could be useful for designing educational settings and curricula.

Recent years have seen a shift in interests, with a steep increase in research on early childhood. This shift was triggered by a new stress on studying development in the period before major changes appear. Psychologists reasoned that if particular competencies are already in place in school-age children, their foundations must have been laid in early childhood. In keeping with this view, researchers began studying how the intellectual and social skills that are prevalent in the school years make their initial appearance in the early years of childhood.

The articles in this section describe some of the developmental changes of early childhood, including cognitive changes (Judy S. DeLoache, Kevin F. Miller, and Karl S. Rosengren; Angeline Lillard); patterns of family interaction that influence moral development (Peggy J. Miller, Angela R. Wiley, Heidi Fung, and Chung-Hui Liang); and changes in the social behaviors of young children (Albert Bandura, Dorothea Ross, and Sheila A. Ross; JoAnn Farver and Carollee Howes; Eleanor E. Maccoby). Together, these articles describe the developmental changes that help set the stage for the child's entry into the social and intellectual world of middle childhood.

Recent changes in family composition and work patterns in many societies have led to a need for preschool children to be cared for outside the home during the day. This social trend has raised many questions about what settings and experiences are best able to meet children's needs during the preschool years. The final article in this section, by John M. Love and colleagues, uses a contextual approach to examine the impact of child-care on development in early childhood.

18 The Credible Shrinking Room: Very Young Children's Performance with Symbolic and Nonsymbolic Relations

JUDY S. DELOACHE • KEVIN F. MILLER • KARL S. ROSENGREN

A unique and important characteristic of human intelligence is the ability to create, understand, and manipulate symbols. A symbol is an arbitrary arrangement of things–letters, numbers, images, or objects–that refers to something else. Because symbols are arbitrary, we must learn what a particular symbol refers to in order to make sense of it and use it effectively. Although our brain is capable of processing symbols, we are not born with knowledge about the symbols we encounter in everyday life. Rather, we develop knowledge of these symbols over the course of early childhood.

Developmental psychologists Judy DeLoache, Kevin Miller, and Karl Rosengren have studied children's skill at understanding symbols by asking 2½-year-olds to find a toy in a room after seeing a tiny version of the toy hidden in a scale model of the room. In the study described in the following article, the researchers used a clever manipulation that allowed them to test the dual representation hypothesis, a prominent view of early symbolic understanding. This hypothesis asserts that young children have difficulty understanding symbols because this understanding requires them to deal simultaneously with two levels of representation: the symbol itself and the object to which it refers. DeLoache and colleagues reason that this complex understanding may emerge gradually over the period of early childhood.

The results of this study may surprise you. Because our understanding of symbols like those studied in this research emerges early in life, few of us remember what it was like to think like the young children in this study. However, the findings reported in this article have been replicated by other researchers. The cognitive change involved here is important for later development, in that much of learning, especially in school, relies on the ability to understand and use symbols.

Becoming a proficient symbol user is a universal developmental task in the first years of life, but detecting and mentally representing symbolic relations can be quite challenging for young children. To test the extent to which symbolic reasoning per se is problematic, we compared the performance of 2½-year-olds in symbolic and nonsymbolic versions of a search task. The children had to use their knowledge of the location of a toy hidden in a room to draw an inference about where to find a miniature toy in a scale model of the room (and vice versa). Children in the nonsymbolic condition believed a shrinking machine had caused the room to become the model. They were much more successful than children in the symbolic condition, for whom the model served as a symbol of the room. The results provide strong support for the role of dual representation in symbol understanding and use.

Reprinted with permission of Blackwell Publishers from DeLoache, J. S., Miller, K. F., & Rosengren, K. S. (1997). The credible shrinking room: Very young children's performance with symbolic and nonsymbolic relations. *Psychological Science, 8,* 308–313.

Acknowledgments The research reported here was supported in part by Grant HD-25271 from the National Institute of Child Health and Human Development. This article was completed while the first author was a fellow at the Center for Advanced Study in the Behavioral Sciences with financial support from the John D. and Catherine T. MacArthur Foundation. Grant No. 95-32005-0. We thank R. Baillargeon and G. Clore for helpful comments on this article and K. Anderson and N. Bryant for assistance in the research.

Nothing so distinguishes humans from other species as the creative and flexible use of symbols. Abstract concepts, reasoning, scientific discovery, and other uniquely human endeavors are made possible by language and a panoply of symbolic tools, including numbers, alphabets, maps, models, and various notational systems. The universality and centrality of symbolic representation in human cognition make understanding its origins a key developmental issue.

How do children master the symbolic artifacts of their culture? They must start by recognizing that certain entities should be interpreted and responded to primarily in terms of what they stand for—their referents—rather than themselves. This is obviously a major challenge in the case of completely arbitrary symbol–referent relations. Nothing about the appearance of a numeral or a printed word suggests what it represents. Hence, it is not surprising that children have to be explicitly taught and only gradually learn the abstract relations between numerals and quantities and between printed and spoken words.

In contrast, it is generally taken for granted that highly iconic symbols (i.e., symbols that resemble their referents) are understood easily and early. Recent research, however, reveals that this assumption is unwarranted: A high degree of similarity between a symbol and its referent is no guarantee that young children will appreciate the symbol–referent relation. For example, several studies have established that very young children often fail to detect the relation between a realistic scale model and the room it represents (DeLoache, 1987, 1989, 1991; DeLoache, Kolstad, & Anderson, 1991; Dow & Pick, 1992; Marzolf & DeLoache, 1994; Uttal, Schreiber, & DeLoache, 1995). Most 2½-year-old children give no evidence of understanding that the model and room are related or that what they know about one space can be used to draw an inference about the other. Children just a few months older (3-year-olds) readily exploit this symbol–referent relation.

Why is a highly iconic relation that is so transparent to older children and adults so opaque to very young children? Many theorists have characterized symbols as possessing dual reality (Gibson, 1979; Gregory, 1970; Potter, 1979). According to the *dual representation* hypothesis (DeLoache, 1987, 1991, 1995a, 1995b), it is the double nature of symbols that poses particular difficulty for young children. To understand and use a symbol, one must mentally represent both the symbol itself and its relation to the referent. Thus, one must achieve dual representation, thinking about the concrete features of the symbol and the abstract relation between it and something else at the same time.

According to this hypothesis, the more salient the concrete aspects of a symbol are, the more diffi-

cult it is to appreciate its abstract, symbolic nature. Thus, young children's attention to a scale model as an interesting and attractive object makes it difficult for them to simultaneously think about its relation to something else. The philosopher Langer (1942) seemed to have something similar in mind when she noted that a peach would make a poor symbol because people care too much about the peach itself.

The research reported here constitutes an extremely stringent test of this hypothesis. We compared 2½-year-old children's performance in two tasks in which they had to detect and exploit the relation between a scale model and a room. In both tasks, children had to use their knowledge of where a toy was hidden in one space to infer where to find an analogous toy in the other space. In one task, there was a symbolic relation between the model and the room, whereas the other task involved a nonsymbolic relation between the same two entities. If achieving dual representation is a key obstacle in early symbolic reasoning, then performance should be superior in the nonsymbolic task, which does not require dual representation. We made this prediction even though the nonsymbolic task involved convincing children of an impossible scenario–that a machine could cause the room to shrink into the model.

Our reasoning was that if a child believes that the model is the large room after having been shrunk, then there is no symbolic relation between the two spaces; to the credulous child, the model simply *is* the room (albeit dramatically different in size). Thus, if the room is shrunk after a large toy has been hidden in it, finding a miniature toy in the model is, from the child's perspective, primarily a memory task. Dual representation is not necessary. Note that in both tasks, children must use the correspondence between the hiding places in the two spaces; their memory representation of the toy hidden behind a full-sized chair in the room must lead them to search behind the miniature chair in the model. In the symbolic task, the child knows there are two chairs, so he or she must represent the relation between them. In the nonsymbolic task, however, the child thinks there is only one chair. Superior performance in the nonsymbolic, shrinking-room task would thus provide strong support for the dual representation hypothesis.

METHOD

SUBJECTS

The subjects included 15 children (29–32 months, $M = 30$ months) in the symbolic condition and 17 (29–33 months, $M = 31$ months) in the nonsymbolic condition. Names of potential subjects came from files of birth announcements in the local newspaper, and the majority of the children were middle class and white.

MATERIALS

The same two spaces were used for both tasks. The larger space was a tentlike portable room (1.9 m × 2.5 m) constructed of plastic pipes supporting white fabric walls (1.9 m high) with a brown cardboard floor. The smaller space was a scale model (48.3 cm × 62.9 cm, with walls 38.1 cm high) of the portable room, constructed of the same materials. The room held several items of furniture (fabric-covered chair, dresser, set of shelves, basket, etc.); the model contained miniature versions of these items that were highly similar in appearance (e.g., same fabric on the chairs) to their larger counterparts. The relative size and spatial arrangement of the objects were the same in the two spaces, and the model was always in the same spatial orientation as the room. This model and room have been used in several previous studies (DeLoache et al., 1991; Marzolf & DeLoache, 1994). Figures 1a, 1b, and 1c show the arrangement of the room and model for the two tasks.

PROCEDURE

Symbolic task In this task (which was very similar to that used in the previously cited model studies), each child was given an orientation that began with the introduction of two troll dolls referred to as "Big Terry" (21 cm high) and "Little Terry" (5 cm). The correspondence between the room (described as "Big Terry's room") and the model ("Little Terry's room") and between all of the objects within them was fully and explicitly described and demonstrated by the experimenter.

On the first of four experimental trials, the child watched as the experimenter hid the larger doll somewhere in the room (e.g., behind the chair, in the basket). The child was told that the smaller toy would be hidden in the "same place" in the model. The child waited (10–15 s) as the miniature toy was hidden in the model in the adjoining area (Fig. 1a) and was then encouraged to retrieve it. The experimenter reminded the child of the corresponding locations of the two

toys: "Can you find Little Terry? Remember, he's hiding in the same place in his little room where Big Terry's hiding in his big room." If the child failed to find the toy on his or her first search, increasingly direct prompts were given until the child retrieved the toy. On the second trial, the hiding event occurred in the model instead of the room. Thus, the child watched as the miniature toy was hidden in the model, and he or she was then asked to retrieve the larger toy from the room. The space in which the hiding event occurred again alternated for the third and fourth trials.[1]

To succeed, children in the symbolic task had to realize that the room and model were related. If they did, they could figure out where to search for the target toy, even though they had not actually seen it being hidden. If they failed to represent the model–room relation, they had no way of knowing where to search. Based on numerous previous studies with this basic task, we expected a low level of performance from our 2½-year-old subjects (DeLoache, 1987, 1989, 1991; DeLoache et al., 1991; Dow & Pick, 1992; Marzolf & DeLoache, 1994).

Nonsymbolic task The initial arrangement for this task is shown in Figure 1b. In the orientation to the task, each child was introduced to "Terry" (the larger troll doll) and to "Terry's room" (the portable room). In the ensuing practice trial, the child watched as the experimenter hid the troll in the room and then waited for a count of 5 before searching. The children always succeeded in this simple memory-based retrieval (100% correct).

Next, the child was shown a "machine that can shrink toys" (actually an oscilloscope with flashing green lights—the solid rectangle in Fig. 1b). The troll doll was placed in front of it, a switch was turned on, and the child and experimenter retreated to an adjoining area and closed the door to the lab. During a delay of approximately 10 s, the child heard a tape of computer-generated tones, which were described as the "sounds the shrinking machine makes while it's working." When the sounds stopped, the child returned to the lab to find a miniature troll (5 cm high) in the place the larger one had previously occupied. Figures 1d and 1e depict the shrinking machine with the troll before and after the shrinking event.

---

1. There were two major differences between the current symbolic task and the standard model task used in previous research: First, the hiding event alternated from trial to trial between model and room. In the standard task, it always occurs in one space or the other for a given child. In studies in which half the children see the hiding event in the room and the other half in the model, there has never been any difference in performance as a function of this variable. Second, in the standard task, children always perform two retrievals: For example, after seeing the toy being hidden in the model, they first search for the larger toy in the room and then return to the model to retrieve the toy they originally observed being hidden. However, the performance of the 2½-year-olds tested in the current study did not differ from that of a group tested in the standard model task using all the same materials.

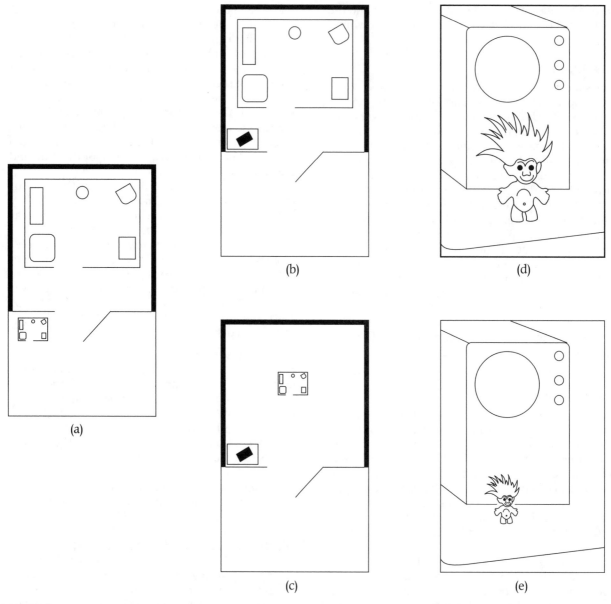

FIGURE 1

Physical arrangements for the symbolic and nonsymbolic tasks. For the symbolic task (a), the portable room was located in a large lab, surrounded on three sides by opaque curtains (represented by heavy lines); the model was located in an adjoining area. The nonsymbolic task began with the arrangement shown in (b); before the first shrinking event, the portable room was located in the lab, partially surrounded by curtains, just as it was for the symbolic task. The only difference was the presence of the shrinking machine, represented by the dark rectangle, sitting on a table. In the aftermath of the shrinking event, depicted in (c), the model sat in the middle of the area previously occupied by the portable room. The sketches in (d) and (e) show Terry the Troll before and after the demonstration shrinking event.

The child was then told that the machine could also make the troll get larger, and the process was repeated in reverse, ending with the large troll again standing in front of the machine. For the final part of the orientation, the same shrinking and enlarging demonstrations were performed with "Terry's room."

The shrinking machine was aimed at the room, and the child and experimenter waited in the adjoining area, listening to a longer (38-s) tape of the same computer sounds. When the door to the lab was opened, the scale model was revealed sitting in the middle of the area previously occupied by the room (Fig. 1c). The sight of the small model in place of the large room was very dramatic. The process was then repeated in reverse, resulting in the room replacing the model.[2]

On the first of four trials, the child watched as the larger doll was hidden in the room (the same hiding places were used as in the symbolic task), and the child was instructed to remember where it was hidden. After a 38-s delay, again spent waiting in the adjoining area listening to the sounds of the shrinking machine, the child entered the lab, where the model had replaced the portable room. The child was encouraged to find the doll: "Can you find Terry? Remember where we hid him? That's where he's hiding." The miniature troll was, of course, hidden in the model in the place that corresponded to where the child had seen the larger troll being hidden in the room. On two of the four trials, the room and large troll were shrunk, alternating with two trials in which the model and miniature troll were enlarged. A different hiding place was used on each trial.

To assess the extent to which the children accepted our shrinking-machine scenario, the experimenter and each child's accompanying parent independently rated the child on a 5-point scale, with 1 indicating that the child "firmly believed" that the machine really did shrink the objects and 5 indicating that the child "firmly did not believe" it. The average ratings were 1.1 and 1.5 for the experimenter and parents, respectively. There was only one child that the observing adults judged to be at all skeptical. The children generally reacted to the shrinking events with interest and pleasure, but not astonishment. Several children made revealing comments, such as "I want to make it big [little] again," and, while listening to the sounds of the shrinking machine, "It's working to make it big." In addition, when the children later told other family members about the session, they typically talked about the troll or the room "getting little." None ever described the situation as pretend or as a trick. We therefore feel confident that our subjects believed that the model and room were actually the same thing, which means that the shrinking-room task was, as intended, nonsymbolic (involving an identity rather than a symbolic relation).[3]

We wish to emphasize that it is unlikely that the a priori prediction of superior performance in the non-

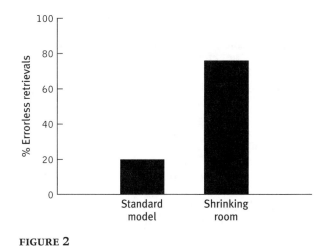

FIGURE 2

Mean number of errorless retrievals (searching first in the correct location) in the symbolic and nonsymbolic tasks.

symbolic task would be made on any basis other than the dual representation hypothesis. Indeed, various aspects of the procedures would lead to the opposite expectation. For example, getting and keeping toddlers motivated in experimental situations is always a challenge; and the shrinking-room task was more complicated, required more verbal communication, and took longer than the standard symbolic task. In addition, the delay between the hiding event and the opportunity to search for the toy was substantially longer in the shrinking-room task (ca. 50–60 s) than in the standard symbolic task (ca. 10–15 s). Delays between hiding and retrieval are known to cause the performance of even older children to deteriorate dramatically in the standard model task (Uttal et al., 1995).

RESULTS

The critical question was whether performance in the nonsymbolic (shrinking-room) condition would be superior to performance in the symbolic (model) condition. Figure 2 shows the mean number of errorless retrievals (searching first at the correct location) achieved in the two tasks.

---

2. An elaborate scenario supported the shrinking and enlarging events. When the child first saw the artificial room, it was surrounded on three sides by black curtains, which were visible only on the sides in front of the portable room (Fig. 1b). For each shrinking event, as soon as the child had left the lab, one assistant turned on a tape recorder to begin the shrinking-machine sounds (thereby concealing any noises made in the lab). Two other assistants pulled the artificial room behind the curtains, and the first placed the model, with the miniature troll in the appropriate position, in the center of the space formerly occupied by the room. In the enlarging events, the model was replaced by the room.

3. The parents of all the participants in this study were fully informed of the procedures to be followed, and a parent was present throughout each experimental session. The children's assent was always obtained before the sessions began. After the completion of their sessions, the children in the nonsymbolic (shrinking-room) condition were debriefed: They were shown the two dolls and the model and room together, and the experimenter explained that the machine did not really shrink or enlarge them.

The children in the symbolic task achieved a mean of only 0.8 errorless retrievals over four trials ($SE = 0.2$), a rate not different from chance. (We conservatively estimated chance at 25%, based on our use of four hiding places; however, it is actually lower because there are additional possible hiding places.) Individual performance in this task was similarly poor: Six of the 15 children never found the toy, and 6 retrieved it only once. No child succeeded on more than two of the four trials. These children understood that they were supposed to search for a hidden toy on each trial, and they were happy to do so, but they apparently failed to realize that their knowledge of one space could be applied to the other.

The poor performance of the children in the symbolic task (19%) is exactly what would be expected from previous model studies. In research in our own and other labs using a variety of different models and rooms, 2½-year-olds reliably average around 20% successful retrievals.

In contrast, children in the nonsymbolic task were very successful. Performance in the nonsymbolic (shrinking-room) condition was well above chance—3.1 errorless retrievals ($SE = 0.2$)—and significantly better than the performance of the children in the symbolic condition. Twelve of the 17 subjects achieved three or more errorless retrievals, and 7 of those had perfect scores. The difference between the two tasks was the only significant result in a 2 (task) × 2 (gender) analysis of variance, $F(1, 28) = 51.5$, $p < .0001$. Performance did not differ on trials in which the hiding event occurred in the room and the child searched in the model versus trials in which the hiding and search spaces were the reverse.

The main result of this study has been replicated, both in an additional study with 2½-year-olds and in two studies in which the same logic was applied to a different age group. Using two different, more difficult versions of the model task, we found the same pattern of results with 3-year-olds as occurred with the 2½-year-olds in the present study—significantly better performance in the nonsymbolic, shrinking-room version than in the symbolic model task (DeLoache, 1995a; Marzolf, 1994).

DISCUSSION

We conclude that a major challenge to detecting and using symbolic relations stems from their inherent dual reality and the necessity of achieving dual representation (DeLoache, 1987, 1995a, 1995b). The model task was more difficult than the shrinking-room task because the former required dual representation, whereas the latter eliminated the need for it. The research reported here provides strong support for a theoretical account of early symbol understanding

and use in which young children's ability to use symbols is considered to be limited by several factors, a key one being the difficulty of achieving dual representation (DeLoache, 1995a, 1995b). Relatively limited information processing capacity makes it difficult for younger children to keep two representations active at the same time, and limited cognitive flexibility makes it especially difficult for them to mentally represent a single entity in two different ways.

The study reported here provides especially strong support against criticism of this theoretical account of early symbol use. It has been claimed that the use of a symbol such as a scale model requires nothing more than simply detecting some kind of correspondence between the symbol and referent (Blades & Spencer, 1994; Lillard, 1993; Perner, 1991). One claim is that the child succeeds on each trial by noticing that the current hiding place of the miniature toy corresponds to the full-sized hiding place of the larger toy, without ever appreciating the higher level relation between the two spaces.

The simple correspondence view cannot explain the current results. For one thing, it offers no account of how children's performance depends on the kind of relation that must be represented. In both tasks, corresponding items in the two spaces must be mentally linked; memory for the object concealing the original toy must support a search at the corresponding object. The challenge in the nonsymbolic task is simply to recognize that object in its new form. The challenge in the symbolic task is to represent the relation between that object and the other one it stands for.

Furthermore, simply detecting the correspondence between matching items does not support successful performance in the symbolic task. In a recent study (DeLoache, 1995a), 2½-year-old children readily matched the items in the room to the corresponding items in the model, yet still failed the subsequent standard model task. Establishing object correspondences is thus necessary but not sufficient for reasoning from one space to the other. Although the simple correspondence account has the appearance of parsimony, because it posits a lower level explanation than dual representation, it cannot account for results presented here and elsewhere in support of dual representation (DeLoache, 1991; Marzolf & DeLoache, 1994).

At the most general level, the research reported here indicates that it is the nature of a child's mental representation of the relation between two entities that governs the child's ability to reason from one to the other. Very young children can reason successfully based on an identity relation, even when it results from the complex and novel scenario of a shrinking machine. They fail to appreciate a symbolic relation between the same two entities, even though it is explained and demonstrated. Despite the importance and universality of symbolization, very young children are quite conservative when it comes to interpreting novel objects as symbols.

The dual representation hypothesis, which received strong support from the study reported here, has important practical implications. For example, it calls into question the assumption commonly made by educators that children will readily comprehend the meaning of manipulables—concrete objects used to instantiate abstract mathematical concepts (Uttal, Scudder, & DeLoache, 1997). One must take care to ensure that children appreciate the relation between, for example, the size of blocks and numerical quantities before using the blocks for teaching purposes. Similar doubt is cast on the widespread practice of using anatomically explicit dolls to interview young children in child-abuse investigations. Young children's difficulty with dual representation suggests that the relevant self–doll relation may not be clear to them; if so, using dolls may not be helpful and might even be counterproductive. Recent research has supported this conjecture: Several studies have reported no advantage to using dolls to interview 3-year-old children about events they have experienced (Bruck, Ceci, Francoeur, & Renick, 1995; DeLoache, Anderson, & Smith, 1995; DeLoache & Marzolf, 1995; Goodman & Aman, 1990; Gordon et al., 1993).

One other aspect of the results reported here merits attention. The 2½-year-old children had no difficulty dealing with the size transformations supposedly effected by the shrinking machine. This finding is consistent with research showing that very young children represent and rely on geometric features of a space (Hermer & Spelke, 1994). The children's ability to mentally scale the two spaces in the present research may have been assisted by the fact that the size transformations preserved the geometric properties of the original space, including its overall shape, the relative sizes and positions of the objects, and the distances among them.

Spatial representations other than scale models also pose problems for young children. Only with difficulty can 3-year-olds use a simple map to locate a hidden object, and their ability to do so is easily disrupted (Bluestein & Acredolo, 1979). Older preschool children often fail to interpret aerial photographs consistently (Liben & Downs, 1992); they may, for example, describe one feature of an aerial photo correctly as a river but another as a piece of cheese. Thus, figuring out the nature and use of spatial symbols is a persistent challenge for young children.

The current study, along with other research on the early understanding and use of symbols, makes it clear that one can never assume that young children will detect a given symbol–referent relation, no matter how transparent that relation seems to adults or older children. Young children may perceive and form a meaningful interpretation of both the symbol and the entity it stands for without representing the relation between them.

REFERENCES

Blades, M., & Spencer, C. (1994). The development of children's ability to use spatial representations. In H. Reese (Ed.), *Advances in child development and behavior* (Vol. 25, pp. 157–199). New York: Academic Press.

Bluestein, N., & Acredolo, L. (1979). Developmental change in map reading skills. *Child Development, 50,* 691–697.

Bruck, M., Ceci, S. J., Francoeur, E., & Renick, A. (1995). Anatomically detailed dolls do not facilitate preschoolers, reports of a pediatric examination involving genital touching. *Journal of Experimental Psychology: Applied, 1,* 95–109.

DeLoache, J. S. (1987). Rapid change in the symbolic functioning of very young children. *Science, 238,* 1556–1557.

DeLoache, J. S. (1989). Young children's understanding of the correspondence between a scale model and a larger space. *Cognitive Development, 4,* 121–139.

DeLoache, J. S. (1991). Symbolic functioning in very young children: Understanding of pictures and models. *Child Development, 62,* 736–752.

DeLoache, J. S. (1995a). Early symbolic understanding and use. In D. Medin (Ed.), *The psychology of learning and motivation* (Vol. 33, pp. 65–114). New York: Academic Press.

DeLoache, J. S. (1995b). Early understanding and use of symbols. *Current Directions in Psychological Science, 4,* 109–113.

DeLoache, J. S., Anderson, K., & Smith, C. M. (1995, April). *Interviewing children about real-life events.* Paper presented at the annual meeting of the Society for Research in Child Development, Indianapolis, IN.

DeLoache, J. S., Kolstad, D. V., & Anderson, K. N. (1991). Physical similarity and young children's understanding of scale models. *Child Development, 62,* 111–126.

DeLoache, J. S., & Marzolf, D. P. (1995). The use of dolls to interview young children. *Journal of Experimental Child Psychology, 60,* 155–173.

Dow, G. A., & Pick, H. L. (1992). Young children's use of models and photographs as spatial representations. *Cognitive Development, 7,* 351–363.

Gibson, J. J. (1979). *The ecological approach to visual perception.* Boston: Houghton Mifflin.

Goodman, G. S., & Aman, C. (1990). Children's use of anatomically detailed dolls to recount an event. *Child Development, 61,* 1859–1871.

Gordon, B. N., Ornstein, P. A., Nida, R. E., Follmer, A., Crenshaw, M. C., & Albert, G. (1993). Does the use of dolls facilitate children's memory of visits to the doctor? *Applied Cognitive Psychology, 7,* 459–474.

Gregory, R. L. (1970). *The intelligent eye.* New York: McGraw-Hill.

Hermer, L., & Spelke, E. (1994). A geometric process for spatial reorientation in young children. *Nature, 370,* 57–69.

Langer, S. K. (1942). *Philosophy in a new key.* Cambridge, MA: Harvard University Press.

Liben, L. L., & Downs, R. M. (1992). Developing an understanding of graphic representations in children and adults: The case of GEO-Graphics. *Cognitive Development, 7,* 331–349.

Lillard, A. S. (1993). Pretend play skills and the child's theory of mind. *Child Development, 64,* 348–371.

Marzolf, D. P. (1994, April). *Representing and mapping relations in a symbolic task.* Paper presented at the International Conference on Infant Studies, Paris.

Marzolf, D. P., & DeLoache, J. S. (1994). Transfer in young children's understanding of spatial representations. *Child Development, 64,* 1–15.

Perner, J. (1991). *Understanding the representational mind.* Cambridge, MA: Bradford Books/MIT Press.

Potter, M. C. (1979). Mundane symbolism: The relations among objects, names, and ideas. In N. R. Smith & M. B. Franklin (Eds.), *Symbolic functioning in childhood* (pp. 41–65). Hillsdale, NJ: Erlbaum.

Uttal, D. H., Schreiber, J. C., & DeLoache, J. S. (1995). Waiting to use a symbol: The effects of delay on children's use of models. *Child Development, 66,* 1875–1891.

Uttal, D. H., Scudder, K. V., & DeLoache, J. S. (1997). Manipulatives as symbols: A new perspective on the use of concrete objects to teach mathematics. *Journal of Applied Developmental Psychology, 18,* 37–54.

QUESTIONS

1. What are symbols, and why are they difficult for young children to understand?
2. What are iconic symbols, and at which age do children begin to understand this type of symbol?
3. What is the dual representation hypothesis?
4. What features of a symbol make it more difficult for young children to understand its abstract and representational nature?
5. What tasks did the investigators develop to test the dual representation hypothesis in young children?
6. What effect did shrinking the room have on the performance of the 2½-year-olds in this study?
7. Do you agree with the reasoning that if children believe that the model is actually a large room that has been shrunk, they do not need symbolic representation to find the toy?
8. What developmental changes do the authors suggest may explain the increase in understanding of symbols that occurs over early childhood?
9. What do you think this study suggests about young children's interest in and understanding of toys that are exact models or replicas of large-scale objects?
10. What implications do these findings have for the use of anatomically correct dolls in interviewing young children in legal cases involving sexual abuse?

19 Personal Storytelling as a Medium of Socialization in Chinese and American Families

PEGGY J. MILLER • ANGELA R. WILEY • HEIDI FUNG • CHUNG-HUI LIANG

From very early in life, children are told stories about themselves and their families. In recent years, developmental psychologists have become increasingly interested in how parents' personal storytelling may contribute to children's socialization. In the following article, Peggy J. Miller and her coauthors describe their research on storytelling practices in European-American and Taiwanese middle-class families with 2½-year-old children. The researchers took great pains to conduct their study in such a way that they could trace the cultural values that help organize the content and form of parent–child storytelling. Although the number of families that participated was relatively small (six families in Taiwan and six families in the United States), the information collected from each family was extensive. Of particular interest to the investigators were the ways in which parents in these two communities told their children stories about past transgressions by the children. A transgression was defined as any behavior that violated either a social or a moral rule.

Prior research by Miller and her colleagues had shown that parents in Taiwan and the United States place different emphases on their children's past transgressions in their personal storytelling. In addition, when transgressions are discussed in these two communities, parents frame them for children in ways that correspond with broader socialization goals in their respective settings. Whereas Taiwanese parents are more evaluative and promote more self-critical analyses by children, European-American parents tend to characterize transgressions more favorably and to encourage more positive self-evaluations by children. In this article, the researchers follow up on these earlier observations by examining structural features of parent–child storytelling. Their goal was to identify more explicitly the similarities and differences in parent–child storytelling in these two communities. To this end, they conducted a detailed analysis of the content, function, and structure of parent–child interaction during personal storytelling. The results indicate that, beginning early in a child's life, personal storytelling by caregivers imparts important information about the values of the family and of the cultural community.

The goal of this study was to determine how personal storytelling functions as a socializing practice within the family context in middle-class Taiwanese and middle-class European American families. The data consist of more than 200 naturally occurring stories in which the past experiences of the focal child, aged 2,6, were narrated. These stories were analyzed at 3 levels: content, function, and structure. Findings converged across these analytic levels, indicating that personal storytelling served overlapping yet distinct socializing functions in the 2 cultural cases. In keeping with the high value placed on didactic narrative within the Confucian tradition, Chinese families were more likely to use personal storytelling to convey moral and social standards. European American families did not treat stories of young children's past experiences as a didactic resource but instead employed stories as a medium of entertainment and affirmation. These findings suggest not

Reprinted with permission of Blackwell Publishers from Miller, P. J., Wiley, A. R., Fung, H., & Liang, C. H. (1997). Personal storytelling as a medium of socialization in Chinese and American families. *Child Development, 68*, 557–568.

Acknowledgments This research was supported, in part, by a grant from the Spencer Foundation awarded to P. J. Miller and by grant no. CUHK 320/95H awarded to H. Fung by the Research Grants Council, Hong Kong Government. An earlier version of this work was presented at the biennial meeting of the Society for Research in Child Development in Indianapolis, Indiana, March 1995. We wish to thank the families who participated in this study.

only that personal storytelling operates as a routine socializing practice in widely different cultures but also that it is already functionally differentiated by 2,6.

> If he does not learn when he is young, what will he be when old? [*The Three Character Classic*]

> When you know your faults, you must correct them. [*The Thousand Character Classic*]

> Men at their birth are naturally good. Their natures are much the same; their habits become widely different. If foolishly there is no teaching, the nature will deteriorate. The right way in teaching is to attach the utmost importance to thoroughness. [*The Three Character Classic*]

INTRODUCTION

It has been well established during the last decade that middle-class European American children are able to narrate their past experiences in conversation from a remarkably early age (e.g., Fivush, Gray, & Fromhoff, 1987; Nelson, 1993a; Peterson & McCabe, 1983). These findings have not only provided new insights into the origins of autobiographical memory (e.g., Fivush & Hamond, 1990; Nelson, 1993a, 1993b) but have sparked increasing interest in the role that personal storytelling plays in socializing young children into the meaning systems of their culture (e.g., Bruner, 1990; Engel, 1995; Fivush, 1993; Miller, 1994; Miller & Moore, 1989; Nelson, 1989). Although there is growing evidence that youngsters from diverse sociocultural traditions in the United States participate in personal storytelling (Eisenberg, 1985; Heath, 1983; Miller, Mintz, Hoogstra, Fung, & Potts, 1992; Miller, Potts, Fung, Hoogstra, & Mintz, 1990; Miller & Sperry, 1988; Sperry & Sperry, 1996), the record with respect to non-Western cultures is virtually nonexistent. In addition, little is known about how personal storytelling is actually practiced as part of everyday family life in any cultural group. This article addresses both of these gaps by way of comparative study of personal storytelling in middle-class Taiwanese and middle-class European American families. We seek to understand how personal storytelling functions as a socializing practice within the family context, focusing on the third year of life.

Taiwanese culture offers a particularly interesting case for comparison with European American culture in that it is deeply rooted in the Confucian tradition, one of the world's most durable ideological systems. Contemporary historians maintain that Confucian values are still alive in Taiwan and other Chinese cultures despite the massive economic, political, and social changes that have occurred in this century

(Dennerline, 1988; Spence, 1992). Moreover, a number of scholars have argued that we cannot fully understand Chinese childrearing without understanding Confucian values (Chao, 1994; Chu, 1972; Wu, 1981), and reviews of the literature conclude that Confucian teachings concerning childrearing are still evident today in patterns of childhood socialization (Ho, 1986; Wu, 1996). Within the Confucian tradition, shame is seen as a virtue, and a high value is placed on teaching, strict discipline, and acceptance of social obligations. According to Wu (1996), a key principle of Confucian parenting is that children be taught and disciplined from an early age, as soon as they can talk and walk. An important socialization goal is the development of filial piety. Filial piety refers to the principle that one conduct oneself so as to bring honor and not disgrace to the family name and encompasses such precepts as devotion and obedience to parents, taking care of one's aged parents, performing the ceremonial duties of ancestral worship, and avoiding harm to one's body (Ho, 1996).

For centuries, filial piety was taught through narrative exemplars of extraordinary filial deeds, written collections of which are still in use in Taiwan (Wu, 1981). Similarly, ancient "primers" such as *The Thousand Character Classic* and *The Three Character Classic* are widely available in Taiwanese bookstores. These texts have been used for hundreds of years to teach children to read and to impart moral lessons and knowledge of Chinese history. Woven throughout these collections of adages are stories of exemplary deeds. For example, *The Three Character Classic* contains a series of stories illustrating the diligence of scholars, followed by an explicit exhortation to the young reader to emulate these examples. These and other classic texts attest to the high value placed on didactic narrative within the Confucian tradition. To our knowledge, however, no one has investigated whether this reliance on didactic narrative to educate the young extends to personal storytelling within the family context.

This article builds upon an earlier investigation in which we began to address this question (Miller, Fung, & Mintz, 1996). Focusing on personal storytelling with 2½-year-olds, we found that Chinese caregivers and children from Taiwan were more likely than their European American counterparts to tell stories about the child's past transgressions, to repeatedly invoke moral and social rules, and to structure their stories so as to establish the child's transgression as the point of the story. Discourse analysis revealed that even in those rare instances in which a European American child's past transgression was narrated, a qualitatively different interpretation of the child's past experience was constructed, one that acknowledged yet downplayed the child's wrongdoing. We concluded that the Chinese families were operating with an explicitly evaluative, overtly self-critical interpretive framework, whereas the European American families were using an implicitly evaluative, overtly self-affirmative framework. The latter seemed to go to considerable lengths to portray the child in a favorable light, possibly as a way of protecting or enhancing the child's self-esteem.

The implicitly evaluative, overtly self-affirmative framework seems to overlap with what Harwood, Miller, and Irizarry (1995) call "self-maximization". They found that self-maximization, which included the component of self-confidence or self-esteem, was used by European American mothers to describe qualities they hoped their children would possess as adults. Although the mainstream American emphasis on self-esteem and self-expression has come under increased scrutiny in recent years, particularly as it applies to educational practice (Damon, 1995; Katz, 1993; Tobin, 1995), little is known about the practices that caregivers use to promote young children's self-esteem within the family context. Emphasizing the positive in narrations of children's past experiences may be one such practice.

The purpose of the current study was to extend and deepen the work reported by Miller et al. (1996), thereby fleshing out the emerging picture of similarities and differences in the ways in which personal storytelling is actually practiced with 2-year-olds in middle-class Taiwanese and middle-class European American families. Specifically, we expected that Chinese 2-year-olds and their caregivers would be more likely than their European American counterparts to us personal storytelling didactically, that is, to impart moral and social standards. We addressed this question at three levels of analysis. At the content level, were Chinese families more likely to narrate stories of the child's past transgressions? An affirmative answer to this question would corroborate Miller et al.'s (1996) finding with a much larger corpus of naturally occurring narrations of personal experience. At the functional level, were Chinese stories more likely to be occasioned by an immediately preceding transgression by the child? At the structural level, were Chinese stories more likely to end with a didactic coda that drew out the implications of the child's past actions for the present or future?

METHOD

The study is part of a larger comparative project designed to investigate how personal storytelling is used to socialize young children within the family context in a variety of communities (Miller, 1996; Miller et al., 1992, 1996). Ethnographic fieldwork was combined with extensive audio and video recording of naturally occurring talk in the home. Researchers spent at least 2 years in the field and collected both cross-sectional and longitudinal observations, encompassing the period from 2,6 to 5,0 and involving at least a dozen families at each research site.

PARTICIPANTS

This article is based on data from six Chinese families in Taipei, Taiwan, and six American families in Longwood (a pseudonym), a European American community in Chicago. The focal children were 2,6 ($M = 2,6$, $range = 2,5$ to $2,9$), and each sample was balanced by gender of child. All of the children had at least one sibling. The samples were comparable in that both consisted of two-parents families who lived in large cities, owned their own homes, and were economically secure. The parents were college educated. All of the focal children had mean length of utterances of at least 2.5 morphemes, computed according to Brown (1973). All participants are referred to by pseudonyms.

RESEARCH SITES

Despite these similarities, the children in this study inhabited very different worlds. (See Miller et al., 1996, for a more detailed description of the research sites.)

Taipei. Taipei, the largest city in Taiwan, Republic of China, has undergone extraordinarily rapid change in the second half of this century. When the Chinese nationalists arrived on the island in 1949, Taiwan was a rural society. In what has come to be known as the "economic miracle," an agrarian economy was transformed into an industrialized economy in matter of decades. By 1990 Taiwan had become a consumer society, with an average per capita income exceeding US$8,000, a low rate of unemployment, a relatively equitable distribution of income, and a trade surplus envied by other nations (Simon & Kau, 1992). In the political sphere change has been slower but no less dramatic. Martial law was lifted in 1987, and presidential elections were held in 1996, completing the transition from the Kuomintang dictatorship to a democratic form of government.

The parents in our study are members of the first "middle-class" generation in Taiwan. The sample includes children whose grandparents came to Taiwan from mainland China as well as those whose grandparents were native-born Taiwanese. Most of the parents had a close relative who resided in the United States or Canada. Although half of the parents spoke fluent Taiwanese, all used Mandarin Chinese, the country's official language, with their children. In addition to representing the ethnic and linguistic diversity characteristic of contemporary Taipei, the families also encompass religious diversity. Folk religion, Christianity, and Buddhism were all practiced, sometimes within the same family.

Due to continuing migration from outlying areas, space is at a premium in Taipei. Middle-class families live in small apartments, and families tend not to have strong ties to particular locales. Taipei is not organized into neighborhoods, and there is little residential segregation by class or ethnicity. Within the context of very rapid urban growth, a variety of pragmatic factors—such as cost, preference for new versus old buildings, access to housing owned by a relative, access to good schools or mass transportation—seem to guide residential choice. Although two-generation households are quickly becoming the norm, replacing the traditional three-generation household, the families in our study maintained close ties to grandparents and other family members. The children were taken care of by their mothers or by a female relative if the mother worked outside the home. The early years of life were spent in close physical and emotional proximity to this primary caregiver. Although focal children had their own bed in a room shared with a sibling, they slept with the caregiver.

Caregivers held high standards for their children's conduct. Two-year-olds were expected to successfully negotiate a home environment that was not childproofed, offering the temptations of open cabinets and fragile objects. They were expected to listen attentively to their elders, comprehend what was said, and behave accordingly. Misdeeds were dealt with promptly, and rules of conduct were rehearsed. Caregivers also corrected grammar and mispronunciations and rehearsed rhymes and poems. They made sure that 2-year-olds knew their full name, parents' names, address, and phone number. Literacy skills were actively cultivated. Parents read to the children and taught them to draw, and some used flash cards to teach Chinese characters or numbers. All of the children were toilet trained by 1,6, and several of the mothers reported that they had begun toilet training at 6 months of age. When the first author visited the families and gave each child a wrapped present decorated with small candies, she was astonished at their self-control. In keeping with proper etiquette, even the 2-year-olds waited until the guests departed to open their gifts.

Longwood.   Longwood is located within the city of Chicago and forms a distinct neighborhood. It has been a home to Irish Americans for nearly a century, and many of its residents have deep roots in the community. Holidays such as St. Patrick's Day are observed with great enthusiasm and include an annual neighborhood parade. The neighborhood is known locally for the beauty of its streets and homes, several of which are on the national historic registry. Civic organizations have worked actively to preserve the special character and small-town ambience of the neighborhood. Many Longwood residents participate in a cohesive social network based on a common cultural heritage and active involvement in one of the three local Catholic churches. Most send their children to the local Catholic school which they themselves attended. Thus, the Longwood families, in contrast to their counterparts in Taipei, were tied by cultural tradition, religion, family history, and active commitment to a community that had a distinct identity within the larger urban environment.

Most Longwood families live in spacious single-family dwellings situated on quiet, tree-lined streets. The interiors of the homes reflect a child-centered emphasis. Each family had a playroom or family room, and each child, even the youngest, had his or her own space and property. Children either had their own bedrooms, or two same-sex siblings shared a bedroom.

The mothers in the sample expressed the belief that young children should be cared for routinely by their own mothers. Several also stated that they chose to stay home with their children because they did not want to miss the opportunity to observe and influence their children's development. Like the "mainstream" mothers described by Ochs and Schieffelin (1984), the Longwood mothers engaged in a variety of practices that accommodated the environment to the child: these included childproofing, use of child-scaled objects and furniture, and abundant provision of toys. These practices are likely related to a concern for the vulnerability of the child's status and the protection of the child's emotional as well as physical well-being. Toilet training was undertaken with a relaxed attitude and was accomplished in most cases by 3 years of age. The Longwood mothers talked and listened to their children, read to them, and pretended with them. These were not just enjoyable experiences, they felt, but ways in which they could provide the kind of focused attention that children need to develop optimally and to feel happy and good about themselves. In discussing a popular preschool teacher, several mothers spoke admiringly of her ability to foster children's self-esteem.

Longwood preschoolers were expected to follow rules of appropriate conduct. When children misbehaved in minor ways—refusing to share with a playmate, quarreling with a sibling, hanging on the dining room curtains—parents intervened promptly and repeatedly if necessary. At the same time, most parents expressed respect for young children's willfulness and appreciated the clever ways in which their youngsters attempted to get what they wanted. When a serious behavior problem occurred, such as hitting or biting another person or an uncontrollable temper tantrum, parents resorted to "time out" procedures or revoked a privilege or treat. For the most part, however, these incidents were not dwelled on by parents and, once settled, were no longer the focus of attention.

In sum, the two groups of children whom we studied in 1988–1991 were not "typical" Taiwanese or "typical" Americans and should not be taken as such. They were members of families who occupied a relatively privileged position within their respective societies, and they created a particular cultural idiom at a particular moment in history. Although Longwood has changed over the decades, what stands out is the extent to which its identity and continuity with the past have been preserved. Families take pride in their traditional values and child- and family-centered way of life, rooted in long-term prosperity. In Taipei, the balance between change and continuity is tipped in the other direction. The Chinese children inhabited a world that differed substantially from those in which their parents and grandparents grew up. Yet, as we shall see, traditional Chinese values were still visible, sturdy and intricate, in everyday narrative practices.

PROCEDURE

Because we were interested in the way that personal storytelling was practiced as part of everyday family life, we took several steps to insure the cultural and ecological validity of our observations. First, we assigned researchers to cultures with which they were familiar—a Taiwanese researcher worked with the Taiwanese families and an American researcher worked with the American families. This "matching" of researchers and field sites meant that researchers could draw on their cultural expertise in recruiting and interacting with the families in a manner that was culturally appropriate. Second, the study was conducted in two phases, a fieldwork phase, followed by a series of video-recorded observations in the home. During the fieldwork phase, the researchers familiarized themselves with the communities through informal observation and collection of documentary materials and recruited families for the observational phase. Most recruitment in both cultural cases was accomplished through informal networks of friends and family. During the fieldwork phase, the researcher also made repeated visits to the homes of the families who agreed to participate in the observational phase of the study; this was done so that researcher and families could become comfortable with one another prior to the first observation session.

The first observation session occurred when the focal child was 2,6. (This article is based only on this initial observation session.) Each observation consisted of two 2-hr video recordings of family interaction in the home scheduled within a few days of one another. Observations occurred at a time that was convenient for the primary caregiver, usually a weekday morning or afternoon. The primary caregiver was always present; often siblings were present as well. Fathers were usually working.

The caregivers were told that we wanted to learn more about how young children learn to communicate as part of ordinary family life, including how they learn to tell stories, to play, and to convey emotions. The researchers did not attempt to script family–child interactions, elicit narrations, or direct the caregivers to elicit narrations from the child. A good deal of thought was given to the problem of how the researchers should participate with the families. We decided that for the researcher to adopt a determinedly silent stance or to act invisible would undermine rather then promote the ecological and cultural validity of the observations of narrative talk (see Miller & Hoogstra, 1992). Instead, each researcher tried to participate as a family friend who had stopped by for a casual visit; at the same time she was careful not to "push" narrative talk. Within these parameters, the researchers were left to their own ingenuity in negotiating a culturally appropriate way of interacting with the families, drawing again upon their cultural intuitions. Elsewhere, we have described some of the ways in which the Chinese and American researchers differed in their participation (Miller, 1996; Miller et al., 1996).

TRANSCRIPTION AND IDENTIFICATION OF NARRATIONS

The first step in organizing the data involved extracting the naturally occurring stories of personal experience from the ongoing flow of recorded talk and interaction. We defined narrations of personal experience as events involving the focal child and at least one other family member in which the focal child's past experiences were recounted in temporal order. These stories referred to a nonimmediate past event (i.e., an event that occurred prior to the taping session) or class of past events in which the focal child was portrayed as a protagonist. Narrations included both "co-narrations" in which the child (as co-narrator) contributed at least two substantive, on-topic utterances and co-narrators referred to the child in the second person and "stories about the child" which were told in the third person, often with no verbal contribution by the child, who participated as onlooker or co-present other. Miller et al. (1996) found that these two subtypes did not differ in terms of types of interpretive frameworks used. Moreover, the analyses below did not differentiate these two subtypes; therefore, except for the initial description of the basic corpus of stories, we present findings for the combined subtypes.

In each cultural sample, two coders independently viewed and coded four 30-min randomly chosen segments of videotaped speech and interaction. (The Chinese data were coded by Chinese coders, and the American data were coded by American coders.) First, each coder simply identified each episode of a narration. The proportion of agreement for the Chinese sample was 1.00 ($N = 18$), whereas agreement between American coders was .94 ($N = 16$). Second, a more stringent estimate of intercoder reliability addressed the boundaries of the stories. At this level, coders identified the opening and final utterance of each story. The opening utterance was defined as the first utterance that referred to the past event or class of past events. The final utterance was the last utterance that referred directly to the specific past event or class of past events. The proportion of agreement for boundaries was .94 ($N = 36$) for the Chinese sample and .83 ($N = 32$) for the American sample.

The present study is based on the complete corpus of narrations extracted from 24 hr of observations for each cultural group. The narrations, including preceding and succeeding interactions, were transcribed in English for the European American families and in Mandarin Chinese for the Chinese families, using the CHILDES system (MacWhinney, 1991). Each transcript was checked and rechecked at least three times by two different transcribers.

CODING OF NARRATIONS

Three codes, corresponding to analyses at the levels of content, function, and structure, respectively, were applied to all co-narrations. In each case, at least one-quarter of all stories were coded for intercoder reliability estimates. Intercoder agreement ranged from .83 to 1.00. (Again, the Chinese data were coded by Chinese coders and the American data by American coders, with repeated joint coding sessions to ensure that the same definitions were followed for the two data sets.)

Content coding: Narrated transgressions. Narrated transgressions were those narrations in which the focal child was portrayed as committing a violation of a social or moral rule in the past event, as interpreted from the perspective of at least one of the narrating participants. Transgressive interpretations were conveyed through a variety of linguistic and paralinguistic means. In the absence of such textual evidence, the story was not counted as a narrated transgression. For example, if the narrators indicated that the focal child broke another child's toy but said that he or she did so accidentally, the narration was not coded as a narrated transgression. Narrated transgressions were identified on the basis of the following kinds of tex-

tual evidence: (1) Explicit evaluation of the child's past act (e.g., "How *naughty!*" said of LongLong by his mother, referring to an event in which LongLong did not let his parents do their shopping; Pat's brother began a story with "When me and Pat were being *bad* boys"); (2) Implicit evaluation of the child's past act, as indicated by intonation, stress, and/or implicit verbal characterizations (e.g., Angu's mother, speaking in a *disapproving tone of voice*, told of a past incident, saying, "In the middle of the night, when you were about to go to bed, you then took pens to draw on my wall!"; Karin's mother, speaking in an *exasperated tone of voice*, said, "*Oh, man*, all day long in the middle of the night, I'll hear Wee Sing," in reference to the child getting up in the middle of the night to watch a video); (3) Explicit reference to the violated rule in the past event (e.g., after his grandmother recounted an incident in which YoYo cried inappropriately, YoYo said, "*Now, I don't cry at all*"; After recounting how Karin sucked her thumb, Karin's mother said, "What does Daddy say?" Karin: "*Get that thumb out of that mouth!*").

Function coding: Occasioning transgressions. Whereas the "narrated transgression" code applied to the child's behavior in the past event, this code applied to the child's behavior in the present. We wanted to know whether narrations of the child's past transgressions were occasioned by the child's transgression in the here and now, that is, immediately preceding the narration itself. In other words, did the interactants take the child's present transgression as an opportunity to remind the child of a past transgression? Again, only transgressions that were interpreted as such by at least one of the participants were coded as occasioning transgressions. Transgressive interpretations were conveyed through the same linguistic and paralinguistic means described for "narrated transgressions." For example, when LongLong began to ride his bicycle on a comforter, his mother scolded him and tried to get him to stop (occasioning transgression); she then reminded him of an earlier incident in which he had misbehaved in a similar way, by putting his bike on the bed (narrated transgression).

This analysis was conducted in two steps. First, every narration in the Chinese and European American corpus that was coded "narrated transgression" ($N = 40$) was examined to determine whether it was immediately preceded by an occasioning transgression, and the proportion of narrated transgressions that was preceded by an occasioning transgression was computed. Second, 32 randomly selected Chinese narrations that did not contain a narrated transgression and 32 randomly selected European American narrations that did not contain a narrated transgression were coded for occasioning transgressions. The proportion of narrations without narrated transgressions that was preceded by an occasioning transgression was computed for each cultural case.

Structure coding: endings. The endings of narrations were categorized as follows.

1. *Didactic coda.* Following the final utterance that refers to the past event, there was a connected unit or coda, consisting of one or more utterances in which the story was brought back into present or future time. There was general topic continuity but a shift in temporal reference to the present or future. More specifically, a didactic coda draws out the implication of the story in the present or for the future in a way that explicitly refers to social or moral rules. For example, Angu's caregiver ended a narration about the child's misbehavior by saying, "Saying dirty words is not good"; a narration involving YoYo and his grandmother ended as follows: Child: "Now I don't cry at all." Grandmother: "Oh, now you don't cry at all, ya." Child: "Hmm." Grandmother: "Oh, good boy."

2. *Attribute of the focal child.* The story ended by mention of some general attribute of the child which the narrative exemplified. Like the coda, this was likely to involve a temporal adverb or (in English) a tense shift to the present, future, or timeless frame but specifically involved some enduring quality attributed to the child. For example, Megan's mother had been talking about how Megan and her sister were quite different, ending the story by saying, "She's becoming more and more independent now." A very similar example occurred for MeiMei.

3. *New topic.* Endings in this category were characterized by topic shifts or interruptions. In either case, the topic of talk shifted from the past event to some present or future-related topic or another story about some other past event. For example, YoYo and his grandmother co-narrated a story about a time that YoYo cried when his father left. YoYo changed the topic by saying, "Now, now Mom is gone."

RESULTS

BASIC DESCRIPTIVE INFORMATION

The naturalistic home observations revealed that every family in the study routinely narrated the past experiences of their 2½-year-old child, yielding a total corpus of 204 narrations. As can be seen in Table 1, narrations occurred at similar frequencies in the Taipei and Longwood families, with median rates per hour of about four stories. The Chinese narrations were somewhat shorter on average than the European American narrations. In the Chinese case, .38 of the narrations were co-narrations in which the focal child was a co-narrator and .62 were stories about the child in which the focal child was an onlooker or co-present other. In the American case, .51 of the narra-

TABLE 1 BASIC DESCRIPTIVE INFORMATION: NARRATIONS OF PERSONAL EXPERIENCE		
Measures	**Taipei**	**Longwood**
Frequency:		
Overall	92	112
Mean/family	15.3	18.7
Median/family	15.5	16.0
Rate/hour:		
Mean/family	3.8	4.7
Median/family	3.9	4.0
Length:*		
Overall	1,116	1,811
Mean/narration	12.1	16.2

*Length in utterances.

tions were co-narrations and .49 were stories about the child. Because the following analyses did not differentiate co-narrations and stories about the child, results are presented for total narrations (with co-narrations and stories about the child combined).

NARRATED TRANSGRESSIONS

The first analysis addressed the content of the narrations. As expected, we found that the Chinese families were much more likely than the European American families to tell stories about the 2-year-old's past transgressions: the average proportions of narrated transgressions were .35 in Taipei, compared with .07 in Longwood. Although there was individual variation within each cultural group, the overlap in the distributions was small: the range was .00 to .56, with a median of .31 for the Taipei families, compared with a range of .00 to .20, with a median of .04 for the Longwood families. Although these patterns strongly differentiated the Taipei and Longwood narrations in the expected direction, it should be noted that the majority of narrations in both cultural cases did not refer to the child's past transgressions.

Further analysis of the content of the narrated transgressions ($N = 32$) produced by the Taipei families revealed that .20 involved emotional displays, such as crying or anger judged inappropriate by the caregiver, and .38 occurred in public (e.g., insulting another child at a restaurant, playing on a forbidden computer at dad's office, interrupting a church service). In addition, .28 of the narrated transgressions actually involved two or more transgressions within a single narration, and there were three instances in which a given transgression was re-narrated twice in succession.

Although narrated transgressions occurred very infrequently ($N = 8$) in the Longwood case, it is interesting to note that there was some overlap with the Chinese in the nature of the infractions. Writing on the wall, eating too much "bad" food, and playing in a way that was too rowdy or dangerous occurred in both cultural cases. At the same time, there seemed to be a qualitative difference such that the Longwood children's transgressions were narrated in ways that rendered them peripheral to the main action of the story or marked them as nonserious. In the longest and most elaborate of the American transgression stories, Tommy started to misbehave in a store, but spontaneously corrected his misdeed without parental intervention and received his reward, a ride on a mechanical horse, "and we were in the shoe department looking for shoes for Maureen [focal child's sister] and he took his shoes off and he said as he took his shoe off, 'Oops, I won't be able to ride the horse.' ... but then he put his shoe right back on and he was real good in Venture so he could ride that horse." Although the child's transgression is narrated, the point of the story is that the child behaved well and was rewarded.

Occasioning Transgressions

The second analysis was a functional analysis that addressed the circumstances that occasioned the narration. As expected, the Taipei families were much more likely than their Longwood counterparts to tell stories about the child's past transgressions immediately after the child committed a transgression in the here and now. Half ($N = 16$) of the Chinese narrations that contained a narrated transgression were preceded by an occasioning transgression, compared with only one of the eight European American narrations that contained a narrated transgression. For example, a Chinese child knocked about a bowl filled with pudding, smashing and spilling it and making a lot of noise in the process. The caregiver warned the child, "Don't be like this. I don't like you being like this. You still have to behave yourself," thereby marking the child's behavior as a rule infraction. The caregiver then launched into a story about a past transgression in which the child misbehaved in church and had to be removed. The single Longwood narration that was occasioned by a transgression revolved around the child's thumb sucking. The mother tried to get the child to stop sucking her thumb. When this was unsuccessful, she began a story about the child's past thumb sucking, and her father's disapproval of it. The entire affair was handled humorously, with the father being quoted in a low voice as saying, "Get that

thumb outta that mouth!" This story provides a good example of how a narrated transgression is keyed nonseriously.

Examination of narrations that did not make reference to the focal child's past transgression revealed that in both cultural cases, none of these stories was occasioned by a present transgression.

Endings

The final analysis focused on how the narrations ended. As expected, we found that the Chinese narrations were more likely than their European American counterparts to end with a didactic coda in which the present or future implications of a rule or rule violation were articulated. Didactic codas occurred in .09 of the Chinese narrations compared with none of the American narrations. Examples of didactic codas include the following:

Example 1: *Mother:* Do you still want to go there again?
Child: Next time I won't do it again.

Example 2: *Mother:* You can only get it if you go to the class.
Child: (looks at mother but says nothing)
Mother: You can get it only if you go to the class.

Example 3: *Mother:* Saying dirty words is not good.
Child: Wooooo.
Mother: Is it right? Saying dirty words is not good.

Example 4: *Child:* Now I don't cry at all.
Grandmother: Oh, now you don't cry at all, ya.
Child: Hmn.
Grandmother: Oh, good boy.

The Taipei families were also more likely than the Longwood families to end their narrations by abstracting an attribute of the child from the story. Attribute endings accounted for .24 of the Chinese narrations, compared with .06 of the European American narrations. For example, after recounting a past experience in which the focal child pointed out the misbehaviors of another child, a Chinese caregiver said, "Ay-yo! So precocious. She is good at blaming people. Aren't you?" Other qualities attributed to the Taipei children were poor memory, shy, little but plays big tricks, bossy, troublemaker, independent, able to concentrate for a long time, feels uncomfortable about misbehaving. Attributes applied to the Longwood children included shy, independent, intuitive, verbally precocious, and a helper. Note that there is some overlap between the two cultural cases in the content of the attributes but that the Longwood attributions were more strongly skewed in the favorable direction.

The remaining narrations simply ended by way of changes in topic or attention, interruption, or other everyday contingencies, including getting knocked on the head by a sibling! In the Chinese families, .67 of the narrations ended in these ways, compared with .94 for the European American families. Once again, it should be noted that although the didactic categories differentiated the Taipei and Longwood families in the expected direction, this difference coexisted with an important similarity in that the majority of narrations in both cultural cases did not end didactically.

DISCUSSION

The results of this study indicate that both middle-class Chinese families and middle-class European American families engaged routinely in personal storytelling with their 2-year-old children. Although the rates at which personal storytelling occurred in the home were remarkably similar in Taipei and Longwood, personal storytelling emerged as more didactic for the Chinese at all levels of analysis—content, function, and structure. The findings of this study thus provide strong support for our expectation that Chinese families would be more likely than European American families to use personal storytelling to impart moral and social standards. They suggest that the Confucian reliance on didactic narrative to educate the young may extend to informal storytelling within the family context.

Corroborating our earlier report (Miller et al., 1996), Chinese families were much more likely than their European American counterparts to tell stories about the child's past transgressions. There are two possible explanations for this contrast. One possibility is that the greater frequency of transgression stories for the Chinese reflects a higher rate of behaviors that are perceived as misdeeds by caregivers. This possibility is supported by ethnographic evidence that Chinese caregivers held high expectations for their young children's conduct (Miller et al., 1996) and felt that they would be remiss as parents if they did not teach their children proper behavior from an early age (Fung, 1994). Although caregivers in Longwood were also concerned with their children's misbehaviors and intervened promptly and repeatedly when necessary, their expectations were more relaxed (Miller et al., 1996). Children were toilet trained much later than the Chinese children, houses were childproofed, and caregivers engaged in a variety of practices that seemed to reflect accommodation to the perceived needs of children. The European American caregivers also expressed appreciation for the child's willfulness.

A second explanation, which is in no way incompatible with the first, is that young children's transgressions were more "storyworthy" in the Chinese than in the American case. Chinese caregivers may be more likely to see the child's past transgressions as a didactic resource for conveying the rules of appropriate conduct to the child. This possibility is supported by the finding that the Chinese caregivers and children were more likely to construct story endings in which the didactic implications of the story were developed. This possibility also fits nicely with the notion of *jihui jiaoyu* or "opportunity education" articulated by the Chinese parents (Fung, 1994). This notion encompasses two interlinked ideas: that it is more effective to situate a moral lesson in the child's concrete experience than to preach in the abstract and that parents should take every opportunity to provide such concrete lessons. The results of our functional analysis indicate that the Chinese caregivers used stories in exactly this way: Half of the stories of the child's past transgressions were occasioned by a transgression in the present. In other words, caregivers treated the child's here-and-now transgressions as opportunities to remind the child of a previous transgression, thereby reinforcing and personalizing moral lessons through concrete exemplars. This strategy of moral socialization requires that parents be alert to, and keep account of, their children's misdeeds.

Caregivers in Longwood seemed to be up to something very different. This is especially well illustrated by an American transgression story in which no one could remember what the child had done wrong. An older sibling and the focal child co-narrated a past experience in which a desired toy was withheld because they had been "bad boys." But neither child could remember why they had been punished. When the mother, who had been out of the room momentarily, returned and tuned into the conversation, she commented ironically, "My kids being bad?!" thereby keying the story nonseriously. She confirmed that the incident had occurred, adding that it happened a week ago, but could not remember the children's misdeed.

This example, as well as the low rate of transgression stories, suggests that the European American families did not treat children's past transgressions as a didactic resource. Instead, stories of young children's past experiences seemed to function as a medium of entertainment and affirmation. Even in those rare instances in which a child's transgression was narrated, as in the Venture store example cited earlier, caregivers did not dwell on the child's misdeeds. This practice of downplaying transgressions in the narrative medium seems to be part of a wider set of practices that Longwood caregivers used to protect their children's self-esteem—conducting serious disciplining in private, putting the best face on the child's shortcomings or even recasting shortcomings as strengths. This does not mean, however, that the European American parents were indifferent to their youngsters' misbehavior;

rather, they seemed to prefer to handle infractions when they occurred, a practice recommended by American childrearing manuals. In the most recent edition of *Dr. Spock's Baby and Child Care*, Spock and Rothenberg (1992) say, "Though children do the major share in civilizing themselves through love and imitation, it still leaves plenty for parents to do, as all of us know. In automobile terms, the child supplies the power but the parents have to do the steering" (p. 435). The authors go on to elaborate on the steady, matter-of-fact guidance that parents need to provide: "The parents have to be saying, 'We hold hands when we cross the street,' 'You can't play with that, it may hurt someone,' 'Say thank you to Mrs. Griffin,' 'Let's go in now, because it belongs to Harry and he wants it,' 'It's time to go to bed so you'll grow big and strong,' etc. etc." (p. 435). Note that all of these examples refer to parental guidance that was offered simultaneously with the targeted child behavior.

In trying to delineate as clearly as possible the ways in which the Chinese and European American narrative practices differed, it is very important not to overstate these differences or formulate them in dichotomous terms. It is important to emphasize that the majority of narrations of the children's past experiences in both Taipei and Longwood did not invoke transgressions. Two-year-olds and their families created accounts of holidays or family excursions–birthday parties, shopping, the fair, the zoo, McDonald's for the European American children; the night market, the zoo, riding on trains and horses for the Chinese children. Both groups also talked about experiences of physical harm, such as illnesses or nosebleeds, and about times when they were afraid. Thus, the striking cultural difference in the priority given to a transgressive interpretation of the young children's past experiences must be seen against the backdrop of substantial overlap in the content of narrated experience.

Also, it should be emphasized that just as the Longwood families found ways to enforce moral and social rules, the Taipei families found ways to portray their children favorably and to express affection. Children were hugged, praised, and given small treats or presents. A parent might cook the child's favorite dishes or patiently teach him or her how to do a difficult puzzle. Mothers slept with their children to be available when needed. From a European American perspective, what may be hard to appreciate is the extent to which a critical parental voice blends with a voice of parental love, a point that Chao's (1994) work with immigrant Chinese also demonstrates. This blending of voices is expressed in the idiom, "The deeper the love, the greater the correction" (*Ai zhi shen, ze zhi qie*). Parents often use this expression with older children by way of justifying a punishment. A related expression is, "It's the child who's getting spanked, but it's the mother who really hurts"

(*Da zai er shen, tong zai niang xin*). Chinese care-givers seem to express their love through a didactic idiom in which the child's transgressions are repeatedly invoked and corrected.

The following excerpt provides an excellent example. In this co-narration, the child's grandmother reviews with him an incident that happened earlier in the day in which his mother spanked him for knocking down a screen. The grandmother focuses her didactic efforts on the child's response to having committed the misdeed–namely, that he said, "Don't hit me!" to his mother–which itself constituted a misdeed from her perspective. She patiently takes him through the incident, pointing out where he went wrong and rehearsing with him what he should have said to his mother after knocking down the screen. She explains that if he admits his misdeeds in the future, his mother will not spank him.

(As the co-narration begins, the grandmother is holding the child in her arms. After the first few words, he gets up and stands by his grandmother.)
Grandma: Oh, right. This morning when Mom was spanking you, what did you say? You said, "Don't hit me!" Right?
Child: Hmn. (Nods)
Grandma: Then, what did I tell you to say?
Child: "I won't push the screen down."
Grandma: Oh right. So, what would you say to Mom?
Child: I would say to Mom, "Don't have the screen pushed down." (Child moves closer and speaks in a very low tone into Grandma's ear)
Grandma: Oh, you would talk to Mom, saying, "Mama, I won't push the screen down."
Child: Hmn.
Grandma: So, Mom wouldn't hit you.
Child: Hmn.
Grandma: Right? Hmn. If you asked Mom, "You don't hit me," Mom would have hit you, right?
Child: Hmn. (Nods)
Grandma: So you would directly say to Mom in this way, "Mom, I won't push the screen down." Then how would Mom have reacted?
Child: [Unintelligible]
Grandma: What?
Child: [Unintelligible]
Grandma: Then she wouldn't hit you, right?
Child: Hmn. (Nods)
Grandma: Oh. So, next time when Mom is going to spank you, which sentence is better for you to say to her?
Child: Hmn. Hmn. (Moving close to Grandma's ear) "I won't have [unintelligible] won't have the screen pushed down."
Grandma: Oh, right. Now you have choices. You say, "Mom, I won't push the screen down." In that

way, Mom won't spank you. So next time when Mom is spanking you, you shouldn't say, "You don't hit me. (High pitch) You don't hit me." (High pitch) You shouldn't say that way.
Child: (Laughs)
Grandma: You say, "Don't hit me." (Raises her voice) Mom will hit more. Right? Instead, you say to Mom, "I won't push the screen down." What will Mom do to you?
Child: Will give me [unintelligible] a tender touch (in Taiwanese).
Grandma: What?
Child: A tender touch (in Taiwanese).
Grandma: A tender touch (in Taiwanese), oh, give you a tender touch (in Taiwanese). OK. (Laughs loudly and holds child in her arms.)

This co-narration ends as it began, with the grandmother holding the child in her arms. Throughout the co-narration, the grandmother's efforts to correct the child seem motivated by her concern not only to correct him but also to promote his well-being and restore harmonious relations between himself and his mother.

We conclude with a few reflections about the methods used in this study. A limitation of the study is that it is based on only six families from each cultural group. Clearly, future work is needed to corroborate these findings with larger samples. At the same time, we argue that studies that involve in-depth, highly contextualized description of a small number of cases can contribute information that cannot be obtained by other methods, information that is essential to understanding socialization cross-culturally. A good example in the present study is the functional analysis in which the events preceding the stories were examined to determine what occasioned the stories. This kind of analysis, which is precluded by the more typical approach of eliciting stories from children and caregivers, is crucial in determining what families are actually doing with stories. Although examination of naturally occurring narrations within the flow of social life is highly labor intensive, this effort is warranted for other reasons as well. By documenting the routine discursive practices that families use in their homes it is possible to expose the intricate patterning of similarities and differences in socialization across cultures without subduing the complexity of particular meaning in each. This approach thereby mitigates the widespread tendency to dichotomize cultural contrasts while also generating culturally valid categories for future work.

REFERENCES

Brown, R. (1973). *A first language.* Cambridge, MA: Harvard University Press.

Bruner, J. (1990). *Acts of meaning.* Cambridge, MA: Harvard University Press.

Chao, R. K. (1994). Beyond parental control and authoritarian parenting style: Understanding Chinese parenting through the cultural notion of training. *Child Development, 65,* 1111–1119.

Chu, C. L. (1972). Cong shehui geren yu wenhua de guanxi lun zhongguo ren de chigan quxiang [On the shame orientation of the Chinese from the interrelationship among society, individual, and culture]. In I. Y. Lee & K. S. Yang (Eds.), *Zhongguo ren de xingge: Keji zonghe xing de taolun* [Symposium on the character of the Chinese: An interdisciplinary approach] (pp. 85–125). Taipei: Institute of Ethnology, Academia Sinica.

Damon, W. (1995). *Greater expectations: Overcoming the culture of indulgence in America's homes and schools.* New York: Free Press.

Dennerline, J. (1988). *Qian Mu and the world of Seven Mansions.* New Haven, CT: Yale University Press.

Eisenberg, A. R. (1985). Learning to describe past experiences in conversation. *Discourse Processes, 8,* 177–204.

Engel, S. (1995). *The stories children tell: Making sense of the narratives of childhood.* New York: Freeman.

Fivush, R. (1993). Emotional content of parent-child conversations about the past. In C. A. Nelson (Ed.), *Memory and affect in development: Minnesota symposia on child psychology* (Vol. 26, pp. 39–77). Hillsdale, NJ: Erlbaum.

Fivush, R., Gray, J. T., & Fromhoff, F. A. (1987). Two-year-olds talk about the past. *Cognitive Development, 2,* 393–409.

Fivush, R., & Hamond, N. (1990). Autobiographical memory across the preschool years: Towards reconceptualizing childhood amnesia. In R. Fivush & J. A. Hudson (Eds.), *Knowing and remembering in young children* (pp. 223–248). New York: Cambridge University Press.

Fung, H. (1994). *The socialization of shame in young Chinese children.* Unpublished doctoral dissertation, University of Chicago.

Harwood, R. L., Miller, J. G., & Irizarry, N. L. (1995). *Culture and attachment: Perceptions of the child in context.* New York: Guilford.

Heath, S. B. (1983). *Ways with words: Language, life and work in communities and classrooms.* New York: Cambridge University Press.

Ho, D. Y. F. (1986). Chinese patterns of socialization: A critical review. In M. H. Bond (Ed.), *The psychology of the Chinese people* (pp. 1–37). Hong Kong: Oxford University Press.

Ho, D. Y. F. (1996). Filial piety and its psychological consequences. In M. H. Bond (Ed.), *The handbook of Chinese psychology* (pp. 155–165). Hong Kong: Oxford University Press.

Katz, L. G. (1993, November). Are we confusing self-esteem and narcissism? *Young Children,* p. 2.

MacWhinney, B. (1991). *The CHILDES Project: Tools for analyzing talk.* Hillsdale, NJ: Erlbaum.

Miller, P. J. (1994). Narrative practices: Their role in socialization and self-construction. In U. Neisser & R. Fivush (Eds.), *The remembering self: Construction and accuracy in the self-narrative* (pp. 158–179). New York: Cambridge University Press.

Miller, P. J. (1996). Instantiating culture through discourse practices: Some personal reflections on socialization and how to study it. In R. Jessor, A. Colby, & R. A. Shweder (Eds.), *Ethnography and human development: Context and meaning in social inquiry* (pp. 183–204). Chicago: University of Chicago Press.

Miller, P. J., Fung, H., & Mintz, J. (1996). Self-construction through narrative practices: A Chinese and American comparison of early socialization. *Ethos, 24,* 1–44.

Miller, P. J., & Hoogstra, L. (1992). Language as tool in the socialization and apprehension of cultural meanings. In T. Schwartz, G. White, & C. Lutz (Eds.), *New directions in psychological anthropology* (pp. 83–101). New York: Cambridge University Press.

Miller, P. J., Mintz, J., Hoogstra, L., Fung, H., & Potts, R. (1992). The narrated self: Young children's construction of self in relation to others in conversational stories of personal experience. *Merrill-Palmer Quarterly, 38,* 45–67.

Miller, P. J., & Moore, B. B. (1989). Narrative conjunctions of caregiver and child: A comparative perspective on socialization through stories. *Ethos, 17,* 428–449.

Miller, P. J., Potts, R., Fung, H., Hoogstra, L., & Mintz, J. (1990). Narrative practices and the social construction of self in childhood. *American Ethnologist, 17,* 292–311.

Miller, P. J., & Sperry, L. L. (1988). Early talk about the past: The origins of conversational stories of personal experience. *Journal of Child Language, 15,* 293–315.

Nelson, K. (Ed.). (1989). *Narratives from the crib.* Cambridge, MA: Harvard University Press.

Nelson, K. (1993a). Events, narratives, memory: What develops? In C. A. Nelson (Ed.), *Memory and affect in development:*

Minnesota symposia on child psychology (Vol. 26, pp. 1–24). Hillsdale, NJ: Erlbaum.

Nelson, K. (1993b). The psychological and social origins of autobiographical memory. *Psychological Sciences, 4,* 7–14.

Ochs, E., & Schieffelin, B. B. (1984). Language acquisition and socialization: Three developmental stories and their implications. In R. A. Shweder & R. A. LeVine (Eds.), *Culture theory: Essays on mind, self, and emotion* (pp. 276–320). New York: Cambridge University Press.

Peterson, C., & McCabe, A. (1983). *Developmental psycholinguistics: Three ways of looking at a child's narrative.* New York: Plenum.

Simon, D. F., & Kau, M. Y. M. (1992). *Taiwan: Beyond the economic miracle.* Armonk, NY: Sharpe.

Spence, J. D. (1992). *Chinese roundabout: Essays in history and culture.* New York: Norton.

Sperry, L. L., & Sperry, D. E. (1996). The early development of narrative skills. *Cognitive Development, 11,* 443–465.

Spock, B., & Rothenberg, M. B. (1992). *Dr. Spock's baby and child care* (6th ed.). New York: Pocket Books.

Tobin, J. (1995). The irony of self-expression. *American Journal of Education, 103,* 233–258.

Wu, D. Y. H. (1981). Child abuse in Taiwan. In J. E. Korbin (Ed.), *Child abuse and neglect: Cross-cultural perspectives* (pp. 139–165). Berkeley: University of California Press.

Wu, D. Y. H. (1996). Chinese childhood socialization. In M. H. Bond (Ed.), *The handbook of Chinese psychology* (pp. 143–154). Hong Kong: Oxford University Press.

QUESTIONS

1. Why are developmental psychologists interested in the storytelling practices of parents and young children?
2. Why did these researchers think that comparing the storytelling practices of European-American and Taiwanese families would be particularly interesting?
3. What are some of the Confucian principles that appear to be important in child socialization practices in Asian and Asian-American families?
4. What findings from earlier research conducted by Miller, Fung, and Mintz (1996) inspired the present study?
5. What behavioral expectations were used to illustrate the assertion that Taiwanese parents hold high standards for their children's conduct?
6. What features of family or home in the European-American households were used to support the claim that this community is child-centered?
7. How did the investigators conduct their research? In particular, what steps did they take to ensure that the families would be comfortable participating in this study and would provide the necessary information?
8. Which components of the parent–child narrations were chosen to be coded? Why were the researchers interested in these particular components of the narrations?
9. What similarities and differences emerged in the parent-child storytelling in Taipei and in Longwood?
10. What does parent–child storytelling indicate about cultural values in these two communities, and how do the types of stories told in each community help to support and maintain those values?

20 Developing a Cultural Theory of Mind: The CIAO Approach

ANGELINE LILLARD

People are aware that they have thoughts—that is, that something goes on in their minds that contains some kind of information. In addition to knowing that we have thoughts ourselves, we are also aware that other people have thoughts. Acquiring this knowledge is an important achievement of childhood. It has enormous implications for social, emotional, and cognitive development. Accordingly, developmental psychologists are very interested in the development of this type of understanding, which is known as a child's theory of mind. A related and equally important question pertains to the consequences of this understanding: What does it mean for human behavior that we come to know that our mind operates in a certain way and that others have similar mental experiences?

A number of explanations of the development of theory of mind in childhood have been proposed. Some theories propose a biological basis for this understanding, not unlike the biological basis that is proposed for language development. Other explanations rely more on social information processing, suggesting that a child develops an understanding of mind by having experiences with other people and trying to figure out their mental states. Still another possibility is that understanding of mind is a type of concept development that is constructed through the interaction of children's mental states and their everyday experiences.

In the following article, Angeline Lillard reviews these different approaches to the development of a theory of mind and argues that culture is also an important part of this developmental process. Although it appears that there are universal aspects of theory of mind—for example, all psychologically healthy humans seem capable of such understanding—there is also substantial variation across cultures in the emphasis that people place on mental states in their reasoning about the self and others. Lillard proposes a model, which she refers to by the acronym CIAO, that incorporates several factors that she sees as critical to explaining the development of theory of mind. These factors are: culture (C); mental examination, or introspection (I); recognition of relations in the behaviors of the self and others, or analogies (A); and age-related changes in these processes, or ontogeny (O).

The study of children's knowledge about minds is an extremely active area of developmental psychology. This article discusses the reach of this research and the theoretical views guiding it. It then presents some cultural variations (within the United States) in behavior explanation and explains the relevance of that variation to developmental theory. A theory of early mind reading that is presented incorporates culture, introspection, analogy, and ontogeny (CIAO).

The ability to posit mental states in other people is among the most subtly remarkable of human feats. Rather than simply detecting behavioral regularities ("A person looking at candy usually proceeds to get candy"), most people readily assume that others have internal mental states ("She sees candy, she wants candy, and she intends to get candy"). And whereas almost all people do this (the really striking exceptions being those with autism), it may be the case that no animals do. Although chimpanzees appear to

Reprinted with permission of Blackwell Publishers from Lillard, A. (1999). Developing a cultural theory of mind: The CIAO approach. *Current Directions in Psychological Science, 8*, 57–61.

Acknowledgments I am grateful to Barbara Spellman and Daniel Wegner for comments on an earlier version of this manuscript, and to the National Science Foundation for providing support for the research discussed here (Grant No. DGE-9550152).

engage in purposeful deception in the wild, well-controlled studies suggest that they have simply detected behavioral regularities (Povinelli & Giambrone, 2000).

Imputing intentions and other mental states is referred to as having a *theory of mind* (Premack & Woodruff, 1978). Understanding of minds is theory-like at least in the sense that mental states are not tangible, and therefore may exist only in theory, as some philosophers argue. A second reason for considering this knowledge a theory is that, like all theories, knowledge of mind appears to have a coherent, causal-explanatory structure, and concepts are defined in terms of other concepts specific to that body of knowledge (Wellman, 1990). For example, surprise is crucially defined in relation to belief or expectation.

Theory-of-mind research has taken developmental psychology by storm in the past decade. One might expect that such fury would run itself dry. Instead, theory of mind is surfacing across the field, because many developmental issues can be profitably viewed from this perspective. In infancy, for example, social referencing* depends on knowing that emotions can be about objects and events. Learning new words depends in part on deciphering what adults refer to, given the infinite choices. Pretend play depends on being able to deal in imagined worlds. In childhood and beyond, successful peer interaction depends in part on correctly interpreting the peer's intentions ("Did he bump into me on purpose?"). Providing reliable court testimony depends in part on knowing what it means to remember, and to lie. Because of its broad relevance, the theory-of-mind perspective could even stand a chance of unifying some disparate areas of research under a single conceptual framework, a unification lost when the developmental stages proposed by Jean Piaget, once very influential, became derailed.

Mental Representation

Theory-of-mind research concerns many issues. A particularly active area of research focuses on children's understanding of mental concepts and activities, like pretense, emotions, and, especially, belief. Understanding belief is a hallmark of understanding minds, because representing the world is quite possibly the most important feature of minds. People respond not to the world as it is, but to the world as they believe it to be. Many of Shakespeare's plays, for example, hinge on this understanding: Lear's belief that the faithful Cordelia is only his "sometime

daughter," Romeo's fatal misconception that Juliet is dead, the comedies' mistaken identities. These plays are paradigmatic of our fascination with how people view the world, and how belief drives action.

The *false-belief* task is a common way to assess when in development children come to understand that minds represent the world (Wimmer & Perner, 1983). In one version of this task, children are told of a boy who hides his candy in a drawer. While he is out, his mother moves it to a cupboard. The children are asked where the boy now thinks his candy is. Children ages 4 and older usually realize the boy thinks it is still where he left it. Remarkably, children under 4 usually do not: They often claim that the boy thinks it is in the new location. An active line of inquiry concerns the source of this error, with some research examining contributions of language skills, or a possible bias to report reality. Although such factors probably do contribute, a recent meta-analysis is consistent with the notion that a conceptual acquisition, such as realizing that belief is independent of reality, importantly underpins the ability to perform false-belief tasks correctly (Wellman, Cross, & Watson, 1999).

Theories of Development

Given the interest in children's knowledge about the mind, there is also much interest in theories about how that knowledge develops. Three dominant theories of development are also theories about the process of mind reading. In the nativist-modular theory, humans are equipped with an innate processing device, similar to Chomsky's language-acquisition device (LAD), whose function is to postulate mental states. When the child sees someone carrying out an action, the processor pops out a mental state, like "trying to do X" (Scholl & Leslie, 1999). Development occurs as additional elements of the processor come on line.

A second theory is that people understand minds by simulating. Upon seeing someone in a situation, a child imagines himself or herself in that situation, and experiences a mental state. The child then assumes the other person experiences that mental state (Harris, 1995). Development occurs as the simulator more accurately renders the other's situation.

The third proposal, dubbed the theory theory, is that people gradually build a theorylike body of knowledge about minds, and interpret behavior with reference to this theory (Wellman, 1990). When a child sees someone drop an ice-cream cone and then cry, the child theorizes that when one loses a trea-

---

*Social referencing means checking how a trusted person reacts emotionally to something and then adopting the same stance oneself.

sured object, sadness ensues. Theory theory allows that several processes might inform the child's theory. For example, the process of introspection, which plays heavily in simulation, might create a link between crying and sadness. Further, an innate "starting state" (Gopnik & Meltzoff, 1997) might get infants off on the right foot in formulating their understanding. Indeed, a fourth developmental theory, social-cultural construction, can also be incorporated: Some mentalistic understandings might come from culture-specific experiences. One such source is explicit tutorials in imaginary constructs. Among many African tribes, for example, witches are believed to cause events, like AIDS or fires. Presumably such beliefs are coached by elders in the culture. Thus, important aspects of three other theoretical approaches are incorporated into the theory theory. Two unique points of this approach are that our knowledge about minds has a theorylike structure and that theories change in response to evidence (e.g., an initial theory that actions stem from desires only may later be replaced by a theory that actions stem from beliefs and desires).

THE CONTRIBUTION OF CULTURE

Throughout much of the literature on children's theories of mind, and a parallel literature in philosophy concerning the process by which we read minds, runs an assumption that "our" theory of mind is universal.* Common are sentiments that "a fascination with mind and psychological states is fundamental to human intellectual functioning" (Mitchell & Lewis, 1994, p.1) and that the crux of understanding other people the world over is analyzing behavior in terms of beliefs and desires.

In a review of other cultures' ideas about minds, I suggested that there may be some universals, but that cultural variation exists and is relevant to evaluating and refining developmental theories (Lillard, 1998). Behavior attribution, or how people explain action, is one area of cultural variation. We usually explain why others do things with reference to their minds, but the predominance of this particular way of explaining behaviors may be unique to us. An example of cultural variation in behavior attribution comes from work by Miller (1984), who asked urban U.S. and Indian respondents to explain various behaviors. Explanations were analyzed in terms of whether they referred more to dispositions of the actor or more to situational constraints. Eight-year-olds in the two cultures responded similarly, choosing to name disposi-

tion and situation reasons about equally. But among older respondents, the cultures diverged, with Americans becoming increasingly dispositional, and Indians increasingly situational, with age.

Even within the United States there are cultural differences on this measure. My colleagues and I examined rural and urban American children and found striking differences (Lillard, Zeljo, & Harlan, 1998). The urban children used psychological explanations frequently and early; about 60% of their explanations for others' good and bad behaviors were psychological even at age 7 (e.g., "He helped me to catch bugs, because he and I like to catch bugs"). In contrast, the rural children averaged only 20% psychological explanations, and instead used mostly situational explanations ("She helped me pick up my books, because if she didn't I would have missed the bus"). In this way, rural American children resembled Asian adults. Asian situationism has been traced to Confucian values, and American internalism to the Western philosophical tradition. Yet a sizable group within America, even a group that shares Western European heritage, apparently tends to construe behaviors as stemming from situational factors.

Future research should elucidate factors contributing to our extreme mentalism. Maybe attending to minds is more important when one lives among a greater variety of people, where social rules vary by individual and so knowing "insides" matters more. Or perhaps mentalism is more important for people who are faced with a greater set of possible choices for how to behave. Regardless of what contributes, the phenomenon of cultural patterns in behavior construal has been demonstrated repeatedly, and its existence has implications for theories of how mentalistic understanding develops.

IMPLICATIONS FOR NATIVIST-MODULAR ACCOUNTS

The fact that many people usually do not explain behaviors with reference to minds seems particularly troubling for nativist-modular accounts, those claiming that a genetically specified mind-reading module, like the LAD,† leads people to automatically compute certain mental states when observing behavior. If this is correct, why do rural U.S. children give mostly situational explanations? Modularity theorists might respond that the rural children arrived at intention explanations for every behavior, just as the urban children did, but that this module output was

---

*Precisely delineating the group that holds this theory is an exercise I do not take up here, but it might loosely include Europeans and Americans, or it might include only academic social scientists working in the European-American tradition.
†Of course, the LAD concept is itself hotly contested in developmental psycholinguistics.

overridden or ignored. But it does not make sense that an innately specified module's output could be routinely overridden by cultural influence; the LAD would have little force if most language groups could willy-nilly override the laws of universal grammar and typically used noncanonical grammatical forms. And it strains common sense that urban, more educated, higher income respondents would be more apt to use modular output than would be rural respondents (who, incidentally, are probably more representative of the majority of human beings).

In retreat, one might say that the module at issue is actually a general explanation-finding module. Perhaps people have an innate, modular structure that outputs causes for phenomena, and one type of cause it might output is mental, and another is situational. Early input would cause neural switches to be set, resulting in some cultures attributing mental causes where others attribute physical ones. The problem with such a model is that settings should be fixed for

life, as grammar is supposedly fixed by switches in the LAD. Regardless of what culture one is from, one can use all sorts of explanations, even for a single event. The frequencies with which various types of explanations are provided vary by culture, more so than the existence of various types. Either theorists have to postulate a new type of innately specified module, one with much less force than the LAD, or they have to question the very existence of innately specified mind-reading modules.

THE CIAO MODEL: CULTURE, INTROSPECTION, ANALOGY, ONTOGENY

What seems to make more sense than the nativist-modular approach is that children are learning ways of describing behavior in their cultures. The CIAO (culture, introspection, analogy, ontogeny) model

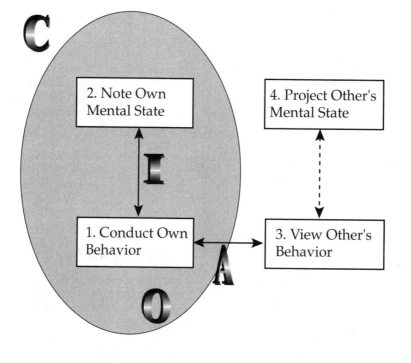

C   Culture
I   Introspection
A   Analogy
O   Ontogeny

FIGURE 1
The CIAO model of the ontogeny of mind reading.

("ciao" being an Italian form of interpersonal acknowledgment) depicted in Figure 1 provides one formulation. In the figure, the shaded area (O) refers to the infant's ontogenesis, or biologically guided development. Within the confines of ontogeny, the infant conducts behaviors and notices his or her own mental states (introspection, I). The infant also notices analogies (A) between his or her own and others' behaviors, and assumes the same mental state exists in the other people as exists in himself or herself (see Meltzoff & Moore, 1995). Meltzoff and his colleagues' notion that infants can, in some limited respect, introspect and draw analogies between self and other is therefore central to the model. Meltzoff et al. have discussed introspection and analogy particularly with reference to imitation, stating that during imitative acts, the infant might think, "I intend to produce these acts, the adult performs these same acts, they are not chance events; therefore the adult intends his acts'" (Meltzoff & Moore, 1995, p. 89).

The proposal that introspection and analogy guide theory-of-mind development is supported by important new unpublished work from Amanda Woodward and Jessica Sommerville, at the University of Chicago. In this study, the more reaching experience 5-month-olds had, the more likely they were to (apparently) attribute goals to others. (For details of the method, see Woodward, 1998.) Perhaps it is the case that when the infant engages in reaching behaviors, the infant introspects, noticing his or her own intention to get something; when the infant observes others reaching, he or she draws a self–other analogy, and sees the other as also intending to get something. Obviously, and as reflected in the CIAO model, ontogeny sets a boundary on when reaching behavior begins, and hence on when the infant might begin (if the introspection-analogy possibility is correct) to posit goals in others.

But the CIAO model highlights the importance of culture, depicted by the surround of Figure 1. Culture penetrates interpersonal understanding in many ways. For example, in some cultures, infants are given many toys, which inspire much reaching; in others, infants' arms are swaddled tightly to their sides, preventing reaching. Those infants who are more inspired and permitted, because of cultural practices, to reach out and get objects could come to attribute object-directed goals to other people earlier than would other infants. A host of effects, some related to theory of mind, might follow from precocity in this domain.

In sum, one way to think about how infants come to attribute mental states is via the CIAO model: In a cultural surround, infants introspect and draw an analogy between self and other. What is experienced and how changes with ontogeny. Because of the biological (I, A, and O) roots of this process, people everywhere can posit mental states. Because of the cultural roots, not everyone does it as much as we do. Perhaps there is some iota of truth to Bloom's (1998) claim that Shakespeare invented the human as we know it. We continue to read Shakespeare and his legacy, and we are strongly disposed to view people mainly in psychological terms. Although social understanding is probably built on foundations that are similar the world over, cultural influences intersect with those foundations from birth.

REFERENCES

Bloom, H. (1998). *Shakespeare: The invention of the human.* New York: Riverhead.

Gopnik, A., & Meltzoff, A. (1997). *Words, thoughts, and theories.* Boston: MIT Press.

Harris, P.L. (1995). From simulation to folk psychology. In M. Davies & T. Stone (Eds.), *Folk psychology: The case for development* (pp. 207–221). Cambridge, England: Blackwell.

Lillard, A.S. (1998). Ethnopsychologies: Cultural variations in theory of mind. *Psychological Bulletin, 123,* 3–33.

Lillard, A.S., Zeljo, A., & Harlan, D. (1998). *Developing cultural schemas.* Unpublished manuscript, University of Virginia, Charlottesville.

Meltzoff, A.N., & Moore, M.K. (1995). A theory of the role of imitation in the emergence of self. In P. Rochat (Ed.), *The self in infancy* (pp. 73–93). Amsterdam: Elsevier.

Miller, J.G. (1984). Culture and the development of everyday social explanation. *Journal of Personality and Social Psychology, 46,* 961–978.

Mitchell, P., & Lewis, C. (1994). Critical issues in children's early understanding of the mind. In C. Lewis & P. Mitchell (Eds.), *Children's early understanding of mind* (pp.1–16). Hillsdale, NJ: Erlbaum.

Povinelli, D., & Giambrone, S. (2000). Inferring other minds: Failure of the argument by analogy. *Philosophical Topics, 27,* 161–201.

Premack, D., & Woodruff, G. (1978). Does the chimpanzee have a theory of mind? *Behavioral and Brain Sciences, 1,* 515–526.

Scholl, A.M., & Leslie, A.M. (1999). Modularity, development, and 'theory of mind.' *Mind and Language, 14,* 131–153.

Wellman, H.M. (1990). *The child's theory of mind.* Cambridge, MA: Bradford.

Wellman, H.M., Cross, D., & Watson, J.K. (1999). *Development of theory of mind: The truth about false belief.* Unpublished manuscript, University of Michigan, Ann Arbor.

Wimmer, H., & Perner, J. (1983). Beliefs about beliefs. *Cognition, 13,* 103–128.

Woodward, A.L. (1998). Infants selectively encode the goal object of an actor's reach. *Cognition, 69,* 1–34.

QUESTIONS

1. What is a theory of mind?
2. What are the implications of a theory of mind for social functioning?
3. What is the false-belief task, and why is it used to assess the development of a theory of mind?
4. How does a nativist-modular theory explain the development of a theory of mind?
5. What is the theory theory, and why is it called this?
6. Does behavioral attribution vary across cultures? If so, what does this variation tell us about the role that culture may play in the development of a theory of mind?
7. What types of explanations do rural children in the United States provide regarding the intentions behind behaviors? Why do you think these children's explanations are more similar to explanations provided by Asian adults than to those of urban children in the United States?
8. Describe the four elements of the CIAO model.
9. What did Woodward and Somerville demonstrate in their research about the relation of reaching behavior and young infants' understanding of the goals of others? What does this result have to do with the development of a theory of mind?
10. What do you think evidence of different emphases on a theory of mind across cultures implies: that in some cultures people have deficits in this ability or that other cultural factors, such as preferences or organization, promote different patterns of reasoning about mental states?

21 Transmission of Aggression Through Imitation of Aggressive Models

ALBERT BANDURA · DOROTHEA ROSS · SHEILA A. ROSS

The following article describes research that investigated observational learning—specifically, what and how children learn when they are exposed to other people who are performing aggressive actions. This experiment is a classic in the field of psychology because of the clarity of its design, the strength of its findings, and the nature of its implications for child development. Before this research was conducted, psychologists, including Bandura and his colleagues, had discovered that children were quick to imitate the behaviors of an adult model in the presence of the model. However, another important question is whether children will imitate aggressive behaviors later, when the adult model is no longer present—a process called delayed imitation. Although one could study delayed imitation of many types of behaviors, the learning of aggressive behavior as a result of exposure to an aggressive model is of particular concern to psychologists and the public at large.

The researchers attempted to identify exactly which factors may contribute to children's learning when they observe aggressive behaviors performed by an adult model. For instance, they studied whether children are more likely to attend to and learn the behaviors of same-gender adult models. The investigators also examined whether boys are more likely than girls to learn aggressive behaviors from a same-gender adult model because these behaviors are considered more acceptable for males than for females.

One impressive feature of this research is the care that was taken in setting up the experimental conditions so that observational learning of aggressive behaviors could be clearly assessed. As a result of these efforts, this study came up with provocative results that have significant implications regarding how children learn aggressive behaviors. It also raised questions about how society can steer children toward prosocial behaviors in the midst of abundant depictions of violence and aggression on television, in video games, and in other media to which young children are regularly exposed.

A previous study, designed to account for the phenomenon of identification in terms of incidental learning, demonstrated that children readily imitated behavior exhibited by an adult model in the presence of the model (Bandura & Huston, 1961). A series of experiments by Blake (1958) and others (Grosser, Polansky, & Lippitt, 1951; Rosenblith, 1959; Schachter & Hall, 1952) have likewise shown that mere observation of responses of a model has a facilitating effect on subjects' reactions in the immediate social influence setting.

While these studies provide convincing evidence for the influence and control exerted on others by the behavior of a model, a more crucial test of imitative learning involves the generalization of imitative response patterns to new settings in which the model is absent.

Reprinted from Bandura, A., Ross, D., & Ross, S. A. (1961). Transmission of aggression through imitation of aggressive models. *Journal of Abnormal and Social Psychology, 63,* 575–582. Article in the Public Domain.

This investigation was supported by Research Grant M-4398 from the National Institute of Health, United States Public Health Service.

The authors wish to express their appreciation to Edith Dowley, Director, and Patricia Rowe, Head Teacher, Stanford University Nursery School for their assistance throughout this study.

In the experiment reported in this paper children were exposed to aggressive and nonaggressive adult models and were then tested for amount of imitative learning in a new situation in the absence of the model. According to the prediction, subjects exposed to aggressive models would reproduce aggressive acts resembling those of their models and would differ in this respect both from subjects who observed nonaggressive models and from those who had no prior exposure to any models. This hypothesis assumed that subjects had learned imitative habits as a result of prior reinforcement, and these tendencies would generalize to some extent to adult experimenters (Miller & Dollard, 1941).

It was further predicted that observation of subdued nonaggressive models would have a generalized inhibiting effect on the subjects' subsequent behavior, and this effect would be reflected in a difference between the nonaggressive and the control groups, with subjects in the latter group displaying significantly more aggression.

Hypotheses were also advanced concerning the influence of the sex of model and sex of subjects on imitation. Fauls and Smith (1956) have shown that preschool children perceive their parents as having distinct preferences regarding sex appropriate modes of behavior for their children. Their findings, as well as informal observation, suggest that parents reward imitation of sex appropriate behavior and discourage or punish sex inappropriate imitative responses, e.g., a male child is unlikely to receive much reward for performing female appropriate activities, such as cooking, or for adopting other aspects of the maternal role, but these same behaviors are typically welcomed if performed by females. As a result of differing reinforcement histories, tendencies to imitate male and female models thus acquire differential habit strength. One would expect, on this basis, subjects to imitate the behavior of a same-sex model to a greater degree than a model of the opposite sex.

Since aggression, however, is a highly masculine-typed behavior, boys should be more predisposed than girls toward imitating aggression, the difference being most marked for subjects exposed to the male aggressive model.

METHOD

SUBJECTS

The subjects were 36 boys and 36 girls enrolled in the Stanford University Nursery School. They ranged in age from 37 to 69 months, with a mean age of 52 months.

Two adults, a male and a female, served in the role of model, and one female experimenter conducted the study for all 72 children.

EXPERIMENTAL DESIGN

Subjects were divided into eight experimental groups of six subjects each and a control group consisting of 24 subjects. Half the experimental subjects were exposed to aggressive models and half were exposed to models that were subdued and nonaggressive in their behavior. These groups were further subdivided into male and female subjects. Half the subjects in the aggressive and nonaggressive conditions observed same-sex models, while the remaining subjects in each group viewed models of the opposite sex. The control group had no prior exposure to the adult models and was tested only in the generalization situation.

It seemed reasonable to expect that the subjects' level of aggressiveness would be positively related to the readiness with which they imitated aggressive modes of behavior. Therefore, in order to increase the precision of treatment comparisons, subjects in the experimental and control groups were matched individually on the basis of ratings of their aggressive behavior in social interactions in the nursery school.

The subjects were rated on four five-point rating scales by the experimenter and a nursery school teacher, both of whom were well acquainted with the children. These scales measured the extent to which subjects displayed physical aggression, verbal aggression, aggression toward inanimate objects, and aggressive inhibition. The latter scale, which dealt with the subjects' tendency to inhibit aggressive reactions in the face of high instigation, provided a measure of aggression anxiety.

Fifty-one subjects were rated independently by both judges so as to permit an assessment of inter-rater agreement. The reliability of the composite aggression score, estimated by means of the Pearson product-moment correlation, was .89.

The composite score was obtained by summing the ratings on the four aggression scales; on the basis of these scores, subjects were arranged in triplets and assigned at random to one of two treatment conditions or to the control group.

EXPERIMENTAL CONDITIONS

In the first step in the procedure subjects were brought individually by the experimenter to the experimental room and the model who was in the hallway outside the room, was invited by the experimenter to come and join in the game. The experimenter then escorted the subject to one corner of the room, which was structured as the subject's play area. After seating the child at a small table, the experimenter demonstrated how the subject could design pictures with potato prints and picture stickers provided. The potato prints included a variety of geometrical forms; the stickers were attractive multicolor pictures of animals, flowers, and western figures to be pasted on a pastoral scene. These activities were selected since they had been established, by previous studies in the nursery school, as having high interest value for the children.

After having settled the subject in his corner, the experimenter escorted the model to the opposite corner of the room which contained a small table and chair, a tinker toy set, a mallet, and a 5-foot inflated Bobo doll. The experimenter explained that these were the materials provided for the model to play with and, after the model was seated, the experimenter left the experimental room.

With subjects in the *nonaggressive condition*, the model assembled the tinker toys in a quiet, subdued manner, totally ignoring the Bobo doll.

In contrast, with subjects in the *aggressive condition*, the model began by assembling the tinker toys but after approximately a minute had elapsed, the model turned to the Bobo doll and spent the remainder of the period aggressing toward it.

Imitative learning can be clearly demonstrated if a model performs sufficiently novel patterns of responses which are unlikely to occur independently of the observation of the behavior of a model and if a subject reproduces these behaviors in substantially identical form. For this reason, in addition to punching the Bobo doll, a response that is likely to be performed by children independently of a demonstration, the model exhibited distinctive aggressive acts which were to be scored as imitative responses. The model laid Bobo on its side, sat on it and punched it repeatedly in the nose. The model then raised the Bobo doll, picked up the mallet and struck the doll on the head. Following the mallet aggression, the model tossed the doll up in the air aggressively and kicked it about the room. This sequence of physically aggressive acts was repeated approximately three times, interspersed with verbally aggressive responses such as, "Sock him in the nose . . . ," "Hit him down . . . ," "Throw him in the air . . . ," "Kick him . . . ," "Pow . . . ," and two nonaggressive comments, "He keeps coming back for more" and "He sure is a tough fella."

Thus in the exposure situation, subjects were provided with a diverting task which occupied their attention while at the same time insured observation of the model's behavior in the absence of any instructions to observe or to learn the responses in question. Since subjects could not perform the model's aggressive behavior, any learning that occurred was purely on an observational or covert basis.

At the end of 10 minutes, the experimenter entered the room, informed the subject that he would now go to another game room, and bid the model goodbye.

AGGRESSION AROUSAL

Subjects were tested for the amount of imitative learning in a different experimental room that was set off from the main nursery school building. The two experimental situations were thus clearly differentiated; in fact, many subjects were under the impression that they were no longer on the nursery school grounds.

Prior to the test for imitation, however, all subjects, experimental and control, were subjected to mild aggression arousal to insure that they were under some degree of instigation to aggression. The arousal experience was included for two main reasons. In the first place, observation of aggressive behavior exhibited by others tends to reduce the probability of aggression on the part of the observer (Rosenbaum & deCharms, 1960). Consequently, subjects in the aggressive condition, in relation both to the nonaggressive and control groups, would be under weaker instigation following exposure to the models. Second, if subjects in the nonaggressive condition expressed little aggression in the face of appropriate instigation, the presence of an inhibitory process would seem to be indicated.

Following the exposure experience, therefore, the experimenter brought the subject to an anteroom that contained these relatively attractive toys: a fire engine, a locomotive, a jet fighter plane, a cable car, a colorful spinning top, and a doll set complete with wardrobe, doll carriage, and baby crib. The experimenter explained that the toys were for the subject to play with but, as soon as the subject became sufficiently involved with the play material (usually in about 2 minutes), the experimenter remarked that these were her very best toys, that she did not let just anyone play with them, and that she had decided to reserve these toys for the other children. However, the subject could play with any of the toys that were in the next room. The experimenter and the subject then entered the adjoining experimental room.

It was necessary for the experimenter to remain in the room during the experimental session; otherwise a number of the children would either refuse to remain alone or, would leave before the termination of the session. However, in order to minimize any influence her presence might have on the subject's behavior, the experimenter remained as inconspicuous as possible by busying herself with paper work at a desk in the far corner of the room and avoiding any interaction with the child.

TEST FOR DELAYED IMITATION

The experimental room contained a variety of toys including some that could be used in imitative or nonimitative aggression, and others that tended to elicit predominantly nonaggressive forms of behavior. The aggressive toys included a 3-foot Bobo doll, a mallet and peg board, two dart guns, and a tether ball with a face painted on it which hung from the ceiling. The nonaggressive toys, on the other hand, included a tea set, crayons and coloring paper, a ball, two dolls, three bears, cars and trucks, and plastic farm animals.

In order to eliminate any variation in behavior due to mere placement of the toys in the room, the play material was arranged in a fixed order for each of the sessions.

The subject spent 20 minutes in this experimental room during which time his behavior was rated in terms of predetermined response categories by judges who observed the session through a one-way mirror in an adjoining observation room. The 20-minute session was divided into 5-second intervals by means of an electric interval timer, thus yielding a total number of 240 response units for each subject.

The male model scored the experimental sessions for all 72 children, Except for the cases in which he served as model, he did not have knowledge of the subjects' group assignments. In order to provide an estimate of interscorer agreement, the performances of half the subjects were also scored independently by a second observer. Thus one or the other of the two observers usually had no knowledge of the conditions to which the subjects were assigned. Since, however, all but two of the subjects in the aggressive condition performed the models' novel aggressive responses while subjects in the other conditions only rarely exhibited such reactions, subjects who were exposed to the aggressive models could be readily identified through their distinctive behavior.

The responses scored involved highly specific concrete classes of behavior and yielded high interscorer reliabilities, the product–moment coefficients being in the .90s.

RESPONSE MEASURES

Three measures of imitation were obtained:

Imitation of physical aggression: This category included acts of striking the Bobo doll with the mallet, sitting on the doll and punching it in the nose, kicking the doll, and tossing it in the air.

Imitative verbal aggression: Subject repeats the phrases, "Sock him," "Hit him down," "Kick him," "Throw him in the air," or "Pow."

Imitative nonaggressive verbal responses: Subject repeats, "He keeps coming back for more," or "He sure is a tough fella."

During the pretest, a number of the subjects imitated the essential components of the model's behavior but did not perform the complete act, or they directed the imitative aggressive response to some

object other than the Bobo doll. Two responses of this type were therefore scored and were interpreted as partially imitative behavior.

Mallet aggression: Subject strikes objects other than the Bobo doll aggressively with the mallet.

Sits on Bobo doll: Subject lays the Bobo doll on its side and sits on it, but does not aggress toward it.

The following additional nonimitative aggressive responses were scored:

Punches Bobo doll: Subject strikes, slaps, or pushes the doll aggressively.

Nonimitative physical and verbal aggression: This category included physically aggressive acts directed toward objects other than the Bobo doll and any hostile remarks except for those in the verbal imitation category; e.g., "Shoot the Bobo," "Cut him," "Stupid ball," "Knock over people," "Horses fighting, biting."

Aggressive gun play: Subject shoots darts or aims the guns and fires imaginary shots at objects in the room.

Ratings were also made of the number of behavior units in which subjects played nonaggressively or sat quietly and did not play with any of the material at all.

RESULTS

COMPLETE IMITATION OF MODELS' BEHAVIOR

Subjects in the aggression condition reproduced a good deal of physical and verbal aggressive behavior resembling that of the models, and their mean scores differed markedly from those of subjects in the nonaggressive and control groups, who exhibited virtually no imitative aggression (see Table 1).

Since there were only a few scores for subjects in the nonaggressive and control conditions (approximately 70% of the subjects had zero scores), and the assumption of homogeneity of variance could not be made, the Friedman two-way analysis of variance by ranks was employed to test the significance of the obtained differences.

The prediction that exposure of subjects to aggressive models increases the probability of aggressive behavior is clearly confirmed (see Table 2). The main effect of treatment conditions is highly significant both for physical and verbal imitative aggression. Comparison of pairs of scores by the sign test shows that the obtained over-all differences were due almost entirely to the aggression displayed by subjects who had been exposed to the aggressive models. Their scores were significantly higher than those of either the nonaggressive or control groups, which did not differ from each other (Table 2).

Imitation was not confined to the model's aggressive responses. Approximately one-third of the sub-

TABLE 1   MEAN AGGRESSION SCORES FOR EXPERIMENTAL AND CONTROL SUBJECTS

| | Experimental groups | | | | |
| | Aggressive | | Nonaggressive | | |
Response category	F Model	M Model	F Model	M Model	Control groups
Imitative physical aggression					
Female subjects	5.5	7.2	2.5	0.0	1.2
Male subjects	12.4	25.8	0.2	1.5	2.0
Imitative verbal aggression					
Female subjects	13.7	2.0	0.3	0.0	0.7
Male subjects	4.3	12.7	1.1	0.0	1.7
Mallet aggression					
Female subjects	17.2	18.7	0.5	0.5	13.1
Male subjects	15.5	28.8	18.7	6.7	13.5
Punches Bobo doll					
Female subjects	6.3	16.5	5.8	4.3	11.7
Male subjects	18.9	11.9	15.6	14.8	15.7
Nonimitative aggression					
Female subjects	21.3	8.4	7.2	1.4	6.1
Male subjects	16.2	36.7	26.1	22.3	24.6
Aggressive gun play					
Female subjects	1.8	4.5	2.6	2.5	3.7
Male subjects	7.3	15.9	8.9	16.7	14.3

TABLE 2   SIGNIFICANCE OF THE DIFFERENCES BETWEEN EXPERIMENTAL AND CONTROL GROUPS IN THE EXPRESSION OF AGGRESSION

| | | | | Comparison of pairs of treatment conditions | | |
| | | | | Aggressive vs. Nonaggressive | Aggressive vs. Control | Non-aggressive vs. Control |
Response category	χ^2_r	Q	φ	p	p	p
Imitative responses						
Physical aggression	27.17		<.001	<.001	<.001	.09
Verbal aggression	9.17		<.02	.004	.048	.09
Nonaggressive verbal responses		17.50	<.001	.004	.004	ns
Partial imitation						
Mallet aggression	11.06		<.01	.026	ns	.005
Sits on Bobo		13.44	<.01	.018	.059	ns
Nonimitative aggression						
Punches Bobo doll	2.87		ns			
Physical and verbal	8.96		<.02	.026	ns	ns
Aggressive gun play	2.75		ns			

jects in the aggressive condition also repeated the model's nonaggressive verbal responses while none of the subjects in either the nonaggressive or control groups made such remarks. This difference, tested by means of the Cochran Q test, was significant well beyond the .001 level (Table 2).

PARTIAL IMITATION OF MODELS' BEHAVIOR

Differences in the predicted direction were also obtained on the two measures of partial imitation.

Analysis of variance of scores based on the subjects' use of the mallet aggressively toward objects other than the Bobo doll reveals that treatment conditions are a statistically significant source of variation (Table 2). In addition, individual sign tests show that both the aggressive and the control groups, relative to subjects in the nonaggressive condition, produced significantly more mallet aggression, the difference being particularly marked with regard to female subjects. Girls who observed nonaggressive models performed a mean number of 0.5 mallet aggression responses as compared to mean values of 18.0 and 13.1 for girls in the aggressive and control groups, respectively.

Although subjects who observed aggressive models performed more mallet aggression ($M = 20.0$) than their controls ($M = 13.3$), the difference was not statistically significant.

With respect to the partially imitative response of sitting on the Bobo doll, the over-all group differences were significant beyond the .01 level (Table 2). Comparison of pairs of scores by the sign test procedure reveals that subjects in the aggressive group reproduced this aspect of the models' behavior to a greater extent than did the nonaggressive ($\phi = .018$) or the control ($p = .059$) subjects. The latter two groups, on the other hand, did not differ from each other.

NONIMITATIVE AGGRESSION

Analyses of variance of the remaining aggression measures (Table 2) show that treatment conditions did not influence the extent to which subjects engaged in aggressive gun play or punched the Bobo doll. The effect of conditions is highly significant ($\chi^2_r = 8.96$, $p < .02$), however, in the case of the subjects' expression of nonimitative physical and verbal aggression. Further comparison of treatment pairs reveals that the main source of the overall difference was the aggressive and nonaggressive groups which differed significantly from each other (Table 2), with subjects exposed to the aggressive models displaying the greater amount of aggression.

INFLUENCE OF SEX OF MODEL AND SEX OF SUBJECTS ON IMITATION

The hypothesis that boys are more prone than girls to imitate aggression exhibited by a model was only partially confirmed. t tests computed for subjects in the aggressive condition reveal that boys reproduced more imitative physical aggression than girls ($t = 2.50$, $p < .01$). The groups do not differ, however, in their imitation of verbal aggression.

The use of nonparametric tests, necessitated by the extremely skewed distributions of scores for subjects in the nonaggressive and control conditions, preclude an over-all test of the influence of sex of model per se, and of the various interactions between the main effects. Inspection of the means presented in Table 1 for subjects in the aggression condition, however, clearly suggests the possibility of a Sex × Model interaction. This interaction effect is much more consistent and pronounced for the male model than for the female model. Male subjects, for example, exhibited more physical ($t = 2.07$, $p < .05$) and verbal imitative aggression ($t = 2.51$, $p < .05$), more nonimitative aggression ($t = 3.15$, $p < .025$), and engaged in significantly more aggressive gun play ($t = 2.12$, $p < .05$) following exposure to the aggressive male model than the female subjects. In contrast, girls exposed to the female model performed considerably more imitative verbal aggression and more nonimitative aggression than did the boys (Table 1). The variances, however, were equally large and with only a small N in each cell the mean differences did not reach statistical significance.

Data for the nonaggressive and control subjects provide additional suggestive evidence that the behavior of the male model exerted a greater influence than the female model on the subjects' behavior in the generalization situation.

It will be recalled that, except for the greater amount of mallet aggression exhibited by the control subjects, no significant differences were obtained between the nonaggressive and control groups. The data indicate, however, that the absence of significant differences between these two groups was due primarily to the fact that subjects exposed to the nonaggressive female model did not differ from the controls on any of the measures of aggression. With respect to the male model, on the other hand, the differences between the groups are striking. Comparison of the sets of scores by means of the sign test reveals that, in relation to the control group, subjects exposed to the nonaggressive male model performed significantly less imitative physical aggression ($p = .06$), less imitative verbal aggression ($p = .002$), less mallet aggression ($p = .003$), less nonimitative physical and verbal aggression ($p = .03$), and they were less inclined to punch the Bobo doll ($p = .07$).

While the comparison of subgroups, when some of the over-all tests do not reach statistical significance, is likely to capitalize on chance differences, nevertheless the consistency of the findings adds support to the interpretation in terms of influence by the model.

NONAGGRESSIVE BEHAVIOR

With the exception of expected sex differences, Lindquist (1956) Type III analyses of variance of the nonaggressive response scores yielded few significant differences.

Female subjects spent more time than boys playing with dolls ($p < .001$), with the tea set ($p < .001$), and coloring ($p < .05$). The boys, on the other hand, devoted significantly more time than the girls to exploratory play with the guns ($p < .01$). No sex differences were found in respect to the subjects' use of the other stimulus objects, i.e., farm animals, cars, or tether ball.

Treatment conditions did produce significant differences on two measures of nonaggressive behavior that are worth mentioning. Subjects in the nonaggressive condition engaged in significantly more nonaggressive play with dolls than either subjects in the aggressive group ($t = 2.67$, $p < .02$), or in the control group ($t = 2.57$, $p < .02$).

Even more noteworthy is the finding that subjects who observed nonaggressive models spent more than twice as much time as subjects in aggressive condition ($t = 3.07$, $p < .01$) in simply sitting quietly without handling any of the play material.

DISCUSSION

Much current research on social learning is focused on the shaping of new behavior through rewarding and punishing consequences. Unless responses are emitted, however, they cannot be influenced. The results of this study provide strong evidence that observation of cues produced by the behavior of others is one effective means of eliciting certain forms of responses for which the original probability is very low or zero. Indeed, social imitation may hasten or shortcut the acquisition of new behaviors without the necessity of reinforcing successive approximations as suggested by Skinner (1953).

Thus subjects given an opportunity to observe aggressive models later reproduced a good deal of physical and verbal aggression (as well as nonaggressive responses) substantially identical with that of the model. In contrast, subjects who were exposed to nonaggressive models and those who had no previous exposure to any models only rarely performed such responses.

To the extent that observation of adult models displaying aggression communicates permissiveness for aggressive behavior, such exposure may serve to weaken inhibitory responses and thereby to increase the probability of aggressive reactions to subsequent frustrations. The fact, however, that subjects expressed their aggression in ways that clearly resembled the novel patterns exhibited by the models provides striking evidence for the occurrence of learning by imitation.

In the procedure employed by Miller and Dollard (1941) for establishing imitative behavior, adult or peer models performed discrimination responses following which they were consistently rewarded, and the subjects were similarly reinforced whenever they matched the leaders' choice responses. While these experiments have been widely accepted as demonstrations of learning by means of imitation, in fact, they simply involve a special case of discrimination learning in which the behavior of others serves as discriminative stimuli for responses that are already part of the subject's repertoire. Auditory or visual environmental cues could easily have been substituted for the social stimuli to facilitate the discrimination learning. In contrast, the process of imitation studied in the present experiment differed in several important respects from the one investigated by Miller and Dollard in that subjects learned to combine fractional responses into relatively complex novel patterns solely by observing the performance of social models without any opportunity to perform the models' behavior in the exposure setting, and without any reinforcers delivered either to the models or to the observers.

An adequate theory of the mechanisms underlying imitative learning is lacking. The explanations that have been offered (Logan, Olmsted, Rosner, Schwartz, & Stevens, 1955; Maccoby, 1959) assume that the imitator performs the model's responses covertly. If it can be assumed additionally that rewards and punishments are self-administered in conjunction with the covert responses, the process of imitative learning could be accounted for in terms of the same principles that govern instrumental trial-and-error learning. In the early stages of the developmental process, however, the range of component responses in the organism's repertoire is probably increased through a process of classical conditioning (Bandura & Huston, 1961; Mowrer, 1950).

The data provide some evidence that the male model influenced the subjects' behavior outside the exposure setting to a greater extent than was true for the female model. In the analyses of the Sex × Model interactions, for example, only the comparisons involving the male model yielded significant differences. Similarly, subjects exposed to the nonaggressive male model performed less aggressive behavior than the controls, whereas comparisons involving the female model were consistently nonsignificant.

In a study of learning by imitation, Rosenblith (1959) has likewise found male experimenters more effective than females in influencing children's behavior. Rosenblith advanced the tentative explanation that the school setting may involve some social deprivation in respect to adult males which, in turn, enhances the male's reward value.

The trends in the data yielded by the present study suggest an alternative explanation. In the case of a highly masculine-typed behavior such as physical aggression, there is a tendency for both male and female subjects to imitate the male model to a greater degree than the female model. On the other hand, in the case of verbal aggression, which is less clearly sex linked, the greatest amount of imitation occurs in relation to the same-sex model. These trends together with the finding that boys in relation to girls are in general more imitative of physical aggression but do not differ in imitation of verbal aggression, suggest that subjects may be differentially affected by the sex of the model but that predictions must take into account the degree to which the behavior in question is sex-typed.

The preceding discussion has assumed that maleness-femaleness rather than some other personal characteristics of the particular models involved, is the significant variable—an assumption that cannot be tested directly with the data at hand. It was clearly evident, however, particularly from boys' spontaneous remarks about the display of aggression by the female model, that some subjects at least were responding in terms of a sex discrimination and their prior learning about what is sex appropriate behavior (e.g., "Who is that lady. That's not the way for a lady to behave. Ladies are supposed to act like ladies . . . " "You should have seen what that girl did in there. She was just acting like a man. I never saw a girl act like that before. She was punching and fighting but no swearing.") Aggression by the male model, on the other hand, was more likely to be seen as appropriate and approved by both the boys ("Al's a good socker, he beat up Bobo. I want to sock like Al.") and the girls ("That man is a strong fighter, he punched and punched and he could hit Bobo right down to the floor and if Bobo got up he said, 'Punch your nose.' He's a good fighter like Daddy.")

The finding that subjects exposed to the quiet models were more inhibited and unresponsive than subjects in the aggressive condition, together with the obtained difference on the aggression measures, suggests that exposure to inhibited models not only decreases the probability of occurrence of aggressive behavior but also generally restricts the range of behavior emitted by the subjects.

"Identification with aggressor" (Freud, 1946) or "defensive identification" (Mowrer, 1950), whereby a person presumably transforms himself from object to agent of aggression by adopting the attributes of an aggressive threatening model so as to allay anxiety, is widely accepted as an explanation of the imitative learning of aggression.

The development of aggressive modes of response by children of aggressively punitive adults, however, may simply reflect object displacement without involving any such mechanism of defensive identification. In studies of child training antecedents of aggressively antisocial adolescents (Bandura & Walters, 1959) and of young hyperaggressive boys (Bandura, 1960), the parents were found to be nonpermissive and punitive of aggression directed toward themselves. On the other hand, they actively encouraged and reinforced their sons' aggression toward persons outside the home. This pattern of differential reinforcement of aggressive behavior served to inhibit the boys' aggression toward the original instigators and fostered the displacement of aggression toward objects and situations eliciting much weaker inhibitory responses.

Moreover, the findings from an earlier study (Bandura & Huston, 1961), in which children imitated to an equal degree aggression exhibited by a nurturant and a nonnurturant model, together with the results of the present experiment in which subjects readily imitated aggressive models who were more or less neutral figures suggest that mere observation of aggression, regardless of the quality of the model–subject relationship, is a sufficient condition for producing imitative aggression in children. A comparative study of the subjects' imitation of aggressive models who are feared, who are linked and esteemed, or who are essentially neutral figures would throw some light on whether or not a more parsimonious theory than the one involved in "identification with the aggressor" can explain the modeling process.

SUMMARY

Twenty-four preschool children were assigned to each of three conditions. One experimental group observed aggressive adult models; a second observed inhibited nonaggressive models; while subjects in a control group had no prior exposure to the models. Half the subjects in the experimental conditions observed same-sex models and half viewed models of the opposite sex. Subjects were then tested for the amount of imitative as well as nonimitative aggression performed in a new situation in the absence of the models.

Comparison of the subjects' behavior in the generalization situation revealed that subjects exposed to aggressive models reproduced a good deal of aggression resembling that of the models, and that their mean scores differed markedly from those of subjects in the nonaggressive and control groups. Subjects in the aggressive condition also exhibited significantly more partially imitative and nonimitative aggressive behavior and were generally less inhibited in their behavior than subjects in the nonaggressive condition.

Imitation was found to be differentially influenced by the sex of the model with boys showing more aggression than girls following exposure to the male model, the difference being particularly marked on highly masculine-typed behavior.

Subjects who observed the nonaggressive models, especially the subdued male model, were generally less aggressive than their controls.

The implications of the findings based on this experiment and related studies for the psychoanalytic theory of identification with the aggressor were discussed.

REFERENCES

Bandura, A. Relationship of family patterns to child behavior disorders. Progress Report, 1960, Stanford University, Project No. M-1734, United States Public Health Service.

Bandura, A., & Huston, Aletha C. Identification as a process of incidental learning. *J. abnorm. soc. Psychol.*, 1961, 63, 311–318.

Bandura, A., & Walters, R. H. *Adolescent aggression.* New York: Ronald, 1959.

Blake, R. R. The other person in the situation. In R. Tagiuri & L. Petrullo (Eds.), *Person perception and interpersonal behav-ior.* Stanford, Calif: Stanford Univer. Press, 1958, Pp. 229–242.

Fauls, Lydia B., & Smith, W. D. Sex-role learning of five-year olds. *J. genel. Psychol.*, 1956, 89, 105–117.

Freud, Anna. *The ego and the mechanisms of defense.* New York: International Univer. Press, 1946.

Grosser, D., Polansky, N., & Lippitt, R. A laboratory study of behavior contagion. *Hum. Relat.*, 1951, 4, 115–142.

Lindquist, E. F. *Design and analysis of experiments.* Boston: Houghton Mifflin, 1956.

Logan, F., Olmsted, O. L., Rosner, B. S., Schwartz, R. D., & Stevens, C. M. *Behavior theory and social science.* New Haven: Yale Univer. Press, 1955.

Maccoby, Eleanor E. Role-taking in childhood and its consequences for social learning. *Child Develpm.*, 1959, 30, 239–252.

Miller, N. E., & Dollard, J. *Social learning and imitation.* New Haven: Yale Univer. Press, 1941.

Mowrer, O. H. (Ed.) Identification: A link between learning theory and psychotherapy. In, *Learning theory and personality dynamics.* New York: Ronald, 1950. Pp. 69–94.

Rosenbaum, M. E., & DeCharms, R. Direct and vicarious reduction of hostility. *J. abnorm. soc. Psychol.*, 1960, 60, 105–111.

Rosenblith, Judy F. Learning by imitation in kindergarten children. *Child Develpm.*, 1959, 30, 69–80.

Schachter, S., & Hall, R. Group-derived restraints and audience persuasion. *Hum. Relat.*, 1952, 5, 397–406.

Skinner, B. F. *Science and human behavior.* New York: Macmillan, 1953.

QUESTIONS

1. Why do the authors call delayed imitation a more crucial indicator of learning than imitation in the presence of a model?
2. What was the main hypothesis the researchers put forward in this experiment?
3. Why were two model conditions tested, one that involved an aggressive model and one that involved a nonaggressive model?
4. According to Bandura, Ross, and Ross, what role does gender play in imitative learning?
5. What was the age range of the children in this study, and why do you think this age group was selected for this research?
6. Which specific child behaviors were assessed before children were exposed to the models in this study, and why was it important to pre-assess children on these behaviors and then use these scores to match children in the experimental and control groups?
7. Why was it important for the model to exhibit several distinctive aggressive actions toward the Bobo doll in the child's presence?
8. What did the researchers do to arouse the children's aggression, and why was this important to this study?
9. How did children in the aggressive and nonaggressive groups differ in their imitation of the models' behavior? Did the children's gender relate to any of these behaviors?
10. What are some of the implications of these results for social policy regarding the exposure of children to violent models in television, movies, video games, and other media?

22 Cultural Differences in American and Mexican Mother–Child Pretend Play

JoAnn Farver • Carollee Howes

Piaget, Vygotsky, Freud, Erikson, and many other early psychologists were very interested in children's play. Their interest stemmed from the belief that play provides children with abundant opportunities for psychological development. These opportunities range from practicing cognitive and social skills to learning how to regulate emotions.

Until recently, research on children's play has concentrated on the play behaviors of middle-class children in Western communities. However, in the past few years, research by developmental psychologists has expanded to include studies of children's play in many communities throughout the world. This research has revealed much similarity in children's play, suggesting that it may be linked to some basic developmental processes. However, some variation in children's play across cultural communities has also been found. These variations come from many sources, including cultural values, practices of social interaction, and the resources available to support and guide children's play.

In the following article, JoAnn Farver and Carollee Howes compare the play behaviors of mothers and toddlers in two cultural communities: the United States and Mexico. Their research focuses on pretend play. This type of play, which is also called dramatic play, allows children to improve their skill at symbolic representation, to imagine their own future roles, and to experience the roles and feelings of others in a playful and nonthreatening way. Farver and Howes went to great effort to include families in Mexico and the United States that were similar along several crucial dimensions, including the family's social class and the target child's position in the family. They also collected different types of data, from observations and interviews, about the children's play behaviors. These efforts resulted in a comprehensive description of the main differences in children's play patterns in these two cultural groups. In addition, the investigators were able to connect these differences to the broader cultural values and practices of these communities.

Toddler-age children's play with their mothers (n = 60) was videotaped in the U.S. and Mexico. Episodes were examined for pretend play, mutual involvement in social play, joint involvement in cooperative social pretend play, and maternal play behaviors. Contextual features were observed, recorded, and analyzed using an activity setting model. Mothers were interviewed about their value of children's play behavior. Although children's pretend play and mother–child mutual involvement increased with age in the two cultures, American mother–child pairs accounted for the greater proportion of interactive social play and pretend play episodes. There were also cultural differences in behaviors that mothers used to structure play and in mothers'

Reprinted from Farver, JoAnn M., & Howes, Carollee, "Cultural Differences in American and Mexican Mother–Child Pretend Play," in *Merrill-Palmer Quarterly, Vol. 39,* No. 3 (July 1993), copyright Wayne State University Press, with the permission of Wayne State University Press.

The research is based on a dissertation submitted by J. M. Farver in partial fulfillment of the requirements for the doctoral degree in the Graduate School of Education, University of California, Los Angeles. The study was supported by grants from the University of California, Los Angeles, Chicano Studies Program, and the Organization of American States, Washington, DC. The authors gratefully acknowledge the families who participated in this study. A special thanks to the Menzie family, and to the Mexican field assistants, Patricia Rodriques, Victor Guerrero, and Evelyn Aron, who helped with coding the data and establishing reliability. Correspondence may be sent to J. M. Farver, Department of Psychology, SGM 501, University of Southern California, Los Angeles, CA 90089-1061.

value of children's play. The findings suggest that mothers guide the development of their children's play according to their particular cultural norms, which poses a theoretical challenge to the current notion that mothers are the primary facilitators of children's early pretend play.

American and Mexican young children's pretend play with their mothers was investigated, with the primary objective of understanding how culture influences the way in which mothers and their children engage in and express pretend play. Most research on children's early symbolic development and play behavior has been based on white, middle-class Western samples. As result, cultural and social-class differences in children's play have been interpreted as signs of deficiency rather than variation (Feitelson, 1977; Smilansky, 1968). In the present study, the data base was broadened by comparing mother–child play in two different cultural contexts to allow general inferences to be made about the role of culture in development. The study also provides information about similarities and variations in developmental processes across particular contexts in which development occurs.

According to Western theorists, young children's pretend play originates in early interaction with parents. Werner and Kaplan (1963) claimed that it is the child's initial desire to share the object world with the mother that motivates the earliest attempts at communication and marks the beginning of internalized symbolic processes. According to this theory, early pretend play begins during the child's active experimentation with objects and in the seeking of confirmation of the developing symbols from the mother. In Western studies of early play behavior, it is proposed that mothers facilitate young children's beginning attempts at pretense. As mothers provide suggestions and communicate the rules of playing pretend, children incorporate the maternal guidance into play sequences and gradually begin to construct pretend scripts and enact roles. During play, mothers and children coordinate their actions and, with maternal assistance, children can perform beyond their existing level of competence (Haight & Miller, 1991; Miller & Garvey, 1984; O'Connell & Bretherton, 1984; Slade, 1987).

Although research indicates that mothers structure or scaffold children's early pretend play, it is unclear whether these findings are generalizable to mothers and children in different cultures. In other societies, children may have few opportunities to play with their mothers. Mothers may not have time to spend in specific child-centered activities involving play. Children's play may not be considered to be a valuable, productive activity, or entering and managing children's play may be culturally inappropriate adult behavior. Cultural variations in mother–child communication styles also may influence their collaboration in play. Such culture-specific factors may affect a mother's inclination to play with her child, her scaffolding behavior, and the partner's involvement in pretend play.

To examine the influence of culture in shaping mother–child pretend play, an activity setting approach was used here. This approach is derived from Soviet activity theory (Leont'ev, 1981) and the Whiting behavior-setting concept (Whiting & Edwards, 1988), and is elaborated in Weisner and Gallimore's work (Tharp & Gallimore, 1988; Weisner, Gallimore, & Jordan, 1988). The model emphasizes the Vygotsky (1978) notion that children's development cannot be understood apart from the wider social milieu. Ecological factors as well as the economic and social organization of a community influence families' daily routines, individuals with whom they interact, activities in which they engage, and scripts that guide their behavior (Whiting & Edwards, 1988).

To compare American and Mexican mother–child play along similar contextual or environmental dimensions, variables that potentially influence mother–child interaction and play behavior were isolated. Features of American and Mexican activity settings, as derived from the research literature, are elaborated in Table 1.

Based on differences in the American and Mexican activity setting features, it was predicted that American children, reared in single family homes where mothers are available and customary play companions, display more symbolic level play with objects and engage in more frequent and more complex episodes of shared pretend play with their mothers than do Mexican children, who live in extended families and have rare opportunities to formally play with their mothers.

A second hypothesis is that cultural differences in childrearing goals and practices and the mother's value of play activity affect the behaviors which mothers use to scaffold children's pretend play. American mothers, who value play, emphasize the early development of cognitive skill, and promote children's independent effort, were expected to make frequent suggestions for fantasy play, to support their children's efforts at pretense, and to use an implicit style of guidance (defined as providing verbal support and following their children's lead in play). Mexican mothers, who place little or no value on play and emphasize direction, modeling, and imitation in shared daily activity, were expected to make few suggestions for fantasy play, to rarely use praise or approval as reinforcement, and to use an explicit style of guidance (defined as organizing and directing play activity).

TABLE 1   FEATURES OF AMERICAN AND MEXICAN ACTIVITY SETTINGS

	American	Mexican
Personnel available	Mothers[a] Toddlers Siblings	Mothers[f] Toddlers Siblings Extended family Neighbors Older children
Nature of tasks and activities performed	Formal play with educational outcomes[b] Mother joins child's activities	Informal play in work contexts[g] Child joins mother's activities
Purpose of tasks	Prepare for school[c]	Prepare for work[h]
Cultural goals, values, and beliefs	Independence[d] Individual autonomy Self-confidence Cognitive skills	Interdependence[i] Family orientation Cooperation Social skills
Scripts governing interactions	Parents help child learn[e] Child learns through adult's efforts at teaching in play	Parents model desired behavior[j] Child learns by observing and imitating adult behavior in work

[a]Rogoff, Mistry, Göncü, & Mosier, 1991; Whiting & Edwards, 1988.
[b]Haight & Miller, 1991; Miller & Garvey, 1984; Whiting & Edwards, 1988.
[c]Bradley & Caldwell, 1984; Levenstein, 1986, in press; LeVine, 1980; White, 1980.
[d]Hoffman, 1988; Lawton, Fowell, Schuler, & Madsen, 1984; LeVine, 1980; Richman, Miller, & Solomon, 1988; Whiting & Edwards, 1988.
[e]Levenstein, 1986, in press; LeVine, 1980.
[f,g,h]Romney & Romney, 1966; Whiting & Edwards, 1988; Zukow, 1989.
[i]Bronstein-Burrows, 1981; Díaz-Guerrero, 1975; Falicov & Karrer, 1980; Holtzman, 1982; Holtzman, Díaz-Guerrero, Swartz, & Tapia, 1969; Kagan, 1981; Kagan & Ember, 1975; Keefe, Padrilla, & Carlos, 1979; Peñalosa, 1968; Ramírez, 1967; Ramírez & Price-Williams, 1974.
[j]Bronstein-Burrows, 1981; Ramírez & Castañeda, 1974.

METHOD

SUBJECTS

The participants were 60 children and their mothers: 30 Anglo-American and 30 Mexican, 10 from each culture, at ages 18, 24, and 36 months. Half of each age group were girls. Criterion for selection was that the child was at least a second-born. American families were contacted by flyers posted at neighborhood parks and by word of mouth. Mexican families were recruited by an assistant who was a resident of the community.

The American sample of white, working-class families came from an economically depressed county in northern California. Nuclear family households contained from two to five children ($M = 2.45$), ranging in age from 6 months to 12 years. Fathers were employed in the building trades, as truck drivers, retail store clerks, and similar occupations. Mothers did not work outside the home. Most mothers reported that, given their level of training and education, they could not earn enough money to both afford childcare and make a significant contribution to family income.

The Spanish-speaking Mexican Mestizo sample came from a town of about 5,000 residents located on the Pacific Coast 1,700 miles south of the U. S. border. Households consisted of intact families (i.e., both parents were living in the home) with two to five children ($M = 3.3$ children), ranging in age from infancy to 10 years. The nuclear families were embedded in an extended kinship cluster that included grandparents and/or paternal siblings and their children.

The Mexican community was selected because the predominant socioeconomic status closely approximated the American working-class sample. Although no universal measure of social class is comparable across societies, Mexican sociologists claim that parallels can be drawn between the American class system and the Mexican (Alba, 1982; Balán, 1973; Eckstein, 1989; Suárez, 1978). Mexican sociologists distinguish working-class status from white-collar professionals who are considered to be middle-class (*clase media*), and the lower class (*clase humilde*) landless peasants (*campesinos*), informal sector day laborers, unskilled and semiskilled workers, who inhabit squatter settlements and tenements (*vecindades*), by using indices of skilled labor union affiliation, work stability, home ownership, desire for upward mobility, and primary-level education of 6 years (Balán, 1973; Eckstein, 1989; Suárez, 1978).

Mexican fathers in this sample were employed in unionized (*syndicados*) construction-related jobs (tile setters, masons, and concrete finishers), as automobile mechanics, wrought iron workers, craftsmen, or truck drivers. Mothers were occupied with household maintenance. During interviews and conversations, parents expressed the desire to improve their economic standing and occupational opportunities and education for their children. Most older siblings were enrolled in or had attended the community's "kinder" program (preschool for 4- and 5-year-olds).

All Mexican families held the title to their land. Their houses were lowcost, but solidly built and of middle-class style, with separate rooms for cooking, sleeping, and everyday living. Houses were furnished with stoves, refrigerators, and television sets, and nearly all had indoor plumbing.

PROCEDURE

Qualitative and quantitative research methods were used in both cultures. The qualitative data collection began first and continued throughout the study with the intent to describe ethnographically the family life, childrearing practices, and the characteristics of the activity settings that the children typically inhabited.

To minimize subjects' reactivity to the observer's presence in the Mexican setting, the researcher spent considerable time in the community prior to data collection. Each family was observed in and around their homes for a total of 8 hours. Observations were unstructured so that family behavior might be as self-motivated and spontaneous as possible. The observer attempted to be unobtrusive while recording detailed field notes of their daily routines and activities.

Field notes were compiled and analyzed using the grounded theory method developed by sociologists Glaser and Strauss (1967), an inductive approach that consists of jointly collecting, categorizing, coding, and analyzing the data to allow theories to emerge. These emerging theories then can be systematically tested, provisionally verified, discarded, or reformulated simultaneously as data collection proceeds. The strength of this approach is that it allows the researcher to uncover patterns in participant behavior as it occurs in context. Thus, the researcher does not enter the setting with preconceived notions, possibly ignoring important variables.

In the quantitative procedure, mothers and children of both cultures were videotaped as they played with a bag of wooden shapes in their home for about 20 min. The wooden shapes included human, animal, and tree figures, various arched and flat rectangular pieces, square blocks, and a wooden train connected by magnets. The purpose of the shapes was to provide opportunities for pretense without introducing "toys" from the American culture to the Mexican and vice versa. Because the shapes were novel in Mexico, and, by maternal report, very different from toys and blocks in the American homes, children in both cultures were allowed to play with the shapes for 20 min prior to the videotaping. In both cultures, mothers were told that the study was about how mothers and children play. Mothers were asked to "Play with your child in anyway you want" (*"Juege con su nino de la manera en que usted le gusta"*).

At the end of the data collection, mothers were interviewed about their views of children's play. All observations, interviews, and videotaping of the children and their families in both cultures were conducted by the first author.

CODING AND MEASURES

Videotapes were fully transcribed and then segmented into play episodes. An episode began when either partner touched an object or verbally interacted with the partner in the immediate environment. An episode ended when participants were no longer involved in play (e.g., either partner's attention was directed away for more than 30 s, or either partner moved away) or the theme of the play changed. The use of a different shape constituted a change in theme, unless the shapes were used in relationship to each other. For example, placing an animal shape on a tall stack of blocks was considered related to the ongoing theme of "stacking blocks." Sustained attention to, or introduction of, another shape into play, or an announced suggestion for a different play theme signaled the beginning of a new episode.

Level of Play with Objects. Each episode was coded once for the focal child's highest level of object play by using a scale adopted from that of O'Connell and Bretherton (1984). *Exploratory play* consisted of all manipulative behaviors such as handling, throwing, banging, or mouthing the objects, or touching one shape to another. *Combinational play* included putting objects together, stacking the shapes, making spatial configurations, or grouping shapes by function or color. *Symbolic play* was coded when children used the shapes to represent other objects or activities, and included conventional or functional uses of the shapes, such as giving a horse shape a "ride" on the train, object substitution (using a block for a bed), and the use of an independent agent (making the human shapes walk or talk).

Mutual Involvement in Social Play.   Each episode was coded for the presence or absence of mutual involvement in social play by using a measure adopted from a study by Howes (1980). Mutual involvement was coded when partners directed social bids to each other (smiled, vocalized, offered or received object, helped with task) and/or engaged in complementary and reciprocal activities with mutual awareness (e.g., child offered a shape, mother took it and offered it back).

Joint Involvement in Cooperative Social Pretend Play.   Episodes containing symbolic level play were selected and coded for partners' joint involvement in cooperative pretend play by using a measure adopted from that of Howes (1985). Cooperative pretend play was coded when both partners performed fantasy actions in the context of ongoing social play, which indicated that they assumed complementary pretend roles (e.g., mother–baby).

Maternal Behaviors in Play.   Fifteen maternal play behaviors, derived from observations of the activity settings and judged to be salient in the two cultures, were coded for the number of times each occurred during an episode. These behaviors were clustered to form four broad maternal scaffolding behaviors. Labeling objects, directing play, correcting child, setting stage for play, attracting child's attention, and providing a model were clustered to represent *explicit guidance.* These were times when mothers explicitly organized and directed play activity and children followed their lead. Requesting help, giving help, joining child's play, describing child's behavior, and describing own behavior, were combined to represent *implicit guidance.* Here, mothers provided interpretative commentary, kept their partner informed about what they were doing, and followed their children's lead in play. Praising and encouraging independence were clustered to form *support child's effort.* Suggesting symbolic play and using paralinguistic cues to animate play objects were combined to represent *suggest fantasy play.*

Reliability.   Videotapes were coded by the bilingual first author and a bicultural, bilingual assistant who was uninformed of the children's ages and the goals of the study. The first author trained the assistant by using six videotapes (one for each age level in each culture). To establish reliability, six additional tapes were randomly selected and coded independently by the first author and the assistant. Cohen's kappas for rater agreement on identifying episodes, coding level of object play, mother–child involvement in social play, and cooperative pretend play, and determining the 15 maternal behaviors and their clustering and coding, ranged from .91 to .96 for the American dyads, and from .82 to .90 for the Mexican dyads. Similar reliability checks performed midway and at the end of the coding ranged from .95 to .97.

Because the data were collected by the first author, careful attention was given to training and establishing reliability with the assistant. To avoid experimenter bias, the assistant's codings of the videotapes were used in the data analysis.

MATERNAL INTERVIEWS

During the interviews, mothers were asked open-ended questions about the value that they placed on children's play behavior and who was their child's most common play partner. In both cultures, mothers' responses about the most important value of play fell into three main types: child's amusement, mutual enjoyment, and educational benefits. The four common play partners were mothers, fathers, siblings, and unrelated children. Mothers rated the importance of play on a 3-point scale: *not important, somewhat important,* and *very important.*

Cohen's kappas for agreement between the first author and the assistant on categorizing and coding of the three maternal interview questions ranged from .97 to .99 for the American sample, and from .94 to .98 for the Mexican sample.

RESULTS

NUMBER OF EPISODES

There were 782 mother–child play episodes in the two cultures (U.S., $M = 12.06$, $SD = 4.33$; Mexico, $M = 11.76$, $SD = 2.95$). An analysis of variance (ANOVA) comparing the number of episodes by age and culture was not significant.

SYMBOLIC LEVEL PLAY, MUTUAL INVOLVEMENT, AND COOPERATIVE PRETEND PLAY

Proportions were calculated for the frequencies of symbolic level object play, mother–child mutual involvement in social play, and mother–child coopera-

TABLE 2 PROPORTION OF TOTAL EPISODES OF SYMBOLIC LEVEL PLAY, MOTHER–CHILD MUTUAL INVOLVEMENT, AND COOPERATIVE PRETEND PLAY BY AGE AND CULTURE

| | Age in Months | | | | | | F | | |
| | 18 | | 24 | | 36 | | | | |
	%	SD	%	SD	%	SD	Culture	Age	Age × Culture
Symbolic play									
U.S.	.34	(.22)	.42	(.35)	.58	(.27)	9.71**	6.75**	1.43
Mexico	.04	(.05)	.37	(.27)	.34	(.19)			
Mutual involvement									
U.S.	.65	(.39)	.88	(.11)	1.00	(.02)	6.27**	4.28*	1.60
Mexico	.63	(.15)	.74	(.19)	.71	(.34)			
Cooperative pretend									
U.S.	.01	(.05)	.02	(.06)	.44	(.41)	3.79*	5.54**	5.01**
Mexico	.00	(.00)	.11	(.31)	.05	(.12)			

Note. In all cases, Scheffé tests indicated age 36 mo. > 18 mo.
*$p < .05$. **$p < .01$.

tive social pretend play by dividing each measure by the total number of episodes. To avoid violating the assumptions of ANOVAS proportional variables, an arcsine transformation was conducted. Proportions were compared using three separate 3(Age) × 2 (Culture) × 2(Sex) ANOVAs. Because no main effects or interactions were found for sex, it was dropped from further analyses.

Significant main effects appeared for age and culture. Proportions of symbolic level play, $F(2, 44) = 6.75$, $p < .01$; partner's mutual involvement, $F(2, 44) = 4.28$, $p < .01$; and cooperative pretend play, $F(2, 44) = 5.54$, $p < .05$, all increased with age. Scheffé post hoc tests ($p < .05$) comparing age groups showed more symbolic level play, partner involvement, and cooperative pretend play among 36-month-olds than 18-month-olds. American children accounted for the greater proportion of symbolic play with objects, $F(1, 44) = 9.71$, $p < .01$. American mother–child dyads had a greater proportion of episodes with mutual involvement, $F(1, 44) = 6.27$, $p < .05$, and cooperative pretend play, $F(1, 44) = 3.79$, $p < .05$, than did Mexican dyads.

MATERNAL PLAY BEHAVIORS

To examine the behaviors that mothers used to structure children's play and to understand how maternal behaviors differ by age and culture, four ANOVAs, 3(Age) × 2(Culture), were conducted. No significant main effects or interactions were found for age. However, significant main effects appeared for culture. American mothers used more implicit guidance (U.S., $M = 40.00$, $SD = 21.09$; Mexico, $M = 19.80$, $SD = 13.25$), $F(1, 58) = 19.31$, $p < .001$; supported child's effort (U.S., $M = 6.30$, $SD = 5.71$; Mexico, $M = 1.57$, $SD = 3.92$), $F(1, 58) = 13.54$, $p < .001$; and suggested fantasy (U.S., $M = 16.83$, $SD = 15.02$; Mexico, $M = 8.50$, $SD = 10.53$), $F(1, 58) = 6.92$, $p < .01$, than did Mexican mothers. Mexican mothers used more explicit guidance (Mexico, $M = 53.46$, $SD = 24.42$; U.S., $M = 36.26$, $SD = 16.69$), $F(1, 58) = 10.44$, $p < .01$, than did American mothers.

MATERNAL INTERVIEWS

Answers in each category were summed and compared by culture. The majority of the American mothers believed that play was very important and provided educational benefits for children. The most common play partners were mothers and siblings. In contrast, the majority of the Mexican mothers believed that play was a relatively unimportant activity that provided amusement for children rather than educational benefits. The most common play partners were siblings and other children.

In summary, many American mothers interpreted the play task as a teaching opportunity whereas some simply played. Mothers who saw their role as a teacher tended to sit back from the play activity while offering commentary on the child's actions and providing suggestions for play. Other mothers used a question-and-answer format to talk about the physical properties of the shapes and used praise to reward correct answers. All mothers made frequent

TABLE 3 CULTURAL DIFFERENCES IN FREQUENCIES OF MATERNAL BELIEFS ABOUT PLAY, ITS IMPORTANCE, AND MOST COMMON PLAY PARTNERS		
	Culture	
	U.S. (n = 30)	**Mexico** (n = 30)
Value of Play		
Child's amusement	2	27
Mutual enjoyment	8	0
Educational benefits	20	3
Importance		
None	0	27
Somewhat	5	3
Very	25	0
Play Partners		
Mother	18	0
Father	2	0
Siblings	10	20
Unrelated children	0	10

suggestions for play and provided assistance when necessary or requested by their child. Mothers who tended to play rather than teach their child suggested symbolic play themes, engaged in role play, and animated human figures and vehicle shapes using paralinguistic cues. In contrast, a few Mexican mothers made suggestions for symbolic play and animated the shapes, whereas others drew their children's attention to the properties of the shapes and then handed them individually to their children to examine.

Some American mothers reported that they frequently played with their children because it was mutually enjoyable, whereas others said they believed that children derived some benefit from it. In contrast, Mexican mothers rarely sat down to play formally with their children. Although the Mexican mothers in this study did not discourage children's play, and said they enjoyed their children's playful efforts at modeling their behavior, they did not attach any particular value to play activity nor did they believe it was important for them to play with their children.

DISCUSSION

The results support the initial assumption that cultural variations in activity-setting components are associated with not only the frequency and the expression of mother–child play, but also the con-

texts in which play occurs. In the American setting, where play activity is valued for its educational benefits, mothers spent time directly organizing children's play activities by providing objects and ideas for play as well as engaging in the play itself. Mothers' facilitation of the play contexts seemed to enhance their children's expression of symbolic level play and the frequency of joint cooperative pretend play.

In contrast, mother–child play was not a common feature of the Mexican setting. In the Mexican community, unlike the American community, children's symbolic or pretend play behavior does not originate in interaction with adults. When asked to play, these Mexican mothers readily complied, but their play became explicit teaching which was based on a work model rather than a play activity setting model. Mexican mother–child interactive play took place in the context of shared work activity rather than in more structured, child-centered pretend play situations that are characteristic of American culture. For example, in the American setting mothers and their children were observed dressing dolls and putting them in baby-doll carriages, whereas, in the Mexican context, mothers and children played with real babies.

This finding is a challenge to the emphasis that Western researchers have placed on the mother–child relationship in facilitating children's early efforts at pretense. Results from a subsequent comparison of mother– and sibling–child play in the same two settings (Farver, 1993) suggest that, in this particular Mexican environment, play develops in the context of sibling interaction. Sibling caretaking and mixed-age group play experiences may provide opportunities for Mexican older siblings to develop skills in directing play with younger siblings. In turn, younger children may begin to acquire skills and knowledge by participating in play activities with more competent partners. The scaffolding or supporting of play provided by a more skilled partner may be essential to the development of children's play, but who does the scaffolding and how it gets done may be culture-specific.

Differences found in the mother–child play and social interaction among the Mexican families should not be construed as cultural deficiencies. Instead, cultural differences apparent in the maternal play behaviors may be related to culture-specific childrearing practices that serve adaptive functions. In both cultures, mothers modified their children's play behavior toward goals and values that were consistent with their patterns of coping with the surrounding environment.

The issue of a possible confound of social class and culture is an important one. Based on the work of Mexican sociologists, relative to the current class structure within Mexico today these families can be considered working class. Although the living conditions of the Mexican families are more "humble" than those of the American families, based on the data reported here it is suggested that cultural values and childrearing practices, rather than material conditions, influence mother–child play.

The use of a single, 20-min quantitative procedure raises two issues. The first concerns the interdependence of the setting and the individual. That is, by asking mothers to play with unfamiliar toys are they being removed from their context and, therefore, do their activities become meaningless? A subsequent analysis of mother–child play with the same subjects in a natural play context suggests not. This research yielded results similar to the structured mother–child "toy play" procedure presented here (Farver, 1991).

The second issue concerns the representativeness of a short 20-min play session. The data reported here were only one part of a larger study examining children's play alone and with multiple partners in toy (shape) play and free-play contexts. Two hours of videotaped play for each child are the bases of the generalizations made here.

In spite of the attempts to balance social class, to collect qualitative observations to inform the quantitative data, and to use "culture free" toys, alternative interpretations of the results are possible. The sample size was small and the communities discussed here represent only two examples of Mexican and American societies. Also, a considerable range of intracultural variability and a great variety of individual differences exist in any cultural group. Therefore, these results need to be replicated in other samples.

REFERENCES

Alba, F. (1982). *The population of Mexico: Trends, issues, and policies*. NJ: Transaction Press.

Balán, J. (1973). *Migration, occupational structure and social mobility*. Mexico City: National Autonomous University of Mexico Press.

Bradley, R., & Caldwell, B. (1984). The relation of infants' home environment to achievement test performance in first grade: A follow-up study. *Child Development, 55*, 803–809.

Bronstein-Burrows, P. (1981). Patterns of parent behavior: A cross-cultural study. *Merrill-Palmer Quarterly, 27*, 129–143.

Diáz-Guerrero, R. (1975). *Psychology of the Mexican: Culture and personality*. Austin: University of Texas Press.

Eckstein, S. (1989). *The poverty of revolution*. Princeton, NJ: Princeton University Press.

Falicov, C. J., & Karrer, B. M. (1980). Cultural variations in the family life cycle: The Mexican-American family. In E. Carter & M. Goldrick (Eds.), *The family life cycle: A framework for family therapy*. New York: Gardner.

Farver, J. (1991, April). Free play activities of American and Mexican mother–child pairs. In L. Beizer & P. Miller (Chairs), *Cultural dimensions of pretend play in infancy and early childhood*. Symposium conducted at the meeting of the Society for Research in Child Development, Seattle, WA.

Farver, J. (1993). Cultural differences in scaffolding play: A comparison of American and Mexican mother–child and sibling–child pairs. In K. MacDonald (Ed.), *Parent–Child Play: Descriptions and Implications*. Albany, NY: SUNY Press.

Feitelson, D. (1977). Cross-cultural studies of representational play. In B. Tizard & D. Harvey (Eds.), *The biology of play*. Suffolk, England: Levenham Press.

Glaser, B., & Strauss, A. (1967). *The discovery of grounded theory*. New York: Aldine.

Haight, W., & Miller, P. (1991, April). Belief systems that frame and inform middle-class parents' participation in their young children's pretend play. In L. Beizer & P. Miller (Chairs), *Cultural dimensions of pretend play in infancy and early childhood*. Symposium conducted at the meeting of the Society for Research in Child Development, Seattle, WA.

Hoffman, L. (1988). Cross-cultural differences in childrearing goals. In R. LeVine, P. Miller, & M. Maxwell (Eds.), *Parental behavior in diverse societies: New directions for child development*. San Francisco: Jossey-Bass.

Holtzman, W. (1982). Cross-cultural comparisons of personality development in Mexico and the United States. In D. Wagner & H. Stevenson (Eds.), *Cultural perspectives on child development*. San Francisco: Freeman.

Holtzman, W., Díaz-Guerrero, R., Swartz, J., & Tapia, L. (1969). Cross-cultural longitudinal research on child development: Studies of American and Mexican school children. In J. P. Hill (Ed.), *Minnesota Symposia on Child Psychology*. Minneapolis: University of Minnesota Press.

Howes, C. (1980). Peer play scale as an index of complexity of social interaction. *Developmental Psychology, 16*, 371–372.

Howes, C. (1985). Sharing fantasy: Social pretend play in toddlers. *Child Development, 56*, 1253–1258.

Kagan, S. (1981). Ecology and the acculturation of cognitive and social styles among Mexican-American children. *Hispanic Journal of Behavioral Sciences, 3*, 111–144.

Kagan, S., & Ember, P. (1975). Maternal response to success and failure of Anglo-American, Mexican-American and Mexican children. *Child Development, 46*, 452–458.

Keefe, S., Padrilla, A., & Carlos, M. (1979). The Mexican-American extended family as an emotional support system. *Human Organization, 38*, 144–152.

Lawton, J., Fowell, N., Schuler, A., & Madsen, M. (1984). Parents' perceptions of actual and ideal childrearing practices. *Journal of Genetic Psychology, 145*, 77–87.

Leont'ev, A. N. (1981). The problem of activity in psychology. In J. Wertsch (Ed.), *The concept of activity in Soviet psychology*. Armonk, NY: Sharpe.

Levenstein, P. (1986). Mother–child interaction and children's educational achievement. In A. Gottfried & C. Brown (Eds.), *Play interactions: The contributions of play materials and parental involvement to children's development*. Boston: Lexington.

Levenstein, P. (1993). The necessary lightness of mother–child play. In K. MacDonald (Ed.), *Parent–Child Play: Descriptions and Implications*. Albany: SUNY Press.

Levine, R. A. (1980). *Anthropology and child development: New directions for child development*. San Francisco: Jossey-Bass.

Miller, P., & Garvey, C. (1984). Mother–baby role play: Its origins in social support. In I. Bretherton (Ed.), *Symbolic play*. New York: Academic Press.

O'Connell, B., & Bretherton, I. (1984). Toddlers' play, alone and with mothers. In I. Bretherton (Ed.), *Symbolic play*. New York: Academic Press.

Peñalosa, P. (1968). Mexican family roles. *Journal of Marriage and the Family, 30*, 680–689.

Ramírez, M. (1967). Identification with Mexican family values and authoritarianism in Mexican-Americans. *Journal of Social Psychology, 73*, 3–11.

Ramírez, M., & Castañeda, A. (1974). *Cultural democracy, bicognitive development and education*. New York: Academic Press.

Ramírez, M., & Price-Williams, D. (1974). Cognitive styles in children: Two Mexican communities. *Interamerican Journal of Psychology, 8*, 93–101.

Richman, A., Miller, P., & Solomon, M. (1988). The socialization of infants in suburban Boston. In R. LeVine, P. Miller, & M. Maxwell (Eds.), *Parental behavior in diverse societies: New directions for child development*. San Francisco: Jossey-Bass.

Rogoff, B., Mistry, J., Göncü, A., & Mosier, C. (1991). Cultural variation in the role relations of toddlers and their families. In M. Bornstein (Ed.), *Cultural approaches to parenting*. Hillsdale, NJ: Erlbaum.

Romney, K., & Romney, R. (1966). *The Mixtecans of Juxtlahuaca*. New York: Wiley.

Slade, A. (1987). A longitudinal study of maternal involvement and symbolic play. *Child Development, 58*, 367–375.

Smilansky, S. (1968). *The effect of sociodramatic play on disadvantaged school children*. New York: Wiley.

Suárez, E. C. (1978). *Stratification and social mobility in Mexico City*. Mexico City: National Autonomous University of Mexico Press.

Tharp, R., & Gallimore, R. (1988). *Rousing minds to life*. Cambridge: Cambridge University Press.

Vygotsky, L. (1978). *Mind in society*. Cambridge: Cambridge University Press.

Weisner, T., Gallimore R., & Jordan, C. (1988). Unpacking cultural effects on classroom learning: Native Hawaiian peer assistance and child generated activity. *Education and Anthropology Quarterly, 19*, 327–353.

Werner, H., & Kaplan, B. (1963). *Symbol formation*. New York: Wiley.

White, B. L. (1980). *A parent's guide to the first three years*. Trenton: Prentice-Hall.

Whiting, B., & Edwards, C. P. (1988). *Children of different worlds: The formation of social behavior*. Cambridge: Harvard University Press.

Zukow, P. (1989). *Sibling interaction across cultures*. New York: Springer-Verlag.

QUESTIONS

1. What is the main reason given by Farver and Howes for expanding research on young children's play to include children from different cultural settings?
2. What is pretend play, and why is it important to child development?
3. According to traditional Western theories of development, how does children's pretend play originate?
4. What is an activity-setting approach to research in child development?
5. Examine the features of American and Mexican activity settings for child development. What are the common features in these two communities? What features differ?
6. What did Farver and Howes do to minimize the impact of observing the families in the Mexican setting? Do you think these efforts were important to make? Why?
7. What are the different ways that mothers and other family members assist children during pretend play in the United States and Mexico?
8. How is children's play different in these two communities? Are there any similarities?
9. What do the mothers in these two communities believe about the importance of play in children's development and about their own role in child's play?
10. How do the different play patterns that were observed in these two communities relate to the cultural values prevalent in each setting? What does this tell you about the role of play in the socialization of children?

23 Gender and Group Process: A Developmental Perspective

ELEANOR E. MACCOBY

Gender-related differences in human behavior have been of interest to psychologists for generations. One of the main questions asked by developmental psychologists is: How do these differences originate? Observing the behavior of young children is one of the best ways to answer this question. Many gender-related behaviors begin to appear during the preschool and early school years.

Eleanor Maccoby has spent her career studying young children's social relationships and development, and she has taken particular interest in the topic of gender differences in social situations and relationships. One observation she finds especially intriguing is that gender-related behaviors are more evident when children are observed in groups than when they are tested individually. This pattern suggests that something about social experience is critical to the expression, and perhaps the development, of gender-related behaviors.

To pursue this topic, the following article explores the role of social relationships in the development and organization of gender-related behaviors. In particular, it focuses on the group activities of girls and boys from early childhood through preadolescence. Several factors pertaining to group influence on the development of gender-related behaviors are discussed, including group composition, group size, patterns of social interaction in boy and girl groups, and behavioral preferences and themes that emerge in gender-segregated play. Maccoby argues that affiliations with peers throughout childhood play a pivotal role in the development and maintenance of gender-related behaviors. This idea is provocative because it is contrary to the longstanding view that parents, not peers, are the major influence on children's gender-typed behaviors.

Until recently, the study of gender development has focused mainly on sex typing as an attribute of the individual. Although this perspective continues to be enlightening, recent work has focused increasingly on children's tendency to congregate in same-sex groups. This self-segregation of the two sexes implies that much of childhood gender enactment occurs in the context of same sex dyads or larger groups. There are emergent properties of such groups, so that certain sex-distinctive qualities occur at the level of the group rather than at the level of the individual. There is increasing research interest in the distinctive nature of the group structures, activities, and interactions that typify all-male as compared with all-female groups, and in the socialization that occurs within these groups. Next steps in research will surely call for the integration of the individual and group perspectives.

Among researchers who study the psychology of gender, a central viewpoint has always been that individuals progressively acquire a set of behaviors, interests, personality traits, and cognitive biases that are more typical of their own sex than of the other sex. And the individual's sense of being either a male or a female person (*gender identity*) is thought to be a core element in the developing sense of self. The acquisition of these sex-distinctive characteristics has been called *sex typing,* and much research has focused on how and why the processes of sex typing occur. A favorite strategy has been to examine differences among individuals in how sex typed they are at a given age, searching for factors associated with a person's becoming more or less "masculine" or more or less "feminine" than other individuals. In early work, there was a heavy emphasis on the family as the major context in which sex typing was believed to take place. Socialization

Reprinted with permission of Blackwell Publishers from Maccoby, E. E. (2002). Gender and group process: A developmental perspective. *Current Directions in Psychological Science, 11,* 55–58.

pressures from parents were thought to shape the child toward "sex-appropriate" behaviors, personality, and interests and a firm gender identity.

On the whole, the efforts to understand gender development by studying individual differences in rate or degree of sex typing, and the connections of these differences to presumed antecedent factors, have not been very successful. The various manifestations of sex typing in childhood—toy and activity preferences, knowledge of gender stereotypes, personality traits—do not cohere together to form a cluster that clearly represents a degree of sex typing in a given child. And whether or not a given child behaves in a gender-typical way seems to vary greatly from one situation to another, depending on the social context and other conditions that make an individual's gender salient at a given moment. Only weak and inconsistent connections have been found between within-family socialization practices and children's sex-typed behavior (Ruble & Martin, 1998). And so far, the study of individual variations in sex typing has not helped us to understand the most robust manifestation of gender during childhood: namely, children's strong tendency to segregate themselves into same-sex social groups. Although work on gender development in individual children continues and shows renewed vigor, a relatively new direction of interest is in children's groups. This current research and theorizing considers how gender is implicated in the formation, interaction processes, and socialization functions of childhood social groupings.

In some of this work, the dyad or larger group, rather than the individual child, is taken as the unit of analysis. Through the history of theoretical writings by sociologists and social psychologists, there have been claims that groups have emergent properties, and that their functioning cannot be understood in terms of the characteristics of their individual members (Levine & Moreland, 1998). Accumulating evidence from recent work suggests that in certain gender configurations, pairs or groups of children elicit certain behaviors from each other that are not characteristic of either of the participants when alone or in other social contexts (Martin & Fabes, 2001). Another possibility is that the group context amplifies what are only weak tendencies in the individual participants. For example, in their article "It Takes Two to Fight," Coie and his colleagues (1999) found that the probability of a fight occurring depended not only on the aggressive predispositions of the two individual boys involved, but also on the unique properties of the dyad itself. Other phenomena, such as social approach to another child, depend on the sex of the approacher and the approachee taken jointly, not on the sex of either child, when children's sociability is analyzed at the level of the individual (summarized in Maccoby, 1998). It is important, then, to describe and analyze children's

dyads or larger groups as such, to see how gender is implicated in their characteristics and functioning.

GENDER COMPOSITION OF CHILDREN'S GROUPS

Beginning at about age 3, children increasingly choose same-sex playmates when in settings where their social groupings are not managed by adults. In preschools, children may play in loose configurations of several children, and reciprocated affiliation between same-sex pairs of children is common, while such reciprocation between pairs of opposite sex is rare (Strayer, 1980; Vaughan, Colvin, Azria, Caya, & Krzysik, 2001). On school playgrounds, children sometimes play in mixed-sex groups, but increasingly, as they move from age 4 to about age 12, they spend a large majority of their free play time exclusively with others of their own sex, rarely playing in a mixed-sex dyad or in a larger group in which no other child of their own sex is involved. Best friendships in middle childhood and well into adolescence are very heavily weighted toward same-sex choices. These strong tendencies toward same-sex social preferences are seen in the other cultures around the world where gender composition of children's groups has been studied, and are also found among young nonhuman primates (reviewed in Maccoby, 1998).

GROUP SIZE

Naturally occurring face-to-face groups whose members interact with one another continuously over time tend to be small—typically having only two or three members, and seldom having more than five or six members. Some gender effects on group size can be seen. Both boys and girls commonly form same-sex dyadic friendships, and sometimes triadic ones as well. But from about the age of 5 onward, boys more often associate together in larger clusters. Boys are more often involved in organized group games, and in their groups, occupy more space on school playgrounds. In an experimental situation in which same-sex groups of six children were allowed to utilize play and construction materials in any way they wished, girls tended to split into dyads or triads, whereas boys not only interacted in larger groups but were much more likely to undertake some kind of joint project, and organize and carry out coordinated activities aimed at achieving a group goal (Benenson, Apostolaris, & Parnass, 1997). Of course, children's small groups—whether dyads or clusters of four, five, or six children—are nested within still larger group structures, such as cliques or "crowds."

Group size matters. Recent studies indicate that the interactions in groups of four or more are different from what typically occurs in dyads. In larger groups, there is more conflict and more competition, particularly in all-male groups; in dyads, individuals of both sexes are more responsive to their partners, and a partner's needs and perspectives are more often taken into account than when individuals interact with several others at once (Benenson, Nicholson, Waite, Roy, & Simpson, 2001; Levine & Moreland, 1998). The question of course arises: To what extent are certain "male" characteristics, such as greater competitiveness, a function of the fact that boys typically interact in larger groups than girls do? At present, this question is one of active debate and study. So far, there are indications that group size does indeed mediate sex differences to some degree, but not entirely nor consistently.

INTERACTION IN SAME-SEX GROUPS

From about age 3 to age 8 or 9, when children congregate together in activities not structured by adults, they are mostly engaged in some form of play. Playtime interactions among boys, more often than among girls, involve rough-and-tumble play, competition, conflict, ego displays, risk taking, and striving to achieve or maintain dominance, with occasional (but actually quite rare) displays of direct aggression. Girls, by contrast, are more often engaged in what is called collaborative discourse, in which they talk and act reciprocally, each responding to what the other has just said or done, while at the same time trying to get her own initiatives across. This does not imply that girls' interactions are conflict free, but rather that girls pursue their individual goals in the context of also striving to maintain group harmony (summary in Maccoby, 1998).

The themes that appear in boys' fantasies, the stories they invent, the scenarios they enact when playing with other boys, and the fictional fare they prefer (books, television) involve danger, conflict, destruction, heroic actions by male heroes, and trials of physical strength, considerably more often than is the case for girls. Girls' fantasies and play themes tend to be oriented around domestic or romantic scripts, portraying characters who are involved in social relationships and depicting the maintenance or restoration of order and safety.

Girls' and boys' close friendships are qualitatively different in some respects. Girls' friendships are more intimate, in the sense that girl friends share information about the details of their lives and concerns. Boys typically know less about their friends' lives, and base their friendship on shared activities.

Boys' groups larger than dyads are in some respects more cohesive than girls' groups. Boys in groups seek and achieve more autonomy from adults than girls do, and explicitly exclude girls from their activities more commonly than girls exclude boys. Boys more often engage in joint risky activities, and close ranks to protect a group member from adult detection and censure. And friendships among boys are more interconnected; that is, friends of a given boy are more likely to be friends with each other than is the case for several girls who are all friends of a given girl (Markovitz, Benenson, & Dolenszky, 2001). The fact that boys' friendships are more interconnected does not mean that they are closer in the sense of intimacy. Rather, it may imply that male friends are more accustomed to functioning as a unit, perhaps having a clearer group identity.

HOW SEX-DISTINCTIVE SUBCULTURES ARE FORMED

In a few instances, researchers have observed the process of group formation from the first meeting of a group over several subsequent meetings. An up-close view of the formation of gendered subcultures among young children has been provided by Nicolopoulou (1994). She followed classrooms of preschool children through a school year, beginning at the time they first entered the school. Every day, any child could tell a story to a teacher, who recorded the story as the child told it. At the end of the day, the teacher read aloud to the class the stories that were recorded that day, and the child author of each story was invited to act it out with the help of other children whom the child selected to act out different parts. At the beginning of the year, stories could be quite rudimentary (e.g., "There was a boy. And a girl. And a wedding."). By the end of the year, stories became greatly elaborated, and different members of the class produced stories related to themes previously introduced by others. In other words, a corpus of shared knowledge, meanings, and scripts grew up, unique to the children in a given classroom and reflecting their shared experiences.

More important for our present purposes, there was a progressive divergence between the stories told by girls and those told by boys. Gender differences were present initially, and the thematic content differed more and more sharply as time went on, with boys increasingly focusing on themes of conflict, danger, heroism, and "winning," while girls' stories increasingly depicted family, nonviolent themes. At the beginning of the year, children might call upon others of both sexes to act in their stories, but by the end of the year, they almost exclusively called upon children of their own sex to enact the roles in their stories. Thus, although all the children in the class were exposed to the stories told by both sexes, the girls picked up on one set of themes and the boys on another, and two distinct subcultures emerged.

Can this scenario serve as a prototype for the formation of distinctive male and female "subcultures" among children? Yes, in the sense that the essence of these cultures is a set of socially shared cognitions, including common knowledge and mutually congruent expectations, and common interests in specific themes and scripts that distinguish the two sexes. These communalities can be augmented in a set of children coming together for the first time, since by age 5 or 6, most will already have participated in several same-sex groups, or observed them in operation on TV, so they are primed for building gender-distinct subcultures in any new group of children they enter. Were we to ask, "Is gender socially constructed?" the answer would surely be "yes." At the same time, there may well be a biological contribution to the nature of the subculture each sex chooses to construct.

SOCIALIZATION WITHIN SAME-SEX GROUPS

There has long been evidence that pairs of friends—mostly same-sex friends—influence one another (see Dishion, Spracklen, & Patterson, 1996, for a recent example). However, only recently has research focused on the effects of the amount of time young children spend playing with other children of their own sex. Martin and Fabes (2001) observed a group of preschoolers over a 6-month period, to obtain stable scores for how much time they spent with same-sex playmates (as distinct from their time spent in mixed-sex or other-sex play). They examined the changes that occurred, over the 6 months of observation, in the degree of sex typing in children's play activities. Martin and Fabes reported that the more time boys spent playing with other boys, the greater the increases in their activity level, rough-and-tumble play, and sex-typed choices of toys and games, and the less time they spent near adults. For girls, by contrast, large amounts of time spent with other girls was associated with increasing time spent near adults, and with decreasing aggression, decreasing activity level, and increasing choices of girl-type play materials and activities. This new work points to a powerful role for same-sex peers in shaping one another's sex-typed behavior, values, and interests.

WHAT COMES NEXT?

The recent focus on children's same-sex groups has revitalized developmental social psychology, and promising avenues for the next phases of research on gender development have appeared. What now needs to be done?

1. Investigators need to study both the variations and the similarities among same-sex groups in their agendas and interactive processes. The extent of generality across groups remains largely unexplored. The way gender is enacted in groups undoubtedly changes with age. And observations in other cultures indicate that play in same-sex children's groups reflects what different cultures offer in the way of materials, play contexts, and belief systems. Still, it seems likely that there are certain sex-distinctive themes that appear in a variety of cultural contexts.

2. Studies of individual differences need to be integrated with the studies of group process. Within each sex, some children are only marginally involved in same-sex groups or dyads, whereas others are involved during much of their free time. And same-sex groups are internally differentiated, so that some children are popular or dominant while others consistently occupy subordinate roles or may even be frequently harassed by others. We need to know more about the individual characteristics that underlie these variations, and about their consequences.

3. Children spend a great deal of their free time in activities that are not gender differentiated at all. We need to understand more fully the conditions under which gender is salient in group process and the conditions under which it is not.

REFERENCES

Benenson, J.F., Apostolaris, N. H., & Parnass, J. (1997). Age and sex differences in dyadic and group interaction. *Developmental Psychology, 33*, 538–543.

Benenson, J.F., Nicholson, C., Waite, A., Roy, R., & Simpson, A. (2001). The influence of group size on children's competitive behavior. *Child Development, 72*, 921–928.

Coie, J.D., Dodge, K.A., Schwartz, D., Cillessen, A.H.N., Hubbard, J.A., & Lemerise, E.A. (1999). It takes two to fight: A test of relational factors, and a method for assessing aggressive dyads. *Developmental Psychology, 36*, 1179–1188.

Dishion, T.J., Spracklen, K.M., & Patterson, G.R. (1996). Deviancy training in male adolescent friendships. *Behavior Therapy, 27*, 373–390.

Levine, J.M., & Moreland, R.L. (1998). Small groups. In D.T. Gilbert, S.T. Fiske, & G. Lindzey (Eds.), *Handbook of social psychology* (Vol. 2, pp. 415–469). Boston: McGraw-Hill.

Maccoby, E. E. (1998). *The two sexes: Growing up apart, coming together.* Cambridge, MA: Harvard University Press.

Markovitz, H., Benenson, J.F., & Dolenszky, E. (2001). Evidence that children and adolescents have internal models of peer interaction that are gender differentiated. *Child Development, 72*, 879–886.

Martin, C. L., & Fabes, R.A. (2001). The stability and consequences of young children's same-sex peer interactions. *Developmental Psychology, 37,* 431–446.

Nicolopoulou, A. (1997). Worldmaking and identity formation in children's narrative play-acting. In B. Cox & C. Lightfoot (Eds.), *Sociogenic perspectives in internalization* (pp. 157–187). Hillsdale, NJ: Erlbaum.

Ruble, D. N., & Martin, C. L. (1998). Gender development. In W. Damon & N. Eisenberg (Eds.), *Handbook of child psychology* (5th ed., Vol. 3, pp. 933–1016). New York: John Wiley & Sons.

Strayer, F.F. (1980). Social ecology of the preschool peer group. In W. A. Collins (Ed.), *Minnesota Symposium on Child Psychology: Vol. 13. Development of cognitions, affect and social relations* (pp. 165–196). Hillsdale, NJ: Erlbaum.

Vaughn, B. E., Colvin, T. N., Azria, M.R., Caya, L., & Krzysik, L. (2001). Dyadic analyses of friendship in a sample of preschool-aged children attending Headstart. *Child Development, 72,* 862–878.

Questions

1. What is sex typing, and what are some of its manifestations in childhood?
2. What social experiences have traditionally been considered the most critical to sex typing in children? Does research support this view?
3. What does Maccoby mean when she says that groups have emergent properties?
4. What patterns of gender-related affiliations appear between 3 and 12 years of age?
5. Are groups of boys different from groups of girls? How?
6. Researchers have found that children's behaviors are more sex-typed when they play with a child of the same sex than with a child of the other sex. Why do you think this happens?
7. What did Nicolopoulou's study reveal about the emergence of boy and girl subcultures?
8. What are the behavioral consequences of boys playing more with boys and girls playing more with girls throughout childhood?
9. Are greater competitiveness among boys and more cooperativeness among girls due to gender differences in group size in childhood or to some other factor?
10. What implications do the results of Maccoby's research have for the question of whether children should be in same-sex or mixed-sex classrooms in the early years of school?

24 Child Care Quality Matters: How Conclusions May Vary with Context

JOHN M. LOVE · LINDA HARRISON · ABRAHAM SAGI-SCHWARTZ · MARINUS H. VAN IJZENDOORN · CHRISTINE ROSS · JUDY A. UNGERER · ET AL.

Over the past 30 years, women in the United States and other developed countries have entered the paid labor force in record numbers. The majority of these women have young children who are in need of supervision and care while their mothers are at work. This reality has posed enormous challenges for families and society. From the perspective of developmental psychology, two important questions arise. On the one hand, we know from research that early attachment to primary caregivers is critical to the child's well-being; does care outside the home disrupt the formation or stability of this primary relationship? On the other hand, we also know from research that stimulation that is appropriately targeted toward the child's current capabilities can foster social, cognitive, and language development; can outside child-care benefit children by enhancing opportunities for the development of language, social skills, and other cognitive abilities? The answers to these questions not only will help parents decide how to balance the care of their young children with the economic needs of their family but also will determine the shape of child-care in years to come.

In the following article, a team of investigators describes how they examined the relationship between early child-care and psychological outcomes for children in three national contexts: Australia, Israel, and the United States. The goal of this research was to home in on the question of how the quality of the care a child experiences outside the home relates to the amount of time that children spend in such settings. Although research on the impact of early child-care on development is still an active area of study, much has been learned over the last decade. As a result, developmental psychologists are increasingly able to provide helpful information for parents, care providers, and policymakers regarding this important psychological and societal issue.

Three studies examined associations between early child care and child outcomes among families different from those in the National Institute of Child Health and Human Development (NICHD) Early Child Care Research Network study. Results suggest that quality is an important influence on children's development and may be an important moderator of the amount of time in care. Thus, the generalizability of the NICHD findings may hinge on the context in which those results were obtained. These studies, conducted in three national contexts, with different regulatory climates, ranges of child care quality, and a diversity of family characteristics, suggest a need for more complete estimates of how both quality and quality of child care may influence a range of young children's developmental outcomes.

Accumulated evidence suggests that for children in child care, the quality of that care is important for their development (Lamb, 1998; Love, Schochet, & Meckstroth, 1996), but findings differ with respect to the nature of the relationship of quality and quality of care with various developmental outcomes. Although higher quality care has been associated with improved cognitive and language skills across a range of studies (e.g., see Campbell, Pungello, Miller-John-

Reprinted with permission of Blackwell Publishers from Love, J. M., Harrison, L., Sagi-Schwartz, A., van Ijzendoorn, M. H., Ross, C., Ungerer, J. A., Raikes, H., Brady-Smith, C., Boller, K., Brooks-Gunn, J., Constantine, J., Kisker, E. E., Paulsell, D., & Chazan-Cohen, R. (2003). Child care quality matters: How conclusions may vary with context. *Child Development, 74,* 1021–1033.

son, Burchinal, & Ramey, 2001; National Institute of Child Health and Human Development [NICHD] Early Child Care Research Network, 2000b, 2003b), associations between care quality and social-emotional development have been more mixed. The latest report from the NICHD Early Child Care Research Network (2003b), consistent with its previous reports, concludes that more time spent in "any of a variety of nonmaternal care arrangements" leads children to display more externalizing behavior problems, and that this relationship holds regardless of quality and other factors (NICHD Early Child Care Research Network, 2003a). Given the potential implications of such findings for understanding children's social-emotional development and contributing to child care policy, it is critical to assess the extent to which the NICHD findings might generalize to other child care contexts.

In this article, we bring together research on this issue from three perspectives: (a) the Sydney Family Development Project (SFDP), (b) the Haifa–NICHD merged data, and (c) the Early Head Start program evaluation in the United States. These perspectives contribute to the child care debate by extending the levels of observed child care quality beyond the more restricted range of the NICHD study, expanding the diversity of families included in the research and breaking the correlation between quality of care and socioeconomic status (SES) found in the NICHD study. The Haifa study adds a sample of families using much lower quality child care across all SES groups; the Australian study adds a sample of families from different SES groups using generally higher quality government-regulated care relative to the average quality of care in the United States; and the Early Head Start study adds a sample of low-income families experimentally offered care of higher quality than is generally available to families with infants and toddlers in the United States, and who are more diverse than the NICHD study families.

The child care settings of the three studies also exist within different regulatory contexts: both regulated (moderately high quality) and nonregulated settings in Sydney, homogenous and high standards in Haifa, and homogenous and high standards in Early Head Start. The three studies include diverse measures of child care quality as well as a range of outcome measures that span children's cognitive and social-emotional domains (from attachment security to language to aggressive behavior problems).

Together our three perspectives capitalize on this diversity, and together they investigate how quantity and quality of child care may relate to children's development. We begin with the Sydney study, move to the merged Haifa-NICHD data, and then turn to the United States to look at child care in the federal Early Head Start program.

AN AUSTRALIAN PERSPECTIVE ON QUALITY, QUANTITY, AND STABILITY IN CHILD CARE

The first perspective is based on a 6-year longitudinal study of the use and effects of child care in an Australian sample of 147 primiparous mothers. Like the study conducted by the NICHD Early Child Care Research Network, the SFDP used a correlational design to assess the relationships of type, amount, and stability of children's child care experiences to developmental outcomes at key points: infant-mother attachment at 12 months, behavior problems at 30 months and 5 years, and teacher-rated adjustment to school at 6 years. The results, however, indicate a different relationship between child care and development than that reported by the NICHD study. We believe this is due, in part, to differing levels of child care quality in the Australian and U. S. contexts.

Like the United States, Australia has achieved a high level of workforce participation among women of child-bearing age (46% with children under 5 years, Australian Bureau of Statistics, 1998; 65% within 18 months after giving birth, Glezer, 1998); however, unlike the United States, this has been linked to government child care policies that have actively encouraged mothers to return to the workforce. Significant funds at both state and federal levels are directed to child care services for children from birth to 12 years, and to preschool programs for children aged 3 to 5 years. State regulations require child care centers to meet minimum child-staff ratios (e.g., New South Wales, 5:1 for children under 2 years, 8:1 for 2- to 3-year-olds, 10:1 for 3- to 5-year-olds) and to employ specialist staff with early childhood qualifications (e.g., 3- to 4-year university degree, 2- to 3-year technical college diploma). Similar standards operate in Australian Family Day Care services, where the child-adult ratio is 5:1 for children under 5 years, and caregivers receive regular training and supervision by qualified early childhood staff. At the federal level, the Quality Improvement and Accreditation System requires centers to meet criterion-based standards of care for families to receive government subsidies for the cost of care (National Childcare Accreditation Council [NCAC], 1993). Fee reductions apply to most families, on an income-to-needs basis, and provide a major incentive for child care operators to become accredited. Australia's national system of formal, government-regulated child care services arguably achieves a uniformly higher level of quality than is found in the United States (e.g., Wangmann, 1995) and, accordingly, could be expected to show a different relationship with children's development than has been reported in studies in the United States.

Despite these provisions, however, not all child care is provided through the formal system, especially during the first 2 years of life, when informal care with relatives, friends, babysitters, or nannies is more typical (e.g., from birth to 1 year, 37% informal vs. 8.5% formal; age 1 to 2 years, 46% informal vs. 24% formal; Australian Bureau of Statistics, 1999). Although similar informal arrangements have been noted in U.S. studies (NICHD Early Child Care Research Network, 1997a), the reasons may not be the same, perhaps because American parents do not receive government financial support for the full cost of child care and may choose informal care as a cheaper option (Scarr & Eisenberg, 1993). Australian families are eligible for financial assistance, which suggests that the decision to use informal care arrangements may be based on personal preference rather than cost. In regard to quality, Australia requires informal child care providers to be registered but as yet has no regulatory systems to support or supervise caregivers. As a result, child-adult ratios, caregiver qualifications, and other factors potentially influencing quality are determined solely by the caregivers themselves. Without regulatory standards, informal settings are likely to be more variable in quality than are formal services and, therefore, less predictive of outcomes for children.

The informal and formal sectors of Australia's child care system provide a useful dichotomy for describing child care quality and comparing the effects of home-based care of variable quality with centers and Family Day Care homes of uniformly moderate to high quality. As such, Australian research has the capacity to extend what has been reported for quality versus quantity of child care in the NICHD study.

COMMONALITIES AND DIFFERENCES BETWEEN THE SFDP AND THE NICHD STUDY

Participants in the SFDP differed from those in the NICHD study in that all the SFDP children were first-born, and mothers were selected to be representative of a larger community sample ($n = 453$) on broad indexes of personality functioning (see Harrison & Ungerer, 2002a). The range of mothers' educational levels (less than high school to postgraduate) was comparable to the range in the NICHD sample (NICHD Early Child Care Research Network, 1997b).

Families' use of child care was similar to that of the NICHD families. By age 12 months, 72% of children were receiving regular nonmaternal care, 18% attended fewer than 10 hr per week, 32% attended part-time (11–30 hr per week), and 22% attended full-time (> 30 hr per week). At 30 months, 86% were in regular care (24% informal, 62% formal). By 3 years, 97% of children were in care, and many (46%) had entered preschool. Cross-age correlations showed

that average weekly hours during the first 12 months were consistent with weekly hours at 30 months, 3 years, and 4 years, $rs = .50$ to $.63$, $p < .001$.

Assessments of children's developmental outcomes matched those in the NICHD longitudinal study. We included security of infant–mother attachment at 12 months (Strange Situation; Ainsworth, Blehar, Waters, & Wall, 1978), mother-reported behavior problems at 30 months and 5 years (Child Behavior Checklist [CBCL]; Achenbach, 1991), and teacher ratings of adjustment to school at 6 years. Teacher-child conflict was assessed (Student–Teacher Relationship Scale: Pianta, 1990) along with other measures of behavioral and social competence (Teacher–Child Rating Scale: Hightower et al., 1989; Classroom Behavior Inventory: Schaefer, Edgerton, & Aaronson, 1978; Teacher Rating Form; Prosocial Behavior Scale; Klein & Abu Taleb, 1993).

The SFDP research questions focused on quality (formal vs. informal care) and quantity of early child care (i.e., from birth to 30 months of age), and stability of care over time (i.e., from birth to 6 years). Changes in care arrangements at three periods (birth to 12 months, 12 to 30 months, 30 months to 6 years) were used to construct a measure describing consistent patterns of more or less stable care. To assess the predictive relationships between child care factors and child outcomes, effects were assessed after controlling for family SES, maternal psychological well-being, marital relationship quality, social support, and child gender and temperament characteristics. For attachment security, maternal sensitivity also was included as a predictor (see Harrison & Ungerer, 2002a). As the questions related to the experience of nonmaternal care, children who were in exclusive maternal care were not included in the analyses.

LONGITUDINAL FINDINGS FROM THE SFDP: EFFECTS OF QUALITY, QUANTITY, AND STABILITY OF CARE

Infant–mother attachment security at 12 months. Secure versus insecure attachment outcomes were compared for the 85 infants who received regular child care during the first year—52 in informal settings versus 33 in formal care. (Sixty children in maternal care were not included in these analyses.) Security was associated with formal care (Family Day Care: 100% secure; center care: 63% secure) rather than informal care (56% secure). Of the children in part-time or full-time care, 70% had secure attachments, whereas only 39% of children attending care for fewer than 10 hr per week were secure (Harrison & Ungerer, 1997). The association between security and formal care was confirmed by logistic regression tests, controlling for hours of care, maternal education, social support, and child difficult temperament

(Wald coefficient = 5.24, $p = .02$; model $\chi^2 = 19.69$, $N = 85$, $df = 5$, $p = .001$; with maternal sensitivity, Wald coefficient = 3.53, $p = .06$; model $\chi^2 = 23.87$, $N = 78$, $df = 6$, $p = .001$). Quantity of care was not a significant predictor in these analyses.

Behavior problems at 30 months and 5 years. Mothers' scores for the child's internalizing, externalizing, and total behavior problems at age 30 months and 5 years showed no associations with type or quantity of early care, $rs(115) = -.01$ to $.08$, *ns*.

Adjustment to school at 6 years. Teacher ratings provided a measure of teacher–child relationship conflict and summary ratings of children's social-emotional development (acting out, hostility, considerateness, prosocial behavior), personal adjustment (outgoing with peers, extrovert, shy or anxious, introvert), and adjustment to the learning demands of school (task orientation, creativity, intelligent behavior, distractibility). Relationships between child care factors and child outcomes were tested using hierarchical regression analyses, controlling for family and child characteristics (Harrison & Ungerer, 2002b). Results showed that teacher–child conflict was associated with patterns of more unstable care over time ($\Delta R^2 = .039$, $p < .05$), but that it was not related to quantity or type of early care. Ratings of social-emotional adjustment were also related to stability of care ($\Delta R^2 = .031$, $p < .05$), being lowest in the group of children whose care had been consistently more unstable and highest in the group whose care had a more stable pattern. Personal adjustment ratings were higher when children had attended formal in contrast to informal care during the first 30 months ($\Delta R^2 = .061$, $p < .01$). Competence in learning was predicted by type of care (higher ratings for formal vs. informal care) and by quantity of care (lower ratings for longer hours of care), together explaining 6.3% of the variance (overall $R^2 = .199$, $p < .01$).

How and Why SFDP and NICHD Early Child Care Research Findings Differ

Longitudinal results from the SFDP, based on teachers' and mothers' reports, provide a useful comparison with findings reported by the NICHD Early Child Care Research Network. Although there are many similarities between SFDP and NICHD children's experiences of care over time, the relationships of dimensions of care with developmental outcomes differ. We attribute this to different systems of child care provision and regulation. The present report from NICHD attributes poorer outcomes for social-emotional development to longer hours of care in general and, in particular, to more time in center-based care. In contrast, the SFDP study found no relationship between quantity of care and mother-reported problem behavior, social adjustment to school, or teacher–child conflict. Rather, it

was stability of care over time that contributed to social-emotional aspects of development. Children who had experienced a consistent pattern of more changes in care were rated by teachers as having more conduct problems and less effective social skills. From an attachment perspective (Bowlby, 1969/1978), repeated changes of care, which place additional demands on children to form new relationships and create the stress of losing existing relationships, are a poor basis for developing emotional resourcefulness or social competence. This may be especially salient as children make the transition to school, where they are required to adapt to large numbers of children and proportionally fewer adults than they experienced in child care.

Quality of care, described by formal, regulated care versus informal, unregulated care, was found to be an important predictor of child outcomes in the SFDP. Children who had attended formal settings before age 30 months (85% of whom had received some center care) were rated by their school teachers as more outgoing and extroverted and less shy and anxious than children whose care had been in informal, nonregulated arrangements. Formal care was also associated with teachers' higher ratings for competencies in learning. These findings support a theoretical position that higher quality care (i.e., care programs that meet required standards for equipment, space, and programming, and are provided by appropriately qualified staff) will support children's learning and development (e.g., see National Association for the Education of Young Children, 1987; NCAC, 1993).

The SFDP results provided some evidence for the negative effects of longer hours of child care and, in this sense, were consistent with the NICHD report. Quantity of care was negatively associated with teachers' ratings for competence in learning, regardless of care type. (Note, however, that competence scores were highest for children who had attended formal care for fewer hours, and lowest for children receiving more hours of informal care.) Our results do not support the suggestion that behavior problems (linked to quantity of care) interfere with readiness to learn, but they indicate that problems of attention (task orientation, distractibility) and interest (creativity, intelligent behavior) were linked to longer hours of care.

Quality Child Center Care Is Important: A Mega-Analysis of the NICHD and the Haifa Study of Early Child Care

How Generalizable Is the NICHD Study?

The present report by the NICHD Early Child Care Research Network (this issue) states that amount of early nonmaternal care—not quality of care—is the crucial predictor of later social-emotional adjustment. The main question is whether this finding pertains to the restricted quality range of nonmaternal care provisions in the United States, and to how generalizable it is to settings with much lower or much higher standards of care. Because the Haifa Study of Early Child Care was developed in parallel to the NICHD project and covered nonmaternal care of much lower quality standards (Sagi, Koren-Karie, Gini, Ziv, & Joels, 2002), we can now test the generalizability of some of the earlier NICHD findings in a broader range of quality standards by comparing and combining the two data sets.

COMMONALITIES AND DIFFERENCES BETWEEN THE HAIFA AND THE NICHD STUDIES

Both the Haifa and the NICHD studies addressed questions concerning ecologically relevant predictors of social-emotional adjustment among infants who experienced various types and quality of early care, and in both studies, all SES groups were included. Because public child care centers in Israel are part of a nationwide network, however, infants from both lower- and middle-class families are placed in the same centers, whereas SES tends to be confounded with quality of group care in the United States. In both studies the investigators focused on mother characteristics, infant characteristics and development, mother–child interaction, mother–father relationship, the environment, and the structure and quality of various types of group care. Moreover, the samples are very large ($N = 1,153$, United States; $N = 758$, Israel), with a low attrition rate and recruited in two different developed Western cultures, both of which place a high premium on education. A major outcome variable studied was quality of the infant-mother attachment (for more details on the U.S. study, see NICHD Early Child Care Research Network, 1997a; for more details on the Israeli study, see Sagi et al., 2002).

Various child care correlates were found in the NICHD study to neither adversely affect nor promote the security of infants' attachment to their mothers at the 15-month age point. However, certain child care conditions, in combination with certain home environments, did increase the probability that infants would be insecurely attached to their mothers. More specifically, infants who received poor quality of care, received more than 10 hr of care per week, or were in more than one child care setting during the first 15 months of life were more likely to be insecurely attached only if their mothers were lower in sensitivity (NICHD Early Child Care Research Network, 1997a).

In the Haifa study, child care, especially center care, increased the likelihood of the infants' attachment insecurity to their mothers (Sagi et al., 2002). More specifically, a significantly larger proportion of insecure-ambivalent infants was found in center care (46%) than in each of the following groups: family child care (28%), paid individual care (27%), individual care with a relative (19%), and maternal care (26%). Furthermore, the data clearly showed that it is the very high infant–caregiver ratio (average of 8:1) that accounted for this increased level of attachment insecurity among center care infants when compared with other professional care (viz., family or paid individual care). Because of the large sample size, it was possible to examine the sole effects of type and quality of care by controlling for a vast array of potentially intervening maternal and child characteristics in parallel with the NICHD study. None of these variables was found to mediate or to minimize the negative effects that were discovered only for center care. Thus, early infant center care in Israel, with its very high infant–caregiver ratio, challenged infants' security of attachment to their mothers.

In an additional analysis of the Haifa data (Aviezer, Sagi, & Koren-Karie, 2003), the expected link between maternal sensitivity and infant attachment security was found only for infants in individual care but not for infants in center care, despite the fact that mothers of children in individual care arrangements and mothers of children in center care were equally sensitive. This analysis suggests that the lack of associations between maternal sensitivity and infant attachment security might contribute to the lower security rates found for center care children. Thus, childrearing context may override the expected influence of maternal sensitivity. Indeed, in center care, the proportion of sensitive mothers with insecurely attached infants was similar to the proportion of insensitive mothers with insecurely attached infants, whereas the proportion of sensitive mothers with secure infants in individual care settings was significantly higher than the proportion of sensitive mothers with insecure infants. Hence, maternal sensitivity did not predict attachment security for center care children.

It should be noted that the moderating influence of center care on the formation of attachment relations in the Haifa study is different from the moderating effect of center care that was found in the NICHD study (NICHD Early Child Care Research Network, 1997a). In the NICHD study, maternal behavior was more salient for children in low-quality facilities of nonmaternal care, and the expected associations between maternal sensitivity and infant attachment were more emphasized. The Israeli data for children in low-quality nonmaternal care suggest that maternal behavior was less salient for these infants, who might be so overwhelmed by the low quality of the center care setting that they may no longer experience their mothers' childrearing behavior as good enough.

Based on the structural characteristics of center care in the two studies (e.g., child–caregiver ratio), it is safe to conclude that center care in the Haifa study represented considerably lower quality of care (which was confirmed by direct observations) relative to center care in the NICHD Early Child Care Research Network (1997a; Sagi et al., 2002). In the NICHD study, the social structure as well as more defined state restrictions concerning certification of center care facilities may have prevented the researchers from investigating facilities with extremely low quality. Some child care facilities in deprived and dangerous inner-city areas may have been inaccessible to the researchers, and noncertified centers may have been hesitant to make themselves available for government-subsidized research. Although Israel is a developed Western country with a high education level, the early care system has received inappropriate public attention, resulting in a very-low-quality system of center care for infants. Thus, in combining the two studies for the purpose of secondary analyses, we create a broader continuum of quality of center care and thus make it less likely that restriction of range will influence the generalizability of the findings.

A "Mega-Analysis" on Combined Data from the Haifa and NICHD Studies

Combining data from the two studies, we focused on amount of care and child-caregiver ratio as important indicators of early care. Amount of care and child-caregiver ratio were defined identically in both studies (for details, see NICHD Early Child Care Research Network, 1997a; Sagi et al., 2002). Child-adult ratio is a distal index of quality of care. We were not able to use a more proximal assessment of quality of care here because the measure used in the NICHD study for assessing qualitative aspects in caregiver-infant interaction (Observational Record of the Caregiving Environment; ORCE) was a unique tool developed by the NICHD Early Child Care Research Network, which became accessible to the scientific community only at a later stage. The Haifa study had to develop its own quality assessments. In the Haifa study, however, child-caregiver ratio is strongly linked to quality of care (Koren-Karie, Sagi, & Egoz-Mizrachi, 1998; Sagi et al., 2002). Also, the NICHD Early Child Care Research Network (2000a) has recently found that positive caregiving was associated with smaller child–caregiver ratios. The NICHD study assessed positive caregiving in five types of care: centers, child care homes, and care provided by in-home sitters, grandparents, and fathers (it should be noted that in most publications the NICHD network presents paternal care as another type of nonmaternal care, in the same league as professional caregiving arrangements). Thus, child–caregiver ratio, which is a standard index in both the Haifa and the NICHD studies, is a useful index of quality of care in our secondary analysis. Our analyses on the combined Haifa and NICHD studies are restricted to infant–mother attachment as an outcome variable, and no data are available to conduct a longitudinal secondary data analysis with the combined sample.

Summary of Major Findings

The present analysis is based on a combined sample ($n = 294$) of all center care cases in both studies ($n = 143$, United States; $n = 151$, Israel). From Table 1 it can be derived that the child–caregiver ratio in the Haifa study was twice as large as the ratio in the NICHD study. In both studies, most infants were involved in center child care full time, with an average of about 5.5 hr per week longer involvement in the Israeli case. In Israeli center child care, the percentage of securely attached infants was significantly lower (54%) than in the NICHD centers (67%). In the NICHD study as well as in the Haifa study, child–caregiver ratio and amount of care did not correlate significantly with attachment security (secure vs. nonsecure as a dichotomous variable). Only in the combined sample did we find a significant correlation between child-caregiver ratio and attachment security ($r = -.13$, $p < .05$), indicating that a larger ratio was associated with less infant attachment security. Because amount of care was also significantly related to child–caregiver ratio, we included both predictors in a logistic regression on attachment security. In the combined sample, this regression proved to be significant ($\chi^2 = 6.02$, $n = 267$, $df = 2$, $p = .049$). Only child–caregiver ratio contributed significantly to this regression equation (Wald coefficient = 4.09, $df = 1$, $p = .043$). Amount of care did not significantly contribute to the logistic regression. In the separate NICHD and Haifa samples, the logistic regressions with amount of care and child–caregiver ratio did not significantly explain the variance in attachment security.

In a broader range of center care quality, we found that a higher child–caregiver ratio was indeed associated with less attachment security, whereas amount of care was not a significant predictor. In the separate NICHD and Haifa samples, a similar result failed to emerge. We suggest that the generalizability of the NICHD findings hinges on the specific context in which these results have been obtained, and on the resulting restriction of range for crucial variables. The NICHD finding of a small association between center care quality and child outcomes should be

TABLE 1 DESCRIPTION OF THE SEPARATE NICHD AND HAIFA CENTER CARE SAMPLES, AND THE COMBINED SAMPLE

Variable	NICHD			Haifa			Combined			
	M	SD	N	M	SD	N	M	SD	N	T
Child–caregiver ratio	4.00	1.38	124	8.00	1.96	151	6.20	2.64	275	19.17**
Amount of care	37.24	11.24	141	42.73	6.15	150	40.07	9.38	291	5.21**
Attachment security	0.67	0.47	137	0.54	0.50	151	0.60	0.49	288	−2.35*

	Amount	Security	Amount	Security	Amount	Security
Child–caregiver ratio	−.01	.04	−.02	−.06	.16*	−.13*
Amount of care		.07		−.03		−.01
	$123 < n < 137$		$150 < n < 151$		$269 < n < 285$	

Note. NICHD is the National Institute of Child Health and Human Development.
*$p < .05$.
**$p < .001$.

limited to the specific population of centers from which the NICHD study sample was derived–until empirically demonstrated otherwise. Although our findings in the combined sample are limited in time (infancy) and in number and type of variables (child–caregiver ratio, amount of care, security of attachment), our case illustrates the risks of premature generalizations to other contexts, in particular when the causal processes leading to a significant association between quantity of care and child outcomes, such as security or aggression, still are obscure. Counterintuitive findings that are not based on a priori predictions from a theoretical framework should be interpreted with caution, although such findings may turn out to be among the most important and exciting in our field of inquiry. But let us first establish their truth value in other contexts and construct an adequate theoretical framework to account for them, before jumping to (policy) conclusions. The absence of evidence for a significant contribution of child care quality to children's social development, especially aggression, should be considered a finding in search of replication and explanation.

INFANT AND TODDLER CHILD CARE IN THE CONTEXT OF EARLY HEAD START: QUANTITY, QUALITY, AND CHILDREN'S DEVELOPMENT

The third perspective on the effects of child care on children's development comes from the national evaluation of the federal Early Head Start program in the United States. Like the NICHD study, the Early Head Start evaluation examined the developmental progress of children during the first 3 years of life. Many of the children were in nonparental child care during those early years. In contrast to the NICHD study, however, the Early Head Start study focused exclusively on children from low-income families. Moreover, because of the Early Head Start intervention, many of the children received good-quality, center-based child care, which few of the NICHD children from low-income families experienced. Early Head Start was launched in 1995 by the Administration for Children and Families (ACF), in the U.S. Department of Health and Human Services and was designed as a two-generation program serving low-income pregnant women and families with infants and toddlers up to the age of 3. Early Head Start grantees design programs to achieve benefits for both children and their parents by providing home- or center-based child development services, combining these approaches, or implementing other locally designed options. Detailed findings about the programs' implementation (Administration for Children and Families [ACF], 2002b) and effects through age 3 (ACF, 2002a) can be found in the project's technical reports, which also include detailed descriptions of the study design, instruments, data collection procedures, and analytic methods.

Important for the context of this research are the high standards the federal Head Start Bureau sets for child care quality. The Head Start Program Performance Standards established a clear set of expectations for the quality of center-based child development services. The standards require (a) a child–staff ratio of 4:1 and a maximum group size of eight infants and toddlers in center-based child care settings, and (b) child care staff to have a Child Development Associate credential within 1 year of being hired as an infant-toddler teacher (U.S. Department of Health and Human Services, 1996). These standards exceed those reported for the settings of the Australian and Israeli studies, as well as for standards set by most states within the United States, which is the context for the NICHD research.

METHOD

ACF selected 17 programs to participate in the national evaluation; these sites span all regions of the country and are in both urban and rural settings. A total of 3,001 families applying to these Early Head Start programs between July 1996 and September 1998 were randomly assigned either to the program or to a control group, which could access all services in the community except Early Head Start. Early Head Start families were diverse: 63% were Hispanic, African American, or other non-White groups; 48% had not earned a high school diploma; 38% were teenage parents; and 23% were neither employed nor in school. Parent interviews and assessments of children's development were conducted when the children were approximately 14, 24, and 36 months old. Assessments when children were 24 months old included measures of cognitive development (the Bayley Scales of Infant Development Mental Development Index, BSID–MDI; Bayley, 1993), language development (the MacArthur Communicative Development Inventory language production scale, CDI; Fenson et al., 1993), and aggressive behavior (the Child Behavior Checklist, CBCL; Achenbach, 1992); see Administration on Children, Youth, and Families (2001, chap. 4) for details. At 36 months of age, child assessments included the BSID–MDI, the Peabody Picture-Vocabulary Test–Third Edition (PPVT–III; Dunn & Dunn, 1997), and the CBCL aggressive behavior scale (Achenbach & Rescorla, 2000; see ACF, 2002a, chap. 5).

We asked parents about their use of child care (along with other services) at several points after program enrollment. Child care quality was assessed by trained observers in 2- to 3-hr visits to the child care settings children were in around the time that the 14-, 24-, and 36-month interviews were completed with the children's parents. Settings observed were those that children were in for at least 10 hr per week for at least the 2 weeks preceding the interview and that were not in the child's own home (unless that in-home care was provided by a nonrelative). When children were 14 and 24 months old, observations of center-based care were conducted using the Infant-Toddler Environment Rating Scale (ITERS; Harms, Cryer, & Clifford, 1990). When children were 36

months old, we used the Early Childhood Environment Rating Scale–Revised (ECERS-R; Harms, Clifford, & Cryer, 1998). These scales consist of 35 items that assess the quality of care. (The shortened version of the ITERS we used excluded three items from the adult needs category–opportunities for professional growth, adult meeting area, and provisions for parents.) Item scores range from 1 to 7, in which 1 is described as *inadequate care*, 3 as *minimal care*, 5 as *good care*, and 7 as *excellent care*. Child-teacher ratios and group sizes were also recorded.

FINDINGS: THE OVERALL IMPACTS OF EARLY HEAD START ON CHILDREN

The national evaluation found that the program had favorable impacts on a wide range of outcomes for children (as well as their families). Early Head Start improved cognitive and language development of children at 24 and 36 months of age, with program children scoring significantly higher than control children on the BSID–MDI and the CDI or PPVT–III. (We are reporting only those program-control differences that were statistically significant in the regression-adjusted impact analyses that controlled for a large number of family background characteristics; see ACF, 2002a.) Early Head Start also produced favorable impacts on aspects of social-emotional development at 36 months, broadening the range of impacts on these behaviors that were found at 24 months. At both 24 and 36 months, levels of aggressive behavior were significantly lower for Early Head Start children than for control-group children.

At the time these positive program impacts were becoming manifest, most Early Head Start children were in regular child care arrangements, and child care use increased as the children got older. In the four center-based programs, for example, the percentage in some type of child care for at least 30 hr per week increased from 66% at 14 months to 74% at 36 months. Moreover, Early Head Start increased the use of child care relative to the control group at all three ages by 7 to 10 percentage points (all differences significant at $p < .01$) and increased the percentage of children in good-quality care even more (see Table 2). Thus, the overall positive impacts of Early Head Start on children's development occurred while substantial numbers of children were enrolled in child care. (Details of the child care analyses described here can be found in a special policy report prepared by the authors; see ACF, 2003.)

The favorable impacts across a variety of dimensions of children's development cannot be attributed solely to the children's child care experiences, however, because not all children in Early Head Start were in child care settings. Furthermore, the Early Head

TABLE 2   EARLY HEAD START PROGRAM AND CONTROL GROUP DIFFERENCES IN CHILD CARE USE AND QUALITY, BY AGE

Analysis	14 months		24 months		36 months	
	Program	Control	Program	Control	Program	Control
Percentage of all children in any child care arrangement	66.4	56.5**	60.5	51.3**	84.4	77.7**
N	997	916	820	749	715	608
Percentage of children in good-quality classrooms[a]	23	8**	34	12**	33	21**
N	533	512	505	474	573	521
Percentage of children in good-quality classrooms in 4 center-based sites[a]	26	9**	37	12**	35	16**
N	268	252	256	224	254	211
Percentage of children in classrooms that met Head Start performance standards for child-adult ratios in 4 center-based sites[b]	72	29**	62	15**	28	7**
N	268	252	256	224	254	211
Mean quality rating of centers used, at center-based sites[c]	4.8	3.9**	4.9	3.8**	4.7	4.1**
SD	1.0	1.3	1.0	1.2	1.0	1.3
N	168	52	162	48	153	72
Mean child-adult ratio in 4 center-based sites	2.8	3.9**	3.2	5.5**	5.6	6.8**
SD	1.0	1.7	1.1	2.6	3.0	2.7
N	102	45	159	47	152	72

Note. From analyses conducted by Mathematica Policy Research and reported in *The Role of Early Head Start Programs in Addressing the Child Care Needs of Low-Income Families With Infants and Toddlers: Influences on Child Care Use and Quality* (Administration for Children and Families, 2003).
[a]Good quality is defined as Infant-Toddler Environment Rating Scale (ITERS) or Early Childhood Environment Rating Scale–Revised (ECERS–R) rating ≥ 5.0 at all sites with sufficient observations. [b]Head Start performance standards specify a child:staff ratio of 4:1 in groups no larger than 8 between birth and age 3. [c]Quality is defined by ratings on the ITERS at 14 and 24 months of age and ECERS–R at 36 months. **Program-control difference significantly different, $p < .01$.

Start intervention included family- and child-development services, as described earlier, and the favorable overall impacts of this random-assignment study must be attributed to the full package of services received. Nevertheless, good-quality child care was an important aspect of the services received and thus is responsible for a share of the favorable impacts of the program.

FINDINGS: THE CONTRIBUTION OF GOOD-QUALITY CHILD CARE TO THE EARLY HEAD START IMPACTS ON CHILDREN

We took two approaches to identifying the effects of good-quality child care on the development of Early

Head Start children. Neither approach has the methodological strength of the overall random assignment design, but both suggest that, rather than doing harm, experience in good-quality child care can play a role in improving outcomes for children from economically disadvantaged families.

First, we focus on the four Early Head Start programs that offered full-day, full-year, center-based child development programs. Children typically attended these centers operated by Early Head Start for substantial periods each week, ranging from 51% at 24 months to 68% at 36 months attending for 30 hr or more per week. (The children experienced even greater amounts of time in all types of nonparental care.)

The quality of child care in the four Early Head Start center-based programs was higher than is typical for center-based infant-toddler care in the United States, and for low-income children more specifically. Observational ratings showed that Early Head Start children at these sites were in classrooms that scored an average of 4.8 on the ITERS for 14-month-olds and 4.9 for 24-month-olds. The classrooms scored 4.7 on the ECERS–R for 36-month-olds. (Note that these averages for Early Head Start children include some children who, for a variety of reasons, were in community centers not operated by the program. Observations of all classrooms operated by Early Head Start centers across all sites showed a mean ITERS or ECERS–R rating of 5.0, 5.2, and 5.1 for 14-, 24-, and 36-month-old children, respectively.) The Early Head Start program quality was significantly higher than the quality that control group children experienced in the same communities. Control group children using center care in these communities were in classrooms rated significantly lower–an average of 3.8 to 3.9 for 14- and 24-month-olds on the ITERS, and 4.1 for 36-month-olds on the ECERS–R (see Table 2). In addition, as Table 2 shows, child–adult rations were 2.8 at 14 months, 3.2 at 24 months, and 5.6 at 36 months, again significantly better than ratios in classrooms attended by control group children. Early Head Start children in the four Early Head Start sites offering center-based child development services clearly received higher quality care as a result of their enrollment in the program.

Because of different measures, we cannot compare these quality ratings directly with the NICHD study classrooms, but national studies typically have found substantially lower ITERS scores than we observed in Early Head Start centers. The scores have ranged from 3.2 to 3.6 in infant and toddler classrooms in several sites across the United States (Cost, Quality, and Child Outcomes Study Team, 1995; Whitebook, Howes, & Phillips, 1989).

The evaluation found that, when impacts on children's development were estimated separately by the program's approach to child development services, center-based programs were as effective as programs offering home-based or mixed-approach services (ACF, 2002a). This evidence certainly suggests that the large amount of good-quality center-based child care offered by Early Head Start was not detrimental to children and, indeed, contributed to positive outcomes found for the program as a whole.

Our second approach to the child care–child development link focuses on children in the Early Head Start program group who received center care. All children in this sample received the full Early Head Start intervention and were in center care during at least one of the three periods (14, 24, or 36 months of age). The analyses relate child care quality and intensity at 14, 24, and 36 months to three key child outcomes at 24 and 36 months of age. Child care quality was measured by the ITERS or ECERS–R and by the child–adult ratio. Intensity was measured by average hours in center child care. We relate these measures of child care to children's cognitive development (BSID–MDI scores), language development (CDI at 24 months or PPVT–III at 36), and aggressive behavior (CBCL aggressive behavior problem scores). Using ordinary least squares regression analyses, mean child care quality and intensity scores at 14 and 24 months were used to predict 24-month outcomes, and mean quality and intensity scores at 14, 24, and 36 months were used to predict 36-month outcomes. All regression analyses controlled for child gender, child age at time of assessment, mother's race or ethnicity, mother's education and marital status, whether mother was teenage (under 19 years of age) at the time of the child's birth, and whether the site was urban.

Among the Early Head Start children who attended child care centers, those in higher quality center-based care showed enhanced developmental outcomes. Mean child care quality over time predicted higher scores on the 24-month BSID–MDI and 36-month PPVT–III. Mean child–adult ratio over time did not significantly predict child outcomes. Mean hours in center care over time predicted higher scores on the 24- and 36-month BSID–MDI and the 36-month PPVT–III. Neither the quality nor the amount of child care predicted child aggressive behavior at 24 or 36 months.

Consistent with previous research, these findings demonstrate that the quality of the child care centers that Early Head Start children attended was positively associated with children's cognitive and language development. Moreover, spending more time in center-based child care was associated with higher cognitive and language scores at 24 and 36 months. We found no evidence that more time in child care was associated with lower child well-being or higher rates of aggressive behavior (ACF, 2003).

SUMMARY AND CONCLUSIONS

This article has described three recent studies that examine associations between early child care and child outcomes among families who are different from those profiled in the NICHD Study of Early Child Care. The three studies suggest that quality of child care is an important factor influencing children's development and that quality may be an important moderator of the amount of time in care, particularly when the child care contexts differ from those of the NICHD research. Taken together, these studies point to a limited generalizability of the

NICHD Early Child Care Research Network's findings. Although some of our results corroborate the NICHD study findings, other outcomes raise questions as to whether the associations between early child care quality and social-emotional development reported by the NICHD network would hold in a more diverse sample of children and families, and in a wider range of child care settings.

In the SFDP, children in care for longer periods before 30 months of age were rated lower by their teachers on adjustment to the learning demands of school at age 6, which appears consistent with the current NICHD finding that extensive early experience in child care may be associated with later behavior problems. In the SFDP, however, being in formal (i.e., higher quality) care was associated with higher ratings on learning competencies, suggesting that quality of care may balance the risk associated with time in care. In contrast to the NICHD report, social-emotional problems were related to stability rather than quantity of care. We suggest that, in a context in which standards for good-quality care are enforced through government regulatory mechanisms, the risk for behavior problems may be explained by factors other than time in care.

In the Haifa study, child care, especially center care, increased the likelihood of the infants' attachment insecurity to their mothers. We suggest that this is because early infant child care, with its very high infant–caregiver ratio, interfered with the traditional link often reported in the literature between maternal sensitivity and infants' security of attachment to their mothers. Analyses of the combined Haifa–NICHD data showed a significant association between child–caregiver ratio (as an index of quality) and children's attachment security but no relation between amount of care and attachment security. Contrary to the suggestion that, in the case of social-emotional development, only child care quantity matters, evidence was found for the significance of child care quality. We suggest that, when the range of quality of care is broadened—either upward or downward, as was the case in the combined Haifa–NICHD data set—quality of child care becomes more salient than time in care in influencing children's development.

Finally, in the Early Head Start study, with its experimental design, children from low-income families (who would be expected to be at higher risk for behavior problems than those in the NICHD sample) experienced a wide range of positive impacts, including reduced aggressive behavior problems. These positive gains in cognitive, language, and social-emotional development occurred for children enrolled in a program that provided high levels of good-quality center child care. The experimental evidence raises serious questions about concluding that an increased amount of child care is detrimental for children's development, at least in the first 3 years of life. In addition, for the sample of Early Head Start children in center-based child care, spending more time in center-based child care was associated with higher cognitive and language scores at 24 and 36 months. We found no evidence that more time in child care was associated with higher rates of aggressive behavior problems. We suggest that this may be a function of both the sample characteristics (100% low income) and the generally good levels of quality care the children experienced.

In summary, the three perspectives provided by our research provide strikingly consistent evidence for the importance of child care quality in the development of young children. We suggest that the generalizability of the NICHD study findings hinges on the specific context in which these results have been obtained. Our data stress the need to take into account the potentially restricted range for child care quality in each investigation. The NICHD Study of Early Child Care is the most impressive investigation on child care to date, and the consortium members should be highly commended for their careful, creative, and painstaking work on one of the most crucial issues in child development. Naturally, such seminal research triggers scientific debate, which underlines the importance of this unprecedented collaborative effort. We hope that the cumulative effect of the data reported here—collected in different countries, with different ranges of child care quality, in different regulatory contexts, and with a diversity of family characteristics—is to provide more complete estimates of the manner in which both quality and quantity of child care may influence a range of young children's developmental outcomes.

References

Achenbach, T. (1991). *Manual for the Child Behavior Checklist/4–18 and 1991 profile.* Burlington: University of Vermont.

Achenbach, T. M. (1992). *Child Behavior Checklist for ages 2–3.* Burlington: University of Vermont.

Achenbach, T. M., & Rescorla, L. A. (2000). *Manual for the ASEBA preschool forms and profiles* Burlington: University of Vermont.

Administration for Children and Families (2002a). *Making a difference in the lives of infants and toddlers and their families: The impacts of Early Head Start.* Washington, DC: U. S. Department of Health and Human Services.

Administration for Children and Families (2002b). *Pathways to quality and full implementation in Early Head Start.* Washington, DC: U.S. Department of Health and Human Services.

Administration for Children and Families (2003). *The role of Early Head Start programs in addressing the child care needs of low-income families with infants and toddlers: Influences on child care use and quality.* Washington, DC: U.S. Department of Health and Human Services.

Administration on Children, Youth and Families. (2001). *Building their futures: How Early Head Start programs are enhancing the lives of infants and toddlers of low-income families. Volumes I–II.* Washington, DC: U.S. Department of Health and Human Services.

Ainsworth, M., Blehar, M., Waters, E., & Wall, S. (1978). *Patterns of attachment.* Hillsdale, NJ: Erlbaum.

Australian Bureau of Statistics. (1998). *Australian social trends 1998.* Canberra: Commonwealth of Australia.

Australian Bureau of Statistics. (1999). *Child care, Australia, 1999.* Canberra: Commonwealth of Australia.

Aviezer, O., Sagi, A., & Koren-Karie, N. (2003). Ecological constraints on the formation of infant–mother attachment relations: When maternal sensitivity becomes ineffective. *Infant Behavior and Development, 26,* 285–299.

Bayley, N. (1993). *Bayley Scales of Infant Development, second edition: Manual.* New York: Psychological Corporation.

Bowlby, J. (1978). *Attachment and loss: Vol. 1. Attachment.* Middlesex, England: Penguin (Original work published 1969).

Campbell, F. A., Pungello, E. P., Miller-Johnson, S., Burchinal, M., & Ramey, C. T. (2001). The development of cognitive and academic abilities: Growth curves from an early childhood educational experiment. *Developmental Psychology, 37,* 231–242.

Cost, Quality, and Child Outcomes Study Team (1995). *Cost, quality, and child outcomes in child care centers; Public report.* Denver: University of Colorado at Denver.

Dunn, L. M., & Dunn, L. M. (1997). *Peabody Picture Vocabulary Test-third edition.* Circle Pines, MN: American Guidance Service.

Fenson, L., Dale, P. S., Reznick, J. S., Thal, D., Bates, E., Hartung, J. P., et al. (1993). *The MacArthur Communicative Development Inventories: User's guide and technical manual.* San Diego, CA: Singular.

Glezer, H. (1988). *Maternity leave in Australia: Employee and employer experiences: Report of a survey.* Melbourne: Australian Institute of Family Studies.

Harms, T., Clifford, R., & Cryer, D. (1998). *Early Childhood Environment Rating Scale–Revised.* New York: Teachers College Press.

Harms, T., Cryer, D., & Clifford, R. (1990). *Infant/Toddler Environment Rating Scale.* New York: Teachers College Press.

Harrison, L., & Ungerer, J. A. (1997). Child care predictors of infant–mother attachment security at age 12 months. *Early Child Development and Care, 137,* 31–46.

Harrison, L. J., & Ungerer, J. A. (2002a). Maternal employment and infant–mother attachment security at 12 months postpartum. *Developmental Psychology, 38,* 758–773.

Harrison, L. J., & Ungerer, J. A. (2002b, December). *The Sydney Family Development Project: Family and child care predictors of school adjustment at age six.* Paper presented in the symposium, Longitudinal Studies of Early Childhood in Australia, J. Bowes (Chair), at the Australian Association for Research in Education conference, Brisbane.

Hightower, A. D., Work, C., Cowen, E., Lotyczewski, B., Spinell, A., Guare, J., et al. (1989). The Teacher-Child Rating Scale: A brief objective measure of elementary school children's school behaviour and competence. *School Psychology Review, 15,* 393–409.

Klein, E. L., & Abu Taleb, T. F. (1993, March). *Self concept and prosocial behavior in kindergarten.* Paper presented at the biennial meeting of the Society for Research in Child Development, New Orleans.

Koren-Karie, N., Sagi, A., & Egoz-Mizrachi, N. (1998, July). *Quality of infant group care in Israel.* Paper presented at the biennial meeting of the International Society for the Study of Behavioral Development, Bern, Switzerland.

Lamb, M. E. (1998). Nonparental child care: Context, quality, correlates. In W. Damon, I. E. Sigel, & K. A. Renninger (Eds.), *Handbook of child psychology, volume 4: Child psychology in practice* (5th ed., pp. 73–134). New York: Wiley.

Love, J. M., Schochet, P. A., & Meckstroth, A. L. (1996). *Are they in any real danger? What research does—and doesn't—tell us about child care quality and children's well-being.* Princeton, NJ: Mathematica Policy Research.

National Association for the Education of Young Children. (1987). *Accreditation criteria and procedures.* Washington, DC: Author.

National Childcare Accreditation Council (1993). *Putting children first. Quality Improvement and Accreditation System handbook.* Sydney, Australia: Author.

National Institute of Child Health and Human Development Early Child Care Research Network (1997a). The effects of infant child care on infant–mother attachment security. Results of the NICHD study of early child care. *Child Development, 68,* 860–879.

National Institute of Child Health and Human Development Early Child Care Research Network (1997b). Familial factors associated with the characteristics of nonmaternal care for infants. *Journal of Marriage and the Family, 59,* 389–408.

National Institute of Child Health and Human Development Early Child Care Research Network (2000a). Characteristics and quality of child care for toddlers and preschoolers. *Applied Developmental Science, 4,* 116–135.

National Institute of Child Health and Human Development Early Child Care Research Network (2000b). The relation of child care to cognitive and language development. *Child Development, 71,* 960–980.

National Institute of Child Health and Human Development Early Child Care Research Network (2001). Before Head Start: Income and ethnicity, family characteristics, child care experiences, and child development. *Early Education and Development, 12,* 545–576.

National Institute of Child Health and Human Development Early Child Care Research Network (2003a). Does amount of time spent in child care predict socioemotional adjustment during the transition to kindergarten? *Child Development, 74,* 976–1005.

National Institute of Child Health and Human Development Early Child Care Research Network. (2003b). Does quality of child care affect child outcomes at age 4½? *Developmental Psychology, 39,* 451–469.

Pianta, R. C. (1990). *The Student–Teacher Relationship Scale*. Unpublished manuscript, University of Virginia.

Sagi, A., Koren-Karie, N., Gini, M., Ziv, Y., & Joels, T. (2002). Shedding further light on the effects of various types and quality of early child care on infant-mother attachment relationship: The Haifa study of early child care. *Child Development, 73,* 1166–1186.

Scarr, S., & Eisenberg, M. (1993). Child care research: Issues, perspectives, and results. *Annual Review of Psychology, 44,* 613–644.

Schaefer, E., Edgerton, M., & Aaronson, M. (1978). *Child Behavior Inventory*. Unpublished manuscript, University of Carolina.

U.S. Department of Health and Human Services (1966, November). Head Start Program: Final rule. *Federal Register, 61 (215),* 57186–57227.

Wangmann, J. (1995). *Towards integration and quality assurance in children's services*. Melbourne: Australian Institute of Family Studies.

Whitebook, M., Howes, C., & Phillips, D. (1989). *Who cares? Child care teachers and the quality of care in America: Final report: National Child Care Staffing Study*. Berkeley, CA: Child Care Employee Project.

QUESTIONS

1. Why did these investigators want to examine the quality and quantity of child care more carefully than other researchers had done?
2. What types of psychological outcomes have been the focus of research on the impact of child care on development?
3. Which three national settings were included in this research, and why was it interesting to compare the impact of child care on psychological development in these settings?
4. In this research, what dimensions of child care were considered in the definition of quality of care?
5. What were the primary differences between Australia and the United States in the effects of quality, quantity, and stability of child care, and how did the researchers explain these differences?
6. What were the relationships between child care and children's attachment to their mothers in Israel and the United States? How did the researchers explain these patterns?
7. In one analysis, why did the investigators combine the data from the United States and Israel? What was the main result from this analysis regarding the relationship between child–caregiver ratio and security of attachment?
8. Why did the researchers want to compare children in the United States who participate in the NICHD study of child care and children in the Early Head Start Program?
9. What psychological outcomes were found for children who participate in the Early Head Start Program?
10. Taken together, what do this research and the research conducted by NICHD tell us about the impact of early child care on psychological development?

PART IV

Middle Childhood

Middle childhood, from age 7 to 12, is universally recognized as an exciting period of children's lives. This is the time when children lose their baby teeth, get involved in activities that take them away from constant adult supervision, and begin to be held responsible for actions. These changes are made possible by increased physical skills, which allow children to help out more at home and at school. Also, their increased intellectual abilities support children as they engage in more complex activities. Cognitive change during middle childhood is not an all-or-nothing process, however, and the article by Robert S. Siegler that opens this section discusses variability in children's thinking during this period.

Children's social life and behavior also change dramatically during middle childhood. They now spend more time with other children, mostly age mates; these interactions may provide opportunities for cognitive development, which is the topic of the article by Ruth T. Duran and Mary Gauvain. Children also begin to have more complex social relationships, such as friendships, which are discussed in the article by Thomas J. Berndt. At this time, children also begin to display social behaviors with peers that align with gender roles, such as patterns of aggression, which are discussed in the article by Nicki B. Crick and Jennifer K. Grotpeter.

After the family, school is the most important social institution with which children are involved. Cultural variation in academic performance during middle childhood suggests that opportunities to develop cognitive skills in the classroom differ greatly; the article by James W. Stigler and Harold W. Stevenson discusses this issue. There is also cultural variation in informal instruction, especially in the role that older siblings play in children's learning, the topic of the article by Ashley E. Maynard. Finally, an article on intelligence by Ulric Neisser and colleagues is included in this section because, although this topic is not unique to middle childhood, it is an increasingly important facet of the child's experience during those years.

Together, these articles characterize middle childhood as a period in which children's developing cognitive skills are increasingly integrated with the social and intellectual life of the community in which they live. Moreover, as children move toward maturity, they experience increased expectations and social responsibilities.

25 Cognitive Variability: A Key to Understanding Cognitive Development

ROBERT S. SIEGLER

Intellectual development entails significant change in the way that individuals think and approach problems. Although understanding how and when such change occurs is important for a complete description of cognitive development, relatively little research on cognitive change has been done. One reason is that it is difficult to study. In addition, some implicit assumptions about cognitive development may have impeded the study of change. For example, it is often assumed that at every age children's thinking has certain characteristics and that all of children's thinking at this age will reflect this characteristic. However, this assumption has recently been called into question by the developmental psychologist Robert Siegler, who has discovered that children's thinking at any given age is far more variable than anyone had previously thought.

Variability in children's thinking has been examined from the theoretical approach known as information processing. This approach conceives of intellectual growth as the gradual learning of new and more complex skills. Much of this research focuses on the development and use of strategies that aid people when they solve problems. What Siegler discovered when he looked closely at children's use of strategy was that more than one way of solving a problem is often available to children. Moreover, variability in strategy use often precedes cognitive change. These observations led Siegler to suggest that variability may be the key for unlocking one of the most difficult and interesting questions in developmental psychology: How does change occur?

In the following article, Siegler summarizes his position on the role of variability in cognitive development and discusses data that support this point of view. This perspective holds promise for developmental psychology, which has long struggled with describing mechanisms or processes of change. Perhaps, as Siegler suggests, progress on this front has been impeded by a too-narrow depiction of what children know at any given point in development.

Among the most remarkable characteristics of human beings is how much our thinking changes with age. When we compare the thinking of an infant, a toddler, an elementary school student, and an adolescent, the magnitude of the change is immediately apparent. Accounting for how these changes occur is perhaps the central goal of researchers who study cognitive development.

Alongside this agreement about the importance of the goal of determining how change occurs, however, is agreement that we traditionally have not done very well in meeting it. In most models of cognitive development, children are depicted as thinking or acting in a certain way for a prolonged period of time, then undergoing a brief, rather mysterious, transition, and then thinking or acting in a different way for another prolonged period. For example, on the classic conservation-of-liquid quantity problem, children are depicted as believing for several years that pouring water into a taller, thinner beaker changes the

Reprinted with permission of Blackwell Publishers from Siegler, R. S. (1994). Cognitive variability: A key to understanding cognitive development. *Current Directions in Psychological Science, 3,* 1–5.

Preparation of this article was made possible by grants from the Spencer Foundation, the National Institutes of Health, and the Mellon Foundation to the author. Special thanks go to Kevin Crowley for his careful readings and excellent suggestions regarding the article.

amount of water; then undergoing a short period of cognitive conflict, in which they are not sure about the effects of pouring the water; and then realizing that pouring does not affect the amount of liquid. How children get from the earlier to the later understanding is described only superficially.

Critiques of the inadequacy of such accounts have been leveled most often at stage models such as Piaget's. The problem, however, is far more pervasive. Regardless of whether the particular approach describes development in terms of stages, rules, strategies, or theories; regardless of whether the focus is on reasoning about the physical or the social world; regardless of the age group of central interest, most theories place static states at center stage and change processes either in the wings or offstage altogether. Thus, 3-year-olds are said to have nonrepresentational theories of mind and 5-year-olds representational ones; 5-year-olds to have absolute views about justice and 10-year-olds relativistic ones; 10-year-olds to be incapable and 15-year-olds capable of true scientific reasoning. The emphasis in almost all cognitive-developmental theories has been on identifying sequences of one-to-one correspondences between ages and ways of thinking or acting, rather than on specifying how the changes occur.

If developmentalists are so interested in change processes, why would the topic be given such cursory treatment in most contemporary theories? Part of the problem is that studying change is inherently difficult. It poses all the conceptual and methodological demands of studying performance at any one time, and imposes the added demands of determining what is changing and how the change is being accomplished.

An additional part of the difficulty, however, may be self-imposed. In our efforts to describe differences among age groups in as simple, dramatic, and memorable terms as possible, we may unwittingly have made understanding change more difficult than it needs to be. In particular, portraying children's thinking and knowledge as monolithic for several years at a time creates a need to explain the wide gulfs between the successive hypothesized understandings—even though such gulfs may not exist. The typical depictions make change a rare, almost exotic, event that demands an exceptional explanation. If children of a given age have for several years had a particular understanding, why would they suddenly form a different understanding, and why would they regularly form it at a particular age? The problem is exacerbated by the fact that for many of the competencies of interest, generally relevant experience is available at all ages and specifically relevant experience at none. Children see liquids poured into containers of different dimensions at all ages—and are not ordinarily told at any age that the amount of liquid remains the same after pouring as before. Why, then, would

they consistently have one concept of liquid quantity conservation at age 5 and a different one at age 7?

Recognition of the unwelcome side effects of the one-to-one depictions of cognitive growth has led to a new generation of research that focuses directly on changes in children's thinking. This research has documented large-scale variability in children's thinking and suggests that the variability contributes directly to cognitive growth.

PERVASIVE VARIABILITY

Variability in children's thinking exists at every level—not just between children of different ages, or between different children of the same age, but also within an individual solving a set of related problems, within an individual solving the same problem twice, and even within an individual on a single trial.

VARIABILITY WITHIN AN INDIVIDUAL SOLVING RELATED PROBLEMS

Detailed analyses of tasks on which one-to-one correspondences between age and way of thinking have been postulated indicate that children's thinking is generally much more variable than past depictions have suggested. To cite an example from language development, rather than young children passing through a stage in which they always overregularize past tense forms (e.g., saying "goed" and "eated" rather than "went" and "ate"), children at all ages between 2½ and 5 years produce both substantial numbers of overregularized forms and substantial numbers of correct ones. The variability throughout this age range is present for a single child followed throughout the period, as well as for groups of children sampled at a single age. Adding to the variability, children often produce more than one incorrect form of a given verb; on different occasions, a given child will say, "I ate it," "I eated it," and "I ated it."[1]

Similar variability has been found in the development of memory strategies. Contrary to the widely cited model that 5-year-olds do not rehearse and 8-year-olds do, trial-by-trial assessments indicate that the majority of children of both ages sometimes do and sometimes do not rehearse.[2] The percentage of trials on which they rehearse increases with age, but, again, there is variability throughout the age range.

Conceptual development evidences the same pattern. Despite claims that 5-year-olds think of number conservation solely in terms of the lengths of the rows, trial-by-trial assessments indicate that most 5-year-olds sometimes rely on the lengths of the rows, sometimes rely on the type of transformation, and sometimes use other strategies such as counting or pairing.[3] Again, the frequency of reliance on these ways of thinking changes with age, but most 5-year-olds' judgments and verbal explanations indicate several different ways of thinking about the concept.

Development of problem-solving skills provides yet more evidence for such within-subject cognitive variability. Contradicting models in which preschoolers are said to use the sum strategy (counting from 1) to solve simple addition problems and in which first through third graders are said to use the min strategy (counting from the larger addend, as when solving 3 + 6 by counting "6, 7, 8, 9") to solve them, children of all these ages use a variety of strategies. In one study, most children presented a set of addition problems used at least three different strategies on different problems, and most children examined in a more extensive microlongitudinal study used at least five distinct strategies.[4]

Variability Within an Individual Solving a Single Problem Twice

The variability within individual children cannot be reduced to children using different strategies on different problems. Even presented the identical problem twice within a single session, or on 2 successive days, children use different strategies on roughly one third of the pairs of trials in addition, time-telling, and block-building tasks.[5] This variability within individuals within problems cannot be explained by learning; in these studies, children used the strategy that appeared more advanced almost as often for the first presentation of a problem as for the second (roughly 45% vs. 55%).

Variability Within a Single Trial

In the limiting case, variability has been found even within an individual solving a particular problem on a single trial. This type of variability has been reported by investigators interested in the relation between children's hand gestures and verbal explanations. In these studies, children often express one type of understanding through the gestures and a quite different understanding through the explanations.[6] For example, on number conservation problems, children may express a reliance on relative lengths of the rows in their hand gestures, while at the same time verbally expressing reliance on the type of transformation, or vice versa.

These findings suggest that cognitive change is better thought of in terms of changing distributions of ways of thinking than in terms of sudden shifts from one way of thinking to another. The types of descriptions of change that emerge from such analyses are illustrated in Figures 1 and 2. Figure 1 shows changes in 3 children's addition strategies over a 3-month period;[4] Figure 2 shows changes in a child's map-drawing strategies over a 2-year period.[7] Similar changes in distributions of strategies have been found in studies of conceptual understanding, memory strategies, problem solving, and language. In all these domains, cognitive development involves changing distributions of approaches, rather than discontinuous movements from one way of thinking to another.

Variability and Cognitive Change

Variability is not just an incidental feature of thinking; it appears to play a critical role in promoting cognitive change. Several types of evidence converge on this conclusion. One comes from observations of children in the process of discovering new strategies. Both the trials immediately before a discovery and the trial on which the discovery is made frequently involve especially variable behavior—disfluencies, unclear references, long pauses, and unusual gestures.[4] A second type of empirical evidence linking variability to cognitive change involves analyses of which children are most likely to make discoveries. Children whose verbal explanations and gestures reflect different initial misunderstandings of number conservation and of numerical equivalence problems (a + b + c = __ + c) are more likely to make discoveries subsequently than are children whose explanations and gestures reflect the same initial misunderstanding.[6] Similarly, children whose pretest explanations reflect varied ways of thinking are more likely to learn from instruction regarding the meaning of the equal sign in mathematics than are children whose pretest explanations reflect crisp, specific misunderstandings.[8]

A different type of evidence for the contribution of variability to cognitive change comes from formal models of development. Theorists who differ in many particular assumptions have found that modeling change requires both mechanisms that produce variability and mechanisms that produce adaptive choices among the variants. Connectionist models of development are based on connection strengths among processing units varying at all points in learning, from initial, randomly varying strengths to final, asymptotic level; change occurs through redistributions of the varying connection strengths. Dynamic systems models also treat variability as a fundamental property of development; they aim to explain how local variability gives to global regularities. Similarly, recent symbolic-processing models of development focus on how varying strategies, analogies, and other higher order units come to be used increasingly in the situations in which they are most effective. At a less formal level, operant conditioning models, evolutionarily based models, and generate-and-test models are all based on the assumption that change occurs

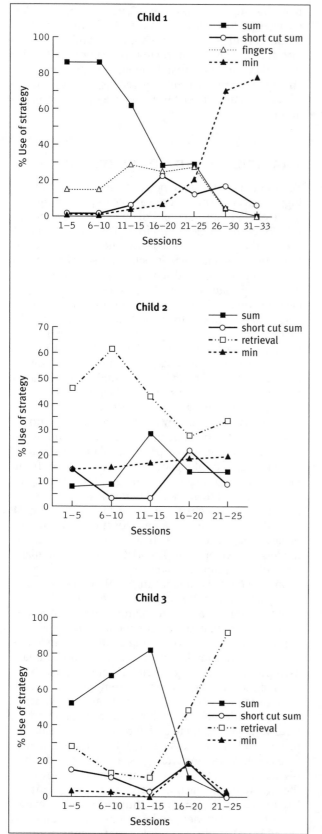

through selection processes operating on omnipresent, spontaneously produced variability in behavior.[9]

A striking empirical finding about the variability in children's thinking, and one that is important for its ability to contribute to cognitive development, is the constrained quality of the variations that children generate. Far from conforming to a trial-and-error model, in which all types of variations might be expected, the new approaches that children attempt consistently conform to the principles that define legal strategies in the domain (except when children are forced to solve problems for which they do not possess any adequate strategy). For example, in a 30-session study of preschoolers' discovery of new addition strategies, none of the children ever attempted strategies that violated the principles underlying addition.[4] They invented legitimate new strategies, such as the min strategy, but never illegitimate ones, such as adding the smaller addend to itself or counting from the larger addend the number of times indicated by the first addend. The question is how they limit their newly generated strategies to legal forms.

One possibility is that even before discovering new strategies, children often understand the goals that legitimate strategies in the domain must satisfy. Such understanding would allow them, without trial and error, to discriminate between legitimate new strategies that meet the essential goals and illegitimate strategies that do not. A very recent study revealed that children possessed such knowledge in both of the domains that were examined—simple addition and tic-tac-toe.[10] In simple addition, children who had not yet discovered the min strategy nonetheless judged that strategy (demonstrated by the experimenter) to be as smart as the strategy they themselves most often used—counting from 1—and significantly smarter than an equally novel but illegitimate strategy that the experimenter demonstrated. In tic-tac-toe, children rated a novel strategy that they did not yet use—forking—as even smarter than the strategy they themselves usually employed—trying to complete a single row or column. Ability to anticipate the value of untried strategies may promote

FIGURE 1

Changes in distributions of addition strategies of 3 children over roughly 30 sessions conducted over a 3-month period. Notice the variability that is present within each child's performance within each block of sessions, as well as the changes in distributions of strategy use over the course of the study (data from Siegler and Jenkins[4]).

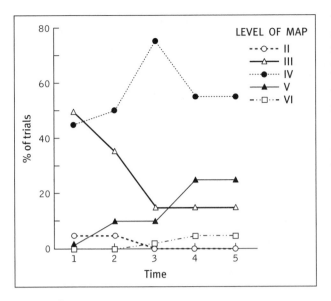

FIGURE 2

Changes in distributions of map-drawing approaches across five sessions, conducted over a 2-year period. Higher numbers indicate more advanced levels of map drawing; thus, Level IV maps are more advanced than Level III ones (data from Feldman[7]).

cognitive growth by filtering out unpromising possibilities and thus channeling innovations in potentially useful directions.

CONCLUSIONS

Thinking is far more variable than usually depicted. In the past, researchers have usually ignored such variability or viewed it as a bother. This stance has led to subjects being given practice periods, not so the especially variable behavior in those periods can be studied, but so that it can be discarded, in order that it not obscure the more orderly patterns in later performance. When such variability has been explicitly noted at all, it has usually been viewed as an unfortunate limitation of human beings, a kind of design defect, something to be overcome through practice. Computers, robots, and other machines not subject to this flaw can perform many tasks more accurately than people can. Presumably, people's performance would also be enhanced if it were less variable.

This view of variability as detracting from efficient performance misses at least half the story, though. The variability of cognition and action allows us to discover a great deal about the environments toward which the thinking and action are directed. Our difficulty in reproducing the way we pronounced a word in an unfamiliar foreign language may lead to some even less adequate pronunciations in the short run, but in the longer run may lead us to generate and then learn better pronunciations. Likewise, our inability to give a colloquium in the same words twice, even when we want to, may lead to some parts being less clear than in the best of our previous presentations, but it also allows us to observe audience reaction to new lines of argument and to learn which ones are best received. In general, cognitive variability may lead to performance never incorporating on any one occasion all the best features of previous performance, but also may be critical to our becoming increasingly proficient over time.

If cognitive variability does indeed facilitate learning, it would be adaptive if such variability were most pronounced when learning, rather than efficient performance, is most important—that is, in infancy and early childhood. This appears to be the case. Across many domains, expertise brings with it decreasingly variable performance. To the extent that young children are "universal novices," their lack of expertise alone would lead to their performance being more variable than that of older children and adults. A number of cognitive neuroscientists have hypothesized that above and beyond such effects of practice, the process of synaptogenesis, which results in children from roughly birth to age 7 having far more synaptic connections than older children and adults, may contribute both to the high variability of early behavior and to young children's special ability to acquire language, perceptual skills, and other competencies under abnormal organismic and environmental conditions.[11] That is, young children's greater variability at the neural level seems to allow them to learn useful behaviors under a greater range of circumstances. The general lesson seems to be that explicitly recognizing the great variability of infants' and young children's thinking, and attempting to explain how it is generated and constrained, will advance our understanding of the central mystery about cognitive development—how change occurs.

NOTES

1. S. A. Kuczaj, The acquisition of regular and irregular past tense forms, *Journal of Verbal Learning and Verbal Behavior, 16,* 589–600 (1977).
2. K. McGilly and R. S. Siegler, The influence of encoding and strategic knowledge on children's choices among serial recall strategies, *Developmental Psychology, 26,* 939–941 (1990).
3. R. S. Siegler, *A microgenetic study of number conservation,* manuscript in preparation, Carnegie Mellon University, Pittsburgh (1993).

4. R. S. Siegler and E. Jenkins, *How Children Discover New Strategies* (Erlbaum, Hillsdale, NJ, 1989).

5. R. S. Siegler and K. McGilly, Strategy choices in children's time-telling, in *Time and Human Cognition: A Life Span Perspective*, I. Levin and D. Zakay, Eds. (Elsevier Science, Amsterdam, 1989); R. S. Siegler and J. Shrager, Strategy choices in addition and subtraction: How do children know what to do? in *The Origins of Cognitive Skills*, C. Sophian, Ed. (Erlbaum, Hillsdale, NJ, 1984); A.C. Wilkinson, Partial knowledge and self-correction: Developmental studies of a quantitative concept, *Developmental Psychology, 18*, 876–893 (1982).

6. R. B. Church and S. Goldin-Meadow, The mismatch between gesture and speech as an index of transitional knowledge, *Cognition, 23*, 43–71 (1986); S. Goldin-Meadow and M. W. Alibali, Transitions in concept acquisition: Using the hand to read the mind, *Psychological Review, 100*, 279–297 (1993).

7. D. H. Feldman, *Beyond Universals in Cognitive Development* (Ablex, Norwood, NJ, 1980).

8. T. Graham and M. Perry, Indexing transitional knowledge, *Developmental Psychology, 29, 779–788* (1993).

9. For examples of these perspectives, see D. T. Campbell, Evolutionary epistemology, in *The Philosophy of Karl Popper*, Vol. 14, P. A. Schilpp, Ed. (Open Court, La Salle, IL, 1974); J. L. McClelland and E. Jenkins, Nature, nurture, and connections: Implications of connectionist models for cognitive development, in *Architectures for Intelligence*, K. Van Lehn, Ed. (Erlbaum, Hillsdale, NJ, 1991); L. B. Smith and E. Thelen, Eds., *A Dynamic Systems Approach to Development: Applications* (Bradford Books, Cambridge, MA, 1993); B. F. Skinner, Selection by consequences, *Science, 213*, 501–504 (1981).

10. R. S. Siegler and K. Crowley, Goal sketches constrain children's strategy discoveries, *Cognitive Psychology* (in press).

11. P. S. Goldman-Rakic, development of cortical circuitry and cognitive function, *Child Development*, 58, 609–622 (1987); W.T. Greenough, J.E. Black, and C. Wallace, Experience and brain development, *Child Development, 58*, 539–559 (1987).

QUESTIONS

1. According to Siegler, why have researchers who study cognitive development rarely focused on processes of intellectual change?

2. What is one example that Siegler uses to support his claim that variability exists when an individual tries to solve similar types of problems?

3. Are you surprised that children sometimes use different strategies to solve the same problem on two different trials? Why? What assumption about cognitive development does this observation challenge?

4. Look closely at Figure 1. Which child would you say shows the most variability in the addition strategies that he or she uses, and which child shows the least variability? On the basis of Siegler's research, which child would you say is closest to having a breakthrough or change in his or her understanding of addition?

5. When children discover new strategies, do the trials immediately preceding and during the discovery involve little or much variability? Why?

6. Why does Siegler think it is important that variations in the strategies that children use to solve a problem are not simply different random attempts based on trial and error?

7. Why is it interesting that children who did not yet use the forking strategy in playing tic-tac-toe nevertheless rated it as better (or smarter) than the strategy they usually did use?

8. What may be the neurological basis for cognitive variability between birth and 7 years of age?

9. How, according to Siegler, might variability in thinking lead to cognitive change?

10. How could information about variability in children's problem-solving approaches be helpful to teachers who work with children as they learn mathematics and other content areas that often involve the use of strategies?

26 The Role of Age versus Expertise in Peer Collaboration during Joint Planning

RUTH T. DURAN • MARY GAUVAIN

Over the last two decades, many researchers have tried to understand the social foundations of cognitive development. The underlying assumption of this research is that social experience provides opportunities for children to learn new ways of solving problems. They learn by observing how other people solve problems or by getting assistance from other people with whom they work. Some of the research on the social context of cognitive development has concentrated on joint problem solving involving adults and children; other research has examined peer collaboration involving children of the same or similar ages.

The following article by Ruth T. Duran and Mary Gauvain is about peer collaboration and cognitive development, a topic that was of much interest to both Piaget and Vygotsky. Despite their similar interest in peer collaboration, Piaget and Vygotsky did not hold the same view on this topic. Piaget thought that collaboration between children who are nearly equal in their understanding promotes cognitive development because when such children disagree about their different understandings, this conflict improves the understanding of the less knowledgeable partner. In contrast, Vygotsky emphasized collaboration between novices and experts and the support that guidance and instruction provide for intellectual growth.

A chief difficulty in studying the influence of expertise on children's learning during peer collaboration on a cognitive task is that expertise is often confounded with child age. The fact that child age is usually an index of social status further complicates the picture. This article describes research that teases these variables apart. The results indicate that age and expertise make different contributions to the social process of cognitive development when peers work together.

This study examined the role of age and expertise in influencing collaboration during joint planning. The collaborative patterns of 7-year-old expert planners working with 5-year-old novice planners were compared to 5-year-old experts collaborating with same-age novices on delivery tasks requiring reverse sequencing strategies. Novices who planned with same-age experts had more involvement in the task than novices in cross-age dyads, and individual posttest performance of the novices was related to the extent to which novices were involved in the collaborative task.

Furthermore, the posttest performance of children who planned with same-age experts, but not older experts, was significantly better than same-age children in a related study using this same task who did not previously collaborate with a peer. Results suggest that cognitive gains are achieved when children collaborate with peers who are more expert in the problem-solving activity, particularly when there is substantial involvement by the novice, and that this is more likely for 5-year-old children when partners are of the same age rather than of different ages. The relation of social facilitation to

Reprinted from *Journal of Experimental Child Psychology, Vol. 55,* Duran, R., & Gauvain, M., The role of age versus expertise in peer collaboration during joint planning, pp. 227–242, copyright 1993, with permission from Elsevier.

This article is based on a senior thesis submitted by the first author to Claremont McKenna College in partial fulfillment of the requirements of a B.A. degree. We are grateful to the children of Condit School, Mary B. Eyre Children's School, and Sycamore Elementary for giving us a chance to work with and learn from them. We also acknowledge the assistance of Laurie Jones, Mark Costanzo, and Paul Huard on this project. Comments by Phil Costanzo and Alex Siegel greatly improved our understanding of the data and are much appreciated.

cognitive development is discussed, with particular attention to the role of social comparison processes in explaining the age patterns found.

Over the past two decades the contribution of peer interaction to children's cognitive development has received increased attention as researchers acknowledge the value of peer experiences on learning and problem solving. Peer interaction facilitates learning because partners often contribute new information, define and restructure a problem in a way that is familiar, and generate discussions that lead to the selection of the most effective problem-solving strategy (Azmitia & Perlmutter, 1989). Thus, through mutual feedback, evaluation, and debate, peers motivate one another to abandon misconceptions and search for better solutions. The present study is intended to broaden our understanding of the effects of peer collaboration on children's thinking by examining age and expertise as mediators of social influence on children's planning skills. Of particular interest is whether age-related status affects cognitive interaction by a novice and expert on a planning task.

Much of the recent research on peer collaboration identifies two theories to account for the facilitation of cognition: Piaget's structural perspective and Vygotsky's sociohistorical perspective. Piaget (1948) and Vygotsky (1978) shared the view that children are active participants in their development, and both emphasized that children learn and develop their thinking processes by interacting with both objects and people. Although Piaget's primary concern was the development of the individual in relation to the physical properties of the world, he did believe that discussion between children plays a role in cognitive development and proposed that cognitive conflict between peers was a mechanism for the social facilitation of cognition. For Piaget, peer interaction is conducive to cognitive development because of the relatively symmetrical nature of peer interaction, i.e., relatively little cognitive and social distance between peers, compared to asymmetric interactions, i.e., those occurring between children and adults or between peers of higher cognitive or social status (Azmitia & Perlmutter, 1989). According to Piaget (1948), children are likely to conform to rules that they do not fully understand because of this asymmetry in adult–child interactions and will tend to agree with the adult, who has more power and knowledge, without examining the ideas themselves. When a peer has a different perspective, no asymmetry of power exists, and thus partners are more likely to participate in the problem-solving process.

Vygotsky (1978) placed greater emphasis on the role of asymmetrical relationships, focusing on the role of guidance by a person who has achieved a level of expertise beyond that of the child. During guided participation (Rogoff, 1990), more experienced social members use sociocultural tools, like language, to encourage thinking in less experienced members beyond what they are capable of on their own. Vygotsky's emphasis on interaction with more mature partners, such as adults or skilled peers, is therefore, essential to his theory (Tudge & Rogoff, 1989).

To help clarify these theoretical differences, researchers have investigated the influence of peers with varying expertise on children's learning. Researchers have found that cognitive development can be attained both by pairing children of different skills, e.g., nonconservers with conservers (e.g., Murray, 1982; Perret-Clermont, 1980), as well as by pairing children at approximately the same cognitive level (Glachan & Light, 1982). Yet Azmitia (1988) found that children at the same level make little progress. And Ellis and Rogoff (1986) showed that more capable peers are not necessarily effective teachers in promoting certain skills. Thus, despite extensive investigations in recent years regarding the influence of peer collaboration on cognitive development, the merit of conflict versus guidance is still under scrutiny. This inquiry is not independent of concerns about the relative skill or expertise of the partners in promoting cognitive growth. Unfortunately, these issues are difficult to disentangle since age and expertise are often confounded in research on peer interaction.

In fact, in many studies individual differences in expertise are assumed to correspond to age differences (Ellis & Gauvain, 1992). Although this may be a reasonable assumption, expertise on particular tasks should not necessarily be assumed to correlate with age, especially ages that are somewhat close developmentally, e.g., 5- and 7-year-old children. Preassessments of children's ability on tasks independent of age are essential to establishing skill level and assigning children to dyads.

A related concern is the influence of differential age on peer involvement during interaction. Recall that Piaget cautioned that interaction with adults may be less effective than with peers due to inherent restrictions of the adult–child status differential. Such cautions may also be relevant to peer interaction in which peers are of the same versus different ages. Research in social development indicates quite clearly that child age is correlated with social status and dominance (Blurton Jones, 1972; Grusec & Lytton, 1988). This suggests that even in peer collaboration, age-related status may play an important role in how partners participate in the interaction. Since age and expertise, even when preassessed, are typically confounded in peer collaboration research, it remains unclear as to how age-related status may affect peer interaction.

In order to reconcile Piaget and Vygotsky's views it is necessary to explore further the variables involved in social interaction such as the relative age and expertise of the social partners and the different mechanisms influencing the social facilitation of cognition. One of the goals of the present study is to examine the processes proposed by Vygotsky and Piaget, such as cognitive conflict and guidance by an expert, that may promote cognitive development, with particular attention to the differential influence of age and expertise on the process and outcome of peer collaboration during joint planning. The study focuses on joint planning because research suggests that children's metacognitive skills, such as planning, are likely to benefit from social interaction (e.g., Hartup, 1985; Rogoff, Gauvain, & Gardner, 1987; Wertsch, McNamee, McLane, & Budwig, 1980).

In the present study, the role of collaboration between children and their more experienced peers in affecting skill in planning was investigated. In particular, the influence of age on novice and expert involvement in the task was studied by comparing the interactional process when children planned with an expert of the same age versus one who was older. Based on findings from earlier research (see Azmitia & Perlmutter, 1989), we expected that novices would improve their planning skills when planning with experts, and the benefits attained from interaction would transfer to the novice's subsequent individual performance. However, it was also expected that the relative ages of the partners would influence the degree to which the novice participated in the task. Novices collaborating with same-age experts were expected to be more involved in the process of planning because, as research in social development suggests, collaboration between children of the same age is less marked by dominance and is therefore less emotionally threatening than corrective advice from adults or older children (Damon, 1984). Because previous research has not established the mechanisms of social interaction that promote cognitive development, this study also investigated the different mechanisms of social interaction. In particular, this study examined conflict between the partners, observational learning by the novice, and guidance by the expert. These processes may influence the likelihood that children will learn through collaboration, however, their use may be related to whether the partners are of the same or different ages.

METHOD

SUBJECTS

Seventy 5- and 7-year-old children from three elementary schools serving middle-income populations were pretested to obtain 16 5-year-old novice planners ($M = 5.5$ years; range = 5.2–5.9 years), 8 5-year-old expert planners ($M = 5.5$ years; range = 5.2–5.9

years), and 8 7-year-old expert planners ($M = 7.5$ years; range = 7.2–7.9 years). During the interactive sessions, novice planners were assigned randomly to either a 5- or 7-year-old expert planner of the same sex. Thus, in the final group there were 8 mixed ability, cross-age dyads and 8 mixed ability, same-age dyads with an equal number of boys and girls in each condition.

TASKS AND MATERIALS

Three tasks, designed by Gauvain (1992), were used for the planning tasks. Each task involved sequencing and delivering five items to locations in a village drawn on 22 × 28-in. (55.9 × 71.1 cm) poster board using a small delivery truck. Solution of the problems required a reverse sequencing strategy, i.e., the delivery vehicles were constructed so that only the next item to be delivered could be removed at any time. Consequently, each problem required advance planning of the entire sequence of items for delivery to be successfully accomplished. The tasks combine some of the elements of planning tasks used by Gauvain and Rogoff (1989) in their research on planning skills and by Boder (1978) in his research on the development of children's skill at reverse sequencing. Each child participated in an individual pretest and a collaborative session, and novices also participated in an individual posttest.

Pretest Task.   The pretest involved delivering mail to houses. This drawing on the poster board contained a post office, a one-way street sign, an oval street route, and five homes (three orange and two blue homes) lined along the one-way road. Materials included five letters (three orange and two blue) that corresponded to the homes according to color and a red toy wagon for delivering the letters from the post office to the homes (Fig. 1).

Collaborative Task.   Children planning collaboratively were asked to deliver farm items to areas in a farm scene depicted on a poster board. Task materials included a poster board on which was drawn a diagram of a farm with pictures of three sheep pens, two pig pens, and a field indicating where three shrubs and two trees were to be planted. Animal pens and planting fields were identified with stickers of the items. Wooden blocks in the shape of the animals (three sheep and two pigs) and the plants (three shrubs and two trees) were delivered to assigned areas in the farm using a wooden truck designed to fit the blocks. Two deliveries were conducted using this scene. The first delivery involved the trees and shrubs and the second the pigs and sheep (Fig. 2).

Posttest Task.   The scene depicted on the poster board for the posttest contained two hat stores, three

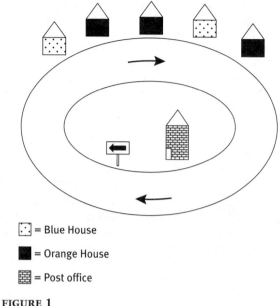

= Blue House

= Orange House

= Post office

FIGURE 1
Mail delivery task used in the pretest.

cat stores, and a warehouse. Cards labeled with stickers of hats or cats and the same wagon used in the pretest were also used (Fig. 3).

PROCEDURE

The children were asked to perform three planning tasks. The first task, the mail delivery, was the easiest of the four and was used as the pretest. Based on

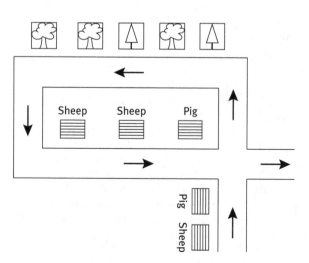

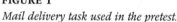

FIGURE 2
Farm delivery task used in the interactional session.

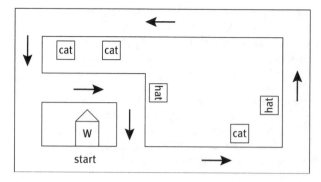

FIGURE 3
Warehouse delivery task used in the posttest.

their performance, the children were identified as either an expert (the child successfully completed the pretest in three or fewer delivery attempts) or a novice (more than three delivery attempts were needed) using normative scores for these tasks obtained from a study that examined the development of children's planning skills (Gauvain, 1992). Children were considered novice planners if their pretest performance exceeded the mean number of trials required for successful completion of the task for their age group. Novices were then paired randomly with either a 5-year-old expert planner or a 7-year-old expert planner for the Farm Delivery. After the collaborative task, the novice was given a posttest similar to, but more difficult than, the pretest. The collaborative sessions took place the same day as the posttest. All of the sessions were videotaped at the children's school in a quiet space where the child could not be distracted or observed by others.

Pretest Task: Mail Delivery.   The experimenter placed the poster board on the table in front of the child. The experimenter explained that the drawing contained a small village, and pointed out the post office, one-way road, and houses, and then asked the child to identify the two types of houses. The child was also asked to trace a finger along the direction of travel indicated for the one-way road. Then the experimenter explained to the child that he or she was to deliver a letter to each of the houses, and the color of the letter was to match the color of the house. The letters were then placed at the post office in random order and the child was shown a wagon and told that it was to be used for the delivery. The experimenter then explained the rules for mail delivery: (1) only one letter from the wagon, the top one, may be removed at a time; (2) the road is one-way so the wagon cannot be backed up; (3) the mail is to be delivered to all the houses in one trip; and (4) if during delivery the child discovers that the arrangement of the letters in the wagon is incorrect, all the letters and the wagon are to be brought back to the Post Office, rearranged, and delivered again. The experimenter asked the child if he or she understood the rules and asked if there were any questions. If the child violated the rules during the delivery, the experimenter reiterated them and asked the child to continue. Upon completion, the experimenter told the child that he or she did a good job.

Collaborative Session: Farm Delivery.   The experimenter placed the poster board on the table facing the children, and told the children that in this task they were to deliver items to a farm. The experimenter described the illustrations on the board: the road, especially the one-way signs, and the fields and pens. The procedure for delivery was explained, with the experimenter pointing out that there would be two different deliveries. First the children were to deliver the trees and shrubs (Delivery One) and then they would deliver the animals (Delivery Two). The experimenter then introduced the items to be delivered and explained that only one item was to go to each delivery point. The experimenter identified where each item went and explained to the children that they were to deliver to the front of the fields and pens. The children were then shown the delivery truck and the experimenter explained how to load and unload items. The starting position for the truck was identified, and then the rules were explained: (1) the road is one-way and therefore the truck cannot back up; (2) the truck is low on gas, so it can go around the road once for each delivery; (3) the children are to work together; and (4) if, during a delivery, they feel that the truck is loaded incorrectly, they are to collect all the items and return to the starting position and reload the truck. The experimenter asked the children if they understood the rules and procedure and asked if there were any questions. The children were then instructed to begin the task. If the children violated the rules, the experimenter repeated them, and then instructed the children to continue with the task. Upon completion, the children were complimented on their work.

Posttest Task: Warehouse Delivery.   The novice was asked to do one more delivery task. The experimenter placed the poster board used in the posttest in front of the child and introduced the illustrations, including the road, especially the one-way markings, the warehouse, and stores. The experimenter pointed out that there were two different types of stores, those that sold cats and those that sold hats. The child was then given cards with stickers of cats or hats on them and asked to deliver them to the stores using the toy wagon. The same rules in the mail delivery task applied in the posttest and were repeated. If the child violated the rules, the experimenter explained the rules

again, and asked the child to continue. After the posttest was completed, the child was complimented on his or her work.

CODING

Performance was coded for plan effectiveness and for the use of planning strategies. The extent of each partners' involvement in the task during the interactional trial was coded, as was the interactional process used by the children to convey or ascertain planning relevant information. Mechanisms of social interaction included observational learning, i.e., the amount of time the novices observed the expert performing the task; guidance by the expert, including physical intervention, directives and suggestions, and positive support; and conflicting statements or disagreements. Three (19%) of the 16 tapes were coded independently by two coders, yielding ϕ correlation reliabilities ranging from .64 to 1.0.

Plan Effectiveness.   To assess the children's pretest, interaction, and posttest performance, the number of delivery attempts made, including the final successful delivery and any partial or instructional attempts, were recorded. Thus, the higher the number of delivery attempts, the less effective the planning performance. On the pretest, children who delivered the mail in three or less trials were considered experts, while those children who took more than three trials were considered novices. This was based on the performance in another study (Gauvain, 1992) of a sample of 5-year-olds on this same pretest in which the average number of trials for successful completion was 3.16 ($SD = 2.8$, $n = 16$).

Planning Strategies.   This includes statements regarding task strategy and was coded during joint planning. Strategy statements include both general task strategy statements, such as how to do the task in an efficient or planful way, and specific strategy statements, concerning strategic handling of individual task moves. Examples of general task strategy statements are "Let's put the last one on first" or "You have to load it the opposite way to deliver it right." Statements such as "What about this one next?" and "The tree goes here" are examples of specific task strategies.

Partners' Task Involvement.   Each of the items selected for loading in the Farm Delivery Task was coded according to whether the novice on his or her own, the expert on his or her own, or the novice and expert together chose the item, loaded the item into the truck, and delivered the item.

Interactional Process.   Three different measures reflecting the various theoretical emphases in the peer literature were used to assess the interactional process the partners used to convey or ascertain task-relevant information. *Observational learning* was the total number of seconds novices spent observing their expert partners perform the task. *Guidance by the expert* was coded as either physical intervention, which was any physical interference by the expert of the novice's activity by manipulating an object or person, e.g., the expert putting his or her hand on the novice's hand; directives and suggestion, that is the expert verbally telling or suggesting to the novice what to do; and positive support, which included positive statements and physical gestures by the expert that recognize progress by the novice on the task and/or promote continuance. *Conflict* included statements of disagreements about the choice, arrangement, or handling of an item.

RESULTS

Analysis of variance (ANOVA) was used to compare the performance and social interactional processes of children collaborating with same-age expert peers versus older expert peers.

PLANNING DURING COLLABORATION

There were no differences in planning effectiveness, i.e., the number of delivery attempts children required to perform the tasks successfully, between the two groups in either farm delivery. Peers in same-age dyads required an average of 1.5 trials to complete Delivery One and 4.1 trials to complete Delivery Two successfully. Peers in cross-age dyads required an average of 1.4 trials to complete Delivery One and 2.7 to complete Delivery Two successfully.

The most interesting differences emerged in relation to partner involvement and the interactional process. Novices planning with same-age experts were more involved in the three task operations, choosing, loading, and delivering items ($M = 40.25$, $SD = 25.94$), during the two trials of the interaction than novices working with older experts ($M = 19.87$, $SD = 15.89$), $F(1, 16) = 5.43$, $p < .05$. (Because the conditions of homogeneity of variance was violated, a log base-10 transformation was used in this analysis.) Novices in same-age dyads were responsible, on average, for 32% of these task operations and novices in cross-age dyads were responsible for an average of 26% of these task operations. (Table 1 contains the means for these variables by group for each of the two farm deliveries.) Experts in same-age dyads were responsible for an average of 51% of the task operations, and experts in cross-age dyads were responsible, on average, for 55%. The remaining 17 and 18%, respectively, were shared by the two partners. Thus, the hypothesis that novices planning with same-age experts would be more involved in the task than novices planning with older experts was supported.

Vygotsky proposed that the experienced partner would adjust the problem-solving process so that, with experience, the learner would be able to participate in increasingly more complex aspects of the solution. Examination of the novice's participation from

TABLE 1   MEANS (AND STANDARD DEVIATIONS) FOR PERCENTAGE INVOLVEMENT BY NOVICES AND EXPERTS AND INTERACTIONAL PROCESS BY GROUP FOR THE INTERACTION TASK

Group	Same-age dyads		Cross-age dyads	
Variable	Delivery 1	Delivery 2	Delivery 1	Delivery 2
Partners' task involvement				
Novice only	28.6 (11.4)	34.6 (16.1)	29.8 (13.2)	22.9 (17.2)
Expert only	52.4 (15.0)	49.9 (15.3)	51.1 (18.2)	58.5 (19.6)
Both novice and expert	19.0 (10.4)	15.4 (7.7)	19.0 (6.7)	18.6 (7.2)
Guidance by an expert				
Physical intervention	1.4 (.7)	3.2 (3.4)	1.4 (.5)	1.6 (1.4)
Directives and suggestions	2.9 (2.2)	5.6 (5.3)	2.6 (2.2)	3.1 (2.5)
Positive support	1.6 (.7)	5.1 (4.7)	1.5 (.8)	1.2 (.5)
Observational learning				
(in seconds)	22.0 (27.1)	50.0 (98.9)	19.0 (16.7)	18.4 (33.2)
Conflict	2.5 (1.9)	4.2 (4.4)	1.1 (.3)	2.2 (1.3)

Delivery One (the easier of the two deliveries) to Delivery Two of the Farm Task reveals that novices planning with same-age experts increased in their participation from Delivery One, when they were responsible for an average of 29% of the task operations, to Delivery Two, when they were responsible for an average of 35% of the task operations, $t(7) = 1.82$, $p = .05$. In contrast, participation of the novices in cross-age dyads decreased as the task became more difficult, from a mean of 30% to a mean of 23%, $t(7) = -2.61$, $p = .02$.

Although the total amount of guidance by the expert on the Farm Task did not differ between the two groups, when the two deliveries are considered separately, we find that during the second delivery 5-year-old experts provided more positive support ($M = 5.12$, $SD = 4.7$), $F(1, 16) = 5.37$, $p = .05$, for the novices than 7-year-old experts ($M = 1.25$, $SD = .46$). In addition, conflict during the second delivery was somewhat greater in the same-age dyads, $F(1, 16) = 3.23$, $p \neq .09$. (See means for these variables in Table 1.) It appears that same-age experts not only fostered more participation by the novice as he or she gained experience, these experts also supported their agemates more during the joint task. However, novices and experts of the same age also tended to challenge each other more than when partners were of different ages. Finally, due to the variance within the groups, they did not differ in terms of the time spent by the novice observing the expert perform the task.

Same-age dyads were not significantly different from cross-age dyads in number of strategy statements made by the expert. Experts in the same-age dyads produced an average of 14.4 strategy statements and those in cross-age dyads produced an average of 7.7 strategy statements. Novices in same-age dyads produced slightly more strategy statements (an average of 8.4) than novices in cross-age dyads (an average of 4.0), $F(1, 16) = 4.01$, $p = .06$, suggesting that, in addition to greater participation in task operations, collaborating with a same-age peer may also facilitate greater involvement by the novice in strategy formation.

Taken together, these results indicate that peer interaction differs when partners are of the same versus different ages. Novices planning with same-age experts were more involved in the task and experienced more support and challenge from same-age partners who were more expert at the task than did novices planning with older experts. Age-related dynamics appear to be an influential factor in the process of peer cognitive interaction. We now examine the relationship of the interactional process in these two groups to the novices' individual posttest performances to investigate whether these dynamics are related to what novices learn from collaborating with an expert.

RELATION OF COLLABORATION TO POSTTEST PLANNING PERFORMANCE

Pearson correlation coefficients were calculated to determine whether the interaction related to posttest performance and whether these relationships differed across the two groups. It was found that the number of trials required by novices to complete the posttest successfully was related to partner involvement during the interaction. More involvement by the novice in choosing, loading, and delivering items during the collaborative tasks was related to more effective planning on the posttest, $r(16) = -.49$, $p < .05$. (Recall that better planning performance is indicated by fewer trials.) And, mirroring this, greater involvement by the expert during the interaction was related to less effective planning by the novice on the posttest, $r(16) = .56$, $p < .05$.

When the two farm deliveries are considered separately, we find that for the novices in the same-age dyads, the number of trials required to complete the posttest was related to the total instances of guidance by the expert in delivery two, $r(8) = -.78$, $p < .05$. That is, for children in same-age dyads only, the extent to which the expert offered assistance to the novice was related to better performance on the posttest. Thus, Vygotsky's suggestion that interaction with those who are more expert would foster guidance and cognitive support was supported in the same-age dyads only. Since there were no differences between groups in the amount of guidance by the experts, perhaps other factors, such as involvement of the novice, which was greater in same-age dyads, bolstered the effectiveness of the experts' assistance during joint planning.

Further support for the importance of learner involvement in the task emerged in t tests comparing the posttest scores (number of delivery trials to complete the task) of the children in this study with the posttest scores of 5-year-old children in a study using this same task but who did not collaborate with a peer prior to the posttest (Gauvain, 1992). It was found that only the children who collaborated with the same-age experts, but not those who collaborated with older experts, performed significantly better than children who did not collaborate, $t(24) = 2.18$, $p < .05$. The mean number of trials to complete the posttest successfully for 5-year-old children who planned with same-age experts was 2.37 ($SD = 1.30$, $n = 8$) and the mean for the children who planned alone prior to the posttest was 4.75 ($SD = 3.94$, $n = 16$). The mean number of trials for 5-year-old children who planned previously with an older expert was 3.37 ($SD = 1.85$, $n = 8$), which does not differ significantly from the children who planned with the same-age experts or who planned entirely on their own. This suggests that collaboration between novices and experts of the same-age, but not of different ages, may lead to more successful planning than when children plan independently.

Discussion

The purpose of this study was to examine the effects of age versus expertise in facilitating the development of children's planning skills during joint planning. It was hypothesized that the age of the expert partner would influence the involvement of the novice, which in turn would affect the extent of learning. The results support this prediction. Novices who planned with same-age experts were more involved in the task than novices who planned with older experts. Furthermore, novices who collaborated with same-age experts performed significantly better in later individual planning than children who did not collaborate prior to performing the same task. This difference did not appear for novices who planned with older experts. Finally, guidance by the expert, although not significantly different between the two groups, was related to later individual planning for novices who previously planned with same-age experts but not for novices who previously planned with older experts.

These findings support Vygotsky's (1978) general contention that cognitive development may benefit from opportunities available in the social context. However, they extend this view by suggesting factors that may influence this process. Although the results indicate that collaboration between novice and expert planners can lead to the development of the novice's skills, exposure to expertise was not sufficient for explaining the cognitive gains resulting from the social situation. The extent to which the novices were involved in the task influenced learning, however, the extent of novice involvement was affected by the relative age of the social partners. Perhaps novices who planned with same-age experts did not perceive as much social and cognitive distance between themselves and the experts compared to novices who planned with older experts. Children may feel more comfortable collaborating with experts of the same age and even perceive the partner's skills as attainable.

Another possibility, related to the first, is that experts in cross-age dyads dominate the interaction and do not allow their novice partners to participate in the problem-solving process. Recall that the data showed that the experts in the cross-age group were responsible, on average, for 55% of the task operations, while their novice partners were responsible for only 26% of the operations (compared with 51% involvement for experts and 32% for novices in same-age dyads). Furthermore, after examining the novices' participation

from Delivery One, the easier of the two deliveries, to Delivery Two of the interaction, it was found that novices planning with same-age experts increased their participation, whereas participation of the novices in cross-age dyads decreased as the task became more difficult. These patterns, as well as the finding that the 5-year-old experts provided more positive support for their partners in Delivery Two, raise the possibility that the 5-year-old experts were more sensitive to the learner's needs and capabilities, and therefore allowed their novice partners to be more involved in the task as they gained experience. Of course, the related interpretation is that 5-year-old novices are more likely to allow older experts to dominate the interaction than same-age experts. The marginally significant difference in conflict between the two groups, with greater conflict in same-age dyads, supports this interpretation. More frequent bids for dominance by older children and acceptance of these by younger children are reciprocal processes, that, by definition, are more likely to appear in mixed-age pairs.

Of the mechanisms that are hypothesized to facilitate cognitive growth—conflict, guided participation, and observational learning—only guidance by an expert was found to mediate learning. However, guidance was only effective for 5-year-old novices planning with same-age experts, who also had greater involvement in the task. Thus, guided participation in conjunction with increased task involvement facilitated learning for the novice when planning with a same-age, but more expert peer. Piaget hypothesized that conflict between children mediates cognitive growth. In this study, the amount of conflict between social partners was minimal, although it was somewhat greater among same-age peers who did not share the same skill at planning. This suggests that in interactions where partners are not equal in skill but equal in age, mechanisms such as guidance and extent of participation may be more central than conflict for social facilitation to occur.

Although these results further our understanding of the role of social experience in cognitive development, they are less useful for explaining why the conditional effects for age were obtained and whether these effects are specific to the ages studied here or represent a more general finding. Research on the development of social comparison processes by Ruble and colleagues (Feldman & Ruble, 1988; Ruble, Boggiano, Feldman, & Loebl, 1980; Ruble & Frey, 1987) suggests a possible answer to these questions. When children collaborate with more experienced partners, opportunities arise for them to make ability comparisons between themselves and their partners that may be useful for defining their behavior as well as for directing future performances. Studies conducted in Ruble's lab have shown that child age influences the occurrence and the nature of these comparisons.

During social interaction, 5- to 6-year-old children, the same age as the novices in the present study, are primarily oriented toward same-age peers as a source of social comparison, whereas older children and adults are more likely to select "upward" comparisons as a source for self-evaluation. Stated more generally, the meaning of different people in social cognitive processes, like social comparison, is a function of age-related developmental processes. In this research, same-age experts may have constituted an ideal arrangement for mediating social cognitive effects for 5- to 6-year-old novices, thereby reflecting age-specific processes of social comparison rather than more general principles of social facilitation across childhood. To explore this suggestion further, research that varies the ages of the novices in addition to that of the experts is needed. Since the ages of 7 to 9 years have been found (e.g., see Ruble & Frey, 1987) to be particularly important for refining processes of social comparison, such research may reveal whether these ages are also critical junctures in processes of social facilitation.

In sum, this research investigated the influence of peer interaction on cognitive development by examining differences in children's planning when they planned with an expert of the same age or an expert who was older. In previous research on peer collaboration, age and expertise have typically been confounded. Rather than suggesting that simply the presence of an expert partner promotes cognitive development, this study points to age-related status and behaviors as mediating the process and outcome of peer interaction on problem-solving tasks. In addition to the extent of task involvement by the novice and guidance by the expert, which were greater in same-age dyads, facilitation effects for young children may also be driven by opportunities during collaboration for children to make social comparisons. These findings suggest that further understanding of how the sociocognitive processes of guided participation, conflict, and observational learning relate to and integrate with processes of social comparison over the course of development is essential for unpacking the mechanisms whereby social interaction may promote or impede cognitive growth.

REFERENCES

Azmitia, M. (1988). Peer interaction and problem solving: When are two heads better than one? *Child Development*, **59**, 87–96.

Azmitia, M., & Perlmutter, M. (1989). Social influences on children's cognition: State of the art and future directions. In H. Reese (Ed.), *Advances in child development and behavior* (Vol. 22, pp. 89–144). San Diego, CA: Academic Press.

Blurton Jones, N. (1972). *Ethological studies of child behavior.* London: Cambridge University Press.

Boder, A. (1978). Etude de la composition d'un ordre inverse: Hypothese dur la coordination de deux sources de controle du raisonnement. *Archives de Psychologie*, **46**, 87–113.

Damon, W. (1984). Peer education: The untapped potential. *Journal of Applied Developmental Psychology*, **5**, 331–343.

Ellis, S., & Gauvain, M. (1992). Social and cultural influences on children's collaborative interactions. In L. T. Winegar and J. Valsiner (Eds.), *Children's development within social context: Vol. 2. Research and methodology* (pp. 155–180). Hillsdale, NJ: Erlbaum.

Ellis, S., & Rogoff, B. (1986). Problem solving in children's management of instruction. In E. Mueller and C. R. Cooper (Eds.), *Process and outcome in peer relationships* (pp. 301–325). New York: Academic Press.

Feldman, N. S., & Ruble, D. N. (1988). The effect of personal relevance on psychological inference: A developmental analysis. *Child Development*, **59**, 1339–1352.

Gauvain, M. (1992). *The development of planning skills*. Unpublished manuscript, University of California, Riverside.

Gauvain, M., & Rogoff, B. (1989). Collaborative problem solving and children's planning skills. *Developmental Psychology*, **25**, 139–151.

Glachan, M., & Light, P. (1982). Peer interaction and learning: Can two wrongs make a right? In G. Butterworth & P. Light (Eds.), *Social cognition: Studies of the development of understanding* (pp. 238–262). Chicago: University of Chicago Press.

Grusec, J. E., & Lytton, H. (1988). *Social development: History, theory, and research.* New York: Springer-Verlag.

Hartup, W. (1985). Relationships and their significance in cognitive development. In R. Hinde & A. Perret-Clermont (Eds.), *Relationships and cognitive development* (pp. 66–82). Oxford: Oxford University Press.

Mueller, E., & Cooper, C. R. (Eds.). (1986). *Process and outcome in peer relationships.* New York: Academic Press.

Murray, F. B. (1982). Teaching through social conflict. *Contemporary Educational Psychology*, **7**, 257–271.

Perret-Clermont, A. N. (1980). *Social interaction and cognitive development in children.* London: Academic Press.

Piaget, J. (1948). *The moral judgement of the child.* IL: Free Press.

Piaget, J. (1983). Piaget's theory. In W. Kessen (Ed.), *History, theory, and methods*: Vol. 1. *Handbook of Child Psychology* (pp. 294–356). New York: Wiley.

Rogoff, B. (1990). *Apprenticeship in thinking: Cognitive development in social context.* New York: Oxford University Press.

Rogoff, B., Gauvain, M., & Gardner, W. P. (1987). *Children's adjustment of plans to circumstances.* In S. L. Friedman, E. K. Scholnick, & R. R. Cocking (Eds.), *The role of planning in psychological development* (pp. 303–320). London: Cambridge University Press.

Ruble, D. N., Boggiano, A. K., Feldman, N. S., & Loebl, J. H. (1980). A developmental analysis of the role of social comparison in self-evaluation. *Developmental Psychology*, **16**, 105–115.

Ruble, D. N., & Frey, K. S. (1987). Social comparison and self-evaluation in the classroom: Developmental changes in knowledge and function. In J. C. Masters & W. P. Smith (Eds.),

Social comparison, social justice, relative deprivation (pp. 81–104). Hillsdale, NJ: Erlbaum.

Tudge, J. R. H., & Rogoff, B. (1989). Peer influences on cognitive development: Piagetian and Vygotskian perspectives. In M. Bornstein and J. Bruner (Eds.). *Interaction in human development* (pp. 17–40). Hillsdale, NJ: Erlbaum.

Vygotsky, L. S. (1978). *Mind and society.* Cambridge, MA: Harvard University Press.

Wertsch, J. V., McNamee, G. D., McLane J. B., & Budwig, N. A. (1980). The adult–child dyad as a problem-solving system. *Child Development*, **51**, 1215–1221.

QUESTIONS

1. According to Piaget, how might peer collaboration contribute to cognitive development?
2. According to Vygotsky, how do more experienced partners facilitate children's learning during peer collaboration?
3. Why are age and expertise often confounded in cognitive developmental research involving peers?
4. What types of cognitive behaviors were coded, and did the display of these behaviors differ in the two groups of children studied?
5. Why were novices who worked with same-age experts expected to learn more about planning than were novices who worked with older experts?
6. What types of partner involvement appeared in the two social groupings (young novice + young expert vs. younger novice + older expert)?
7. How did guidance and conflict differ in these two groups?
8. How does developmental change in the process of social comparison help explain these results?
9. Whose view of peer collaboration and cognitive development did these results support, Piaget's or Vygotsky's? Explain.
10. If you were to advise a teacher about how to group children in the classroom to promote learning, what type of peer arrangement would the results of this study lead you to suggest?

27 Relational Aggression, Gender, and Social-Psychological Adjustment

NICKI R. CRICK • JENNIFER K. GROTPETER

Traditionally, aggression has been defined in psychological research as any physical act that is directed toward another person and is intended to cause harm. When this definition has been used in research that examines gender differences in aggression among children or adults, results indicate higher rates of aggression among males than females. The reasons for this difference are complex and pertain both to biological and social-experiential differences between males and females. One conclusion that has been drawn from this research is that males are more aggressive than females. However, these results actually indicate that males are more aggressive than females when aggression is defined along physical dimensions. This research does not answer the question of whether males are more aggressive in general than females. It may be that other forms of aggression, such as aggression that is more verbally based or relationally directed, have different gender-related patterns, either with similar rates for males and females or perhaps higher rates for females than for males. This question is the topic of the following article.

In the study described in this article, Nicki Crick and Jennifer Grotpeter broadened the operational definition of aggression to include relational aggression—that is, attempts to harm other children either by damaging their friendships or by excluding them from the peer group. The goals of this research were to study the prevalence of relational aggression in middle childhood and to determine whether gender differences in this form of aggressive behavior exist.

Crick and Grotpeter were also interested in whether relational aggression is related to social and psychological adjustment. Prior research has established a link between physical aggression and maladjustment. Therefore, investigating whether children who are relationally aggressive also have adjustment difficulties is consistent with research on aggression and social dysfunction more generally.

To study relational aggression in middle childhood, peer reports from children in grades 3 to 6 were collected. The children reported on aggressive behaviors among age mates as well as on aspects of their own social-psychological adjustment, such as loneliness, social anxiety, and depression. The results support the hypotheses that relational aggression is a meaningful and distinct type of aggressive behavior among children and that relational aggression is significantly related to gender and social-psychological adjustment. This research is important for several reasons. It broadens the scope of child behaviors that are considered antisocial. It also suggests that aggression may be characteristic of human beings in general and that the characterization of males as aggressive and females as nonaggressive is incorrect.

Prior studies of childhood aggression have demonstrated that as a group, boys are more aggressive than girls. We hypothesized that this finding reflects a lack of research on forms of aggression that are relevant to young females rather than an actual gender difference in levels of overall aggressiveness. In the present study, a form of aggression hypothesized to be typical of girls, relational aggression, was assessed with a peer nomination instrument for a sample of 491 third- through sixth-grade children. Overt aggression (i.e., physical

Reprinted with permission of Blackwell Publishers from Crick, N. R., & Grotpeter, J. K. (1995). Relational aggression, gender, and social-psychological adjustment. *Child Development, 66,* 710–722.

This research was funded by a grant from the University of Illinois Research Board to the first author. Portions of this study were presented at the meeting of the Society for Research in Child Development, March 1993, New Orleans. The authors would like to thank the principals, teachers, and students of Coppenbarger, Garfield, Harris, and Stevenson Elementary Schools for their assistance with the study. Special thanks also to Aaron Ebata for his invaluable comments on earlier drafts of this article.

and verbal aggression as assessed in past research) and social-psychological adjustment were also assessed. Results provide evidence for the validity and distinctiveness of relational aggression. Further, they indicated that, as predicted, girls were significantly more relationally aggressive than were boys. Results also indicated that relationally aggressive children may be at risk for serious adjustment difficulties (e.g., they were significantly more rejected and reported significantly higher levels of loneliness, depression, and isolation relative to their nonrelationally aggressive peers).

Because of the deleterious effects of conduct problems on children's development (see Parker & Asher, 1987, for a review), a great deal of research has been conducted on aggression in the past decade (e.g., see Dodge & Crick, 1990; Parke & Slaby, 1983, for reviews). Although significant advances have been made in our understanding of childhood aggression, one limitation of this research has been the lack of attention to gender differences in the expression of aggression (cf. Robins, 1986). Prior studies demonstrate that, as a group, boys exhibit significantly higher levels of aggression than do girls (see Block, 1983; Parke & Slaby, 1983, for reviews), a difference that persists throughout the life span (Eagly & Steffen, 1986; Hyde, 1986; Kenrick, 1987). Not surprisingly, these findings have been interpreted as an overall lack of aggressiveness in girls' peer interactions. However, an alternative explanation is that the forms of aggression assessed in past research are more salient for boys than for girls. If so, young females may exhibit unique forms of aggression, forms that have been overlooked in past research.

Although specific definitions have varied over the years, aggression has been generally defined by most authors as behaviors that are intended to hurt or harm others (e.g., Berkowitz, 1993; Brehm & Kassin, 1990; Gormly & Brodzinsky, 1993; Myers, 1990; Vander Zanden, 1993). We propose that, when attempting to inflict harm on peers (i.e., aggressing), children do so in ways that best thwart or damage the goals that are valued by their respective gender peer groups. As past research has consistently shown, boys tend to harm others through physical and verbal aggression (e.g., hitting or pushing others, threatening to beat up others). These behaviors are consistent with the types of goals that past research has shown to be important to boys within the peer-group context, specifically, themes of instrumentality and physical dominance (see Block, 1983, for a review). These types of concerns are not as salient for most girls, however. In contrast to boys, girls are more likely to focus on relational issues during social interaction (e.g., establishing close, intimate connections with others) (see Block, 1983, for a review). In the present study, we hypothesized that aggressive behavior among girls would be consistent with their social concerns, similar to the pattern found for boys. Specifically, we hypothesized that girls' attempts to harm others would focus on relational issues and would include behaviors that are intended to significantly damage another child's friendships or feelings of inclusion by the peer group (e.g., angrily retaliating against a child by excluding her from one's play group; purposefully withdrawing friendship or acceptance in order to hurt or control the child; spreading rumors about the child so that peers will reject her). Thus, we expected that girls would be most likely to harm peers through relational aggression (i.e., harming others through purposeful manipulation and damage of their peer relationships) whereas boys would be most likely to harm peers through overt aggression (i.e., harming others through physical aggression, verbal threats, instrumental intimidation).

Although gender differences in the forms of aggression that children exhibit were postulated years ago (Feshbach, 1969), very little relevant research has yet been conducted. In one of the earliest studies on this topic, Feshbach (1969) observed first graders' responses to unfamiliar peers. She found that girls were significantly more likely than boys to respond to the unfamiliar peer with behaviors that, although referred to by the author as "indirect aggression," appear similar to those specifically defined here as relational aggression (e.g., rejection and social exclusion).

This pattern of results has also been documented for older children. In a more recent study, Cairns, Cairns, Neckerman, Ferguson, and Gariepy (1989) asked fourth through ninth graders to describe recent conflicts with peers. Content analysis of children's responses revealed that same-gender conflicts among girls were significantly more likely than boys' conflicts to involve themes of social alienation and manipulation of peer acceptance (i.e., themes that are consistent with relational aggression). Using a Finnish sample of fifth graders, Lagerspetz, Bjorkqvist, and Peltonen (1988) used a peer-rating scale to assess gender differences in children's use of several types of behaviors, some of which were relationally aggressive. Although their instrument confounded relational aggression with nonverbal aggression, their results were similar to those of the previously described research (i.e., girls exhibited significantly higher levels of relational/nonverbal aggression than did boys).

These investigations provide initial support for the hypothesis that relationally aggressive behaviors are present in children's peer interactions and that girls are more likely than boys to exhibit them. However, despite the conduct of hundreds of studies on the general topic of childhood aggression in the past several decades (see Dodge & Crick, 1990; Parke &

Slaby, 1983, for reviews), no systematic research has been conducted on relational aggression. Thus, no information has yet been generated on the correlates of relational aggression or the characteristics of the children who exhibit it (i.e., other than the previously described gender differences). Given the potentially serious consequences of aggression for children's adjustment (see Parker & Asher, 1987, for a review), it seems important to initiate research in this relevant, but unexplored domain. This is particularly true given that this form of aggression may be most characteristic of young females, a group whose behavioral difficulties have received scant attention in past research. The present research was designed as an initial attempt to address these issues.

We had four goals for the present study: (1) to develop a reliable measure of relational aggression, one that did not confound relational aggression with other forms of aggression; (2) to assess gender differences in relational aggression; (3) to assess the degree to which relational aggression is distinct from overt aggression (i.e., physical and verbal aggression as assessed in most of the past research in this area); and (4) to assess whether relational aggression is related to social-psychological maladjustment. We hypothesized that relational aggression would be related to, but also relatively distinct from, overt aggression. Further, we expected girls to be more relationally aggressive than boys. Also, similar to overtly aggressive children (Bukowski & Newcomb, 1984; Coie & Kupersmidt, 1983; Dodge, 1983; Parker & Asher, 1987), we expected relationally aggressive children to be more socially and psychologically maladjusted than their nonaggressive peers.

To address our goals, a peer nomination scale was constructed and used to assess relational aggression and overt aggression. Peers were selected as informants for two reasons. First, peer nominations have been used extensively in past research to identify aggressive children (e.g., Coie & Dodge, 1983; Dodge, 1980; Dodge & Frame, 1982; Perry, Perry, & Rasmussen. 1986). Second, it was thought that relationally aggressive behaviors, because of their relatively indirect nature and focus on peer relationships, might be difficult for those outside the peer group (e.g., teachers, researchers) to reliably observe and evaluate in naturalistic settings (cf. Lagerspetz et al., 1988). Thus, it was judged that peers would be the best informants, a method that has the additional advantage of providing multiple assessments of behavior (i.e., because each child is evaluated by all of his or her classmates as opposed to only one teacher, for example). In addition to the peer nomination instrument, subjects also completed several instruments designed to assess social-psychological adjustment (i.e., peer status, depression, loneliness, social anxiety, social avoidance, and perceptions of peer relations). These aspects of adjustment were chosen because past research has shown them to be predictive of concurrent and/or future socio-emotional difficulties (e.g., Asher & Wheeler, 1985; Crick & Ladd, 1993; Franke & Hymel, 1984; Kovacs, 1985; Parker & Asher, 1987). Thus, they would allow for an assessment of the adjustment risk status of relationally aggressive children.

METHOD

SUBJECTS

A total of 491 third- through sixth-grade children from four public schools in a moderately sized midwestern town participated as subjects.[1] The sample included 128 third (65 girls and 63 boys), 126 fourth (56 girls and 70 boys), 126 fifth (57 girls and 69 boys), and 111 sixth graders (57 girls and 54 boys). Approximately 37% of the sample was African-American, 60% was European-American, and 3% represented other ethnic groups. Each subject had parental consent to participate in the study (consent rate was above 82%).

PEER ASSESSMENT OF RELATIONAL AGGRESSION AND OTHER ASPECTS OF SOCIAL ADJUSTMENT

A peer nomination instrument was used to assess social adjustment. This instrument, which consisted of 19 items, included a peer sociometric and four subscales designed to assess social behavior: relational aggression, overt aggression, prosocial behavior, and isolation. These particular indices were selected because they represent the constructs that have been used most extensively in past research to evaluate children's social adjustment (i.e., peer status, aggression, withdrawal, prosocial behavior) (Crick & Dodge, 1994).

---

1. Due to practical constraints at the participating schools, we were not able to collect complete information for the self-report measures for some of the children who were absent during the class sessions or who skipped a question during testing (i.e., we were able to do make-up sessions with some, but not all, of these subjects). Because we had no reason to suspect bias in the part of the sample with incomplete information, we used all of the available subjects with complete information for a particular analysis. The total number of children who completed each instrument varied from 462 to 491 (refer to the residual degrees of freedom for each analysis to determine the number of subjects for each analysis).

Overt aggression was assessed with a three-item peer nomination scale. The items included in this scale assessed physical and verbal aggression and were drawn from those used in prior research (e.g., Asher & Williams, 1987; Coie & Dodge, 1983; Dodge, 1980; refer to Table 1 for a description of the items). Relational aggression was assessed with a five-item nomination scale that was developed for use in the present project (refer to Table 1 for item descriptions). Items included in this scale describe behaviors that represent purposeful attempts to harm, or threats to harm, another's peer relationships (e.g., telling a friend that you will not like her anymore unless she does what you tell her to do). A pool of relational aggression items, designed to fit the proposed definition, was initially generated by the authors. Selection of the subsequently chosen items and specific wording of each was based on pilot testing with grade-school-age children.

The prosocial behavior scale consisted of five items (e.g., peers who help others), and the isolation scale consisted of four items (e.g., peers who play alone at school, peers who seem lonely at school). The items included in these scales were based on those used in past research (e.g., Asher & Williams, 1987; Crick & Dodge, 1989). The peer sociometric consisted of two items, nominations of liked and disliked peers (positive and negative nominations). These items have been used extensively in past research to assess peer acceptance and rejection (see Crick & Dodge, 1994, for a review).

During the administration of the peer nomination instrument, children were provided with a class roster and were asked to nominate up to three classmates for each of the items. The number of nominations children received from peers for each of the items (for each child, these scores could range from 0 to the total number of children in his or her class minus 1) was summed and then standardized within each classroom. The standardized scores for the overt aggression, relational aggression, prosocial behavior, and isolation scales were summed to yield four total scores (e.g., children's standardized scores for each of the three items on the overt aggression scale were summed to create a total score).

TABLE 1   FACTOR LOADINGS FOR THE PEER NOMINATION INSTRUMENTS

Item	Prosocial/ happy	Overt aggression	Relational aggression	Isolation/ unhappy
Good leader	.789	—	—	—
Does nice things for others	.884	—	—	—
Helps others	.899	—	—	—
Cheers up others	.855	—	—	—
Seems happy at school	.832	—	—	—
Hits, pushes others	—	.906	—	—
Yells, calls others mean names	—	.823	—	—
Starts fights	—	.884	—	—
When mad, gets even by keeping the person from being in their group of friends	—	—	.763	—
Tells friends they will stop liking them unless friends do what they say	—	—	.772	—
When mad at a person, ignores them or stops talking to them	—	—	.837	—
Tries to keep certain people from being in their group during activity or play time	—	—	.727	—
Plays alone a lot	—	—	—	.911
Seems sad at school	—	—	—	.916
Seems lonely at school	—	—	—	.916

Note. All other factor loadings were less than .300 except for two items with loadings of .380 and .376. These were considered insubstantial given the relatively high loadings presented above.

Classification of aggressive groups Children's relational (RAGG) and overt (OAGG) aggression scores were used as continuous variables in subsequent analyses and also to identify groups of aggressive versus nonaggressive children. Children with scores one standard deviation above the sample means for RAGG, OAGG, or both (RAGG *and* OAGG) were considered aggressive, and the remaining children were considered nonaggressive. This procedure allowed for the identification of children high and low in relational aggression and children high and low in overt aggression, resulting in four distinct groups: (1) non-aggressive (RAGG and OAGG both low); (2) overtly aggressive (RAGG low, OAGG high); (3) relationally aggressive (RAGG high, OAGG low); and (4) combined overtly and relationally aggressive (RAGG and OAGG both high). This procedure resulted in the identification of 371 nonaggressive children, 41 overtly aggressive children, 46 relationally aggressive children, and 33 overtly plus relationally aggressive children.

Classification of sociometric status groups The positive and negative sociometric nominations children received from their classmates were used to identify five sociometric status groups, popular, average, neglected, rejected, and controversial children, using the procedure described by Coie and Dodge (1983) (except for those in the average group who were identified using the criteria described by Coie, Dodge, & Coppotelli, 1982). This procedure resulted in the identification of 63 popular, 153 average, 69 neglected, 56 rejected, and 26 controversial status children.

SELF-REPORT SOCIAL-PSYCHOLOGICAL ADJUSTMENT INDICES

Loneliness The Asher and Wheeler (1985) loneliness scale was used to assess children's feelings of loneliness and social dissatisfaction. This scale, an instrument with demonstrated reliability and validity (e.g., Asher & Wheeler, 1985; Asher & Williams, 1987; Crick & Ladd, 1993), consists of 16 items that assess loneliness at school (e.g., I feel alone at school) and eight filler items (e.g., I like music). Possible responses to each item range from 1 (Not at all true about me) to 5 (Always true about me). Children's responses to the loneliness items were summed yielding total scores that could range from 16 (low loneliness) to 80 (high loneliness). Cronbach's alpha for children's responses to the loneliness scale was .91.

Social anxiety and avoidance The Franke and Hymel (1984) social anxiety scale, an instrument with demonstrated reliability and validity (e.g., Crick & Ladd, 1993; Franke & Hymel, 1984), was used to assess social anxiety and social avoidance. This instru-

ment consists of two subscales, social anxiety (e.g., I usually feel nervous when I meet someone for the first time) and social avoidance (e.g., I often try to get away from all the other kids), each of which include six items. Possible responses to each item range from 1 (Not at all true about me) to 5 (Always true about me). Children's responses to the items were summed for each subscale yielding total scores that could range from 6 (low anxiety/avoidance) to 30 (high anxiety/avoidance). Cronbach's alpha for children's responses to the social anxiety and social avoidance scales was .69 and .74, respectively.

Depression The Children's Depression Inventory (CDI) was used to assess children's feelings and symptoms of depression (Kovacs, 1985). This measure consists of 27 items, all of which assess depression. Each item consists of three related statements, and children respond by selecting the one statement that best fits how they feel (e.g., I am sad once in a while vs. I am sad many times vs. I am sad all the time). Items are scored from 0 to 2, with higher scores indicating more evidence of depression. Two modifications were made to this instrument prior to its use in the present study, both of which were motivated by ethical concerns. First, two items were dropped from the measure due to content that was considered too sensitive for use in the participating schools (i.e., an item that focused on suicidal ideation and an item concerned with self-hate). Second, five positively toned filler items that were neutral in content were added to the instrument (e.g., I like swimming a lot vs. I like swimming a little vs. I do not like swimming) in an attempt to balance the negative tone of the CDI items. Cronbach's alpha for children's responses to the 25 depression items was .85.

Perceptions of peer relations An adaptation of the Children's Peer Relations Scale (Crick, 1991) was used to assess children's perceptions of their peer interactions. This instrument is designed to assess six aspects of children's perceptions of their interactions with peers at school: perceived peer acceptance, isolation from peers, negative affect, engagement in caring acts, engagement in overt aggression, and engagement in relational aggression. Specifically, the perceived peer acceptance subscale (three items) assesses the degree to which children feel liked by peers at school (e.g., Some kids have a lot of classmates who like to play with them. How often do the kids in your class like to play with you?). The isolation from peers subscale (two items) assesses the degree to which children perceive themselves as loners at school (e.g., Some kids play by themselves a lot at school. How often do you do this?). The negative affect subscale (three items) assesses the degree to which children feel lonely, sad, or upset at school (e.g., Some kids feel upset at school. How often do you feel this way?). The engagement in caring acts subscale (four items) assesses children's perceptions of the degree to which they direct prosocial behaviors toward their peers (e.g., Some kids try to cheer up other kids who feel upset or sad. How often do you do this?). The engagement in overt aggression subscale (three items) assesses children's perceptions of the degree to which they direct overtly aggressive acts toward their peers (e.g., Some kids hit other kids at school. How often do you do this?). The engagement in relational aggression subscale (five items) assesses children's perceptions of the degree to which they direct relationally aggressive behaviors toward their peers (e.g., Some kids tell their friends that they will stop liking them unless the friends do what they say. How often do you tell friends this?). The last two subscales, engagement in overt and relational aggression, were designed to parallel those included in the peer-nomination measure of aggression.

Possible responses to the items on the Children's Peer Relations Scale range from 1 (Never) to 5 (All the time). Responses to the items in each subscale were summed to yield total scores. Due to substantial item content overlap with other measures used in this study (e.g., CDI), children's negative affect scores were not analyzed. An analysis of internal consistency showed that children's responses to the items were reliable with Cronbach's alpha = .74, .76, .66, .82, and .73 for the perceived acceptance, caring acts, peer isolation, overt aggression, and relational aggression subscales, respectively for the present sample. Support for the construct validity of the Children's Peer Relations Scale (CPRS) has also been demonstrated in past research (e.g., rejected, overtly aggressive children report significantly higher levels of overt aggression on the CPRS relative to peers; rejected, withdrawn children report significantly higher levels of isolation and lower levels of peer acceptance relative to peers) (Crick, 1991).

ADMINISTRATION PROCEDURES

The previously described instruments were completed by subjects during two 60-min group assessment sessions (session A and session B) conducted within children's classrooms. These sessions were conducted by the authors, who employed standardized procedures. During each session, children were trained in the use of the response scales prior to administration of the instruments. Each item of every instrument was read aloud by the administrator, and assistants were available to answer children's questions. Sessions A and B were administered to classrooms in a random order, and the two sessions occurred approximately 1 week apart.

During session A, children completed the peer sociometric and behavior nomination measure, the Asher and Wheeler (1985) loneliness scale, the Franke and Hymel (1984) social anxiety scale, and one additional instrument that was not part of the present study. The peer nomination instrument was always administered first (to help insure that children would not be focused on the nominations they gave to others at the end of the session), however, the order of the loneliness and social anxiety scales was determined randomly. During session B, children completed the Children's Peer Relations Scale (Crick, 1991), the Children's Depression Inventory (Kovacs, 1985), and two additional instruments that were not part of the present study. The four instruments included in session B were presented in a random order.

RESULTS

ASSESSMENT OF RELATIONAL AGGRESSION

A principal components factor analysis with VARIMAX rotation of the factors was first conducted on the scores children received from the peer nomination instrument to assess whether relational aggression would emerge as a separate factor, independent of overt aggression. This analysis yielded the four predicted factors (prosocial behavior, overt aggression, relational aggression, and isolation), and these factors accounted for 79.1% of the variation in the scores. Specifically, the prosocial factor accounted for 34.0% of the variation (eigenvalue = 5.10), the overt aggression factor accounted for 23.9% (eigenvalue = 3.59), the relational aggression factor accounted for 13.5% (eigenvalue = 2.02), and the isolation factor accounted for 7.6% (eigenvalue = 1.14). Based on the results of the factor analysis, two items were dropped from the scales. Specifically, one isolation item (i.e., gives in easily to others) was dropped because it had a much lower factor loading than did the other items on this scale (.54 relative to the other items which loaded above .90). Further, one relational aggression item (i.e., tells mean lies or rumors about a person to make other kids not like the person) was dropped because, although it loaded on relational aggression (.64), it also cross-loaded with overt aggression (.49). Factor loadings for the items of the resulting four subscales were relatively high, ranging from .73 to .92 (refer to Table 1). Computation of Cronbach's alpha showed all scales to be highly reliable (alpha = .94, .83, .91, .92 for overt aggression, relational aggression, prosocial behavior, and isolation, respectively).

The relation between relational and overt aggression was further assessed with a correlation coefficient, $r = .54$, $p < .01$. The moderate magnitude of this correlation is what one would expect for two constructs that are hypothesized to be *different* forms of the *same* general behavior (i.e., there should be a moderate association rather than a low or high association). Overall, these analyses provide initial evidence that relational aggression is a distinct construct, and that, although related, it is relatively independent of overt aggression.

GENDER

It was next of interest to assess gender differences in relational aggression. First, a descriptive analysis was conducted of the percentage of boys versus girls who could be classified as either nonaggressive, overtly aggressive, relationally aggressive, or both overtly and relationally aggressive. Results showed that approximately equal numbers of each gender were classified as nonaggressive (73.0% of the boys and 78.3% of the girls). However, boys and girls were not evenly distributed among the remaining three aggressive groups. Rather, the overtly aggressive group consisted primarily of boys (15.6% of the boys vs. 0.4% of the girls); the relationally aggressive group consisted primarily of girls (17.4% of the girls vs. 2.0% of the boys); and the combined group consisted of both boys and girls (9.4% of the boys and 3.8% of the girls). One implication of these findings is that, contrary to prior research, aggressive boys and girls may be identified with almost equal frequency (27% of the boys vs. 21.7% of the girls in this study) when relational as well as overt forms of aggression are assessed.

To assess further the relation between gender and aggression, two analyses of variance were conducted in which gender and grade served as the independent variables and children's scores for the relational aggression and overt aggression scales served as the dependent variables. Both analyses yielded a significant main effect of gender, $F(1, 483) = 7.8$, $p < .01$, for relational aggression and $F(1, 483) = 68.1$, $p < .001$, for overt aggression. Specifically, girls ($M = .42$, SD = 3.4) were significantly more relationally aggressive than boys ($M = -.40$, SD = 2.9) whereas boys ($M = .77$, SD = 3.1) were significantly more overtly aggressive than girls ($M = -1.09$, SD = 1.6). These findings are consistent with the results of the descriptive analyses previously described.

RELATIONAL AGGRESSION AND SOCIAL-PSYCHOLOGICAL ADJUSTMENT

In order to assess the relation between relational aggression and social-psychological adjustment, two sets of analyses were performed. First, analyses of covariance were conducted in which relational aggression group (two levels: relationally aggressive vs. nonrelationally aggressive) and sex served as the independent variables, overt aggression served as the covariate, and the social-psychological adjustment indices served as the dependent variables (i.e., peer nominations of acceptance, rejection, prosocial behavior, and isolation/unhappiness; self-reports of depression, loneliness, social anxiety, social avoidance, and perceptions of peer relations).[2] Due to the moderate correlation between overt and relational forms of aggression, children's overt aggression scores were employed as a covariate to insure that any significant effects obtained were relatively independent of this form of aggression.[3] Student-Newman-Keuls post hoc tests ($p < .05$) were conducted as appropriate to investigate further significant effects (refer to Table 2 for adjusted cell means and standard deviations by relational aggression group).

Peer nominations of status, prosocial behavior, and isolation Analyses of children's peer acceptance and rejection scores yielded a significant main effect of relational aggression group, $F(1, 486) = 12.3$, $p < .01$, for peer rejection. Specifically, relationally aggressive children were significantly more disliked by peers than were their nonrelationally aggressive peers.

---

2. Grade was initially included as an independent variable in these analyses (in order to avoid small cell sizes, the third and fourth graders were combined into one level of grade and the fifth and sixth graders were combined into a second level of grade). However, with two minor exceptions, none of the interactions involving grade were significant, and thus grade was excluded from the presented analyses (i.e., grade main effects for the dependent variables studied here have been assessed in prior research and were not of interest here). Both significant interactions involving grade were from analyses of the Children's Peer Relations Scale. The first was the grade × relational aggression group × sex interaction for the caring subscale. Inspection of cell means showed that the youngest (i.e., third and fourth grade), relationally aggressive males reported less engagement in caring acts than did all other groups. The second interaction was the grade × sex interaction for the peer isolation subscale. Inspection of cell means showed that the youngest girls reported more isolation from peers than did the oldest girls and the boys.

3. A set of 2 (relational aggression group) × 2 (overt aggression group) ANOVAs were also conducted (sex could not be included as a factor because resulting cell sizes were too small in some cases). Results for the relational aggression group were comparable to those reported in the text. Significant effects of overt aggression were also obtained in some cases. Specifically, overtly aggressive children were significantly more rejected than other children. Further, analyses of the self-report instruments showed that, in sharp contrast to relationally aggressive children, whenever overtly aggressive children differed significantly from nonaggressive peers, they reported *higher* levels of social-psychological adjustment (e.g., significantly less social anxiety; higher levels of perceived peer acceptance; lower levels of social isolation) than other children. In addition, overtly aggressive children reported significantly more frequent use of overt aggression than did their peers. These findings provide further support for the distinctiveness of overt and relational aggression.

TABLE 2   CELL MEANS AND STANDARD DEVIATIONS FOR SOCIAL-PSYCHOLOGICAL ADJUSTMENT INDICES BY RELATIONAL AGGRESSION GROUP ADJUSTED FOR OVERT AGGRESSION

	Relational aggression group	
Measure	Nonaggressive	Aggressive
Peer nominations:		
Peer acceptance	.0 (1.0)	.2 (.9)
Peer rejection	.0 (.8)	.4 (1.2)**
Prosocial behavior	.0 (4.5)	−.2 (3.3)
Isolation	−.4 (2.8)	−.1 (2.1)
Self-reports:		
Depression	8.6 (7.4)	10.4 (6.1)*
Loneliness	29.9 (12.1)	34.6 (14.1)**
Social anxiety	18.4 (5.3)	19.5 (4.7)
Social avoidance	12.2 (4.7)	12.5 (4.8)
Perceived peer acceptance	11.8 (3.0)	11.2 (3.2)*
Peer isolation	4.0 (1.9)	4.4 (2.1)*
Caring acts	14.0 (3.3)	13.2 (3.4)
Overt aggression	7.2 (2.9)	7.3 (3.3)
Relational aggression	9.1 (3.4)	9.6 (4.3)

Note. Standard deviations are in parentheses.
*$p < .05$.
**$p < .01$.

Analyses of children's peer-assessed prosocial behavior and isolation yielded a significant main effect of sex, $F(1, 486) = 45.6$, $p < .001$, and a significant interaction of sex and relational aggression group, $F(1, 486) = 8.8$, $p < .01$, for prosocial behavior. Specifically, girls ($M = .62$, SD = 4.8) were viewed by peers as significantly more prosocial than were boys ($M = −.84$, SD = 3.2). However, follow-up tests on the significant interaction indicated that this effect varied as a function of relational aggression group. Specifically, nonaggressive girls ($M = 1.47$, SD = 5.1) were viewed as significantly more prosocial than children in the other three groups, nonaggressive boys ($M = −1.53$, SD = 3.2), aggressive girls ($M = −.22$, SD = 3.3), and aggressive boys ($M = −.15$, SD = 2.9). In contrast, nonaggressive boys were viewed as significantly less prosocial than children in the other three groups. The prosocial scores of relationally aggressive boys and girls were in between these two extremes and did not differ from each other.

Self-reports of social-psychological adjustment The ANOVA conducted on children's loneliness scores yielded a significant main effect of relational aggression group, $F(1, 457) = 10.6$, $p < .01$, and a significant interaction effect, $F(1, 457) = 4.3$, $p < .05$. Specifically,

relationally aggressive children were significantly more lonely than were their nonrelationally aggressive peers. However, follow-up analyses of the interaction effect showed that the main effect was apparent for girls only. That is, relationally aggressive girls ($M = 37.0$, SD = 14.5) reported significantly higher levels of loneliness than did nonrelationally aggressive boys ($M = 31.0$, SD = 12.7) and girls ($M = 28.8$, SD = 11.4). In contrast, the loneliness scores of relationally aggressive boys ($M = 32.2$, SD = 12.5) did not differ from those of their nonaggressive peers. The analysis of children's social anxiety scores and social avoidance scores did not yield significant effects. The analysis of children's responses to the Children's Depression Inventory yielded a significant main effect of relational aggression group, $F(1, 458) = 4.8$, $p < .05$, and a significant main effect of sex, $F(1, 458) = 4.2$, $p < .05$. Specifically, relationally aggressive children reported significantly higher levels of depression than did nonrelationally aggressive children. Also, boys ($M = 9.7$, SD = 7.8) reported significantly higher levels of depression than did girls ($M = 9.3$, SD = 6.5).

Analyses of the subscales of the Children's Peer Relations Scale also yielded significant findings. Specifically, the analysis of children's perceived peer acceptance scores yielded a significant main effect of relational aggression group, $F(1, 464) = 5.7$, $p < .05$, and a significant interaction effect, $F(1, 464) = 4.3$, $p < .05$. Specifically, relationally aggressive children perceived themselves to be more poorly accepted by peers than did their nonaggressive counterparts. However, this effect was qualified by the interaction effect. Specifically, post hoc analyses indicated that relationally aggressive girls ($M = 10.6$, SD = 3.0) reported poorer acceptance by peers than did nonaggressive girls ($M = 12.0$, SD = 3.0), nonaggressive boys ($M = 11.7$, SD = 3.0), and relationally aggressive boys ($M = 11.7$, SD = 2.6). In contrast, the perceived acceptance reported by relationally aggressive boys did not differ from that reported by nonaggressive children.

Analysis of the peer isolation subscale yielded a significant main effect of relational aggression group, $F(1, 464) = 4.9$, $p < .05$, and a significant relational aggression group by sex interaction, $F(1, 464) = 5.4$, $p < .05$. That is, relationally aggressive children reported significantly greater isolation from other children than did their peers. However, this effect was qualified by the interaction effect. Specifically, follow-up tests showed that relationally aggressive girls ($M = 5.0$, SD = 2.0) reported significantly more isolation from peers than did nonaggressive girls ($M = 4.0$, SD = 2.0) and boys ($M = 4.0$, SD = 1.8, for nonaggressive and $M = 3.8$, SD = 1.8 for aggressive boys). Analysis of the caring acts subscale produced a significant main effect of sex, $F(1, 464) = 24.0$, $p < .001$, with girls ($M = 14.6$, SD = 2.9) reporting significantly more engagement in prosocial acts than boys ($M = 12.6$, SD = 3.5).

The ANOVA conducted on children's self-reports of overt aggression and relational aggression yielded a significant main effect of sex for each variable, $F(1, 464) = 13.2$, $p < .001$, and $F(1, 464) = 5.7$, $p < .05$, respectively. Boys reported significantly higher use of overt aggression ($M = 7.6$, SD = 3.1) and of relational aggression ($M = 9.6$, SD = 4.0) than did girls ($M = 7.0$, SD = 2.6 and $M = 9.1$, SD = 2.9 for overt aggression and relational aggression, respectively).

Sociometric status classifications　Because sociometric status group has been considered an important social adjustment indicator in numerous prior studies (see Coie, Dodge, & Kupersmidt, 1990; Parker & Asher, 1987), the second set of analyses was designed to assess the relation between relational aggression and status group membership. Toward this end, an analysis of variance was conducted in which status group (popular, average, neglected, rejected, controversial) served as the independent variable and children's relational aggression scores (i.e., from the peer nomination instrument) served as the dependent variable (note that a covariate was not used for these analyses). This analysis yielded a significant effect for

Status Group	Relational aggression score	Overt aggression score
Popular	−.66 (2.9)	−.95 (1.8)
Average	−.11 (2.9)	−.34 (2.4)
Neglected	−1.36 (1.8)	−.75 (1.9)
Rejected	.76 (3.8)	1.11 (3.5)
Controversial	2.82 (3.0)	1.19 (3.2)

TABLE 3　CELL MEANS AND STANDARD DEVIATIONS FOR RELATIONAL AGGRESSION AND OVERT AGGRESSION BY SOCIOMETRIC STATUS GROUP

Note. Standard deviations are in parentheses.

sociometric status, $F(4, 362) = 11.6$, $p < .001$. A Student-Newman-Keuls post hoc test ($p < .05$) indicated that controversial status children were significantly more relationally aggressive than all other status groups, including rejected children (refer to Table 3 for cell means and standard deviations). However, rejected children were significantly more relationally aggressive than popular and neglected children. Also, neglected children were significantly less relationally aggressive than were average status children. A comparable ANOVA was conducted of children's overt aggression scores for comparison purposes. This analysis also yielded a significant effect of status group, $F(4, 362) = 8.3$, $p < .001$. A Student-Newman-Keuls post hoc test ($p < .05$) indicated that controversial and rejected children were significantly more overtly aggressive than popular, average, and neglected children, a finding that is consistent with past research (see Coie et al., 1990, for a review).

DISCUSSION

Results of the present study provide evidence for the validity of a relational form of aggression. As hypothesized, relational aggression appears to be relatively distinct from overt aggression, and it is significantly related to gender and to social-psychological adjustment in meaningful ways. These findings contribute uniquely to our understanding of children with adjustment difficulties, particularly young females.

As predicted, relational aggression appears to be more characteristic of girls than of boys. Results indicated that (1) as a group, girls were significantly more relationally aggressive than boys and (2) when relatively extreme groups of aggressive and nonaggressive children were identified, girls were more likely than boys to be represented in the relationally aggressive group. Interestingly, a parallel set of findings was obtained for boys and overt aggression. That is, on average, boys were significantly more overtly aggressive than girls and were more likely to be represented in the extreme group of overtly aggressive children, findings that are consistent with prior research on gender differences in aggression (see Block, 1983; Parke & Slaby, 1983, for reviews). The present study provides evidence that the degree of aggressiveness exhibited by girls has been underestimated in these prior studies, largely because forms of aggression relevant to girls' peer groups have not been assessed.

The paucity of research on girls' aggression may exist partly because of the complexity and subtleness of the behaviors involved, characteristics that make them more difficult to study than overt aggression. For example, reliably assessing overt aggression in an interaction where one child hits another is significantly less complex than assessing relational aggression in an interaction where one child seems to exclude a peer from an activity. To competently judge the latter interaction, knowledge is needed that goes beyond the immediate situation (e.g., information about the relationship history of the aggressive child involved so that one can distinguish an excluded friend from a peer who simply never plays with the target child). Thus, when assessing relational aggression, the relevant behaviors may be overlooked unless informants are employed who can access information about friendships and other relationships within the relevant peer group. This issue was addressed in the present study through the use of children's peers as informants, an approach that, based on the current findings, appears promising.

Support for the distinctiveness of relational versus overt aggression was obtained in a number of ways. First, the factor analysis of the peer nomination instrument yielded separate factors for overt and relational aggression, with items that loaded highly on each factor and cross-loaded insubstantially. Second, the classification of children into extreme groups of aggressive children showed that, although some of the children identified as high in aggression exhibited both forms (i.e., the combined group), the majority of aggressive children exhibited solely overt or relational forms of aggression. Specifically, of the 121 children identified as high in aggression, only 27.3% ($n = 33$) exhibited both relational and overt forms of aggression. The majority of aggressive children (72.7%) exhibited either relational or overt aggression, but not both. In addition, as will be discussed in more detail below, relational aggression was significantly related to social-psychological maladjustment, independent of overt aggression. These findings pro-

vide evidence that, although overt and relational aggression are likely related constructs (i.e., because both constitute harmful, aggressive acts), they each provide unique information about children's social behavior.

Findings from the peer assessments as well as from the self-report instruments indicate that, as has been found in past research for overtly aggressive children (Parker & Asher, 1987) relationally aggressive children also experience significant social problems. Specifically, relationally aggressive children were significantly more disliked than other children. In addition, the peer status groups who exhibited the highest levels of relational aggression were the rejected and controversial groups (i.e., classifications that indicate impaired peer relationships; Coie et al., 1990). Moreover, relational aggression was significantly related to social maladjustment (i.e., peer nominations of rejection and self-reports of poor peer acceptance), independent of overt aggression (i.e., the relations were significant even though overt aggression, the best known behavioral predictor of peer rejection, was employed as a covariate). These findings indicate that relational aggression provides unique and important information about children's social difficulties that cannot be accounted for by overt aggression alone.

It is possible that engaging in relationally aggressive behaviors, because of their aversive nature, leads to being disliked by peers. Support for this particular temporal relation between rejection and aggression has been established in past research for overt aggression (Coie & Kupersmidt, 1983; Dodge, 1983). However, it is also conceivable that rejection by one's peers may precede relational aggression. For example, a rejected child may attempt to harm peers' relationships with others in an effort to compensate (or retaliate) for her own lack of success in those relationships. In either case, the association found between relational aggression and rejection significantly enhances our knowledge of the social adjustment difficulties of girls. To date, relatively few studies have focused on the correlates of rejection for girls (cf. Coie & Whidby, 1986), and these studies have not established a relation between aggression and rejection for young females (Coie & Whidby, 1986; French, 1990). The present study provides initial evidence for such a relation.

The significant relation obtained between relational aggression and controversial status group membership is particularly interesting. Controversial children, by definition, are highly disliked by some peers and highly liked by other peers. It is possible that aggressive, controversial status children direct their relationally aggressive behaviors disproportionately among their peers (i.e., so that some peers are frequently victims of these behaviors whereas other peers are never victims of these acts). If so, it seems likely that controversial children may receive disliked nominations from peers who have been the targets of their relationally aggressive acts (e.g., children that they exclude from peer interactions) whereas they may receive liked nominations from peers who have escaped this maltreatment. Relative to other sociometric status groups, much less is known about the peer relationships of controversial children, except that they tend to be more overtly aggressive than their better accepted peers (present study; see Coie et al., 1990, for a review of past studies with similar findings). However, the present pattern of findings for relational aggression suggests that this group of children may play a critical role in controlling the structure and nature of peer group interactions (e.g., controlling who is included in peer activities; deciding who receives social approval). Their popularity with some peers may give these children the "social authority" and control necessary to successfully manipulate peer group relationships. Investigation of these hypotheses in future research seems warranted, particularly since research on controversial children is lacking. One direction for future study would be an assessment of specific perpetrator-victim relationships within the peer group (e.g., to determine whether the disliked nominations received by controversial children are provided by the peers that they victimize).

Findings from the self-report social-psychological adjustment instruments provide further evidence that relational aggression is significantly related to maladjustment (e.g., depression, loneliness, social isolation). These findings indicate that relationally aggressive children feel unhappy and distressed about their peer relationships. These significant relations between psychological maladjustment and relational aggression were apparent even after level of overt aggression was taken into account. It may be that frequent engagement in relationally aggressive behaviors exacerbates, if not generates, feelings of social-psychological distress because these acts potentially limit children's access to peer relationships (e.g., excluding peers results in fewer peers with which to play or interact). However, it may also be that feelings of psychological distress lead to engagement in relational aggression. For example, children who feel lonely or poorly accepted by peers may use relational aggression as a way to retaliate against peers (e.g., "You rejected me, now I'll get even by rejecting you") or to make themselves feel better (e.g., they may feel more competent or in control if they exclude or put down others).

Results also demonstrate that the nature of the relation between social-psychological adjustment and relational aggression varies as a function of sex. That is, the present results indicate that it is stronger or more pervasive for girls than for boys (i.e., for some of the adjustment indices, only the scores of relationally aggressive girls differed from those of their nonaggressive peers). One goal for future research will be to employ longitudinal designs that assess whether relational aggression is predictive of future, as well as concurrent, social-psychological problems.

In sum, results of the present study provide support for the hypothesis that, on average, *both* girls and boys are aggressive but tend to exhibit distinct forms of the behavior (relational aggression for girls and overt aggression for boys). They also indicate that further study of relational aggression is warranted, particularly given that this form of aggression is significantly associated with social-psychological adjustment problems. It will be important in future research to develop further our understanding of the correlates, antecedents, and consequences of relational aggression as well as knowledge of the function it serves in children's peer groups.

REFERENCES

Asher, S. R., & Wheeler, V. A. (1985). Children's loneliness: A comparison of rejected and neglected peer status. *Journal of Consulting and Clinical Psychology, 53,* 500–505.

Asher, S. R., & Williams, G. A. (April, 1987). New approaches to identifying rejected children at school. In G. W. Ladd (Chair), *Identification and treatment of socially rejected children in school settings.* Symposium conducted at the annual meeting of the American Educational Research Association, Washington, DC.

Berkowitz, L. (1993). *Aggression: Its causes, consequences, and control.* New York: Academic Press.

Block, J. H. (1983). Differential premises arising from differential socialization of the sexes: Some conjectures. *Child Development, 54,* 1335–1354.

Brehm, S. S., & Kassin, S. M. (1990). *Social psychology.* Boston: Houghton Mifflin.

Bukowski, W. M., & Newcomb, A. F. (1984). Stability and determinants of sociometric status and friendship choice: A longitudinal perspective. *Developmental Psychology, 20,* 941–952.

Cairns, R. B., Cairns, B. D., Neckerman, H. J., Ferguson, L. L., & Gariepy, J. L. (1989). Growth and aggression: 1. Childhood to early adolescence. *Developmental Psychology, 25,* 320–330.

Coie, J. D., & Dodge, K. A. (1983). Continuities and changes in children's social status: A five-year longitudinal study. *Merrill-Palmer Quarterly, 29,* 261–282.

Coie, J. D., Dodge, K. A., & Coppotelli, H. (1982). Dimensions and types of social status: A cross-age perspective. *Developmental Psychology, 18,* 557–570.

Coie, J. D., Dodge, K. A., & Kupersmidt, J. B. (1990). Peer group behavior and social status. In S. R. Asher & J. D. Coie

(Eds.), *Peer rejection in childhood* (pp. 17–59). New York: Cambridge University Press.

Coie, J. D., & Kupersmidt, J. B. (1983). A behavioral analysis of emerging social status in boys' playgroups. *Child Development*, 54, 1400–1416.

Coie, J. D., & Whidby, J. (April, 1986). *Gender differences in the basis for social rejection in childhood*. Paper presented at the annual meeting of the American Educational Research Association, San Francisco.

Crick, N. R. (April, 1991). *Subgroups of neglected and rejected children*. Paper presented at the biennial meeting of the Society for Research in Child Development, Seattle.

Crick, N. R., & Dodge, K. A. (1989). Children's perceptions of peer entry and conflict situations: Social strategies, goals, and outcome expectations. In B. Schneider, J. Nadel, G. Attili, & R. Weissberg (Eds.), *Social competence in developmental perspective*. Norwell, MA: Kluwer.

Crick, N. R., & Dodge, K. A. (1994). A review and reformulation of social-information-processing mechanisms in children's social adjustment. *Psychological Bulletin*, 115, 74–101.

Crick, N. R., & Ladd, G. W. (1993). Children's perceptions of their peer experiences: Attributions, loneliness, social anxiety, and social avoidance. *Developmental Psychology*, 29, 244–254.

Dodge, K. A. (1980). Social cognition and children's aggressive behavior. *Child Development*, 51, 162–170.

Dodge, K. A. (1983). Behavioral antecedents of peer social status. *Child Development*, 54, 1386–1389.

Dodge, K. A., & Crick, N. R. (1990). Social information processing bases of aggressive behavior in children. *Personality and Social Psychology Bulletin*, 53, 1146–1158.

Dodge, K. A., & Frame, C. L. (1982). Social cognitive biases and deficits in aggressive boys. *Child Development*, 55, 163–173.

Eagly, A. H., & Steffen, V. J. (1986). Gender and aggressive behavior: A meta-analytic review of the social psychological literature. *Psychological Bulletin*, 100, 309–330.

Feshbach, N. D. (1969). Sex differences in children's modes of aggressive responses toward outsiders. *Merrill-Palmer Quarterly*, 15, 249–258.

Franke, S., & Hymel, S. (May, 1984). *Social anxiety in children: The development of self-report measures*. Paper presented at the biennial meeting of the University of Waterloo Conference on Child Development, Waterloo, Ontario.

French, D. C. (1990). Heterogeneity of peer-rejected girls. *Child Development*, 61, 2028–2031.

Gormly, A. V., & Brodzinsky, D. M. (1993). *Lifespan human development*. Orlando, FL: Holt, Rinehart, & Winston.

Hyde, J. S. (1986). Gender differences in aggression. In J. S. Hyde & M. C. Linn (Eds.), *The psychology of gender: Advances through meta-analysis*. Baltimore: Johns Hopkins University Press.

Kenrick, D. T. (1987). Gender, genes, and the social environment: A biosocial interactionist perspective. In P. Shaver & C. Hendrick (Eds.), *Sex and gender: Review of personality and social psychology* (Vol. 7). Beverly Hills, CA: Sage.

Kovacs, M. (1985). The Children's Depression Inventory. *Psychopharmacology Bulletin*, 21, 995–998.

Lagerspetz, K. M. J., Bjorkqvist, K., & Peltonen, T. (1988). Is indirect aggression more typical of females? Gender differences in aggressiveness in 11- to 12-year-old children. *Aggressive Behavior*, 14, 403–414.

Myers, D. G. (1990). *Social Psychology*. New York: McGraw-Hill.

Parke, R. D., & Slaby, R. G. (1983). The development of aggression. In E. M. Hetherington (Ed.), P. H. Mussen (Series Ed.), *Handbook of child psychology: Vol. 4. Socialization, personality, and social development* (pp. 547–642). New York: Wiley.

Parker, J., & Asher, S. R. (1987). Peer acceptance and later personal adjustment: Are low-accepted children "at risk"? *Psychological Bulletin*, 102, 357–389.

Perry, D. G., Perry, L. C., & Rasmussen, P. (1986). Cognitive social learning mediators of aggression. *Child Development*, 57, 700–711.

Robins, L. N. (1986). The consequences of conduct disorder in girls. In D. Olweus, J. Block, & M. Radke-Yarrow (Eds.), *Development of antisocial and prosocial behavior: Research, theories, and issues*. New York: Academic Press.

Vander Zanden, J. W. (1993). *Human development*. New York: McGraw-Hill.

QUESTIONS

1. How have prior findings regarding higher rates of physical aggression in boys been used to describe aggression among girls? What is the problem with this interpretation?
2. What is relational aggression, and why is it considered a form of aggression?
3. Why did Crick and Grotpeter hypothesize higher rates of relational aggression among girls than boys?
4. Why were peers and not teachers or parents used as informants in this research?
5. What is sociometric status and how did it relate to the use of relational aggression by children in this study?
6. How did Crick and Grotpeter establish that physical aggression and relational aggression are distinct forms of aggression?

7. Who was more aggressive, boys or girls, on each of the three dimensions studied: overt physical aggression, relational aggression, and combined overt physical and relational aggression?
8. Why do you think children dislike relationally aggressive peers?
9. What social-psychological adjustment difficulties were found among children who were high in relational aggression?
10. What types of interventions do you think could be introduced in schools to help children who are perpetrators or victims of relational aggression?

28 How Asian Teachers Polish Each Lesson to Perfection

JAMES W. STIGLER · HAROLD W. STEVENSON

During middle childhood, much of children's academic work concentrates on the development and refinement of basic skills of reading, writing, and mathematics. It is clear that if children do not develop these skills during this time, they will face many difficulties in school in the years ahead. In recent years, mathematics achievement during the years of middle childhood has become a particular area of concern. Cross-national research indicates that, in general, children in the United States fall far behind children in other nations, especially China and Japan, in mathematics. Given the importance of understanding mathematics both for further learning in this domain as well as for learning science in high school and beyond, this lag is very disturbing.

Many developmental psychologists have attempted to understand these cross-national patterns. The most successful research to date was conducted by James W. Stigler and Harold W. Stevenson, who describe their work in the following article. The researchers focused on children's experiences in the classroom in China, Japan, and the United States. Specifically, they examined educational practices and goals in the three societies. Their observations indicate that both the processes and the outcomes of schooling in those communities support children's learning of mathematics in different ways. In addition, many of the educational practices that are used in China and Japan reflect deeply held cultural values and practices in those societies. As a result, this research suggests that modeling classrooms in the United States after the classrooms in China and Japan would not necessarily benefit U.S. children in the absence of the meaning and direction provided by the broader cultural context.

The research described in this article is important for several reasons. It connects children's experiences in the mathematics classroom to specific learning outcomes. Although this seems like an obvious step, the classroom context, especially across cultures, has rarely been examined in enough detail to establish how different classroom practices affect children's learning. The research is also an excellent example of cultural psychology, in that it studies children and their experiences in relation to the broader social and cultural context in which development occurs. Finally, because it provides insight into different ways that teachers teach mathematics, this research offers some new and interesting ideas about how to approach mathematics instruction.

Although there is no overall difference in intelligence, the differences in mathematical achievement of American children and their Asian counterparts are staggering.[1]

Let us look first at the results of a study we conducted in 120 classrooms in three cities: Taipei (Taiwan); Sendai (Japan); and the Minneapolis metropolitan area. First and fifth graders from representative schools in these cities were given a test of mathematics that required computation and problem solving. Among the one hundred first graders in the three locations who received the lowest scores, fifty-eight were American children; among the one hundred lowest-scoring fifth graders, sixty-seven were

Reprinted with permission from the Spring 1991 issue of the American Educator, the quarterly journal of the American Federation of Teachers.

Note: The research described in this article has been funded by grants from the National Institute of Mental Health, the National Science Foundation, and the W.T. Grant Foundation. The research is the result of collaboration with a large group of colleagues in China, Japan, Taiwan, and the United States who have worked together for the past decade. We are indebted to each of these colleagues and are especially grateful to Shinying Lee of the University of Michigan who has been a major contributor to the research described in this article.

American children. Among the top one hundred first graders in mathematics, there were only fifteen American children. And only one American child appeared among the top one hundred fifth graders. The highest-scoring American classroom obtained an average score lower than that of the lowest-scoring Japanese classroom and of all but one of the twenty classrooms in Taipei. In whatever way we looked at the data, the poor performance of American children was evident.

These data are startling, but no more so than the results of a study that involved 40 first- and 40 fifth-grade classrooms in the metropolitan area of Chicago—a very representative sample of the city and the suburbs of Cook County—and twenty-two classes in each of these grades in metropolitan Beijing (China). In this study, children were given a battery of mathematics tasks that included diverse problems, such as estimating the distance between a tree and a hidden treasure on a map, deciding who won a race on the basis of data in a graph, trying to explain subtraction to visiting Martians, or calculating the sum of nineteen and forty-five. There was no area in which the American children were competitive with those from China. The Chinese children's superiority appeared in complex tasks involving the application of knowledge as well as in the routines of computation. When fifth graders were asked, for example, how many members of a stamp club with twenty-four members collected only foreign stamps if five-sixths of the members did so, 59 percent of Beijing children, but only 9 percent of the Chicago children produced the correct answer. On a computation test, only 2.2 percent of the Chinese fifth graders scored at or below the mean for their American counterparts. All of the twenty Chicago area schools had average scores on the fifth-grade geometry test that were below those of the Beijing schools. The results from all these tasks paint a bleak picture of American children's competencies in mathematics.[2]

The poor performance of American students compels us to try to understand the reasons why. We have written extensively elsewhere about the cultural differences in attitudes toward learning and toward the importance of effort vs. innate ability and about the substantially greater amounts of time Japanese and Chinese students devote to academic activities in general and to the study of math in particular.[3] Important as these factors are, they do not tell the whole story. For that we have to take a close look inside the classrooms of Japan, China, and the United States to see how mathematics is actually taught in the three cultures.

LESSONS NOT LECTURES

If we were asked briefly to characterize classes in Japan and China, we would say that they consist of coherent lessons that are presented in a thoughtful, relaxed, and nonauthoritarian manner. Teachers frequently rely on students as sources of information. Lessons are oriented toward problem solving rather than rote mastery of facts and procedures and utilize many different types of representational materials. The role assumed by the teacher is that of knowledgeable guide, rather than that of prime dispenser of information and arbiter of what is correct. There is frequent verbal interaction in the classroom as the teacher attempts to stimulate students to produce, explain, and evaluate solutions to problems. These characteristics contradict stereotypes held by most Westerners about Asian teaching practices. Lessons are not rote; they are not filled with drill. Teachers do not spend large amounts of time lecturing but attempt to lead the children in productive interactions and discussions. And the children are not the passive automata depicted in Western descriptions but active participants in the learning process.

We begin by discussing what we mean by the coherence of a lesson. One way to think of a lesson is by using the analog of a story. A good story is highly organized; it has a beginning, a middle, and an end; and it follows a protagonist who meets challenges and resolves problems that arise along the way. Above all, a good story engages the reader's interest in a series of interconnected events, which are best understood in the context of the events that precede and follow it.

Such a concept of a lesson guides the organization of instruction in Asia. The curricula are defined in terms of coherent lessons, each carefully designed to fill a forty- to fifty-minute class period with sustained attention to the development of some concept or skill. Like a good story, the lesson has an introduction, a conclusion, and a consistent theme.

We can illustrate what we are talking about with this account of a fifth-grade Japanese mathematics class:

> The teacher walks in carrying a large paper bag full of clinking glass. Entering the classroom with a large paper bag is highly unusual, and by the time she has placed the bag on her desk the students are regarding her with rapt attention. What's in the bag? She begins to pull items out of the bag, placing them, one-by-one, on her desk. She removes a pitcher and a vase. A beer bottle evokes laughter and surprise. She soon has six containers lined up on her desk. The children continue to watch intently, glancing back and forth at each other as they seek to understand the purpose of this display.
>
> The teacher, looking thoughtfully at the containers, poses a question: "I wonder which one would hold the most water?" Hands go up, and the teacher calls on different students to give their

guesses: "the pitcher," "the beer bottle," "the teapot." The teacher stands aside and ponders: "Some of you said one thing, others said something different. You don't agree with each other. There must be some way we can find out who is correct. How can we know who is correct?" Interest is high, and the discussion continues.

The students soon agree that to find out how much each container holds they will need to fill the containers with something. How about water? The teacher finds some buckets and sends several children out to fill them with water. When they return, the teacher says: "Now what do we do?" Again there is a discussion, and after several minutes the children decide that they will need to use a smaller container to measure how much water fits into each of the larger containers. They decide on a drinking cup, and one of the students warns that they all have to fill each cup to the same level—otherwise the measure won't be the same for all of the groups.

At this point the teacher divides the class into their groups (*han*) and gives each group one of the containers and a drinking cup. Each group fills its container, counts how many cups of water it holds, and writes the result in a notebook. When all of the groups have completed the task, the teacher calls on the leader of each group to report on the group's findings and notes the results on the blackboard. She has written the names of the containers in a column on the left and a scale from 1 to 6 along the bottom. Pitcher, 4.5 cups; vase, 3 cups; beer bottle, 1.5 cups; and so on. As each group makes its report the teacher draws a bar representing the amount, in cups, the container holds.

Finally, the teacher returns to the question she posed at the beginning of the lesson: Which container holds the most water? She reviews how they were able to solve the problem and points out that the answer is now contained in the bar graph on the board. She then arranges the containers on the table in order according to how much they hold and writes a rank order on each container, from 1 to 6. She ends the class with a brief review of what they have done. No definitions of ordinate and abscissa, no discussion of how to make a graph preceded the example— these all became obvious in the course of the lesson, and only at the end did the teacher mention the terms that describe the horizontal and vertical axes of the graph they had made.

With one carefully crafted problem, this Japanese teacher has guided her students to discover—and most likely to remember—several important con-

cepts. As this article unfolds, we hope to demonstrate that this example of how well-designed Asian class lessons are is not an isolated one; to the contrary, it is the norm. And as we hope to further demonstrate, excellent class lessons do not come effortlessly or magically. Asian teachers are not born great teachers; they and the lessons they develop require careful nurturing and constant refinement. The practice of teaching in Japan and China is more uniformly perfected than it is in the United States because their systems of education are structured to encourage teaching excellence to develop and flourish. Ours is not. We will take up the question of why and what can be done about this later in the piece. But first, we present a more detailed look at what Asian lessons are like.

COHERENCE BROKEN

Asian lessons almost always begin with a practical problem, such as the example we have just given, or with a word problem written on the blackboard. Asian teachers, to a much greater degree than American teachers, give coherence to their lessons by introducing the lesson with a word problem.

It is not uncommon for the Asian teacher to organize the entire lesson around the solution to this single problem. The teacher leads the children to recognize what is known and what is unknown and directs the students' attention to the critical parts of the problem. Teachers are careful to see that the problem is understood by all of the children, and even mechanics, such as mathematical computation, are presented in the context of solving a problem.

Before ending the lesson, the teacher reviews what has been learned and relates it to the problem she posed at the beginning of the lesson. American teachers are much less likely than Asian teachers to begin and end lessons in this way. For example, we found that fifth-grade teachers in Beijing spent eight times as long at the end of the class period summarizing the lessons as did those in the Chicago metropolitan area.

Now contrast the Japanese math lesson described above with a fifth-grade American mathematics classroom that we recently visited. Immediately after getting the students' attention, the teacher pointed out that today was Tuesday, "band day," and that all students in the band should go to the band room. "Those of you doing the news report today should meet over there in the corner," he continued. He then began the mathematics class with the remaining students by reviewing the solution to a computation problem that had been included in the previous day's homework. After this brief review, the teacher directed the students' attention to the blackboard, where the day's assignment had been written. From this point on, the teacher spent most of the rest of the period walking about the room monitoring the children's work, talking to individual children about questions or errors, and uttering "shushes" whenever the students began talking among themselves.

This example is typical of the American classrooms we have visited, classrooms where students spend more time in transition and less in academic activities, more time working on their own and less being instructed by the teacher; where teachers spend much of their time working with individual students and attending to matters of discipline; and where the shape of a coherent lesson is often hard to discern.

American lessons are often disrupted by irrelevant interruptions. These serve to break the continuity of the lesson and add to children's difficulty in perceiving the lesson as a coherent whole. In our American observations, the teacher interrupted the flow of the lesson with an interlude of irrelevant comments or the class was interrupted by someone else in 20 percent of all first-grade lessons and 47 percent of all fifth-grade lessons. This occurred less than 10 percent of the time at both grade levels in Sendai, Taipei, and Beijing. In fact, no interruptions of either type were recorded during the eighty hours of observation in Beijing fifth-grade classrooms. The mathematics lesson in one of the American classrooms we visited was interrupted every morning by a woman from the cafeteria who polled the children about their lunch plans and collected money from those who planned to eat the hot lunch. Interruptions, as well as inefficient transitions from one activity to another, make it difficult to sustain a coherent lesson throughout the class period.

Coherence is also disrupted when teachers shift frequently from one topic to another. This occurred often in the American classrooms we observed. The teacher might begin with a segment on measurement, then proceed to a segment on simple addition, then to a segment on telling time, and then to a second segment on addition. These segments constitute a math class, but they are hardly a coherent lesson. Such changes in topic were responsible for 21 percent of the changes in segments that we observed in American classrooms but accounted for only 4 percent of the changes in segments in Japanese classrooms.

Teachers frequently capitalize on variety as a means of capturing children's interest. This may explain why American teachers shift topics so frequently within the lesson. Asian teachers also seek variety, but they tend to introduce new activities instead of new topics. Shifts in materials do not necessarily pose a threat to coherence. For example, the coherence of a lesson does not diminish when the teacher shifts from working with numerals to working with concrete objects, if both are used to represent the same subtraction problem. Shifting the topic, on the other hand, introduces variety, but at the risk of destroying the coherence of the lesson.

CLASSROOM ORGANIZATION

Elementary school classrooms are typically organized in one of three ways: the whole class is working as a unit; the class is divided into a number of small groups; or children work individually. In our observations, we noted when the child was receiving instruction or assistance from the teacher and when the student was working on his own. The child was considered to be receiving instruction whenever the teacher was the leader of the activity, whether it involved the whole class, a small group, or only the individual child.

Looking at the classroom in this manner led us to one of our most pronounced findings: Although the number of children in Asian classes is significantly greater than the number in American classes, Asian students received much more instruction from their teachers than American students. In Taiwan, the teacher was the leader of the child's activity 90 percent of the time, as opposed to 74 percent in Japan, and only 46 percent in the United States. No one was leading instruction 9 percent of the time in Taiwan, 26 percent in Japan, and an astonishing 51 percent of the time in the United States (see Figure 1). Even American first graders actually spent more time on their own than they did participating in an activity led by the teacher.

One of the reasons American children received less instruction is that American teachers spent 13 percent of their time in the mathematics classes not working with any students, something that happened only 6 percent of the time in Japan and 9 percent in Taiwan. (As we will see later, American teachers have to steal class time to attend to the multitude of chores involving preparation, assessment, and administration because so little nonteaching time is available for them during the day.)

A much more critical factor in the erosion of instructional time was the amount of time American teachers were involved with individuals or small groups. American children spend 10 percent of their time in small groups and 47 percent of their time working individually. Much of the 87 percent of the time American teachers were working with their students was spent with these individual students or small groups, rather than with the class as a whole. When teachers provide individual instruction, they must leave the rest of the class unattended, so instructional time for all remaining children is reduced.

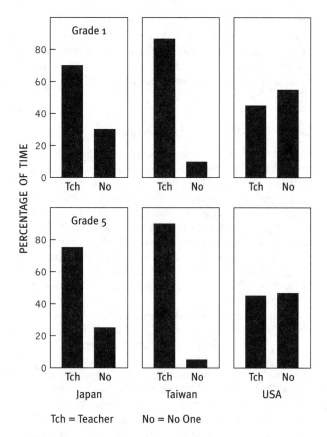

FIGURE 1

Percentage of time students spent in activity led by teacher and by no one.

Children can learn without a teacher. Nevertheless, it seems likely that they could profit from having their teacher as the leader of their activities more than half of the time they are in the classroom. It is the incredibly large amounts of time that American children are left unassisted and the effect that unattended time has on the coherence of the larger lesson that is the problem.

When children must work alone for long periods of time without guidance or reaction from the teacher, they begin to lose focus on the purpose of their activity. Asian teachers not only assign less seatwork than American teachers, they also use seatwork differently. Chinese and Japanese teachers tend to use short, frequent periods of seatwork, alternating between group discussion of problems and time for children to work problems on their own. Seatwork is thereby embedded into the lesson. After they work individually or in small groups on a problem, Asian students are called upon to present and defend the solutions they came up with. Thus, instruction, practice, and evaluation are tightly interwoven into a coherent whole. In contrast, the average length of

seatwork in American fifth-grade classrooms was almost twice as long as it was in Asian classrooms. And, instead of embedding seatwork into the ongoing back and forth of the lesson, American teachers tend to relegate it to one long period at the end of the class, where it becomes little more than a time for repetitious practice. In Chicago, 59 percent of all fifth-grade lessons ended with a period of seatwork, compared with 23 percent in Sendai and 14 percent in Taipei. American teachers often do not discuss the work or its connection to the goal of the lesson, or even evaluate its accuracy. Seatwork was never evaluated or discussed in 48 percent of all American fifth-grade classes we observed, compared to less than 3 percent of Japanese classes and 6 percent of Taiwan classes.

Since Asian students spend so much of their time in whole-group work, we need to say a word about that format. Whole-class instruction in the United States has gotten a somewhat bad reputation. It has become associated with too much teacher talk and too many passive, tuned-out students. But as we will see in more detail as we continue our description of Asian classrooms, whole-class instruction in Japan and China is a very lively, engaging enterprise. Asian teachers do not spend large amounts of time lecturing. They present interesting problems; they pose provocative questions; they probe and guide. The students work hard, generating multiple approaches to a solution, explaining the rationale behind their methods, and making good use of wrong answers.

HANDLING DIVERSITY

The organization of American elementary school classrooms is based on the assumption that whole-group instruction cannot accommodate students' diverse abilities and levels of achievement; thus, large amounts of whole-class time are given up so that the teacher can work individually with students. Asian educators are more comfortable in the belief that all children, with proper effort, can take advantage of a uniform educational experience, and so they are able to focus on providing the same high-quality experience to all students. Our results suggest that American educators need to question their long-held assumption that an individualized learning experience is inherently a higher-quality, more effective experience than is a whole-class learning experience. Although it may be true that an equal amount of time with a teacher may be more effective in a one-on-one situation than in a large-group situation, we must realize that the result of individualized instruction, given realistic financial constraints, is to drastically reduce the amount of teacher instruction every child receives.

HOW WE MADE SURE WE WERE LOOKING AT REPRESENTATIVE SCHOOLS

Frequent reports on television and in books and newspapers purport to depict what happens inside Japanese and Chinese classrooms. These reports usually are based on impressions gathered during brief visits to classrooms—most likely classrooms that the visitor's contacts in Asia have preselected. As a result, it is difficult to gauge the generality of what was seen and reported. Without observing large, representative samples of schools and teachers, it is impossible to characterize the teaching practices of any culture.

The descriptions that we present are based on two large observational studies of first-and fifth-grade classrooms that we conducted in Japan, Taiwan, China, and the United States. In contrast to informal observations, the strength of formal studies such as ours is that the observations are made according to consistent rules about where, when, and what to observe.

In the first study, our observers were in classrooms for a total of over four thousand hours—over a thousand class periods in 20 first- and fifth-grade classrooms in each of three cities: Sendai, Japan; Taipei, Taiwan; and Minneapolis, Minnesota.[1] Our second study took place in two hundred classrooms, forty each in Sendai and Taipei, plus forty in Beijing, China, and eighty in the Chicago metropolitan area of the United States.[2] Care was taken to choose schools that were representative. Our Chicago metropolitan area sample—the urban and suburban areas that make up Cook County—included schools that are predominantly white, black, Hispanic, and ethnically mixed; schools that draw from upper, middle, and lower socioeconomic groups; schools that are public and private; and schools that are urban and suburban.

Observers visited each classroom four times over a one-to two-week period, yielding a total of eight hundred hours of observations. The observers, who were residents of each city, wrote down as much as they could about what transpired during each mathematics class. Tape recordings made during the classes assisted the observers in filling in any missing information. These detailed narrative accounts of what transpired in the classrooms yielded even richer information than we obtained in the first study, where the observers followed predefined categories for coding behavior during the course of observations.

After the narrative records had been translated into English, we divided each observation into segments, which we defined as beginning each time there was a change in topic, materials, or activity. For example, a segment began when students put away their textbooks and began working on a worksheet or when the teacher stopped lecturing and asked some of the students to write their solutions to a problem on the blackboard.

Both studies focused on mathematics classes rather than on classes in subjects such as reading, where cultural differences in teaching practices may be more strongly determined by the content of what is being taught. For example, it is likely that the processes of teaching and learning about the multiplication of fractions transcend cultural differences, whereas teaching children how to read Chinese characters may require different approaches from those used to teach children to read an alphabetic language.

REFERENCES

1. Stevenson, H. W., Stigler, J. W., Lucker, G. W., Lee, S. Y., Hsu, C. C., & Kitamura, S. (1987). Classroom behavior and achievement of Japanese, Chinese, and American children. In R. Glaser (Ed.), *Advances in instructional psychology.* Hillsdale NJ: Erlbaum.
2. Stigler, J. W., & Perry, M. (1990). Mathematics learning in Japanese, Chinese, and American classrooms. In Stigler, J. W., Shweder, R. A., & Herdt, G. (Eds.), *Cultural psychology: Essays on comparative human development.* Cambridge, Cambridge University Press. pp. 328–356.

Japanese and Chinese teachers recognize individual differences among students, but they handle that diversity in a very different way. First, as we will see in more detail later, they have much greater amounts of nonteaching time than do American teachers, and part of that time is available for working with individual students. They may spend extra time with slower students or ask faster students to assist them, but they focus their lesson on teaching all children regardless of apparent differences in ability or developmental readiness. Before we discuss how they do that in a whole-group setting, we need to first address the question of whether American classrooms are more diverse than Asian ones, thus potentially rendering whole-class instruction more difficult.

Whenever we discuss our research on teaching practices, someone in the audience inevitably reminds us that Japan and China are nations with relatively homogeneous populations while the United States is the melting pot of the world. How could we expect that practices used in Asian societies could possibly be relevant for the American context, where diversity is the rule in race, ethnicity, language, and social class?

What impedes teaching is the uneven preparation of children for the academic tasks that must be accomplished. It is diversity in children's educational backgrounds, not in their social and cultural backgrounds, that poses the greatest problems in teaching. Although the United States is culturally more diverse than Japan or China, we have found no more diversity at the classroom level in the educational level of American than of Asian students. The key factor is that, in the United States, educational and cultural diversity are positively related, leading some persons to the inappropriate conclusion that it is ethnic and cultural diversity, rather than educational diversity, that leads to the difficulties faced by American teachers.

It is true, for example, that there is greater variability in mathematics achievement among American than among Japanese children, but this does not mean that the differences are evident in any particular classroom. Variability in the United States exists to a large extent across neighborhoods and schools (rather than within them). Within individual classrooms, the variability in levels of academic achievement differs little between the United States and Japan, Taiwan, or China. It is wrong to argue that diversity within classrooms is an American problem. Teachers everywhere must deal with students who vary in their knowledge and motivation.

Tracking does not exist in Asian elementary schools. Children are never separated into different classrooms according to their presumed levels of intellectual ability. This egalitarian philosophy carries over to organization within the classroom. Children are not separated into reading groups according to their ability; there is no division of the class into groups differentiated by the rate at which they proceed through their mathematics books. No children leave the classroom for special classes, such as those designed for children who have been diagnosed as having learning disabilities.

How do teachers in Asian classrooms handle diversity in students' knowledge and skills? For one thing, they typically use a variety of approaches in their teaching, allowing students who may not understand one approach the opportunity to experience other approaches to presenting the material. Periods of recitation are alternated with periods in which children work for short periods on practice problems. Explanations by the teacher are interspersed with periods in which children work with concrete materials or struggle to come up with their own solutions to problems. There is continuous change from one mode of presentation, one type of representation, and one type of teaching method to another.

Asian teaching practices thrive in the face of diversity, and some practices can depend on diversity for their effectiveness. Asking students to suggest alternative solutions to a problem, for example, works best when students have had experience in generating a variety of solutions. Incorrect solutions, which are typically dismissed by the American teacher, become topics for discussion in Asian classrooms, and all students can learn from this discussion. Thus, while American schools attempt to solve the problems of diversity by segregating children into different groups or different classrooms, and by spending large amounts of regular class time working with individual students, Asian teachers believe that the only way they can cope with the problem is by devising teaching techniques that accommodate the different interests and backgrounds of the children in their classrooms.

Asian teachers also exploit the fact that the same instruction can affect different students in different ways, something that may be overlooked by American teachers. In this sense, Asian teachers subscribe to what would be considered in the West to be a "constructivist" view of learning. According to this view, knowledge is regarded as something that must be constructed by the child rather than as a set of facts and skills that can be imparted by the teacher. Because children are engaged in their own construction of knowledge, some of the major tasks for the teacher are to pose provocative questions, to allow adequate time for reflection, and to vary teaching techniques so that they are responsive to differences in students' prior experience. Through such practices, Asian teachers are able to accommodate individual differences in learning, even though instruction is not tailored to each student.

USE OF REAL-WORLD PROBLEMS AND OBJECTS

Elementary school mathematics is often defined in terms of mathematical symbols and their manipulation; for example, children must learn the place-value system of numeration and the operations for manipulating numerals to add, subtract, multiply, and divide. In addition, children must be able to apply these symbols and operations to solving problems. In order to accomplish these goals, teachers rely primarily on two powerful tools for representing mathematics: language and the manipulation of concrete objects. How effectively teachers use these forms of representation plays a critical role in determining how well children will understand mathematics.

One common function of language is in defining terms and stating rules for performing mathematical operations. A second, broader function is the use of language as a means of connecting mathematical operations to the real world and of integrating what children know about mathematics. We find that American elementary school teachers are more prone to use language to define terms and state rules than are Asian teachers, who, in their efforts to make mathematics meaningful, use language to clarify different aspects of mathematics and to integrate what children know about mathematics with the demands of real-world problems. Here is an example of what we mean by a class in which the teacher defines terms and states rules:

> An American teacher announces that the lesson today concerns fractions. Fractions are defined and she names the numerator and denominator. "What do we call this?" she then asks. "And this?" After assuring herself that the children understand the meaning of the terms, she spends the rest of the lesson teaching them to apply the rules for forming fractions.

Asian teachers tend to reverse the procedure. They focus initially on interpreting and relating a real-world problem to the quantification that is necessary for a mathematical solution and then to define terms and state rules. In the following example, a third-grade teacher in Japan was also teaching a lesson that introduced the notation system for fractions.

> The lesson began with the teacher posing the question of how many liters of juice (colored water) were contained in a large beaker. "More than one liter," answered one child. "One and a half liters," answered another. After several children had made guesses, the teacher suggested that they pour the juice into some one-liter beakers and see. Horizontal lines on each beaker divided it into thirds. The juice filled one beaker and part of a second. The teacher pointed out that the water came up to the first line on the second beaker—only one of the three parts was full. The procedure was repeated with a second set of beakers to illustrate the concept of one-half. After stating that there had been one and one-out-of-three liters of juice in the first big beaker and one and one-out-of-two liters in the second, the teacher wrote the fractions on the board. He continued the lesson by asking the children how to represent two parts out of three, two parts out of five, and so forth. Near the end of the period he mentioned the term "fraction" for the first time and attached names to the numerator and the denominator.

He ended the lesson by summarizing how fractions can be used to represent the parts of a whole.

In the second example, the concept of fractions emerged from a meaningful experience; in the first, it was introduced initially as an abstract concept. The terms and operations in the second example flowed naturally from the teacher's questions and discussion; in the first, language was used primarily for defining and summarizing rules. Mathematics ultimately requires abstract representation, but young children understand such representation more readily if it is derived from meaningful experience than if it results from learning definitions and rules.

Asian teachers generally are more likely than American teachers to engage their students, even very young ones, in the discussion of mathematical concepts. The kind of verbal discussion we find in American classrooms is more short-answer in nature, oriented, for example, toward clarifying the correct way to implement a computational procedure.

Teachers ask questions for different reasons in the United States and in Japan. In the United States, the purpose of a question is to get an answer. In Japan, teachers pose questions to stimulate thought. A Japanese teacher considers a question to be a poor one if it elicits an immediate answer, for this indicates that students were not challenged to think. One teacher we interviewed told us of discussions she had with her fellow teachers on how to improve teaching practices. "What do you talk about?" we wondered. "A great deal of time," she reported, "is spent talking about questions we can pose to the class—which wordings work best to get students involved in thinking and discussing the material. One good question can keep a whole class going for a long time; a bad one produces little more than a simple answer."

In one memorable example recorded by our observers, a Japanese first-grade teacher began her class by posing the question to one of her students: "Would you explain the difference between what we learned in yesterday's lesson and what you came across in preparing for today's lesson?" The young student thought for a long time, but then answered the question intelligently, a performance that undoubtedly enhanced his understanding of both lessons.

CONCRETE REPRESENTATIONS

Every elementary school student in Sendai possesses a "Math Set," a box of colorful, well-designed materials for teaching mathematical concepts: tiles, clock, ruler, checkerboard, colored triangles, beads, and many other attractive objects.

In Taipei, every classroom is equipped with a similar, but larger, set of such objects. In Beijing, where there is much less money available for purchasing such materials, teachers improvise with colored paper, wax fruit, plates, and other easily obtained objects. In all cases, these concrete objects are considered to be critically important tools for teaching mathematics, for it is through manipulating these objects that children can form important links between real-world problems and abstract mathematical notations.

American teachers are much less likely than Chinese or Japanese teachers to use concrete objects. At fifth grade, for example, Sendai teachers were nearly twice as likely to use concrete objects as the Chicago area teachers, and Taipei teachers were nearly five times as likely. There was also a subtle, but important, difference in the way Asian and American teachers used concrete objects. Japanese teachers, for example, use the items in the Math Set throughout the elementary school years and introduced small tiles in a high percentage of the lessons we observed in the first grade. American teachers seek variety and may use Popsicle sticks in one lesson, and in another, marbles, Cheerios, M&Ms, checkers, poker chips, or plastic animals. The American view is that objects should be varied in order to maintain children's interest. The Asian view is that using a variety of representational materials may confuse children, and thereby make it more difficult for them to use the objects for the representation and solution of mathematics problems. Having learned to add with tiles makes multiplication easier to understand when the same tiles are used.

Through the skillful use of concrete objects, teachers are able to teach elementary school children to understand and solve problems that are not introduced in American curricula until much later. An example occurred in a fourth-grade mathematics lesson we observed in Japan. The problem the teacher posed is a difficult one for fourth graders, and its solution is generally not taught in the United States until much later. This is the problem:

> There are a total of thirty-eight children in Akira's class. There are six more boys than there are girls. How many boys and how many girls are in the class?

This lesson began with a discussion of the problem and with the children proposing ways to solve it. After the discussion, the teacher handed each child two strips of paper, one six units longer than the other, and told the class that the strips would be used to help them think about the problem. One slip represented the number of girls in the class and the other represented the number of boys. By lining the strips next to each other, the children could see that the degree to which the longer one protruded beyond the shorter one represented 6 boys. The procedure for solving the problem then unfolded as the teacher, through skillful questioning, led the children to the solution: The number of girls was found by taking the total of both strips, subtracting 6 to make the strips of equal length, and then dividing by 2. The number of boys could be found, of course, by adding 6 to the number of girls. With this concrete visual representation of the problem and careful guidance from the teacher, even fourth graders were able to understand the problem and its solution.

STUDENTS CONSTRUCT MULTIPLE SOLUTIONS

A common Western stereotype is that the Asian teacher is an authoritarian purveyor of information, one who expects students to listen and memorize correct answers or correct procedures rather than to construct knowledge themselves. This may or may not be an accurate description of Asian high school teachers,[4] but, as we have seen in previous examples, it does not describe the dozens of elementary school teachers that we have observed.

Chinese and Japanese teachers rely on students to generate ideas and evaluate the correctness of the ideas. The possibility that they will be called upon to state their own solution as well as to evaluate what another student has proposed keeps Asian students alert, but this technique has two other important functions. First, it engages students in the lesson, increasing their motivation by making them feel they are participants in a group process. Second, it conveys a more realistic impression of how knowledge is acquired. Mathematics, for example, is a body of knowledge that has evolved gradually through a process of argument and proof. Learning to argue about mathematical ideas is fundamental to understanding mathematics. Chinese and Japanese children begin learning these skills in the first grade; many American elementary school students are never exposed to them.

We can illustrate the way Asian teachers use students' ideas with the following example. A fifth-grade teacher in Taiwan began her mathematics lesson by calling attention to a six-sided figure she had drawn on the blackboard. She asked the students how they might go about finding the area of the shaded region. "I don't want you to tell me what the actual area is, just tell me the approach you would use to solve the problem. Think of as many different ways as you can of ways you could determine the area that I have drawn in yellow chalk." She allowed the students several minutes to work in small groups and then called upon a child from each group to describe the group's solution. After each proposal, many of which were quite complex, the teacher asked members of the other groups whether the procedure described could yield a correct answer. After several different procedures had been suggested, the teacher moved on to a second problem with a different embedded figure and repeated the process. Neither teacher nor students actually carried out a solution to the problem until all of the alternative solutions had been discussed. The lesson ended with the teacher affirming the importance of coming up with multiple solutions. "After all," she said, "we face many problems every day in the real world. We have to remember that there is not only one way we can solve each problem."

American teachers are less likely to give students opportunities to respond at such length. Although a great deal of interaction appears to occur in American classrooms—with teachers and students posing questions and giving answers—American teachers generally pose questions that are answerable with a yes or no or with a short phrase. They seek a correct answer and continue calling on students until one produces it. "Since we can't subtract 8 from 6," says an American teacher, "we have to . . . what?" Hands go up, the teacher calls on a girl who says "Borrow." "Correct," the teacher replies. This kind of interchange does not establish the student as a valid source of information, for the final arbiter of the correctness of the student's opinions is still the teacher. The situation is very different in Asian classrooms, where children are likely to be asked to explain their answers and other children are then called upon to evaluate their correctness.

Clear evidence of these differing beliefs about the roles of students and teachers appears in the observations of how teachers evaluate students' responses. The most frequent form of evaluation used by American teachers was praise, a technique that was rarely used in either Taiwan or Japan. In Japan, evaluation most frequently took the form of a discussion of children's errors.

Praise serves to cut off discussion and to highlight the teacher's role as the authority. It also encourages children to be satisfied with their performance rather than informing them about where they need improvement. Discussing errors, on the other hand, encourages argument and justification and involves students in the exciting quest of assessing the strengths and weaknesses of the various alternative solutions that have been proposed.

Why are American teachers often reluctant to encourage students to participate at greater length during mathematics lessons? One possibility is that they feel insecure about the depth of their own mathematical training. Placing more emphasis on students' explanations necessarily requires teachers to relinquish some control over the direction the lesson will take. This can be a frightening prospect to a teacher who is unprepared to evaluate the validity of novel ideas that students inevitably propose.

USING ERRORS EFFECTIVELY

We have been struck by the different reactions of Asian and American teachers to children's errors. For Americans, errors tend to be interpreted as an indication of failure in learning the lesson. For Chinese and Japanese, they are an index of what still needs to be learned. These divergent interpretations result in very different reactions to the display of errors—embarrassment on the part of the American children, calm acceptance by Asian children. They also result in differences in the manner in which teachers utilize errors as effective means of instruction.

We visited a fifth-grade classroom in Japan the first day the teacher introduced the problem of adding fractions with unequal denominators. The problem was a simple one: adding one-third and one-half. The children were told to solve the problem and that the class would then review the different solutions.

After everyone appeared to have completed the task, the teacher called on one of the students to give his answer and to explain his solution. "The answer is two-fifths," he stated. Pointing first to the numerators and then to the denominators, he explained: "One plus one is two; three plus two is five. The answer is two-fifths." Without comment, the teacher asked another boy for his solution. "Two point one plus three point one, when changed into a fraction adds up to two-fifths." The children in the classroom looked puzzled. The teacher, unperturbed, asked a third student for her solution. "The answer is five-sixths." The student went on to explain how she had found the common denominator, changed the fractions so that each had this denominator, and then added them.

The teacher returned to the first solution. "How many of you think this solution is correct?" Most agreed that it was not. She used the opportunity to direct the children's attention to reasons why the solution was incorrect. "Which is larger, two-fifths or one-half?" The class agreed that it was one-half. "It is strange, isn't it, that you could add a number to one-half and get a number that is smaller than one-half." She went on to explain how the procedure the child used would result in the odd situation where, when one-half was added to one-half, the answer yielded is one-half. In a similarly careful, interactive manner, she discussed how the second boy had confused fractions with decimals to come up with his surprising answer. Rather than ignoring the incorrect solutions and concentrating her attention on the correct solution, the teacher capitalized on the errors the children made in order to dispel two common misperceptions about fractions.

We have not observed American teachers responding to children's errors so inventively. Perhaps because of the strong influence of behavioristic teaching that conditions should be arranged so that the learner avoids errors and makes only a reinforceable response, American teachers place little emphasis on the constructive use of errors as a teaching technique. It seems likely, however, that learning about what is wrong may hasten children's understanding of why the correct procedures are appropriate.

WHY NOT HERE?

Few who have visited urban classrooms in Asia would disagree that the great majority of Chinese and Japanese teachers are highly skilled professionals. Their dedication is legendary; what is often not appreciated is how thoughtfully and adroitly they guide children through the vast amount of material that they must master during the six years of elementary school. We, of course, witnessed examples of excellent lessons in American classrooms. And there are of course individual differences among Asian teachers. But what has impressed us in our personal observations and in the data from our observational studies is how remarkably well most Asian teachers teach. It is the *widespread* excellence of Asian class lessons, the high level of performance of the *average* teacher, that is so stunning.

The techniques used by Chinese and Japanese teachers are not new to the teaching profession—nor are they foreign or exotic. In fact, they are the types of techniques often recommended by American educators. What the Japanese and Chinese examples demonstrate so compellingly is that when widely implemented, such practices can produce extraordinary outcomes.

Unfortunately, these techniques have not been broadly applied in the United States. Why? One reason, as we have discussed, is the Asian belief that the whole-group lesson, if done well, can be made to work for every child. With that assumption, Asian teachers can focus on the perfection of that lesson. However, even if American educators shared that belief, it would be difficult for them to achieve anything near the broad-based high quality that we observed in Asian classrooms. This is not the fault of American teachers. The fault lies with a system that prepares them inadequately and then exhausts them physically, emotionally, and intellectually while denying them the collegial interaction that every profession relies upon for the growth and refinement of its knowledge base.

The first major obstacle to the widespread development and execution of excellent lessons in America is the fact that American teachers are overworked. It is inconceivable that American teachers, by themselves, would be able to organize lively, vivid, coherent lessons under a regimen that requires that they teach hour after hour every day throughout the school year. Preparing lessons that require the discovery of knowledge and the construction of understanding takes time. Teaching them effectively requires energy. Both are in very short supply for most American teachers.

Being an elementary school teacher in the United States at the end of the twentieth century is extraordinarily difficult, and the demands made by American society exhaust even the most energetic among them. "I'm dancing as fast as I can," one teacher summarized her feelings about her job, "but with all the things that I'm supposed to do, I just can't keep up."

The full realization of how little time American teachers have when they are not directly in charge of children became clear to us during a meeting in Beijing. We were discussing the teachers' workday. When we informed the Chinese teachers that American teachers are responsible for their classes all day long, with only an hour or less outside the classroom each day, they looked incredulous. How could any teacher be expected to do a good job when there is no time outside of class to prepare and correct lessons, work with individual children, consult with other teachers, and attend to all of the matters that arise in a typical day at school! Beijing teachers teach no more than three hours a day, unless the teacher is a homeroom teacher, in which case, the total is four hours. During the first three grades, the teaching assignment includes both reading and mathematics; for the upper three grades of elementary school, teachers specialize in one of these subjects. They spend the rest of their day at school carrying out all of their other responsibilities to their students and to the school. The situation is similar in Japan. According to our estimate, Japanese elementary school teachers are in charge of classes only 60 percent of the time they are at school.

The large amounts of nonteaching time at school are available to Asian teachers because of two factors. The first concerns the number of teachers typically assigned to Asian schools. Although class sizes are considerably larger in Asia, the student-to-teacher ratio within a school does not differ greatly from that in the United States. By having more students in each class and the same number of teachers in the school, all teachers can have fewer teaching hours. Time is freed up for teachers to meet and work together on a daily basis, to prepare lessons for the next day, to work with individual children, and to attend staff meetings.

The second factor increasing the time available to Japanese and Chinese teachers at school is that they spend more hours at school each day than do American teachers. In our study, for example, teachers in Sendai and Taipei spent an average of 9.5 and 9.1 hours per day, respectively, compared to only 7.3 hours for the American teachers. Asian teachers arrive at school early and stay late, which gives them time to meet together and to work with children who need extra help. Most American teachers, in contrast, arrive at school shortly before classes begin and leave not long after they end. This does not mean a shorter work week for American teachers. What it does mean is that they must devote their evenings to working alone on the next day's lessons, further increasing their sense of isolation.

LEARNING FROM EACH OTHER

The second reason Asian classes are so well crafted is that there is a very systematic effort to pass on the accumulated wisdom of teaching practice to each new generation of teachers and to keep perfecting that practice by providing teachers the opportunities to continually learn from each other.

Americans often act as if good teachers are born, not made. We hear this from both teachers and parents. They seem to believe that good teaching happens if the teacher has a knack with children, gets along well with them, and keeps them reasonably attentive and enthusiastic about learning. It is a commonly accepted truism in many colleges of education that teaching is an art and that students cannot be taught how to teach.

Perhaps because of this belief, students emerge from American colleges of education with little training in how to design and teach effective lessons. It is assumed that teachers will discover this for themselves. Courses in teaching methods are designed to serve a different purpose. On the one hand, they present theories of learning and cognitive development. Although the students are able to quote the major tenets of the theorists currently in vogue, the theories remain as broad generalizations that are difficult to apply to the everyday tasks that they will face as classroom teachers. At the opposite extreme, these methods courses provide education students with lists of specific suggestions for activities and materials that are easy to use and that children should enjoy (for example, pieces of breakfast cereal make handy counters for teaching basic number facts). Teachers are faced, therefore, with information that is either too general to be applied readily or so specific that it has only limited usefulness. Because of this, Ameri-

can teachers complain that most of what they know had to be learned by themselves, alone, on the job.

In Asia, graduates of teacher training programs are still considered to be novices who need the guidance and support of their experienced colleagues. In the United States, training comes to a near halt after the teachers acquire their teaching certificates. American teachers may take additional coursework in the evenings or during summer vacations, or they may attend district or citywide workshops from time to time. But these opportunities are not considered to be an essential part of the American system of teacher training.

In Japan, the system of teacher training is much like an apprenticeship under the guidance of experienced colleagues. The teacher's first year of employment marks the beginning of a lengthy and elaborate training process. By Japanese law, beginning teachers must receive a minimum of twenty days of inservice training during their first year on the job.[5] Supervising the inservice training are master teachers, selected for their teaching ability and their willingness to assist their young colleagues. During one-year leaves of absence from their own classrooms, they observe the beginner in the classroom and offer suggestions for improvement.

In addition to this early tutelage in teaching techniques, Japanese teachers, beginners as well as seasoned teachers, are required to continually perfect their teaching skills through interaction with other teachers. One mechanism is through meetings organized by the vice principal and head teachers of their own school. These experienced professionals assume responsibility for advising and guiding their young colleagues. The head teachers organize meetings to discuss teaching techniques and to devise lesson plans and handouts. These meetings are supplemented by informal districtwide study groups and courses at municipal or prefectural education centers.[6]

A glimpse at what takes place in these study groups is provided in a conversation we recently had with a Japanese teacher. She and her colleagues spend a good deal of their time together working on lesson plans. After they finish a plan, one teacher from the group teaches the lesson to her students while the other teachers look on. Afterward, the group meets again to criticize the teacher's performance and to make suggestions for how the lesson could be improved. In her school, there is an annual "teaching fair." Teachers from other schools are invited to visit the school and observe the lessons being taught. The visitors rate the lessons, and the teacher with the best lesson is declared the winner.

In addition, national television in Japan presents programs that show how master teachers handle particular lessons or concepts. In Taiwan, such demonstrations are available on sets of videotapes that cover the whole curriculum.

Making use of lessons that have been honed over time does not mean that the Asian teacher simply mimics what she sees. As with great actors or musicians, the substance of the curriculum becomes the script or the score; the goal is to perform the role or piece as effectively and creatively as possible. Rather than executing the curriculum as a mere routine, the skilled teacher strives to perfect the presentation of each lesson. She uses the teaching techniques she has learned and imposes her own interpretation on these techniques in a manner that she thinks will interest and motivate her pupils.

Of course, teachers find it easier to share helpful tips and techniques among themselves when they are all teaching the same lesson at about the same time. The fact that Taiwan, Japan, and China each has a national curriculum that provides a common focus is a significant factor in teacher interaction. Not only do we have no national curriculum in the United States, but the curriculum may not be consistent within a city or even within a single school. American textbooks, with a spiral curriculum that repeats topics year after year and with a profusion of material about each topic, force teachers to omit some of each year's material. Even when teachers use the same textbook, their classes differ according to which topics they choose to skip and in the pace with which they proceed through the text. As a result, American teachers have less incentive than Asian teachers to share experiences with each other or to benefit from the successes and failures that others have had in teaching particular lessons.

Adding further to the sense of isolation is the fact that American teachers, unlike other professionals, do not share a common body of knowledge and experience. The courses offered at different universities and colleges vary, and even among their required courses, there is often little common content from college to college. Student teaching, the only other activity in which all budding teachers participate, is a solitary endeavor shared only with the regular classroom teacher and perhaps a few fellow student teachers.

Opportunities for Asian teachers to learn from each other are influenced, in part, by the physical arrangements of the schools. In Japanese and Chinese schools, a large room in each school is designed as a teachers' room, and each teacher is assigned a desk in this room. It is here that they spend their time away from the classroom preparing lessons, correcting students' papers, and discussing teaching techniques. American teachers, isolated in their own classrooms, find it much harder to discuss their work with colleagues. Their desk and teaching materials are in their own classrooms, and the only common space available to teachers is usually a cramped room that often houses supplies and the school's duplicating facilities, along with a few chairs and a coffee machine. Rarely do teachers have enough time in their visits to this room to engage in serious discussions of educational policy or teaching practices.

Critics argue that the problems facing the American teacher are unique and that it is futile to consider what Japanese and Chinese teaching are like in seeking solutions to educational problems in the United States. One of the frequent arguments is that the students in the typical Asian classroom share a common language and culture, are well disciplined and attentive, and are not distracted by family crises and their own personal problems, whereas the typical American teacher is often faced with a diverse, burdened, distracted group of students. To be sure, the conditions encountered by teachers differ greatly among these societies. Week after week, American teachers must cope with children who present them with complex, wrenching personal problems. But much of what gives American classrooms their aura of disarray and disorganization may be traced to how schools are organized and teachers are trained as well as to characteristics of the children.

It is easy to blame teachers for the problems confronting American education, and this is something that the American public is prone to do. The accusation is unfair. We cannot blame teachers when we deprive them of adequate training and yet expect that on their own they will become innovative teachers; when we cast them in the roles of surrogate parents, counselors, and psychotherapists and still expect them to be effective teachers; and when we keep them so busy in the classroom that they have little time or opportunity for professional development once they have joined the ranks of the teaching profession.

Surely the most immediate and pressing task in educating young students is to create a new type of school environment, one where great lessons are a commonplace occurrence. In order to do this, we must ask how we can institute reforms that will make it possible for American teachers to practice their profession under conditions that are as favorable for their own professional development and for the education of children as those that exist in Asia.

REFERENCES

1. The superior academic achievement of Chinese and Japanese children sometimes leads to speculation that they are brighter than American children. This possibility has been supported in a few reports that have received attention in the popular press and in several scientific journals. What has not been reported or widely understood is that, without exception, the studies contending that differences in intelligence are responsible for differences in academic performance have

failed to meet acceptable standards of scientific inquiry. In fact, studies that have reported differences in I.Q. scores between Asian and American children have been flawed conceptually and methodologically. Their major defects are nonequivalent tests used in the different locations and noncomparable samples of children. To determine the cognitive abilities of children in the three cultures, we needed tests that were linguistically comparable and culturally unbiased. These requirements preclude reliance on tests translated from one language to another or the evaluation of children in one country on the basis of norms obtained in another country. We assembled a team with members from each of the three cultures, and they developed ten cognitive tasks falling into traditional "verbal" and "performance" categories. The test results revealed no evidence of overall differences in the cognitive functioning of American, Chinese, and Japanese children. There was no tendency for children from any of the three cultures to achieve significantly higher average scores on all the tasks. Children in each culture had strengths and weaknesses, but by the fifth grade of elementary school, the most notable feature of children's cognitive performance was the similarity in level and variability of their scores. [Stevenson, H. W., Stigler, J. W., Lee, S. Y., Lucker, G. W.,

Kitamura, S., & Hsu, C. C. (1985). Cognitive performance and academic achievement of Japanese, Chinese, and American children. *Child Development*, 56, 718–734.]

2. Stevenson, H. W. (1990). Adapting to school: Children in Beijing and Chicago. *Annual Report*. Stanford CA: Center for Advanced Study in the Behavioral Sciences. Stevenson, H. W., Lee, S., Chen, C., Lummis, M., Stigler, J., Fan, L., & Ge, F. (1990). Mathematics achievement of children in China and the United States. *Child Development*, 61, 1053–1066. Stevenson, H. W., Stigler, J. W., & Lee, S.Y (1986). Mathematics achievement of Chinese, Japanese, and American children. *Science*, 231, 693–699. Stigler, J. W., Lee, S. Y., & Stevenson, H. W. (1990). *Mathematical knowledge*. Reston, VA: National Council of Teachers of Mathematics.

3. Stevenson, H. W., Lee, S. Y., Chen C., Stigler, J. W., Hsu, C. C., & Kitamura, S. (1990). Contexts of achievement. *Monographs of the Society for Research in Child Development*. Serial No. 221, 55, Nos. 1–2.

4. Rohlen, T. P. (1983). *Japan's High Schools*. Berkeley: University of California Press.

5. Dorfman, C. H. (Ed.) (1987). *Japanese Education Today*. Washington, D.C.: U.S. Department of Education.

6. Ibid.

Questions

1. Why do Stigler and Stevenson begin this article by pointing out that there are no overall differences in intelligence between U.S. children and their Asian counterparts?
2. What are the differences in mathematics achievement in the United States, China, and Japan? Are these three countries close or far apart in children's mathematics scores?
3. What are three classroom practices that are different in the United States, Japan, and China, and how do these practices affect what children learn about mathematics in school?
4. Why do mathematics teachers in Japan and China strive to make their lessons coherent, and how do they accomplish this goal?
5. How is instructional time eroded in U.S. classrooms? What can be done to change this pattern?
6. How did Stigler and Stevenson ensure that the schools they observed in each country were representative of that country and that the different classrooms were comparable across the three countries? Why are both these sampling issues important to address in cross-national research on academic performance?
7. Siegler and Stevenson found that the use of real-world problems and objects helps children learn mathematics better than more abstract references. What do you think is the explanation for this difference?
8. Why is it problematic when the majority of class time is spent on individual work as opposed to group instruction or activities?
9. How do differences in cultural values in these countries lead to different interpretations and different uses of children's errors in the classroom for instructional purposes?
10. Which aspects of teacher training and support in the United States would need to be changed to enable teachers to use the techniques practiced by teachers in China and Japan?

29 Friendship Quality and Social Development

Thomas J. Berndt

Children's relationships with peers during middle childhood have been the subject of much research on social and emotional development. Although this topic is interesting in its own right, it also has much practical significance. Children's relationships with peers during childhood and adolescence are among the best predictors of healthy adjustment in adulthood. Therefore, better understanding of how children formulate relationships with peers, especially close relationships, is critical to our understanding of psychological well-being.

The closest relationship that a person has with someone outside the family is friendship, and developmental psychologists have been interested in many questions about children's friendships. For example, does the nature of children's friendships change over the course of development? In other words, do children at different ages seek different qualities in their closest companions? Are the effects of friendship on child development direct, in that they offer an improved quality of social experience with peers, as well as indirect, in that they enhance children's academic performance or increase prosocial behaviors? Are some of the friendships that children have more positive, or of a higher quality, than other friendships? And if children have high-quality friendships, do these relationships have different consequences for development than do lower-quality friendships?

In the following article, Thomas Berndt, a developmental psychologist who has conducted extensive research on children's friendships, reviews the literature on this topic. His focus in this article is on how friendship quality in childhood can be understood. He also discusses how psychologists have tried to trace the connections between types of friendship experiences and children's social development and adjustment. As you will see, friendship quality is defined somewhat differently in middle childhood and in adolescence. The impact of friendship on social-psychological adjustment also changes with development. Finally, several examples in this article illustrate how important positive friendships are to adjustment during adolescence. Given that middle childhood immediately precedes adolescence, it is important to think about the contributions that friendships during middle childhood may make to friendship quality and psychological adjustment in adolescence.

A high-quality friendship is characterized by high levels of prosocial behavior, intimacy, and other positive features, and low levels of conflicts, rivalry, and other negative features. Friendship quality has been assumed to have direct effects on many aspects of children's social development, including their self-esteem and social adjustment. Recent research suggests, however, that friendship quality affects primarily children's success in the social world of peers. Friendship quality could also have indirect effects, by magnifying or diminishing the influence of friends on each other's attitudes and behaviors. Having high-quality friendships may lessen children's tendencies to imitate the behavior of shy and withdrawn friends, but little evidence supports the hypothesis that high-quality friendships magnify friends' influence.

Do good friendships enhance children's social development? What if those good friendships are with bad friends, friends who often misbehave in school or show other signs of poor social or psychological adjustment? Do good friendships with friends like those have a positive or a negative influence on children?

Similar questions about the effects of friends and friendships have been discussed in theoretical writings for decades. Only in recent years, however, have

Reprinted with permission of Blackwell Publishers from Berndt, T. J. (2002). Friendship quality and social development. *Current Directions in Psychological Science, 11,* 7–10.

answers to the questions begun to emerge from empirical research. The recent advances have resulted in part from researchers' success in defining, conceptually and operationally, what a good friendship is. In much of the literature, good friendships are now defined as friendships high in quality (e.g., Berndt, 1996).

High-quality friendships may enhance children's development regardless of the characteristics of those friends. Research on this hypothesis can be described as examining the direct effects of friendship quality. But another possibility is that friendship quality most often has indirect effects on children, effects that depend on the friends' characteristics. For example, when friendships are high in quality, the influence of the friends' characteristics may be magnified. I review evidence for both types of effects in this article, but it is necessary to begin by defining the construct of friendship quality more precisely.

A Definition of Friendship Quality

The old proverb says, "A friend in need is a friend indeed." That is, friends help and share with each other. Children agree with adults that these types of prosocial behavior are expected among friends. Children also agree with adults that good friends praise each other's successes and encourage each other after failures, thereby bolstering each other's self-esteem.

Some features of high-quality friendships are recognized by adolescents but not by young children. Adolescents often say that best friends tell each other everything, or disclose their most personal thoughts and feelings. These personal self-disclosures are the hallmark of an intimate friendship. Adolescents also say that friends will stick up for one another in a fight, demonstrating their loyalty.

A few researchers have described various positive features of good friendships, including prosocial behavior, self-esteem support, intimacy, loyalty, plus others, and investigated the associations between these features by asking questions assessing them. For example, to assess intimacy, researchers have asked children how often they tell a particular friend things about themselves that they would not tell most other people (Berndt & Keefe, 1995). Such research has found that children who say that their friendship has a high level of one positive feature, such as intimacy, typically say that their friendship is high in all other positive features. These results suggest that all positive features are linked to a single dimension of friendship quality.

Even best friendships can have negative features. Most children admit that best friends sometimes have conflicts with each other. In addition, children typically think of themselves as equal to their friends, but

equality can be more an ideal than a reality. Children sometimes say that their friends try to boss them around, or dominate them. Children say that their friends "try to prove they're better than me," or engage in rivalry. When asked about actual friendships, children usually report the co-occurrence of conflicts, dominance attempts, and rivalry. Thus, all negative features seem to be linked to a single dimension of friendship quality. Scores on this negative dimension are only weakly correlated with those on the positive dimension (Berndt, 1996), so both dimensions must be considered when defining the quality of a friendship.

Direct Effects of Friendship Quality

Most writers on friendship have assumed that high-quality friendships have positive effects on children: fostering their self-esteem, improving their social adjustment, and increasing their ability to cope with stressors (see Hartup & Stevens, 1999). Moreover, the correlations of friendship quality with indicators of social adjustment are consistent with that assumption. For example, among early adolescents, having friendships with more positive features correlates with greater involvement in school, higher self-perceived social acceptance, and higher general self-esteem (Berndt & Keefe, 1995; Keefe & Berndt, 1996).

Still, a significant correlation between two variables is only weak evidence that one affects the other. To test hypotheses about the effects of friendship quality more conclusively, researchers have assessed children's friendships and their adjustment on two or more occasions months or years apart (e.g., Ladd, Kochenderfer, & Coleman, 1996). Then the researchers have examined whether the quality of children's friendships on the first occasion predicted the changes over time in their adjustment. If so, the researchers tentatively have concluded that friendship quality affected the changes in children's adjustment.

In one study of this type (Ladd et al., 1996), kindergarten children who had high-quality friendships in January of the school year improved by the following May in their liking for school and in their perceptions of their classmates' support. In another study (Berndt, Hawkins, & Jiao, 1999), classmates rated students' sociability and leadership in sixth grade and again in seventh grade. Students whose sixth-grade friendships were high in positive features improved between sixth and seventh grade in peer-rated sociability and leadership, but only if their sixth-grade friendships were stable over time. These findings are consistent with hypotheses about the direct effects of high-quality friendships, but other data are not. In one study (Berndt et al., 1999), my colleagues and I found that friendship quality did not significantly affect the changes over time in students' general self-esteem. In three earlier longitudinal studies (see Keefe & Berndt, 1996), friendship quality also was not significantly related to changes in general self-esteem. These data cast doubt on the hypothesis that good friendships enhance children's self-esteem. Stated more strongly, the repeated failures to confirm the hypothesis that high-quality friendships increase children's self-esteem suggest a need for less sweeping and more specific hypotheses about the benefits of good friendships.

One possibility is that friendships high in positive features affect primarily children's success in the social world of peers. Thus, good friendships can improve children's views of their classmates and improve their classmates' views of them. A speculative explanation for these effects can also be offered. Having a few good friendships may help children make positive contacts with several other classmates. Those positive contacts may then lead to positive relationships that are not as close as best friendships but that affect the children's attitudes toward their classmates and vice versa.

The effects of negative friendship features have also been examined. In one study (Ladd et al., 1996), kindergarten boys who had many conflicts with friends in the middle of a school year exhibited a decrease by the end of the year in liking for school and engagement in classroom activities, but an increase in loneliness. In another study (Berndt & Keefe, 1995), seventh graders whose friendships were high in negative features in the fall of a year reported increased disruptive behavior at school the following spring. Moreover, those students whose friendships were also high in positive features reported the greatest increase in disruptive behavior.

One possible explanation of these findings focuses on the likely effects of negative interactions between friends. Friends who frequently get into conflicts with each other, or who often try to dominate or assert their superiority over one another, are practicing a repertoire of negative social behaviors that may generalize to interactions with other peers and adults. Moreover, the closer a friendship is, the more the friends interact and the more frequently they practice their negative social repertoire. Naturally, the students' negative behaviors provoke negative reactions from classmates and teachers. Those negative reactions encourage the students to disengage from classmates and classroom activities, to feel more lonely, and to like school less.

These explanations are only possibilities because the recent longitudinal studies do not provide evidence on the processes responsible for the effects of friendship quality. Examining these processes must be a major goal of future research (Hartup, 1999). Information about processes would be especially valuable as researchers seek to replace theories about the general effects of friendship quality with theories that explain the effects of each dimension of friendship quality on specific aspects of social development.

INDIRECT EFFECTS OF FRIENDSHIP QUALITY

For decades, researchers from a variety of disciplines have tested the hypothesis that children and adolescents are influenced by the attitudes and behaviors of their peers. Not all studies have provided support for the hypothesis, but the available data convincingly show that close friends influence many facets of children's and adolescents' social behavior and adjustment (Collins & Laursen, 1999). In most studies, researchers have not assessed the quality of the friendships among the peers who were influencing one another. But when the issue has been raised, researchers have often suggested that the magnitude of friends' influence should be affected by the quality of their friendships. In this way, friendship quality can have an indirect effect on children's social development—affecting how much children are influenced by their friends' characteristics.

For example, according to the differential-association theory of delinquent behavior, adolescents who spend time with delinquent friends are expected to commit delinquent acts themselves (see Agnew, 1991). Moreover, delinquent friends are assumed to have more influence the more positive the relationships with those friends are. That is, having high-quality friendships with delinquent friends is assumed to increase the influence of those friends, thereby increasing the degree to which adolescents become like their friends over time.

Many other theories include the hypothesis that friends' influence is magnified when friendships are higher in quality (see Berndt, 1999). For example, social learning theory suggests that observational learning from friends is enhanced when friends have more positive relationships. Other theories suggest that friends' influence should be greater the more friends trust each other, and trust is another facet of the positive dimension of friendship quality.

Given the plausibility of the hypothesis about the magnifying effect of friendship quality, the scarcity of evidence for it is surprising. Some evidence consistent with the hypothesis was obtained in one longitudinal study of adolescents' delinquent behavior (Agnew, 1991). Among all the adolescents whose friends engaged in serious delinquent acts, only those who were closely attached to those friends became more seriously delinquent themselves. However, the comparable effect of attachment to friends who engaged in minor delinquency was nonsignificant. Other studies have yielded equally equivocal support for the hypothesis (Berndt et al., 1999), or no support at all (Berndt & Keefe, 1995; Poulin, Dishion, & Haas, 1999). In short, the general hypothesis that high friendship quality magnifies friends' influence must currently be viewed as doubtful.

Under certain conditions, having high-quality friendships may lessen rather than magnify friends' influence on each other. Consider, in particular, children who have good friendships with peers who are shy and withdrawn. Would those friendships increase the children's tendencies to imitate their friends' shy and withdrawn behavior? Alternatively, would those friendships enhance children's confidence in social situations and make them less prone to social withdrawal?

These questions were addressed in a longitudinal study of early adolescents whose shyness and social withdrawal were judged by their classmates (Berndt et al., 1999). Adolescents whose friends showed above-average shyness and withdrawal became more shy and withdrawn themselves over time only if those friendships were average or low in quality. Having shy and withdrawn friends did not influence changes in students' shyness and withdrawal when those friendships were high in quality. Apparently, the support that the students received from their friends offset any tendencies to imitate the friends' patterns of social behavior.

The hypothesis that variations in friendship quality affect the magnitude of friends' influence on each other can be evaluated only in studies that include measures of friends' characteristics and of friendship quality. Unfortunately, researchers interested in exploring the benefits of friendships have seldom examined what those friends are like, and researchers interested in exploring friends' influence have seldom examined the types of relationships those friends have. Consequently, the evidence necessary for answering questions about indirect effects is very limited. This gap in the literature creates serious problems, because researchers may misjudge either the effects of friendship quality or the influence of friends by not exploring how friends' influence is moderated by friendship quality.

Understanding of indirect effects would increase if researchers more often probed the processes responsible for those effects (Hartup, 1999). Typically, researchers use interviews or questionnaires to assess friendship quality and the characteristics of children and their friends, without ever seeing how the friends behave toward each other. But a few researchers have shown that rich and compelling data can be obtained by observing the social interactions between friends (e.g., Dishion, Andrews, & Crosby, 1995). These observations can reveal both the features of children's friendships and the relations of those features to the friends' influence on each other. Such observational studies can be a valuable complement to interview–questionnaire studies. When used in combination, the two research strategies should greatly expand knowledge about the indirect effects of friendship quality and the processes responsible for those effects.

CONCLUSIONS

Children prize friendships that are high in prosocial behavior, intimacy, and other positive features. Children are troubled by friendships that are high in conflicts, dominance, rivalry, and other negative features. Friendships are high in quality when they have high levels of positive features and low levels of negative features.

High-quality friendships have often been assumed to have positive effects on many aspects of children's social development. However, the direct effects of friendship quality appear to be quite specific. Having friendships high in negative features increases disagreeable and disruptive behaviors, probably because the interactional style that children practice with friends generalizes to interactions with other peers and adults. Having friendships high in positive features enhances children's success in the social world of peers, but it apparently does not affect children's general self-esteem. These findings are surprising because numerous studies with adults suggest that friendships and other supportive relationships enhance many aspects of adults' physical and mental health, including their self-esteem (e.g., Uchino, Uno, & Holt-Lunstad, 1999). If future research confirms that friendship quality has only narrow and specific effects in childhood but has broad and general effects in adulthood, the reasons for this difference should be thoroughly explored.

High-quality friendships may also have indirect effects on children's social development. Most theories of social influence include some form of the hypothesis that children are more strongly influenced by their friends' characteristics the higher the quality of those friendships. An alarming corollary of this hypothesis is that good friendships with bad friends (e.g., friends with poor social or psychological adjustment) should have especially negative effects on children's behavior and development. However, recent research provides equivocal support for this hypothesis. Often, the influence of friends' characteristics has varied little with the quality of these friendships.

More extensive tests of this hypothesis are necessary, for both theoretical and practical reasons. If the hypothesis is not supported in future research, most theories of social influence in childhood will need to be reevaluated. By contrast, if future studies do support the hypothesis, interventions to improve children's friendships will need to be carefully designed to ensure that they do not inadvertently magnify the negative influence of poorly adjusted friends. More generally, a fuller understanding of the joint effects of friendship quality and friends' characteristics will be crucial for enhancing the positive contributions of friendships to children's social development.

REFERENCES

Agnew, R. (1991). The interactive effects of peer variables on delinquency. *Criminology, 29,* 47–72.

Berndt, T. J. (1996). Exploring the effects of friendship quality on social development. In W. M. Bukowski, A. F. Newcomb, & W. W. Hartup (Eds.), *The company they keep: Friendship in childhood and adolescence* (pp. 346–365). Cambridge, England: Cambridge University Press.

Berndt, T. J. (1999). Friends' influence on students' adjustment to school. *Educational Psychologist, 34,* 15–28.

Berndt, T. J., Hawkins, J. A., & Jiao, Z. (1999). Influences of friends and friendships on adjustment to junior high school. *Merrill-Palmer Quarterly, 45,* 13–41.

Berndt, T. J., & Keefe, K. (1995). Friends' influence on adolescents' adjustment to school. *Child Development, 66,* 1312–1329.

Collins, W. A., & Laursen, B. (Eds.). (1999). *Relationships as developmental contexts.* Mahwah, NJ: Erlbaum.

Dishion, T. J., Andrews, D. W., & Crosby, L. (1995). Antisocial boys and their friends in early adolescence: Relationship characteristics, quality, and interactional process. *Child Development, 66,* 139–151.

Hartup, W. W. (1999). Constraints on peer socialization: Let me count the ways. *Merrill-Palmer Quarterly, 45,* 172–183.

Hartup, W. W., & Stevens, N. (1999). Friendships and adaptation across the life span. *Current Directions in Psychological Science, 8,* 76–79.

Keefe, K., & Berndt, T. J. (1996). Relations of friendship quality to self-esteem in early adolescence. *Journal of Early Adolescence, 16,* 110–129.

Ladd, G. W., Kochenderfer, B. J., & Coleman, C. C. (1996). Friendship quality as a predictor of young children's early school adjustment. *Child Development, 67,* 1103–1118.

Poulin, F., Dishion, T. J., & Haas, E. (1999). The peer influence paradox: Friendship quality and deviancy training within male adolescent friendships. *Merrill-Palmer Quarterly, 45,* 42–61.

Uchino, B. N., Uno, D., & Holt-Lunstad, J. (1999). Social support, physiological processes, and health. *Current Directions in Psychological Science, 8,* 145–148.

QUESTIONS

1. What is friendship, and what qualities are important to good friendships?
2. What are some of the differences in what children and adolescents hope to gain from their friendships?
3. In general, what benefits are children assumed to reap from high-quality friendships?
4. What changes over the school year did Ladd et al. (1996) find in kindergarten children who had high-quality friendships? What do these results imply about the connection between peer relations and academic success?
5. Why do you think positive friendships are related to self-esteem in adulthood but not in childhood?
6. What does the lack of findings linking friendship and self-esteem in children suggest about how the role of friendship in child development should be studied?
7. What evidence is there to support the view that negative friendships present problems for children?
8. What types of indirect effects of friendship quality have been identified in research? Do these effects surprise you? Why or why not?
9. Do you think having good friendships with bad friends—that is, friends who are poorly adjusted socially or psychologically—may have especially negative effects on children? Why or why not?
10. Do you think a lack of friends in middle childhood puts children at risk for unhealthy development during this period of growth?

30 Cultural Teaching: The Development of Teaching Skills in Maya Sibling Interactions

ASHLEY E. MAYNARD

In the course of development, children acquire skill at all kinds of everyday activities or tasks that are commonplace in their communities. The acquisition of everyday skills, such as preparing food, bathing, and caregiving, is important to development, but little is known about when and how children actually learn these types of skills. Children's play has been cited as one avenue for such learning. During play, children practice many of the behaviors that they see adults perform in their everyday lives. However, until recently, little attention has been paid to whether instruction also contributes to this type of learning. Some research demonstrates that adults, especially parents, teach children everyday skills. Specifically, research on Vygotsky's notion of the zone of proximal development has described how parents help children learn to use eating utensils in the first few years of life and to get ready for school in the morning when they are in the elementary school years.

By emphasizing adult–child instruction, researchers have overlooked another common and valuable source of instruction in young children's lives: older siblings. Because they often spend much time with younger family members and have more advanced skills than younger children, older siblings may be especially helpful to younger children as they learn about and practice the everyday activities and skills that are important in their community. The following article describes a study of older-sibling instruction in a Mayan community in Mexico. Because sibling caretaking is common in this community, researcher Ashley Maynard reasoned that teaching by older siblings may also be a common feature of young children's experience there. Maynard observed the sibling interactions of children between 2 and 8 years of age and coded the interactions that were teaching episodes. She then examined these episodes more closely to determine the nature and extent of older children's instruction to their younger siblings.

Maynard discovered two interesting aspects of sibling teaching behaviors: As children got older, their verbal and nonverbal instructions improved; and with development, the older children's patterns of instruction increasingly resembled those of the adults in this community. These results suggest that both the content and the form of children's teaching reflect the cultural context of development.

Psychology has considered the development of learning, but the development of teaching in childhood has not been considered. The data presented in this article demonstrate that children develop teaching skills over the course of middle childhood. Seventy-two Maya children (25 boys, 47 girls) ranging in age from 3 to 11 years (M = 6.8 years) were videotaped in sibling caretaking interactions with their 2-year-old brothers and sisters (18 boys, 18 girls). In the context of play, older siblings taught their younger siblings how to do everyday tasks such as washing and cooking. Ethnographic observations, discourse analyses, and quantification of discourse findings showed that children's teaching skills increased over the course of middle childhood. By the

Reprinted with permission of Blackwell Publishers from Maynard, A. E. (2002). Cultural teaching: The development of teaching skills in Maya sibling interactions. *Child Development, 73,* 969–982.

The data presented in this article were submitted in partial fulfillment of the requirements for the doctoral degree in psychology at the University of California, Los Angeles. Portions of these data were presented at the annual meeting of the Jean Piaget Society, Mexico City, Mexico, June 1999 ("Cultural Context and Developmental Theory: Evidence from the Maya of Mexico," P. Greenfield, Chair) and at the annual meeting of the American Anthropological Association, Chicago, Illinois, November 1999 ("The Cultural Study of Children's Play," S. Gaskins, Chair).

age of 4 years, children took responsibility for initiating teaching situations with their toddler siblings. By the age of 8 years, children were highly skilled in using talk combined with manual demonstrations, verbal feedback, explanations, and guiding the body of younger learners. Children's developing competence in teaching helped their younger siblings increase their participation in culturally important tasks.

INTRODUCTION

Children learn about their environments with the help of others in the process of socialization. Adults are said to provide a scaffold of help upon which children can accomplish tasks that they would not be able to accomplish on their own (e.g., Rogoff, 1991; Vygotsky, 1978; Wood, Bruner, & Ross, 1976). Cultural learning (Kruger & Tomasello, 1996; Tomasello, Kruger, & Ratner, 1993) requires contexts in which children can engage their new world, but also requires others to act as teachers. Psychologists have considered the development of learning, but the development of teaching (e.g., the development of skill in scaffolding) has not been considered. Although the capacity to teach is basic to the transmission of human culture, few studies have explored the roots of teaching in childhood.

The theory of cultural learning (Tomasello et al., 1993) was postulated to link children's development to their increasing participation in cultural activities. In cultural learning, the focus is on the attainments of children learners that make them able to internalize important aspects of culture, or in other words, to acquire culture. In cultural teaching, the focus is on the examination of the local discourse practices, the social ecology of development, and the material aspects of the environment that make cultural learning possible. The way that cultural teaching develops in children's daily routines was the central focus of the research presented in this article.

Children acquire patterns of thinking and communicating in their interactions with more competent members of their culture, within the zone of proximal development (Rogoff, 1990; Vygotsky, 1978). Through their increasing participation in interactions with more competent others, children appropriate patterns of behavior and thus acquire the means to become competent members of their communities themselves. An important question concerns the ways in which the ability to provide appropriate help to a less experienced member of the culture develops during childhood.

Numerous studies of children's cognitive and social development in the preschool years have indicated dramatic increases in skills that would be important in the developing ability to teach. During the course of development, children experience major gains in intersubjectivity (Gopnik & Meltzoff, 1994; Trevarthen & Logotheti, 1989), linguistic competence (Goodluck, 1991), and cognitive and sociocognitive attainments (Piaget, 1952, 1967; Rogoff, 1990), all skills that can be used by children as they teach others. One of the most sophisticated teaching skills that must develop is the skill of scaffolding (Rogoff, 1990; Rogoff, Mistry, Göncü, & Mosier, 1993). Children must be able to understand what younger children know and don't know to provide the most appropriate kind of help.

Children's peer interactions can be beneficial to their acquisition of these cognitive and social skills (Corsaro, 1985; Goodwin, 1990; Rogoff, 1990; Vygotsky, 1978). Sometimes peers teach each other as they engage in activities, indicating that they do have some early teaching skills. For example, children's work as peer tutors provides a glimpse into children's skills in teaching (Foster-Harrison, 1995; Johnson & Bailey, 1974). Siblings, especially, can be effective peer teachers of their younger siblings because they are related, are often emotionally close, and are close in age (Meisner & Fisher, 1980).

The goal of the present study was to examine the role of older siblings in teaching their younger siblings to become competent members of their culture by guiding them in cultural activities. It was reasoned that sibling interactions in a sibling caretaking society would provide the greatest opportunity to observe sibling guidance. This is because sibling caretaking is a highly valued form of childcare that allows parents to do other work to support the family economically (Zukow-Goldring, 2002), while older siblings teach younger children to do culturally important tasks, such as weaving (Greenfield, Maynard, & Childs, 2000; Zukow-Goldring, personal communication, October 14, 2000). By studying a community that employs sibling caretaking in the social support of children it is possible to examine the development of sibling teaching as it happens, in its natural environment.

The present research was conducted in a community that employs sibling caretaking in the social support of children—the Zinacantec Maya village, Nabenchauk, in the highlands of Chiapas, Mexico. Previous research on weaving apprenticeship among the Zinacantec Maya has given insight into the teaching and learning practices of this group, focusing on an adult model of apprenticeship (Childs & Greenfield, 1980; Greenfield, 1984; Greenfield, Maynard, & Childs, 1999; Greenfield et al., 2000; Maynard, 1996; Maynard, Greenfield, & Childs, 1999). The present research was designed to examine the developmental roots of that adult model and thus chart the course of the development of teaching.

THE ROLE OF SIBLINGS IN CHILD DEVELOPMENT

The role of siblings in early childhood socialization has received much attention over the last 2 decades (e.g., Abramovitch, Corter, & Lando, 1979; Kendrick & Dunn, 1980; Watson-Gegeo & Gegeo, 1989; Weisner, 1987; Weisner & Gallimore, 1977; Zukow, 1989a; Zukow-Goldring, 2002). Developmental research has focused on the role of siblings in children's intellectual development (Zukow, 1989b), and on the role of siblings in children's social and emotional development (Dunn, 1989; Howe & Ross, 1990; Teti & Ablard, 1989; Whiting & Edwards, 1988; Zukow, 1989a).

There are several social effects of the sibling relationship that might influence both the quality and quantity of sibling teaching. Sibling interactions foster children's ability to comfort, share with, and cooperate with each other (Dunn & Munn, 1986). Children with siblings exhibit more prosocial behaviors—such as perspective taking and sharing—earlier and to a greater degree than children without siblings (Dunn, 1992). Being nurtured by older siblings has been found to predict American children's later social perspective taking (Bryant, 1987) and to have a positive effect on children's school behaviors and adjustment (Gallimore, Tharp, & Speidel, 1978; Weisner, Gallimore, & Jordan, 1988). Children who interact with an extended kin network (including multiple siblings) are precocious in their acquisition of false belief compared with those who interact with a more limited kin group (Lewis, Freeman, Kyriakidou, Maridaki-Kassotaki, & Berridge, 1996). Younger siblings imitate older siblings more than they are imitated (Pepler, Abramovitch, & Corter, 1981), and they receive guidance from older brothers or sisters (Zukow, 1989b) rather than the other way around. These social and perspective-taking skills are likely to be reflected in sibling teaching, especially in a sibling-caretaking community such as Zinacantan, where older siblings are given the role as helpers of their younger siblings. It is likely that the help given to younger siblings is instrumental in the older children's teaching of the younger children. Helping behaviors provide a context for teaching to occur.

Sibling caretaking provides children the opportunity to demonstrate that they are competent cultural members by engaging their charges in appropriate activities (Zukow, 1989b; Zukow-Goldring, 2002). Ethnographers working in agrarian societies all over the world have noted the widespread use of sibling caretaking, starting when the sibling caretaker is as young as age 3 (e.g., Gaskins, 1999; Martini, 1994; Watson-Gegeo & Gegeo, 1989; Weisner & Gallimore, 1977; Whiting & Edwards, 1988; Whiting & Whiting, 1975; Zukow, 1989a; Zukow-Goldring, 2002). In their pioneering study of children in six cultures, Whiting and colleagues (Whiting & Edwards, 1988; Whiting & Whiting, 1975) quantified sibling behaviors and made general descriptions of the roles that siblings in various cultures play while caring for a younger child.

Sibling caretakers do more than address the biological needs of their charges (Zukow-Goldring, 2002). For example, in a study in Central Mexico, Zukow (1989a) described examples of older siblings engaging their younger charges in more advanced play than that which the younger ones had been previously engaged in on their own. In the Marquesas, Martini (1994) found that sibling caretakers socialize each other to become competent at managing stratified social roles, respecting the complex social hierarchy of Marquesan culture. Sibling caretakers introduce younger siblings to new languages, language routines, and appropriate ways to behave (Ochs, 1988; Watson-Gegeo & Gegeo, 1989; Zukow-Goldring, 2002). Thus, siblings have been found to teach each other in very useful ways. In Hawaii and in a Navajo group, children's teaching experiences as sibling caretakers have been translated into improved learning environments in schools (Gallimore et al., 1978; Tharp, 1994; Weisner et al., 1988).

The present study is the first known to describe and examine the development of teaching over a cross-section of ages from 3 to 11 years. A meta-analysis of the literature indicates that most studies have focused at a particular age, chosen for each study. For example, Stewart (1983) studied 8-year-olds who were teaching 6-year-olds to use a toy camera. A few studies compared adult teaching with sibling teaching, when the teacher-siblings were age 6 and the learner-siblings were age 4 (Perez-Granados & Callanan, 1997); and when the teacher-siblings were age 9 and the learner-siblings were age 6 (Cicirelli, 1976). The siblings in Perez-Granados and Callanan's study more often just did the task for their younger sibling, rather than acting as a guide for the sibling to help the sibling accomplish the task by him- or herself. This may be because the sibling role in the U.S. majority culture does not include the sibling as a guide or teacher for the younger one.

In studies in which the focus was on the development of peer teaching or collaboration and not sibling teaching per se, the researchers only tested children in a limited age range: 24 to 42 months (Ashley & Tomasello, 1998); infant toddler peers, 12 to 30 months (Brownell & Carriger, 1991); or 9-year-old children (Ellis & Rogoff, 1982). One study compared siblings and peers as agents of cognitive development by watching the collaborative activities of 9-year-olds with 7-year-olds (Azmitia & Hesser, 1993).

None of this previous work looked at the moment-by-moment socialization practices of siblings, tracing the developmental progression of sibling socialization across a range of ages. In addition, no study has described how siblings at various developmental stages organize events and guide one another in the joint co-construction of activities. The current study was designed to fill this gap by showing how older siblings develop the skills to participate in an apprenticeship process or socialization of younger children.

THE STUDY SITE: NABENCHAUK, ZINACANTÁN

There is a long tradition in the study of apprenticeship in Nabenchauk. For example, Greenfield and Childs (Childs & Greenfield, 1980; Greenfield, 1984) first analyzed the processes of Zinacantec teaching and learning in the domain of weaving. Childs and Greenfield (1980) demonstrated the particular verbal and nonverbal variables that were important as adults taught girls to weave, focusing on commands, explanations, questions, declaratives, and positive and negative reinforcement. Of particular interest is that the command form was the most used discourse form; teachers expected obedience from their pupils. There was little verbal explanation and almost no extrinsic verbal reinforcement, such as praise or criticism. Childs and Greenfield also discussed the highly scaffolded nature of Zinacantec weaving apprenticeship, whereby a teacher helps a learner accomplish a task by providing help that is sensitive to the learner's stage of acquisition.

The Zinacantec model of teaching and learning (Maynard, 1996) is based on the work of Childs and Greenfield (1980) as well as my own ethnographic fieldwork in Nabenchauk. The model includes such features as the expectation of obedience, scaffolded help, observational learning, contextualized talk, teacher and learner bodily closeness, and having more than one teacher for a given task; and reflects an overall pattern of apprenticeship that centers around helping younger members of the culture become more competent participants in cultural activities. This study was designed to chart the development of this cultural model in childhood.

It was hypothesized that children would approach the adult Zinacantec model of teaching (Maynard, 1996) as they matured. Just as the model is acquired and used in the apprenticeship of weaving skills, the current study examined its use in socialization practices. A further goal was to chart its acquisition and use by developing children. Older children's teaching was expected to approach the teaching of adults, with a greater expectation of obedience (demonstrated by the issuance of commands), more scaffolded help, and bodily closeness.

Children's use of effective discursive teaching acts, involving intersubjectivity, linguistic compe-

tence, and cognitive and sociocognitive attainments, was hypothesized to increase with age. For example, children were expected to use more appropriate verbal discourse as they developed stronger communication skills. As another example, children's abilities to simplify a task for another child were expected to increase over middle childhood as they gained a greater ability to take the perspective of another.

In this study, children's interactions were analyzed by discourse analyses, to get a picture of their cognitive and sociocognitive attainments as they were revealed in their social practices (Goodwin & Goodwin, 1992; Wootton, 1997). Discourse analysis involves the microanalytic examination of communication processes in context, which includes settings, tools, and participants. Many researchers in child development have used discourse analysis to explore aspects of development; for example, language development (Ochs, 1988; Wootton, 1997), processes of social interaction in childhood (Goodwin, 1990), language socialization (Ochs & Schieffelin, 1984), and sibling socialization (Zukow, 1986, 1989a; Zukow-Goldring, 1997). A picture of the development of communicative practices over the range of ages in this study was produced by careful analyses, both quantitative and qualitative, of the children's discourse strategies. Quantitative analyses of discourse processes were used to chart the development of the children's verbal and nonverbal teaching abilities. Qualitative examples richly illustrate the quantitative findings, showing how each of the discourse variables is used by children in the different age groups.

METHOD

PARTICIPANTS

Participants were members of 36 Zinacantec households in the hamlet of Nabenchauk, Zinacantán (population approximately 4,500). Each household had an average of five children. The availability of siblings increased the likelihood of observing teaching. Participants were 108 Zinacantec Maya children ranging in age from 20 months to 11 years. Of these, 36 (18 girls and 18 boys) were aged 20 to 36 months ($M = 24$ months); hereafter these are referred to as the focal children. There was just 1 focal child per household. An additional 72 children (25 boys and 47 girls) were siblings who interacted with these focal children. They ranged in age from 3 to 11 years ($M = 6.8$ years). A few cousins and one 6-year-old aunt who interacted with the focal children were included because they were often the child's primary sibling caretaker, sharing the household or the extended-family compound. All the older siblings, first cousins, and the young aunt are hereafter referred to as the "siblings" or "teachers" to simplify description. The teaching behavior of these older children with respect to the focal children was the focus of the present study.

The 72 siblings of the focal children came from a total pool of 93 siblings (age: $M = 8.3$ years) in the required age range who might have interacted with the focal children. The total pool of siblings was derived from the genealogical information collected in family interviews. There were fewer boys than girls in the sample for two reasons. First, Zinacantec boys are not primary sibling caregivers when girls are available, so several boys who were present did not interact with the focal children during the study procedures. Second, some boys were not present because they were away at school or away selling peaches at a market. Fewer girls in the sample went to school or away on selling trips without their nuclear family groups; therefore girls were more likely to be available as sibling caretakers.

PROCEDURE

Participants were recruited on a volunteer basis with the help of an indigenous field assistant who went to the homes of families with 2-year-olds and asked if they would be interested in talking about their possible participation in the study. Recruitment was aided by word-of-mouth discussion of the study in the village.

Participants were observed one time with a video camera in their own homes or courtyards for a period of 1 hr. During videotaping, most mothers carried out their usual domestic routine. Some mothers stayed close by the children and watched the interactions. Mothers were always within earshot of the children, often inside the house while the children were outside.

To reduce the intrusive effect of the observer and the camera, the observer paid at least one visit to the home before conducting the videotaped observation, and did not begin the recording session until at least 10 min after arrival. In the first visit to the home of each family, participants were shown the video camera and how it worked. The observer told the families that the main interest was in watching what the children did during the day. Mothers were interviewed about the ages and schooling experience of each person in the household.

Each family was paid 25 pesos (about U.S. $3.25 at the time of the study) for their participation. In addition, the observer took photographs of family members to give to them as part of payment. Paying the participants may have affected the children's activities: their frequency of play may have increased because the families knew that the children were being watched, and play was a readily available activity for children to do. Even if this was the case, it would not have an effect on the developmental comparisons

that are the focus of this article. Moreover, it is not believed that the content of play changed as a result of the observer's presence or payment to participants. Mothers reported similar play at times outside of the observation session, and many of the same children were seen playing similar activities in their homes and around the village on days other than those during which they were observed.

DATA ANALYSIS

Video data were analyzed using the vPrism software system, which was designed specifically for video analysis of behavior (Stigler, 1988). The first step in the analysis was to extract the teaching episodes from the longer tapes. Teaching was defined as any activity attended to by the younger child that had the possible effect of transmitting cultural knowledge. To track the developmental change in teaching skills, the definition of teaching encompassed both intentional and unintentional teaching. Thus, the younger child had to be paying attention to the activity of the older child, but the older child did not have to engage the younger child explicitly for the segment to be considered a teaching segment. The teaching segments were operationally defined in two ways: (1) any task that an older sibling drew the younger child's attention to, either verbally or nonverbally; or (2) any activity that older children were performing next to or "side-by-side" with the 2-year-old, such that the 2-year-old might learn something about the activity from observation of the older child and from practicing next to the older child and using the older child as a model. Data meeting the second criterion were included to obtain a baseline measure of what kinds of teaching skills the youngest teachers exhibited or did not exhibit. For example, many of the 3- to 5-year-olds engaged in side-by-side activity with their younger siblings. They set out tasks for their younger siblings but, in many cases, did not engage them further, either verbally or nonverbally; the children just performed the activities side-by-side. Older children, however, engaged the younger children, both verbally and nonverbally, carefully guiding them in the tasks.

The teaching session was deemed to have begun when the teacher first tried to get the attention of the focal child to engage him or her in a task or when the older child (teacher) began the task next to the focal 2-year-old, who was paying attention to the older child. Thus, the beginnings of episodes were marked by either verbal or nonverbal actions. The endings of teaching episodes were marked when the focal child left the scene of the teaching episode, when the older sibling (teacher) left the scene of the episode without returning, or when any child shifted tasks, thus beginning a new episode with a different activity.

Almost all interactions between older siblings and 2-year-olds were considered teaching episodes, including episodes that an observer might label "play." The teaching episodes analyzed in this study fit into a larger category of multiage play. The teaching episodes were thus one subclass of the larger category of play.

Play became synonymous with sibling teaching in this study because there was so much teaching in the multiage play. Older children always took on the responsibility of showing the younger child how to do a particular task so that the younger child could participate in the play situation. Therefore, a more precise term for these interactions was "teaching," even though the episodes were still a part of the larger category of play. Some interactions between older siblings and 2-year-olds were not considered teaching; for example, when the older child provided care that did not involve any teaching (e.g., carrying a toddler to the mother to nurse or helping the younger child with toileting). There were also other types of play that did not involve teaching; for example, children age 4 and older played games and engaged in activities (soccer, "curing ceremony," throwing rocks, and so forth) that did not involve 2-year-olds, who were not able to participate without help, due to their limited skills and abilities. Thus, only play with 2-year-olds was included in this study, and that play usually involved older siblings teaching younger ones to do everyday things.

There were 158 teaching episodes in the 36 hr of tape, which produced a total of 12 hr, 8 min, 15 s of teaching episodes that were included in the analyses. Teaching episodes ranged in length from 11.9 s to 32 min, 9 s, with a mean length of 10 min, 7 s. The teaching episodes were transcribed and coded for measures of the development of teaching skills. Children taught everyday tasks such as washing, cooking, taking care of baby dolls, and making tortillas. All teaching episodes involved objects, ranging from dirt and leaves to household items such as tortilla presses and articles of clothing to items purchased specifically for children such as dolls and toy trucks.

MEASURES: VARIABLES USED IN QUANTITATIVE DISCOURSE ANALYSIS

Children's discourse was measured by verbal and nonverbal variables. Several of these variables were used by Childs and Greenfield (1980) in their study of weaving apprenticeship in Zinacantán. The variables also reflected features of the Zinacantec model of teaching and learning. The mutually exclusive and exhaustive codes for the variables are listed (with examples) in Table 1. Each variable reflected some aspect of cognitive development, such as the ability to take the

perspective of the younger child to provide the correct guidance in the task. The verbal discourse variables were commands, explanations and descriptions, feedback on the child's performance, and praise or criticism. The nonverbal discourse variables were simplifying the task nonverbally, and guiding the child's body in the desired task. One variable—talk with demonstration—involved the coordination of both verbal and nonverbal information. Teacher initiation of an episode could be either verbal or nonverbal.

Commands   Commands are an important part of teaching. It was expected that teachers would tell the focal children to perform a task by giving a command. Previous research has found that older siblings produce more directives than do younger siblings when they play together (Tomasello & Mannle, 1985). Moreover, commands are culturally normative in Zinacantec child socialization (Blanco & Chodorow, 1964; Childs & Greenfield, 1980); older siblings may issue commands to younger siblings in their charge. Thus, it was hypothesized that older sibling teachers in this study would give commands to their younger siblings when they taught them to do things. Commands indicate that the older child knows that the other can understand language and assumes that the 2-year-old focal child can follow through on the order and that he knows what the command means.

Talk with demonstration   This variable, which has been used in other studies of children's interactions (e.g., Zukow, 1989b), was identified when teachers demonstrated what they wanted the focal children to do (physically) and simultaneously said something relevant to the action. Talk with demonstration was coded separately from nonverbal task simplification.

Explanations and descriptions   Explanations and descriptions were indicated by teachers' statements of the reason they were doing a particular activity, of the way an activity should be done, or of the outcome or final state of the activity being taught. Childs and Greenfield (1980) found that explanations and descriptions (which they called statements) were rather infrequent in Zinacantec weaving apprenticeship. Explanations and descriptions were included together in one category because they are both kinds of talk about the task being taught. As part of a category of metatalk about activities, explanations and descriptions were hypothesized to develop together.

Feedback   Feedback was indicated by teachers' positive or negative comments that guided focal children's behavior. Feedback included comments such as, "Like that" or "Not like that." Such comments were usually followed by talk with demonstration. Utterances considered as feedback in this study were coded by Childs and Greenfield (1980) as vague positive and negative commands. Feedback was coded separately in the present study because it did not always involve an explicit command for action.

TABLE 1   DISCOURSE MEASURES OF CHILDREN'S TEACHING SKILLS

Measure	Examples
Verbal	
Commands (without a demonstration)	"Wash!" "Put it in there!"
Explanations/ descriptions	"Hold the baby because it has a fever." "We are finished washing!"
Feedback on the child's performance	"Yes, like that!" "No, not like that!"
Praise and criticism	"Dummy!" "[That's] bad!"
Nonverbal	
Task simplification	Child pours water from a large container into a smaller container that is easily held by focal child. When teaching how to make tortillas, child tears leaves off a branch and gives the leaves one at a time to focal child, rather than handing the child the whole branch.
Touching/guiding the child's body	Guiding child's hand in a washing motion. Folding child's legs under her to get her to kneel.
Verbal and nonverbal	
Talk with a demonstration	"Pat [the tortilla] like this" [as teacher pats out a tortilla]. "I'm washing!" [as teacher washes a rag].
Verbal and/or nonverbal	
Teacher initiation of episode	The age and gender of the child who initiated the episode are coded.

Praise and criticism   Separate from feedback, praise and criticism are verbal measures of explicit evaluations, for example, "Good" or "Bad." Childs and Greenfield (1980) had found that there was virtually no praise or criticism in Zinacantec weaving apprenticeship. Likewise, it was expected that there would be little or no overt praise or criticism in the sibling teaching interactions.

Simplifying the task nonverbally for the learner This variable was indicated when teachers broke down a task into simpler parts, for instance, when they managed the teaching situation by presenting simpler parts of a task first.

Guiding the body   This variable indicated the instances when teachers touched the bodies of the focal children to guide them in performing a specific activity. Zukow-Goldring and Ferko (1994) used this variable in their study of the socialization of attention.

Teacher initiation   Teacher initiation was another way of looking at the role of age in teaching. There is a pervasive Zinacantec cultural norm of respect for el-

ders (Vogt, 1969, 1990) that would lead younger children to defer to older children to initiate episodes of play. This measure was also a test of the development of respect for elders; if younger children defer to older children to initiate play episodes, it may indicate respect for their authority.

For the quantitative analysis, frequency counts were taken of each of the measures and then divided by the number of minutes each teacher was involved in a teaching activity to control for overall time spent teaching the younger child.

RELIABILITY

The principal investigator (A.E.M.) coded both the quantitative and qualitative data. An independent coder, fluent in the Tzotzil language and unaware of the hypotheses, coded 25% ($N = 9$) of the videotapes. Interrater agreement for the number of episodes, assessed by percentage agreement, was 95.2% (40 out of 42). There was one disagreement in which the principal investigator indicated two separate shorter episodes and the independent coder indicated only one long episode. The second disagreement was when the principal investigator thought there was an episode of teaching when the independent coder did not.

Interrater agreement for the duration of episodes was assessed by examining the two raters' beginning and end points of every episode in which there was agreement that there was an episode, and comparing the number of seconds of disagreement. For the beginning points of episodes, the disagreements ranged from .66 s to 29 s, with a mean of 10.7 s. For the end points of episodes, the disagreements ranged from 1 to 30 s, with a mean of 11.8 s.

Interrater agreement for the discourse measures was assessed by Cohen's κ. For all the discourse measures taken together, κ = .80 (percentage agreement was 84.6% for all the discourse variables in Table 1 excluding praise/criticism, which occurred too infrequently in the reliability observations for assessment). This κ value was considered to be indicative of excellent reliability (Bakeman & Gottman, 1986).

RESULTS

QUANTITATIVE ANALYSES

For purposes of statistical analysis, the codes for the discourse variables were divided by each teacher's time spent in teaching. There were no differences across the age groups in time spent in teaching, $F(2, 69) = 1.93$, $p = .153$. This nonsignificant difference reflects two features of sibling caretaking in Nabenchauk: its beginning at age 3 or 4 and its importance and prevalence until approximately age 10. The nonsignificant differences in time spent in teaching also made the analysis and interpretation of the discourse variables easy and straightforward: because there were no differences in time spent in teaching—the denominator of all discourse measures of the study—the discussion of the results is focused on the dependent measures in question.

There were natural breaks in the means for most of the variables between ages 5 and 6, and between ages 7 and 8. Therefore, participants were divided into three groups: 3- to 5-year-olds ($n = 19$; $M = 4.26$ years), 6- to 7-year-olds ($n = 20$; $M = 6.25$ years), and 8- to 11-year-olds ($n = 33$; $M = 8.61$ years).

Talk with demonstration, commands, explanations, feedback, guiding the learner's body, and teacher initiation were included in a MANOVA with the factors of age and gender. There were no effects of gender. With the use of the Wilks' criterion, the combined dependent variables were significantly related to the factor of age, $F(12, 108) = 3.40$, $p = .001$. Univariate F tests for each of the six discourse vari-

ables indicated four individually significant effects. There was a significant relation between the factor of age and teacher talk with demonstration, $F(2, 60) = 5.37$, $p < .01$, explanations, $F(2, 60) = 9.22$, $p < .001$, feedback, $F(2, 60) = 6.34$, $p < .01$, and teacher initiation, $F(2, 60) = 3.4$, $p < .05$. The developmental progression from the youngest age group to the oldest age group can be seen in the marked differences between the age groups (Figure 1).

The significant results from the MANOVA were further analyzed by Bonferroni t tests to find specific intergroup differences. For talk with demonstration there was a significant difference between the youngest age group, the 3- to 5-year-olds ($M = .238$), and the oldest age group, the 8- to 11-year-olds ($M = 1.32$), $t(50) = 3.26$, $p < .001$. The two older age groups, 6 to 7 ($M = .526$) and 8 to 11 ($M = 1.32$) were also significantly different from each other, $t(51) = 2.63$, $p < .01$. Middle children ($M = .526$) did not differ significantly from youngest children ($M = .238$), $t(37) = 1.19$, $p = .24$.

There were also significant relations between age and explanations. The oldest age group ($M = .691$) gave explanations or descriptions significantly more than did the middle age group ($M = .171$), $t(51) = 3.00$, $p < .005$, or the youngest age group ($M = 0$), $t(50) = 4.11$, $p < .001$. The middle age group ($M = .171$) also gave explanations significantly more than did the youngest age group ($M = 0$), $t(37) = 2.29$, $p < .05$.

Oldest children ($M = .636$) gave significantly more feedback than did middle children ($M = .092$), $t(51) = 2.81$, $p < .01$, and youngest children ($M = .024$), $t(50) = 3.10$, $p < .005$. Middle children ($M = .092$) gave the same amount of feedback as youngest children ($M = .024$), $t(37) = 1.68$, $p = .10$.

Praise and criticism were evaluative comments coded separately from positive and negative feedback. There was no overt praise in the entire database. There were only two instances of criticism. In one, a 6-year-old girl said, "*Chopol* [That's bad]" in response to her 2-year-old sister's attempt at making a tortilla with leaves. The older child thought the focal child was tearing off the wrong leaves to use for the tortillas. In the other instance of criticism, a 9-year-old girl said, "*Chich* [Dummy]" to the focal child when she did not do a cooking activity properly.

Oldest children ($M = 2.61$) and middle children ($M = 2.60$) initiated significantly more teaching episodes than did youngest children ($M = 1.05$), $t(50) = 2.63$, $p < .01$, and $t(37) = 2.40$, $p < .05$, respectively. Oldest children ($M = 2.61$) and middle children ($M = 2.60$) did not differ significantly from each other, $t(51) = .01$, $p = .993$.

Nonverbal task simplification increased as a function of age, $F(2, 69) = 4.353$, $p < .05$. None of the 3- to 5-year-olds used task simplification in their teaching,

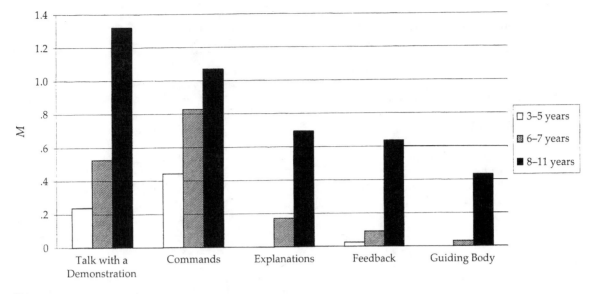

FIGURE 1
Mean use of discourse variables by age group, controlled for time teaching.

whereas 2 (10%) of the 6- to 7-year-olds and 15 (45.5%) of the 8- to 11-year-olds used task simplification to help learners with the tasks.

QUALITATIVE ANALYSES OF THE DISCOURSE VARIABLES BY AGE GROUP: THREE EXAMPLES

As previously discussed, there were significant relations between age group and four of the discourse variables. This section presents examples of teaching episodes with 1 child from each of the three age groups: 8- to 11-, 6- to 7-, and 3- to 5-year-olds. A more complete corpus is found in Maynard (1999). The episodes are matched closely for duration (approximately 2 min each). Each example is of a child teaching a 2-year-old how to wash a baby doll. Each pair of children is from a different nuclear family. In the following transcripts the Tzotzil transcription is presented first, followed by the English gloss. Nonverbal information is also indicated in double parentheses. Tzotzil orthographic conventions and transcription conventions are listed in the Appendix.

Example 1: Age 8 In the first example, 8-year-old Tonik teaches 2-year-old Katal how to wash a baby doll using task simplification, talk with demonstration, and commands.

Tonik: ((Laughs. Brings over a glass of water, to wash the baby doll.))
Taso. Taso.
Take it out. Take it out (of the water).

Xivi.
Like this. ((Katal watches.))

Tonik/Katal: ((Four hands on the glass, in position to pour, but they don't pour together at this time.))
T: Cakel=vi.
You watch=look.
K: ((Watches.))
T: Xitovi. ((Pouring the water herself, Katal watches.)) Like this.
[*K'embo xivi.*
[Pour like this. ((Pouring, laughs.))
T/K: ((Four hands are on the glass.))
T: ((Moves doll into position that is easier for Katal to pour accurately.))
T/K: [((They pour together.))
T: [K'embo'un!
Pour it now!
Caklie.
Like that.
Ihtaso'un.
I took it out.
Cataso'un.
You take it out.
K: e, ee ((Baby-talk sounds; requests more water by reaching for glass.))
T: Cakan to.
You want some more.
((Goes to get more water and comes back.))
Va'i un.
Understand!

Va'i.
Understand. ((Hands Katal the water, still supporting the glass.))

T/K: ((Three hands on glass, two are Tonik's. Water pours out toward the back of the frame.))

T: *Vi'i!*
Look! ((Laughs at the error of water pouring the wrong way.))
Pulo vo'ota, Xunka'.
You draw some water, Xunka'. ((Spoken to other sister who is present.))
Tas caklie. Atintaso.
Take it out like that. Take it out and wash it.

K: ((Washes baby with washing motion of hand.))

T: [*Caklie.*
[Like that.

K: (Reaches for glass.)

T: *Lah xa.* ((Pours from the empty glass, showing that glass is empty.))
It's finished already.
Vi.
Look.

K: ((Washes baby doll with washing motion.))

T: *Ani' un.*
Hurry up! ((To other sister who is drawing water.))
Akbo xa=casutotal anil!
Put the water in already=come back fast! ((Spoken to other sister.))
((Hands Katal an empty glass while they wait.))

T: *Keltik un. Keltik. Xitovi=Xitovi=Xitovi. Taso, caklie.*
Let's watch! Let's watch. Like this=Like this=Like this. Take it out like this.

Xunka': (Comes back with water in a bottle; hands glass to Tonik.)

T: ((Pours water from the bottle into the glass that they have been using to wash.))
((Hands glass to Katal.))
K'embo Xitovi ((Taking glass from Katal.))
Pour like this.
Xitovi. ((Repositions doll to make it easier for herself.))
Like this.
Xitovi. Xitovi.
Like this. Like this. ((Pours water over the doll's head, rubbing doll's head in a washing motion.))
Atintaso.
Take it out and wash it.
((Hands glass and doll to Katal for Katal to do it.))
Xitovi. K'embo.
Like this. Pour it. ((Repositions the doll to make it easier for Katal.))
K'embo xitovi
Pour it like this. ((Pours water on.))

((Hands glass to Katal.))
C'in, K'embo.
Sister, pour it.
Vi un. K'embo.
Look! Pour it.
Caklie. K'embo sciuk sku'.
Like that. Pour it on its blouse also. ((The baby doll is wearing a blouse.))

K: [((Pours water over the baby, with some difficulty.))

T: [*Caklie.*
Like that.
((Puts another bottle in front of Katal, who is looking away.))
Lah xa li'e vi.
It's finished now, look. ((Deciding the doll is clean, she picks it up.))

In this example, Tonik provided a scaffold of help for the focal child by pouring water for her when she noticed that she was having trouble. She narrated much of what she did, showing and telling Katal what to do. Tonik gave commands that guided Katal in each step of the washing. She also provided descriptive elaborations of actions. She said, "Pour it on its blouse also," pointing out that the doll was wearing a blouse, and expanding the washing to include the blouse. Tonik was sensitive to Katal's actions. When Katal picked up the empty glass, Tonik responded by getting her some more water or having another sister draw some water. Tonik also gave Katal some feedback in this example. There were several instances when she affirmed Katal's actions by saying, "Like that."

Example 2: Age 7   In the next example, Xun, age 7, uses talk with demonstration and commands to teach Teresa, age 2, to wash a baby doll.

Xun: *Teresa—*
Teresa ((Holds the baby out to her; they are both touching it.))
Pok'etik nene.
Let's wash baby! ((As he washes the baby himself.))
Vi. Vi. . . . la jole.
Look. Look . . . the head. ((As he pats the head.))
Vi. La pok'etik li yoke. Pok'etik.
Look. We are washing its foot. Let's wash.
((Puts the doll in the bowl of water.))
[((He pats the doll's head, playing with the hair.))

Teresa: [((Watches.))
((Teresa loses interest, moves away from Xun.))

Like 8-year-old Tonik, Xun used talk with demonstration in his teaching: he pointed out parts of the doll he was washing. One major difference between his teaching and that of Tonik was that he did not get Teresa to wash the baby doll herself, whereas Tonik was able to get Katal to do the washing by herself, in carefully simplified parts.

Example 3: Age 4   In the next example, Petu', age 4, teaches Elena, age 2, how to wash a baby doll. She gives one verbal command to Elena, but does not use any of the other discourse skills used by the older children.

Petu': *Pok'o la nene!*
    Wash the baby!
    ((Puts soap and water on the baby doll.))
    [((Washes the baby doll's stomach and back.))
Elena: [((Washes a rag, continues to look at what
    Petu' is doing.))
  P: ((Continues to wash the baby doll.))
  E: *Tutu.* ((Baby-talk name for Petu', who does not
    respond.))
    Tutu.
  P: ((Continues to wash the baby doll.))
  E: ((Wanders off.))

This is an example of the developmental beginning point of teaching. Petu' gave a command to Elena to wash the baby doll, but did not narrate her washing behavior for Elena. She washed the baby doll and allowed Elena to help a little. The episode was short, a little over 1 min, and the teaching was characterized solely by nonverbal demonstration of the activity.

DISCUSSION

There was an overall developmental trend in the use of important discourse skills required for teaching, with children developing toward the Zinacantec model of teaching and learning (Maynard, 1996). As predicted by the study of adult apprenticeship of weaving (Childs & Greenfield, 1980), the children in the present study developed a pattern of teaching that stressed scaffolded help, contextualized verbal explanations and feedback, and obedience, with virtually no praise or criticism. By the age of 8 years, the children in this study used skills that involved an understanding of the other child's perspective, such as simplifying the tasks for the learners. Children also provided necessary and useful information to the young learners, such as appropriate feedback and narrated demonstrations.

The observable characteristics of the children's teaching changed over the three age groups. The 3- to 5-year-olds gave the least amount of verbal instruction. Their teaching behavior was mostly nonverbal: They did the task and let their siblings join in right next to them. They sometimes looked to their charges to see what they were doing, but they did not give explicit instruction as to how to do a task or any particular part of a task. The 3- to 5-year-olds were "side-by-side co-operators"; they usually cooperated with their toddler siblings, but they didn't collaborate or explicitly teach in the way one usually thinks of teaching. Their actions represented the developmental beginning point of teaching.

The 6- to 7-year-olds gave significantly more commands than did the 3- to 5-year-olds. The 6- to 7-year-olds were the "unequal collaborators" or "orchestrators of events"; they were unequal in that they worked with the child to make something happen, but gave a lot of commands and did the task themselves if the 2-year-olds didn't do enough.

The 8- to 11-year-olds demonstrated the skills of adult scaffolding. Their use of commands declined as their use of talk with demonstration increased sharply (Figure 1). They increased their use of evaluations and explanations, and used the body in teaching at helpful moments. They were, by the age of 8 years, already the "guides of development" talked about in so many studies. They were also "administrators of action," coordinating the actions of the younger siblings around them to do a play task. Perhaps the nature of Zinacantec relationships, with a pervasive emphasis on obedience from younger to older people (Vogt, 1969), helps children develop skills of social coordination.

Ethnographic studies of children's relationships in cultures in which sibling caretaking is an important part of childrearing have not examined how it is that children teach each other to do everyday things (e.g., Lancy, 1996; Weisner & Gallimore, 1977; Whiting & Edwards, 1988; Zukow, 1989a, 1989b). The literature widely reports that children are not taught (didactically and with language) to do everyday things. Researchers have suggested that everyday skills develop through participation in joint activities (Lave & Wenger, 1991). For example, Lancy (1996, p. 144) wrote of the Kpelle in Liberia, "No one teaches a girl to wield a hoe." One might have similarly believed that no one teaches a child to make tortillas or to wash in Nabenchauk. The data presented in this study showed that there is some teaching of everyday activities, at least in Nabenchauk. Although it is true that Zinacantec parents do not teach their children to do everyday tasks, didactically and with language, Zinacantec siblings clearly do. Perhaps there are children in other cultures who teach each other to do everyday things. More exceptions may be uncovered by further study, thus changing the prevailing view of the way that children learn everyday tasks.

The present study on children's interactions leads to many more questions about the development of their ability to teach. First, examining children's teaching in its everyday context (without informing the children that their teaching was the focus of the study) might not have pushed the children to be the best teachers they could be. Perhaps a future study could explore children's teaching first in its everyday context and then with an experimental protocol designed to reflect or be compatible with the children's daily routines, to see the children's potential.

Second, the strong sibling relationships may have privileged the teaching interactions reported here. Indeed, Azmitia and Hesser (1993) reported that young children in a collaborative task asked more questions of siblings than of a peer who was the same age as their sibling. The closeness of the relationships in this study may have had an impact on the quality of the teaching. It would be worthwhile to examine children's teaching with both related and unrelated younger children to begin to further our understanding of the impact of the very special sibling caretaking relationship.

Third, this study focused on the teaching behaviors of the older siblings without systematically analyzing the learning behaviors of the younger children. Although the younger children participated in the activities with their older siblings, their behavior was not analyzed by quantitative discourse analysis. It would be important in a future study to obtain an understanding of the teachers' effectiveness by analyzing more closely the participation of the younger children.

CONCLUSION

Related to the development of children's teaching are processes of cultural transmission and child socialization. This study of cultural teaching has informed our knowledge of the transmission of culture. In Nabenchauk, everyday tasks are learned through more than mere "legitimate peripheral participation" (Lave & Wenger, 1991). The present study validated children's contributions to each other's everyday routines in a specific way: by showing the verbal and nonverbal tools that children use to help each other participate in their culture and the developmental trend of these skills. Children create culture at the same time that they are acquiring culture. As they are being socialized by their parents, they are also socializing, in their own way, their younger siblings.

The children in this study developed discourse abilities that they then used to teach their toddler siblings how to do everyday things. These children were learning skills that they will likely perform in adolescence and adulthood, including not only the skills involved in the tasks themselves, but also the skill of guiding learners in everyday tasks. There were aspects of the children's teaching that were clearly re-

lated to their upbringing in Zinacantán, such as the lack of praise and criticism in their teaching. Other factors, such as providing talk with demonstration or simplifying a task for a young learner may be more basic to cultural transmission, and therefore more universal. Future studies of children's teaching in other cultures will inform our knowledge of the social and cognitive skills that children acquire over the course of middle childhood.

APPENDIX:
TZOTZIL ORTHOGRAPHIC CONVENTIONS

All the Tzotzil vowels are included. The reader should note that each Tzotzil vowel is articulated as a separate sound. Only the consonants that do not have the same orthography in English are included in this list. Other consonants (as they are written in this document) sound almost the same in Tzotzil and English and are, therefore, not included.

Vowels

Transcribed phoneme	Example of sound in an English word
a	st*o*p
e	*e*gg
i	sp*ee*d
o	c*o*mb
u	sm*oo*th

Consonants

Transcribed phoneme	Example of sound in an English word
´	Glottal stop; no such consonant in English
x	*sh*op
j	*h*eat
c	*ch*alk

Transcription conventions

For readability, if the same child has the next turn, the name is not repeated next to the turn.

Convention	Meaning
=	Speech that is produced in one stream of air; fast speech
(( ))	Nonverbal behaviors
[	A point of overlap onset between
[	two speakers

REFERENCES

Abramovitch, R., Corter, C., & Lando, B. (1979). Sibling interaction in the home. *Child Development, 51,* 1268–1271.

Ashley J., & Tomasello, M. (1998). Cooperative problem-solving and teaching in preschoolers. *Social Development, 2,* 143–163.

Azmitia, M., & Hesser, J. (1993). Why siblings are important agents of cognitive development: A comparison of siblings and peers. *Child Development, 64,* 430–444.

Bakeman, R., & Gottman, J. M. (1986). *Observing interaction: An introduction to sequential analysis.* New York: Cambridge University Press.

Blanco, M. H., & Chodorow, N.J. (1964). Children's work and obedience in Zinacantán. Manuscript on file, Harvard Chiapas Project, Department of Anthropology, Harvard University, Cambridge, MA.

Brownell, C. A., & Carriger, M. S. (1991). Collaborations among toddler peers: Individual contributions to social contexts. In L. B. Resnick, J. M. Levine, & S. D. Teasley (Eds.), *Perspectives on socially shared cognition* (pp. 365–393). Washington, DC: American Psychological Association.

Bryant, B. (1987). Mental health, temperament, family, and friends: Perspectives on children's empathy and social perspective taking. In N. Eisenberg & J. Strayer (Eds.), *Empathy and its development* (pp. 245–270). New York: Cambridge University Press.

Childs, C. P., & Greenfield, P. M. (1980). Informal modes of learning and teaching: The case of Zinacanteco weaving. In N. Warren (Ed.), *Studies in cross-cultural psychology* (Vol. 2, pp. 269–316). London: Academic Press.

Cicirelli, V. (1976). Mother-child and sibling-siblings interactions on a problem-solving task. *Child Development, 47,* 588–596.

Corsaro, W. A. (1985). *Friendship and peer culture in the early years.* Norwood, NJ: Ablex.

Dunn, J. (1989). Siblings and the development of social understanding in early childhood. In P. G. Zukow (Ed.), *Sibling interaction across cultures. Theoretical and methodological issues* (pp. 106–116). New York: Springer-Verlag.

Dunn, J. (1992). Sisters and brothers: Current issues in developmental research. In F. Boer & J. Dunn (Eds.), *Children's sibling relationships: Developmental and clinical issues* (pp. 1–17). Hillsdale, NJ: Erlbaum.

Dunn, J., & Munn, P. (1986). Siblings and the development of prosocial behaviour. *International Journal of Behavioral Development, 9,* 265–284.

Ellis, S., & Rogoff, B. (1982). The strategies and efficacy of child versus adult teachers. *Child Development, 53,* 730–735.

Foster-Harrison, E. S. (1995). Peer helping in the elementary and middle grades: A developmental perspective. *Elementary School Guidance and Counseling, 30,* 94–104.

Gallimore, R., Tharp, R. G., & Speidel, G. E. (1978). The relationship of sibling caretaking and attentiveness to a peer tutor. *American Educational Research Journal, 15,* 267–273.

Gaskins, S. (1999). Children's daily lives in a Mayan village: A case study of culturally constructed roles and activities. In A. Göncü (Ed.), *Children's engagement in the world: Sociocultural perspectives* (pp. 25–61). New York: Cambridge University Press.

Goodluck, H. (1991). *Language acquisition: A linguistic introduction.* Oxford, U.K.: Blackwell.

Goodwin, C., & Goodwin, M. H. (1992). Assessments and the construction of context. In A. Duranti & C. Goodwin (Eds.), *Rethinking context: Language as an interactive phenomenon* (pp. 147–189). Canbridge, U.K: Cambridge University Press.

Goodwin, M. H. (1990). *He-said-she-said. Talk as social organization among Black children.* Bloomington: Indiana University Press.

Gopnik, A., & Meltzoff, A. N. (1994). Minds, bodies, and persons: Young children's understanding of the self and others as reflected in imitation and theory of mind research. In S. T. Parker & R. W. Mitchell (Eds.), *Self-awareness in humans and animals: Developmental perspectives* (pp. 166–186). Cambridge, U.K.: Cambridge University Press.

Greenfield, P. M. (1984). A theory of the teacher in the learning activities of everyday life. In B. Rogoff & J. Lave (Eds.), *Everyday cognition: Its development in social context* (pp. 117–138). Cambridge, MA: Harvard University Press.

Greenfield, P. M., Maynard, A. E., & Childs, C. P. (1999). *Historical change, cultural apprenticeship, and cognitive representation in Zinacantec Maya children.* Unpublished manuscript.

Greenfield, P. M., Maynard, A. E., & Childs, C. P. (2000). History, culture, learning, and development. *Cross-Cultural Research: The Journal of Comparative Social Science, 34,* 351–374.

Howe, N., & Ross, H. S. (1990). Socialization, perspective-taking, and the sibling relationship. *Developmental Psychology, 26,* 160–165.

Johnson, M., & Bailey, J. S. (1974). Cross-age tutoring: Fifth graders as arithmetic tutors for kindergarten children. *Journal of Applied Behavior Analysis, 7,* 223–232.

Kendrick, C., & Dunn, J. (1980). Caring for second baby: Effects on interaction between mother and firstborn. *Developmental Psychology, 16,* 303–311.

Kruger, A. C., & Tomasello, M. (1996). Cultural learning and learning culture. In D. R. Olson & N. Torrance (Eds.), *The handbook of education and human development. New models of learning, teaching, and schooling* (pp. 369–387). Cambridge, MA: Blackwell.

Lancy, D. (1996). *Playing on the mother ground: Cultural routines for children's development.* New York: Guilford Press.

Lave, J., & Wenger, E. (1991). *Situated learning. Legitimate peripheral participation.* Cambridge, UK.: Cambridge University Press.

Lewis, C., Freeman, N. H., Kyriakidou, C., Maridaki-Kassotaki, K., & Berridge, D. M. (1996). Social influences on false belief access: Specific sibling influences or general apprenticeship? *Child Development, 67,* 2930–2947.

Martini, M. (1994). Peer interactions in Polynesia: A view from the Marquesas. In J. P. Roopnarine, J. E. Johnson, & F. H. Hooper (Eds.), *Children's play in diverse cultures* (pp. 73–103). Albany: State University of New York Press.

Maynard, A. E. (1996). *The Zinacantec model of teaching and learning.* Unpublished masters thesis, University of California, Los Angeles.

Maynard, A. E. (1999). *Cultural teaching: The social organization and development of teaching in Zinacantec Maya sibling interactions.* Unpublished doctoral dissertation, University of California, Los Angeles.

Maynard, A. E., Greenfield, P. M., & Childs, C. P. (1999). Culture, history, biology, and body: Native and nonnative acquisition of technological skill. *Ethos, 27,* 379–402.

Meisner, J. S., & Fisher, V. L. (1980). Cognitive shifts of young children as a function of peer interaction and sibling status. *The Journal of Genetic Psychology, 136,* 247–253.

Ochs, E. (1988). *Culture and language development: Language acquisition and socialization in a Samoan village.* Cambridge, U.K.: Cambridge University Press.

Ochs, E., & Schieffelin, B. B. (1984). Language acquisition and socialization: Three developmental stories and their implications. In R. Shweder & R. LeVine (Eds.), *Culture theory: Essays on mind, self, and emotion* (pp. 276–320). Cambridge, U.K.: Cambridge University Press.

Pepler, D. J., Abramovitch, R., & Corter, C. (1981). Sibling interactions in the home: A longitudinal study. *Child Development, 52,* 1344–1347.

Perez-Granados, D.R., & Callanan, M. A. (1997). Conversations with mothers and siblings: Young children's semantic and conceptual development. *Developmental Psychology, 33,* 120–134.

Piaget, J. (1952). *The origins of intelligence in children.* New York: International Universities Press.

Piaget, J. (1967). *Six psychological studies.* Toronto, Ontario, Canada: Random House.

Rogoff, B. (1990). *Apprenticeship in thinking.* New York: Oxford University Press.

Rogoff, B. (1991). The joint socialization of development by young children and adults. In M. Lewis & S. Feinman (Eds.), *Social influences and socialization in infancy* (pp. 253–280). New York: Plenum Press.

Rogoff, B., Mistry, J., Göncü, A., & Mosier, C. (1993). Guided participation in cultural activity by toddlers and caregivers. *Monographs of the Society for Research in Child Development, 58* (8, Serial No. 236).

Stewart, R. B. (1983). Sibling interaction. The role of the older child as teacher for the younger. *Merrill-Palmer Quarterly, 29,* 47–68.

Stigler, J. W. (1988). Video surverys: New data for the improvement of classroom instruction. In S. G. Paris & H. M. Wellman (Eds.), *Global prospects for education: Development, culture, and schooling* (pp. 129–168). Washington, DC: American Psychological Association.

Teti, D. M., & Ablard, K. E. (1989). Security of attachment and infant–sibling relationships: A laboratory study. *Child Development, 60,* 1519–1528.

Tharp, R. G. (1994). Intergroup differences among Native Americans in socialization and child cognition: An ethnogenetic analysis. In P.M. Greenfield & R.R. Cocking (Eds.), *Cross-cultural roots of minority child development* (pp. 87–105). Hillsdale, NJ: Erlbaum.

Tomasello, M., Kruger, A. C., & Ratner, H. H. (1993). Cultural learning. *Behavioral and Brain Sciences, 16,* 495–552.

Tomasello, M., & Mannle, S. (1985). Pragmatics of sibling speech to one-year-olds. *Child Development, 56,* 911–917.

Trevarthen, C., & Logotheti, K. (1989). Child and culture: Genesis of co-operative knowing. In A. Gellatly, D. Rogers, &

J. A. Sloboda (Eds.), *Cognition and social worlds* (pp. 37–56). Oxford, U.K.: Clarendon Press/Oxford University Press.

Vogt, E. Z. (1969). *Zinacantan: A Maya community in the highlands of Chiapas.* Cambridge, MA: Harvard University Press.

Vogt, E. Z. (1990). *The Zinacantecos of Mexico: A modern Maya way of life* (2nd ed.). New York: Harcourt, Brace, Jovanovich.

Vygotsky, L. S. (1978). *Mind in society.* New York: Cambridge University Press.

Waston-Gegeo, K. A., & Gegeo, D. W. (1989). The role of sibling interaction in child socialization. In P.G. Zukow (Ed.), *Sibling interaction across cultures. Theoretical and methodological issues* (pp. 54–76). New York: Springer-Verlag.

Weisner, T. S. (1987). Socialization for parenthood in sibling caretaking societies. In J. B. Lancaster, J. Altmann, A. S. Rossi, & L. R. Sherrod (Eds.), *Parenting across the life span: Biosocial dimensions.* Hawthorne, NY: Aldine.

Weisner, T. S., & Gallimore, R.(1977). My brother's keeper: Child and sibling caretaking. *Current Anthropology, 18,* 169–190.

Weisner, T. S., Gallimore, R., & Jordan, C. (1988). Unpackaging cultural effects on classroom learning: Native Hawaiian peer assistance and child-generated activity. *Anthropology and Education Quarterly, 19,* 327–353.

Whiting, B. B., & Edwards, C. P. (1988). *Children of different worlds: The formation of social behavior.* Cambridge, MA: Harvard University Press.

Whiting, B. B., & Whiting, J. M. (1975). *Children of six cultures: A psycho-cultural analysis.* Cambridge, MA: Harvard University Press.

Wood, D., Bruner, J. S., & Ross, G. (1976). The role of tutoring in problem solving. *Journal of Child Psychology and Psychiatry, 17,* 89–100.

Wootton, A. J. (1997). *Interaction and the development of mind.* Cambridge, U.K.: Cambridge University Press.

Zukow, P. G. (1986). The relationship between interaction with the caregiver and the emergence of play activities during the one-word period. *British Journal of Developmental Psychology, 4,* 223–234.

Zukow, P. G. (1989a.) *Sibling interaction across cultures. Theoretical and methodological issues.* New York: Springer-Verlag.

Zukow, P. G. (1989b.) Siblings as effective socializing agents: Evidence from Central Mexico. In P. G. Zukow (Ed.), *Sibling interaction across cultures. Theoretical and methodological issues.* (pp.79–105). New York: Springer-Verlag.

Zukow-Goldring, P. G. (1997). A social ecological realist approach to the emergence of the lexicon: Educating attention to amodal invariants in gesture and speech. In C. Dent-Read & P. Zukow-Goldring (Eds.), *Evolving explanations of development: Ecological approaches to organism-environment systems* (pp. 199–250). Washington, DC: American Psychological Association.

Zukow-Goldring, P. (2002). Sibling caregiving. In M. H. Bornstein (Ed.), *Handbook of parenting: Vol. 3. Status and social conditions of parenting* (2nd ed., pp. 253–286). Hillsdale, NJ: Erlbaum.

Zukow-Goldring, P., & Ferko, K. R. (1994). An ecological approach to the emergence of the lexicon: Socializing attention. In V. John-Steiner, C. P. Panofsky, & L. W. Smith (Eds.), *Sociocultural approaches to language and literacy. An interactionist perspective* (pp. 170–190). Cambridge, U.K.: Cambridge University Press.

QUESTIONS

1. What is cultural teaching, and what social and psychological aspects of culture are involved in this process?
2. Why might older siblings be especially important to children as they learn the practices and skills that are valued in their culture?
3. How does sibling caretaking vary across cultures?
4. In what community did Maynard conduct her research, and why was this community especially interesting to study in relation to cultural instruction by siblings?
5. How was teaching defined in this study, and what specific teaching techniques did the child teachers in this study use?
6. In sibling instruction, what is the relation of play to teaching?
7. What age differences were found in children's teaching behaviors? On the basis of these results, would you say that children get better at teaching as they get older? Why or why not?
8. Maynard argues that child teaching develops in such a way that as children get older, their teaching reflects the model of teaching and learning that is valued in their culture. What evidence does she cite to support this view? Do you agree with it?
9. What different types of experiences help children develop the skills needed to perform the everyday tasks that are valued in their community?
10. How is sibling teaching in middle-class homes in the United States similar to and different from the sibling teaching described in this article?

31 Intelligence: Knowns and Unknowns

Ulric Neisser • Gwyneth Boodoo • Thomas J. Bouchard, Jr. •
A. Wade Boykin • Nathan Brody • Stephen J. Ceci • et al.

Of the many individual differences that distinguish one person from another, none has produced a stormier and more prolonged debate than intelligence. Throughout the 20th century, psychologists sought valid measures of intelligence that would not be influenced by family background or cultural origin. Unfortunately, this effort has met with limited success and has fueled an ongoing debate. The following article is part of a report commissioned by the American Psychological Association. The authors are scholars knowledgeable about the construct and study of intelligence. The group was convened to respond to questions raised in the 1990s by the controversial book *The Bell Curve,* in which racial differences in IQ were attributed to biological differences in intellectual capacity.

This report covers a wide range of topics pertinent to the study of intelligence. It discusses what intelligence is and how it is measured. It also discusses a critical aspect of intelligence tests: what behaviors or abilities they predict. The report touches on issues of genetic inheritance and intelligence. It also includes an extensive discussion on group differences in intelligence and how such differences should be interpreted.

As the title of the report indicates, the answers to some of the critical questions about intelligence and intelligence testing are known. The main insight that has been well established by research is that both heredity and environment are involved in organizing and directing human intelligence. The answers to many other questions remain unknown, however. Many of these unknowns concern exactly how nature and nurture interact to produce the individual and group patterns of intelligence that have been documented. Another lingering question pertains to the definition of intelligence itself. Most psychologists agree that the current operational definition is far narrower than the construct of intelligence actually is in human experience. It is clear that these unknowns will set the research agenda in the area of intelligence for decades to come.

In the fall of 1994, the publication of Richard Herrnstein and Charles Murray's book The Bell Curve *sparked a new round of debate about the meaning of intelligence test scores and the nature of intelligence. The debate was characterized by strong assertions as well as by strong feelings. Unfortunately, those assertions often revealed serious misunderstandings of what has (and has not) been demonstrated by scientific research in this field. Although a great deal is now known, the issues remain complex and in many cases still unresolved. Another unfortunate aspect of the debate was that many participants made little effort to distinguish scientific issues from political ones. Research findings were often assessed not so much on their merits or their scientific standing as on their supposed political implications. In such a climate, individuals who wish to make their own judgments find it hard to know what to believe.*

Reviewing the intelligence debate at its meeting of November 1994, the Board of Scientific Affairs (BSA) of the American Psychological Association (APA) concluded that there was urgent need for an authoritative

Copyright 1996 by the American Psychological Association. Reprinted by permission of the authors and the American Psychological Association from *American Psychologist, Vol. 51,* pp. 77–101.

This is a "Report of a Task Force Established by the American Psychological Association."

The Task Force appreciates the contributions of many members of the APA Board of Scientific Affairs (BSA) and the APA Board for the Advancement of Psychology in the Public Interest (BAPPI), who made helpful comments on a preliminary draft of this report. We also wish to acknowledge the indispensable logistical support of the APA Science Directorate during the preparation of the report itself.

report on these issues—one that all sides could use as a basis for discussion. Acting by unanimous vote, BSA established a Task Force charged with preparing such a report. Ulric Neisser, Professor of Psychology at Emory University and a member of BSA, was appointed Chair. The APA Board on the Advancement of Psychology in the Public Interest, which was consulted extensively during this process, nominated one member of the Task Force; the Committee on Psychological Tests and Assessment nominated another; a third was nominated by the Council of Representatives. Other members were chosen by an extended consultative process, with the aim of representing a broad range of expertise and opinion.

The Task Force met twice, in January and March of 1995. Between and after these meetings, drafts of the various sections were circulated, revised, and revised yet again. Disputes were resolved by discussion. As a result, the report presented here has the unanimous support of the entire Task Force.

1. CONCEPTS OF INTELLIGENCE

Individuals differ from one another in their ability to understand complex ideas, to adapt effectively to the environment, to learn from experience, to engage in various forms of reasoning, to overcome obstacles by taking thought. Although these individual differences can be substantial, they are never entirely consistent: A given person's intellectual performance will vary on different occasions, in different domains, as judged by different criteria. Concepts of "intelligence" are attempts to clarify and organize this complex set of phenomena. Although considerable clarity has been achieved in some areas, no such conceptualization has yet answered all the important questions and none commands universal assent. Indeed, when two dozen prominent theorists were recently asked to define intelligence, they gave two dozen somewhat different definitions (Sternberg & Detterman, 1986). Such disagreements are not cause for dismay. Scientific research rarely begins with fully agreed definitions, though it may eventually lead to them.

. . . Several current theorists argue that there are many different "intelligences" (systems of abilities), only a few of which can be captured by standard psychometric tests. Others emphasize the role of culture, both in establishing different conceptions of intelligence and in influencing the acquisition of intellectual skills. Developmental psychologists, taking yet another direction, often focus more on the processes by which all children come to think intelligently than on measuring individual differences among them. There is also a new interest in the neural and biologi-

cal bases of intelligence, a field of research that seems certain to expand in the next few years.

In this brief report, we focus on a limited and rather specific set of questions:

[Note from eds.: Because we have not included the text of this article in its entirety, please see Neisser et al. (1996). Intelligence: Knowns and Unknowns. *American Psychologist, 51*(2), 77–101, for further discussion of these different approaches to intelligence. We include the description of the psychometric approach to aid in interpreting the later sections.]

- What are the significant conceptualizations of intelligence at this time? (Section 1)
- What do intelligence test scores mean, what do they predict, and how well do they predict it? (Section 2)
- Why do individuals differ in intelligence, and especially in their scores on intelligence tests? Our discussion of these questions implicates both genetic factors (Section 3) and environmental factors (Section 4).
- Do various ethnic groups display different patterns of performance on intelligence tests, and if so what might explain those differences? (Section 5)
- What significant scientific issues are presently unresolved? (Section 6)

Public discussion of these issues has been especially vigorous since the 1994 publication of Herrnstein and Murray's *The Bell Curve*, a controversial volume which stimulated many equally controversial reviews and replies. Nevertheless, we do not directly enter that debate. Herrnstein and Murray (and many of their critics) have gone well beyond the scientific findings, making explicit recommendations on various aspects of public policy. Our concern here, however, is with science rather than policy. The charge to our Task Force was to prepare a dispassionate survey of the state of the art: to make clear what has been scientifically established, what is presently in dispute, and what is still unknown. In fulfilling that charge, the only recommendations we shall make are for further research and calmer debate.

THE PSYCHOMETRIC APPROACH

Ever since Alfred Binet's great success in devising tests to distinguish mentally retarded children from those with behavior problems, psychometric instruments have played an important part in European and American life. Tests are used for many purposes, such as selection, diagnosis, and evaluation. Many of the most widely used tests are not intended to measure intelligence itself but some closely related construct: scholastic aptitude, school achievement, specific abilities, etc. Such tests are especially important for selection purposes. For preparatory school, it's the SSAT; for college, the SAT or ACT; for graduate school, the GRE; for medical school, the MCAT; for law school, the LSAT; for business school, the GMAT. Scores on intelligence-related tests matter, and the stakes can be high.

Intelligence Tests.   Tests of intelligence itself (in the psychometric sense) come in many forms. Some use only a single type of item or question: examples include the Peabody Picture Vocabulary Test (a measure of children's verbal intelligence) and Raven's Progressive Matrices (a nonverbal, untimed test that requires inductive reasoning about perceptual patterns). Although such instruments are useful for specific purposes, the more familiar measures of general intelligence—such as the Wechsler tests and the Stanford-Binet—include many different types of items, both verbal and nonverbal. Test-takers may be asked to give the meanings of words, to complete a series of pictures, to indicate which of several words does not belong with the others, and the like. Their performance can then be scored to yield several subscores as well as an overall score.

By convention, overall intelligence test scores are usually converted to a scale in which the mean is 100 and the standard deviation is 15. (The standard deviation is a measure of the variability of the distribution of scores.) Approximately 95% of the population has scores within two standard deviations of the mean, i.e., between 70 and 130. For historical reasons, the term "IQ" is often used to describe scores on tests of intelligence. It originally referred to an "Intelligence Quotient" that was formed by dividing a so-called mental age by a chronological age, but this procedure is no longer used.

Intercorrelations Among Tests.   Individuals rarely perform equally well on all the different kinds of items included in a test of intelligence. One person may do relatively better on verbal than on spatial items, for example, while another may show the opposite pattern. Nevertheless, subtests measuring different abilities tend to be positively correlated: people who score high on one such subtest are likely to be above average on others as well. These complex patterns of correlation can be clarified by factor analysis, but the results of such analyses are often controversial themselves. Some theorists (e.g., Spearman, 1927) have emphasized the importance of a general factor, g, which represents what all the tests have in common; others (e.g., Thurstone, 1938) focus on more specific group factors such as memory, verbal comprehension, or number facility. As we shall see in Sec-

tion 2, one common view today envisages something like a hierarchy of factors with g at the apex. But there is no full agreement on what g actually means: it has been described as a mere statistical regularity (Thomson, 1939), a kind of mental energy (Spearman, 1927), a generalized abstract reasoning ability (Gustafsson, 1984), or an index measure of neural processing speed (Reed & Jensen, 1992).

There have been many disputes over the utility of IQ and g. Some theorists are critical of the entire psychometric approach (e.g., Ceci, 1990; Gardner, 1983; Gould, 1978), while others regard it as firmly established (e.g., Carroll, 1993; Eysenck, 1973; Herrnstein & Murray, 1994; Jensen, 1972). The critics do not dispute the stability of test scores, nor the fact that they predict certain forms of achievement—especially school achievement—rather effectively (see Section 2). They do argue, however, that to base a concept of intelligence on test scores alone is to ignore many important aspects of mental ability.

. . .

2. INTELLIGENCE TESTS AND THEIR CORRELATES

The correlation coefficient, r, can be computed whenever the scores in a sample are paired in some way. Typically this is because each individual is measured twice: he or she takes the same test on two occasions, or takes two different tests, or has both a test score and some criterion measure such as grade point average or job performance. (In Section 3 we consider cases where the paired scores are those of two different individuals, such as twins or parent and child.) The value of r measures the degree of relationship between the two sets of scores in a convenient way, by assessing how well one of them (computationally it doesn't matter which one) could be used to predict the value of the other. Its sign indicates the direction of relationship: when r is negative, high scores on one measure predict low scores on the other. Its magnitude indicates the strength of the relationship. If $r = 0$, there is no relation at all; if r is 1 (or -1), one score can be used to predict the other score perfectly. Moreover, the square of r has a particular meaning in cases where we are concerned with predicting one variable from another. When $r = .50$, for example, r^2 is .25: this means (given certain linear assumptions) that 25% of the variance in one set of scores is predictable from the correlated values of the other set, while the remaining 75% is not.

BASIC CHARACTERISTICS OF TEST SCORES

Stability. Intelligence test scores are fairly stable during development. When Jones and Bayley (1941) tested a sample of children annually throughout childhood and adolescence, for example, scores obtained at age 18 were correlated $r = .77$ with scores that had been obtained at age 6 and $r = .89$ with scores from age 12. When scores were averaged across several successive tests to remove short-term fluctuations, the correlations were even higher. The mean for ages 17 and 18 was correlated $r = .86$ with the mean for ages 5, 6, and 7, and $r = .96$ with the mean for ages 11, 12, and 13. (For comparable findings in a more recent study, see Moffitt, Caspi, Harkness, & Silva, 1993.) Nevertheless, IQ scores do change over time. In the same study (Jones & Bayley, 1941), the average change between age 12 and age 17 was 7.1 IQ points: some individuals changed as much as 18 points. . . .

It is important to understand what remains stable and what changes in the development of intelligence. A child whose IQ score remains the same from age 6 to age 18 does not exhibit the same performance throughout that period. On the contrary, steady gains in general knowledge, vocabulary, reasoning ability, etc. will be apparent. What does *not* change is his or her score in comparison to that of other individuals of the same age. A six-year-old with an IQ of 100 is at the mean of six-year-olds; an 18-year-old with that score is at the mean of 18-year-olds.

Factors and g. As noted in Section 1, the patterns of intercorrelation among tests (i.e., among different kinds of items) are complex. Some pairs of tests are much more closely related than others, but all such correlations are typically positive and form what is called a "positive manifold." Spearman (1927) showed that in any such manifold, some portion of the variance of scores on each test can be mathematically attributed to a "general factor," or *g*. Given this analysis, the overall pattern of correlations can be roughly described as produced by individual differences in *g* plus differences in the specific abilities sampled by particular tests. In addition, however, there are usually patterns of intercorrelation among groups of tests. These commonalities, which played only a small role in Spearman's analysis, were emphasized by other theorists. Thurstone (1938), for example, proposed an analysis based primarily on the concept of group factors.

While some psychologists today still regard *g* as the most fundamental measure of intelligence (e.g., Jensen, 1980), others prefer to emphasize the distinctive profile of strengths and weaknesses present in each person's performance. A recently published review identifies over 70 different abilities that can be distinguished by currently available tests (Carroll, 1993). One way to represent this structure is in terms of a hierarchical arrangement with a general intelligence factor at the apex and various more specialized abilities arrayed below it. Such a summary merely acknowledges that performance levels on different tests are correlated; it is consistent with, but does not prove, the hypothesis that a common factor such as *g* underlies those correlations. Different specialized abilities might also be correlated for other reasons, such as the effects of education. Thus while the *g*-based factor hierarchy is the most widely accepted current view of the structure of abilities, some theorists regard it as misleading (Ceci, 1990). Moreover, as noted in Section 1, a wide range of human abilities—including many that seem to have intellectual components—are outside the domain of standard psychometric tests.

TESTS AS PREDICTORS

School Performance. Intelligence tests were originally devised by Alfred Binet to measure children's ability to succeed in school. They do in fact predict school performance fairly well: the correlation between IQ scores and grades is about .50. They also predict scores on school achievement tests, designed to measure knowledge of the curriculum. Note, however, that correlations of this magnitude account for only about 25% of the overall variance. Successful school learning depends on many personal characteristics other than intelligence, such as persistence, interest in school, and willingness to study. The encouragement for academic achievement that is received from peers, family, and teachers may also be important, together with more general cultural factors (see Section 5).

Years of Education. Some children stay in school longer than others; many go on to college and perhaps beyond. Two variables that can be measured as early as elementary school correlate with the total amount of education individuals will obtain: test scores and social class background. Correlations between IQ scores and total years of education are about .55, implying that differences in psychometric intelligence account for about 30% of the outcome variance. The correlations of years of education with social class background (as indexed by the occupation/education of a child's parents) are also positive, but somewhat lower.

There are a number of reasons why children with higher test scores tend to get more education. They are likely to get good grades, and to be encouraged by teachers and counselors; often they are placed in "college preparatory" classes, where they make friends who may also encourage them. In general, they are likely to find the process of education rewarding in a way that many low-scoring children do not (Rehberg & Rosenthal, 1978). These influences are not omnipotent: some high scoring children do drop out of school. Many personal and social characteristics other than psychometric intelligence determine academic success and interest, and social privilege may also play a role. Nevertheless, test scores are the best single predictor of an individual's years of education. . . .

Social Status and Income.   How well do IQ scores (which can be obtained before individuals enter the labor force) predict such outcome measures as the social status or income of adults? This question is complex, in part because another variable also predicts such outcomes: namely, the socioeconomic status (SES) of one's parents. Unsurprisingly, children of privileged families are more likely to attain high social status than those whose parents are poor and less educated. These two predictors (IQ and parental SES) are by no means independent of one another; the correlation between them is around .33 (White, 1982).

One way to look at these relationships is to begin with SES. According to Jencks (1979), measures of parental SES predict about one-third of the variance in young adults' social status and about one-fifth of the variance in their income. About half of this predictive effectiveness depends on the fact that the SES of parents also predicts children's intelligence test scores, which have their own predictive value for social outcomes; the other half comes about in other ways.

We can also begin with IQ scores, which by themselves account for about one-fourth of the social status variance and one-sixth of the income variance. Statistical controls for parental SES eliminate only about a quarter of this predictive power. One way to conceptualize this effect is by comparing the occupational status (or income) of adult brothers who grew up in the same family and hence have the same parental SES. In such cases, the brother with the higher adolescent IQ score is likely to have the higher adult social status and income (Jencks, 1979). This effect, in turn, is substantially mediated by education: the brother with the higher test scores is likely to get more schooling, and hence to be better credentialled as he enters the workplace. . . .

Job Performance.   Scores on intelligence tests predict various measures of job performance: supervisor ratings, work samples, etc. Such correlations, which typically lie between $r = .30$ and $r = .50$, are partly restricted by the limited reliability of those measures themselves. They become higher when r is statistically corrected for this unreliability: in one survey of relevant studies (Hunter, 1983), the mean of the corrected correlations was .54. This implies that, across a wide range of occupations, intelligence test performance accounts for some 29% of the variance in job performance. . . .

Social Outcomes.   Psychometric intelligence is negatively correlated with certain socially undesirable outcomes. For example, children with high test scores are less likely than lower-scoring children to engage in juvenile crime. In one study, Moffitt, Gabrielli, Mednick, and Schulsinger (1981) found a correlation of $-.19$ between IQ scores and number of juvenile offenses in a large Danish sample; with social class controlled, the correlation dropped to $-.17$. The correlations for most "negative outcome" variables are typically smaller than .20, which means that test scores are associated with less than 4% of their total variance. It is important to realize that the causal links between psychometric ability and social outcomes may be indirect. Children who are unsuccessful in—and hence alienated from—school may be more likely to engage in delinquent behaviors for that very reason, compared to other children who enjoy school and are doing well.

In summary, intelligence test scores predict a wide range of social outcomes with varying degrees of success. Correlations are highest for school achievement, where they account for about a quarter of the variance. They are somewhat lower for job performance, and very low for negatively valued outcomes such as criminality. In general, intelligence tests measure only some of the many personal characteristics that are relevant to life in contemporary America. Those characteristics are never the only influence on outcomes, though in the case of school performance they may well be the strongest.

TEST SCORES AND MEASURES OF PROCESSING SPEED

Many recent studies show that the speeds with which people perform very simple perceptual and cognitive tasks are correlated with psychometric intelligence (for reviews see Ceci, 1990; Deary, 1995; Vernon, 1987). In general, people with higher intelligence test scores tend to apprehend, scan, retrieve, and respond to stimuli more quickly than those who score lower.

. . .

Problems of Interpretation.   Some researchers believe that psychometric intelligence, especially g, depends directly on what may be called the "neural efficiency" of the brain (Eysenck, 1986; Vernon, 1987). They regard the observed correlations between test scores and measures of processing speed as evidence for their view. If choice reaction times, inspection times, and VEP latencies actually do reflect the speed of basic neural processes, such correlations are only to be expected. In fact, however, the observed patterns of correlation are rarely as simple as this hypothesis would predict. Moreover, it is quite possible that high- and low-IQ individuals differ in other ways that affect speeded performance (cf. Ceci, 1990). Those variables include motivation, response criteria (emphasis on speed vs. accuracy), perceptual strategies (cf. Mackenzie et al., 1991), attentional strategies, and—in some cases—differential familiarity with the material itself. Finally, we do not yet know the direction of causation that underlies such correlations. Do high levels of "neural efficiency" promote the development of intelligence, or do more intelligent people simply find faster ways to carry out perceptual tasks? Or both? These questions are still open.

3. THE GENES AND INTELLIGENCE

. . . We focus here on the relative contributions of genes and environments to individual differences in particular traits. To avoid misunderstanding, it must be emphasized from the outset that gene action always involves an environment—at least a biochemical environment, and often an ecological one. (For humans, that ecology is usually interpersonal or cultural.) Thus all genetic effects on the development of observable traits are potentially modifiable by environmental input, though the practicability of making such modifications may be another matter. Conversely, all environmental effects on trait development involve the genes or structures to which the genes have contributed. Thus there is always a genetic aspect to the effects of the environment (cf. Plomin & Bergeman, 1991).

RESULTS FOR IQ SCORES

Parameter Estimates. Across the ordinary range of environments in modern Western societies, a sizable part of the variation in intelligence test scores is associated with genetic differences among individuals. Quantitative estimates vary from one study to another, because many are based on small or selective samples. If one simply combines all available correlations in a single analysis, the heritability (h^2) works out to about .50 and the between-family variance (c^2) to about .25 (e.g., Chipuer, Rovine, & Plomin, 1990; Loehlin, 1989). These overall figures are misleading, however, because most of the relevant studies have been done with children. We now know that the heritability of IQ changes with age: h^2 goes up and c^2 goes down from infancy to adulthood (McCartney, Harris, & Bernieri, 1990; McGue, Bouchard, Iacono, &

Lykken, 1993). In childhood h^2 and c^2 for IQ are of the order of .45 and .35; by late adolescence h^2 is around .75 and c^2 is quite low (zero in some studies). Substantial environmental variance remains, but it primarily reflects within-family rather than between-family differences.

These adult parameter estimates are based on a number of independent studies. The correlation between MZ twins reared apart, which directly estimates h^2, ranged from .68 to .78 in five studies involving adult samples from Europe and the United States (McGue et al., 1993). The correlation between unrelated children reared together in adoptive families, which directly estimates c^2, was approximately zero for adolescents in two adoption studies (Loehlin, Horn, & Willerman, 1989; Scarr & Weinberg, 1978) and .19 in a third (the Minnesota transracial adoption study: Scarr, Weinberg, & Waldman, 1993).

These particular estimates derive from samples in which the lowest socioeconomic levels were underrepresented (i.e., there were few very poor families), so the range of between-family differences was smaller than in the population as a whole. This means that we should be cautious in generalizing the findings for between-family effects across the entire social spectrum. The samples were also mostly White, but available data suggest that twin and sibling correlations in African American and similarly selected White samples are more often comparable than not (Loehlin, Lindzey, & Spuhler, 1975).

Why should individual differences in intelligence (as measured by test scores) reflect genetic differences more strongly in adults than they do in children? One possibility is that as individuals grow older their transactions with their environments are increasingly influenced by the characteristics that they bring to those environments themselves, decreasingly by the conditions imposed by family life and social origins. Older persons are in a better position to select their own effective environments, a form of genotype-environment correlation. In any case the popular view that genetic influences on the development of a trait are essentially frozen at conception while the effects of the early environment cumulate inexorably is quite misleading, at least for the trait of psychometric intelligence.

Implications. Estimates of h^2 and c^2 for IQ (or any other trait) are descriptive statistics for the populations studied. (In this respect they are like means and standard deviations.) They are outcome measures, summarizing the results of a great many diverse, intricate, individually variable events and processes, but they can nevertheless be quite useful. They can tell us how much of the variation in a given trait the genes and family environments explain, and changes in them place some constraints on theories of how this occurs. On the other hand they have little to say about specific mechanisms, i.e., about how genetic and environmental differences get translated into individual physiological and psychological differences. Many psychologists and neuroscientists are actively studying such processes; data on heritabilities may give them ideas about what to look for and where or when to look for it.

A common error is to assume that because something is heritable it is necessarily unchangeable. This is wrong. Heritability does not imply immutability. As previously noted, heritable traits can depend on learning, and they may be subject to other environmental effects as well. The value of h^2 can change if the distribution of environments (or genes) in the population is substantially altered. On the other hand, there can be effective environmental changes that do not change heritability at all. If the environment relevant to a given trait improves in a way that affects all members of the population equally, the mean value of the trait will rise without any change in its heritability (because the differences among individuals in the population will stay the same). This has evidently happened for height: the heritability of stature is high, but average heights continue to increase (Olivier, 1980). Something of the sort may also be taking place for IQ scores—the so-called "Flynn effect" discussed in Section 4. . . .

4. ENVIRONMENTAL EFFECTS ON INTELLIGENCE

The "environment" includes a wide range of influences on intelligence. Some of those variables affect whole populations, while others contribute to individual differences within a given group. Some of them are social, some are biological; at this point some are still mysterious. It may also happen that the proper interpretation of an environmental variable requires the simultaneous consideration of genetic effects. Nevertheless, a good deal of solid information is available.

SOCIAL VARIABLES

It is obvious that the cultural environment—how people live, what they value, what they do—has a significant effect on the intellectual skills developed by individuals. Rice farmers in Liberia are good at estimating quantities of rice (Gay & Cole, 1967); children in Botswana, accustomed to story-telling, have excellent memories for stories (Dube, 1982). Both these groups were far ahead of American controls on the tasks in question. On the other hand Americans and other Westernized groups typically outperform members of traditional societies on psychometric tests, even those designed to be "culture-fair."

Cultures typically differ from one another in so many ways that particular differences can rarely be ascribed to single causes. Even comparisons between subpopulations can be difficult to interpret. If we find that middle-class and poor Americans differ in their scores on intelligence tests, it is easy to suppose that the environmental difference has caused the IQ difference (i.e., that growing up in the middle class produces higher psychometric intelligence than growing up poor). But there may also be an opposite direction of causation: individuals can come to be in one environment or another because of differences in their own abilities. Waller (1971) has shown, for example, that adult sons whose IQ scores are above those of their fathers tend to have higher social-class status than those fathers; conversely, sons with IQ scores below their fathers' tend to have lower social-class status. Since all the subjects grew up with their fathers, the IQ differences in this study cannot have resulted from class-related differences in childhood experience. Rather, those differences (or other factors correlated with them) seem to have had an influence on the status that they achieved. Such a result is not surprising, given the relation between test scores and years of education reviewed in Section 2.

Occupation. In Section 2 we noted that intelligence test scores predict occupational level, not only because some occupations require more intelligence than others but also because admission to many professions depends on test scores in the first place. There can also be an effect in the opposite direction, i.e., workplaces may affect the intelligence of those who work in them. Kohn and Schooler (1973), who interviewed some 3,000 men in various occupations (farmers, managers, machinists, porters, etc.), argued that more "complex" jobs produce more "intellectual flexibility" in the individuals who hold them. Although the issue of direction of effects was not fully resolved in their study—and perhaps not even in its longitudinal follow-up (Kohn & Schooler, 1983)—this remains a plausible suggestion. . . .

Schooling. Attendance at school is both a dependent and an independent variable in relation to intelligence. On the one hand, children with higher test scores are less likely to drop out and more likely to be promoted from grade to grade and then to attend college. Thus the number of years of education that adults complete is roughly predictable from their childhood scores on intelligence tests. On the other hand, schooling itself changes mental abilities, including those abilities measured on psychometric tests. This is obvious for tests like the SAT that are explicitly designed to assess school learning, but it is almost equally true of intelligence tests themselves. . . .

Schools affect intelligence in several ways, most obviously by transmitting information. The answers to questions like "Who wrote Hamlet?" and "What is the boiling point of water?" are typically learned in school, where some pupils learn them more easily and thoroughly than others. Perhaps at least as important are certain general skills and attitudes: systematic problem-solving, abstract thinking, categorization, sustained attention to material of little intrinsic interest, and repeated manipulation of basic symbols and operations. There is no doubt that schools promote and permit the development of significant intellectual skills, which develop to different extents in different children. It is because tests of intelligence draw on many of those same skills that they predict school achievement as well as they do.

To achieve these results, the school experience must meet at least some minimum standard of quality. In very poor schools, children may learn so little that they fall farther behind the national IQ norms for every year of attendance. When this happens, older siblings have systematically lower scores than their younger counterparts. This pattern of scores appeared in at least one rural Georgia school system in the 1970s (Jensen, 1977). Before desegregation, it must have been characteristic of many of the schools attended by Black pupils in the South. In a study based on Black children who had moved to Philadelphia at various ages during this period, Lee (1951) found that their IQ scores went up more than half a point for each year that they were enrolled in the Philadelphia system.

Interventions. Intelligence test scores reflect a child's standing relative to others in his or her age cohort. Very poor or interrupted schooling can lower that standing substantially; are there also ways to raise it? In fact many interventions have been shown to raise test scores and mental ability "in the short run" (i.e., while the program itself was in progress), but long-run gains have proved more elusive. One noteworthy example of (at least short-run) success was the Venezuelan Intelligence Project (Herrnstein, Nickerson, de Sanchez, & Swets, 1986), in which hundreds of seventh-grade children from under-privileged backgrounds in that country were exposed to an extensive, theoretically-based curriculum focused on thinking skills. The intervention produced substantial gains on a wide range of tests, but there has been no follow-up.

Children who participate in "Head Start" and similar programs are exposed to various school-related materials and experiences for one or two years. Their test scores often go up during the course of the program, but these gains fade with time. By the end of elementary school, there are usually no significant IQ or achievement-test differences between children

who have been in such programs and controls who have not. There may, however, be other differences. Follow-up studies suggest that children who participated in such programs as preschoolers are less likely to be assigned to special education, less likely to be held back in grade, and more likely to finish high school than matched controls (Consortium for Longitudinal Studies, 1983; Darlington, 1986; but see Locurto, 1991).

More extensive interventions might be expected to produce larger and more lasting effects, but few such programs have been evaluated systematically. One of the more successful is the Carolina Abecedarian Project (Campbell & Ramey, 1994), which provided a group of children with enriched environments from early infancy through preschool and also maintained appropriate controls. The test scores of the enrichment-group children were already higher than those of controls at age two; they were still some 5 points higher at age 12, seven years after the end of the intervention. Importantly, the enrichment group also outperformed the controls in academic achievement.

Family Environment. No one doubts that normal child development requires a certain minimum level of responsible care. Severely deprived, neglectful, or abusive environments must have negative effects on a great many aspects—including intellectual aspects—of development. Beyond that minimum, however, the role of family experience is now in serious dispute (Baumrind, 1993; Jackson, 1993; Scarr, 1992, 1993). Psychometric intelligence is a case in point. Do differences between children's family environments (within the normal range) produce differences in their intelligence test performance? The problem here is to disentangle causation from correlation. There is no doubt that such variables as resources of the home (Gottfried, 1984) and parents' use of language (Hart & Risley, 1992, 1995) are correlated with children's IQ scores, but such correlations may be mediated by genetic as well as (or instead of) environmental factors.
. . .

BIOLOGICAL VARIABLES

Every individual has a biological as well as a social environment, one that begins in the womb and extends throughout life. Many aspects of that environment can affect intellectual development. We now know that a number of biological factors—malnutrition, exposure to toxic substances, various prenatal and perinatal stressors—result in lowered psychometric intelligence under at least some conditions.

Nutrition. There has been only one major study of the effects of prenatal malnutrition (i.e., malnutrition

of the mother during pregnancy) on long-term intellectual development. Stein, Susser, Saenger, and
Marolla (1975) analyzed the test scores of Dutch 19-
year-old males in relation to a wartime famine that
had occurred in the winter of 1944–45, just before
their birth. In this very large sample (made possible
by a universal military induction requirement), exposure to the famine had no effect on adult intelligence.
Note, however, that the famine itself lasted only a few
months; the subjects were exposed to it prenatally
but not after birth.

In contrast, prolonged malnutrition during childhood does have long-term intellectual effects. These
have not been easy to establish, in part because many
other unfavorable socioeconomic conditions are
often associated with chronic malnutrition (Ricciuti,
1993; but cf. Sigman, 1995). In one intervention
study, however, preschoolers in two Guatemalan villages (where undernourishment is common) were
given ad lib access to a protein dietary supplement
for several years. A decade later, many of these children (namely, those from the poorest socioeconomic
levels) scored significantly higher on school-related
achievement tests than comparable controls (Pollitt,
Gorman, Engle, Martorell, & Rivera, 1993). It is worth
noting that the effects of poor nutrition on intelligence may well be indirect. Malnourished children
are typically less responsive to adults, less motivated
to learn, and less active in exploration than their
more adequately nourished counterparts. . . .

Lead.   Certain toxins have well-established negative
effects on intelligence. Exposure to lead is one such
factor. In one long-term study (Baghurst et al., 1992;
McMichael et al., 1988), the blood lead levels of children growing up near a lead smelting plant were substantially and negatively correlated with intelligence
test scores throughout childhood. No "threshold
dose" for the effect of lead appears in such studies. Although ambient lead levels in the United States have
been reduced in recent years, there is reason to believe that some American children—especially those
in inner cities—may still be at risk from this source (cf.
Needleman, Geiger, & Frank, 1985).

Alcohol.   Extensive prenatal exposure to alcohol
(which occurs if the mother drinks heavily during
pregnancy) can give rise to fetal alcohol syndrome,
which includes mental retardation as well as a range
of physical symptoms. Smaller "doses" of prenatal alcohol may have negative effects on intelligence even
when the full syndrome does not appear. Streissguth,
Barr, Sampson, Darby, and Martin (1989) found that
mothers who reported consuming more than 1.5 oz.
of alcohol daily during pregnancy had children who
scored some 5 points below controls at age four. Prenatal exposure to aspirin and antibiotics had similar
negative effects in this study.

Perinatal Factors.   Complications at delivery and
other negative perinatal factors may have serious
consequences for development. Nevertheless, because they occur only rarely, they contribute relatively little to the population variance of intelligence
(Broman, Nichols, & Kennedy, 1975). Down's syndrome, a chromosomal abnormality that produces serious mental retardation, is also rare enough to have
little impact on the overall distribution of test scores.

The correlation between birth weight and later intelligence deserves particular discussion. In some
cases low birth weight simply reflects premature delivery; in others, the infant's size is below normal for
its gestational age. Both factors apparently contribute
to the tendency of low-birth-weight infants to have
lower test scores in later childhood (Lubchenko,
1976). These correlations are small, ranging from .05
to .13 in different groups (Broman et al., 1975). The
effects of low birth weight are substantial only when
it is very low indeed (less than 1,500 gm). Premature
babies born at these very low birth weights are behind controls on most developmental measures; they
often have severe or permanent intellectual deficits
(Rosetti, 1986).

CONTINUOUSLY RISING TEST SCORES

Perhaps the most striking of all environmental effects
is the steady worldwide rise in intelligence test performance. Although many psychometricians had
noted these gains, it was James Flynn (1984, 1987)
who first described them systematically. His analysis
shows that performance has been going up ever since
testing began. The "Flynn effect" is now very well documented, not only in the United States but in many
other technologically advanced countries. The average gain is about 3 IQ points per decade—more than a
full standard deviation since, say, 1940.

Although it is simplest to describe the gains as increases in population IQ, this is not exactly what
happens. Most intelligence tests are "restandardized"
from time to time, in part to keep up with these very
gains. As part of this process the mean score of the
new standardization sample is typically set to 100
again, so the increase more or less disappears from
view. In this context, the Flynn effect means that if
20 years have passed since the last time the test was
standardized, people who now score 100 on the new
version would probably average about 106 on the
old one.

The sheer extent of these increases is remarkable,
and the rate of gain may even be increasing. The
scores of 19-year-olds in the Netherlands, for example, went up more than 8 points—over half a standard
deviation—between 1972 and 1982. What's more, the
largest gains appear on the types of tests that were

specifically designed to be free of cultural influence (Flynn, 1987). One of these is Raven's Progressive Matrices, an untimed nonverbal test that many psychometricians regard as a good measure of *g*.

These steady gains in intelligence test performance have not always been accompanied by corresponding gains in school achievement. Indeed, the relation between intelligence and achievement test scores can be complex. This is especially true for the Scholastic Aptitude Test (SAT), in part because the ability range of the students who take the SAT has broadened over time. That change explains some portion—not all—of the prolonged decline in SAT scores that took place from the mid-1960s to the early 1980s, even as IQ scores were continuing to rise (Flynn, 1984). Meanwhile, however, other more representative measures show that school achievement levels have held steady or in some cases actually increased (Herrnstein & Murray, 1994). The National Assessment of Educational Progress (NAEP), for example, shows that the average reading and math achievement of American 13- and 17-year-olds improved somewhat from the early 1970s to 1990 (Grissmer, Kirby, Berends, & Williamson, 1994). An analysis of these data by ethnic group, reported in Section 5, shows that this small overall increase actually reflects very substantial gains by Blacks and Latinos combined with little or no gain by Whites.

The consistent IQ gains documented by Flynn seem much too large to result from simple increases in test sophistication. Their cause is presently unknown, but three interpretations deserve our consideration. Perhaps the most plausible of these is based on the striking cultural differences between successive generations. Daily life and occupational experience both seem more "complex" (Kohn & Schooler, 1973) today than in the time of our parents and grandparents. The population is increasingly urbanized; television exposes us to more information and more perspectives on more topics than ever before; children stay in school longer; and almost everyone seems to be encountering new forms of experience. These changes in the complexity of life may have produced corresponding changes in complexity of mind, and hence in certain psychometric abilities.

A different hypothesis attributes the gains to modern improvements in nutrition. Lynn (1990) points out that large nutritionally-based increases in height have occurred during the same period as the IQ gains: perhaps there have been increases in brain size as well. As we have seen, however, the effects of nutrition on intelligence are themselves not firmly established.

The third interpretation addresses the very definition of intelligence. Flynn himself believes that real intelligence—whatever it may be—cannot have increased as much as these data would suggest. Consider, for example, the number of individuals who have IQ scores of 140 or more. (This is slightly above the cutoff used by L. M. Terman [1925] in his famous longitudinal study of "genius.") In 1952 only 0.38% of Dutch test takers had IQs over 140; in 1982, scored by the same norms, 9.12% exceeded this figure! Judging by these criteria, the Netherlands should now be experiencing "a cultural renaissance too great to be overlooked" (Flynn, 1987, p. 187). So too should France, Norway, the United States, and many other countries. Because Flynn (1987) finds this conclusion implausible or absurd, he argues that what has risen cannot be intelligence itself but only a minor sort of "abstract problem solving ability." The issue remains unresolved. . . .

5. GROUP DIFFERENCES

Group means have no direct implications for individuals. What matters for the next person you meet (to the extent that test scores matter at all) is that person's own particular score, not the mean of some reference group to which he or she happens to belong. The commitment to evaluate people on their own individual merit is central to a democratic society. It also makes quantitative sense. The distributions of different groups inevitably overlap, with the range of scores within any one group always wider than the mean differences between any two groups. In the case of intelligence test scores, the variance attributable to individual differences far exceeds the variance related to group membership (Jensen, 1980). . . .

Besides European Americans ("Whites"), the ethnic groups to be considered are Chinese and Japanese Americans, Hispanic Americans ("Latinos"), Native Americans ("Indians"), and African Americans ("Blacks"). These groups (we avoid the term "race") are defined and self-defined by social conventions based on ethnic origin as well as on observable physical characteristics such as skin color. None of them are internally homogeneous. Asian Americans, for example, may have roots in many different cultures: not only China and Japan but also Korea, Laos, Vietnam, the Philippines, India, and Pakistan. Hispanic Americans, who share a common linguistic tradition, actually differ along many cultural dimensions. In their own minds they may be less "Latinos" than Puerto Ricans, Mexican Americans, Cuban Americans, or representatives of other Latin cultures. "Native American" is an even more diverse category, including a great many culturally distinct tribes living in a wide range of environments.

. . .

MEAN SCORES OF DIFFERENT ETHNIC GROUPS

Asian Americans.   In the years since the Second World War, Asian Americans—especially those of Chinese and Japanese extraction—have compiled an outstanding record of academic and professional achievement. This record is reflected in school grades, in scores on content-oriented achievement tests like the SAT and GRE, and especially in the disproportionate representation of Asian Americans in many sciences and professions. Although it is often supposed that these achievements reflect correspondingly high intelligence test scores, this is not the case. In more than a dozen studies from the 1960s and 1970s analyzed by Flynn (1991), the mean IQs of Japanese and Chinese American children were always around 97 or 98; none was over 100. Even Lynn (1993), who argues for a slightly higher figure, concedes that the achievements of these Asian Americans far outstrip what might have been expected on the basis of their test scores.

It may be worth noting that the interpretation of test scores obtained by Asians in Asia has been controversial in its own right. Lynn (1982) reported a mean Japanese IQ of 111 while Flynn (1991) estimated it to be between 101 and 105. Stevenson et al. (1985), comparing the intelligence-test performance of children in Japan, Taiwan, and the United States, found no substantive differences at all. Given the general problems of cross-cultural comparison, there is no reason to expect precision or stability in such estimates. Nevertheless, some interest attaches to these particular comparisons: they show that the well-established differences in school achievement among the same three groups (Chinese and Japanese children are much better at math than American children) do not simply reflect differences in psychometric intelligence. Stevenson, Lee, and Stigler (1986) suggest that they result from structural differences in the schools of the three nations as well as from varying cultural attitudes toward learning itself. It is also possible that spatial ability—in which Japanese and Chinese obtain somewhat higher scores than Americans—plays a particular role in the learning of mathematics. . . .

Hispanic Americans.   Hispanic immigrants have come to America from many countries. In 1993, the largest Latino groups in the continental United States were Mexican Americans (64%), Puerto Ricans (11%), Central and South Americans (13%), and Cubans (5%) (U.S. Bureau of the Census, 1994). There are very substantial cultural differences among these nationality groups, as well as differences in academic achievement (Duran, 1983; United States National Commission for Employment Policy, 1982). Taken together, Latinos make up the second largest and the

fastest-growing minority group in America (Davis, Haub, & Willette, 1983; Eyde, 1992).

In the United States, the mean intelligence test scores of Hispanics typically lie between those of Blacks and Whites. There are also differences in the patterning of scores across different abilities and subtests (Hennessy & Merrifield, 1978; Lesser, Fifer, & Clark, 1965). Linguistic factors play a particularly important role for Hispanic Americans, who may know relatively little English. (By one estimate, 25% of Puerto Ricans and Mexican Americans and at least 40% of Cubans speak English "not well" or "not at all" [Rodriguez, 1992]). Even those who describe themselves as bilingual may be at a disadvantage if Spanish was their first and best-learned language. It is not surprising that Latino children typically score higher on the performance than on the verbal subtests of the English-based Wechsler Intelligence Scale for Children–Revised (WISC–R; Kaufman, 1994). Nevertheless, the predictive validity of Latino test scores is not negligible. In young children, the WISC–R has reasonably high correlations with school achievement measures (McShane & Cook, 1985). For high school students of moderate to high English proficiency, standard aptitude tests predict first-year college grades about as well as they do for non-Hispanic Whites (Pennock-Roman, 1992).

Native Americans.   There are a great many culturally distinct North American Indian tribes (Driver, 1969), speaking some 200 different languages (Leap, 1981). Many Native Americans live on reservations, which themselves represent a great variety of ecological and cultural settings. Many others presently live in metropolitan areas (Brandt, 1984). Although few generalizations can be appropriate across so wide a range, two or three points seem fairly well established. The first is a specific relation between ecology and cognition: the Inuit (Eskimo) and other groups that live in the arctic tend to have particularly high visual-spatial skills. (For a review see McShane & Berry, 1988.) Moreover, there seem to be no substantial sex differences in those skills (Berry, 1974). It seems likely that this represents an adaptation—genetic or learned or both—to the difficult hunting, traveling, and living conditions that characterize the arctic environment.

On the average, Indian children obtain relatively low scores on tests of verbal intelligence, which are often administered in school settings. The result is a performance-test/verbal-test discrepancy similar to that exhibited by Hispanic Americans and other groups whose first language is generally not English. Moreover, many Indian children suffer from chronic middle-ear infection (otitis media), which is "the leading identifiable disease among Indians since record-keeping began in 1962" (McShane & Plas, 1984a,

p. 84). Hearing loss can have marked negative effects on verbal test performance (McShane & Plas, 1984b).

African Americans. The relatively low mean of the distribution of African American intelligence test scores has been discussed for many years. Although studies using different tests and samples yield a range of results, the Black mean is typically about one standard deviation (about 15 points) below that of Whites (Jensen, 1980; Loehlin et al., 1975; Reynolds et al., 1987). The difference is largest on those tests (verbal or nonverbal) that best represent the general intelligence factor *g* (Jensen, 1985). It is possible, however, that this differential is diminishing. In the most recent restandardization of the Stanford-Binet test, the Black/White differential was 13 points for younger children and 10 points for older children (Thorndike, Hagen, & Sattler, 1986). In several other studies of children since 1980, the Black mean has consistently been over 90 and the differential has been in single digits (Vincent, 1991). Larger and more definitive studies are needed before this trend can be regarded as established.

Another reason to think the IQ mean might be changing is that the Black/White differential in *achievement* scores has diminished substantially in the last few years. Consider, for example, the mathematics achievement of 17-year-olds as measured by the National Assessment of Educational Progress (NAEP). The differential between Black and White scores, about 1.1 standard deviations as recently as 1978, had shrunk to .65 *SD* by 1990 (Grissmer et al., 1994) because of Black gains. Hispanics showed similar but smaller gains; there was little change in the scores of Whites. Other assessments of school achievement also show substantial recent gains in the performance of minority children.

In their own analysis of these gains, Grissmer et al. (1994) cite both demographic factors and the effects of public policy. They found the level of parents' education to be a particularly good predictor of children's school achievement; that level increased for all groups between 1970 and 1990, but most sharply for Blacks. Family size was another good predictor (children from smaller families tend to achieve higher scores); here too, the largest change over time was among Blacks. Above and beyond these demographic effects, Grissmer et al. believe that some of the gains can be attributed to the many specific programs, geared to the education of minority children, that were implemented during that period.

Test Bias. It is often argued that the lower mean scores of African Americans reflect a bias in the intelligence tests themselves. This argument is right in one sense of "bias" but wrong in another. To see the first of these, consider how the term is used in probability theory. When a coin comes up heads consis-

tently for any reason it is said to be "biased," regardless of any consequences that the outcome may or may not have. In this sense the Black/White score differential is *ipso facto* evidence of what may be called "outcome bias." African Americans are subject to outcome bias not only with respect to tests but along many dimensions of American life. They have the short end of nearly every stick: average income, representation in high-level occupations, health and health care, death rate, confrontations with the legal system, and so on. With this situation in mind, some critics regard the test score differential as just another example of a pervasive outcome bias that characterizes our society as a whole (Jackson, 1975; Mercer, 1984). Although there is a sense in which they are right, this critique ignores the particular social purpose that tests are designed to serve.

From an educational point of view, the chief function of mental tests is as *predictors* (Section 2). Intelligence tests predict school performance fairly well, at least in American schools as they are now constituted. Similarly, achievement tests are fairly good predictors of performance in college and postgraduate settings. Considered in this light, the relevant question is whether the tests have a "predictive bias" against Blacks. Such a bias would exist if African American performance on the criterion variables (school achievement, college GPA, etc.) were systematically higher than the same subjects' test scores would predict. This is not the case. The actual regression lines (which show the mean criterion performance for individuals who got various scores on the predictor) for Blacks do not lie above those for Whites; there is even a slight tendency in the other direction (Jensen, 1980; Reynolds & Brown, 1984). Considered as predictors of future performance, the tests do not seem to be biased against African Americans.

Characteristics of Tests. It has been suggested that various aspects of the way tests are formulated and administered may put African Americans at a disadvantage. The language of testing is a standard form of English with which some Blacks may not be familiar; specific vocabulary items are often unfamiliar to Black children; the tests are often given by White examiners rather than by more familiar Black teachers; African Americans may not be motivated to work hard on tests that so clearly reflect White values; the time demands of some tests may be alien to Black culture. (Similar suggestions have been made in connection with the test performance of Hispanic Americans, e.g., Rodriguez, 1992.) Many of these suggestions are plausible, and such mechanisms may play a role in particular cases. Controlled studies have shown, however, that none of them contributes substantially to the Black/White differential under discussion here (Jensen, 1980; Reynolds & Brown, 1984;

for a different view see Helms, 1992). Moreover, efforts to devise reliable and valid tests that would minimize disadvantages of this kind have been unsuccessful.

INTERPRETING GROUP DIFFERENCES

If group differences in test performance do not result from the simple forms of bias reviewed above, what is responsible for them? The fact is that we do not know. Various explanations have been proposed, but none is generally accepted. It is clear, however, that these differences—whatever their origin—are well within the range of effect sizes that can be produced by environmental factors. The Black/White differential amounts to one standard deviation or less, and we know that environmental factors have recently raised mean test scores in many populations by at least that much (Flynn, 1987: see Section 4). To be sure, the "Flynn effect" is itself poorly understood: it may reflect generational changes in culture, improved nutrition, or other factors as yet unknown. Whatever may be responsible for it, we cannot exclude the possibility that the same factors play a role in contemporary group differences.

Socioeconomic Factors. Several specific environmental/cultural explanations of those differences have been proposed. All of them refer to the general life situation in which contemporary African Americans find themselves, but that situation can be described in several different ways. The simplest such hypothesis can be framed in economic terms. On the average, Blacks have lower incomes than Whites; a much higher proportion of them are poor. It is plausible to suppose that many inevitable aspects of poverty—poor nutrition, frequently inadequate prenatal care, lack of intellectual resources—have negative effects on children's developing intelligence. Indeed, the correlation between "socioeconomic status" (SES) and scores on intelligence tests is well-known (White, 1982).

Several considerations suggest that this cannot be the whole explanation. For one thing, the Black/White differential in test scores is not eliminated when groups or individuals are matched for SES (Loehlin et al., 1975). Moreover, the data reviewed in Section 4 suggest that—if we exclude extreme conditions—nutrition and other biological factors that may vary with SES account for relatively little of the variance in such scores. Finally, the (relatively weak) relationship between test scores and income is much more complex than a simple SES hypothesis would suggest. The living conditions of children result in part from the accomplishments of their parents: If the skills measured by psychometric tests actually matter for those accomplishments, intelligence is affecting

SES rather than the other way around. We do not know the magnitude of these various effects in various populations, but it is clear that no model in which "SES" directly determines "IQ" will do.

A more fundamental difficulty with explanations based on economics alone appears from a different perspective. To imagine that any simple income- and education-based index can adequately describe the situation of African Americans is to ignore important categories of experience. The sense of belonging to a group with a distinctive culture—one that has long been the target of oppression—and the awareness or anticipation of racial discrimination are profound personal experiences, not just aspects of socioeconomic status. Some of these more deeply rooted differences are addressed by other hypotheses, based on caste and culture.

Caste-like Minorities.   Most discussions of this issue treat Black/White differences as aspects of a uniquely "American dilemma" (Myrdal, 1944). The fact is, however, that comparably disadvantaged groups exist in many countries: the Maori in New Zealand, scheduled castes ("untouchables") in India, non-European Jews in Israel, the Burakumin in Japan. All these are "caste-like" (Ogbu, 1978) or "involuntary" (Ogbu, 1994) minorities. John Ogbu distinguishes this status from that of "autonomous" minorities who are not politically or economically subordinated (like Amish or Mormons in the United States), and from that of "immigrant" or "voluntary" minorities who initially came to their new homes with positive expectations. Immigrant minorities expect their situations to improve; they tend to compare themselves favorably with peers in the old country, not unfavorably with members of the dominant majority. In contrast, to be born into a caste-like minority is to grow up firmly convinced that one's life will eventually be restricted to a small and poorly-rewarded set of social roles.

Distinctions of caste are not always linked to perceptions of race. In some countries lower and upper caste groups differ by appearance and are assumed to be racially distinct; in others they are not. The social and educational consequences are the same in both cases. All over the world, the children of caste-like minorities do less well in school than upper-caste children and drop out sooner. Where there are data, they have usually been found to have lower test scores as well.

In explaining these findings, Ogbu (1978) argues that the children of caste-like minorities do not have "effort optimism," i.e., the conviction that hard work (especially hard schoolwork) and serious commitment on their part will actually be rewarded. As a result they ignore or reject the forms of learning that are offered in school. Indeed they may practice a sort of cultural inversion, deliberately rejecting certain behaviors (such as academic achievement or other forms of "acting White") that are seen as characteristic of the dominant group. While the extent to which the attitudes described by Ogbu (1978, 1994) are responsible for African American test scores and school achievement has not been empirically established, it does seem that familiar problems can take on quite a different look when they are viewed from an international perspective.

African American Culture. According to Boykin (1986, 1994), there is a fundamental conflict between certain aspects of African American culture on the one hand and the implicit cultural commitments of most American schools on the other. "When children are ordered to do their own work, arrive at their own individual answers, work only with their own materials, they are being sent cultural messages. When children come to believe that getting up and moving about the classroom is inappropriate, they are being sent powerful cultural messages. When children come to confine their 'learning' to consistently bracketed time periods, when they are consistently prompted to tell what they know and not how they feel, when they are led to believe that they are completely responsible for their own success and failure, when they are required to consistently put forth considerable effort for effort's sake on tedious and personally irrelevant tasks ... then they are pervasively having cultural lessons imposed on them" (1994, p. 125).

In Boykin's view, the combination of constriction and competition that most American schools demand of their pupils conflicts with certain themes in the "deep structure" of African American culture. That culture includes an emphasis on such aspects of experience as spirituality, harmony, movement, verve, affect, expressive individualism, communalism, orality, and a socially defined time perspective (Boykin, 1986, 1994). While it is not shared by all African Americans to the same degree, its accessibility and familiarity give it a profound influence.

The result of this cultural conflict, in Boykin's view, is that many Black children become alienated from both the process and the products of the education to which they are exposed. One aspect of that process, now an intrinsic aspect of the culture of most American schools, is the psychometric enterprise itself. He argues (Boykin, 1994) that the successful education of African American children will require an approach that is less concerned with talent sorting and assessment, more concerned with talent development.

One further factor should not be overlooked. Only a single generation has passed since the Civil Rights movement opened new doors for African Americans, and many forms of discrimination are still all too fa-

miliar in their experience today. Hard enough to bear in its own right, discrimination is also a sharp reminder of a still more intolerable past. It would be rash indeed to assume that those experiences, and that historical legacy, have no impact on intellectual development.

The Genetic Hypothesis. It is sometimes suggested that the Black/White differential in psychometric intelligence is partly due to genetic differences (Jensen, 1972). There is not much direct evidence on this point, but what little there is fails to support the genetic hypothesis. One piece of evidence comes from a study of the children of American soldiers stationed in Germany after the Second World War (Eyferth, 1961): there was no mean difference between the test scores of those children whose fathers were White and those whose fathers were Black. (For a discussion of possible confounds in this study, see Flynn, 1980.) Moreover, several studies have used blood-group methods to estimate the degree of African ancestry of American Blacks; there were no significant correlations between those estimates and IQ scores (Loehlin, Vandenberg, & Osborne, 1973; Scarr, Pakstis, Katz, & Barker, 1977).

It is clear (Section 3) that genes make a substantial contribution to individual differences in intelligence test scores, at least in the White population. The fact is, however, that the high heritability of a trait within a given group has no necessary implications for the source of a difference between groups (Loehlin et al., 1975). This is now generally understood (e.g., Herrnstein & Murray, 1994). But even though no such implication is *necessary*, some have argued that a high value of h^2 makes a genetic contribution to group differences more *plausible*. Does it?

That depends on one's assessment of the actual difference between the two environments. Consider Lewontin's (1970) well-known example of seeds from the same genetically variable stock that are planted in two different fields. If the plants in field X are fertilized appropriately while key nutrients are withheld from those in field Y, we have produced an entirely environmental group difference. This example works (i.e., h^2 is genuinely irrelevant to the differential between the fields) because the differences between the effective environments of X and Y are both large and consistent. Are the environmental and cultural situations of American Blacks and Whites also substantially and consistently different—different enough to make this a good analogy? If so, the within-group heritability of IQ scores is irrelevant to the issue. Or are those situations similar enough to suggest that the analogy is inappropriate, and that one can plausibly generalize from within-group heritabilities? Thus the issue ultimately comes down to a personal judgment: How different are the relevant life experiences of Whites and Blacks in the United States today? At present, this question has no scientific answer.

6. Summary and Conclusions

. . .

It is customary to conclude surveys like this one with a summary of what has been established. Indeed, much is now known about intelligence. A near-century of research, most of it based on psychometric methods, has produced an impressive body of findings. Although we have tried to do justice to those findings in this report, it seems appropriate to conclude on a different note. In this contentious arena, our most useful role may be to remind our readers that many of the critical questions about intelligence are still unanswered. Here are a few of those questions:

1. Differences in genetic endowment contribute substantially to individual differences in (psychometric) intelligence, but the pathway by which genes produce their effects is still unknown. The impact of genetic differences appears to increase with age, but we do not know why.

2. Environmental factors also contribute substantially to the development of intelligence, but we do not clearly understand what those factors are or how they work. Attendance at school is certainly important, for example, but we do not know what aspects of schooling are critical.

3. The role of nutrition in intelligence remains obscure. Severe childhood malnutrition has clear negative effects, but the hypothesis that particular "micronutrients" may affect intelligence in otherwise adequately-fed populations has not yet been convincingly demonstrated.

4. There are significant correlations between measures of information-processing speed and psychometric intelligence, but the overall pattern of these findings yields no easy theoretical interpretation.

5. Mean scores on intelligence tests are rising steadily. They have gone up a full standard deviation in the last 50 years or so, and the rate of gain may be increasing. No one is sure why these gains are happening or what they mean.

6. The differential between the mean intelligence test scores of Blacks and Whites (about one standard deviation, although it may be diminishing) does not result from any obvious biases in test construction and administration, nor does it simply reflect differences in socioeconomic status. Explanations based on factors of caste and cul-

ture may be appropriate, but so far have little direct empirical support. There is certainly no such support for a genetic interpretation. At present, no one knows what causes this differential.

7. It is widely agreed that standardized tests do not sample all forms of intelligence. Obvious examples include creativity, wisdom, practical sense, and social sensitivity; there are surely others. Despite the importance of these abilities we know very little about them: how they develop, what factors influence that development, how they are related to more traditional measures.

In a field where so many issues are unresolved and so many questions unanswered, the confident tone that has characterized most of the debate on these topics is clearly out of place. The study of intelligence does not need politicized assertions and recriminations; it needs self-restraint, reflection, and a great deal more research. The questions that remain are socially as well as scientifically important. There is no reason to think them unanswerable, but finding the answers will require a shared and sustained effort as well as the commitment of substantial scientific resources. Just such a commitment is what we strongly recommend.

References

Baghurst, P. A., McMichael, A. J., Wigg, N. R., Vimpani, G. V., Robertson, E. F., Roberts, R. J., & Tong, S. L. (1992). Environmental exposure to lead and children's intelligence at the age of seven years: The Port Pirie cohort study. *New England Journal of Medicine, 327*, 1279–1284.

Baumrind, D. (1993). The average expectable environment is not good enough: A response to Scarr. *Child Development, 64*, 1299–1317.

Berry, J. W. (1974). Ecological and cultural factors in spatial perceptual development. In J. W. Berry & P. R. Dasen (Eds.), *Culture and cognition: Readings in cross-cultural psychology* (pp. 129–140). London: Methuen.

Boykin, A. W. (1986). The triple quandary and the schooling of Afro-American children. In U. Neisser (Ed.), *The school achievement of minority children* (pp. 57–92). Hillsdale, NJ: Erlbaum.

Boykin, A. W. (1994). Harvesting talent and culture: African-American children and educational reform. In R. Rossi (Ed.), *Schools and students at risk* (pp. 116–138). New York: Teachers College Press.

Brandt, E. A. (1984). The cognitive functioning of American Indian children: A critique of McShane and Plas. *School Psychology Review, 13*, 74–82.

Broman, S. H., Nichols, P. L., & Kennedy, W. A. (1975). *Preschool IQ: Prenatal and early developmental correlates.* Hillsdale. NJ: Erlbaum.

Campbell, F. A., & Ramey, C. T. (1994). Effects of early intervention on intellectual and academic achievement: A follow-up study of children from low-income families. *Child Development, 65*, 684–698.

Carroll, J. B. (1993). *Human cognitive abilities: A survey of factor-analytic studies.* Cambridge, England: University of Cambridge Press.

Ceci, S. J. (1990). *On intelligence ... more or less: A bioecological treatise on intellectual development.* Englewood Cliffs, NJ: Prentice Hall.

Chipuer, H. M., Rovine, M., & Plomin, R. (1990). LISREL modelling: Genetic and environmental influences on IQ revisited. *Intelligence, 14*, 11–29.

Consortium for Longitudinal Studies. (1983). *As the twig is bent ... lasting effects of preschool programs.* Hillsdale, NJ: Erlbaum.

Darlington, R. B. (1986). Long-term effects of preschool programs. In U. Neisser (Ed.), *The school achievement of minority children* (pp. 159–167). Hillsdale, NJ: Erlbaum.

Davis, C., Haub, C., & Willette, J. (1983). U.S. Hispanics: Changing the face of America. *Population Bulletin, 38*(No. 3).

Deary, I. J. (1995). Auditory inspection time and intelligence: What is the causal direction? *Developmental Psychology, 31*, 237–250.

Driver, H. E. (1969). *Indians of North America.* Chicago: University of Chicago Press.

Dube, E. F. (1982). Literacy, cultural familiarity, and "intelligence" as determinants of story recall. In U. Neisser (Ed.), *Memory observed: Remembering in natural contexts* (pp. 274–292). New York: Freeman.

Duran, R. P. (1983). *Hispanics' education and background: Prediction of college achievement.* New York: College Entrance Examination Board.

Eyde, L. D. (1992). Introduction to the testing of Hispanics in industry and research. In K. F. Geisinger (Ed.), *Psychological testing of Hispanics* (pp. 167–172). Washington. DC: American Psychological Association.

Eyferth, K. (1961). Leistungen verchiedener Gruppen von Besatzungskindern Hamburg-Wechsler Intelligentztest fur Kinder (HAWIK) [The performance of different groups of occupation children in the Hamburg-Wechsler Intelligence Test for Children]. *Archive fur die gesamte Psychologie, 113*, 222–241.

Eysenck, H. (1973). *The measurement of intelligence.* Baltimore: Williams & Wilkins.

Eysenck, H. J. (1986). Inspection time and intelligence: A historical introduction. *Personality and Individual Differences, 7*, 603–607.

Flynn, J. R. (1980). *Race, IQ, and Jensen.* London: Routledge & Kegan Paul.

Flynn, J. R. (1984). The mean IQ of Americans: Massive gains 1932 to 1978. *Psychological Bulletin, 95*, 29–51.

Flynn, J. R. (1987). Massive IQ gains in 14 nations: What IQ tests really measure. *Psychological Bulletin, 101*, 171–191.

Flynn, J. R. (1991). *Asian-Americans: Achievement beyond IQ.* Hillsdale, NJ: Erlbaum.

Gardner, H. (1983). *Frames of mind: The theory of multiple intelligences.* New York: Basic Books.

Gay, J., & Cole, M. (1967). *The new mathematics and an old culture: A study of learning among the Kpelle of Liberia.* New York: Holt, Rhinehart & Winston.

Gottfried, A. W. (Ed.). (1984). *Home environment and early cognitive development: Longitudinal research.* New York: Academic Press.

Gould, S. J. (1978). Morton's ranking of races by cranial capacity: Unconscious manipulation of data may be a scientific norm. *Science, 200*, 503–509.

Grissmer, D. W., Kirby, S. N., Berends, M., & Williamson, S. (1994). *Student achievement and the changing American family.* Santa Monica, CA: RAND Corporation.

Gustafsson, J.-E. (1984). A unifying model for the structure of intellectual abilities. *Intelligence, 8*, 179–203.

Hart, B., & Risley, T. R. (1992). American parenting of language-learning children: Persisting differences in family-child interactions observed in natural home environments. *Developmental Psychology, 28*, 1096–1105.

Hart, B., & Risley, T. R. (1995). *Meaningful differences in the everyday experience of young American children.* Baltimore: P. H. Brookes.

Helms, J. E. (1992). Why is there no study of cultural equivalence in standardized cognitive ability testing? *American Psychologist, 47*, 1083–1101.

Hennessy, J. J., & Merrifield, P. R. (1978). Ethnicity and sex distinctions in patterns of aptitude factor scores in a sample of urban high school seniors. *American Educational Research Journal, 15*, 385–389.

Herrnstein, R. J., & Murray, C. (1994). *The bell curve: Intelligence and class structure in American life.* New York: Free Press.

Herrnstein, R. J., Nickerson R. S., de Sanchez, M., & Swets, J. A. (1986). Teaching thinking skills. *American Psychologist, 41*, 1279–1289.

Hunter, J. E. (1983). A causal analysis of cognitive ability, job knowledge, job performance, and supervisor ratings. In F. Landy, S. Zedeck, & J. Cleveland (Eds.), *Performance measurement and theory* (pp. 257–266). Hillsdale, NJ: Erlbaum.

Jackson, G. D. (1975). On the report of the Ad Hoc Committee on Educational Uses of Tests with Disadvantaged Students: Another psychological view from the Association of Black Psychologists. *American Psychologist, 30*, 88–93.

Jackson, J. F. (1993). Human behavioral genetics, Scarr's theory, and her views on interventions: A critical review and commentary on their implications for African American children. *Child Development, 64*, 1318–1332.

Jencks, C. (1979). *Who gets ahead? The determinants of economic success in America.* New York: Basic Books.

Jensen, A. R. (1972). *Genetics and education.* New York: Harper & Row.

Jensen, A. R. (1977). Cumulative deficit in IQ of Blacks in the rural South. *Developmental Psychology, 13*, 184–191.

Jensen, A. R. (1980). *Bias in mental testing.* New York: Free Press.

Jensen, A. R. (1985). The nature of the black-white difference on various psychometric tests: Spearman's hypothesis. *Behavioral and Brain Sciences, 8*, 193–263.

Jones, H. E., and Bayley, N. (1941). The Berkeley Growth Study. *Child Development, 12,* 167–173.

Kaufman, A. S. (1994). *Intelligent testing with the WISC-III.* New York: Wiley.

Kohn, M. L., & Schooler, C. (1973). Occupational experience and psychological functioning: An assessment of reciprocal effects. *American Sociological Review, 38,* 97–118.

Kohn, M. L., & Schooler, C. (1983). *Work and personality: An inquiry into the impact of social stratification.* Norwood, NJ: Ablex.

Leap, W. L. (1981). American Indian languages. In C. Ferguson & S. B. Heath (Eds.), *Language in the USA.* Cambridge, England: Cambridge University Press.

Lee, E. S. (1951). Negro intelligence and selective migration: A Philadelphia test of the Klineberg hypothesis. *American Sociological Review, 16,* 227–232.

Lesser, G. S., Fifer, G., & Clark, D. H. (1965). Mental abilities of children from different social-class and cultural groups. *Monographs of the Society for Research in Child Development, 30* (Whole No. 102).

Lewontin, R. (1970). Race and intelligence. *Bulletin of the Atomic Scientists, 26,* 2–8.

Locurto, C. (1991). Beyond IQ in preschool programs? *Intelligence, 15,* 295–312.

Loehlin, J. C. (1989). Partitioning environmental and genetic contributions to behavioral development. *American Psychologist, 10,* 1285–1292.

Loehlin, J. C., Horn, J. M., & Willerman, L. (1989). Modeling IQ change: Evidence from the Texas Adoption Project. *Child Development, 60,* 993–1004.

Loehlin, J. C., Lindzey, G., & Spuhler, J. N. (1975). *Race differences in intelligence.* New York: Freeman.

Loehlin, J. C., Vandenberg, S. G., & Osborne, R. T. (1973). Blood group genes and Negro-White ability differences. *Behavior Genetics, 3,* 263–270.

Lubchenko, L. O. (1976). *The high-risk infant.* Philadelphia: Saunders.

Lynn, R. (1982). IQ in Japan and the United States shows a growing disparity. *Nature, 297,* 222–223.

Lynn, R. (1990). The role of nutrition in secular increases in intelligence. *Personality and Individual Differences, 11,* 273–285.

Lynn, R. (1993). Oriental Americans: Their IQ, educational attainment, and socio-economic status. *Personality and Individual Differences, 15,* 237–242.

Mackenzie, B., Molloy, E., Martin, F., Lovegrove, W., & McNicol, D. (1991). Inspection time and the content of simple tasks: A framework for research on speed of information processing. *Australian Journal of Psychology, 43,* 37–43.

McCartney, K., Harris, M. J., & Bernieri, F. (1990). Growing up and growing apart: A developmental meta-analysis of twin studies. *Psychological Bulletin, 107,* 226–237.

McGue, M., Bouchard, T. J., Jr., Iacono, W. G., & Lykken, D. T. (1993). Behavioral genetics of cognitive ability: A life-span perspective. In R. Plomin & G. E. McClearn (Eds.). *Nature, nurture, & psychology* (pp. 59–76). Washington, DC: American Psychological Association.

McMichael, A. J., Baghurst, P. A., Wigg, N. R., Vimpani, G. V., Robertson, E. F., & Roberts, R. J. (1988). Port Pirie cohort study: Environmental exposure to lead and children's abilities at the age of four years. *New England Journal of Medicine, 319,* 468–475.

McShane, D. A., & Berry, J. W. (1988). Native North Americans: Indian and Inuit abilities. In S. H. Irvine & J. W. Berry (Eds.). *Human abilities in cultural context* (pp. 385–426). New York: Cambridge University Press.

McShane, D. A., & Cook, V. J. (1985). Transcultural intellectual assessment: Performance by Hispanics on the Wechsler Scales. In B. B. Wolman (Ed.), *Handbook of intelligence: Theories, measurements, and applications.* New York: Wiley.

McShane, D. A., & Plas, J. M. (1984a). Response to a critique of the McShane & Plas review of American Indian performance on the Wechsler Intelligence Scales. *School Psychology Review, 13,* 83–88.

McShane, D. A., & Plas, J. M. (1984b). The cognitive functioning of American Indian children: Moving from the WISC to the WISC-R. *School Psychology Review, 13,* 61–73.

Mercer, J. R. (1984). What is a racially and culturally nondiscriminatory test? A sociological and pluralistic perspective. In C. R. Reynolds & R. T. Brown (Eds.), *Perspectives on bias in mental testing.* New York: Plenum Press.

Moffitt, T. E., Caspi, A., Harkness, A. R., & Silva, P. A. (1993). The natural history of change in intellectual performance: Who changes? How much? Is it meaningful? *Journal of Child Psychology and Psychiatry, 34,* 455–506.

Moffitt, T. E., Gabrielli, W. F., Mednick, S. A., & Schulsinger, F. (1981). Socioeconomic status, IQ, and delinquency. *Journal of Abnormal Psychology, 90,* 152–156.

Myrdal, G. (1944). *An American dilemma: The Negro problem and modern democracy.* New York: Harper.

Needleman, H. L., Geiger, S. K., & Frank, R. (1985). Lead and IQ scores: A reanalysis. *Science, 227,* 701–704.

Ogbu, J. U. (1978). *Minority education and caste: The American system in cross-cultural perspective.* New York: Academic Press.

Ogbu, J. U. (1994). From cultural differences to differences in cultural frames of references. In P. M. Greenfield & R. R. Cocking (Eds.), *Cross-cultural roots of minority child development* (pp. 365–391). Hillsdale, NJ: Erlbaum.

Olivier, G. (1980). The increase of stature in France. *Journal of Human Evolution, 9,* 645–649.

Pennock-Roman, M. (1992). Interpreting test performance in selective admissions for Hispanic students. In K. F. Geisinger (Ed.), *Psychological testing of Hispanics* (pp. 95–135). Washington, DC: American Psychological Association.

Plomin, R., & Bergeman, C. S. (1991). The nature of nurture: Genetic influence on "environmental" measures. *Behavioral and Brain Sciences, 14,* 373–427.

Pollitt, E., Gorman, K. S., Engle, P. L., Martorell, R., & Rivera, J. (1993). Early supplementary feeding and cognition. *Monographs of the Society for Research in Child Development, 58* (Serial No. 235).

Reed, T. E., & Jensen, A. R. (1992). Conduction velocity in a brain nerve pathway of normal adults correlates with intelligence level. *Intelligence, 16,* 259–272.

Rehberg, R. A., & Rosenthal, E. R. (1978). *Class and merit in the American high school.* New York: Longman.

Reynolds, C. R., & Brown, R. T. (1984). Bias in mental testing: An introduction to the issues. In C. R. Reynolds & R. T. Brown (Eds.), *Perspectives on bias in mental testing* (pp. 1–39). New York: Plenum Press.

Reynolds, C. R., Chastain, R. L., Kaufman, A. S., & McLean, J. E. (1987). Demographic characteristics and IQ among adults: Analysis of the WAIS-R standardization sample as a function of the stratification variables. *Journal of School Psychology, 25,* 323–342.

Ricciuti, H. N. (1993). Nutrition and mental development. *Current Directions in Psychological Science, 2,* 43–46.

Rodriguez, O. (1992). Introduction to technical and societal issues in the psychological testing of Hispanics. In K. F. Geisinger (Ed.), *Psychological testing of Hispanics* (pp. 11–15). Washington, DC: American Psychological Association.

Rosetti, L. (1986). *High risk infants: Identification, assessment, and intervention.* Boston: Little Brown.

Scarr, S. (1992). Developmental theories for the 1990s: Development and individual differences. *Child Development, 63,* 1–19.

Scarr, S. (1993). Biological and cultural diversity: The legacy of Darwin for development. *Child Development, 64,* 1333–1353.

Scarr, S., Pakstis, A. J., Katz, S. H., & Barker, W. B. (1977). Absence of a relationship between degree of White ancestry and intellectual skills within a Black population. *Human Genetics, 39,* 69–86.

Scarr, S., & Weinberg, R. A. (1978). The influence of "family background" on intellectual attainment. *American Sociological Review, 43,* 674–692.

Scarr, S., Weinberg, R. A., & Waldman, I. D. (1993). IQ correlations in transracial adoptive families. *Intelligence, 17,* 541–555.

Sigman, M. (1995). Nutrition and child development: More food for thought. *Current Directions in Psychological Science, 4,* 52–55.

Spearman, C. (1927). *The abilities of man.* New York: Macmillan.

Stein, Z., Susser, M., Saenger, G., & Marolla, F. (1975). *Famine and human development: The Dutch hunger winter of 1944–45.* New York: Oxford University Press.

Sternberg, R. J., & Detterman, D. K. (Eds.). (1986). *What is intelligence? Contemporary viewpoints on its nature and definition.* Norwood, NJ: Ablex.

Stevenson, H. W., Lee, S. Y., & Stigler, J. W. (1986). Mathematics achievement of Chinese, Japanese, and American children. *Science, 231,* 693–699.

Stevenson, H. W., Stigler, J. W., Lee, S. Y., Lucker, G. W., Kitamura, S., & Hsu, C. C. (1985). Cognitive performance and academic achievement of Japanese, Chinese, and American children. *Child Development, 56,* 718–734.

Streissguth, A. P., Barr, H. M., Sampson, P. D., Darby, B. L., & Martin, D. C. (1989). IQ at age 4 in relation to maternal alcohol use and smoking during pregnancy. *Developmental Psychology, 25,* 3–11.

Terman, L. M. (1925). *Genetic studies of genius: Mental and physical traits of a thousand gifted children.* Stanford, CA: Stanford University Press.

Thomson, G. H. (1939). *The factorial analysis of human ability.* Boston: Houghton Mifflin.

Thorndike, R. L., Hagen, E. P., & Sattler, J. M. (1986). *Stanford-Binet intelligence scale: Fourth edition (Technical Manual).* Chicago: Riverside.

Thurstone, L. L. (1938). *Primary mental abilities.* Chicago: University of Chicago Press.

United States Bureau of the Census. (1994). *The Hispanic population of the United States: March 1993* (Current Population Reports, Series P20–475). Washington, DC: Author.

United States National Commission for Employment Policy. (1982). *Hispanics and jobs: Barriers to progress* (Report No. 14). Washington, DC: Author.

Vernon, P. A. (1987). *Speed of information processing and intelligence.* Norwood, NJ: Ablex.

Vincent, K. R. (1991). Black/White IQ differences: Does age make the difference? *Journal of Clinical Psychology, 47,* 266–270.

Waller, J. H. (1971). Achievement and social mobility: Relationships among IQ score, education, and occupation in two generations. *Social Biology, 18,* 252–259.

White, K. R. (1982). The relation between socioeconomic status and academic achievement. *Psychological Bulletin, 91,* 461–481.

QUESTIONS

1. What is intelligence?
2. What is the psychometric approach to intelligence, and what role does this approach currently play in IQ testing?
3. Why is stability considered an important characteristic of an IQ test score?
4. What do IQ tests predict, and what do they not predict?
5. Does IQ relate to cognitive processing in any way? Explain.
6. What does research on environmental effects on intelligence indicate about the nature of human intelligence?
7. Why have overall IQ test scores improved over the past century?

8. How does Lowentin's (1970) example of genetically identical seeds growing in different fields re-late to the debate about racial differences in IQ?
9. How does heredity contribute to intelligence?
10. What are some of the critical issues in interpreting group differences in IQ in the United States today?

PART V

Adolescence

Adolescence is a time of life that is difficult to define. In many ways, it is a cultural construction. That is, whether adolescence is considered a unique stage depends on the culture in which a child lives. The duration of adolescence also varies across cultures. In Western communities, adolescence is fairly long, ranging from about age 11 to the end of the teen years, and sometimes stretching into the early twenties for youth who are still dependent on their parents. In many non-Western communities, adolescence is fairly short and usually ends at puberty with an abrupt transition to adult marital or work responsibilities.

Research on adolescence cuts across many topics. The general tenor of the research for a long time was problem-focused, seeing adolescence as a time of much conflict and difficulty. The articles in this section address this issue in a variety of ways. Jeffrey Jensen Arnett reexamines the question of whether adolescence is indeed a time of storm and stress. Amy A. Wolfson and Mary A. Carskadon investigate assumptions about biological change in adolescence, specifically the sleep/wake cycle. Mark S. Chapell and Willis F. Overton focus on cognitive development in African-American youth, with particular attention to social class and ethnic identity. The article by Matthew F. Bumpus, Ann C. Crouter, and Susan M. McHale concentrates on the parent–adolescent relationship, especially on the influence the children's gender has on the parents' granting of autonomy. Thomas J. Dishion, David W. Andrews, and Lynn Crosby explore the origins of adolescent delinquency by looking closely at the friendships of antisocial boys. Finally, Jodie Roth and Jeanne Brooks-Gunn discuss the policy implications of what adolescents need in order to develop in healthy ways.

All these articles make it clear that adolescence is a time of rapid physical, cognitive, and emotional change, and those changes are greatly influenced by the social and cultural context. Society's expectations for its members who are just on the verge of maturity reflect cultural values and goals, which are evident in the relationships and experiences that adolescents have throughout this period of growth.

32 Adolescent Storm and Stress, Reconsidered

JEFFREY JENSEN ARNETT

The study of adolescence has been filled for decades with controversy. There are disagreements about the cause(s) of adolescence: Is it instigated by biological or social or cognitive changes? There are disagreements about when adolescence begins and when it ends: Does it begin when the first signs of puberty appear, or is it regulated by certain social passages, like entering junior high or high school? Does it end at high school graduation or age 20 or marriage or college graduation? Finally, is adolescence a universal stage of human development, or does it exist in some cultures but not in others?

One longstanding disagreement among psychologists and other scholars concerns the nature of adolescence itself. Historically, many thinkers from ancient Greek philosophers to Shakespeare to anthropologists in the early 20th century have commented on the period of development between childhood and adulthood. In large measure, their comments stress the difficulties associated with this period—both for the adolescents themselves and for those who interact with adolescents, especially parents and teachers. The first American developmental psychologist, G. Stanley Hall, followed up on this general theme when he called adolescence a time of "storm and stress." Hall thought that the difficulties associated with adolescence were inevitable and reflected the normal biological course of this period of growth. Since Hall's writing, this view of adolescence has become the conventional wisdom. But what does the research say about it?

The following article discusses the history of and research on adolescent storm and stress. In particular, researcher Jeffrey Jensen Arnett examines the three elements that are often included in this notion: conflict with parents, mood disruptions, and risk behavior. Arnett describes how psychologists study each of these topics, as well as the consensus on each that is emerging from research. In general, current research supports the idea that adolescence is a time of storm and stress. However, the definition and interpretation of storm and stress have changed substantially over the years. Moreover, we now know that culture plays an important role in this process, in both the attention to and the promotion of adolescent behaviors that conform to this conception. This article is a fascinating reminder that some of the oldest ideas in psychology are the most interesting, as well as the hardest to understand.

G. S. Hall's (1904) view that adolescence is a period of heightened "storm and stress" is reconsidered in light of contemporary research. The author provides a brief history of the storm-and-stress view and examines 3 key aspects of this view: conflict with parents, mood disruptions, and risk behavior. In all 3 areas, evidence supports a modified storm-and-stress view that takes into account individual differences and cultural variations. Not all adolescents experience storm and stress, but storm and stress is more likely during adolescence than at other ages. Adolescent storm and stress tends to be lower in traditional cultures than in the West but may increase as globalization increases individualism. Similar issues apply to minority cultures in American society. Finally, although the general public is sometimes portrayed by scholars as having a stereotypical view of adolescent storm and stress, both scholars and the general public appear to support a modified storm-and-stress view.

Nearly 100 years after G. Stanley Hall (1904) proposed that adolescence is inherently a time of storm

Editor's note: Ann S. Masten served as action editor for this article.

Author's note: I thank Christy Buchanan, Lene Jensen, and Reed Larson for their insightful comments and suggestions.

and stress, his view continues to be addressed by psychologists. For the most part, contemporary psychologists reject the view that adolescent storm and stress is universal and inevitable (e.g., Eccles et al., 1993; Offer & Schonert-Reichl, 1992; Petersen et al., 1993; Steinberg & Levine, 1997). However, the storm-and-stress view is usually invoked by psychologists only in passing, in the course of addressing some other topic. Rarely has the storm-and-stress view been considered directly, and rarely have its merits and limitations been evaluated in depth.

Hall initiated the scientific study of adolescence, and since his time (especially in the past 20 years), research on adolescence has produced a great deal of information that bears on the question of adolescent storm and stress. As the centennial of Hall's (1904) landmark two-volume work approaches, this may be an appropriate time to evaluate the merits of the view for which he is best known today. I argue here that a case can be made for the validity of a modified storm-and-stress view. The claim that adolescent storm and stress is characteristic of all adolescents and that the source of it is purely biological is clearly false. However, evidence supports the existence of some degree of storm and stress—at least for adolescents in the middle-class American majority culture—with respect to conflict with parents, mood disruptions, and risk behavior. Not all adolescents experience storm and stress in these areas, but adolescence is the period when storm and stress is *more likely* to occur than at other ages. I emphasize that there are individual differences among adolescents in the extent to which they exhibit storm and stress and that there are cultural variations in the pervasiveness of adolescent storm and stress.

STORM AND STRESS: A BRIEF HISTORY

Hall (1904) was the first to consider the storm-and-stress issue explicitly and formally in relation to adolescent development, but he was not the first in the history of Western thought to remark on the emotional and behavioral distinctiveness of adolescence. Aristotle stated that youth "are heated by Nature as drunken men by wine." Socrates characterized youth as inclined to "contradict their parents" and "tyrannize their teachers." Rousseau relied on a stormy metaphor in describing adolescence: "As the roaring of the waves precedes the tempest, so the murmur of rising passions announces the tumultuous change. . . . Keep your hand upon the helm," he advised parents, "or all is lost" (Rousseau, 1762/1962, pp. 172–173).

Around the time Rousseau was writing, an influential genre of German literature was developing, known as "sturm und drang" literature—roughly translated as "storm and stress." The quintessential work of the genre was Goethe's (1774/1989) *The Sorrows of Young Werther*, a story about a young man who commits suicide in despair over his doomed love for a married woman. There were numerous other stories at the time that depicted youthful anguish and angst. The genre gave rise to popular use of the term "storm and stress," which Hall (1904) adopted a century later when writing his magnum opus on adolescent development.

Hall (1904) favored the Lamarckian evolutionary ideas that were considered by many prominent thinkers in the early 20th century (Freud and Jung included) to be a better explanation of evolution than Darwin's theory of natural selection. In Lamarck's now-discredited theory, evolution takes place as a result of accumulated experience. Organisms pass on their characteristics from one generation to the next not in the form of genes (which were unknown at the time Lamarck and Darwin devised their theories), but in the form of *memories and acquired characteristics*. Thus, Hall, considering development during adolescence, judged it to be "suggestive of some ancient period of storm and stress" (1904, Vol. 1, p. xiii). In his view, there must have been a period of human evolution that was extremely difficult and tumultuous: the memory of that period had been passed ever since from one generation to the next and was *recapitulated* in the development of each individual as the storm and stress of adolescent development. To Hall, this legacy of storm and stress was particularly evident in adolescents' tendency to question and contradict their parents, in their mood disruptions, and in their propensity for reckless and antisocial behavior.

Although Hall is often portrayed as depicting adolescent storm and stress as universal and biological, in fact his view was more nuanced. He acknowledged individual differences, noting for example that conflict with parents was more likely for adolescents with "ruder natures" (1904, Vol. 2, p. 79). Also, he believed that a *tendency* toward storm and stress in adolescence was universal and biologically based, but that culture influenced adolescents' expression and experience of it. He saw storm and stress as more likely to occur in the United States of his day than in "older lands with more conservative traditions" (1904, Vol. 1, p. xvi). In his view, the storm and stress of American adolescence was aggravated by growing urbanization, with all its temptations to vice, and by the clash between the sedentary quality of urban life and what he saw as adolescents' inherent need for activity and exploration. Hall also believed that adolescent storm and stress in his time was aggravated by the failure of home, school, and religious organizations to recognize the true nature and potential perils of adolescence and to adapt their institutions accordingly, a view not unlike that of many more recent scholars (e.g., Eccles et al., 1993; Simmons & Blythe, 1987).

In the century since Hall's work established adolescence as an area of scientific study, the debate over adolescent storm and stress has simmered steadily and boiled to the surface periodically. Anthropologists, led by Margaret Mead (1928), countered the claim that a tendency toward storm and stress in adolescence is universal and biological by describing non-Western cultures in which adolescence was neither stormy nor stressful. In contrast, psychoanalytic theorists, particularly Anna Freud (1946, 1958, 1968, 1969), have been the most outspoken proponents of the storm-and-stress view. Like Hall, psychoanalytic theorists viewed adolescent storm and stress as rooted in the recapitulation of earlier experiences, but as a recapitulation of ontogenetic Oedipal conflicts from early childhood rather than phylogenetic epochs (Blos, 1962). This recapitulation of Oedipal conflicts provoked emotional volatility (as the adolescent ego attempted to gain ascendancy over resurgent instinctual drives), depressed mood (as the adolescent mourned the renunciation of the Oedipal parent), and conflict with parents (in the course of making this renunciation: Blos, 1962). Furthermore, the resurgence of instinctual drives was regarded as likely to be acted out in "dissocial, even criminal" behavior (Freud, 1968, p. 18).

Anna Freud (1958, 1968, 1969) viewed adolescents who did not experience storm and stress with great suspicion, claiming that their outward calm concealed the inward reality that they must have "built up excessive defenses against their drive activities and are now crippled by the results" (1968, p. 15). She, much more than Hall, viewed storm and stress as universal and immutable, to the extent that its absence signified psychopathology: "To be normal during the adolescent period is by itself abnormal" (1958, p. 267).

In recent decades, two types of studies concerning adolescent storm and stress have appeared. A handful of studies, mostly by Buchanan and Holmbeck (Buchanan, 1998; Buchanan et al., 1990; Buchanan & Holmbeck, 1998; Holmbeck & Hill, 1988; Offer, Ostrov, & Howard, 1981), have focused on public perceptions of adolescence as a time of storm and stress. These studies (using American middle-class samples) have consistently found that most people in the American majority culture perceive adolescence as a time of relative storm and stress. For example, Buchanan et al. (1990) found that the majority of both parents and teachers agreed with statements such as "early adolescence is a difficult time of life for children and their parents/teachers." Buchanan and Holmbeck (1998) reported that college students and parents of early adolescents viewed adolescents as more likely than elementary school children to have problems such as symptoms of internalizing disorders (e.g., anxiousness, insecurity, and depression) and risk taking/rebelliousness (e.g., recklessness, impulsivity, and rudeness). Similarly, the majority of college students surveyed by Holmbeck and Hill (1988) agreed with statements such as "adolescents frequently fight with their parents."

A second type of contemporary study has addressed the actual occurrence of adolescent storm and stress, in the specific areas of conflict with parents (Gecas & Seff, 1990; Steinberg, 1987), emotional volatility (Larson & Richards, 1994), negative affect (Brooks-Gunn & Warren, 1989; Buchanan, Eccles, & Becker, 1992; Petersen et al., 1993), and risk behavior (Arnett, 1992; Moffitt, 1993). Storm and stress tends to be mentioned in these studies not as the primary focus but in the course of addressing another topic. Consistently, these studies reject the claim—usually attributed to Hall—that adolescent storm and stress is universal and find only weak support for the claim that it is biologically based. However, the studies also consistently support a modified storm-and-stress thesis that adolescence is a time when various types of problems are *more likely* to arise than at other ages. The primary goal of this article is to draw together the evidence from these areas and to present an argument for the validity of the modified storm-and-stress thesis.

DEFINING STORM AND STRESS

It is important at this point to address directly the question of what is included under the concept of adolescent storm and stress. Taking historical and theoretical views in combination with contemporary research, the core of the storm-and-stress view seems to be the idea that adolescence is a period of life that is *difficult* (Buchanan et al., 1990)—more difficult in some ways than other periods of life and difficult for adolescents as well as for the people around them. This idea, that adolescence is difficult, includes three key elements:

1. *Conflict with parents.* Adolescents have a tendency to be rebellious and to resist adult authority. In particular, adolescence is a time when conflict with parents is especially high.

2. *Mood disruptions.* Adolescents tend to be more volatile emotionally than either children or adults. They experience more extremes of mood and more swings of mood from one extreme to the other. They also experience more frequent episodes of depressed mood.

3. *Risk behavior.* Adolescents have higher rates of reckless, norm-breaking, and antisocial behavior than either children or adults. Adolescents are more likely to cause disruptions of the social order and to engage in behavior that carries the

potential for harm to themselves and/or the people around them.

This is not an all-inclusive list of the possible elements of adolescent storm and stress. Occasionally, storm and stress has been discussed in terms of other elements such as school difficulties (Eccles et al., 1993) and self-image (Offer & Offer, 1975). However, the three elements discussed here appear consistently in the writings of Hall (1904), the anthropologists (Mead, 1928), the psychoanalysts (Blos, 1962; Freud, 1968, 1969), and contemporary scholars (e.g., Buchanan, 1998; Eccles et al., 1993; Offer & Schonert-Reichl, 1992; Petersen et al., 1993; Steinberg & Levine, 1997). Thus, these three elements are the focus of this article.

Before proceeding, one more comment is in order about the length of adolescence. Hall (1904, Vol. 1, p. xix) viewed adolescence and its accompanying storm and stress as lasting through the early twenties. Other observers of adolescent storm and stress, from Aristotle to the present, have applied their comments not just to early adolescence but to a middle and late adolescence/emerging adulthood extending through the late teens and early twenties (see Kett, 1977). Here, I too consider the evidence related to the storm-and-stress view for an extended adolescent age range. Different elements of storm and stress have different peaks—conflict with parents in early adolescence (Paikoff & Brooks-Gunn, 1991), mood disruptions in midadolescence (Petersen et al., 1993), and risk behavior in late adolescence and emerging adulthood (Arnett, 1992, 1999). Each of these elements represents a different kind of difficulty to be experienced, for adolescents as well as for those around them. It is in combination that they create a perception of adolescence as a difficult period of life.

I now consider each of the three elements of the storm-and-stress view, in order of their developmental peak during adolescence: conflict with parents, mood disruptions, and risk behavior.

CONFLICT WITH PARENTS

Hall (1904) viewed adolescence as a time when "the wisdom and advice of parents and teachers is overtopped, and in ruder natures may be met by blank contradiction" (Vol. 2, p. 79). He viewed this as due not only to human evolutionary history but also to the incompatibility between adolescents' need for independence and the fact that "parents still think of their offspring as mere children, and tighten the rein where they should loosen it" (Vol. 2, p. 384). Contemporary studies have established that conflict with parents increases in early adolescence, compared with preadolescence, and typically remains high for a couple of years before declining in late adolescence

(Laursen, Coy, & Collins, 1998; Paikoff & Brooks-Gunn, 1991; Smetana, 1989). A recent meta-analysis by Laursen et al. (1998) concluded that within adolescence, conflict frequency is highest in early adolescence and conflict intensity is highest in midadolescence. One naturalistic study of early adolescents' conflicts with parents and siblings reported a rate of 2 conflicts every three days, or 20 per month (Montemayor & Hanson, 1985). During the same time that the number of daily conflicts between parents and their early adolescent children increases (compared with preadolescence), declines occur in the amount of time they spend together and in their reports of emotional closeness (Larson & Richards, 1994). Conflict is especially frequent and intense between mothers and early adolescent daughters (Collins, 1990).

This conflict makes adolescence difficult not just for adolescents but for their parents. Parents tend to perceive adolescence as the most difficult stage of their children's development (Buchanan et al., 1990; Pasley & Gecas, 1984; Small, Cornelius, & Eastman, 1983). However, it should be added that there are substantial individual differences, and there are many parents and adolescents between whom there is little conflict, even if overall rates of conflict between parents and children rise in adolescence. Conflict between parents and adolescents is more likely when the adolescent is experiencing depressed mood (Cole & McPherson, 1993), when the adolescent is experiencing other problems such as substance abuse (Petersen, 1988), and when the adolescent is an early-maturing girl (Buchanan et al., 1992).

Almost without exception, contemporary scholars emphasize that higher rates of conflict with parents in adolescence do not indicate a serious or enduring breach in parent–adolescent relationships (e.g., Hill & Holmbeck, 1987; Montemayor, 1986; Offer & Offer, 1975; Rutter, Graham, Chadwick & Yule, 1976; Steinberg & Levine, 1997). Even amidst relatively high conflict, parents and adolescents tend to report that overall their relationships are good, that they share a wide range of core values, and that they retain a considerable amount of mutual affection and attachment. The conflicts tend to be over apparently mundane issues such as personal appearance, dating, curfews, and the like (Smetana, 1988). Even if they disagree on these issues, they tend to agree on more serious issues such as the value of honesty and the importance of education.

This point seems well-established by research, but it does not mean that adolescence is not a difficult time for both adolescents and their parents as a result of their minor but frequent conflicts. A useful connection could be made here to the literature on stress. This literature provides substantial evidence that it does not take cataclysmic events such as loss of employment or the death of a loved one to induce the experience of high stress. On the contrary, many people experience a high degree of stress from an accumulation of minor irritations and aggravations, the "daily hassles" of life (Kohn, Lafreniere, & Gurevich, 1991; Taylor, 1991). Thus, for parents and adolescents, it may be true that their frequent conflicts tend to concern relatively mundane day-to-day issues. However, it may be that the "hassle" of these frequent conflicts is substantially responsible for perceptions that adolescence is a difficult time.

Furthermore, the principal issues of conflict between adolescents and their parents may not be as trivial as they seem on the surface. Conflicts between adolescents and their parents often concern issues such as when adolescents should begin dating and whom they should date, where they should be allowed to go, and how late they should stay out. All of these issues can serve as proxies for arguments over more serious issues such as substance use, automobile driving safety, and sex. By restricting when adolescents can date and with whom, parents indirectly restrict adolescents' sexual opportunities. By attempting to restrict where adolescents can go and how late they should stay out, parents may be attempting to limit adolescents' access to alcohol and drugs, to shield adolescents from the potentially dangerous combination of substance use and automobile driving, and to restrict adolescents' opportunities for sexual exploration.

Sexual issues may be especially likely to be argued about in this indirect way, through issues that seem mundane (and therefore safe for discussion) on the surface. No clear mores currently exist in American society concerning the sexual behavior of unmarried young people in their teens (Michael, Gagnon, Laumann, & Kolata, 1994). Because of this lack of social consensus, parents of adolescents are left with many questions that admit no easy answers. Few would agree that sexual intercourse is permissible for 13 year olds, but beyond this the questions grow more complex. Is kissing OK for 13 year olds? When do necking and petting become permissible? At what age should dating be allowed, in light of the fact that it may lead to kissing, necking, petting, and more? If intercourse is not permissible for 13 year olds, what about for 16 or 17 year olds? For the most part, American parents prefer not to discuss these issues—or any other sexual issues—directly with their children (Jones et al., 1986). Yet even parents who believe in giving their adolescents a substantial degree of autonomy may not feel that they can simply leave sexual decisions to their adolescents, particularly in a time when AIDS and other sexually transmitted diseases are prevalent (Eccles et al., 1993). The result is that parents and their adolescents argue about seemingly trivial issues (such as whether dating should be allowed as early as age 13 or whether a 17 year old's curfew should be at midnight or at 1 a.m.) that may be proxies for arguments over complex and sensitive sexual issues.

Some scholars (e.g., Steinberg, 1990) have suggested that conflict between adolescents and their parents is actually beneficial to adolescents' development, because it promotes the development of individuation and autonomy within the context of a warm relationship. This may be true, but high conflict may make adolescence a difficult time for adolescents and their parents even if the conflict ultimately has benefits.

MOOD DISRUPTIONS

The claim of a link between adolescence and extremes of emotion (especially negative) is perhaps the most ancient and enduring part of the storm-and-stress view. Hall (1904) viewed adolescence as "the age of . . . rapid fluctuation of moods" (Vol. 1, p. xv), with extremes of both elation and depressed mood. What does contemporary research tell us about whether adolescence is distinguished by high emotional volatility and a tendency toward negative moods? In general, studies that have assessed mood at frequent intervals have found that adolescents do indeed report greater extremes of mood and more frequent changes of mood, compared with preadolescents or adults. Also, a number of large longitudinal studies concur that negative affect increases in the transition from preadolescence to adolescence (see Buchanan et al., 1992, for a review).

One of the most interesting and enlightening lines of research on this topic in recent years has involved studies using the Experience Sampling Method (ESM; e.g., Csikszentmihalyi & Larson, 1984; Larson & Ham, 1993; Larson & Richards, 1994). Also known as the "beeper method," this research entails having adolescents (and others) carry beepers throughout the day and having them record their thoughts, behavior, and emotions when they are beeped at random times. This method has provided an unprecedented look into the daily lives of adolescents, including how their emotions vary in the course of a day and how these variations compare with the emotions recorded by preadolescents and adults using the same method.

The results of this research indicate that there is truth to the storm-and-stress claim that adolescence is a time of greater mood disruptions. Adolescents report experiencing extremes of emotion (positive as well as negative, but especially negative) more often than their parents do (Larson & Richards, 1994; also see Larson, Csikszentmihalyi, & Graef, 1980). They report feeling "self-conscious" and "embarrassed" two to three times more often than their parents and are also more likely to feel awkward, lonely, nervous, and ignored. Adolescents also report greater mood disruptions when compared with preadolescents. Comparing preadolescent fifth graders with adolescent ninth graders, Larson and Richards (1994) described the emotional "fall from grace" that occurs in that interval, as the proportion of time experienced as "very happy" declines by 50%, and similar declines take place in reports of feeling "great," "proud," and "in control." The result is an overall "deflation of childhood happiness" (p. 85) as childhood ends and adolescence begins.

Larson and Richards (1994) saw this increase in mood disruptions as due to cognitive and environmental factors rather than pubertal changes. They noted that there is little relationship in their data between pubertal stage and mood disruptions. Rather, adolescents' newly developed capacities for abstract reasoning "allow them to see beneath the surface of situations and envision hidden and more long-lasting threats to their well-being" (p. 86). Larson and Richards also argued that the experience of multiple life changes and personal transitions during adolescence (such as the onset of puberty, changing schools, and beginning to date) contributes to adolescents' mood disruptions. However, Larson and Richards emphasized that it is not just that adolescents experience potentially stressful events, but *how* they experience and interpret them, that underlies their mood disruptions. Even in response to the same or similar events, adolescents report more extreme and negative moods than preadolescents or adults.

In addition to the ESM studies, other studies have found negative moods to be prevalent in adolescence, especially for girls. In their review of adolescent depression, Petersen et al. (1993) described a "midadolescence peak" (p. 157) that has been reported in studies of age differences in depressed mood, indicating that adolescents have higher rates of depressed mood than either children or adults. Petersen et al. analyzed 14 studies of nonclinical samples of adolescents and concluded that depressed mood ("above which a score is thought to be predictive of clinical depression," p. 157) applied to over one third of adolescents at any given time.

Adolescents vary in the degree to which they experience mood disruptions. A variety of factors have been found to make mood disruptions in adolescence more likely, including low popularity with peers, poor school performance, and family problems such as marital discord and parental divorce (Petersen et al., 1993). The more negative life events adolescents experience, the more likely they are to experience mood disruptions (Brooks-Gunn & Warren, 1989). Although these individual differences should be kept in mind, overall the results of research indicate support for the storm-and-stress view that adolescence is more likely than other age periods to be a time of emotional difficulty.

RISK BEHAVIOR

At the beginning of a scene in "The Winter's Tale," Shakespeare (1623/1995) has an older man deliver a soliloquy about the youth of his day. "I would that there were no age between ten and three-and-twenty, or that youth would sleep out the rest," he grumbles, "for there is nothing in between but getting wenches with child, wronging the ancientry, stealing, fighting . . . " (Act III, Scene 3). This lament should ring familiar to anyone living in Western societies in recent centuries and to people in many other societies as well. Adolescence has long been associated with heightened rates of antisocial, norm-breaking, and criminal behavior, particularly for boys. Hall (1904) included this as part of his view of adolescent storm and stress, agreeing that "a period of semicriminality is normal for all healthy [adolescent] boys" (Vol. 1, p. 404).

Contemporary research confirms that in the United States and other Western countries, the teens and early twenties are the years of highest prevalence of a variety of types of risk behavior (i.e., behavior that carries the potential for harm to self and/or others). This pattern exists for crime as well as for behavior such as substance use, risky automobile driving, and risky sexual behavior (Arnett, 1992; Moffitt, 1993). Unlike conflict with parents or mood disruptions, rates of risk behavior peak in late adolescence/emerging adulthood rather than early or middle adolescence (Arnett, 1999). Rates of crime rise in the teens until peaking at age 18, then drop steeply (Gottfredson & Hirschi, 1990). Rates of most types of substance use peak at about age 20 (Johnston, O'Malley, & Bachman, 1994). Rates of automobile accidents and fatalities are highest in the late teens (U.S. Department of Transportation, 1995). Rates of sexually transmitted diseases (STDs) peak in the early twenties (Stein, Newcomb, & Bentler, 1994), and two thirds of all STDs are contracted by people who are under 25 years old (Hatcher, Trussell, Stewart, & Stewart, 1994).

The variety of respects in which adolescents engage in risk behavior at greater rates than children or adults lends further validity to the perception of adolescence as a difficult time, a time of storm and stress. Although adolescents generally experience their participation in risk behavior as pleasurable (Arnett, 1992; Lyng, 1993), suffering the consequences of such behavior—contact with the legal system, treatment for an STD, involvement in an automobile accident, and so forth—is likely to be experienced as difficult. Furthermore, it is understandable that parents may find it difficult to watch their children pass through the ages when such behavior is most likely to occur.

In this area, as with conflict with parents and mood disruptions, it is important to recognize individual differences. Adolescents vary a great deal in the extent to which they participate in risk behavior. To some extent, these differences are forecast by behavior prior to adolescence. Persons who exhibit behavior problems in childhood are especially likely to engage in risk behavior as adolescents (Moffitt, 1993). Individual differences in characteristics such as sensation seeking and impulsivity also contribute to individual differences in risk behavior during adolescence (Arnett, 1992; Zuckerman, 1983). Nevertheless, although not all adolescents engage in risk behavior, the majority of adolescents take part occasionally in risk behavior of one kind or another (Arnett, 1992; Moffitt, 1993). This lends substantial credence to the view that adolescence is a period of storm and stress.

WHY STORM AND STRESS?

Even if we accept the argument that adolescence is a time of heightened tendency toward storm and stress, the question of why this should be so remains. To what extent do the roots of storm and stress lie in the biological changes that take place in the course of puberty? To what extent are the roots cultural, with adolescent storm and stress being especially pronounced in cultures that value individualism?

Current evidence indicates that biological changes make some contribution. With respect to mood disruptions, reviews of the effects of hormones on adolescents' moods have concluded that the dramatic hormonal changes that accompany puberty contribute to emotional volatility (Buchanan et al., 1992) and negative moods (Brooks-Gunn, Graber, & Paikoff, 1994), particularly in early adolescence when the rate of hormonal change is steepest. However, scholars in this area emphasize that the hormonal contribution to adolescent mood disruptions appears to be small and tends to exist only in interaction with other factors (Brooks-Gunn et al., 1994; Brooks-Gunn & Warren, 1989; Susman, 1997).

More generally, with respect to mood disruptions as well as with respect to conflict with parents and risk behavior, too little is known about the role of biological factors to make definitive statements at this point about the role they may play in adolescent storm and stress. Numerous possibilities exist concerning biological influences on storm and stress and the interaction between biological and cultural factors. For example, recently a phenomenon called *delayed phase preference* has been identified (Carskadon, Vieria, & Acebo, 1993), which is a tendency, based in the biological changes of puberty, for adolescents to prefer staying up until relatively late at night and sleeping until relatively late in the morning. Does the cultural practice of requiring adolescents to get up in the early morning to attend school—even earlier than young children—result for some adolescents in a sleep-deprived state that may contribute to mood disruptions and more frequent conflict with parents? Other possible biological contributors to adolescent storm and stress include genes that may become active in adolescence and increase the likelihood of mood disruptions, as well as biological bases for developmental changes in characteristics such as emotional regulation (mood disruptions), aggressiveness (conflict with parents), and sensation seeking (risk behavior).

Even with the limitations that exist in the knowledge of biological contributions to adolescent storm and stress, it is clear that the biological changes of puberty do not make adolescent storm and stress universal and inevitable. This is easily and unmistakably demonstrated by the fact that not all cultures experience the same levels of adolescent storm and stress, and some evidently do not experience it at all. Margaret Mead's (1928) original assertion to this effect has more recently been confirmed by Schlegel and Barry (1991), in their analysis of adolescence in 186 "traditional" (preindustrial) cultures worldwide. They reported that most traditional cultures experience less storm and stress among their adolescents, compared with the West.

A key difference between traditional cultures and the West, as Schlegel and Barry (1991) observed, is the degree of *independence* allowed by adults and expected by adolescents. In the majority cultures of the West, because of cultural values of individualism, it is taken for granted by adolescents and their parents (as well as by most Western social scientists) that children should become independent from their parents during the course of adolescence and should attain full independence by the end of adolescence. A substantial amount of adolescent storm and stress arises from regulating the pace of adolescents' growing independence (Steinberg, 1987). Differences of opinion over the proper pace of this process are a source of conflict between adolescents and their parents, and part of parents' perception of adolescence as difficult results from their concern that adolescents' growing independence may lead to participation in risk behavior (Pasley & Gecas, 1984). In contrast, independence for adolescents is less likely to be expected by adolescents and their parents in traditional cultures, so it is less likely to be a source of adolescent storm and stress (Dasen, 2000).

Even in traditional cultures, adolescent storm and stress is not unknown. Biological changes in combination with changing family obligations and changing economic responsibilities are common to adolescence virtually everywhere and inherently involve new challenges and—for some adolescents, at least—difficulty (Dasen, 2000). Some ethnographies on adolescence describe conceptions in traditional cultures of adolescence as a time of mood disruptions (e.g., Davis & Davis, 1989; Kirkpatrick, 1987). It should also be noted that differences exist among traditional cultures, with cultures that exclude adolescent boys from the activities of men being more likely to have problems with their adolescent boys than cultures in which boys take part daily in men's activities (Schlegel & Barry, 1991). Nevertheless, adolescent storm and stress is generally more common in the industrialized societies of the West than in traditional cultures.

However, all over the world, traditional cultures are becoming integrated into the global economy and are being influenced by Western (especially American) cultures through growing economic ties and through exposure to Western movies, music, and television (Barber, 1995). Within traditional cultures, adolescents are often the most enthusiastic consumers of Western media (Barber, 1995; Schlegel, 2000), and evidence shows that adolescents may embrace the individualism of the West more readily than their parents do (Feldman, Mont-Reynaud, & Rosenthal, 1992). A potentially rich topic for research in the coming years would be to monitor changes in the degree of adolescent storm and stress in traditional cultures as globalization proceeds.

The limited evidence available so far indicates that adolescents in traditional cultures often are able to maintain their traditional values and practices—including low conflict with parents and low rates of risk behavior—even as they become avid consumers of Western popular culture (Feldman et al., 1992; Feldman, Rosenthal, Mont-Reynaud, Leung, & Lau, 1991; Schlegel, 2000). However, it remains to be seen whether adolescents' adherence to traditional ways and their low levels of storm and stress will be sustained as globalization increasingly changes the nature of their daily experience. For adolescents in traditional cultures, the results of globalization include more time in school, more time with peers, less time spent with their parents and other adults, and more time for media-oriented leisure (Schlegel, 2000). All of these changes mean greater independence for adolescents, greater emphasis on their individual development, and less emphasis on their obligations to others. If it is true that cultural values of individualism lie at the heart of adolescent storm and stress, then it seems likely that adolescence in traditional cultures will become more stormy and stressful in the ways described here as the influence of the West increases (Dasen, 2000).

This does not mean that storm and stress is likely to increase in all respects for all adolescents in traditional cultures. Individual differences will undoubtedly exist, as they do in the West. Indeed, increased individualism means broadening the boundaries of socialization, so that a greater range of individual differences is allowed expression (Arnett, 1995). Furthermore, the increased individualism fostered by globalization is likely to result in benefits for adolescents, along with increased storm and stress. Cultural changes toward globalization and individualism are likely to mean that adolescents in traditional cultures will have a greater range of educational and occupational opportunities than previously and that these choices will be less constrained by gender and other factors (Dasen, 2000; Noble, Cover, & Yanagishita, 1996). However, the cost may be greater adolescent storm and stress. It is even possible that storm and stress will become more characteristic of adolescence in traditional cultures than in the West, because adolescents in rapidly changing societies will be confronted with multiple changes not only in their immediate lives but in their societies as well (Dasen, 2000).

Similar issues exist within American society. Currently, there is evidence that adolescent storm and stress may be more likely in the majority culture—the largely White middle class—than in other cultures that are part of American society. For example, parent–adolescent conflict has been found to be more frequent in White middle-class families than in Mexican American families (Suarez-Orozco & Suarez-Orozco, 1996). In the same way that values of individualism make adolescent storm and stress more likely in the American majority culture compared with non-Western traditional cultures, a similar difference in values may make storm and stress more likely in the American majority culture than in certain minority cultures that are part of American society. And in the same way that adolescence in traditional cultures may become more stormy and stressful as the influence of the West increases, adolescents in American minority cultures may exhibit storm and stress to the extent that they adopt the individualistic values of the American majority culture.

Thus, it might be expected that adolescent storm and stress will increase with the number of generations an adolescent's family has been in the United States. Among Asian American adolescents, for example, it has been found that the greater the number of generations their families have been in the United States, the more likely the adolescents are to exhibit aspects of storm and stress (Fletcher & Steinberg, 1994; Steinberg, 1996; also see Rosenthal, 1984). However, as with the issues involving traditional cultures, the direct exploration of storm-and-stress issues involving adolescents in American minority cultures has been minimal thus far and represents a promising area for further investigation.

SCHOLARS AND STEREOTYPES

When adolescent storm and stress is discussed by contemporary scholars on adolescence, it is generally in the context of the scholars expressing concern over the "stereotype" or "myth" of adolescent storm and stress that is perceived to exist among parents, teachers, and the general public (Buchanan et al., 1990; Holmbeck & Hill, 1988; Offer & Schonert-Reichl, 1992; Petersen et al., 1993; Steinberg & Levine, 1997). Scholars contrast these popular perceptions of adolescence as a difficult time with their own research findings that adolescence is not difficult for all adolescents in all respects and that the biological changes of puberty are not strongly related to any storm and stress that does exist in adolescence.

One of the implications of the argument presented here is that the findings of the scholars and the conception of adolescence held by nonscholars in American society may not be so far apart after all. With respect to conflict with parents, mood disruptions, and risk behavior, the results of scholars' research indicate that adolescence is stormy and stressful for many American adolescents and for the people around them. It is true that this research also indicates that there are substantial individual differences in these difficulties and that storm and stress is by no means universal and inevitable. However, there is no indication that most people in the American public see storm and stress as universal and inevitable. On the contrary, the studies that have investigated perceptions of storm and stress inquire about people's perceptions of adolescents *in general*. People's responses endorsing storm-and-stress statements indicate simply that they see storm and stress as characteristic of adolescents taken as a group, not that it is characteristic of all adolescents without exception (Buchanan, 1998; Buchanan et al., 1990; Buchanan & Holmbeck, 1998; Holmbeck & Hill, 1988).

People tend to see adolescence as a time of life that is more likely than other times of life to involve difficulties such as conflict with parents, mood disruptions, and risk behavior, and scholars' research supports this modified storm-and-stress view of adolescence rather than contradicting it. Contemporary scholars disagree not so much with the American public or even with G. Stanley Hall (1904), but mainly with the psychoanalytic theorists of the past, particularly Anna Freud (1946, 1958, 1968, 1969), who can truly be said to have claimed that adolescent storm and stress is universal and inevitable. The one storm-and-stress issue on which scholars and the general public seem genuinely to disagree is the meaning and significance of parent–adolescent conflict, which scholars concede is common but tend to deprecate as being over trivial and mundane issues. However, as I have argued, there may be more merit to the popular view on this topic than scholars have acknowledged.

One reason for scholars' concern over public beliefs about adolescent storm and stress is that they fear such beliefs could have negative consequences. Some scholars speculate that storm-and-stress beliefs may lead parents to adopt authoritarian parenting techniques as a way of thwarting the storm and stress they anticipate in their adolescents (Holmbeck, 1996). Others fear that if storm and stress is regarded as normative, adolescents with serious problems will not get the attention and help they need because their problems will be dismissed as normal for adolescence (Offer & Schonert-Reichl, 1992; Petersen et al., 1993). These concerns are legitimate and are well-taken. However, there are also concerns that arise from underrating the likelihood of storm and stress, and benefits that can result from expecting adolescence to be a time of storm and stress. Although it is true that if adolescence is expected to be a time of "turmoil" there may be adolescents whose problems go unrecognized and untreated, it is also true that if adolescence is expected to be no more difficult than childhood, then adolescents who are experiencing normal difficulties may be seen as pathological and in need of treatment.

Also, expecting adolescence to be difficult could have positive effects. Anticipating adolescent storm and stress may inspire parents and teachers to think ahead about how to approach potential problems of adolescence if they arise. Furthermore, parents, teachers, adolescents, and others who expect adolescence to be difficult may be pleasantly surprised when a particular adolescent shows few or no difficulties, as will be the case for many adolescents because there are considerable individual differences in the storm and stress they experience (Buchanan, 1998).

CONCLUSION

Adolescent storm and stress is not simply a myth that has captured the popular imagination but a real part of life for many adolescents and their parents in contemporary American society. Although the extreme portrayal of adolescent storm and stress by certain psychoanalytic theorists (Freud, 1958, 1968, 1969) is a caricature of normal adolescent development, there is support for Hall's (1904) view that a tendency toward some aspects of storm and stress exists in adolescence. In their conflicts with parents, in their mood disruptions, and in their higher rates of a variety of types of risk behavior, many adolescents exhibit a heightened degree of storm and stress compared with other periods of life. Their parents, too, often experience difficulty—from increased conflict when their children are in early adolescence, from mood disruptions during midadolescence, and from anxiety over the increased possibility of risk behavior when their children are in late adolescence. However, storm and stress in adolescence is not something written indelibly into the human life course. On the contrary, there are cultural differences in storm and stress, and within cultures there are individual differences in the extent to which adolescents exhibit the different aspects of it.

Finally, to view adolescence as a time of storm and stress is not to say that adolescence is characterized only by storm and stress. Even amidst the storm and stress of adolescence, most adolescents take pleasure in many aspects of their lives, are satisfied with most of their relationships most of the time, and are hopeful about the future (Offer & Schonert-Reichl, 1992). G. S. Hall (1904) saw adolescence as stormy and stressful, but also as "the birthday of the imagination" (Vol. 1, p. 313) and "the best decade of life" (Vol. 1, p. xviii), when "the life of feeling has its prime" (Vol. 1, p. 59). The paradox of adolescence is that it can be at once a time of storm and stress and a time of exuberant growth.

REFERENCES

Arnett, J. (1992). Reckless behavior in adolescence: A developmental perspective. *Developmental Review, 12,* 339–373.

Arnett, J. J. (1995). Broad and narrow socialization: The family in the context of a cultural theory. *Journal of Marriage and the Family, 57,* 617–628.

Arnett, J. (1999). *Emerging adulthood: A conception of development from the late teens through the twenties.* Manuscript submitted for publication.

Barber, B. R. (1995). *Jihad vs. McWorld: How globalism and tribalism are reshaping the world.* New York: Ballantine.

Blos, P. (1962). *On adolescence: A psychoanalytic interpretation.* New York: Free Press.

Brooks-Gunn, J., Graber, J. A., & Paikoff, R. L. (1994). Studying links between hormones and negative affect: Models and measures. *Journal of Research on Adolescence, 4,* 469–486.

Brooks-Gunn, J., & Warren, M. P. (1989). Biological and social contributions to negative affect in young adolescent girls. *Child Development, 60,* 40–55.

Buchanan, C. M. (1998). *Parents' category-based beliefs about adolescence: Links to expectations for one's own child.* Manuscript submitted for publication.

Buchanan, C. M., Eccles, J., & Becker, J. (1992). Are adolescents the victims of raging hormones? Evidence for activational effects of hormones on moods and behavior at adolescence. *Psychological Bulletin, 111,* 62–107.

Buchanan, C. M., Eccles, J. S., Flanagan, C., Midgley, C., Feldlaufer, H., & Harold, R. D. (1990). Parents' and teachers' beliefs about adolescents: Effects of sex and experience. *Journal of Youth & Adolescence, 19,* 363–394.

Buchanan, C. M., & Holmbeck, G. N. (1998). Measuring beliefs about adolescent personality and behavior. *Journal of Youth & Adolescence, 27,* 609–629.

Carskadon, M., Vieria, C., & Acebo, C. (1993). Association between puberty and delayed phase preference. *Sleep, 16,* 258–262.

Cole, D. A., & McPherson, A. E. (1993). Relation of family subsystems to adolescent depression: Implementing a new family assessment strategy. *Journal of Family Psychology, 7,* 119–133.

Collins, W. A. (1990). Parent–child relationships in the transition to adolescence: Continuity and change in interaction, affect, and cognition. In R. Montemayor, G. R. Adams, & T. P. Gullotta (Eds.), *From childhood to adolescence: A transitional period?* (pp. 85–106). Newbury Park, CA: Sage.

Csikszentmihalyi, M., & Larson, R. W. (1984). *Being adolescent: Conflict and growth in the teenage years.* New York: Basic Books.

Dasen, P. (2000). Rapid social change and the turmoil of adolescence: A cross-cultural perspective. *International Journal of Group Tensions, 29,* 17–49.

Davis, S. S., & Davis, D. A. (1989). *Adolescence in a Moroccan town.* New Brunswick, NJ: Rutgers.

Eccles, J. S., Midgely, C., Wigfield, A., Buchanan, C. M., Reuman, D., Flanagan, C., & MacIver, D. (1993). Development during adolescence: The impact of stage-environment fit on young adolescents' experiences in schools and in families. *American Psychologist, 48,* 90–101.

Feldman, S. S., Mont-Reynaud, R., & Rosenthal, D. A. (1992). When East moves West: The acculturation of values of Chinese adolescents in the U. S. and Australia. *Journal of Research on Adolescence, 2,* 147–175.

Feldman, S. S., Rosenthal, D. A., Mont-Reynaud, R., Leung, K., & Lau, S. (1991). Ain't misbehavin': Adolescent values and family environments as correlates of adolescent misconduct in Australia, Hong Kong, and the United States. *Journal of Research on Adolescence, 1,* 109–134.

Fletcher, A., & Steinberg, L. (1994, February). *Generational status and country of origin as influences on psychological adjustment of Asian-American adolescents.* Paper presented at the biennial meeting of the Society for Research on Adolescence, San Diego, CA.

Freud, A. (1946). *The ego and the mechanisms of defense.* New York: International Universities Press.

Freud, A. (1958). Adolescence. *Psychoanalytic Study of the Child, 15,* 255–278.

Freud, A. (1968). Adolescence. In A. E. Winder & D. Angus (Eds.), *Adolescence: Contemporary studies* (pp. 13–24). New York: American Book.

Freud, A. (1969). Adolescence as a developmental disturbance. In G. Caplan & S. Lebovici (Eds.), *Adolescence: Psychosocial perspectives* (pp. 5–10). New York: Basic Books.

Gecas, V., & Seff, M. A. (1990). Families and adolescents: A review of the 1980s. *Journal of Marriage and the Family, 52,* 941–958.

Goethe, J. W. von. (1989). *The sorrows of young werther, by Johann Wolfgang von Goethe* (M. Hulse, Trans.). London: Penguin. (Original work published 1774)

Gottfredson, M. R., & Hirschi, T. (1990). *A general theory of crime*. Stanford, CA: Stanford University Press.

Hall, G. S. (1904). *Adolescence: Its psychology and its relation to physiology, anthropology, sociology, sex, crime, religion, and education* (Vols. I & II). Englewood Cliffs, NJ: Prentice-Hall.

Hatcher, R. A., Trussell, J., Stewart, F., & Stewart, G. (1994). *Contraceptive technology*. New York: Irvington.

Hill, J., & Holmbeck, G. (1987). Disagreements about rules in families with seventh-grade girls and boys. *Journal of Youth & Adolescence, 16*, 221–246.

Holmbeck, G. N. (1996). A model of family relational transformations during the transition to adolescence: Parent-adolescent conflict and adaptation. In J. A. Graber, J. Brooks-Gunn, & A. C. Petersen (Eds.), *Transitions through adolescence: Interpersonal domains and context* (pp. 167–199). Mahwah, NJ: Erlbaum.

Holmbeck, G., & Hill, J. (1988). Storm and stress beliefs about adolescence: Prevalence, self-reported antecedents, and effects of an undergraduate course. *Journal of Youth & Adolescence, 17*, 285–306.

Johnston, L. D., O'Malley, P. M., & Bachman, J. G. (1994). *National survey results on drug use from the Monitoring the Future study, 1975–1993* (NIH Publication No. 94-3810). Washington, DC: U.S. Government Printing Office.

Jones, E. F., Forrest, J. D., Goldman, N., Henshaw, S., Lincoln, R., Rosoff, J. I., Westoff, C. F., & Wulf, D. (1986). *Teenage pregnancy in industrialized countries*. New Haven, CT: Yale University Press.

Kett, J. F. (1977). *Rites of passage: Adolescence in America, 1790 to the present*. New York: Basic Books.

Kirkpatrick, J. (1987). *Taure'are'a*: A liminal category and passage to Marquesan adulthood. *Ethos, 15*, 382–405.

Kohn, P. M., Lafreniere, K., & Gurevich, M. (1991). Hassles, health, and personality. *Journal of Personality and Social Psychology, 61*, 478–482.

Larson, R. W., Csikszentmihalyi, M., & Graef, R. (1980). Mood variability and the psycho-social adjustment of adolescents. *Journal of Youth & Adolescence, 9*, 469–490.

Larson, R., & Ham, M. (1993). Stress and "storm and stress" in early adolescence: The relationship of negative life events with dysphoric affect. *Developmental Psychology, 29*, 130–140.

Larson, R., & Richards, M. H. (1994). *Divergent realities: The emotional lives of mothers, fathers, and adolescents*. New York: Basic Books.

Laursen, B., Coy, K. C., & Collins, W. A. (1998). Reconsidering changes in parent-child conflict across adolescence: A meta-analysis. *Child Development, 69*, 817–832.

Lyng, S. (1993). Dysfunctional risk taking: Criminal behavior as edgework. In N. J. Bell & R. W. Bell (Eds.), *Adolescent risk taking* (pp. 107–130). Newbury Park, CA: Sage.

Mead, M. (1928). *Coming of age in Samoa*. New York: Morrow.

Michael, R. T., Gagnon, J. H., Laumann, E. O., & Kolata, G. (1994). *Sex in America*. Boston: Little, Brown.

Moffitt, T. (1993). Adolescence-limited and life-course persistent antisocial behavior: A developmental taxonomy. *Psychological Review, 100*, 674–701.

Montemayor, R. (1986). Family variation in adolescent storm and stress. *Journal of Adolescent Research, 1*, 15–31.

Montemayor, R., & Hanson, E. (1985). A naturalistic view of conflict between adolescents and their parents and siblings. *Journal of Early Adolescents, 5*, 23–30.

Noble, J., Cover, J., & Yanagishita, M. (1996). *The world's youth*. Washington, DC: Population Reference Bureau.

Offer, D., & Offer, J. B. (1975). *From teenage to young manhood*. New York: Basic Books.

Offer, D., Ostrov, E., & Howard, K. I. (1981). The mental health professional's concept of the normal adolescent. *Archives of General Psychiatry, 38*, 149–153.

Offer, D., & Schonert-Reichl, K. A. (1992). Debunking the myths of adolescence: Findings from recent research. *Journal of the American Academy of Child & Adolescent Psychiatry, 31*, 1003–1014.

Paikoff, R., & Brooks-Gunn, J. (1991). Do parent–child relationships change during puberty? *Psychological Bulletin, 110*, 47–66.

Pasley, K., & Gecas, V. (1984). Stresses and satisfactions of the parental role. *Personnel and Guidance Journal, 2*, 400–404.

Petersen, A. C. (1988). Adolescent development. *Annual Review of Psychology, 39*, 583–607.

Petersen, A. C., Compas, B. E., Brooks-Gunn, J., Stemmler, M., Ey, S., & Grant, K. E. (1993). Depression in adolescence. *American Psychologist, 48*, 155–168.

Rosenthal, D. A. (1984). Intergenerational conflict and culture: A study of immigrant and nonimmigrant adolescents and their parents. *Genetic Psychology Monographs, 109*, 53–75.

Rousseau, J. J. (1962). *The Emile of Jean Jacques Rousseau*. (W. Boyd, Ed. & Trans.). New York: Teachers College Press, Columbia University. (Original work published 1762)

Rutter, M., Graham, P., Chadwick, F., Yule, W. (1976). Adolescent turmoil: Fact or fiction? *Journal of Child Psychiatry and Psychology, 17*, 35–56.

Schlegel, A. (2000). The global spread of adolescent culture. In L. Crockett & R. K. Silbereisen (Eds.), *Negotiating adolescence in a time of social change* (pp. 71–88). Cambridge, England: Cambridge University Press.

Schlegel, A., & Barry, H., III. (1991). *Adolescence: An anthropological inquiry*. New York: Free Press.

Simmons, R., & Blythe, D. (1987). *Moving into adolescence: The impact of pubertal change and school context*. Hawthorn, NY: Aldine de Gruyter.

Small, S. A., Cornelius, S., & Eastman, G. (1983, August). *Parenting adolescent children: A period of adult storm and stress?* Paper presented at the 91st Annual Meeting of the American Psychological Association, Anaheim, CA.

Smetana, J. G. (1988). Concepts of self and social convention: Adolescents' and parents' reasoning about hypothetical and actual family conflicts. In M. Gunnar & W. A. Collins (Eds.), *Minnesota Symposium on Child Psychology* (Vol. 21, pp. 79–122). Hillsdale, NJ: Erlbaum.

Smetana, J. G. (1989). Adolescents' and parents' reasoning about actual family conflict. *Child Development, 60*, 1052–1067.

Stein, J. A., Newcomb, M. D., & Bentler, P. M. (1994). Psychosocial correlates and predictors of AIDS risk behaviors, abortion, and drug use among a community sample of young adult women. *Health Psychology, 13*, 308–318.

Steinberg, L. (1987). Family processes in adolescence: A developmental perspective. *Family Therapy, 14*, 77–86.

Steinberg, L. (1990). Autonomy, conflict, and harmony in the family relationship. In S. Feldman & G. Elliott (Eds.), *At the threshold: The developing adolescent* (pp. 255–276). Cambridge, MA: Harvard University Press.

Steinberg, L. (1996). *Beyond the classroom: Why school reform has failed and what parents need to do.* New York: Simon & Schuster.

Steinberg, L., & Levine, A. (1997). *You and your adolescent: A parents' guide for ages 10 to 20.* New York: Harper Perennial.

Suarez-Orozco, C., & Suarez-Orozco, M. (1996). *Transformations: Migration, family life and achievement motivation among Latino adolescents.* Palo Alto, CA: Stanford University Press.

Susman, E. J. (1997). Modeling developmental complexity in adolescence: Hormones and behavior in context. *Journal of Research on Adolescence, 7*, 283–306.

Taylor, S. E. (1991). *Health psychology* (2nd ed.). New York: McGraw-Hill.

U. S. Department of Transportation. (1995). *Understanding youthful risk taking and driving.* (DOT Publication No. HS 808-318). Springfield, VA: National Technical Information Service.

Zuckerman, M. (Ed.). (1983). *Biological bases of sensation seeking, impulsivity, and anxiety.* Hillsdale, NJ: Erlbaum.

QUESTIONS

1. Do all adolescents experience storm and stress? Which adolescents does Arnett think are most likely to experience storm and stress?
2. What early thinkers, before G. Stanley Hall, commented on adolescence as a stormy and stressful time, and what types of behaviors did they write about?
3. Did Hall think that the tendency for adolescents to experience storm and stress is universal, or did he think that culture influences it?
4. Describe the three key elements of adolescent storm and stress.
5. When are conflicts between adolescents and their parents at their most frequent? Is there a developmental explanation for this pattern?
6. What is the Experience Sampling Method, and how is it used to study adolescent emotions and mood disruptions?
7. What factors are related to an adolescent's inclination to take risks?
8. Are biological changes at puberty the cause of storm and stress in adolescence? Why or why not?
9. Why do you think non-Western adolescents are their societies' most enthusiastic consumers of Western media products (movies, music, etc.)? What cultural consequences might this behavior have?
10. In your view, is the public justified in considering adolescence a time of storm and stress?

33 Sleep Schedules and Daytime Functioning in Adolescents

AMY R. WOLFSON • MARY A. CARSKADON

The typical high school begins its day at about 7:30 or 8:00 A.M., and students often shuffle into class very tired. Teachers, noticing their students' fatigue, tell them that they should go to bed earlier and get more sleep. Adolescents have complained for years that school begins too early in the day, but these complaints have been dismissed because the sleep habits of adolescents are seen as the cause of the problem. Furthermore, these sleep habits are seen as voluntary—that is, adolescents choose to stay up late and budget too little time during the week for sleep. This "choice" is also seen as leading to a sleep debt for which adolescents try to compensate by sleeping late on weekends. Is this interpretation of adolescent sleep-related behaviors correct?

Recent research on biological changes during adolescence, including the study of the circadian timing system, casts doubt on the view that adolescents regulate their sleep/wake cycle to any great degree. This research suggests that the sleep/wake/fatigue cycle that adolescents experience is actually part of the normal process of pubertal maturation. In the following article, Amy R. Wolfson and Mary A. Carskadon describe their large-scale survey of the sleep/wake patterns of adolescents. They discovered that the sleep needs of adolescents change over the high school years and are different from the sleep needs of adults. They also found that the sleep/wake schedules of adolescents and adults are different and that the ideal sleep/wake pattern for adolescents is undermined by societal demands, particularly school starting times. The clash between adolescent sleep needs and the schedule imposed on adolescents by their high schools has a significant impact on the daily functioning of adolescents.

These findings suggest that it is necessary to reexamine adolescent behavior in light of the biological and social requirements of this period of development. This research has significant implications for social practices and polices related to the sleep/wake cycle, especially the time at which the school day begins.

Sleep and waking behaviors change significantly during the adolescent years. The objective of this study was to describe the relation between adolescents' sleep/wake habits, characteristics of students (age, sex, school), and daytime functioning (mood, school performance, and behavior). A Sleep Habits Survey was administered in homeroom classes to 3,120 high school students at 4 public high schools from 3 Rhode Island school districts. Self-reported total sleep times (school and weekend nights) decreased by 40–50 min across ages 13–19, ps < .001. The sleep loss was due to increasingly later bedtimes, whereas rise times were more consistent across ages. Students who described themselves as struggling or failing school (C's, D's/F's) reported that on school nights they obtain about 25 min less sleep and go to bed an average of 40 min later than A and B students, ps < .001. In addition, students with worse grades reported greater weekend delays of sleep schedule than did those with better grades. Furthermore, this study examined a priori defined adequate sleep habit groups versus less than adequate sleep habit groups on their daytime functioning. Students in the short school-night

Reprinted with permission of Blackwell Publishers from Wolfson, A. R., & Carskadon, M. A. (1998). Sleep schedules and daytime functioning in adolescents. *Child Development, 69,* 875–887.

Acknowledgments. This study was supported by funds from the National Institutes of Health, MH 45945. We thank Camille Brown, Catherine Darley, Francois Garand, Liza Kelly, Eric Kravitz, Christopher Monti, Orna Tzischinsky, and Beth Yoder for their assistance in gathering and coding data, and Christine Acebo and Ronald Seifer for their assistance regarding data analysis and interpretation of results. We would also like to thank the participating school districts in Rhode Island.

total sleep group (< 6 hr 45 min) and/or large week-end bedtime delay group (> 120 min) reported increased daytime sleepiness, depressive mood, and sleep/wake behavior problems, ps < .05, versus those sleeping longer than 8 hr 15 min with less than 60 min weekend delay. Altogether, most of the adolescents surveyed do not get enough sleep, and their sleep loss interferes with daytime functioning.

INTRODUCTION

Adolescence is a time of important physical, cognitive, emotional, and social change when the behaviors in one developmental stage are constantly challenged by new abilities, insights, and expectations of the next stage. Sleep is a primary aspect of adolescent development. The way adolescents sleep critically influences their ability to think, behave, and feel during daytime hours. Likewise, daytime activities, changes in the environment, and individual factors can have significant effects on adolescents' sleeping patterns. Over the last 2 decades, researchers, teachers, parents, and adolescents themselves, have consistently reported that they are not getting enough sleep (Carskadon, 1990a; Carskadon, Harvey, Duke, Anders, & Dement, 1980; Price, Coates, Thoresen, & Grinstead, 1978; Strauch & Meier, 1988).

Although laboratory data demonstrate that adolescents probably do not have a decreased need for sleep during puberty (Carskadon, 1990a; Carskadon et al., 1980; Carskadon, Orav, & Dement, 1983), survey and field studies show that teenagers usually obtain much less sleep than school-age children, from 10 hr during middle childhood to less than 7.5–8 hours by age 16 (Allen, 1992; Carskadon, 1982, 1990a; Williams, Karacan, & Hursch, 1974). Although sleeping less than when younger, over 54% of high school students in a Swiss study (Strauch & Meier, 1988) endorsed a *wish for more sleep*.

A consistent finding in studies of adolescent sleep patterns is that they tend to stay up late. Price et al. (1978), for example, found that 60% of the eleventh and twelfth graders whom they surveyed stated that they "enjoyed staying up late." Another large survey study found that 45% of tenth to twelfth graders go to bed after midnight on school nights, and 90% retire later than midnight on weekends (Carskadon & Mancuso, 1988). Another consistent report (Bearpark & Michie, 1987; Petta, Carskadon, & Dement, 1984; Strauch & Meier, 1988) is that weekend total sleep times average 30–60 min more than school-night sleep times in 10- to 13/14-year-olds, and this difference increases to over 2 hr by age 18. Such data are usually interpreted as indicating that teenagers do not get enough sleep on school nights and then ex-tend sleep on weekend nights to pay back a sleep debt. The most obvious explanation for the adolescent sleep debt appears to be a pattern of insufficient school-night sleep resulting from a combination of early school start times, late afternoon/evening jobs and activities, academic and social pressures, and a physiological sleep requirement that does not decrease with puberty (Carskadon, 1990b; Manber et al., 1995; Wolfson et al., 1995).

Many factors contribute to or are affected by increased daytime sleepiness and inconsistent sleep schedules during the junior high and senior high school years. In the sections below, we review several key issues.

PUBERTY: SLEEP NEED, DAYTIME SLEEPINESS, AND CIRCADIAN PHASE DELAY

Several important changes directly affecting sleep patterns occur during the pubertal years. One feature that seems not to change or to change in an unexpected direction is sleep need. A 6-year longitudinal summer sleep laboratory study of Carskadon and colleagues (1980) held the opportunity for sleep constant at 10 hr in children who were 10, 11, or 12 years old at their first 3 night assessment. The research hypothesis was that with age, the youngsters would sleep less, reaching a normal adult sleep length of 7.5 or 8 hr by the late teens. In fact, the sleep quantity remained consistent at approximately 9.2 hours across all pubertal stages. Thus, these data clarified that sleep need is not reduced during adolescence. The longitudinal study of Carskadon and colleagues (1980) simultaneously demonstrated that daytime sleep tendency was increased at midpuberty. In other words, even though the amount of nocturnal sleep consumed by the adolescents did not decline during puberty, their midday sleepiness increased significantly at midpuberty and remained at that level (Carskadon et al., 1980, 1983). This finding was based on physician assessment of puberty using Tanner staging (Tanner, 1962) and a sensitive laboratory measure of sleepiness, the Multiple Sleep Latency Test (MSLT; Carskadon et al., 1986).

A significant change in the timing of behavior across adolescent development is a tendency to stay up later at night and to sleep in later in the morning than preadolescents, that is, to delay the phase of sleep (Carskadon, Vieira, & Acebo, 1993; Dahl & Carskadon, 1995). One manifestation of this process is that adolescents' sleep patterns on weekends show a considerable delay (as well as lengthening) versus weekdays, with sleep onset and offset both occurring significantly later. This sleep phase shift is attributed to psychosocial factors and to biological changes that take place during puberty. For example, in the longitudinal study described above, as children reached puberty, they were less likely to wake up on their own, and laboratory staff needed to wake them up (Carskadon et al., 1980). In fact, they likely would have slept more than 9 hr if undisturbed.

Carskadon and her colleagues have shown that this adolescent tendency to phase delay may be augmented by a biological process accompanying puberty. An association between self-reported puberty scores (Carskadon & Acebo, 1993) and phase preference (morningness/eveningness) scores of over 400 pre- and early pubertal sixth graders showed a delay of phase preference correlated with maturation stage (Carskadon et al., 1993). Morningness/eveningness is a construct developed to estimate phase tendencies from self-descriptions. Morning persons tend to arise early in the morning and have difficulty staying up late whereas night persons have difficulty getting up early in the morning and prefer staying up late. Whereas most people are somewhere between these extremes, the cohort value shifts during adolescence (Andrade, Benedito-Silva, & Domenice, 1993; Ishihara, Honma, & Miyake, 1990). A recent study examined the circadian timing system more directly in early adolescents by measuring the timing of melatonin secretion, for the first time demonstrating a biological phase delay in association with puberty and in the absence of psychosocial factors (Carskadon, Acebo, Richardson, Tate, & Seifer, 1997).

ENVIRONMENTAL CONSTRAINT: SCHOOL START TIME

Many U.S. school districts start school earlier at academic transitions, for example, elementary to junior high school and junior high school to senior high school. Earlier high school start time is a major externally imposed constraint on teenagers' sleep-wake schedules; for most teens waking up to go to school is neither spontaneous nor negotiable. Early morning school demands often significantly constrict the hours available for sleep. For example, Szymczak, Jasinska, Pawlak, and Swierzykowska (1993) followed Polish students aged 10 and 14 years for over a year and found that all slept longer on weekends and during vacations as a result of waking up later. These investigators concluded that the school duty schedule was the predominant determinant of awakening times for these students. Similarly, several surveys of high school students found that students who start school at 7:30 A.M. or earlier obtain less total sleep on school nights due to earlier rise times (Allen, 1991; Allen & Mirabile, 1989; Carskadon & Mancuso, 1988).

In a preliminary laboratory/field study, we evaluated the impact of a 65 min advance in school start time on 15 ninth graders across the transition to tenth grade (Carskadon, Wolfson, Tzischinsky, & Acebo, 1995; Wolfson et al., 1995). The initial findings demonstrated that students slept an average of 40 min less in tenth grade compared with ninth grade due to earlier rise times, and they displayed an increase in MSLT measured daytime sleepiness. In addition, evening type students had more difficulty adjusting to the earlier start time than did morning types, and higher scores on the externalizing behavior problems scale (Youth Self-Report; Achenbach, 1991) were associated with less total sleep and later bedtimes (Brown et al., 1995; Wolfson et al., 1995).

DAYTIME BEHAVIORS

Very little research has assessed the relation between adolescents' sleep patterns and their daytime behaviors. Although studies have concluded that associations between sleep/wake patterns and daytime functioning exist, the direction of this relation is not clear. Clinical experience shows that adolescents who have trouble adapting to new school schedules and other changes (e.g., new bedtimes and rise times, increased activities during the day, increased academic demands) may develop problematic sleeping behaviors leading to chronic sleepiness. Several studies indicate an association between sleep and stress. For example, a number of studies have found that sleep-disturbed elementary school-age children experience a greater number of stresses (e.g., maternal absence due to work/school; family illness/accident; maternal depressed mood) than non-sleep-disturbed children (Kataria, Swanson, & Trevathan, 1987). Likewise, sleepy elementary school-age children may have poorer coping behaviors (e.g., more difficulty recognizing, appraising, and adapting to stressful situations) and display more behavior problems at home and in school (Fisher & Rinehart, 1990; Wolfson et al., 1995).

ACADEMIC PERFORMANCE

Sleepy adolescents—that is, those with inadequate sleep—may also encounter more academic difficulties. Several surveys of sample sizes ranging from 50 to 200 high school students reported that more total sleep, earlier bedtimes, and later weekday rise times are associated with better grades in school (Allen, 1992; Link & Ancoli-Israel, 1995; Manber et al., 1995). Epstein, Chillag, and Lavie (1995) surveyed Israeli elementary, junior high, and senior high school students and reported that less total sleep time was associated with daytime fatigue, inability to concentrate in school, and a tendency to doze off in class. Persistent sleep problems have also been associated with learning difficulties throughout the school years (Quine,

1992). Studies of excessive sleepiness in adolescents due to narcolepsy or sleep apnea have also reported negative effects on learning, school performance, and behavior (Dahl, Holttum, & Trubnick, 1994; Guilleminault, Winkle, & Korobkin, 1982).

SUMMARY OF FACTORS IMPOSING ON ADOLESCENTS' SLEEP/WAKE PATTERNS

The interplay among sleep/wake schedules, circadian rhythms, and behavior during adolescence results in an increasing pressure on the nocturnal sleep period, producing insufficient sleep in many teenagers and, ultimately, changes in daytime functioning (Carskadon, 1995). For preadolescents, parents are more likely to set bedtimes, school begins later in the morning, and societal expectations favor long sleep. Prepubescent children are thus more likely to have earlier bedtimes and to wake up before the school day begins (Petta et al., 1984). In contrast, due to behavioral factors (social, academic, work-related), environmental constraints (school schedule), and circadian variables (pubertal phase delay), teenagers have later bedtimes, earlier rise times, and therefore, decreased time available to sleep (Carskadon, 1995). As a result, adolescents get to bed late, have difficulty waking up in the morning, and struggle to stay alert and to function successfully during the daytime.

Unfortunately, previous studies of adolescents' lifestyles (e.g., Hendry, Glendinning, Shucksmith, Love, & Scott, 1994) have failed to factor in these important developmental changes in sleep/wake patterns, and unanswered questions remain regarding the developmental changes in adolescent sleep/wake habits, the impact of adolescents' sleep habits on their daytime functioning (e.g., school performance), and the influence of the environment (e.g., school schedules) on teenagers' sleep. The present study examines more closely adolescents' sleep/wake habits and their association with several daytime behaviors using data from a large-scale survey. Such data are useful to assess generalizability of findings; furthermore, a large sample provides an opportunity to accentuate meaningful findings by setting the effect size (Cohen, 1988) and by examining extreme groups from the larger sample (Kagan, Resnick, & Gibbons, 1989).

The chief goal of this study is to document the association between adolescents' sleep/wake habits and daytime sleepiness, high school grades, depressed mood, and other daytime behaviors. Our study has three objectives: (1) to describe age, sex, and school differences in sleep/wake patterns; (2) to characterize the relation between self-reported high school grades and sleep/wake schedules; and (3) to compare daytime functioning in students on schedules we define a priori as *adequate* versus those adopting *less than adequate* schedules.

METHOD

MEASURES

In the fall of 1994, an eight page School Sleep Habits Survey was administered in homeroom classes to high school students at four public high schools from three Rhode Island school districts. School start times ranged from 7:10 A.M. to 7:30 A.M. All students who wanted to complete the survey did so unless their parent/guardian refused consent. The survey items queried students about usual sleeping and waking behaviors over the past 2 weeks. Chief variables include school-night and weekend night total sleep time (TST), bedtime, and rise time. To assess *sleep schedule regularity*, two additional sleep variables were derived: *weekend delay* is the difference between weekend bedtime and school-night bedtime, and *weekend oversleep* is the difference between weekend total sleep time and school-night total sleep time.

The survey also covered school performance (self-reported grades in school) and scales assessing daytime sleepiness, sleep/wake behavior problems (Carskadon, Seifer, & Acebo, 1991), and depressive mood (Kandel & Davies, 1982). School performance was assessed by asking students, "Are your grades mostly A's, A's and B's, B's, B's and C's, C's, C's and D's, D's, or D's and F's?" These data were collapsed into four categories (mostly A's or A's/B's; mostly B's or B's/C's; mostly C's or C's/D's; mostly D's/F's).

The sleepiness scale consisted of total responses to items asking whether the respondent had struggled to stay awake (fought sleep) or fallen asleep in 10 different situations in the last 2 weeks, such as in conversation, while studying, in class at school, and so on (Carskadon et al., 1991). The respondent was asked to rate his or her answer on a scale of 1 to 4 (1 = no to 4 = both struggled to stay awake and fallen asleep). Scores on the sleepiness scale range from 10 to 40 and coefficient alpha was .70.

The sleep/wake behavior problems scale included 10 items asking frequency of indicators of erratic sleep/wake behaviors over the course of the last 2 weeks (e.g., arrived late to class because you overslept, stayed up past 3:00 A.M., needed more than one reminder to get up in the A.M., had an extremely hard time falling asleep, and so on; Carskadon et al., 1991). High school students were asked to rate the frequency of the particular behavior on a 5 point scale from everyday/night to never (5 = everyday, 1 = never). Scores range from 10 to 50, and coefficient alpha for the sleep/wake behaviors scale was .75.

The depressive mood scale (Kandel & Davies, 1982) queried the high school students as to how often they were bothered or troubled by certain situations in the last 2 weeks. It consists of six items (e.g., feeling unhappy, sad, or depressed; feeling hopeless about the future), and three response categories were provided, ranging from not at all to somewhat too much (e.g., scored 1 to 3, respectively). The index of depressive mood was based on a total score and has high internal reliability (coefficient alpha was .79 for this sample and .79 in the original study; Kandel & Davies, 1982). The Pearson correlation between the Kandel and Davies six item, depressive mood scale and the SCL-90 scale is .72, and prior studies demonstrated that the scale has high test-retest reliability with adolescent samples ($r = .76$) over 5–6 month intervals (Kandel & Davies, 1982).

PARTICIPANTS

The survey was completed anonymously by 3,120 students, 395 students at School A (rural), 1,077 at School B (urban), 745 at School C (suburban), and 903 at School D (suburban) (48% boys, 52% girls). The sample in Schools B and C comprised grades 10–12, whereas Schools A and D had ninth to twelfth graders. Approximately 8% of the students from schools A, C, and D and 17% from School B were eligible for free or reduced price lunches (State of Rhode Island Department of Education, 1994). Overall, the response rate was 88%. The students' ages ranged from 13 to 19 years (age 13–14, $n = 336$, age 15, $n = 858$, age 16, $n = 919$, age 17–19, $n = 988$). Over 91% of the students from Schools A, C, D reported that they were European American, whereas School B was more diverse (75% European American, 25% multiracial). On average, 81% of the students from all four schools reported that they live with both parents; 46% have older siblings, and 63% have younger siblings living in their homes. Eighty-six percent of their mothers *and* fathers were employed.

STATISTICAL METHODS

The findings are presented in three sections: (1) changes in sleep/wake habits according to age, sex, and school; (2) relation between high school grades and sleep/wake habits; and (3) an analysis of the differences in daytime functioning for students in extreme groups on several sleep parameters: short versus long school-night total sleep time, short versus long weekend oversleep, and small versus large weekend delay.

In the first two sections, multivariate analyses of variance (MANOVA) were used to examine age, sex, school, and grades in relation to the sleep/wake variables: total sleep time, bedtime, rise time, weekend delay, and weekend oversleep. Three multivariate analyses were computed: (1) school-night sleep variables, (2) weekend sleep variables, and (3) weekend delay and weekend oversleep. When significant multivariate effects were found, univariate effects were then examined using Bonferroni tests to determine significant group mean differences.

The large sample size in this study raises the possibility of finding many *statistically* significant results that have very small effect sizes, thus running the risk of overinterpreting inconsequential relations. To address this potential problem, we use an effect size criterion in addition to a statistical significance criterion for discussion and interpretation of those results most likely to prove meaningful in the long run. In the results section that follows, we restrict our discussion to those significant findings that also have effect sizes between what Cohen (1988) characterizes as small and medium. Specifically, a correlation of .20 is the effect size criterion, which is slightly smaller than the midpoint of Cohen's small ($r = .10$) and medium ($r = .30$) effects in terms of variance explained. For analysis of group differences, effects where two groups differ by more than one-third of the sample standard deviation are considered. Again, this is slightly lower than the midpoint between small ($d = .20$) and medium ($d = .50$) effect sizes (Cohen, 1988). (Note that we do not calculate exact effect sizes for our more complex analyses but simply wish to have a reasonable criterion for further consideration of effects most likely to have generalizable implications.) All *statistically* significant results, regardless of effect size, are noted in the tables that accompany the text.

RESULTS

SLEEP/WAKE PATTERNS CHANGE ACROSS HIGH SCHOOL AGE GROUPS

Our analysis of age-related affects grouped data by four age ranges; Table 1 presents means, standard deviations, and *F* values for the sleep variables according to age. All school-night sleep variables were affected by age, multivariate $F(9, 6571) = 22.49$, $p < .001$. Specifically, average total sleep time decreased by approximately 40 min across the four age groups, $p < .001$, average school-night bedtimes were about 45 min later, $p < .001$, and average rise times about 10 min later, $p < .001$. Reported weekend sleep habits also showed age-related changes, multivariate $F(9, 6327) = 21.28$, $p < .001$. Average weekend total sleep time declined by about 50 min across the age groups, $p < .001$, as weekend night bedtimes shifted increasingly later, $p < .001$, differing by about 1 hr between the youngest and oldest teenagers. Weekend rise

TABLE 1   MEANS AND STANDARD DEVIATIONS FOR SCHOOL-NIGHT AND WEEKEND SLEEP VARIABLES BY AGE

Sleep/Wake Variable	13–14 Years ($\underline{n}$ = 336)	15 Years ($\underline{n}$ = 858)	16 Years ($\underline{n}$ = 919)	17–19 Years ($\underline{n}$ = 988)	F Value	Bonferroni
School-night TST	462 (67)	449 (66)	435 (68)	424 (66)	24.13***	14, 15 > 16 > 17
School-night bedtime	10:05 P.M. (49)	10:20 P.M. (55)	10:37 P.M. (58)	10:51 P.M. (58)	53.54***	14 < 15 < 16 < 17
School-night rise time	5:59 A.M. (24)	6:00 A.M. (25)	6:05 A.M. (29)	6:10 A.M. (31)	19.47***	14, 15 < 16 < 17
Weekend TST	567 (100)	564 (104)	549 (108)	518 (114)	32.53***	14, 15 > 16 > 17
Weekend bedtime	11:54 P.M. (94)	12:06 A.M. (83)	12:30 A.M. (82)	12:49 A.M. (80)	42.33***	14, 15 < 16 < 17
Weekend rise time	9:22 A.M. (85)	9:40 A.M. (104)	9:46 A.M. (107)	9:32 A.M. (107)	ns	. . .
Weekend oversleep	104 (102)	115 (112)	112 (116)	95 (114)	5.80**⁻	. . .
Weekend delay	89 (71)	88 (66)	92 (65)	95 (68)	ns	. . .

Note : TST refers to total sleep time (minutes). Weekend oversleep is the difference between weekend and school-night total sleep times and weekend delay is the difference between weekend and school-night bedtimes. Standard deviations in parentheses, are in minutes; TST, weekend oversleep, and weekend delay are in minutes as well.

**p < .01; ***p < .001; –does not meet effect size criterion (e.g., effects where two groups differ by more than one-third of the sample standard deviation).

times did not change with age. Overall, weekend delay and weekend oversleep changed between ages 13 and 19, multivariate $F (6, 5060) = 3.93$, $p < .01$. Although this multivariate F is statistically significant, age group differences for weekend delay and weekend oversleep were too small (on the order of .1 SD) to meet our effect size criterion.

Although all four high schools had similarly early school start times (between 7:10 A.M. and 7:30 A.M.), students' school-night sleep habits varied among the schools, multivariate $F (9, 6571) = 12.76$, $p < .001$, due to differences in rise times, $p < .001$. In particular, students who attended the school with the earliest school start time (7:10) reported earlier rise times than students at the other schools (School A: $M = 5:53$ versus Schools B, C, D: $Ms = 6:04–6:09$, $ps < .01$). Although school differences occurred in reported average total sleep times and bedtimes, these group differences did not meet effect size criterion. Weekend sleep also varied among schools, multivariate $F (9, 6327) = 4.74$, $p < .001$; however, univariate differences for total sleep time, bedtime, and rise time did not meet our effect size criterion. Additionally, small differences among the schools on weekend

delay and weekend oversleep were not meaningful based on the effect size criterion.

Few sex differences were identified. Female students reported different school-night sleep habits than their male peers, multivariate $F (3, 2700) = 41.36$, $p < .001$, due to female students reporting waking up earlier than males: females, $M = 5:58$ versus males, $M = 6:10$, $F (1, 2702) = 100.81$, $p < .001$. Boys and girls did not differ on reported school-night bedtimes, nor total sleep times. Overall, female students had greater weekend delays and weekend oversleeps than the male students, multivariate $F (2, 2530) = 6.67$, $p < .001$; however, univariate differences did not meet the effect size criterion. Female and male high school students did not report significant differences in weekend total sleep times, bedtimes, or rise times. The overall sample distributions of sleep patterns are displayed in Figure 1.

ACADEMIC PERFORMANCE AND SLEEP HABITS

Table 2 [on page 310] presents the analyses of sleep habits based on self-reported academic performance.

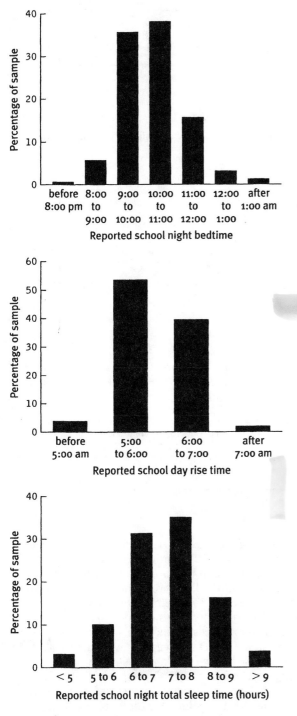

FIGURE 1

Sample distributions of sleep patterns

grades. Post hoc analysis showed that these differences distinguished students reporting C's and worse from those reporting mostly B's or better. Students' weekend sleep habits also differed according to self-reported grades, multivariate $F(9, 6327) = 18.79$, $p < .001$. Specifically, A and B students reported earlier bedtimes and earlier rise times than did C and D/F students, $ps < .001$; however, self-reported grades did not distinguish the students on reported weekend total sleep. Finally, students with worse grades reported greater weekend delays of sleep schedule than did those with better grades, multivariate $F(6, 5060) = 18.22$, $p < .001$. Thus, C and D/F students reported going to bed on average about 2.3 hr later on weekends than on school nights versus a difference of about 1.8 hr for the A and B students, $ps < .001$. Students with D/F's reported longer weekend oversleeps than A, B, or C students; however, these differences did not meet the effect size criterion.

DAYTIME FUNCTIONING OF STUDENTS WHO ADOPT *ADEQUATE* VERSUS *LESS THAN ADEQUATE* SLEEP HABITS

Data presented in the previous sections demonstrate that older high school students sleep less and have later bedtimes than younger students, and those who report a poor academic performance are more likely to sleep less, go to bed later, and have more irregular sleep/wake habits. These descriptive findings, however, do not explain whether especially short amounts of sleep and/or irregular schedules are associated with changes in daytime functioning. To describe more thoroughly the high school students who are obtaining minimal sleep and/or who have irregular sleep schedules, we examined a priori defined groups based on sleep variables that have been cited previously as having an impact on behavior, deriving our values from empirical data (Carskadon et al., 1980, 1983; Carskadon, Keenan, & Dement, 1987). Other potentially important factors (e.g., history of sleep disorders), may covary with these, but data from our survey focused on total sleep and school-night versus weekend schedule changes.

The *extreme* groups of students were defined as follows: long ($\geq$ 8 hr 15 min) versus short ($\leq$ 6 hr 45 min) school-night total sleep time; large ($\geq$ 120 min) versus small ($\leq$ 60 min) weekend delay; or high (> 120 min) versus low (< 60 min) weekend oversleep. High school students who had longer total sleep times, small weekend delays, or low weekend oversleeps were defined as having adopted *adequate* sleep habits, whereas students with shorter sleep times, large weekend delays or high weekend oversleeps were defined as having adopted *less than adequate* sleep habits. We compared these *extreme*

In general, students with higher grades reported longer and more regular sleep, multivariate $F(9, 6571) = 8.91$, $p < .001$. Specifically, they reported more total sleep, $p < .001$, and earlier bedtimes, $p < .001$, on school nights than did students with lower

TABLE 2   MEANS AND STANDARD DEVIATIONS FOR SCHOOL-NIGHT AND WEEKEND SLEEP VARIABLES BY GRADES

	Self-Reported Grades					
Sleep/Wake Variables	Mostly A's or A's/B's ($\underline{n}$ = 1,238)	Mostly B's or B's/C's ($\underline{n}$ = 1,371)	Mostly C's or C's/D's ($\underline{n}$ = 390)	Mostly D's/F's ($\underline{n}$ = 61)	F Value	Bonferroni
School-night TST	442 (62)	441 (66)	424 (74)	408 (94)	16.66***	A, B > C, D/F
School-night bedtime	10:27 P.M. (53)	10:32 P.M. (56)	10:52 P.M. (65)	11:22 P.M. (81)	24.58***	A, B < C, D/F
School-night rise time	6:02 A.M. (25)	6:05 A.M. (29)	6:10 A.M. (34)	6:09 A.M. (31)	ns	. . .
Weekend TST	547 (100)	547 (109)	534 (124)	549 (137)	ns	. . .
Weekend bedtime	12:06 A.M. (78)	12:29 A.M. (82)	1:09 A.M. (97)	1:33 A.M. (93)	51.32***	A < B < C, D/F
Weekend rise time	9:21 A.M. (97)	9:43 A.M. (103)	9:59 A.M. (113)	10:33 A.M. (160)	24.10***	A < B < C, D/F
Weekend oversleep	105 (101)	108 (114)	109 (130)	137 (159)	3.32*–	A, B, C < D/F
Weekend delay	99 (68)	117 (72)	137 (77)	133 (80)	26.53***	A < B < C, D/F

Note: TST refers to total sleep time (minutes). Weekend oversleep is the difference between weekend and school-night total sleep times, and weekend delay is the difference between weekend and school-night bedtimes. Standard deviations, in parentheses, are in minutes; TST, weekend oversleep, and weekend delay are in minutes as well.

*p < .05; **p < .01; ***p < .001; –does not meet effect size criterion (e.g., effects where two groups differ by more than one-third of the sample standard deviation).

groups on daytime and nighttime functioning. Table 3 displays means, standard deviations, and *F* values for depressive mood, sleepiness, and sleep/wake behavior problems for each of the sleep variable groups. (The demographic breakdown of these groups reflected the larger sample on age, sex, and school attendance.) Separate analyses of variance were calculated for each dependent variable (depressive mood, level of sleepiness, and sleep/wake behavior problems), with school-night total sleep time, weekend delay, weekend oversleep, and sex as independent variables. Age was analyzed as a covariate in these analyses.

Overall, adolescents who were in the groups defined as *less than adequate* sleep habits reported increased behavioral difficulties in comparison to those we defined as *adequate sleepers* . Thus, students in the short total sleep group reported more sleep/wake behavior problems, such as arrived late to class because of oversleeping, tired or dragged out nearly every day, needed more than one re-

minder to get up, *p*s < .01, higher levels of depressive mood, *p*s < .001, and greater sleepiness, *p*s < .001, than those in the long sleep group. Similarly, adolescents in the large weekend delay group described more sleep/wake behavior problems, *p*s < .01, and greater daytime sleepiness, *p*s < .05, but no difference in depressed mood from those with small weekend delays. One exception was that the female students with large weekend delays reported increased depressive mood levels, *p* < .05. Adolescents in the high weekend oversleep group reported more sleep/wake behavior problems, *p* < .001, but no differences in depressed mood or sleepiness from those in the low oversleep group. No sex differences were found in self-reported sleep/wake behavior problems; however, females reported higher levels of depressed mood: females, M = 11.04, SD = 2.91 versus males, M = 9.20, SD = 2.68, *p* < .001, and daytime sleepiness: females, M = 15.26, SD = 3.59 versus males, M = 14.67, SD = 4.16, *p* ≤ .01, than did males.

TABLE 3 MEANS, STANDARD DEVIATIONS, AND ANALYSIS OF VARIANCE FOR DAYTIME BEHAVIOR SCALES FOR ADEQUATE VERSUS LESS THAN ADEQUATE SLEEPERS

| Daytime Functioning Variables | Weekend Delay | | Weekend Oversleep | | School-Night TST | | F Values Sleep Variables | | | | | |
| | | | | | | | Delay | | Oversleep | | TST | |
	≤60 (n = 887)	≥120 (n = 928)	<60 (n = 972)	>120 (n = 1,411)	≥495 (n = 959)	≤405 (n = 1,207)	M	F	M	F	M	F
Depressive mood	10.13	10.35	9.92	10.42	9.48	10.79	ns	3.89*	ns	ns	10.80***	12.94***
	(2.94)	(2.97)	(2.85)	(2.99)	(2.76)	(3.00)						
Sleepiness	14.63	15.29	14.76	15.23	14.03	15.86	4.37*	6.45**	ns	ns	19.79***	29.77***
	(3.71)	(3.98)	(3.82)	(3.81)	(3.51)	(4.01)						
Sleep/wake behavior problems	19.10	21.80	19.33	21.22	18.48	22.17	13.17***	47.20***	17.83***	7.93**	16.15***	28.70***
	(6.61)	(7.16)	(6.83)	(7.18)	(6.63)	(7.01)						

Note: Weekend delay small = ≤60 min, large = ≥120 min; weekend oversleep short = <60 min, long = >120 min, and school-night TST long = ≥8 hr 45 min, short = ≤6 hr 15 min. M = effect for males, F = effect for females.

*p < .05; **p < .01; ***p < .001.

DISCUSSION

The principal aim of this research was to assess the relation between adolescents' sleep/wake habits and their daytime functioning. The relatively high response rate (88%) obtained in this school-based study allows us to consider our findings representative of adolescents enrolled in moderate to large public high schools in this geographical region. The use of a self-report questionnaire enabled us to gather timely information from a large student population.

HIGH SCHOOL STUDENTS' SLEEP LOSS AND IRREGULAR SLEEP/WAKE SCHEDULES

In particular, this sample of over 3,000 high school students reported lower total sleep (school and weekend nights) across ages 13–19. On school nights, the mean total sleep decreased from 7 hr 42 min to 7 hr 4 min. Similarly, average weekend total sleep decreased from 9 hr 20 min to 8 hr 38 min. The sleep loss is due to increasingly later bedtimes in older teens, whereas rise times remain more consistent. The sleep habits of the students attending the four different high schools showed minimal differences, with the exception of school day rise time, which was significantly earlier for students attending the school with the earliest start time. Although the difference between 7:10 and 7:30 may appear slight, the impact on sleep patterns was meaningful.

Remarkably few differences were found between male and female high school students' sleep/wake patterns. Female adolescents reported that they woke up 12 min earlier than their male peers on school mornings, a finding consistent with an earlier survey of high school students (Carskadon, 1990b) and a study of junior high school students in Taiwan (Gau & Soong, 1995). In the Gau et al. sample, however, the junior high school girls also reported less total sleep than the boys. We speculate that adolescent girls may be getting up earlier because they require more time to prepare for school and/or for family responsibilities.

Taken together, we conclude that most of these adolescents do not get enough sleep. Our laboratory data indicate that optimal sleep length is about 9.2 hr in adolescents (Carskadon et al., 1980). Although individual differences in sleep need are likely, we note that 87% of our sample responded that they need more sleep than they get (median self-reported sleep need = 9 hr). Forty percent of the students reported that they went to bed after 11:00 P.M. on school nights, and 91% went to bed after 11:00 P.M. (67% after midnight) on weekends. Furthermore, 26% reported that they usually sleep 6.5 hr or less, and only 15% reported sleeping 8.5 hr or more on school nights (median = 7.5 hr). Nearly 70% of the students reported weekend delays of 60 min or more; on average, they reported oversleeping on weekends by nearly 1 hr and 50 min. Ninety-one percent of these high school students rise at 6:30 A.M. or earlier on school mornings, and 72% awaken at 9:00 A.M. or later on weekends.

These high school students' reported sleep/wake schedules are consistent with the major trends in the field: (1) self-reported nocturnal sleep time declines across the adolescent years; (2) bedtimes during high school become later; and (3) teenagers show large variations between weekend and school-night sleep schedules (e.g., Carskadon, 1990a; Strauch & Meier, 1988; Szymczak et al., 1993). In comparison to data from Rhode Island high school students surveyed 8 years earlier, these students reported on average approximately 15–20 min less sleep per night on school nights, principally reflecting earlier rising times (Carskadon, 1990a). The developmental and secular trends raise concerns about patterns that may have negative effects on teenagers' waking behavior.

Not assessed in this survey is the impact of family factors on sleep patterns. In the past, we have shown that parents tend to relinquish control of bedtime while increasing involvement with rising time as youngsters pass into adolescence (Carskadon, 1990a). In this particular sample, only 5.1% of students reported that parents set bedtimes on school nights; thus, the great majority of these youngsters set their own bedtime agenda. Over 80% of youngsters in this survey come from two-parent households in which both parents are employed, and we saw no differences between this cohort and those from single-parent homes on the major sleep variables. We propose that the biological and psychosocial processes favoring sleep delay in teens collides with early rising times mandated by schools and that even in the most well-regulated families the capacity for adequate adjustments may be limited.

SLEEP/WAKE HABITS AND SCHOOL PERFORMANCE

Our data support and extend findings from Kowalski and Allen (1995) and Link and Ancoli-Israel (1995) that students who described themselves as struggling or failing school (i.e., obtaining C's, D's/F's) report that they obtain less sleep, have later bedtimes, and have more irregular sleep/wake schedules than students who report better grades (i.e., A's, B's). In the Link and Ancoli-Israel survey of 150 high school students, students with self-reported higher grade point averages (GPA) slept more at night and reported less daytime sleepiness than students with lower GPAs. One explanation for these results is that students who get more sleep and maintain more consistent school/weekend sleep schedules obtain better grades because of their ability to be more alert and to pay greater attention in class and on homework. In contrast, Gau et al. (1995) found that younger students (junior high school age) on a highly competitive academic track reported shorter school and weekend night total sleep times, later bedtimes, and decreased daytime alertness than students in an alternative, less competitive program. Our data do not show a one-to-one relation between sleep patterns and grades. Certainly some students are able to function in school quite well with short amounts of sleep but may pay a price in other ways. Many students, however, may be too impaired by insufficient sleep to cope optimally with school demands. A major limitation of all of these studies is that they involve self-report; additional laboratory and field research are needed to clarify the direction of the relations among sleep loss, irregular sleep schedules, and academic performance and to assess other moderating and mediating variables, such as coping strategies, family rules, class schedules, and type of academic work.

ADDITIONAL CONSEQUENCES OF POOR SLEEP/WAKE HABITS

We have attempted to describe more thoroughly certain consequences of insufficient sleep and irregular sleep/wake schedules on adolescents' functioning by comparing extreme groups of students who reported patterns we defined as *adequate* versus *less than adequate* sleep/wake patterns. Students with short school-night sleep reported increased levels of depressed mood, daytime sleepiness, and problematic sleep behaviors in comparison to longer sleepers. Likewise, students with more irregular sleep schedules had more behavior problems. These data suggest that high school students with inadequate total sleep and/or irregular school-night to weekend sleep/wake schedules may struggle with daytime behavior problems. We interpret these findings to indicate that poor sleep habits influence behavior and mood, acknowledging that in certain youngsters the cause-effect arrow may go in the opposite direction.

Researchers are just beginning to compile evidence relating emotional well-being to sleep patterns. Our findings showing that teenagers with very short and irregular sleep/wake patterns have more daytime difficulties support the work of Morrison, McGee, and Stanton (1992), who compared four groups of 13- and 15-year-olds in New Zealand: those with no sleep problems, those indicating they needed more sleep only, those reporting difficulties falling asleep or maintaining sleep, and those with multiple sleep problems. These investigators found that adolescents in the sleep-problem groups were more anxious, had

higher levels of depression, and had lower social competence than those in the no-sleep-problem group. Similarly, Carskadon et al. (1991) found that a pattern of short sleep in college-bound high school seniors was associated with reports of sleepiness and sleep problems in males and females, and with anxiety and depression in females. Moreover, in a study calling for ninth to twelfth graders to reduce their habitual sleep by 2 hr over 5 consecutive nights, dysphoric mood changes occurred during the reduced sleep period on both daily and weekly depressive mood scales (Carskadon et al., 1989).

We hypothesize that if adolescents had the opportunity to obtain more sleep each night, they would experience fewer fluctuations in daily mood and fewer behavioral difficulties. In essence, we propose that adolescent moodiness may be in part a repercussion of insufficient sleep. The tendency for some adolescents to have reduced nocturnal sleep times and irregular schedules may have consequences that extend beyond daytime sleepiness to feelings of depression. On the other hand, depressed adolescents may be more inclined toward insufficient sleep and irregular schedules (Dahl et al., 1996). Additional in-depth laboratory and field assessment studies to probe the interplay between context, sleep/wake patterns, and daytime functioning of adolescents may enable us to tease apart some of these factors.

CAVEATS AND IMPLICATIONS

We are very concerned about the important information that we have obtained from this large sample of high school students; however, certain caveats pertain. First, it is difficult to evaluate how representative the sample was, although the congruence between our findings and those from prior research (e.g., Carskadon, 1990a; Strauch & Meier, 1988) strongly suggest that the sample was quite typical. Whether our results hold for adolescents drawn from a wider socioeconomic and cultural background is an important issue for future studies. Second, the results of this study are based entirely on the adolescents' self-reports and suffer limitations because data are retrospective, based only on the last 2 weeks, and subjective. Multiple sources of measurement such as parent and teacher ratings, school record data, standardized test batteries, and sleep laboratory recordings would provide a more comprehensive and possibly more reliable assessment than the current study. Our previous experience in laboratory studies indicate that such self-report data are well correlated with data obtained from daily sleep diaries or continuous activity monitoring, although we have not made a formal comparison. On the other hand, in a study of tenth grade students that included 2 weeks of diaries and activity monitoring followed by a laboratory assessment, we found an average sleep length on school nights of 6 hr, 53 min ($SD = 39$), very similar to self-report (Carskadon, Acebo, Wolfson, Tzischinsky, & Darley, 1997).

Third, because the survey was conducted in one geographic area, some caution should be taken in generalizing the findings. Fourth, because the study design was cross-sectional, no conclusions about long-term development and ramifications of inadequate sleep can be drawn. Future investigations should gather several weeks of sleep and behavioral data and consider following high school students over several years. Finally, because the data are cross-sectional it is difficult to demonstrate causal direction. Models that include parameters different than those included in the present study (e.g., home structure, parenting styles, school schedules, and so forth) could also account for variation in grades and/or sleep/wake schedules. Nevertheless, the present study extends the research on adolescent sleep in several ways: (1) to a large population of public, high school students; (2) to a broader understanding of the association between sleep/wake habits, emotional well-being, and school performance in high school students from ages 13 to 19; and (3) to a clearer conceptualization of the risks for adolescents who obtain short amounts of sleep and/or experience erratic weekday-weekend sleep schedules on their daytime performance and mood.

Although self-report surveys have clear limitations, the implications of these data seem undeniable. First, schools need to take an active role and to examine sleep in the context of academic grades, test scores, truancy, behavioral difficulties, and other aspects of daytime functioning and adolescent development. Second, investigators in other fields who are concerned with adolescent development and well-being need to add the insights regarding adolescents' sleep into their studies and clinical work. Third, researchers, practitioners, and educators need to take interdisciplinary approaches to understanding and promoting the academic, health, and behavioral well-being of adolescents.

Adolescents confront a multitude of vulnerabilities, uncertainties, and changes. This developmental period is extremely eventful in terms of physiological, cognitive, and psychosocial development. Undoubtedly, most adolescents require more than 7 hr, 20 min (sample mean) of sleep to cope optimally with academic demands, social pressures, driving, and job responsibilities. Although adolescents may be differentially affected by pubertal changes in sleep/wake patterns, school start times, and academic responsibilities, the excessive sleepiness consequent to insufficient, erratic sleep is a potentially serious factor for adolescent development and behavioral

well-being. The magnitude of the problem has been unrecognized because adolescent sleepiness is so widespread that it almost seems normal (Carskadon, 1990a). Steinberg and Darling (1994), Petersen, Silbereisen, and Soerensen (1993) and others have emphasized the importance of studying the context of adolescent development. The development of adolescent sleeping patterns cannot be understood without taking into account school schedules and other contexts; likewise, adolescent development (psychosocial, cognitive, emotional) cannot be fully examined without considering sleep/wake factors.

REFERENCES

Achenbach, T. (1991). *Manual for the Youth Self-Report and 1991 profile* . Burlington: University of Vermont Department of Psychiatry.

Allen, R. (1991). School-week sleep lag: Sleep problems with earlier starting of senior high schools. *Sleep Research, 20,* 198.

Allen, R. (1992). Social factors associated with the amount of school week sleep lag for seniors in an early starting suburban high school. *Sleep Research, 21,* 114.

Allen, R., & Mirabile, J. (1989). Self-reported sleep-wake patterns for students during the school year from two different senior high schools. *Sleep Research, 18,* 132.

Andrade, M. M., Benedito-Silva, E. E., & Domenice, S. (1993). Sleep characteristics of adolescents: A longitudinal study. *Journal of Adolescent Health, 14,* 401–406.

Bearpark, H. M., & Michie, P. T. (1987). Prevalence of sleep/wake disturbances in Sydney adolescents. *Sleep Research, 16,* 304.

Brown, C., Tzischinsky, O., Wolfson, A., Acebo, C., Wicks, J., Darley, C., & Carskadon, M. A. (1995). Circadian phase preference and adjustment to the high school transition. *Sleep Research, 24,* 90.

Carskadon, M. A. (1982). The second decade. In C. Guilleminault (Ed.), *Sleeping and waking disorders: Indications and techniques* . Menlo Park: Addison-Wesley.

Carskadon, M. A. (1990a). Patterns of sleep and sleepiness in adolescents. *Pediatrician, 17,* 5–12.

Carskadon, M. A. (1990b). Adolescent sleepiness: Increased risk in a high-risk population. *Alcohol, Drugs, and Driving, 5/6,* 317–328.

Carskadon, M. A. (1995). Sleep's place in teenagers' lives. *Proceedings of the Biennial Meeting of the Society for Research in Child Development,* p. 32 (abstract).

Carskadon, M. A., & Acebo, C. (1993). A self-administered rating scale for pubertal development. *Journal of Adolescent Health Care, 14,* 190–195.

Carskadon, M. A., Acebo, C., Richardson, G. S., Tate, B. A., & Seifer, R. (1997). Long nights protocol: Access to circadian parameters in adolescents. *Journal of Biological Rhythms, 12,* 278–289.

Carskadon, M. A., Acebo, C., Wolfson, A., Tzischinsky, O., & Darley, C. (1997). REM sleep on MSLTS in high school students is related to circadian phase. *Sleep Research, 26,* 705.

Carskadon, M. A., Dement, W. C., Mitler, M. M., Roth, T., Westbrook, P. R., & Keenan, S. (1986). Guidelines for the Multiple Sleep Latency Test (MSLT): A standard measure of sleepiness. *Sleep, 9*, 519–524.

Carskadon, M. A., Harvey, K., Duke, P., Anders, T. F., & Dement, W. C. (1980). Pubertal changes in daytime sleepiness. *Sleep, 2*, 453–460.

Carskadon, M. A., Keenan, S., & Dement, W. C. (1987). Nighttime sleep and daytime sleep tendency in preadolescents. In C. Guilleminault (Ed.), *Sleep and its disorders in children.* New York: Raven Press.

Carskadon, M. A., & Mancuso, J. (1988). Sleep habits in high school adolescents: Boarding versus day students. *Sleep Research, 17,* 74.

Carskadon, M. A., Orav, E. J., & Dement, W. C. (1983). Evolution of sleep and daytime sleepiness in adolescents. In C. Guilleminault & E. Lugaresi (Eds.), *Sleep/wake disorders: Natural history, epidemiology, and long-term evolution* (pp. 201–216). New York: Raven Press.

Carskadon, M. A., Rosekind, M. R., Galli, J., Sohn, J., Herman, K. B., & Davis, S. S. (1989). Adolescent sleepiness during sleep restriction in the natural environment. *Sleep Research, 18*, 115.

Carskadon, M. A., Seifer, R., & Acebo, C. (1991). Reliability of six scales in a sleep questionnaire for adolescents. *Sleep Research, 20*, 421.

Carskadon, M. A., Vieira, C., & Acebo, C., (1993). Association between puberty and delayed phase preference. *Sleep, 16*, 258–262.

Carskadon, M. A., Wolfson, A., Tzischinsky, O., & Acebo, C. (1995). Early school schedules modify adolescent sleepiness. *Sleep Research, 24*, 92.

Cohen, J. (1988). *Statistical Power Analysis for the Behavioral Sciences*. Hillsdale, NJ: Erlbaum.

Dahl, R. E., & Carskadon, M. A. (1995). Sleep in its disorders in adolescence. In R. Ferber & M. Kryger (Eds.), *Principles and practice of sleep medicine in the child*. Philadelphia: WB Saunders.

Dahl, R. E., Holttum, J., & Trubnick, L. (1994). A clinical picture of childhood and adolescent narcolepsy. *Journal of the American Academy of Child and Adolescent Psychiatry, 33*, 834–841.

Dahl, R. E., Ryan, N. D., Matty, M. K., Birmaher, B., Alshabbout, M., Williamson, D. E., & Kupfer, D. J. (1996). Sleep onset abnormalities in depressed adolescents. *Biological Psychiatry, 39*, 400–410.

Epstein, R., Chillag, N., & Lavie, P. (1995). Sleep habits of children and adolescents in Israel: The influence of starting time of school. *Sleep Research, 24a*, 432.

Fisher, B. E., & Rinehart, S. (1990). Stress, arousal, psychopathology and temperament: A multidimensional approach to sleep disturbance in children. *Personality and Individual Differences, 11*, 431–438.

Gau, S-F., & Soong, W-T. (1995). Sleep problems of junior high school students in Taipei. *Sleep, 18*, 667–673.

Guilleminault, C., Winkle, R., & Korobkin, R. (1982). Children and nocturnal snoring: Evaluation of the effects of sleep related respiratory resistive load and daytime functioning. *European Journal of Pediatrics, 139*, 165–171.

Hendry, L. B., Glendinning, A., Shucksmith, J., Love, J., & Scott, J. (1994). The developmental context of adolescent lifestyles. In R. K. Silbereisen & T. Eberhard (Eds.), *Adolescence in context: The interplay of family, school, peers, and work in adjustment* (pp. 66–81). New York: Springer-Verlag.

Ishihara, K., Honma, Y., & Miyake, S. (1990). Investigation of the children's version of the morningness-eveningness questionnaire with primary and junior high school pupils in Japan. *Perceptual and Motor Skills, 71*, 1353–1354.

Kagan, J., Resnick, J. S., & Gibbons, J. (1989). Inhibited and uninhibited types of children. *Child Development, 60*, 838–845.

Kandel, D. B., & Davies, M. (1982). Epidemiology of depressive mood in adolescents. *Archives of General Psychiatry, 39*, 1205–1212.

Kataria, S., Swanson, M. S., & Trevathan, G. E. (1987). Persistence of sleep disturbances in preschool children. *Pediatrics, 110*, 642–646.

Kowalski, N., & Allen, R. (1995). School sleep lag is less but persists with a very late starting high school. *Sleep Research, 24*, 124.

Link, S. C., & Ancoli-Israel, S. (1995). Sleep and the teenager. *Sleep Research, 24a*, 184.

Manber, R., Pardee, R. E., Bootzin, R. R., Kuo, T., Rider, A. M., Rider, S. P., & Bergstrom, L. (1995). Changing sleep patterns in adolescence. *Sleep Research, 24*, 106.

Morrison, D. N., McGee, R., & Stanton, W. R. (1992). Sleep problems in adolescence. *Journal of the American Academy of Child and Adolescent Psychiatry, 31*, 94–99.

Peterson, A. C., Silbereisen, R. K., & Soerensen, S. (1993). Adolescent development: A global perspective. In W. Meeus, M. de Goede, W. Kox, & K. Hurrelmann (Eds.), *Adolescence, careers and cultures* (pp. 1–34). New York: De Gruyter.

Petta, D., Carskadon, M. A., & Dement, W. C. (1984). Sleep habits in children aged 7–13 years. *Sleep Research, 13*, 86.

Price, V. A., Coates, T. J., Thoresen, C. E., & Grinstead, O. A. (1978). Prevalence and correlates of poor sleep among adolescents. *American Journal of Diseases of Children, 132*, 583–586.

Quine, L. (1992). Severity of sleep problems in children with severe learning difficulties: Description and correlates. *Journal of Community and Applied Social Psychology, 2*, 247–268.

State of Rhode Island Department of Education. (1994). *Rhode Island Public Schools 1994 District Profiles*. Providence: Rhode Island Department of Elementary and Secondary Education.

Steinberg, L., & Darling, N. (1994). The broader context of social influence in adolescence. In R. K. Silbereisen & T. Eberhard (Eds.), *Adolescence in context: The interplay of family, school, peers, and work in adjustment* (pp. 25–45). New York: Springer-Verlag.

Strauch, I., & Meier, B. (1988). Sleep need in adolescents: A longitudinal approach. *Sleep, 11*, 378–386.

Szymczak, J. T., Jasinska, M., Pawlak, E., & Swierzykowska, M. (1993). Annual and weekly changes in the sleep-wake rhythm of school children. *Sleep, 16*, 433–435.

Tanner, J. M. (1962). *Growth in adolescence*. Oxford: Blackwell.

Williams, R., Karacan, I., & Hursch, C. (1974). *EEG of human sleep*. New York: Wiley & Sons.

Wolfson, A. R., Tzischinsky, O., Brown, C., Darley, C., Acebo, C., & Carskadon, M. (1995). Sleep, behavior, and stress at the transition to senior high school. *Sleep Research, 24*, 115.

QUESTIONS

1. What biological changes in sleep schedules and sleep demands occur in adolescence?
2. What is the adolescent sleep debt, and what biological and environmental factors contribute to this pattern?
3. How does the need for sleep change from childhood to adolescence? What do you think this change suggests about the maturational process during the adolescent years?
4. According to Wolfson and Carskadon, what changes occur in adolescent sleep schedules from age 13 to age 19?
5. How does the adolescent sleep pattern affect academic performance?
6. Do high school students who get less than adequate amounts of sleep suffer? If so, how?
7. Why is the fact that the sleep patterns of adolescents were similar across the four high schools studied important for understanding this process?
8. Why do you think female (but not male) students who experienced large weekend bedtime delays reported more depression?
9. How do you think family factors make disruptive patterns of adolescent sleep better or worse?
10. What policy implications are suggested by these findings? Do you think such changes would be easy or difficult to implement? Why?

34 Development of Logical Reasoning and the School Performance of African American Adolescents in Relation to Socioeconomic Status, Ethnic Identity, and Self-Esteem

MARK S. CHAPELL · WILLIS F. OVERTON

Among the many changes that occur in adolescence, cognitive or intellectual changes rank high in importance. They permit adolescents to think in more complex, abstract, and hypothetical ways than ever before. When Jean Piaget characterized adolescent thought as formal operational, he meant that adolescents are capable of performing logical operations that are formal, or abstract, in nature. As a result, abstract mathematics and scientific reasoning become possible for adolescents. Following up on Piaget's assertion, researchers have documented developmental change from early to late adolescence in logical reasoning skills. However, this research has mainly included adolescents of European-American ancestry. Consequently, little is known about this development in youth from other cultural groups either within or outside the United States.

In the following article, Mark S. Chapell and Willis F. Overton address this shortcoming. They conducted a study of the logical reasoning skills of African-American adolescents from the sixth grade up to the college years. In addition, Chapell and Overton were interested in how family social class relates to the development of logical reasoning in African-American adolescents. They also probed two theoretical models regarding the expression of cognitive abilities in African-American youth. Ogbu's *cultural-ecological theory* concentrates on the relation between ethnic identity and cognitive performance. It suggests that as African-American youth develop a stronger ethnic identity, they become disillusioned with behaviors associated with advanced cognitive performance and therefore their performance on cognitive tasks deteriorates. Steele's *stereotype-threat theory* focuses on the connection between self-esteem and cognitive performance, and suggests that negative stereotypes of intellectual inferiority impinge on the performance of African-American adolescents on cognitive tasks. Chapell and Overton's study provides empirical information relevant to both of these provocative views. It also offers interesting insight into how the social and cultural experiences of African-American adolescents may contribute to the development of logical reasoning skills.

This study explored the deductive reasoning and school performance of 330 African American adolescents and the relation of reasoning and school performance to socioeconomic status (SES), ethnic identity, and self-esteem. As expected, there was a systematic increase in selection task reasoning performance across adolescence, and high SES students outscored low SES students in reasoning performance and school grades.

Ogbu's cultural-ecological theory, which predicts an inverse relationship between cognitive performance and ethnic identity strength, was not supported because better reasoning performance was associated instead with stronger ethnic identity. Steele's stereotype threat theory, which predicts that there will be an association between global self-esteem and school grades in early adolescent African Americans that subsequently decreases across

Reprinted from the *Journal of Black Psychology, Vol. 28* (2002), pp. 295–317, copyright 2002 by Sage Publications, Inc.
Authors' Note: *Part of this study, based on Mark S. Chapell's doctoral dissertation, was presented at the annual meeting of the American Psychological Society in Miami, Florida, June 2000.*

adolescence, was partially supported. Self-esteem and grades were strongly related in 6th graders, not significantly related in 10th and 12th graders, yet strongly related in college students.

Researchers (Fisher, Jackson, & Villaruel, 1998; Lerner & Galambos, 1998; Steinberg & Morris, 2000) have noted that the empirical literature addressing the normative psychological development of American ethnic minority adolescents is very limited, "In fact, the majority of studies published in the leading scientific journals of child and adolescent development have virtually ignored development within non-European, non-middle class children and families" (Fisher et al., 1998, p. 1150). This trend has continued despite the proliferation of theories (Cooper & Denner, 1998) that express the importance of context and culture for developmental processes.

One area of development where there have been few studies of ethnic minority adolescents is the development of reasoning, an important type of thinking that involves inference, the process where propositions known as premises that have been accepted provide the evidence for arriving at and accepting further propositions known as conclusions (Overton, 1994). There are two major types of reasoning processes: inductive and deductive. Inductive reasoning involves an inference process that proceeds from particular to general propositions, where premises provide probable but not certain evidence for conclusions. Deductive reasoning involves an inference process that moves from general to particular propositions, where general premises provide absolutely certain evidence for the truth of particular conclusions. The first focus of this study is on the development of deductive reasoning in African American adolescents.

The main line of investigation into deductive reasoning (Cheng & Holyoak, 1985; Cosmides, 1989; Evans, 1996; Overton, 1990) has used versions of the four-card selection task (Wason, 1968), a measure consisting of propositional logic problems that test the individual's ability to deduce correct conclusions from given rules. Investigators using the selection task have found that deductive reasoning competence first develops during early adolescence and that by late adolescence a high level of proficiency in solving deductive reasoning problems is generally achieved (Chapell & Overton, 1998; Foltz, Overton, & Ricco, 1995; Overton, Ward, Noveck, Black, & O'Brien, 1987; Reene & Overton, 1989; Ward & Overton, 1990). These results support cognitive developmental theory (Inhelder & Piaget, 1958), which predicts that both inductive and deductive reasoning develop during and across adolescence.

To date, developmental studies of deductive reasoning have been conducted exclusively with Euro-

pean American adolescents. Three published studies of deductive reasoning ability measured by selection task performance have used samples of ethnic minority adolescents (Bell, Brown, & Bryant, 1993; DeShon, Smith, Chan, & Schmitt, 1998; Smith & Drumming, 1989). However, these were nondevelopmental studies because they involved only African American college students. To further test the main prediction from cognitive developmental theory that deductive reasoning competence develops during and across adolescence, this study explored the development of deductive reasoning in African American 6th, 10th, and 12th graders and college students. It was hypothesized, consistent with the pattern of deductive reasoning performance found in European Americans, that there would be a clear developmental progression of deductive reasoning performance across adolescence in African Americans.

The first purpose of this study was to explore the development of deductive reasoning in African American adolescents to diversify and broaden the scope of cognitive developmental research. According to current developmental theory, however, "To understand individual growth and development, the changing relations among biological, psychological, and social contextual levels that comprise the process of developmental change must be examined concurrently" (Fisher et al., 1998, p. 1153). Consistent with this view, studies have shown that there are significant individual differences in the expression of deductive reasoning competence and that deductive reasoning performance is influenced by contextual factors such as familiarity of problem content (Overton et al., 1987) and parenting styles and test anxiety (Chapell & Overton, 1998). Therefore, the second purpose of this study was to explore two factors that may significantly influence the cognitive performance of African American adolescents: socioeconomic status (SES) and ethnic identity.

Researchers have noted that studies that do include participants other than middle-class European Americans often confound race and social class effects by comparing low SES African Americans with higher SES European Americans (Graham, 1992). For instance, in the study cited above, DeShon et al. (1998) compared the deductive reasoning performance of European American college students to that of African Americans whose average family income was lower. This SES inequality also has typified studies using only African American participants, as Graham (1992) pointed out, "Furthermore, with the growing gap between the affluent and the impoverished within the population of American Blacks, it is just as important that race-homogeneous studies not err in the direction of ignoring socioeconomic distinctions between African American subjects" (p. 634). Given the consistent finding that high SES individuals outscore low SES individuals on cognitive tests (Neisser et al., 1996; Suzuki & Valencia, 1997; Williams & Ceci, 1997), this study explored the hypothesis that high SES African American students would have better deductive reasoning performance than low SES students.

OGBU'S CULTURAL-ECOLOGICAL THEORY

African American adolescents generally perform more poorly on cognitive tests and receive lower grades in school than European Americans (Jencks & Phillips, 1998; Neisser et al., 1996; Steinberg, Dornbusch, & Brown, 1992; Williams & Ceci, 1997). This performance gap has most frequently been attributed to ethnic differences in genetic factors related to intelligence, ineffectual parenting practices, and aspects of the linguistic and cognitive styles of African American culture considered disadvantageous to cognitive test performance (Ogbu, 1986, 1993). Ogbu (1986) has long contended that all of these views suffer from ethnocentric bias, and Ogbu's alternative cultural-ecological model maintains that the missing factor in the African American cognitive performance equation is their lower caste-like status as an involuntary minority group created by and historically subordinated to a dominant European American majority.

Ogbu (1986) maintains that African Americans develop and possess the same cognitive capacities as European Americans, including the capacity to "remember, generalize, form concepts, operate with abstractions, and reason logically" (p. 34). However, Ogbu distinguishes the availability of these cognitive capacities from their application, "Cognitive competencies or cognitive skills, on the other hand, arise from the different ways different populations use the common human cognitive capacities to solve specific cognitive problems they face in their particular environments and in their historical experiences" (Ogbu, 1987, p. 157).

In the case of African Americans, Ogbu (1986, 1987, 1988, 1993) maintains that because of their long history of inferior education and exclusion from middle-class, white-collar jobs that require advanced cognitive skills, African Americans have systematically been deterred from expressing their universal cognitive capacities. Rather, as a reaction to centuries of racial discrimination, Ogbu theorizes that many African Americans have become disillusioned about their future job prospects and the actual value of schooling and have developed a disinterested attitude leading to depressed cognitive performance and scholastic underachievement. Fordham and Ogbu (1986) further proposed that African Americans have developed a sense of collective identity that stands in active opposition to that of European Americans. As a result, behaviors related to cognitive performance, such as speaking standard English, taking math and science courses, studying hard and testing well, are seen by African Americans as attempts to "act White," which cross "cultural and cognitive boundaries" and betray the African American group identity. Some high-achieving African American students have been found to gain success in school at the cost of forsaking their ethnic identity and becoming "raceless" (Fordham, 1988), but pressure to "stay Black" is so intensely felt that many African American adolescents are thought to prefer to maintain their ethnic identities by consciously or unconsciously testing poorly and underachieving.

Studies designed to test Ogbu's theory based on information and data gathered 20 or more years ago (Fordham, 1988, 1996; Fordham & Ogbu, 1986; Mickelson, 1990; Ogbu, 1974) supported the predicted relationships between perceived racial discrimination barriers such as "job ceilings," the maintenance of an oppositional ethnic identity, and depressed African American school performance. Recent studies have provided more mixed results, finding that African American adolescents reported peer support for academic success, no "acting White" stigmatization by peers for doing well in school (Ainsworth-Darnell & Downey, 1998; Cook & Ludwig, 1998; Ogbu & Simons, 1994; Spencer, Noll, Stoltzfus, & Harpalani, 2001), and that high ethnic identity scores were associated instead with increased school engagement and better grades (Taylor, Casten, Flickinger, Roberts, & Fulmore, 1994). The present study adds to the investigation of Ogbu's theory by testing the hypotheses that African American sixth graders through college students with high ethnic identity scores would have lower deductive reasoning performance and grade point averages (GPAs) than those with low ethnic identity scores.

STEELE'S STEREOTYPE THREAT THEORY

A second major theoretical model, the stereotype threat theory of Steele (1992, 1997, 1998, 1999), also has proposed that the cognitive performance of African American adolescents is negatively influenced by a history of racial discrimination and prejudice. Steele and Aronson (1995) state, "Whenever African American students perform an explicitly scholastic or intellectual task, they face the threat of confirming or being judged by a negative societal stereotype—a suspicion—about their group's intellectual ability and competence" (p. 797). According to Steele, stereotype threat is experienced as a negative emotional reaction that can interfere with performance in academic evaluation situations, affecting individuals from groups whose abilities have been negatively stereotyped.

Steele further suggests that faced with the continual threat of being judged by or confirming this negative stereotype of intellectual inferiority, over time, African American adolescents may gradually come to devalue school performance and underperform. According to this "school disidentification" hypothesis, "If the poor school achievement of ability-stigmatized groups is mediated by disidentification, then it might be expected that among the ability stigmatized, there would be a disassociation between school outcomes and overall self-esteem" (Steele, 1997, p. 623). Thus, African American adolescents chronically subjected to the added stress of stereotype threat in academic evaluation situations may eventually disengage from school and devalue school performance to protect their self-esteem.

Although Ogbu's cultural-ecological theory and Steele's stereotype threat theory both ascribe African American cognitive underperformance to the negative impact of racial prejudice and discrimination, these models offer distinctly different explanations as to how African American students interpret and respond to these negative conditions. Thus, for instance, whereas Ogbu suggests that African American students interpret testing well and performing well in school as "acting White," constituting a threat to their ethnic group identity to be avoided by performing poorly, Steele suggests that the strain of being judged by or confirming the negative stereotype of Black intellectual inferiority in academic evaluation situations threatens the personal identity and self-esteem of African American students, leading them to gradually disidentify with school, resulting in underachievement.

Osborne (1995, 1997) first tested Steele's school disidentification hypothesis using data from the National Education Longitudinal Study and, as predicted, found a pattern of growing disidentification with school performance in African Americans, with the positive correlation between global self-esteem and school GPA in 8th graders decreasing in both male and female 10th graders and becoming nonsignificant in 12th-grade men. In the current cross-sectional study, Steele's school disidentification thesis was explored further by hypothesizing that the correlation between global self-esteem and GPA would decline in African Americans across all of adolescence, from the 6th grade through college.

In summary, the main developmental hypothesis tested in this study was that deductive reasoning performance would increase across adolescence in African Americans. It was also predicted that (a) high SES African American students would have significantly better deductive reasoning performance than

low SES students, (b) adolescents with high ethnic identity scores would have significantly lower reasoning scores and GPAs than those with low ethnic identity scores, and (c) the correlation between self-esteem and GPA would decline across adolescence.

METHOD

PARTICIPANTS

A total of 330 African American students participated voluntarily, including 62 6th graders (28 men, 34 women), 66 10th graders (34 men, 32 women), 87 12th graders (32 men, 55 women), and 115 college undergraduates (32 men, 83 women). The middle school and high school participants were drawn from public schools located in a major eastern city. The ethnic composition of the middle school was 99% African American, with 70% of the students described by the school district as low income. The high school was 98% African American, with 80% low income students. The college participants attended a public university in a major eastern city with a total enrollment of 26,000 that was 60% European, 26% African American, 10% Asian, and 3% Hispanic.

This sample was not randomly selected but was a sample of convenience including all students who volunteered to participate. Given that approximately 15% of African American high school students drop out before completing their degrees (National Center for Educational Statistics, 1997), some during the middle school years and some during high school, the issue of how to maintain the comparability of the sample from the 6th grade through college was a problem requiring careful attention. To help strengthen the internal validity of the study, the 6th graders were chosen from a middle school with a high (90%) grade promotion rate. The 10th and 12th graders were drawn from the high school's top college preparatory track, and the 12th graders had all been accepted at a college. However, neither the middle school nor high school used were selective in admissions but were schools whose students performed at city-wide averages on standardized tests ("Report Card on the Schools," 1997), and this balance of selectiveness and nonselectiveness was used to maximize comparability without sacrificing the representativeness of this urban African American sample and the generalizability of this study's findings.

DESIGN AND PROCEDURE

Participants in groups of 10 to 30 were administered a general information measure, including questions about age, sex, and grade in school or year in college, followed by measures of GPA (Dornbusch, Ritter,

Leiderman, Roberts, & Fraleigh, 1987), SES (Steinberg, Mounts, Lamborn, & Dornbusch, 1991), Rosenberg's (1979) Self-Esteem Scale, Overton's (1990) version of the selection task, and Phinney's (1992) Multigroup Ethnic Identity Measure.

The administration of all measures was performed by the European American first author during school time in school classrooms. Graham (1992) reviewed studies and concluded that there is no evidence suggesting that European American researchers negatively influence the cognitive performance of African Americans. However, Graham also recommended that in studies such as the current one, which did not involve African American researchers, the possibility of limitations due to unknown, potential researcher–participant effects should be acknowledged.

MEASURES

School GPA   Student GPA was measured using a self-report scale (Dornbusch et al., 1987), consisting of a question asking the participant to select the category describing the usual grades the student gets in school. The categories are as follows: mostly As, about half As and Bs, mostly Bs, about half Bs and half Cs, mostly Cs, about half Cs and half Ds, mostly Ds, and mostly below D. A numerical scale was then related to these responses, with 4.0 representing the "mostly As category," 3.5 representing the "about half As and half Bs" category, and so forth. In previous studies with large multi-ethnic samples, Dornbusch et al. (1987) and Steinberg, Lamborn, Darling, Mounts, and Dornbusch (1994) reported high correlations of $r = .76$ and $r = .80$, respectively, between student GPA measured with the self-report measure and actual student grades taken from school records.

SES   SES was operationalized as the mean educational level of the parents or guardians with whom the participants resided (Steinberg et al., 1991). Parental education has been found to be the most stable component of a family's social class (see Steinberg et al., 1991, for a discussion). This measure asks participants to indicate the highest of eight levels of education completed by each of their parents or guardians, including some grade school, finished grade school, some high school, finished high school, some college or 2-year degree, 4-year college degree, some school beyond college, and professional or graduate school. Each level on this scale is given 1 point, yielding a total score ranging from 1 to 8 points. Scores for both parents are summed and averaged to yield the participant's SES score. Two social class categories were created, with those whose parental education level was below the sample median classified as low SES and those above the median classified as high SES.

TABLE 1   SELECTION TASK CONDITIONAL PROPOSITION STATEMENTS

If a person is swimming in the public pool, then a lifeguard is present.[a]

If a student is watching television, then the student's homework is finished.

If a person is drinking beer, then the person is 21 years of age.

If a person is driving a motor vehicle, then the person must be over 16 years of age.

If a student is caught running in the halls, then the student must be punished.

If a person is retired from work, then the person is over 55 years of age.

If a student strikes a teacher, then the student is suspended.

If a person has a handgun, then the handgun must be registered.

If a drunken driver kills someone, then the driver must be charged with murder.

If a child with AIDS attends school, then the child has the community's approval

If a girl under 14 years old has an abortion, then she must have her parents' permission.

[a]This was a warm-up problem.

Self-esteem   Global self-esteem was assessed using Rosenberg's (1979) 10-item Self-Esteem Scale ($\alpha = .82$). Rosenberg's measure is considered the most psychometrically sound measure of global self-esteem and has been used extensively with African American adolescents (Gray-Little & Hafdahl, 2000). Participants respond to each of 10 statements on a 4-point Likert-type scale ranging from *strongly disagree* (1) to *strongly agree* (4). This scale contains both positively and negatively worded items regarding the respondent's opinion of his or her self-worth. The total self-esteem score is obtained by reversing negatively worded items, summing all item scores, and obtaining the mean. Scores range from a maximum of 4 (indicating high self-esteem) to a low of 1 (indicating low self-esteem).

Selection task   The selection task (Overton, 1990) is composed of a series of 10 conditional propositions (see Table 1). Formal deductive understanding of an implication ("If p, then q") requires the recognition that particular instances of the antecedent and consequent clauses of a sentence are either permissible, not permissible, or indeterminate. The selection task requires this recognition and coordination between permissible and impermissible instances; thus, it is a valid measure of deductive reasoning. The validity of this measure is further supported by evidence showing a close relationship between deductive reasoning on Overton's selection task and on other tasks (Foltz et al., 1995).

Selection task test booklets were constructed containing 10 problems presented in the conditional "if p, then q" form, such as, "If a person is drinking beer, then the person must be over 21." In each problem, participants were required to establish the logical conditions under which these rules would be broken. A general solution score, giving partial credit for partial solutions, was the first dependent measure. For each problem, participants received one point for each of the following: choosing "p," choosing "not q," not choosing "not p," and not choosing "q," yielding a total possible score with a range of 0 to 40 points across the 10 problems. The correct logical response to selection task problems is the selection of the "p" and the "not q" alternatives while not selecting the "not p" or the "q" alternatives. This selection combination, called the complete falsification solution, was used as a second dependent variable. A score of 1 point was given for each problem when this solution is selected and 0 points for any other response, yielding a score range of 0 to 10 points. Finally, the consistency with which participants selected the complete falsification solution across the 10 problems was assessed. As established in prior research (Chapell & Overton, 1998; Overton et al., 1987; Ward & Overton, 1990), a consistency criterion of 6 complete falsification solutions out of 10 problems was used to indicate the attainment of formal deductive reasoning competence.

Ethnic identity Phinney's (1992) Multigroup Ethnic Identity Measure (MEIM) is a 14-item questionnaire ($\alpha = .78$) that has consistently demonstrated good reliability in many studies across a wide range of ethnic groups, including African Americans (Phinney, 1992; Phinney, Cantu, & Kurtz, 1997; Phinney & Chavira, 1995; Phinney, Ferguson, & Tate, 1997). The MEIM assesses three aspects of ethnic identity: positive ethnic attitudes and sense of belonging (5 items), ethnic identity achievement based on exploration and commitment (7 items), and ethnic behaviors or practices (2 items). Each item is rated on a 4-point scale from *strongly agree* to *strongly disagree*. Scores range from 4 points (indicating high ethnic identity) to 1 point (indicating low ethnic identity). The total MEIM score is derived by reversing negative items, summing across items, and obtaining the mean. High MEIM scores indicate a strong ethnic identity and low scores indicate a weak ethnic identity. Two categories were created, with participants whose ethnic identity scores were below the sample median classified as low ethnic identity and those above the median classified as high ethnic identity.

RESULTS

Prior to testing hypotheses, descriptive statistics for the main variables were computed for the entire sample and for each grade level (see Tables 2 and 3). In addition, a preliminary analysis via MANOVA examined for gender differences. There were no significant differences on any dependent variable based on gender, $F(6, 305) = .98$, $p = .96$, and univariate ANOVAs further confirmed that there were no significant differences on any individual variable based on gender.

DEVELOPMENT OF LOGICAL REASONING

To test the main cognitive developmental and contextual hypotheses, a 4 (grade) × 2 (SES) × 2 (ethnic identity) ANOVA, adjusted for unequal cell sizes, was

---

TABLE 2   MEANS, STANDARD DEVIATIONS, AND RANGES OF THE VARIABLES

	M	SD	Range	N
Age (years)	17.72	3.70	12–27	330
GPA	2.95	.64	1.5–4.0	314
SES	4.81	1.31	1.0–8.0	322
Self-esteem	3.40	.44	2.3–4.0	314
Ethnic identity	3.27	.48	1.8–4.0	330
General scores	31.10	6.38	16–40	330
Falsifications	4.44	3.80	0–10	330

Note: GPA = grade point average, SES = socioeconomic status.

	Grade							
	6th		10th		12th		College	
	M	SD	M	SD	M	SD	M	SD
Age (years)	12.70	.47	15.40	.77	17.90	.95	21.50	2.60
GPA	2.82	.70	3.04	.89	2.88	.52	3.02	.56
SES	4.62	1.20	4.84	1.30	4.64	1.20	5.01	1.40
Self-esteem	3.01	.38	3.40	.41	3.46	.40	3.62	.40
Ethnic identity	2.99	.46	3.09	.49	3.30	.39	3.48	.45
General scores	27.20	6.00	29.80	6.30	32.20	6.00	33.00	5.80
Falsifications	2.44	3.10	4.20	3.50	4.64	3.90	5.57	3.80

Note: GPA = grade point average, SES = socioeconomic status. There were no significant between-grade differences in GPA, $F(3, 310) = 1.17$, $p = .32$, or SES, $F(3, 318) = 2.09$, $p = .11$. The modal parental SES level was the completion of high school.

computed on the general solution scores (see Table 4). Given an a priori alpha level of .05 for all statistical tests, there were significant main effects for grade, $F(3, 304) = 9.01$, $p < .001$, (effect size $f = .28$); SES, $F(1, 304) = 3.94$, $p < .05$, ($f = .10$); and ethnic identity, $F(1, 304) = 6.72$, $p < .05$, ($f = .13$). (According to Cohen [1977], effect sizes of $f = .10$ are considered small, whereas those in the .25 range are moderate.) Scheffé tests showed that, as expected, college students ($p < .001$), 12th graders ($p < .001$), and 10th graders ($p < .05$) had higher reasoning scores than 6th graders. There were no other significances between grade differences. High SES students significantly outscored low SES students, $p < .05$. High ethnic identity stu-

dents outscored low ethnic identity students, $p < .01$. There were no significant interactions.

To further test these hypotheses, a 4 (grade) × 2 (SES) × 2 (ethnic identity) ANOVA was computed on the complete falsification solution scores (see Table 5). There was a significant main effect for grade level, $F(3, 304) = 6.88$, $p < .001$ ($f = .24$). Scheffé tests showed that, as expected, college students ($p < .001$), 12th graders ($p < .05$), and 10th graders ($p < .05$) had higher reasoning scores than 6th graders. There were no other significances between grade differences and no significant interactions.

The final analyses of reasoning performance compared the consistency with which participants at each

	Grade							
	6th		10th		12th		College	
	M	SD	M	SD	M	SD	M	SD
Grade	27.2	6.0	29.8	6.3	32.2	6.0	33.0	5.8
SES								
Low	27.2	5.7	28.7	7.4	31.4	5.6	32.8	5.6
High	27.1	6.7	31.1	5.8	33.2	6.4	33.3	6.0
Ethnic identity								
Low	25.6	5.6	28.7	6.2	32.5	6.1	31.5	6.5
High	29.2	6.1	31.8	6.8	31.5	5.9	33.2	5.5

Note: SES = socioeconomic status.

TABLE 5   COMPLETE FALSIFICATIONS BY GRADE, SES, AND ETHNIC IDENTITY LEVEL

	Grade							
	6th		10th		12th		College	
	M	SD	M	SD	M	SD	M	SD
Grade	2.4	3.1	4.2	3.5	4.6	3.9	5.6	3.8
SES								
Low	2.1	3.0	4.0	3.5	4.4	3.7	5.5	3.6
High	3.0	3.3	4.3	3.6	5.3	4.1	5.6	3.9
Ethnic identity								
Low	1.9	2.7	3.5	3.2	4.7	4.1	4.6	4.1
High	3.0	3.5	4.6	3.8	4.9	3.8	5.6	3.6

Note: SES = socioeconomic status.

grade level, SES level, and ethnic identity level gave the logically correct complete falsification solution. Based on the consistency criterion of 6 of 10 complete falsifications, 18% of 6th graders, 39% of 10th graders, 45% of 12th graders, and 56% of college students were rated as formal deductive reasoners. More college students ($z = 4.88$, $p < .001$), 12th graders ($z = 3.44$, $p < .001$), and 10th graders ($z = 2.62$, $p < .01$) were formal deductive reasoners than were 6th graders. There were also more formal deductive reasoners among college students than 10th graders ($z = 2.21$, $p < .05$). There were no other significant differences between grades and no significant differences in reasoning performance among college freshmen, sophomores, juniors, and seniors, but more college seniors (63%) were formal deductive reasoners than were 12th graders (45%), ($z = 2.28$, $p < .05$). Finally, more high SES students (50%) were formal deductive reasoners than low SES students (29%), χ^2 (1, $N = 322$) = 13.72, $p < .001$, and more high ethnic identity students (45%) were formal deductive reasoners than were low ethnic identity students (33%), χ^2 (1, $N = 330$) = 4.82, $p < .05$.

DIFFERENCES IN REASONING PERFORMANCE AND GPA RELATED TO ETHNIC IDENTITY LEVEL

Contrary to prediction from Ogbu's theory, as shown in the analyses above, high ethnic identity students had significantly higher reasoning scores than did those with low ethnic identity, whether using general solution scores, complete falsifications, or the deductive reasoning consistency criterion. To further test Ogbu's theory, a 4 (grade) × 2 (SES) × 2 (ethnic iden-

tity) ANOVA was computed on student GPAs (see Table 6). There was a significant effect for SES, $F(1, 298)$ = 4.05, $p < .05$ ($f = .14$), and post hoc analyses confirmed that high SES students had better GPAs than did low SES students, $p < .05$, but there were no other significant effects or interactions.

RELATION BETWEEN SELF-ESTEEM AND GPA

To test Steele's stereotype threat theory, the final analyses in this study examined the relationship between global self-esteem and school GPA. The correlation of these factors in the whole sample was significant and positive, $r = .27$, $p < .01$ (see Table 7). When analyzed by separate grade levels, however, a different pattern emerged, a pattern of decreasing correlations between self-esteem and GPA from 6th graders through 12th graders, consistent with Steele's school disidentification hypothesis. For 6th graders, the correlation between self-esteem and GPA was significant, $r = .45$, $p < .001$. For 10th and 12th graders, this correlation was not significant, $r = .18$, $p = .15$, and $r = .14$, $p = .21$, respectively. This study extended the investigation of Steele's disidentification hypothesis to include African American college students. Contrary to expectation, there was a strong positive correlation between global self-esteem and GPA in this sample of 115 college students, $r = .51$, $p < .001$. Tests confirmed that the self-esteem and GPA correlations for 10th and 12th graders were significantly different from the correlation for 6th graders, $z = 1.67$ and $z = 2.03$, respectively, $p < .05$, and for the college students, $z = 2.54$ and $z = 2.93$, respectively, $p < .01$. There were no significant differences between the

TABLE 6 STUDENT GPA BY GRADE, SES, AND ETHNIC IDENTITY LEVEL

	Grade							
	6th		10th		12th		College	
	M	SD	M	SD	M	SD	M	SD
Grade	2.82	.70	3.04	.89	2.88	.52	3.02	.56
SES								
Low	2.78	.69	2.77	.95	2.87	.49	2.88	.51
High	2.88	.74	3.32	.80	2.98	.54	3.13	.59
Ethnic identity								
Low	2.80	.73	2.92	.89	2.72	.48	2.87	.63
High	2.79	.71	3.13	.92	2.96	.53	3.08	.53

Note: SES = socioeconomic status.

correlations for the 10th and 12th graders or between those for the 6th graders and college students.

DISCUSSION

As hypothesized, consistent with cognitive developmental theory and the results of prior research with European American adolescents, this study found that deductive reasoning performance increased systematically across adolescence in African Americans. Of 6th graders, 18% were consistently competent, formal deductive reasoners, compared to 39% of 10th graders, 45% of 12th graders, and 56% of college students. These results suggest that the ability to reason logically develops across adolescence, but more definitive conclusions require further studies, particularly longitudinal investigations that can provide more direct evidence of reasoning development than

cross-sectional studies. Taken as a whole, though, the findings of this initial study of the development of deductive reasoning in African American adolescents agree with and lend considerable weight to the conclusion reached by Smith and Drumming (1989) in their deductive reasoning study with African American college students: "On balance, the results of this study challenge monolithic notions of cognitive development that universally ascribe deficits in reasoning ability to Blacks" (p. 236).

Despite the solid developmental progression of reasoning performance evidenced by the African American students in this study, the average level of selection task performance in each grade was lower than that reported in earlier studies using samples of mainly European American students (Chapell & Overton, 1998; Reene & Overton, 1989). Chapell and Overton (1998) found that 48% of 6th graders, 70% of 10th graders, and 80% of 12th graders were formal

TABLE 7 INTERCORRELATIONS AMONG THE VARIABLES

	1	2	3	4	5	6	7
1. Age	—	.07	.06	.41***	.30***	.31***	.27***
2. GPA		—	.32***	.27**	.24**	.30***	.23**
3. SES			—	.01	.14*	.17**	.16**
4. Self-esteem				—	.39***	.12	.11
5. Ethnic identity					—	.30***	.24***
6. General solution scores						—	.88***
7. Complete falsification scores							—

Note: GPA = grade point average, SES = socioeconomic status.
*p < .05. **p < .01. ***p < .001.

deductive reasoners. Reene and Overton (1989) also reported a higher rate of performance in their 3-year longitudinal study with cohorts of 6th graders and 8th graders. Reene and Overton found that 17% of their 6th-grade cohort were formal deductive reasoners in the 6th grade, increasing to 38% by 7th grade and 53% by 9th grade, whereas 38% of the 8th-grade cohort were formal deductive reasoners in 8th grade, increasing to 60% by 9th grade and 67% by 10th grade. It is important to note, however, that in both of these studies the participants were from upper-middle-class families. Given that high SES individuals consistently outscore low SES individuals on a variety of cognitive tests (Williams & Ceci,1997), it seems fair to suggest that part of the deductive reasoning performance differences found between these two studies and the current study may be related to SES differences.

Indeed, given the well-established association between social class and cognitive performance, the relationship of SES differences to reasoning performance was investigated in this study. As hypothesized, high SES African American students signigicantly outperformed low SES students, with 50% of high SES students rated as formal deductive reasoners, compared to 29% of low SES students. High SES students also had significantly higher grades in school than did low SES students. These results agree with and add to previous research, which has shown that higher SES adolescents consistently perform better on IQ and achievement tests than do lower SES students (Neisser et al., 1996; Suzuki & Valencia, 1997; Williams & Ceci, 1997), a performance advantage related to the lower school quality, lower support at home for school success, reduced access to educational resources, and higher levels of stress that are more often experienced by low SES students (McLoyd, 2000; Steinberg,1999). The findings of this study based on SES differences must be interpreted with caution, however, because the measure of SES used in this study relied exclusively on a parental education criterion, and whereas this is one basic index of SES, standard SES measures generally examine at least one other factor, such as parental occupation, employment status, or income (Entwisle & Astone, 1994).

OGBU'S CULTURAL ECOLOGICAL THEORY

Ogbu's influential theory predicts that adolescents with more developed ethnic identities will have lower reasoning scores and GPAs than those with less developed ethnic identities because reasoning and school tests will be seen as part of the White cultural frame of reference and resistance to "acting White" will depress performance. These hypotheses

were not supported in this study with primarily inner-city Black youth; to the contrary, a more developed ethnic identity was related to better reasoning performance and no relationship was found between ethnic identity level and GPA. In this study, participants apparently did not view solving a demanding set of reasoning problems or doing well in school as threats to their ethnic identity, requiring poor performance to avoid crossing "cultural and cognitive boundaries."

One possible explanation for the positive relationship between reasoning performance and ethnic identity, and the lack of any negative relationship between ethnic identity and GPA found in this study, is that social conditions in America are not the same in 2000 as they were in the early 1970s, when Ogbu (1974) originally formulated his theory. Ogbu has long contended that African Americans have been prevented from fully using their cognitive capacities due to substandard schooling and racist exclusion from middle-class jobs reserved for European Americans. However, over the past 30 years, the educational and employment opportunity outlook for Blacks in America has gradually improved, due in part to long-term effects of hard-won civil rights and antidiscrimination legislation, better access to higher education, and affirmative action (Garibaldi, 1997). African American adolescents today may realistically aspire to go to college and obtain middle-class jobs and may thus see performance on cognitive tests as more of a real means for achieving success than did previous generations.

This view is supported by the fact that the percentage of African Americans age 25 to 29 having completed high school is the highest in history (88.7%), as is the percentage of African American high school graduates having completed some college (57.8%) (National Center for Educational Statistics, 2000). Further evidence supporting this view is the trend over the past 30 years toward closing the gap between European American and African American cognitive test scores (Grissmer, Flanagan, & Williamson, 1998; Hedges & Nowell, 1998; Williams & Ceci, 1997), a convergence particularly evident in college graduates (Myerson, Rank, Raines, & Schnitzler, 1998). Taken as a whole, perhaps the issue of performing well on cognitive tests for African Americans circa 2000 is becoming somewhat less of a hard choice between individual achievement and ethnic group solidarity. It is important to note, however, that this study investigated only one key part of Ogbu's theory, namely, the relationship between African American adolescents' ethnic identity and their cognitive performance, and a more comprehensive test of Ogbu's far-reaching model was beyond both the scope and aims of this study.

STEELE'S STEREOTYPE THREAT THEORY

Based on Steele's (1992, 1997, 1998, 1999) stereotype threat theory, due to having to cope with the stressful threat of being judged by or confirming the racist, negative stereotype of African American intellectual inferiority, it was expected that African Americans would distance themselves from school performance during adolescence. Thus, global self-esteem might be significantly correlated with GPA in 6th graders but not in high school and college students. This school disidentification hypothesis was partially supported because the correlation between self-esteem and GPA decreased from a strong positive relationship in 6th graders to a nonsignificant relationship in 10th and 12th graders. This study extended the investigation of the school disidentification hypothesis to college students and, against expectation, there was a strong positive correlation between global self-esteem and GPA in this sample of 115 African American undergraduates. It is important to note here that there were no significant differences in either SES or GPA among the 6th-, 10th-, 12th-grade, and college students who participated in this study.

One possible explanation for this association between GPA and self-esteem in African American college students is suggested by the work of Myerson et al. (1998). Using cognitive ability test data collected in the National Longitudinal Survey of Youth, Myerson et al. compared the performance of 120 African Americans and 600 European Americans from 8th grade through college completion. After controlling for differences in school attrition rates, SES, and age, European American test scores were found to increase substantially during high school, where as African American scores did not. In sharp contrast, between the time of high school graduation and college graduation, test scores of African Americans increased at a rate four times greater than those of European Americans. Thus, whereas European Americans had higher average test scores than African Americans from 8th grade through college, the size of this gap was reduced from 1.1 standard deviations at high school graduation to just 0.4 standard deviations by the end of college. Myerson et al. suggested that the large and widening test score gap between European Americans and African Americans in high school, and the substantial closing of this gap in college, might be due to disparity in the quality of high school education and the subsequent equal quality of the college education experienced by these groups.

Many African Americans attend de facto segregated secondary schools of lower quality than those attended by European Americans and have lower academic performance, even after controlling for SES differences (Garibaldi, 1997; Yancey & Saporito, 1997).

African Americans often receive lower quality education than European Americans, even in integrated schools (Fisher et al., 1998). Once in college, however, African Americans and European Americans experience more comparable education (National Center for Educational Statistics, 1995). In the current study, African Americans may have become disidentified from academic success in high school, as suggested by the lack of association between self-esteem and GPA in the 10th and 12th graders. However, the correlation between self-esteem and academic achievement was as strong in college students as in 6th graders, suggesting a possible pattern of resilient recovery during college analogous to that described by Myerson et al. (1998).

These interpretations must be tempered by the fact that the measure of GPA used in this study was a self-report scale that, although widely used (as in Osborne's 1995 and 1997 studies cited above) and highly correlated with actual grades taken from school records in previous studies (Dornbusch et al., 1987; Steinberg et al., 1994), also has been found to slightly overstate the GPA of students who were averaging a C or less in school. What is less ambiguous is that further investigation into the relationship of African American college student global self-esteem and GPA is needed to test the school disidentification hypothesis of Steele's increasingly influential stereotype threat theory. Whereas the negative impact of stereotype threat on African American college students' test performance and disidentification from school has been well demonstrated under experimental conditions using various cognitive tests (Major, Spencer, Schmader, Wolfe, & Crocker, 1998; Steele & Aronson, 1998), to date there have been no large-scale studies published examining the relationship between global self-esteem and college GPA in African American college students and students from other ethnic groups.

SUMMARY

In conclusion, the main developmental finding of this study was that African Americans showed a clear pattern of progress in deductive reasoning performance from early through late adolescence. On average, the 6th-grade, preteen participants were not consistently logical reasoners, whereas the high school students reasoned better than the 6th graders but not as well as the college students, who were entering adulthood having developed consistently strong logical reasoning skills. This study also found that cognitive performance was significantly related to contextual factors, with high SES students consistently outscoring low SES students in reasoning and grades.

Ogbu's cultural-ecological theory, which predicts an inverse relationship between cognitive performance and ethnic identity strength in African American adolescents, was not supported because better reasoning performance was associated instead with stronger ethnic identity. Steele's stereotype threat school disidentification thesis, which predicts that African American global self-esteem and GPA would be associated in early adolescence but become dissociated thereafter, was partially supported. Self-esteem and GPA were strongly related in 6th graders, not significantly related in high school students, yet strongly related in college students.

REFERENCES

Ainsworth-Darnell, J. W., & Downey, D. B. (1998). Assessing the oppositional culture explanation for racial/ethnic differences in school performance. *American Sociological Review, 63*, 536–553.

Bell, Y. R., Brown, R., & Bryant, A. R. (1993). Traditional and culturally-relevant presentations of a logical reasoning task and performance among African-American students. *Western Journal of Black Studies, 17*, 173–178.

Chapell, M. S., & Overton, W. F. (1998). Development of logical reasoning in the context of parental style and test anxiety. *Merrill-Palmer Quarterly, 44*, 141–156.

Cheng, P. W., & Holyoak, K. J. (1985). Pragmatic reasoning schemas. *Cognitive Psychology, 17*, 391–416.

Cohen, J. (1977). *Statistical power analysis for the behavioral sciences.* New York: Academic Press.

Cook, P. J., & Ludwig, J. (1998). The burden of "acting White": Do Black adolescents disparage academic achievement? In C. Jencks & M. Phillips (Eds.), *The Black–White test score gap* (pp. 375–400). Washington, DC: Brookings Institution.

Cooper, C. R., & Denner, J. (1998). Theories linking culture and psychology: Universal and community-specific processes. *Annual Review of Psychology, 49*, 559–584.

Cosmides, L. (1989). The logic of social exchange: Has natural selection shaped how humans reason? Studies with the Wason selection task. *Cognition, 31*, 187–276.

DeShon, R. P., Smith, M. R., Chan, D., & Schmitt, N. (1998). Can racial differences in cognitive test performance be reduced by presenting problems in a social context? *Journal of Applied Psychology, 83*, 438–451.

Dornbusch, S. M., Ritter, P. L., Leiderman, P. H., Roberts, D. F., & Fraleigh, M. J., (1987). The relation of parenting style to adolescent school performance. *Child Development, 58*, 1244–1257.

Entwisle, D. R., & Astone, N. M. (1994). Some practical guidelines for measuring youth's race/ethnicity and socioeconomic status. *Child Development, 65*, 1521–1540.

Evans, J. St. B. T. (1996). Deciding before you think: Relevance and reasoning in the selection task. *British Journal of Psychology, 87*, 223–240.

Fisher, C. B., Jackson, J. F., & Villaruel, F. A. (1998). The study of African American and Latin American children and youth.

In W. M. Damon (Series Ed.) & R. M. Lerner (Vol. Ed.), *Handbook of child psychology: Vol. 1. Theoretical models of human development* (5th ed., pp. 1145–1207). New York: John Wiley.

Foltz, C., Overton, W. F., & Ricco, R. B. (1995). Adolescent development from inductive to deductive problem solving. *Journal of Experimental Child Psychology, 59*, 179–195.

Fordham, S. (1988). Racelessness as a factor in Black students' school success: Pragmatic strategy or pyrrhic victory? *Harvard Educational Review, 58,* 54–84.

Fordham, S. (1996). *Blacked out: Dilemmas of race, identity and success at Capital High.* Chicago: University of Chicago Press.

Fordham, S., & Ogbu, J. (1986). Black student's school success: Coping with the burden of "acting white." *Urban Review, 18*, 176–206.

Garibaldi, A. M. (1997). Four decades of progress . . . and decline: An assessment of African American educational attainment. *Journal of Negro Education, 66*, 105–120.

Graham, S. (1992). "Most of the subjects were White and middle-class." *American Psychologist, 47*, 629–639.

Gray-Little, B., & Hafdahl, A. R. (2000). Factors influencing racial comparisons of self-esteem: A quantitative review. *Psychological Bulletin, 126*, 26–54.

Grissmer, D., Flanagan, A., & Williamson, S. (1998). Why did the Black–White score gap narrow in the 1970s and 1980s? In C. Jencks & M. Phillips (Eds.), *The Black–White test score gap* (pp. 182–226). Washington, DC: Brookings Institution.

Hedges, L. V., & Nowell, A. (1998). Black–White test score convergence since 1965. In C. Jencks & M. Phillips (Eds.), *The Black–White test score gap* (pp. 149–181). Washington, DC: Brookings Institution.

Inhelder, B., & Piaget, J. (1958). *The growth of logical thinking from childhood to adolescence.* New York: Basic Books.

Jencks, C., & Phillips, M. (Eds.), (1998). *The Black–White test score gap.* Washington, DC: Brookings Institution.

Lerner, R. M., & Galambos, N. L. (1998). Adolescent development: Challenges and opportunities for research, programs, and policies. *Annual Review of Psychology, 49*, 413–446.

Major, B., Spencer, S., Schmader, T., Wolfe, C., & Crocker, J. (1998). Coping with negative stereotypes about intellectual performance: The role of psychosocial disengagement. *Personality and Social Psychology Bulletin, 24*, 34–50.

McLoyd, V. C. (2000). Poverty. In A. Kazdin (Ed.), *Encyclopedia of psychology.* New York: Oxford University Press.

Mickelson, R. A. (1990). The attitude–achievement paradox among Black adolescents. *Sociology of Education, 63,* 44–61.

Myerson, J., Rank, M. R., Raines, R. Q., & Schnitzler, M. A. (1998). Race and general cognitive ability: The myth of diminishing returns to education. *Psychological Science, 9*, 139–142.

National Center for Educational Statistics. (1995). *Minority undergraduate participation in postsecondary education.* Washington, DC: U.S. Department of Education, Office of Educational Research and Improvement.

National Center for Educational Statistics. (1997). *Dropout rates in the United States: 1996.* Washington, DC: U.S. Department of Education, Office of Educational Research and Improvement.

National Center for Educational Statistics. (2000). *The condition of education 2000*. Washington, DC: U.S. Department of Education, Office of Educational Research and Improvement.

Neisser, U., Boodoo, G., Bouchard, T. J., Jr., Boykin, A. W., Brody, N., Ceci, S.J., et al. (1996). Intelligence: Knowns and unknowns. *American Psychologist, 51*, 77–101.

Ogbu, J. U. (1974). *The next generation: An ethnography of education in an urban neighborhood*. New York: Academic Press.

Ogbu, J. U. (1986). The consequences of the American caste system. In U. Neisser (Ed.), *The school achievement of minority children* (pp. 19–56). Hillsdale, NJ: Lawrence Erlbaum.

Ogbu, J. U. (1987). Cultural influences on plasticity in human development. In J. J. Gallagher & C. T. Ramey (Eds.), *The malleability of children* (pp. 155–169). Bahimore: Brooks.

Ogbu, J. U. (1988). Cultural diversity and human development. In D. T. Slaughter (Ed.), *Black children and poverty: A developmental perspective* (pp. 11–28). San Francisco: Jossey-Bass.

Ogbu, J. U. (1993). Differences in cultural frame of reference. *International Journal of Behavioral Development, 16*, 483–506.

Ogbu, J. U., & Simons, H. D. (1994). *Cultural models of school achievement: A quantitative test of Ogbu's theory*. Berkeley: University of California Press. (ERIC Document Reproduction Service No. ED376515)

Osborne, J. W. (1995). Academics, self-esteem, and race: A look at the underlying assumptions of the disidentification hypothesis. *Personality and Social Psychology Bulletin, 21*, 728–735.

Osborne, J. W. (1997). Race and academic disidentification. *Journal of Educational Psychology, 89*, 728–735.

Overton, W. F. (1990). Competence and procedures: Constraints on the development of logical reasoning. In W. F. Overton (Ed.), *Reasoning, necessity, and logic: Developmental perspectives* (pp. 1–32). Hillsdale, NJ: Lawrence Erlbaum.

Overton, W. F. (1994). Reasoning. In V.S. Ramachandran (Ed.), *Encyclopedia of human behavior: Vol. 4* (pp. 13–24). New York: Academic Press.

Overton, W. F., Ward, S. L., Noveck, I. A., Black, J., & O'Brien, D. P. (1987). Form and content in the development of deductive reasoning. *Developmental Psychology, 21*, 692–701.

Phinney, J. S. (1992). The Multigroup Ethnic Identity Measure: A new scale for use with diverse groups. *Journal of Adolescent Research, 2*, 156–176.

Phinney, J. S. Cantu, C., & Kurtz, D. (1997). Ethnic and American identity as predictors of self-esteem among African American, Latino, and White adolescents. *Journal of Youth and Adolescence, 26*, 165–185.

Phinney, J. S., & Chavira, V. (1995). Parental ethnic socialization and adolescent coping with problems related to ethnicity. *Journal of Research on Adolescence, 5*, 31–53.

Phinney, J. S., Ferguson, D. L., & Tate, J. D. (1997). Intergroup attitudes among ethnic minority adolescents: A causal model. *Child Development, 68*, 955–969.

Reene, K. J., & Overton, W. F. (1989, June). *Longitudinal investigation of adolescent deductive reasoning*. Paper presented at the biennial meeting of the Society for Research in Child Development, Kansas City, Missouri.

Report card on the schools: Do ours make the grade. A region-wide look at public education. (1997, September 14). *The Philadelphia Inquirer*, pp. L1-L20.

Rosenberg, M. (1979). *Conceiving the self*. New York: Basic Books.

Smith, W. I., & Drumming, S.T. (1989). On the strategies that Blacks employ in deductive reasoning. *Journal of Black Psychology, 16*, 1–22.

Spencer, M. B., Noll, E., Stoltzfus, J., & Harpalani, V. (2001). Identity and school adjustment: Revisiting the "acting White" assumption. *Educational Psychologist, 36*, 21–30.

Steele, C. M. (1992, April). Race and the schooling of Black Americans. *Atlantic Monthly*, pp. 68–78.

Steele, C. M. (1997). A threat in the air: How stereotypes shape intellectual identity and performance. *American Psychologist, 52*, 613–629.

Steele, C. M. (1998). Stereotyping and its threat are real. *American Psychologist, 53*, 680–681.

Steele, C. M. (1999). Thin ice: "Stereotype threat" and Black college students. *Atlantic Monthly*, pp. 44–54.

Steele, C. M., & Aronson, J. (1995). Stereotype threat and the intellectual test performance of African Americans. *Journal of Personality and Social Psychology, 69*, 797–811.

Steele, C. M., & Aronson, J. (1998). Stereotype threat and the test performance of academically successful African Americans. In C. Jencks & M. Phillips (Eds.), *The Black-White test score gap* (pp. 401–427). Washington, DC: Brookings Institution.

Steinberg, L. (1999). *Adolescence* (5th ed.). New York: McGraw-Hill.

Steinberg, L., Dornbusch, S. M., & Brown, B. B. (1992). Ethnic differences in adolescent achievement: An ecological perspective. *American Psychologist, 47*, 723–729.

Steinberg, L., Lamborn, S. D., Darling, N., Mounts, N. S., & Dornbusch, S. M. (1994). Overtime changes in adjustment and competence among adolescents from authoritative, authoritarian, indulgent, and neglectful families. *Child Development, 65*, 754–770.

Steinberg, L., & Morris, A. S. (2000). Adolescent development. *Annual Review of Psychology, 52*, 83–110.

Steinberg, L., Mounts, N. S., Lamborn, S. D., & Dornbusch, S. M. (1991). Authoritative parenting and adolescent adjustment across varied ecological niches. *Journal of Research on Adolescence, 1*, 19–36.

Suzuki, L. A., & Valencia, R. R. (1997). Race-ethnicity and measured intelligence: Educational implications. *American Psychologist, 52*, 1103–1114.

Taylor, R. D., Casten, R., Flickinger, S. M., Roberts, D., & Fulmore, C. (1994). Explaining the school performance of African-American adolescents. *Journal of Research on Adolescence, 4*, 21–44.

Ward, S. L., & Overton, W. F. (1990). Semantic familiarity, relevance, and the development of deductive reasoning. *Developmental Psychology, 26*, 488–493.

Wason, P. C. (1968). Reasoning about a rule. *Quarterly Journal of Experimental Psychology, 20,* 273–281.

Williams, W. M., & Ceci, S. J. (1997). Are Americans becoming more or less alike? Trends in race, class, and ability differences in intelligence. *American Psychologist, 52,* 1226–1235.

Yancey, W. L., & Saporito, S. J. (1997). Racial and economic segregation and educational outcomes: One tale, two cities. In R. D. Taylor & M. C. Wang (Eds.), *Social and emotional adjustment and family relations in ethnic minority families* (pp. 159–179). Mahwah, NJ: Lawrence Erlbaum.

QUESTIONS

1. What is reasoning, and what are the two major types of reasoning processes?
2. What is the developmental course of deductive reasoning?
3. Why did the researchers concentrate on deductive reasoning in African-American adolescents?
4. What was the hypothesis of this research regarding the relation between socioeconomic status and deductive reasoning in African-American youth? What was the basis of this hypothesis?
5. According to Ogbu, why are cognitive differences often found in research that compares African-American and European-American adolescents?
6. What is stereotype-threat theory, and how does it explain cognitive differences in African-American and European-American adolescents?
7. Are this study's findings about the development of reasoning by African-American adolescents consistent with research on this topic conducted among European-American adolescents?
8. What relation between SES and deductive reasoning did this study reveal?
9. According to this study, how did ethnic identity relate to adolescents' reasoning scores? Does this result support or contradict Ogbu's cultural-ecological theory?
10. Was Steele's stereotype-threat theory supported by this research? Explain why or why not.

35 Parental Autonomy Granting During Adolescence: Exploring Gender Differences in Context

MATTHEW F. BUMPUS • ANN C. CROUTER • SUSAN M. MCHALE

As children proceed through adolescence, their competence in a wide range of areas increases. In response, parents adjust the responsibilities that they expect adolescents to assume. One of the ways in which parents support adolescent changes in competence is by granting their children more autonomy, or independence, in their daily lives. Although developmental psychologists are interested in adolescent autonomy and how it develops, the contributions that parents and, more generally, the family make to this process are not well understood. Of particular interest along these lines is whether family socialization practices related to the development of autonomy are different for girls and boys.

In the following article, Matthew Bumpus, Ann Crouter, and Susan McHale describe their research on parental granting of autonomy in early adolescence. They investigated this issue from an ecological perspective, focusing on features of the family context that may play important roles in this process. Such factors include the family's composition, in particular whether the first-born child is a son or daughter; the parents' attitudes about gender, especially traditional gender roles; and the adolescent's maturity, specifically the child's pubertal status. The research design was multi-informant: Mothers, fathers, and their first-born and second-born adolescent children participated. Two aspects of autonomy granting were assessed: the child's participation in decision making in the family and parental knowledge of the adolescent's daily activities.

The researchers found that parental autonomy granting is influenced by several contextual factors, including the adolescent's gender, birth order, sibling sex composition, and the parents' attitudes about traditional female roles. The complexity of these findings reflects the complexity of the phenomenon studied. As children get older, parents create new opportunities for them to develop and practice emerging skills. However, families differ in the timing and patterning of these opportunities. The findings are particularly interesting in relation to traditional gender-role expectations. The societal constraints that are often imposed on girls in early adolescence are at odds with the fact that girls tend to mature quicker than boys during these years. This research suggests that different families create different solutions to this dilemma and that certain family factors relate to these processes in predictable ways.

This study investigated the ways in which 2 indicators of parental autonomy granting, adolescents' decision-making input and parental knowledge of adolescents' daily experiences, differed as a function of contextual factors (i.e., parents' gender role attitudes or sibling dyad sex composition) and boys' and girls' personal qualities (i.e., gender, pubertal status, developmental status, or birth order) in a sample of 194 families with firstborn (M = 15.0 years) and second-born (M = 12.5 years) adolescents. Firstborns were granted more autonomy than second-borns, especially in families with firstborn girls and second-born boys. Girls in families marked by traditional maternal gender role attitudes were granted fewer autonomy opportunities. Post-

Copyright 2002 by the American Psychological Association. Reprinted by permission of the authors and the American Psychological Association from *Developmental Psychology, Vol. 37*, pp. 163–173.

This research was supported by Grant R01-HD29409 from the National Institute of Child Health and Human Development. Portions of this research were presented at the annual meeting of the National Council on Family Relations, Milwaukee, Wisconsin, November 1998.

*menarcheal second-born girls were granted more op-
portunities for autonomy than were premenarcheal second-born girls, but only in families with less traditional
maternal gender role attitudes.*

The convergence of biological, cognitive, and social
changes during adolescence serves as an impetus for
restructuring the parent–adolescent relationship
(Collins, 1990; Collins, Gleason, & Sesma, 1997; Hill &
Holmbeck, 1986; Holmbeck, Paikoff, & Brooks-Gunn,
1995; Steinberg, 1990). Parents may be prompted to
treat their offspring in a more adultlike manner by
granting them more behavioral autonomy (Eccles et
al., 1991; Paikoff & Brooks-Gunn, 1991; Steinberg &
Silverberg, 1986), a style that tends to have positive
implications for adolescents (Brody, Moore, & Glei,
1994; Fuligni & Eccles, 1993; Holmbeck & O'Donnell,
1991). As Baumrind (1991, p. 125) maintained,
"Parental practices that change in the direction of
greater responsiveness and independence-granting
are expected to facilitate the development of competence following puberty." Although this notion has received empirical support, very little is known about
the conditions under which parents afford their adolescents high or low levels of autonomy (Silverberg &
Gondoli, 1996).

Adolescent gender is one possible determinant of
parental autonomy granting. Early adolescence is a
developmental period in which youth are increasingly likely to behave and be treated in sex-typed
ways (Crouter, Manke, & McHale, 1995; Galambos,
Almeida, & Petersen, 1990; Hill & Lynch, 1983; Huston & Alvarez, 1990). Hill and Lynch's (1983) *gender
intensification hypothesis* holds that during adolescence (especially early adolescence), sex-typed differences between boys and girls increase because of
pressures to conform to traditional notions of masculinity and femininity. Boys, according to Hill and
Lynch, often are encouraged to be independent and
assertive, whereas girls often are socialized to be expressive and compliant. The gender intensification
hypothesis has received some support from investigations focused on sex differences in domains such as
math and science achievement (Linn & Petersen,
1986; Updegraff, McHale, & Crouter, 1996) and adolescents' sex role attitudes (Galambos et al., 1990).
Another way to address this question, however, targets sex typing from an ecological perspective (Bronfenbrenner, 1979). Rather than focusing on normative
patterns of gender role development in adolescence,
an ecologically oriented approach calls for an examination of the conditions under which parents treat
their adolescent sons and daughters along sex-typed
lines. In one of the few studies examining sex typing
in adolescence using such an approach, Crouter et al.
(1995) found evidence consistent with the gender in-

tensification hypothesis in two domains: adolescents'
participation in housework and involvement with
same-sex versus opposite-sex parents. Sex-typed patterns were especially evident in families in which the
adolescent's younger sibling was of the opposite sex
(which, the authors proposed, enabled parents to
"pair off" with same-sex offspring) and parents' division of labor was more traditional. These findings led
Crouter et al. (1995) to conclude that "gender intensification depends in part on the dimension of family
socialization that is examined and on the nature of
the familial context" (pp. 324–325). Similarly, Updegraff et al. (1996) noted declines in girls' math and
science achievement across the transition to seventh
grade—but only in families in which fathers were relatively uninvolved in child-oriented activities.

The present study also took an ecological approach and focused on the conditions under which
sex typing was evident in two dimensions of parental
socialization—the extent to which adolescents are involved in making decisions in the family domain and
parents' knowledge about their adolescents' daily experiences and activities—both of which may reflect the
extent to which parents grant their adolescents opportunities to behave in autonomous ways. We also were
interested in three factors that may moderate the impact of adolescent gender on adolescents' decision
making and parental knowledge: parents' attitudes
about gender, adolescents' pubertal status, and the
sex composition of the adolescent sibling dyad.

PARENTAL AUTONOMY-GRANTING PROCESSES

ADOLESCENTS' DECISION-MAKING INPUT

An important component of family relations during
adolescence is the opportunity for adolescents to have
increased input in decisions about issues that affect
their daily lives (Fuligni & Eccles, 1993; Holmbeck et
al., 1995; Silverberg & Gondoli, 1996; Steinberg, 1990).
Enabling adolescents to have input when decision-
making opportunities arise has been identified as an
important way in which families can provide an appropriate fit with their adolescents' developing needs
for independence in a supportive context (Eccles et al.,
1993). Parental encouragement of adolescents' participation in decision making also may promote appropriate levels of individuality and autonomy by
demonstrating to adolescents that their points of view
are important (Brody et al., 1994). Indeed, high levels
of family decision-making input have been linked to
positive outcomes, including lower levels of potentially unhealthy reliance on peers (Fuligni & Eccles,
1993) and increases over time in positive self-concept
(Holmbeck & O'Donnell, 1991).

Does the extent to which adolescents are involved in family decision making differ in ways that are sex typed? A consistent finding in the literature on adolescent decision making is that girls are described as having more decision-making input than boys (Brown & Mann, 1990; Flanagan, 1990; Fuligni & Eccles, 1993; Holmbeck & O'Donnell, 1991; Jacobs, Bennett, & Flanagan, 1993), a pattern inconsistent with the notion that during adolescence, girls tend to be socialized in ways that encourage compliance and discourage independence. However, no known studies have explored the possibility that under certain conditions—for example in families where parents hold traditional attitudes about gender—girls may have less decision-making input.

PARENTAL KNOWLEDGE OF ADOLESCENTS' DAILY ACTIVITIES AND EXPERIENCES

Parental monitoring, generally conceptualized as parents' attention to and tracking of their children's whereabouts and activities (Dishion & McMahon, 1998), is an important family process; low levels of monitoring have been associated with a variety of negative adolescent outcomes, including substance use and delinquency (Mekos, Hetherington, & Reiss, 1996; Metzler, Noell, Biglan, Ary, & Smolkowski, 1994; Patterson & Stouthamer-Loeber, 1984; Steinberg, Fletcher, & Darling, 1994). A related construct, and the focus in this study, is the extent to which parents are knowledgeable about their adolescents' activities, companions, and whereabouts. Parental monitoring and parental knowledge tend to be scripted according to gender (Crouter, Helms-Erikson, Updegraff, & McHale, 1999). Girls tend to be monitored more closely than boys (Dishion & McMahon, 1998), mothers are more knowledgeable than fathers, and parents tend to be more knowledgeable about the activities and experiences of their same-sex versus opposite-sex children (Crouter et al., 1999).

Few longitudinal studies have delineated patterns of parental monitoring or parental knowledge during adolescence. However, we speculate that a normative pattern for parents, as their adolescents' lives become less centered on the family, may be to gradually back off and, as a result, become less knowledgeable about their offspring's daily experiences and activities over the course of adolescence. This tendency may be especially pronounced for parents of boys. Indeed, Hill and Lynch (1983) proposed that a facet of gender intensification during early adolescence is the tendency for parents to become more protective of their daughters (and therefore to supervise them more closely) while permitting more independence in sons. We were interested in the conditions under which parents' knowledge vis-à-vis their adolescents would exhibit gender-typed patterns (i.e., higher levels of knowledge about girls than about boys).

MODERATING FACTORS

What factors might exacerbate or minimize the tendency for parents to treat their adolescents in sex-typed ways in the areas of decision making and parental knowledge? We focused on three factors that may shape the expression of sex-typed socialization: parents' attitudes about gender, adolescents' pubertal status, and the sex composition of the adolescent sibling dyad.

PARENTS' ATTITUDES ABOUT GENDER

A handful of studies have demonstrated that patterns of socialization consistent with gender intensification are more common in families with a traditional division of labor (Crouter et al., 1995; Updegraff et al., 1996). Attitudes may operate in the same manner. We speculated that mothers and fathers with traditional attitudes about women's roles would view independence and initiative as important for adolescent sons but less important for daughters and would therefore create a family environment marked by (a) lower levels of decision-making input for girls but not boys (see McHale, Crouter, & Tucker, 1999, for a study focused on similar issues during middle childhood) and (b) higher levels of parental knowledge vis-à-vis girls but not boys. Furthermore, given that patterns of sex typing are particularly evident in families with brothers and sisters (Crouter et al., 1995; McHale et al., 1999; Stocker & McHale, 1992), we expected that parents' traditionality would be associated with within-family differences (favoring sons over daughters) in decision-making input and parental knowledge in families with mixed-sex sibling dyads.

ADOLESCENTS' PUBERTAL STATUS

Another factor that may moderate the impact of gender on parental autonomy-granting processes is adolescents' pubertal status, an area of study that has received much attention from researchers interested in family dynamics during adolescence (Brooks-Gunn & Reiter, 1990; Buchanan, Eccles, & Becker, 1992; Paikoff & Brooks-Gunn, 1991). The development of secondary sex characteristics and other physical changes associated with puberty alerts family members to adolescents' physical maturity. Whereas some parents respond to this change by treating adolescents in a more adultlike manner (Collins, 1990; Eccles et al., 1993; Hill, 1988), other, more traditional parents may react to pubertal changes by treating girls and boys in more sex-typed ways. In a longitudinal study focused on gender intensification in early adolescence, Galambos et al. (1990) found that overall patterns indicative of gender intensification were not moderated by adolescents' pubertal status. The outcome variables of interest in their study, however, were adolescents' masculinity, femininity, and sex role attitudes; the role of pubertal status may be more easily detected when examining parental socialization processes and may be more apparent in some family contexts than others.

We made two predictions about the role of puberty as a potential moderator of gender role socialization. Given the tendency for puberty to be linked to more adultlike relationships with parents, we expected firstborn and second-born adolescents' level of physical development to be positively associated with their decision-making input and negatively associated with their parents' knowledge about their activities and whereabouts. We were also interested in the possibility that under certain conditions, parents might respond in different ways to their adolescents' physical development. Some parents might be uneasy about their adolescent daughters' emerging sexuality, resulting in increased vigilance and monitoring and, in turn, (a) decreased opportunities for adolescents to participate in decision making and (b) high levels of parental knowledge. Further, as noted, this pattern of protectiveness might be exacerbated when parents hold traditional views about women's roles (Hill & Lynch, 1983). We therefore expected adolescents' pubertal status and parents' attitudes about gender to interact in moderating the impact of gender on family process outcomes, leading to (a) low levels of girls' decision-making input and (b) high levels of parental knowledge vis-à-vis daughters when families held traditional attitudes and girls were more physically mature. We made no predictions regarding the potential impact of boys' pubertal status on the parental autonomy-granting processes of interest but were interested in whether the opposite pattern would be apparent. Traditional parents might encourage more independence in physically mature boys.

SIBLING SEX COMPOSITION

Few studies have considered the possibility that parental autonomy granting may be influenced by the characteristics of adolescents' siblings. Crouter et al. (1995) noted that patterns of gender intensification were exacerbated when adolescents had a younger sibling of the opposite sex; in such family contexts, parents might be more likely to socialize their boys toward masculine roles and their girls toward feminine roles. However, their study included only data on firstborns' experiences; it is unclear whether the sex of one's older sibling would be similarly important for a second-born sibling. Nevertheless, we expected that sex-typed patterns of socialization—specifically, high levels of parental knowledge and low levels of decision-making input for girls—would be especially apparent in families with mixed-sex sibling dyads.

WITHIN-FAMILY COMPARISONS

In addition to the three between-family factors, we were interested in two types of within-family comparisons. The norm in research on family relations during adolescence has been to focus on the experiences of one target adolescent from the perspective of one parent, usually the mother. We incorporated data from four family members—mothers, fathers, and two adolescent siblings—a design that allowed us to compare the experiences of siblings at different developmental levels: firstborns in middle adolescence (approximately 15 years old) and second-borns in early adolescence (approximately 12 years old). In addition, by comparing mothers and fathers on the autonomy-granting variables of interest (parents' knowledge of adolescents' daily activities and adolescents' decision-making input), we were able to examine the possibility that parents may differ in their patterns of sex typing.

OLDER SIBLINGS VERSUS YOUNGER SIBLINGS

Increasing input into decision making has been discussed as an important facet of adolescents' adaptive development (Silverberg & Gondoli, 1996). Some evidence from short-term longitudinal studies shows that low levels of decision-making input can have negative developmental implications for adolescents (Fuligni & Eccles, 1993; Holmbeck & O'Donnell, 1991), but whether there are normative, age-related changes in decision-making input has not been demonstrated. We explored the nature of decision-making input by looking at families with two siblings at different stages of adolescence: a firstborn in middle adolescence and a second-born in early adolescence. We expected to find that older adolescents would have more decision-making input than their younger siblings, a pattern that would be consistent with studies showing that other indicators of autonomy increase from early adolescence to middle adolescence (Collins & Luebker, 1994; Greenberger, 1984; Steinberg & Silverberg, 1986), although in this cross-sectional study, developmental status is confounded with birth order.

With regard to parental knowledge or parental monitoring, Crouter et al. (1999), in the only other study comparing the parental knowledge or parental monitoring of older and younger siblings, found that parents knew more about the daily experiences of their younger children than they did about their older children. Although Crouter et al. (1999) studied a school-aged sample, we expected the same result in adolescence because youth in middle adolescence typically spend less time with other family members than do younger adolescents (Larson, Richards, Moneta, Holmbeck, & Duckett, 1996).

MOTHERS VERSUS FATHERS

We were also interested in making within-family comparisons between mothers and fathers regarding their perceptions of adolescents' decision-making input and their knowledge of their adolescents' daily activities and experiences. We expected moderate to high correlations between mothers' and fathers' perceptions of their adolescents' decision-making input (because presumably parents are reporting on the same phenomenon) and modest correlations between mothers' and fathers' knowledge of their adolescents' daily activities (Crouter et al., 1999). We also expected mean differences between mothers and fathers in these domains. Research on parenting during adolescence has shown that fathers tend to be less warm and more restrictive than mothers (Parke, 1995). Also, because fathers generally spend less time with adolescents than do mothers (Larson et al., 1996: Montemayor & Brownlee, 1987; Parke, 1995), fathers may be both less aware of instances when adolescents are active in the decision-making process and less knowledgeable about adolescents' daily lives than mothers are (Crouter et al., 1999). On the basis of these notions, we predicted that fathers, when compared with mothers, would perceive their adolescents as having fewer opportunities for decision-making input and would be less knowledgeable about their adolescents' daily experiences and activities.

Finally, we were interested in exploring the ways in which sex-typed patterns of decision making and parental knowledge were predicted by combinations of within-family and between-family factors. For example, differences in mothers' versus fathers' perceptions of adolescents' decision making (a within family difference) might be exacerbated in families with certain dyadic sex combinations (a between-family factor). In this instance, the tendency for fathers, more than mothers, to be involved with same-sex versus opposite-sex offspring (Collins & Russell, 1991; Parke, 1995; Siegal, 1987) might result in greater similarity between mothers and fathers of sons than between mothers and fathers of daughters.

METHOD

PARTICIPANTS

Data for this study were drawn from the first phase of a 3-year longitudinal study designed to examine the connections between adolescent development and family dynamics. To recruit the sample, we sent letters describing the study and eligibility criteria to the homes of all families with 8th, 9th, or 10th graders enrolled in 18 local school districts. Families who were eligible and interested in the study returned a postcard and were subsequently invited to participate. Eligible families met the following criteria: The firstborn adolescent was in one of the targeted grades and had at least one sibling 1 to 4 years younger, and families were maritally intact. In addition, we sought families in which both parents were employed at least part time. The original sample ($N = 197$) was composed primarily of working- and middle-class families from small cities, towns, and rural areas. Financial restrictions precluded us from requesting return postcards from all families whether or not they fit our criteria. Thus, we cannot establish the response rate of eligible families. We do know, however, that of the eligible families who returned postcards indicating tentative interest, over 90% agreed to participate once they had discussed the study with project staff.

Three families were excluded from these analyses: one family with a developmentally disabled older sibling, one family with a mother and stepfather who were inadvertently included despite our screening, and one family whose data were incomplete. The reduced sample (see Table 1) included 45 older-sister/younger-sister pairs, 45 older-sister/younger-brother pairs, 50 older-brother/younger-sister pairs, and 54 older-brother/younger-brother pairs. Roughly three fourths of the second-born adolescents in our sample were younger than the youngest firstborn participant (13.1 years). With the exception of four biracial families, all family members were White. All parents were employed at least part time except for two families in which the mother was not employed and one family in which the father was not employed. Fathers' and mothers' occupational prestige was measured by means of National Opinion Research Center codes (Nakao & Treas, 1994). Examples of occupations near mothers' and fathers' mean level of prestige include farm manager, real estate agent, and public relations specialist. In this sample, mothers' occupations tended to be more prestigious than those of fathers, $t(190) = 1.77$, $p < .08$, whereas fathers' work hours and incomes were higher than those of mothers: $t(192) = 9.53$, $p < .001$, and $t(189) = 8.61$, $p < .001$, for hours and income, respectively.

TABLE 1 SAMPLE CHARACTERISTICS (N = 194)

Characteristic	M	SD	Range
Age (in years)			
Mothers	39.94	3.89	31–50
Fathers	41.84	4.23	32–57
Firstborns	14.96	0.71	13–16
Second-borns	12.50	1.01	10–14
Education (in years)			
Mothers	14.34	2.12	11–18
Fathers	14.27	2.30	9–20
Firstborns	9.26	0.69	8–10
Second-borns	6.75	1.02	5–9
Work hours			
Mothers	37.03	14.61	0–129
Fathers	50.90	13.02	0–100
Job prestige			
Mothers	49.52	12.96	21.16–74.77
Fathers	47.30	13.01	22.33–86.05
Income			
Mothers	$20,930	$14,590	$0–$100,000
Fathers	$41,430	$31,496	$0–$300,000
Family size	4.58	0.80	4–9
Marriage duration (in years)	17.64	3.18	4–30

Note: Four mothers and two fathers refused to report their annual income. Job prestige is missing for 2 mothers and 1 father who were not employed. Job prestige was measured with National Opinion Research Center codes.

PROCEDURES

Data were collected by means of two procedures. First, during in-home interviews, 4 family members (mother, father, firstborn adolescent [$M = 15.0$ years], and second-born adolescent [$M = 12.5$ years]) were interviewed separately about their family relationships, attitudes, and personal adjustment. Measures from the home interviews used in these analyses included family members' reports of adolescents' decision-making input, mothers' and fathers' reports of their own gender role attitudes, and adolescents' reports of their pubertal status.

In a second procedure, families were telephoned on 7 different evenings (5 weeknights and 2 weekend nights) during the several weeks after the home interviews. Both adolescents were interviewed during every call. Mothers and fathers each were interviewed on 2 weeknights and 1 weekend night. The seventh call, during a weeknight, included both parents. Telephone interviews focused on family members' daily activities, as well as the extent to which parents were knowledgeable about their children's daily activities, companions, and whereabouts.

HOME INTERVIEW MEASURES

Adolescents' decision-making input was assessed with a questionnaire adapted from Dornbusch et al. (1985). Parents and adolescents considered eight domains—chores, appearance, homework and schoolwork, social life, bedtime and curfew, health, participation in activities, and money—and indicated the person or persons who typically made decisions for the target adolescent over the past year. For each domain, respondents selected one of the following: youth alone, mother, father, both parents, father and youth, mother and youth, parents and youth, other person(s), or nobody. A 3-point scale was developed by collapsing responses based on the extent to which the adolescent was involved in making decisions. A score of 1 was given if the adolescent typically had no opportunity to make decisions in that domain (i.e., responses of "mother," "father," or "both parents" make decisions). A score of 2 signified that the adolescent typically made decisions along with one or both parents (i.e., "mother and youth," "father and youth," or "parents and youth" make decisions). A score of 3 was given if the adolescent typically made independent decisions in the given domain (i.e., "youth alone" makes decisions). Responses of "other person(s)" or "nobody" were quite rare and therefore were omitted and replaced by the mean of the remaining items. Responses were summed across domains to create total decision-making input scores regarding firstborn and second-born adolescents for fathers, mothers, and the adolescent in question. Cronbach's alphas for firstborn adolescents' decision-making input were .72, .76, and .51 for mothers', fathers', and firstborns' reports, respectively. For second-borns, alphas were .74 for mothers' report, .67 for fathers' report, and .58 for second-borns' report.

Mothers' and fathers' gender role attitudes were measured with the Attitudes Toward Women Scale (Spence & Helmreich, 1978), which consists of 15 items (e.g., "in general, the father should have greater authority than the mother in making decisions about raising children") measured on a 4-point scale ranging from *strongly agree* to *strongly disagree*. Responses were summed so that a higher score indicated more traditional attitudes about men's and women's roles. Cronbach's alphas were .79 for mothers and .71 for fathers. The correlation between mothers' and fathers' gender role attitudes was moderate ($r = .26$, $p < .001$), not high enough to justify using an average of mothers' and fathers' reports. Instead, we considered parents' gender role attitudes separately, using first a median split on mothers' gender role attitudes to create two groups of families. One in which mothers held more traditional attitudes ($n = 96$, mean traditionality score = 31.3) and one in which maternal attitudes were less traditional ($n = 98$, $M = 21.5$). We then created two groups of families based on fathers' gender role attitudes. We divided the groups (for more traditional attitudes, $n = 131$, $M = 31.3$; for less traditional attitudes, $n = 63$, $M = 22.6$) using the same cutoff score for fathers as we had for mothers, so the groups would be comparable.

Adolescents reported on their physical development during the home interviews. Because there was insufficient variability among firstborns' pubertal status, we focused only on the physical development of second-borns. We assessed pubertal status with the Physical Development Scale (Petersen, Crockett, Richards, & Boxer, 1988), a five-item measure of adolescents' pubertal status. Boys completed items pertaining to growth in height, body hair growth, skin changes, voice change, and facial hair growth; girls responded to items pertaining to growth in height, body hair growth, skin changes, breast development, and menarcheal status. For each item, adolescents rated their development on a 4-point scale that ranged from 1 (*not begun*) to 4 (*complete*). Cronbach's alpha was .81 for second-born girls and .71 for second-born boys. Median splits conducted separately on boys and girls yielded groups that were less physically developed (girls: $n = 52$, $M = 7.1$: boys: $n = 43$, $M = 6.8$) and more physically developed (girls: $n = 41$, $M = 12.0$; boys: $n = 56$, $M = 10.2$). For adolescent girls, however, menarcheal status may be a more reliable indicator of their pubertal development than the self-report items, so we also divided second-born girls into two groups on the basis of their reports of whether they had ($n = 29$) or had not ($n = 66$) experienced menarche. We then created two groups of boys that paralleled the premenarcheal and postmenarcheal groups of girls by conducting a split at the upper tertile of the physical development scale (more physically developed: $n = 30$, $M = 11.2$; less physically developed: $n = 69$, $M = 7.6$).

TELEPHONE INTERVIEW MEASURE

To assess parental knowledge, we first asked parents 24 questions (6 questions per night) about the firstborns' and the second-borns' experiences, whereabouts, and activities on the day of the call (Crouter et al., 1999). We then asked adolescent offspring the same questions. Parental knowledge scores were calculated as the extent to which parents' and adolescents' responses matched. Each question consisted of

two parts: a general question (e.g., "Did [adolescent] talk to any friends on the phone today?") and a follow-up question that asked only if the parent or adolescent reported that a particular event had happened that day. If, for example, the adolescent reported that she had talked to a friend on the phone during the day of the call, the follow-up question "What friend(s) did [adolescent] talk to?" was asked. If parent and adolescent disagreed about whether an event took place, the parent was given a score of 0 for that item. If the parent and adolescent agreed that the event occurred that day but differed in their reports about the details, the parent was given a score of 1 for that item. Parents received 2 points (full credit) if they agreed with the adolescent that the event in question did not take place that day or if they agreed with the adolescent that the event did occur and also agreed about the details. Intercoder reliability, established in another sample, was quite high (Crouter et al., 1999). Questions were not repeated across a parent's calls and were asked in different sequences for mothers and fathers, so parents could not anticipate the questions they would receive on any given interview. Total knowledge scores were calculated as the percentage of matching answers, with high scores indicating high levels of knowledge about adolescents' experiences.

RESULTS

PRELIMINARY ANALYSES

We first examined the correlations among family members regarding both decision-making input and parental knowledge. For both firstborns' and second-borns' decision-making input, mothers' and fathers' reports were moderately correlated: for firstborns, $r = .29$, $p < .001$; for second-borns, $r = .33$, $p < .001$. However, adolescents' reports of their decision-making input were uncorrelated with parents' reports (firstborn–mother, $r = .07$, firstborn–father, $r = .09$, second-born–mother, $r = .12$, second-born–father, $r = .03$; all $ps > .05$). Furthermore, with the exception of the mother–second-born dyad, mothers and fathers viewed adolescents as having less decision-making input than the adolescents themselves reported. As a result, we were suspicious that parents and adolescents were interpreting the decision-making measure differently, so we elected to use mothers' and fathers' reports, but not adolescents' reports, in the analyses that follow. With regard to parental knowledge, mothers' and fathers' scores regarding their firstborns' activities and experiences were moderately correlated ($r = .28$, $p < .001$), and mothers' and fathers' knowledge scores vis-à-vis second-borns were unrelated ($r = .08$, $p > .05$).

Mother–Father and Firstborn–Second-born Differences

To examine mother–father and firstborn–second-born differences in decision-making input and parental knowledge, we conducted two parallel mixed-model analyses of variance. Dependent variables in one analysis were mothers' and fathers' perceptions of their firstborns' and second-borns' decision-making input; in the second analysis, mothers' knowledge and fathers' knowledge of their firstborns' and second-borns' daily activities and experiences were the dependent variables. Parent and sibling were treated as within-family factors, which allowed us to examine mother versus father and firstborn versus second-born differences. All significant effects were followed up with Tukey tests. A parent effect emerged for both decision-making input, $F(1,193) = 18.35$, $p < .001$, and parental knowledge, $F(1, 193) = 54.11$, $p < .001$. As predicted, fathers ($M = 14.61$, $SD = 2.18$) perceived adolescents as having less decision-making input than did mothers ($M = 15.40$, $SD = 2.23$), and mothers ($M = 77.23$, $SD = 8.99$) were more knowledgeable than fathers ($M = 70.61$, $SD = 10.47$), in keeping with earlier research on families with children in middle childhood (e.g., Crouter, MacDermid, McHale, & Perry-Jenkins, 1990). Sibling effects were also significant for decision-making input, $F(1,193) = 80.65$, $p < .001$, and parental knowledge, $F(1, 193) = 6.88$, $p < .01$. Parents concurred that firstborn adolescents had more opportunities for decision making ($M = 15.53$, $SD = 2.06$) than did their second-born adolescent offspring ($M = 14.47$, $SD = 1.88$), and parents were more knowledgeable about second-born adolescents ($M = 74.82$, $SD = 8.29$, averaged across mothers and fathers) than about firstborn adolescents ($M = 73.01$, $SD = 9.46$).

For decision-making input, a Parent × Sibling interaction, $F(1, 186) = 66.49$, $p < .001$, qualified the parent and sibling effects. Fathers, compared with mothers, perceived a much wider gap between their firstborns' and second-borns' decision-making input (fathers vis-à-vis firstborns, $M = 15.56$, $SD = 2.68$; fathers vis-à-vis second-borns, $M = 13.66$, $SD = 2.30$; mothers vis-à-vis firstborns, $M = 15.51$, $SD = 2.48$; mothers vis-à-vis second-borns, $M = 15.29$, $SD = 2.37$). Put another way, mothers' and fathers' perceptions of their firstborns' decision-making input did not differ, but fathers perceived significantly less decision-making input for second-borns than did mothers.

Analyses Involving Potential Moderators: Plan of Analysis

We used an analysis of covariance (ANCOVA)-oriented approach for the analyses that follow. For the questions of interest in this study, mixed-model ANCOVAs

were more efficient than multiple regression because mothers' and fathers' reports of both firstborns' and second-borns' experiences could be considered in a single analysis. Statistical power is increased as a result. In addition, within-family effects (i.e., mother–father or firstborn–second-born differences) and between-family effects are tested simultaneously.

Dependent variables in one set of analyses were mothers' and fathers' perceptions of firstborns' and second-borns' decision-making input. In a parallel set of analyses, mothers' knowledge and fathers' knowledge of their firstborns' and second-borns' activities and experiences were the dependent variables. Parent and sibling were treated as within-family factors in each analysis. Two between-family factors in each analysis were sibling sex constellation (e.g., older-girl–younger-girl) and mothers' gender role attitudes (traditional vs. less traditional). Firstborns' and second-borns' ages were entered as covariates in all analyses that follow. Follow-up tests of significant effects were conducted with Tukey tests.

Because cell sizes precluded our considering both parents' gender role attitudes in the same model, parallel analyses examining first mothers' and then fathers' attitudes were conducted. The analyses focusing on fathers' attitudes, however, revealed no associations with decision making or parental knowledge. Thus, the results described here are based on analyses of mothers' attitudes only.

Because pubertal status was measured differently for boys and girls, we performed these analyses separately for second-born boys and girls, with a series of 2 (pubertal status) × 2 (mothers' gender role attitudes) × 2 (sex of parent) mixed-model ANCOVAs that treated parent as a within-family factor and adolescents' age as a covariate.

The Role of the Sibling Sex Constellation

We expected to see sex-typed socialization patterns emerge primarily in families with mixed-sex sibling dyads, such that the tendency for firstborns to experience more autonomy than their younger siblings would be exacerbated in families with firstborn boys and second-born girls and would be minimized in families with firstborn girls and second-born boys.

Decision-making input   At the main effects level, sibling sex composition was not related to decision-making input. However, sex composition was associated with within-family differences in firstborns' and second-borns' decision making, as evidenced by a significant Sibling × Sex Constellation interaction, $F(3, 184) = 2.66$, $p < .05$. As Table 2 suggests, the difference between firstborn and second-born adolescents' decision-making input was especially pronounced in

TABLE 2   ADJUSTED MEANS AND STANDARD ERRORS FOR FIRSTBORNS', SECOND-BORNS', AND WITHIN-DYAD DIFFERENCES IN DECISION-MAKING INPUT BY DYAD SEX CONSTELLATION

Variable	Girl–girl		Girl–boy		Boy–girl		Boy–boy	
	M	**SE**	**M**	**SE**	**M**	**SE**	**M**	**SE**
Firstborns	15.6	0.3	15.9	0.3	15.1	0.3	15.6	0.3
Second-borns	14.5	0.3	14.2	0.3	14.3	0.3	14.8	0.3
Difference	$1.12_{a,b}$	0.3	1.63_a	0.3	0.78_b	0.3	0.83_b	0.3

Note: Scores reflect the mean of mothers' and fathers' report. Difference = second-borns' scores subtracted from firstborns' scores. Means with different subscripts differ significantly at $p < .05$ by the Tukey test. Higher scores indicate more decision-making input for adolescents.

favor of the older sibling among families with firstborn girls and second-born boys. In these families, the gap between firstborns' and second-borns' decision-making input was larger than the gap in firstborn-boy/second-born-boy or firstborn-boy/second-born-girl families.

Parental knowledge   Sibling sex composition was not related to parental knowledge at the level of a between-subjects main effect; however, a significant Sibling × Sex Constellation effect emerged, $F(3, 184) = 4.93$, $p < .01$ (see Table 3). Follow-up tests revealed that differential parental knowledge of firstborns versus second-borns was present in families with opposite-sex (but not same-sex) sibling dyads. The gap between parents' knowledge of firstborns and second-borns was more pronounced (in the direction of more knowledge vis-à-vis the second-born) in families with firstborn girls and second-born boys than in families with firstborn boys and second-born girls. This effect was qualified by a Sex of Parent × Sibling × Sex Constellation effect, $F(3, 184) = 12.06$, $p < .001$. Examining mothers' and fathers' knowledge separately (see Table 3) clarified this within-family effect. Mothers' knowledge did not differ as a function of sex constellation; however, sex constellation effects emerged for fathers' knowledge of firstborns, $F(3, 184) = 3.55$, $p < .02$, and second-borns, $F(3, 184) = 3.61$, $p < .02$. Fathers with older daughters and younger sons were less knowledgeable regarding their firstborns' experiences, whereabouts, and activities than were other fathers. Conversely, fathers with older sons and younger daughters were less knowledgeable about their second-borns than were fathers with older daughters and younger sons. In other words, fathers with both daughters and sons tended to be less knowledgeable about their daughters than were other fathers.

Summary   Analyses focused on the sex composition of the sibling dyad revealed consistent, but unexpected, patterns. Discrepancies between firstborns and second-borns in decision-making input and parental knowledge were largest (in the direction of more autonomy for firstborns) in families with firstborn girls and second-born boys. At least with regard to parental knowledge, this discrepancy was due to fathers' particularly low levels of knowledge regarding firstborn girls with younger brothers.

MOTHERS' GENDER ROLE ATTITUDES

We made two predictions about the role of mothers' gender role attitudes. First, we predicted an interaction between gender role attitudes and adolescents' sex such that mothers' traditionality would be linked to low levels of autonomy for daughters but not sons. We further expected the pattern of granting autonomy to sons but not daughters in traditional families with mixed-sex sibling dyads.

Decision-making input   An overall main effect emerged for mothers' gender role attitudes, $F(1, 184) = 9.35$, $p < .01$. Adolescents with less traditional mothers had more decision-making input (adjusted $M = 15.38$, $SE = 0.18$) than did adolescents whose mothers held more traditional attitudes ($M = 14.58$, $SE = 0.19$). An additional between-family effect qualified the main effect: A Mothers' Gender Role Attitudes × Sex Constellation interaction, $F(1, 184) = 3.03$, $p < .05$, revealed that the link between mothers' attitudes and adolescents' decision making was different depending on the sex constellation of the sibling dyad. As Table 4 illustrates, adolescents in families with firstborn and second-born girls had less decision-making input when mothers were more traditional than when mothers were less traditional. Decision making did not differ as a function of mothers' attitudes in any of the other three sex constellations.

Parental knowledge   Analyses focused on parental knowledge revealed a trend for parents in families

TABLE 3   ADJUSTED MEANS AND STANDARD ERRORS OF FATHERS', MOTHERS', AND WITHIN-DYAD DIFFERENCES IN PARENTAL KNOWLEDGE BY DYAD SEX CONSTELLATION

| | Mothers' knowledge | | | | | | | |
| | Girl–girl | | Girl–boy | | Boy–girl | | Boy–boy | |
Variable	M	SE	M	SE	M	SE	M	SE
Firstborns	75.8	1.8	75.7	1.7	77.3	1.6	75.7	1.6
Second-borns	79.8	1.5	76.2	1.5	78.4	1.4	79.1	1.4
Difference	3.98	1.8	0.48	1.8	1.04	1.6	3.41	1.6
	Fathers' knowledge							
	Girl–girl		Girl–boy		Boy–girl		Boy–boy	
Variable	M	SE	M	SE	M	SE	M	SE
Firstborns	71.8_a	1.9	64.8_b	1.9	72.0_a	1.7	71.2_a	1.7
Second-borns	71.6	1.9	76.1_a	1.9	67.6_b	1.7	71.8	1.7
Difference	-0.25_b	1.9	11.24_a	1.9	-4.40_b	1.7	0.65_b	1.7

Note: Means with different subscripts within a given row differ significantly at $p < .05$ by the Tukey test. Higher scores indicate more parental knowledge.

with traditional maternal attitudes to be more knowledgeable about their adolescents' activities ($M = 74.97$, $SE = 0.77$) than parents in families with less traditional maternal attitudes ($M = 73.14$, $SE = 0.76$), $F(1, 184) = 2.85$, $p < .10$.

Summary   In families where mothers held more traditional attitudes, adolescent offspring experienced fewer decision-making opportunities than those from less traditional families; this pattern was only apparent, however, in families with firstborn girls and second-born girls. Parents in families in which mothers held more traditional attitudes toward gender roles also tended to be more knowledgeable regarding their

adolescents' experiences and activities than parents in families where mothers held more traditional views.

THE ROLE OF ADOLESCENTS' PUBERTAL DEVELOPMENT

We predicted that more pubertally advanced adolescent girls would be granted more autonomy than less advanced girls. However, we also expected this association to be qualified by an interaction with mothers' gender role attitudes, such that menarche would be linked to higher levels of autonomy only

TABLE 4   ADJUSTED MEANS AND STANDARD ERRORS FOR SIBLING DYAD AVERAGES IN DECISION-MAKING INPUT BY MOTHERS' GENDER ROLE ATTITUDES AND DYAD SEX CONSTELLATION

| Gender role attitude | Girl–girl | | Girl–boy | | Boy–girl | | Boy–boy | |
	M	SE	M	SE	M	SE	M	SE
Less traditional	16.0_a	0.34	15.4	0.42	15.0	0.37	15.1	0.32
More traditional	14.0_b	0.43	14.7	0.36	14.3	0.34	15.3	0.37

Note: Scores reflect the mean of mothers' and fathers' report regarding both firstborns and second-borns. Means with different subscripts differ significantly at $p < .05$ by the Tukey test. Higher scores indicate more decision-making input for adolescents.

TABLE 5   ADJUSTED MEANS AND STANDARD ERRORS FOR PARENTS' KNOWLEDGE OF SECOND-BORN DAUGHTERS AS A FUNCTION OF MOTHERS' GENDER ROLE ATTITUDES AND DAUGHTERS' MENARCHEAL STATUS

Mothers' gender role attitudes	Adolescents' menarcheal status	n	Parents' knowledge	
			M	SE
More traditional	Premenarcheal	32	76.23_a	1.52
More traditional	Postmenarcheal	13	74.40_a	2.43
Less traditional	Premenarcheal	34	75.96_a	1.51
Less traditional	Postmenarcheal	16	66.36_b	2.35

Note: Scores were calculated as means of mothers' and fathers' knowledge scores. Means with different subscripts differ significantly at $p < .05$ by the Tukey test. Higher scores indicate more parental knowledge.

in families in which mothers held less traditional attitudes.

Decision-making input   We found no significant associations between adolescents' decision-making input and their pubertal status.

Parental knowledge   Second-born boys' pubertal status was unrelated to parents' knowledge; second-born girls' status, as measured by a median split on the physical development measure, was similarly unrelated to parental knowledge. However, a significant between-family effect for second-born girls' menarcheal status revealed that mothers and fathers were more knowledgeable about girls who had reached menarche, $F(1, 89) = 6.17$, $p < .02$ (see Table 5). This effect was qualified by a Menarcheal Status × Mothers' Attitudes interaction, $F(1, 89) = 4.30$, $p < .05$. As Table 5 illustrates, parents in families with less traditional maternal attitudes were more knowledgeable about premenarcheal daughters than about postmenarcheal daughters. In contrast, when mothers held more traditional attitudes, parents' knowledge of their second-born girls' activities and whereabouts did not differ as a function of menarcheal status.

DISCUSSION

In this study, we set out to examine the ways in which two indicators of parental autonomy granting—adolescents' decision-making input and parental knowledge of adolescents' daily experiences—differed as a function of contextual factors and boys' and girls' personal characteristics. We found little evidence for universal gender role socialization patterns that were consistent with Hill and Lynch's (1983) ideas; instead, this investigation joins a handful of other studies that

have examined contextual factors that may moderate the ways in which gender is experienced in families with adolescents (e.g., Crouter et al., 1995; Updegraff et al., 1996). Our data included reports from multiple family members regarding two adolescents at different developmental levels in each family, a design that permits within-family and between-family comparisons. This study provides a starting point for future examinations. It will be important to investigate whether the patterns detected here are present in samples that are more diverse in terms of race, ethnicity, and family structure. In addition, longitudinal investigations focused on gender role socialization during adolescence are needed to more clearly delineate the circumstances under which patterns of gender role socialization are present.

Mothers' and fathers' perceptions of decision making and their knowledge of adolescents' daily experiences differed for older and younger adolescents. First, while holding both firstborns' and second-borns' ages constant, we found that mothers and fathers were more knowledgeable about younger adolescents than older adolescents. In this study, however, developmental status is confounded with ordinal position. This confound necessitates considering explanations that point to developmental status as well as interpretations that target ordinal position. A developmental status interpretation is that parents know less about their older adolescents because in the middle adolescent years, compared with early adolescence, youth spend less time with parents (Larson et al., 1996). One ordinal position interpretation is that parents know less about firstborns because of parental expectations about the role of firstborns in the family; older adolescents may be seen as deserving of more autonomy because of their firstborn status in the family.

We also found that fathers viewed younger adolescents as having less decision-making input than they did older adolescents. Perhaps father are slower than mothers to recognize and respond to the developmental needs of young adolescents by including them in the decision-making process. Mothers are generally more supportive and emotionally close to adolescents than are fathers (Collins & Russell, 1991), which may, in turn, make mothers more sensitive to the fact that the numerous changes associated with early adolescence necessitate alterations in the nature of the parent–adolescent relationship as well (Holmbeck, Paikoff, & Brooks-Gunn, 1995). This interpretation is consistent with research by Collins (1990) showing that mothers were more perceptive than fathers of declines in their adolescent offspring's communicativeness.

We were also interested in the ways in which adolescents' decision-making input and parental knowledge differed as function of the sex composition of the adolescent sibling dyad. Given that girls tend to have more input into decision making than boys (Brown & Mann, 1990; Flanagan, 1990; Fuligni & Eccles, 1993; Holmbeck & O'Donnell, 1991; Jacobs et al., 1993), we expected that adolescents in families with firstborn and second-born girls would have more decision-making opportunity than adolescents in other families. We found no such between-family differences in decision making as a function of sex composition; rather, the gap between firstborns' and second-borns' decision-making input, while present in all family groups, was especially large in families with firstborn girls and second-born boys. In contrast, the difference in decision making between firstborns and second-borns was least pronounced in families with firstborn boys. We wondered whether the decision-making opportunities typically afforded firstborn girls would generalize such that their younger siblings would also be granted high levels of opportunity for decision making; this was clearly not the case, particularly when the younger siblings in question were boys. Why parents grant their firstborn daughters (but not their second-born sons) high levels of decision-making input is unclear, but several processes may be at work. Perhaps parents involve adolescents in decision making in conjunction with adolescents' physical or cognitive development, a plausible interpretation given that girls typically mature earlier than boys (Brooks-Gunn & Reiter, 1990). Boys' relative immaturity may be magnified in families with (relatively mature) firstborn girls, leading parents to grant less autonomy to their younger sons. Another possibility is that because boys have higher levels of problem behavior than girls, parents may be restrictive of their second-born sons in anticipation of problem behavior as their sons approach and enter adolescence, a pattern that may be exacerbated if the parents have a firstborn daughter (and therefore no prior experience with sons).

With regard to parental knowledge, a similar within-family pattern emerged. Mothers were consistently more knowledgeable about second-borns than about firstborns; however, fathers with both sons and daughters were more knowledgeable about their sons' experiences than their daughters' experiences, regardless of ordinal position. In this study, lower paternal knowledge about girls was evident only when fathers had both sons and daughters. Fathers' knowledge of their sons' daily experiences, in contrast, was similar regardless of sibling composition. One explanation for this pattern is that perhaps fathers with both a son and a daughter are more likely than other fathers to pair off with the son at the expense of time with the daughter. In any event, these findings are consistent with research indicating that fathers, more than mothers, may be especially invested in parenting their same-sex offspring (Collins & Russell, 1991; Siegal, 1987) but extend beyond the majority of studies addressing this question by examining parents' behaviors toward sons and daughters in the same family. Taken together, our findings suggest that firstborn daughters with younger brothers may be especially likely to be granted high levels of autonomy by parents.

The tendency for daughters to be granted more autonomy than their brothers, as in the patterns described above, is inconsistent with the notion that parents' greater restrictiveness toward daughters versus sons is a normative pattern during adolescence. In this study, however, we were also interested in the possibility that family context, specifically parents' attitudes about gender, would moderate any associations between adolescent gender and parental autonomy granting. In general, we found that adolescents from families in which mothers' attitudes were more traditional were granted less autonomy, but these associations were qualified by sibling sex constellation. Decision-making input differed as a function of mothers' attitudes only in families with sister–sister pairs. In addition, parents were less knowledgeable about their second-born daughters who were postmenarcheal—but only in families where mothers held less traditional attitudes. In sum, these findings show that girls' opportunities for autonomy may be more likely than boys' to hinge on the traditionality of their mother's attitudes.

These patterns of findings raise several questions. First, why do mothers' gender role attitudes (but not fathers' attitudes) matter for adolescents' decision-making input and parental knowledge? A marital power perspective (McHale, Crouter, McGuire, & Updegraff, 1995) would hold that husbands and wives who possess more resources relative to their spouse tend to have more influence on family decisions and functioning; in this study, mothers' occupational prestige was slightly higher than that of fathers. Perhaps the combination of high occupational prestige and fewer hours at work (giving mothers more opportunity for interaction with adolescents) helps explain the importance of mothers' attitudes in moderating the socialization processes investigated here.

A second question of interest concerns the finding that traditional maternal attitudes are especially important in families with firstborn and second-born girls; only in these families did adolescents' decision-making input differ as a function of mothers' traditionality. We expected to find traditionality associated with within-family differences, with more autonomy for sons and less for their sisters. Perhaps mothers' attitudes are particularly influential in families with firstborn and second-born daughters because these are female-oriented environments in which mothers' opinions may hold more sway. The role of mothers' and fathers' relative influence deserves attention in future studies focused on autonomy-granting processes during adolescence.

Finally, controlling for chronological age, we found that parents were less knowledgeable about the activities and whereabouts of postmenarcheal younger daughters than of their premenarcheal counterparts. No such association was detected, however, when we replicated the analyses using median splits on a self-report physical development measure as a grouping factor. It is possible that for parents, menarche, more than any other physical characteristic, is a particularly powerful indicator of girls' developmental status. We also found that in families with traditional maternal attitudes, postmenarcheal daughters were granted less autonomy than their counterparts in less traditional family contexts. Parents with traditional attitudes toward gender roles may be most inclined to take a protective stance toward their physically maturing female offspring. Note, however, that the analogous pattern did not emerge for boys. Parents with traditional attitudes toward gender roles did not grant their sons high levels of autonomy.

In sum, this study illustrates the inherent complexities of conducting ecologically oriented research on parenting processes. We set out to explore the ways in which parental autonomy granting intersected with patterns of gender role socialization, using Hill and Lynch's (1983) ideas about gender intensification as a guiding theoretical framework. We found, in a pattern that is inconsistent with notions of gender intensification, that in general, daughters were granted more autonomy than sons, particularly when the girls had younger brothers. However, in some families, for instance, when mothers held traditional attitudes about gender, girls were granted lower levels of autonomy. These results are further evidence that gender intensification may not be a universal phenomenon but rather emerges under some conditions and not others. An important step for future investigations in this domain will be to examine whether low levels of autonomy place girls in families with traditional notions about gender roles at risk for negative developmental consequences.

References

Baumrind, D. (1991). Effective parenting during the early adolescent transition. In P. A. Cowan & E. M. Hetherington (Eds.), *Advances in family research* (Vol. 2, pp. 111–163). Hillsdale, NJ: Erlbaum.

Brody, G., Moore, K., & Glei, D. (1994). Family processes during adolescence as predictors of parent–young adult attitude similarity: A six-year longitudinal analysis. *Family Relations, 43*, 369–373.

Bronfenbrenner, U. (1979). *The ecology of human development.* Cambridge, MA: Harvard University Press.

Brooks-Gunn, J., & Reiter, E. O. (1990). The role of pubertal processes. In S. S. Feldman & G. R. Elliott (Eds.), *At the threshold: The developing adolescent* (pp. 16–53). Cambridge, MA: Harvard University Press.

Brown, J. E., & Mann, L. (1990). The relationship between family structure and process variables and adolescent decision-making. *Journal of Adolescence, 13*, 25–37.

Buchanan, C. M., Eccles. J. S., & Becker, J. B. (1992). Are adolescents the victims of raging hormones: Evidence for activational effects of hormones on moods and behavior at adolescence. *Psychological Bulletin, 111*, 62–107.

Collins, W. A. (1990). Parent–child relationships in the transition to adolescence: Continuity and change in interaction, affect, and cognition. In R. Montemayor. G. Adams, & T. Gullotta (Eds.), *Advances in adolescent development: From childhood to adolescence: A transitional period?* (Vol. 2. pp. 85–106). Newbury Park. CA: Sage.

Collins, W. A., Gleason, T., & Sesma, A. (1997). Internalization, autonomy, and relationships: Development during adolescence. In J. E. Grusec & L. Kuczynski (Eds.), *Parenting and children's internalization of values: A handbook of contemporary theory* (pp. 78–99). New York: Wiley.

Collins, W. A., & Luebker, C. (1994). Parent and adolescent expectancies: Individual and relational significance. In J. G. Smetana (Ed.), *New directions for child development* (Vol. 66, pp. 65–80). San Francisco: Jossey-Bass.

Collins, W. A., & Russell, G. (1991). Mother–child and father–child relationships in middle childhood and adolescence: A developmental analysis. *Developmental Review. 11*, 99–136.

Crouter, A. C., Helms-Erikson, H., Updegraff, K., & McHale. S. M. (1999). Conditions underlying parents' knowledge about children's daily lives in middle childhood: Between- and within-family comparisons. *Child Development, 70*, 246–259.

Crouter, A. C., MacDermid, S. M., McHale, S. M., & Perry-Jenkins, M. (1990). Parental monitoring and perceptions of children's school performance and conduct in dual-earner and single-earner families. *Developmental Psychology, 26*, 649–657.

Crouter, A. C., Manke, B. A., & McHale, S. M. (1995). The family context of gender intensification in early adolescence. *Child Development, 66,* 317–329.

Dishion, T. J., & McMahon, R. J. (1998). Parental monitoring and the prevention of child and adolescent problem behavior: A conceptual and empirical formulation. *Clinical Child and Family Psychology Review, 1,* 61–75.

Dornbusch, S. M., Carlsmith. J. M., Bushwall, S. J., Ritter, P. L., Leiderman, H., Hastort, A. H., & Gross, R. T. (1985). Single parents, extended households, and the control of adolescents. *Child Development, 56,* 326–341.

Eccles, J., Buchanan, C., Flanagan, C., Fuligni, A., Midgley, C., & Yee, D. (1991). Control versus autonomy during adolescence. *Journal of Social Issues, 47,* 53–68.

Eccles, J. S., Midgley, C., Wigfield, A., Buchanan, C. M., Reuman, D., Flanagan, C., & Maciver, D. (1993). The impact of stage–environment fit on young adolescents' experiences in schools and in families. *American Psychologist, 48,* 90–101.

Flanagan, C. (1990). Changes in family work status: Effects on parent–adolescent decision-making. *Child Development, 61,* 163–177.

Fuligni, A. J., & Eccles, J. S. (1993). Perceived parent-child relationships and early adolescents' orientation toward peers. *Developmental Psychology, 29,* 622–632.

Galambos, N. L., Almeida, D. M., & Petersen, A. C. (1990). Masculinity, femininity, and sex role attitudes in early adolescence: Exploring gender intensification. *Child Development, 61,* 1905–1914.

Greenberger, E. (1984). Defining psychosocial maturity in adolescence. In P. Karoly & J. Steffen (Eds.), *Adolescent behavior disorders: Foundations and contemporary concerns* (pp. 54–81). Lexington, MA: Heath.

Hill, J. P. (1988). Adapting to menarche: Familial control and conflict. In M. R. Gunnar & W. A. Collins (Eds.), *21st Minnesota Symposium on Child Psychology* (pp. 43–77). Hillsdale, NJ: Erlbaum.

Hill, J. P., & Holmbeck, G. N. (1986). Attachment and autonomy in adolescence. In G. J. Whitehurst (Ed.), *Annals of child development* (Vol. 3, pp. 145–189). Greenwich, CT: JAI Press.

Hill, J. P., & Lynch, M. E. (1983). The intensification of gender-related role expectations during early adolescence. In J. Brooks-Gunn & A. C. Petersen (Eds.), *Girls at puberty: Biological and psychosocial perspectives* (pp. 201–228). New York: Plenum.

Holmbeck, G. N., & O'Donnell, K. (1991). Discrepancies between perceptions of decision-making and behavioral autonomy. In R. L. Paikoff (Ed.), *Shared views in the family during adolescence: New directions for child development* (Vol. 51, pp. 51–69). San Francisco: Jossey-Bass.

Holmbeck, G. N., Paikoff, A., & Brooks-Gunn, J. (1995). Parenting adolescents. In M. Bornstein (Ed.), *The handbook of parenting* (Vol. 1, pp. 91–118). Mahwah, NJ: Erlbaum.

Huston, A. C., & Alvarez, M. M. (1990). The socialization context of gender role development in early adolescence. In R. Montemayor, G. R. Adams, & T. P. Gullotta (Eds.), *From childhood to adolescence: A transitional period?* (pp. 156–179). Newbury Park, CA: Sage.

Jacobs, J. E., Bennett, M. A., & Flanagan, C. (1993). Decision-making in one-parent and two-parent families: Influence and information selection. *Journal of Early Adolescence, 13,* 245–256.

Larson, R. W., Richards, M. H., Moneta, G. Holmbeck, G., & Duckett, E. (1996). Changes in adolescents' daily interactions with their families from ages 10 to 18: Disengagement and transformation. *Developmental Psychology, 32,* 744–754.

Linn, M. C., & Petersen, A. C. (1986). A meta-analysis of gender differences in spatial ability: Implications for math and science achievement. In J. S. Hyde & M. C. Linn (Eds.), *The psychology of gender: Advances through meta-analysis* (pp. 67–101). Baltimore: Johns Hopkins University Press.

McHale, S. M., Crouter, A. C., McGuire, S. A., & Updegraff, K. A. (1995). Congruence between mothers' and fathers' differential treatment of siblings: Links with family relations and children's well-being. *Child Development, 66,* 116–128.

McHale, S. M., Crouter, A. C., & Tucker, C. J. (1999). Family context and gender role socialization in middle childhood: Comparing girls to boys and sisters to brothers. *Child Development, 70,* 990–1004.

Mekos, D., Hetherington, E. M., & Reiss, D. (1996). Sibling differences in problem behavior and parental treatment in nondivorced and remarried families. *Child Development, 67,* 2148–2165.

Metzler, C. W., Noell, J., Biglan, A., Ary, D., & Smolkowski, K. (1994). The social context of risky sexual behavior among adolescents. *Journal of Behavioral Medicine, 17,* 419–438.

Montemayor, R., & Brownlee, J. (1987). Fathers, mothers, and adolescents: Gender-based differences in parental roles during adolescence. *Journal of Youth and Adolescence, 16,* 281–292.

Nakao, K., & Treas, J. (1994). Updating occupational prestige and socioeconomic scores: How the new measures measure up. *Sociological Methodology, 24,* 1–72.

Paikoff, R. L., & Brooks-Gunn, J. (1991). Do parent–child relationships change during puberty? *Psychological Bulletin, 110,* 47–66.

Parke, R. D. (1995). Fathers and families. In M. H. Bornstein (Ed.), *Handbook of parenting* (Vol. 3. pp. 27–63). Mahwah, NJ: Erlbaum.

Patterson, G. R., & Stouthamer-Loeber, M. (1984). The correlation of family management practices and delinquency. *Child Development, 55,* 1299–1307.

Petersen, A. C., Crockett, L., Richards, M., & Boxer, A. (1988). A self-report measure of pubertal status: Reliability, validity, and initial norms. *Journal of Youth and Adolescence, 17,* 117–133.

Siegal, M. (1987). Are sons and daughters treated more differently by fathers than by mothers? *Developmental Review, 7,* 183–209.

Silverberg, S. B., & Gondoli, D. M. (1996). Autonomy in adolescence: A contextual perspective. In G. R. Adams, R. Montemayor, & T. P. Gullotta (Eds.), *Advances in adolescent development* (Vol. 8, pp. 12–61). Thousand Oaks. CA: Sage.

Spence, J. T., & Helmreich, R. L. (1978). *Masculinity and femininity: Their psychological dimensions. correlates, and antecedents.* Austin: University of Texas Press.

Steinberg, L. (1990). Interdependence in the family: Autonomy, conflict, and harmony in the parent–adolescent relationship. In S. S. Feldman & G. L. Elliott (Eds.), *At the threshold: The developing adolescent* (pp. 255–276). Cambridge, MA: Harvard Press.

Steinberg, L., Fletcher, A., & Darling, N. (1994). Parental monitoring and peer influences on adolescent substance use. *Pediatrics, 93,* 1–5.

Steinberg, L., & Silverberg, S. (1986). The vicissitudes of autonomy in adolescence. *Child Development, 57,* 841–851.

Stocker, C. M., & McHale, S. M. (1992). The nature and family correlates of preadolescents' perceptions of their sibling relationships. *Journal of Social and Personal Relationships, 9,* 179–195.

Updegraff, K. A., McHale, S. M., & Crouter, A. C. (1996). Gender roles in marriage: What do they mean for girls' and boys' school achievement? *Journal of Youth and Adolescence, 25,* 73–88.

QUESTIONS

1. What is the gender intensification hypothesis?
2. What psychological outcomes are related to adolescent participation in family decision making?
3. What is parental monitoring, and how is it related to adolescent children's gender?
4. What three moderating factors did the researchers study in relation to the participation of boys and girls in family decision making and parental monitoring?
5. Why did the researchers want to conduct within-family comparisons of parental patterns of autonomy granting in adolescence?
6. How did adolescents' decision-making input in the family differ according to their mothers' attitudes concerning gender roles? Did the children's gender contribute to this pattern? How?
7. What types of contextual factors in the family were important for explaining the autonomy-granting patterns revealed in this research?
8. How do the researchers interpret the autonomy-granting differences that were found for first- and second-born children?
9. What differences were identified in the ways in which mothers and fathers involved their adolescents in family decision making?
10. According to the researchers, why was the gap in decision-making input especially wide in families in which the first-born child was a girl and the second-born child was a boy?

36

Antisocial Boys and Their Friends in Early Adolescence: Relationship Characteristics, Quality, and Interactional Process

THOMAS J. DISHION • DAVID W. ANDREWS • LYNN CROSBY

Violence toward other people and willful destruction of property are disturbing crimes that shatter people's trust in one another, especially when such acts are committed by youth. What are the explanations for and origins of antisocial adolescent behaviors? Developmental psychologists have examined the roles played by the family, school experience, and poverty. Some psychologists have focused on the contribution of the peer group to adolescent problem behaviors. While there is substantial evidence for the disruptive effect of antisocial behavior on peer relations more generally, very little is known about how the friendships of antisocial children differ from those of well-adjusted children.

In the following article, Thomas Dishion, David Andrews, and Lynn Crosby describe their research on the origins and characteristics of the close friendships of antisocial boys during the early years of adolescence. Among the questions the researchers tried to answer is whether antisocial youth, who are known to lack the basic social skills needed to develop a supportive friendship network, have friends and, if so, what those friends tend to be like. Dishion and his colleagues also examined the nature of these friendships: how they are formed, how long they last, how satisfying they are for antisocial youth, and what types of behaviors characterize them. Finally, the researchers were interested in how these friendships contribute to the individual development and adjustment of antisocial youth, especially whether they increase the likelihood of delinquent behavior.

The findings of this study challenge conventional wisdom. Antisocial adolescent boys do have friendships, and these relationships serve a number of social and psychological functions. However, such friendships differ from the friendships experienced by well-adjusted youth in several ways. These differences are particularly evident in the types of behaviors that antisocial friends exhibit toward one another. Although friendships are often seen as helpful to individual development in childhood and adolescence, it seems that certain friendships may increase maladaptive behavior and put antisocial boys at even greater risk for delinquent behavior. This research also suggests that a better understanding of the social experiences that antisocial youth have with their friends may result in improved intervention programs for these individuals.

Reprinted with permission of Blackwell Publishers from Dishion, T. J., Andrews, D. A., & Crosby, L. (1995). Antisocial boys and their friends in early adolescence: Relationship characteristics, quality, and interactional process. *Child Development, 66,* 139–151.

This research would not have been possible were it not for the dedicated efforts of the OYS staff supervised by Deborah Capaldi. Education leaders (Charles Stevens, Robert Lady, and Robert Hammond) within the community where this research was conducted were vital to this and other projects ongoing at the Oregon Social Learning Center. Julie Rusby (author of PPC manual) deserves special acknowledgment for her care in supervising the coding of videotapes upon which these data are based. This research was supported by grants to Gerald Patterson (MH 37940, Center for Studies of Violent Behavior and Traumatic Stress, NIMH, U.S. PHS) and Thomas Dishion (DA07031, National Institute of Drug Abuse, U.S. PHS).

This study examines the close friendships of early adolescent boys in relation to antisocial behavior. 186 13–14-year-old boys and their close friends were interviewed, assessed at school, and videotaped in a problem-solving task. Similarity was observed between the demographic characteristics and antisocial behavior of the boys and their close friends. There was a tendency for the close friends of antisocial boys to live within the same neighborhood block and to have met in unstructured, unsupervised activities. Direct observations of interactions with close friends revealed a reliable correlation between antisocial behavior, directives, and negative reciprocity. Positive interactions within the friendship were uncorrelated with antisocial behavior and relationship quality. Implications of these findings for clinical and developmental theory are discussed.

INTRODUCTION

Studies about peer factors associated with child antisocial behavior offer a paradox to developmental and clinical researchers. On the one hand, it is well established that antisocial children are rejected by peers (Coie & Kupersmidt, 1983; Dishion, 1990; Dodge, 1983) and lack basic skills required for developing a supportive friendship network (Putallaz & Gottman, 1979). On the other hand, sociological studies of adolescents reveal a remarkably high level of correlation between deviant peers, delinquent behavior, and drug use (Elliott, Huizinga, & Ageton, 1985; Kandel, 1973). It appears that most antisocial children do develop friendships (Giordano, Cernkovich, & Pugh, 1986), but at the cost of escalating problem behavior in adolescence.

The troubled child's development of friendships with other antisocial children is an important developmental adaptation. From an ethnological view of behavioral development, much is to be learned from these adaptations (e.g., Hinde, 1989; Hinde & Stevenson-Hinde, 1986). According to this view, relationships are embedded within a social nexus, where factors unique to the individual shape the relationship, and the relationship, in turn, shapes the individual. The focus of this report, then, is to better understand the origins and characteristics of the close friendships of antisocial boys, and the potential influences of these relationships on individual development. Data from the Oregon Youth Study (OYS) (Capaldi & Patterson, 1987; Patterson, Reid, & Dishion, 1992) were used for this purpose.

As early as middle childhood, antisocial children tend to associate with other antisocial and/or rejected peers. It is unclear as to whether this is by choice or through default (Cairns & Cairns, 1991). There is support for the idea that children are attracted to those most like themselves (i.e., social choice), particularly with respect to aggressive behavior in middle childhood (Cairns, Cairns, Neckerman, Gest, & Gariepy, 1988) and drug use in adolescence (Kandel, 1973). Kandel (1978) and others have referred to mutual attraction processes in friendship formation as "homophily." As also hypothesized in Kenny's Social Relations Model (1988), perceptions of self–other agreement and trait congruence may be the passageway through which friendship forms.

Friendships among antisocial children may also form, in part, because of social forces such as peer rejection (Dishion, Patterson, Stoolmiller, & Skinner, 1991), ability tracking in schools (Kellam, 1990), or other features of communities such as neighborhood demographics (Simcha-Fagan & Schwartz, 1986). Rejected children tend to play with younger children and other rejected children and to report friendships with children outside the school setting (Ladd, 1983). Adult supervision of peer relationships may also be a key factor (Dishion et al., 1991; Steinberg & Silverberg, 1986).

Whether antisocial children "find" each other by choice or default, the family background of antisocial children provides a perspective on the specific interpersonal characteristics they are likely to bring to their friendships. Many investigators have shown that harsh, inconsistent, and negative parenting practices are prognostic of current (e.g., Patterson, 1986) and future (e.g., Farington, 1978; McCord, McCord, & Howard, 1969) antisocial behavior. According to the coercion model (Patterson, 1982; Patterson et al., 1992), aversive child behavior is strengthened via escape conditioning within reciprocal parent–child exchanges (Gardner, 1989; Patterson, 1982). Children learn to escalate aversive behavior in order to control (and reduce) their parents' efforts to set limits. We expected this overlearned coercive pattern to emerge at some point in the antisocial child's friendships. The friend's reactions to coercive acts help determine the stability of the pattern in the new relationship. The best test of this hypothesis is an analysis of the sequential structure of interaction. In such an analysis, we expected negative reciprocity to be associated with the dyad's level of antisocial behavior.

While Raush (1965) found "hyperaggressive" boys engaging in high rates of negative exchanges when interacting with other children defined as the same, the data were not examined sequentially and the interactants were not friends. Austin and Draper (1984) did look at close friends of rejected children and found aggressive children to be bossy with their close friends. Given the high overlap between peer rejection and antisocial behavior, this finding may also apply to the antisocial child. Panella and Henggeler (1986) studied the interactions of conduct-disordered, anxious, and well-adjusted boys with their close friends and found no differences in rates of negative behavior.

The coercion model (Patterson, 1982; Patterson et al., 1992) also hypothesizes that antisocial behavior disrupts prosocial skill development and leaves antisocial children less socially competent. Theorists have argued for decades that critical social skills are developed within childhood friendships (e.g., Hartup, 1983; Sullivan, 1953; Youniss, 1980). High levels of peer rejection limit extended contact among prosocial peers, thereby reducing the antisocial child's opportunity to model positive relationship skills. From this perspective, indices of interpersonal skill such as positive behavior and prosocial reciprocity are negatively correlated with the dyad's level of antisocial behavior. However, recent research has not fully supported this contention. Giordano's (Giordano et al., 1986) in-depth interviews negated some of the stereotypes of delinquent friendships. Although a tendency for conflict was correlated with delinquent behavior, more positive features (e.g., caring and trust) of friendship were uncorrelated. Similarly, Panella and Henggeler (1986) revealed that conduct-disordered children were not different from well-adjusted children in rates of positive behavior but were different on coders' global ratings of social competence.

Due to the limitations in social competence and higher levels of conflict, the general quality of the friendships may be compromised, as indicated by the participants themselves. Although investigators have documented less stability (e.g., Berndt, 1992) and satisfaction (Parker & Asher, 1989) in school friendships of both the antisocial and rejected child, it is not clear that these outcomes are associated with interpersonal behavior styles. In addition, school-based studies of friendships may overemphasize weaknesses of children whose close friends do not include classmates or schoolmates.

In summary, much is known about the disruptive effect of antisocial behavior on children's peer relations in school and their association with other antisocial peers. Very little is known, however, about the origins, characteristics, quality, and interpersonal style of close friendships of antisocial children compared to well-adjusted children. To this end, adolescent boys, some of whom display high rates of antisocial behavior, were asked to bring in their close friends, with whom they were observed interacting in a videotaped problem-solving task; they were also interviewed on the origins and nature of their friendship. These data were then used to address the following questions:

1. What is the relation between antisocial behavior and the friendship characteristics of adolescent boys? Specifically, at a more macro-level, what

are the behavioral, demographic, and relationship quality characteristics associated with antisocial friendships?

2. To what extent is antisocial behavior associated with interpersonal deficits or excesses as indicated by direct observation rates, sequential patterns, and observer impressions?

METHOD

SAMPLE

The original sample consisted of 206 13–14-year-old boys participating in the fifth year of the longitudinal Oregon Youth Study (OYS) (Patterson, 1986; Patterson & Bank, 1985; Patterson et al., 1992). Two cohorts of 102 and 104 boys and their families were recruited from 1983 to 1985 to participate in the study. The boys and their families were from 10 elementary schools in a Northwest community with a population of 150,000 to 200,000. Ten elementary schools were selected because of the high density of neighborhood delinquency reported in their area.

The resulting sample was 90% European-American and of lower socioeconomic status, with a relatively high percentage of unemployed parents (Capaldi & Patterson, 1987). When the study boys were 9 to 10 years old, 42% of the families were two-parent biological families, 32% were single-parent families, and 26% were step-parent families. At ages 13 to 14 (Wave 5), the percentages had changed to 37% two-parent families, 29% single-parent families, and 34% step-parent families. Additional demographic information on the OYS families at the time of recruitment is presented in Table 1.

The results of this report focused on data resulting from the Wave 5 assessment (i.e., yearly assessment) of OYS, which included structured interviews with boys and parents, school data collection (teacher ratings and school records), and official records of police contact. In addition, the boys were asked to bring a friend to the research center to participate in the observational phase of the study. During the family interview, the boys were asked to nominate "a child with whom you spend the most amount of time" to participate with them in the study. The boys' parents were also asked to give the name of a peer with whom their child spent most of his time. Parent and child nominations were then compared, and peers were selected to participate if they were nominated by the study child and confirmed by his parent(s).

There were 20 boys from the original OYS sample of 206 who did not participate in the Peer Interaction Task (PIT). Of these subjects, three did not participate in any phase of Wave 5, four refused to participate in the PIT, seven reported not having friends, and six

TABLE 1 DEMOGRAPHICS OF OREGON
YOUTH STUDY COHORTS 1 AND 2

	Cohort 1	Cohort 2
Family socioeconomic status (%):[a]		
Lower (Categories 1, 2)	50	45
Working (Category 3)	26	29
Middle (Categories 4, 5)	23	26
Employment status (%):		
Unemployed	34	30
Family income (%):		
0–4,999	11	16
5,000–9,999	22	20
10,000–14,999	15	17
15,000–19,999	14	14
20,000–24,999	16	14
25,000–29,999	8	10
30,000–39,999	13	6
40,000+	3	2
Family structure (%):		
Single parent	31	39
Number of children (%):		
1–2	52	58
3–4	37	32
5 or more	12	11
Mean age of mother (years)	34	34
Mean age of father (years)	36	37

[a]Hollingshead (1975).

2 and 3. Solve a problem related to getting along with parents that occurred for the study boy and his friend within the last month.

4 and 5. Solve a problem related to getting along with peers that occurred for the study boy and his friend within the last month.

Each of the above segments lasted 5 min. The order of the tasks *following* activity planning was counterbalanced, and the parent, peer tasks were staggered.

The resulting 25 min of videotaped interactions were coded by a set of observers (unaware of the adjustment status of the boys) using the Peer Process Code (PPC) (Dishion et al., 1989). The PPC is a microsocial coding system that records peer interaction in real time, capturing the interpersonal content and affective valence of the discussion. The videotapes were first previewed and then directly coded by using a handheld microcomputer.

Eighteen percent ($n = 32$) of the videotaped friend dyadic interactions were randomly selected to be coded independently by two observers. Using an entry-by-entry approach, there was 86.4% agreement on the content of the code (basic code category) and 73.4% on the affective valence. Percent agreement on content and affect codes ranged from .37 to .91. An overall weighted kappa (Cohen, 1960) of .69 was found on the combined content and valence of each entry, with kappa scores ranging from .37 to .78.

Four a priori behavior scores were developed from a 24-category coding system for the purposes of this research: Positive Engagement, Converse, Directives, and Negative Engagement. These scores included 19 of the 24 coding categories. Four codes not included in these behavior clusters were Comply, Not Comply, Agree, Disagree. These categories were coded only following a command, and thus were highly correlated with commands and ipsative with one another. In addition, Manipulation of Objects was not included in the four clusters, since it was quite low in base rate and deemed irrelevant to interpersonal process.

The specific description of each of the behavior scores follows. In addition to the overall percent agreement on the PPC code, interobserver consistency was examined for each of the observation indicators described below. Consistency is represented by the zero-order correlation between the scores of two observers on each observation indicator taken during 32 reliability sessions. Note that interobserver consistency was computed for a dyad version of the behavior clusters, which was the score used in the analyses that follow. Table 3 (below) reveals substantial correlation between the two boys on the following cluster scores.

Positive engagement Positive engagement includes the following content categories recorded in

were excluded because they brought siblings to the PIT. Because these boys are involved in a long-term longitudinal study, it was possible to identify the fourth-grade sociometric status (Coie, Dodge, & Coppotelli, 1982) of boys not participating in the PIT: (4) Rejected; (1) Neglected; (7) Average (combined with undefined); (3) Popular; (1) Controversial. An unreliable trend suggested higher rates of rejection (25%) among boys not engaging in the task compared to the overall sample (15%).

PEER INTERACTION TASK (PIT)

The already-defined PIT was designed to elicit a wide range of interactive behaviors between the participating boy and his friend. The boys were videotaped in a 25-min session during which they were asked to:

1. Plan an activity together (something they could potentially do together within the next week).

neutral or positive valence: Positive Verbal, Unqualified Positive Regard, Self-Disclose, Positive Nonverbal, Touch/Hold, and Physical Interact. In addition, neutral content categories in positive affect were included: Talk, Vocal, and Neutral Nonverbal (interobserver $r = .81$).

Directives   The following categories in neutral or positive affective valence comprise the Directive score: Request, Request Ambiguous, Command, and Command Ambiguous (interobserver $r = .92$).

Negative engagement   This score includes behaviors that were developed to describe aversive behavior, regardless of the valence: Negative Verbal, Verbal Attack, Coerce, Coerce Ambiguous, Negative Nonverbal, and Physical Aggressive. Also included were neutral and positive content codes (listed above) displayed in negative affective valence (interobserver $r = .85$).

Converse   Converse captures on-task, interpersonal-neutral behavior and includes the following content codes in neutral affective valence: Talk, Vocal, and Neutral Nonverbal (interobserver $r = .72$).

Global ratings of social skill   Observers provided global ratings on Social Skills (e. g., took turns speaking) on nine items (alpha = .85). One item from the original ratings from the study boy was dropped due to low loading (loading <.30) on a principal components factor analysis. The correlation between the two boys' social skills ratings was .79.

Global ratings of noxious behavior   Noxious behavior (e. g., used aggressive gestures) was represented by five items (alpha = .76). The correlation between the study boy's and the friend's noxious behavior ratings was .75.

FRIENDSHIP CHARACTERISTICS

In the friendship interview, the boys were individually asked a series of questions regarding their friendship. Questions used in this study were, "How long have you known each other?" "Where did the two of you first meet?" and "How close do you live to each other?" Data from this interview were used only if the two boys agreed in their response.

One year following the friendship interview, the study boys were asked to report the status of the friendship. Their responses were coded to represent the following relationship 1-year outcomes: (*a*) unfriendly, (*b*) drifted apart, (*c*) nonvolitional separation, (*d*) no change, and (*e*) better friends.

TEACHER RATINGS OF SOCIAL PREFERENCE

Teacher estimates of sociometric status (social preference) for the study boy and his friend were computed by using the scoring method developed by Coie et al. (1982). A teacher's social preference score was computed from ratings (usually different teachers) of the proportion of other students who "liked" the boys and those who "disliked" the boys. These teacher estimates of social preference for the study boy correlated .43 ($p < .001$) with the peer nomination score of social preference (Coie et al., 1982) collected 4 years earlier in the fourth grade.

RELATIONSHIP SATISFACTION

Three reliable dimensions of relationship satisfaction were derived from the Friendship Quality Questionnaire (Lathrop, Dishion, & Capaldi, 1987) using both principal component analysis and item analyses (Cronbach, 1951): Conflict, Quality, and Evaluation. The scales and their psychometric properties are described below.

The Conflict scale assessed disagreements and estrangement within the friendship (e.g., "How often do you get on each other's nerves?"). Four items produced satisfactory internal consistency (alpha = .78). The Quality scale originally consisted of four items, but two were dropped due to low item total correlations. The two items that remained assessed the boys' sense of trust and happiness in their friendship (e.g., "How happy are you with this friendship?"), yielding satisfactory internal consistency ($r = .68$). The Evaluation scale used a semantic differential format to assess the boys' evaluation of their friend's character (e.g., "Friend is good/bad"). This scale produced high internal consistency ($r = .88$). These three scales were standardized and combined into a single score of Dyadic Relationship Satisfaction. The internal consistency of this composite score based on Conflict, Evaluation, and Quality scales was .78.

ANTISOCIAL BEHAVIOR

Each boy's antisocial behavior was assessed using teacher, self, and interviewer impressions. Teacher ratings of the boys' antisocial behavior were derived from 19 items (e.g., "disobedient at school," "steals") from the Child Behavior Checklist (Achenbach & Edelbrock, 1986). In addition, teachers were asked to rate, "How often does he exert a negative influence on his friends?" In the interview, the boys reported on their delinquent behavior using the minor delinquent offenses of the survey instrument developed by Elliott and colleagues (Elliott et al., 1985). This instrument assessed the number of times the boys committed each delinquent act (e.g., "How many times in the last year have you damaged or destroyed school property?"). These act frequencies were summed into a total score for this indicator. In addition, the interviewers provided impression ratings of each boy separately (e.g., "adolescent seemed involved in delinquent and antisocial behavior"). The three indicators of antisocial behavior were standardized and aggregated into a composite score for the study boy and his friend.

Juvenile court records A search was conducted of local juvenile court records for any police contact with study boys and their friends. Date and nature of all police contacts become a matter of computer records. For these analyses, only contacts for reasons of delinquency were considered.

ANALYTIC PROCEDURES

The following questions were addressed in the analysis. (1) What are the origins, characteristics, and quality of early adolescent boys' friendships as related to antisocial behavior? Here the data from the friendship interview and data on the two boys were compared using correlational, analysis of variance, and nonparametric strategies. The status of the friendship 1 year later was also assessed as an indicator of the quality of the relationship with respect to antisocial behavior and dyad relationship satisfaction. (2) The interactional processes within the relationship were examined simply by correlating rates of behavior and observer impressions with the boys' antisocial behavior. Then lag 1 sequential scores were computed for each possible sequence given the four behavior clusters following procedures outlined by Gottman and

Roy (1990), where Allison-Liker Z scores (Allison & Liker, 1982) represented whether a sequential contingency was statistically reliable. Homogeneous groups were formed to provide an assessment of whether the sequential structure varied for antisocial dyads compared to well-adjusted dyads.

RESULTS

RELATIONSHIP CHARACTERISTICS

Two questions were asked in relation to the origin of the boys' friendship. Each boy was asked how they met and how far apart they lived from one another. There were 135 dyads who agreed in their response as to how they met and 164 dyads where the boys agreed on how far away from each other they lived. Of the 135 dyads agreeing on how they met, 73% met in school or some other organized activity, and 17% met in their neighborhood or in an unsupervised community setting. Of the 164 dyads agreeing on the distance that they lived from one another, 71% were living within three blocks of one another and 29% were living farther away than three blocks.

To determine whether the origin of the boys' friendships was related to the quality of the relationship and their level of deviance, these scores were analyzed in respect to where the boys met and how close they lived to each other (see Table 2). Dyadic

TABLE 2 SUMMARIES OF DYADIC ANTISOCIAL AND RELATIONSHIP QUALITY TRAITS BY FRIENDSHIP CHARACTERISTICS

Value	Dyad Antisocial		Dyad Relationship Satisfaction		Cases
	Mean	Standard Deviation	Mean	Standard Deviation	
"Where did you first meet?"					
In my neighborhood and other unorganized activity	.329	1.27	−.063	1.05	36
In school and organized activity	−.194	.90	.119	1.00	99
"How close do you live to each other?"					
Within 2–3 blocks	.369	1.24	−.551	1.11	47
Farther than 2–3 blocks	−.163	.85	.233	.87	117
Status of relationship after 1 year:					
Unfriendly	1.108	.96	−.731	.88	9
Drifted apart	.144	1.03	−.023	1.12	27
Nonvolitional	.085	1.02	−.187	.98	56
No change	−.286	.826	.088	.92	49
Better friends	−.231	.896	.352	1.01	36

scores of antisocial behavior and relationship satisfaction were used for this analysis. There was a significant multivariate effect found for the boys' deviance and relationship satisfaction for both where they met (Wilks's lambda = .95, $p < .043$) and how close they lived to each other (Wilks's lambda = .86, $p < .0001$). Inspection of the univariate effects in Table 2 reveals that the greatest effect was for antisocial dyads to have met outside of school, $F(1, 133) = 7.10$, $p < .01$, and live within the same neighborhood, $F(1, 162) = 9.93$, $p < .002$. As one might expect, there tended to be less satisfaction within the relationships of boys in the same neighborhood, $F(1, 162) = 23.02$, $p < .0001$, suggesting that these were friendships of convenience.

Given that boys tended to bring in friends who lived close by, the level of similarity between the boys on basic demographic characteristics and social behavior was not surprising. The study boy and friend were close in age, with a nonsignificant mean age difference of .90 years and a range of .02 to 3.52 years. Other social behavior and demographic characteristics of the study boy and his friend were compared using Pearson product moment correlation coefficients (see Table 3) and chi-square analysis.

The demographic profiles for the study boy and his friend were modestly associated. Family income correlated .25 ($p < .0001$) for the two boys. The association between the two boys on parental status was statistically marginal ($\chi^2 = 6.3$, $p < .18$).

The adjustment of the study boys and their friends was strongly correlated (see Table 3). The multimethod, multiagent antisocial construct scores generated for both boys were significantly correlated ($r = .41$, $p < .0001$). A modest correlation was found between the boys' and their friends' social preference scores as rated by teachers. In addition, the boys' arrest records were cross-tabulated and subjected to a chi-square test ($\chi^2 = 5.2$, $p < .03$). More study boys (28%) had police records than did friends (12%), but 72% of the dyads were similar in arrest status. It is noteworthy in these analyses that the level of covariation in adjustment status between the two boys was not influenced by monomethod bias (Cook & Campbell, 1979). Ratings for the two boys were derived from different reporting agents in all cases.

As one might expect from interaction literature (Cairns, 1979), the boys' performance on each of the four behavior clusters was highly correlated. Significant correlations ($p < .001$) were found for each of the microsocial behavior clusters, with coefficients ranging from .45 to .69. Given this level of correlation among the two boys' behavior in the peer interaction task, it seems reasonable to consider their behavior as a dyadic process rather than as independent individual behavior. Thus, when looking at predictive validity, we considered the dyad rate-per-minute of

TABLE 3   CORRELATIONS BETWEEN STUDY BOYS AND FRIENDS ON PROBLEM BEHAVIOR, MICRO-SOCIAL EXCHANGE PATTERNS, AND DEMOGRAPHIC DATA

Measurements	Correlation
Macro-social:	
Antisocial construct score	.410***
Relationship satisfaction	.330***
Social preference	.205**
Micro-social:	
Rates-per-minute:	
Directives	.446***
Converse	.687***
Positive engagement	.629***
Negative engagement	.571***
Demographics:	
Family income	.237***

*$p < .05$.
**$p < .01$.
***$p < .001$.

Negative Engagement, Positive Engagement, Converse, and Directives as described above. The zero-order correlation between the dyad's level of antisocial behavior ($r = -.36$) and relationship satisfaction certainly suggests that deviant peer relationships are somewhat compromised. Antisocial behavior was also correlated with the other social characteristics of the boys (see Table 4). Teacher ratings of social preference of the study boy and his friends correlated negatively with the dyad's antisocial behavior ($-.40$ and $-.22$. respectively) and positively with relationship satisfaction (.29) reported by the study boy.

The most telling measure of the quality of the boys' friendship was the outcome as determined 1 year later. In the next assessment wave, they were asked whether their friendship had ended on an unfriendly basis, drifted apart, ended for other reasons (nonvolitional), stayed the same, or improved (they had become better friends). The means and standard deviations for the boys' relationship satisfaction and antisocial behavior are provided in Table 2. A MANOVA analysis revealed that the 1-year outcome covaried with dyadic antisocial behavior and relationship quality (Wilks's lambda = .87, $p < .002$). Analysis of univariate effects showed that antisocial behavior, $F(4, 172) = 5.04$, $p < .001$, and relationship satisfaction, $F(4, 172) = 2.98$, $p < .03$, were independently prognostic of the course of the friendship. Scheffé post hoc comparisons did not confirm the impres-

TABLE 4 FRIENDSHIP CHARACTERISTICS, ANTISOCIAL BEHAVIOR, AND RELATIONSHIP SATISFACTION

	Dyad Antisocial	Dyad Relationship Satisfaction
Years as friends	−.137*	−.076
Social preference:		
Study boy	−.399***	.292***
Friend	−.215**	.100
Microsocial behavior:		
Negative engagement	.091	−.212**
Positive engagement	.016	.090
Directives	.328***	−.156*
Converse	−.073	.074
Coder impressions:		
Social skills	−.213**	.266***
Noxious behavior	.284***	−.212**

*$p < .05.$
**$p < .01.$
***$p < .001.$

sions that those friendships that ended on an unfriendly basis were marked by the lowest relationship satisfaction and the highest antisocial behavior of all groups, but mean differences were in this direction. This finding suggests that the friendships of antisocial boys tend to be of shorter duration, which may be an outcome of their interactive styles—the question to which we now turn.

INTERACTIONAL PROCESS

Direct observations provide a more detailed and objective picture of the boys' relationships. The extent to which there was a correlation between the boys' antisocial behavior and interactions with their friends was assessed by examining the rate-per-minute of Negative Engagements, Positive Engagements, Directives, and Converse. Generally speaking, the level of covariation was modest (see Table 4). It should be noted that predictive validity did not improve appreciably when considering the correlations of the dyad antisocial scores with those of individual boys. The boys' tendency to give commands was most correlated with their antisocial behavior ($r = .33$). Coder impressions of dyadic social skills and noxious behavior were also reliably correlated with the boys' antisocial behavior. The rate-per-minute of Negative Engagement and Directives were correlated nega-

tively with relationship satisfaction, although there was no statistically reliable correlation between positive engagement and, conversely, with overall relationship satisfaction. Clearly, it was the abrasive behavior within friendships that compromised relationship quality, with positive interpersonal behavior showing no predictive validity.

The sequential patterns of the boys in their friendships were also analyzed. Consistent with the dyadic focus, we combined the two boys' behaviors to create "bidirectional nonparallel streams" (Wampold, 1989), referring to decision rules regarding computation of dyadic sequential structure. For example, in computing the sequence "Converse (antecedent) to Positive Engagement (consequence)," we considered either the boy or his friend as providing the antecedent. Nonparallel refers to the fact that we considered the following two interactions as operate sequences: "Converse to Positive Engagement" and "Positive Engagement to Converse."

The advantage of an Allison-Liker Z score is that the distributions are such that a Z score of 1.96 reflects a statistically significant contingency between an antecedent and a consequence sequence. This can be interpreted at the individual or group level (Gottman & Roy, 1990).

In general, little covariation was found between the strength of these sequential patterns and the boys' antisocial behavior and relationship satisfaction. Only the Positive Engagement to Negative Engagement score was correlated with dyadic antisocial construct scores ($r = −.17$, $p < .02$). As one might suspect, the positive reciprocity sequential score was positively correlated with relationship satisfaction ($r = −.17$, $p < .002$).

To further investigate the relation between interaction patterns and antisocial behaviors, a subsample of highly antisocial dyads was compared to a subsample of the well-adjusted dyads. For this analysis, there was a concern for developing distinctive, homogeneous groups. High antisocial dyads ($n = 9$) were selected as those dyads where both the study boy and his friend had an official police contact, and their antisocial constructs scores were above the mean. The selected low antisocial dyads ($n = 9$) were ones in which neither boy had a police contact, and they were the lowest ranking of this dyad type in terms of antisocial behavior. Using these criteria, two groups of nine dyads were selected for additional sequential analysis.

When considering these aggregated groups (Fig. 1), we again found that there were more similarities than differences. Both groups showed significant sequential contingencies (see Z scores in Fig. 1) on Converse and Positive Engagement reciprocity. Consistent with many studies of social interaction (Cairns, 1979), these interactions were carried by the boys' recipro-

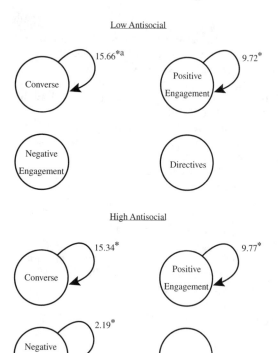

Low Antisocial

High Antisocial

⤴ Reciprocity transitions (e.g., Converse →Converse)

[a]Allison and Liker Z scores representing a significant sequential category.

*$p < .05$

FIGURE 1

The sequential structure of interpersonal process in high and low antisocial dyads.

cating, facilitative behavior. Since Directives were quite low in base rate, we found no reciprocity (Z score = 2.19, $p < .05$) in Directives. The only difference between the two groups was that the high antisocial dyads showed significant negative reciprocity, whereas the well-adjusted dyads did not reciprocate negative behavior. However, the high antisocial dyads did. The finding is consistent with the coercion model, which emphasizes the role of negative reciprocity within families as an etiological factor.

DISCUSSION

Considering these findings with those of previous studies, it appears that a multitude of factors may account for establishing friendship clusters, including geographical proximity, activity involvement, homophily, rejection by school peers, and academic fail-

ure. In addition, families with similar demographic characteristics tend to live within the same neighborhoods (Lewis, 1978). In this sense, some of the commonality observed within these friendship dyads is probably due to broader community or societal factors that influences families.

The majority of peer relations studies conducted to date have focused on school-based networks. Attention to broader community networks and social influences is needed, as friends who meet in school and organized activities are less at risk for problematic behavior. Research is needed that seeks out person-context-process interactions on how children get selected into peer networks (Bronfenbrenner, 1989). In order to accomplish these studies, we need to study children's peer relations across multiple contexts that include not only school but also neighborhoods, organized activities, and unsupervised community settings (e. g., Steinberg & Silverberg, 1986). In this way, we can better understand which children end up in settings that detract from or enhance their social trajectories, as well as the interpersonal processes that explain these various outcomes.

The data in this report corroborate some assumptions about the societal cost of child antisocial affiliations and underscore the need for studying interpersonal process. The relationships of antisocial dyads were somewhat low in quality, of relatively short duration, were perceived by the boys as marginally satisfactory, and tended to end acrimoniously. Consistent with Giordano's findings (Giordano et al., 1986), it was not the lack of positive behaviors that accounted for compromised relationship quality, but rather the presence of bossiness and coercive behavior. Thus, antisocial friendships provided another context within which to practice coercion. Although friendships and marriages are a world apart, one cannot help comparing these findings with those from the marital interaction literature, where it is the presence of coercion (i.e., negative reciprocity) that places a couple into the qualitative state of "distressed" and heading for divorce (Gottman, 1979). Similarities in findings with regard to the disruptive effect of coercion on parent–child, child–child, and husband–wife interactions suggest that the ethnological framework (e.g., Hinde, 1989) for relationships has considerable merit. Studies of interpersonal processes within close relationships reveal similarities in maladaptive patterns. However, at the level of the individual, it is clear that each relationship has a "life of its own." For example, Andrews and Dishion (1994) found that for these boys, negative reciprocity within the friendship was uncorrelated with the same sequential pattern in the parent–child relationship. However, simply summing the level of negative reciprocity across relationships and time was the best predictor of the boy's overall level of antisocial behavior. In this sense, children's socioemotional adjustment is embedded within a matrix of relationship adaptations (Hinde, 1989). Antisocial behavior cannot be fully understood by considering any individual relationship process in a single context (Bronfenbrenner, 1989).

We found that coder impressions of the boys' noxious behavior and lack of social skill were correlated with the boys' antisocial behavior, much more than "objective" behavior counts of the direct observations. Cairns and Green (1979) discussed the relative advantages and disadvantages of "macro" ratings versus "micro" behavioral observation. As evidenced in this report and in research by Panella and Henggeler (1986), global ratings provide better predictive validity, since they are more sensitive to the nuances of context and delivery that contribute to the interpretation of any specific interpersonal act. For example, micro-social coding typically ignores the topic content and congruence of the interaction. However, micro-social coding provides information on duration and sequence which allows the study of interpersonal processes. For example, sequential analysis of the antisocial versus well-adjusted dyads revealed that the structure of the interchanges within the two homogeneous groups was different in respect to negative reciprocity. This level of analysis is not possible in less expensive global ratings but is essential for a process-oriented developmental theory (Patterson, 1982).

These data challenge conventional notions about the intervention needs of antisocial youth. It does not appear that they have deficits in positive behavior with their friends. Although coder impressions indicated social skill deficits, it is conceivable that the coder attributions may be based on the boys' abrasive behavior and/or the discussion of inappropriate or antisocial topics. In this respect, it seems that clinical interventions might focus on the following: (a) reduce their tendency to reciprocate in kind to a negative behavior, and (b) improve their skills at negotiating control within close relationships.

Scanning the ecology of these boys' lives, however, suggests that caution is in order before concluding that such interventions would provide the royal road to good adjustment (Berndt, 1992). At the onset of adolescence, antisocial boys tend to coalesce into antisocial peer groups (Dishion et al., 1991). Thus, it is conceivable that improving the friendships of some of these youngsters may result in deviant peer networks that are more satisfactory, more stable, and perhaps more maladaptive in the long run. On the other hand, improving their performance in relationships early in development might promote friendships with prosocially skilled peers.

This study focuses on friendships among young adolescent males who are primarily European-American and live within a suburban, metropolitan area. The findings cannot be generalized, at this time, to other ethnic groups, community settings, or to the friendship characteristics of girls and their antisocial behavior. As discussed above, there is a clear need to increase research on multiethnic families living in diverse areas, which include inner-city settings (Rutter, 1978), to fully clarify the impact of the ecology of the developmental processes that leads to antisocial behavior (Dishion, French, & Patterson, 1995).

REFERENCES

Achenbach, T. M., & Edelbrock, C. (1986). *Manual for the teacher's report form and teacher version of the Child Behavior Profile.* Burlington: University of Vermont Press.

Allison, P. D., & Liker, J. K. (1982). Analyzing sequential categorical data on dyadic interaction: Comment on Gottman. *Psychological Bulletin, 91,* 393–403.

Andrews, D. W., & Dishion, T. J. (1994). The microsocial structure underpinnings of adolescent problem behavior. In M. Lamb & R. Ketterlinus (Eds.), *Adolescent problem behavior* (pp. 187–207). Hillsdale, NJ: Erlbaum.

Austin, A. M. B., & Draper, D. C. (1984). Verbal interactions of popular and rejected children with their friends and non-friends. *Child Study Journal, 14,* 309–323.

Berndt, T. (1992, March). *Stability in friendships: How much, for which adolescents, and why does it matter?* Paper presented at the biennial meeting of the Society for Research in Adolescence, Washington, DC.

Bronfenbrenner, U. (Ed.). (1989). Ecological systems theory. In P. Vasta (Ed.), *Annals of child development: Vol. 6. Six theories of child development: Revised formulations and current issues* (pp. 187–249). London: JAI.

Cairns, R. B. (1979). *The analysis of social interaction: Methods, issues, and illustrations.* Hillsdale, NJ: Erlbaum.

Cairns, R. B., & Cairns B. D. (1991). Social cognition and social networks: A developmental and treatment of childhood aggression. In D. J. Pepler & K. H. Rubin (Eds.), *The development and treatment of childhood aggression* (pp. 249–278). Hillsdale, NJ: Erlbaum.

Cairns, R. B., Cairns, B. D., Neckerman, H. J., Gest, S. D., & Gariepy, J. L. (1988). Social networks and aggressive behavior: Peer support or peer rejection. *Developmental Psychology, 24,* 815–823.

Cairns, R. B., & Green, J. A. (1979). How to assess personality and social patterns: Observations or ratings? In R. B. Cairns (Ed.), *The analysis of social interaction: Methods, issues, and illustrations* (pp. 213–230). Hillsdale, NJ: Erlbaum.

Capaldi, D., & Patterson, G. R. (1987). An approach to the problem of recruitment and retention rates for longitudinal research. *Behavioral Assessment, 9,* 169–177.

Cohen, J. A. (1960). A coefficient of agreement for nominal scales. *Educational and Psychological Measurement, 20,* 37–46.

Coie, J. D., Dodge, K. A., & Coppotelli, H. (1982). Dimensions and types of social status: A cross-age perspective. *Developmental Psychology, 18,* 557–570.

Coie, J. D., & Kupersmidt, J. B. (1983). A behavioral analysis of emerging social status in boys' groups. *Child Development,* 54, 1400–1416.

Cook, T. D., & Campbell, D. T. (1979). *Quasi-experimentation: Design and analysis issues for field settings.* Boston: Houghton Mifflin.

Cronbach, L. J. (1951). Coefficient alpha and the internal structure of tests. *Psychometrika,* 16, 297–334.

Dishion, T. J. (1990). Peer context of troublesome behavior in children and adolescents. In P. Leone (Ed.), *Understanding troubled and troublesome youth* (pp. 128–153). Beverly Hills, CA: Sage.

Dishion, T. J., Crosby, L., Rusby, J. C., Shane, D., Patterson, G. R., & Baker, J. (1989). *Peer process code: Multidimensional system for observing adolescent peer interaction.* Unpublished manual. Available from the Oregon Social Learning Center, 207 East Fifth Avenue, Suite 202, Eugene, OR 97401.

Dishion, T. J., French, D., & Patterson, G. R. (1995). The development and ecology of child antisocial behavior. In D. Cicchetti & D. Cohen (Eds.), *Developmental psychopathology, Vol. 2.* (pp. 421–471) New York: Wiley.

Dishion, T. J., Patterson, G. R., Stoolmiller, M., & Skinner, M. (1991). Family, school, and behavioral antecedents to early adolescent involvement with antisocial peers. *Developmental Psychology,* 27, 172–180.

Dodge, K. A. (1983). Behavioral antecedents: A peer social status. *Child Development,* 54, 1386–1399.

Elliott, D. S., Huizinga, D., & Ageton, S. S. (1985). *Explaining delinquency and drug use.* Beverly Hills, CA: Sage.

Farrington, D. P. (1978). The family backgrounds of aggressive youths. In L. A. Herson, M. Berger, & D. Shaffer (Eds.), *Aggression and antisocial behavior in childhood and adolescence* (pp. 73–93). Oxford: Pergamon.

Gardner, F.M. (1989). Inconsistent parenting: Is there evidence for a link with children's conduct problems? *Journal of Abnormal Child Psychology,* 17, 223–233.

Giordano, P. C., Cernkovich, S. A., & Pugh, M. D. (1986). Friendships and delinquency. *American Journal of Sociology,* 91, 1170–1202.

Gottman, J. M. (1979). *Marital interaction: Experimental investigations.* New York: Academic Press.

Gottman, J. M., & Roy, A. K. (1990). *Sequential analysis: A guide for behavioral researchers.* Cambridge: Cambridge University Press.

Hartup, W. W. (1983). Peer relations. In E. M. Hetherington (Ed.), P. H. Mussen (Series Ed.), *Handbook of child psychology: Vol. 4. Socialization, personality, and social development* (pp. 104–196). New York: Wiley.

Hinde, R. A. (1989). Ethological and relationship approaches. In R. Vasta (Ed.), *Annals of child development: Vol. 6. Six theories of child development: Revised formulations and current issues* (pp. 251–285). Hillsdale, NJ: Erlbaum.

Hinde, R. A., & Stevenson-Hinde, J. (1986). Relating childhood relationships to individual characteristics. In W. Hartup & Z. Rubin (Eds.), *Relationships and development* (pp. 71–89). Hillsdale, NJ: Erlbaum.

Hollingshead. A. B. (1975). *Four-Factor Index of Social Status.* Unpublished manuscript, Department of Sociology, Yale University, New Haven, CT.

Kandel, D. B. (1973). Adolescent marijuana use: Role of parents and peers. *Science,* 181, 1067–1081.

Kandel, D. B. (1978). Homophily, selection, and socialization in adolescent friendships. *American Journal of Sociology, 84,* 427–436.

Kandel, D.B. (1986). Process of peer influence on adolescence. In R. K. Silbereisen (Ed.), *Development as action in context* (pp, 33–52). Berlin: Springer Verlag.

Kellam. S. (1990). Developmental epidemiological framework for family research on depression and aggression. In G. R. Patterson (Ed.), *Depression and aggression in family interaction* (pp. 11–48). Hillsdale, NJ: Erlbaum.

Kenny, D. A. (1988). Interpersonal perception: A social relations analysis. *Journal of Social and Personal Relationships,* 5, 247–261.

Ladd, G. W. (1983). Social networks of popular, average, and rejected children in school settings. *Merrill-Palmer Quarterly,* 29, 283–307.

Lathrop, M., Dishion, T. J., & Capaldi, D. (1987). *Friendship quality questionnaire.* Unpublished instrument. Eugene: Oregon Social Learning Center.

Lewis, M. S. (1978). Nearest neighbor analysis of epidemiological and community variables. *Psychological Bulletin,* 85, 1302–1308.

McCord, W., McCord, J., & Howard, A. (1969). Family interaction as antecedent to the direction of male aggressiveness. *Journal of Abnormal and Social Psychology,* 66, 239–242.

Panella, D., & Henggeler, S. W. (1986). Peer interactions of conduct-disordered, anxious-withdrawn, and well-adjusted black adolescents. *Journal of Abnormal Child Psychology,* 14, 1–11.

Parke, R., & Bhavnagri, N. P. (1988). Parents as managers of children's peer relationships. In D. Belle (Ed.), *Children's social networks and social supports.* New York: Wiley.

Parker J. G., & Asher, S. R. (1989, April). *Peer relations and social adjustment: Are friendship and group acceptance distinct domains?* Paper presented at the biennial meeting of the Society for Research in Child Development, Kansas City, MO.

Patterson, G. R. (1982). *Coercive family process.* Eugene, OR: Castalia.

Patterson, G. R. (1986). Maternal rejection: Determinant or product for deviant child behavior? In W. Hartup & Z. Rubin (Eds.), *Relationships and development* (pp. 73–94). Hillsdale, NJ: Erlbaum.

Patterson, G. R., & Bank, L. (1985). Bootstrapping your way in the nomological thicket. *Behavioral Assessment,* 8, 49–73.

Patterson, G. R., Reid, J. B., & Dishion, T. J. (1992). *Antisocial boys.* Eugene, OR: Castalia.

Putallaz, M., & Gottman, J. M. (1979). Social skills and group acceptance. In S. R. Asher & J. M. Gottman (Eds.), *The development of children's friendships.* Cambridge: Cambridge University Press.

Raush, H. L. (1965). Interaction sequences. *Journal of Personality and Social Psychology, 2,* 487–499.

Rutter, M. (1978). Family, area, and school influences in the genesis of conduct disorders. In L. A. Hersov, M. Berger, & D. Shaffer (Eds.), *Aggression and antisocial behavior in childhood and adolescence* (pp. 95–114). New York: Pergamon.

Simcha-Fagan, O., & Schwartz, J. E. (1986). Neighborhood and delinquency: An assessment of contextual effects. *Criminology, 24,* 667–703.

Steinberg, L., & Silverberg, S. B. (1986). The vicissitudes of autonomy in early adolescence. *Child Development, 57,* 841–851.

Sullivan, H. S. (1953). *The interpersonal theory of psychiatry.* New York: Norton.

Wampold, B. E., (1989). Kappa as a measure of pattern in sequential data. *Quality and Quantity, 22,* 19–35.

Youniss, J. (1980). *Parents and peers in social development: A Sullivan-Piagetian perspective.* Chicago: University of Chicago Press.

QUESTIONS

1. With whom do antisocial adolescent boys tend to socialize, and what explanations are offered for their choice of friends?
2. What types of parenting practices are associated with antisocial behavior in youth?
3. What are coercive behaviors, and how do they contribute to the development of antisocial behavior?
4. How are the coercive behavior patterns learned at home evident in the friendship patterns of antisocial youth?
5. How might antisocial behavior interfere with the development of social skills?
6. How do antisocial adolescent boys choose their friends, and what types of peers do they tend choose as friends?
7. How satisfied are antisocial boys with their friendships? Does this finding surprise you?
8. What differences were found in the interaction patterns of the pairs of highly antisocial friends and the pairs of well-adjusted friends?
9. Do you think these behavioral styles characterize all the relationships of antisocial boys, or are they restricted to their close friendships?
10. What do this study's results suggest regarding an appropriate and effective intervention program for antisocial boys?

---

37 What Do Adolescents Need for Healthy Development?: Implications for Youth Policy

JODIE ROTH · JEANNE BROOKS-GUNN

Research and policy statements regarding adolescent development are often problem-oriented, stating or implying that one of the main purposes of programs aimed at adolescents is simply to keep them out of trouble. Not only is this negative bias inaccurate (research does not support the assumption that all or even the majority of adolescents have or cause problems); it also ignores two of the principal features of adolescence: (1) adolescents are extraordinarily capable (after all, the many cognitive, social, and emotional advances made in infancy and childhood come to fruition during adolescence) and (2) adolescents are on the verge of taking on the huge set of responsibilities that come with adulthood, although they still have much to learn.

In the following article, Jodie Roth and Jeanne Brooks-Gunn discuss four questions: What do adolescents need to develop successfully? How do adolescents meet the challenges unique to this period of development? How do the settings in which adolescents live contribute to their healthy development? And what types of programs can and should be developed that will promote positive youth development? Roth and Brooks-Gunn cover many facets of adolescent experience: the family, the peer group, the school, and the workplace. Adolescents rely on positive experiences in each of these settings to develop the complex set of dispositions and skills that underlie psychological well-being.

This article concludes with a poignant discussion that is introduced by a disturbingly apt and deeply troubling question: Is there a war on teenagers? Despite all the psychological research as well as first-person testimonials from parents, teachers, and others who work with youth, our society emphasizes and inflates the negative aspects of this period of development. No one believes that preventive programs should not be made available for youth whenever they are needed. But it is important in the midst of these efforts that societal resources also be committed to supporting and promoting the positive side of youth and its development.

National interest in how youth develop in healthy ways and how we can facilitate this process has intensified in recent years. This Social Policy Report summarizes what we know about healthy adolescent development and what this knowledge means for our ability to improve the lives of youth by raising and answering three questions.

1. What do adolescents need to develop successfully? Successful adolescent development includes the promotion of positive as well as prevention of negative actions, feelings, and thoughts. This can be done through the opportunities and supports, or assets, offered in families, schools, and communities.

Reprinted by permission of the Society for Research in Child Development from Roth, J., & Brooks-Gunn, J. (2000). What do adolescents need for healthy development? *Social Policy Report, XIV*, 3–19.
Support for this paper came from the Robert Wood Johnson Foundation. Additional support was provided by the U. S. Department of Education, Office of Educational Research and Improvement. We would also like to thank the NICHD Research Network on Child and Family Wellbeing for their support and the Lilly Endowment Program on Youth and Caring for their leadership. We are grateful for the guidance and support of our collaborators, William Foster and Lawrence Murray from the National Center on Addiction and Substance Abuse at Columbia University. The insights from Ruby Takanishi and Joy Dryfoos are also appreciated. We would like to thank Rebecca Fauth for her assistance with the preparation of this manuscript.

2. How do the settings in which adolescents live, study, and play enhance (and, in cases, impede) their wellbeing? The research on the often overlapping worlds of the teenager—the family, peer group, school, work, and neighborhood settings—shows the influence of these different settings. The important aspects of the family setting are characterized by TLC.

TIME,

LIMIT setting, Listening, and Laughter

CONNECTEDNESS/Caring and Communication.

The influence of the peer group lies in FRIENDs, offering opportunities for

FRIENDSHIP, risks for not

RESISTING negative influences, chances for developing shared or new

INTERESTS,

EXAMPLES of different attitudes and behaviors (and their consequences), the influential power in

NUMBERS, and the danger of associating with

DEVIANT youth.

The ABC's of the school world include the importance of a developmentally

APPROPRIATE school environment for youth, particularly young adolescents, the influence of the

BEHAVIOR of others in the school, and the powerful role of

CONNECTION, to the institution of school as well as to teachers and other students.

The ideal adolescent WORKplace would offer youth the chance to

WIDEN their horizons, particularly in terms of future careers, develop

ORGANIZATIONAL skills, learn about

RESPONSIBILITY, and gain valuable

KNOWLEDGE.

Neighborhoods impact youth behavior and emotions through their

Place, Space, and Face.

3. What are the implications of what we know about the worlds of adolescents for the development of youth programs? Beneficial youth programs promote successful adolescent development by creating opportunities and supports influential in youths' worlds. Successful programs mimic successful families and schools by providing TLC and ABC's, encourage the benefits of FRIENDs while helping participants avoid their harm, and structure activities to capture the best of teen WORKplaces. Community-wide efforts to enhance youths' lives rest on the recognition of the important intersection of the Place, Space, and Face of neighborhoods.

Successful programs view adolescents as resources to be developed. We as a nation cannot hope to pro-

mote the healthy development of all our youth without a change in Americans' negative views towards adolescents.

ADOLESCENT HEALTH AS A NATIONAL CONCERN

The national initiative *Healthy People 2000* (U.S. Department of Health and Human Services, 1991) spurred a serious discussion as to how to help our nation's youth navigate the transition from adolescence to adulthood without engaging in unhealthy and risky behaviors. Throughout the past decade, scholars, policy makers, and practitioners have been asking how youth develop in healthy ways and how this process may be facilitated (e.g., Carnegie Council on Adolescent Development, 1989, 1994, 1996). Indeed, interest in these topics has intensified in recent years, as witnessed by the *Healthy People 2010* initiative (U.S. Department of Health and Human Services, 2000) and the first ever White House Conference on Teenagers held in May, 2000.

This social policy report summarizes research on adolescents to address four questions about helping youth grow into adulthood. First, what are the ingredients for successful adolescent development? In a nutshell, adolescents who are merely problem-free are not fully prepared for their future (Pittman, 1991). Second, what are some of the special challenges of adolescence and how do youth negotiate transitions at this time of life? Third, since adolescents' lives are touched by family, friends, school, work, and community, what do we know about how these spheres influence their development? Fourth, what are the implications of these findings for designing and implementing youth programs that are beneficial and appealing for adolescents? We provide recommendations for altering perceptions of teenagers in communities in the last section, in order to stress promoting the positive, not just preventing the problems (Moore & Halle, 2000).

WHAT ARE THE INGREDIENTS FOR SUCCESSFUL ADOLESCENT DEVELOPMENT?

Generally speaking, positive (successful) youth development encompasses all our hopes and aspirations for a nation of healthy, happy and competent adolescents on their way to productive and satisfying adulthoods. Scholars at research and policy centers, on national committees, in the government, at foundations, and in youth programs have reached general consensus on what constitutes healthy development.

Lerner, Fisher, and Weinberg (2000) summarize the ingredients into the "five C's" (p. 15). These positive attributes encompass: **competence** in academic, social, and vocational areas; **confidence** or a positive self identity; **connection** or healthy relations to community, family, and peers; **character** or positive values, integrity, moral commitment; and **caring** and compassion. The focus is on wellbeing, rather than just on problems.

Promoting the positive also is replacing preventing the negative in youth programming. The work of the Search Institute in Minneapolis, Minnesota, has propelled this paradigm shift by providing concrete descriptions of the assets necessary for positive development. Benson (1997) describes the 40 internal and external assets believed, based on literature reviews and survey data, to be the universal building blocks of positive development. He defines positive development rather generally, based on the absence of negative outcomes, as the engagement in prosocial behaviors and avoidance of health-compromising and future-jeopardizing behaviors (suggesting the importance of including promotion and prevention in our program effort).

The 20 external assets envelop youth with familial and extra-familial networks that provide support, empowerment, boundaries and expectations, and constructive use of time. The 20 internal assets serve to nurture, within individuals, positive commitments, values, and identities, as well as social competencies. The external assets describe the necessary ingredients in youths' environment for positive development. The internal assets illustrate personal qualities which encourage positive development.

Much of this work rests on the findings from research investigating which events cause adolescents to follow different pathways, and what factors can alter the trajectory of both healthy and risky behaviors. That is, do risk and protective factors interact to facilitate or hinder healthy adolescent development (e.g., Werner & Smith, 1992)? Along these lines, the co-occurrence of health-compromising behaviors and risky lifestyles are also studied in terms of barriers to wellbeing (e.g., Jessor, 1993).

Other scholars focus on how different facets of personality, such as creativity, humor, honesty, hope, and tolerance develop and impact adolescents' preparation for adulthood (Moore, Evans, Brooks-Gunn, & Roth, 2001). The goal of this type of research is to develop ways to measure our progress as a nation in achieving positive youth outcomes. This effort stands in contrast to our current tracking of undesired outcomes, such as school dropout or teenage pregnancy (Annie E. Casey Foundation, 1999).

The emergence of youth development programs incorporates this shift into practice. Youth development programs go beyond traditional prevention or intervention programs by stressing skill and competency development rather than focusing on preventing specific problem behaviors. These programs strive to influence an adolescent's developmental path toward positive outcomes. Although no consensus exists as to exactly what constitutes a youth development program, they are best characterized by their approach to youth as resources to be developed rather than as problems to be managed, and their efforts to help youth become healthy, happy, and productive by increasing exposure to external assets, opportunities, and supports (Pittman, 1991; Roth, Brooks-Gunn, Murray, & Foster, 1998). This shift does not exclude prevention efforts. Instead, it recognizes that preventing problem behaviors does not necessarily equip adolescents with the tools for a responsible and productive adulthood (Quinn, 1999).

WHAT ARE THE CHALLENGES OF THE ADOLESCENT YEARS?

Adolescence, a time of bodily changes, expanding independence, and growing self-discovery, is sometimes characterized as a series of challenges. Each challenge carries the possibility of risk, opportunity, or both. Scholars of adolescent development refer to these challenges as developmental transitions, or critical junctures along the path that connects children to their transformed physical, mental, and social adult selves (Graber, Brooks-Gunn, & Petersen, 1996; Schulenberg, Maggs, & Hurrelmann, 1997). Each transition requires some change in adolescents' roles, how they make sense of themselves and their world, and how others view them. Despite the multiple physical changes and social challenges facing adolescents, it would be misleading to view adolescence as a time of total upheaval.

Contrary to popular opinion, the vast majority of youth emerge from the second decade of life without lasting problems. Most individuals navigate transitions equipped with the competencies needed to meet new challenges and take on new roles while further developing the skills necessary for these new roles (Graber et al., 1996). However, many do not enter adulthood with all of the competencies they will need. Individual differences in the experience or negotiation of a transition are associated with development prior to the transition, timing of the transition, the individual's experience of the transition, and the context in which the transition occurs (Rutter, 1989). The numerous changes during adolescence appear to be overwhelming only for some adolescents—those with less optimal peer and family relationships, poorer coping skills, and academic difficulties during middle childhood (Feldman & Elliot, 1990; Lerner et al., 1996; Paikoff & Brooks-Gunn,

1991). Thus, circumstances from different environments—the family, peers, school—impact adolescents' preparation for, and success at, navigating the transitions inherent in their development.

WHAT IS KNOWN ABOUT THE MULTIPLE WORLDS OF ADOLESCENCE?

Children and youth live in various overlapping worlds—family, peers, school, workplace, neighborhood, community, region, and country. These worlds shape a youth's development through sustained, consistent, intersecting interactions (or lack of) with the adolescent (Bronfenbrenner & Morris, 1998). We know a lot about the worlds of the family and school, but less about the neighborhood or community. How these worlds support or clash with one another as youth move among them is not very well understood. There is growing interest in how a *particular* type of family, school, or community influences adolescents (development within distinctive ecological niches, such as the inner city). In addition, there is an expanding literature specifically relating contextual influences to health-related behavior (Jessor, 1998; Millstein, Petersen, & Nightingale, 1993; Schulenberg et al., 1997). This literature describes how individuals and circumstances within the different contexts can serve as either opportunities or barriers to health-related behaviors.

We briefly review what is known about these worlds as places that support and sometimes thwart the wellbeing of youth. Recent attention to the influence of youth programs on development suggests that they too should be viewed as one of the many worlds of adolescents' development (Larson, 2000). Thus, we also show how these findings may be applied to improving youth programs as a context for positive lives. To highlight the most salient characteristics within settings, we attach a (hopefully) memorable phrase for each. For the family, it is TLC; for the peers, it is FRIENDS; for the school setting, it is the ABC's; for the workplace, it is WORK; and for the neighborhood setting, it is Place, Space, and Face.

TLC FROM THE FAMILY

Contrary to popular belief, the importance of the family does not disappear during adolescence. Families provide their children with TLC, which is more than tender loving care. In our scheme, it is TIME, LIMIT SETTING, and CONNECTEDNESS/CARING. The research consistently shows how families influence their adolescents' developmental paths through the provision, or lack, of TLC.

Time Demographic changes in American families, such as increased maternal employment and single parenthood, has lead to a decrease in the amount of time youth spend with their parents, particularly in the after-school hours (Hofferth & Sandberg, 1998). In addition, increased autonomy, including more unsupervised time alone and with peers, is viewed as developmentally appropriate in American society. This time fosters independence, provides opportunities for self-sufficiency, and develops a sense of efficacy (Collins, 1990). In one study, the percentage of their waking hours that white adolescents spent with families fell from 33% to 14% between 5th and 12th grades (Larson, Richards, Moneta, Holmbeck, & Duckett, 1996).

The effects for adolescents of spending less time with their family depend on what they are doing during that time. The negative effects of unsupervised time, particularly with peers, has been emphasized by the widely publicized FBI statistics that violent juvenile crime peaks on weekdays between the hours of two and eight o'clock (Sickmund, Snyder, & Poe-Yamagata, 1997). Time away from parents provides increased opportunity for experimentation in other health-compromising behaviors as well. Data from the National Longitudinal Study on Adolescent Health, a study of a nationally representative (cross-sectional) sample of over 12,000 7th through 12th graders, presented at the White House Conference on Teenagers, used the frequency of family meals as a proxy for time with parents. Youth who did not eat dinner with a parent five or more days a week showed dramatically higher rates of smoking, drinking, marijuana use, getting into fights, and initiation of sexual activity (Council of Economic Advisors, 2000). These trends are behind recent government initiatives to create more constructive activities for youth during the non-school hours.

The implications for youth programs are clear. Programs that offer only limited contact with adolescents cannot expect to alter behavior. In our review of 15 methodologically sound evaluations of community-based programs for at-risk youth, we found that longer-term, more intensive programs that engage youth throughout adolescence appear to be the most effective (Roth et al., 1998). Not surprisingly, spending time with adolescents is necessary to develop a trusting relationship. The importance of such a relationship is discussed below in the section on connection.

Limit Setting Increased autonomy for adolescents does not necessarily mean less supervision than in the childhood years. Supervision and limit setting remain critical. For example, adolescents with less parental supervision show greater susceptibility to peer influences encouraging health-compromising behaviors. Consistent, firm control and monitoring can be provided from a distance. Monitoring can take the form of telephone calls to youth, or conversations with the parents of the youth's friends. Caring and monitoring together seem to result in the least risk-taking in youth (Galambos & Maggs, 1991). These effects may be, in part, the result of youth feeling more comfortable talking to their parents (Kerr & Stattin, 2000). Thus, monitoring through communication is important, not merely strict control.

The level of supervision or parental monitoring necessary for healthy development may differ as a function of adolescents' peer and neighborhood environments. Early research on parent styles (e.g., Baumrind, 1971) found that an authoritative style, defined as democratic, firm, and loving, was the most beneficial for children and adolescents. But, a higher degree of limit setting may be necessary for youth living in dangerous neighborhoods with low community control (Sampson & Morenoff, 1997) and higher levels of problem behavior among peers (Mason, Cauce, Gonzales, & Hiraga, 1996).

The on-site supervision and monitoring that youth programs do provide for adolescents is part of their appeal for parents and community leaders. Successful programs not only engage youth in constructive, competency-building activities, but also set clear rules about expected behavior while at the program (Roth et al., 1998). Additionally, staff at effective programs tend to become actively involved in monitoring participants' behavior, even when they are not at the program site. For example, staff may act as liaisons to the adolescents' school in order to observe participants' performance and behavior, and intervene when necessary.

However, too much supervision, or control, may be counterproductive. Research from the Public/Private Ventures initiative on mentoring found that how mentors approach their role contributed to the longevity of the mentoring relationship. Adolescents in matches lasting a year or longer showed the largest number of improvements. Progressively fewer positive outcomes were found for youth in relationships that ended earlier (Grossman & Rhodes, 2002). Mentors who jumped into the relationship by trying to immediately reform their mentees, making unilateral decisions about the type of activities and relationship, were frequently unable to develop mutually satisfying relationships. Approximately 70% of the matches with these types of mentors met only sporadically and ended within 9 months. On the other hand, matches in which mentors did not attempt to change their mentees, but instead focused on building a trusting relationship by letting youth drive the pace and activities, lasted longer and were more successful. These findings dovetail with the notion that monitoring needs to be coupled with communication and respect, rather than linked with control.

Connectedness   The type of family setting most conducive to healthy development changes from childhood to adolescence. For example, feelings of connectedness, or a close parent–child relationship, are important during the childhood period. Some independence, or separation from parents, is a hallmark of adolescent development. Yet, connectedness remains salient; evidence suggests greater maturity for adolescents whose parents combine separation with connectedness, and increased risk-taking when separation is not coupled with connectedness (Galambos & Ehrenberg, 1997). Family connectedness, defined as feeling close, loved, and understood by one or both parents, was associated with more optimal outcomes for each of the five health-related outcomes studied in the Adolescent Health Study (emotional distress, suicidality, violence, substance use, and sexual behaviors) regardless of race, ethnicity, family structure, or poverty status (Resnick et al., 1997).

Parental connectedness may be more important for some youth than others (for example, younger adolescents and youth with few close friends, Scales & Leffert, 1999). However, the fundamental salience of parental caring appears across all groups of adolescents. Parents' connectedness and involvement with adolescents (aged 14 to 16) may be more associated with better grades and educational expectations than with delinquency and substance use (Herman, Dornbusch, Herron, & Herting, 1997). In contrast, delinquency may be more influenced by limit setting.

The youth program literature also identifies caring adults or relationships as critical. In our review, we identified the adolescent–adult relationship as a critical element of success (Roth et al., 1998). Other compilations of "best practices" reach the same conclusion (Catalano, Berglund, Ryan, Lonczak, & Hawkins, 1999; James & Jurich, 1999). Not surprisingly, the qualities of the adult relationship that appear to be consequential are similar to those in effective families: closeness, communication, monitoring, and engagement in youths' lives. Programs that provide a family-like environment, in which adolescents can feel safe and where caring adults support and empower them to develop their competencies, were judged by adolescents to be the most successful (McLaughlin, 2000).

Although not the only way, many programs match youth with mentors to provide the opportunity for a one-on-one relationship with a supportive adult. Despite their popularity, research on the effectiveness of programmatically supported mentoring relationships is just becoming available. We found only one rigorous evaluation of a mentoring-only program—Big Brothers/Big Sisters (BB/BS). Participants in BB/BS received slightly higher grades, skipped half as many days of school, cut fewer classes, and felt more competent about doing their schoolwork than did youth in the control group. Although BB/BS did not focus on reducing problems, participants were less likely to start using illegal drugs, initiate drug or alcohol use, or engage in violence after 18 months of participation (Tierney, Grossman, & Resch, 1995).

This evaluation provides evidence for the value of caring relationships between adults and youths created and supported by programs. However, the benefits from mentoring programs do not occur automatically. The critical ingredient appears to be the development of trust between two strangers facilitated by the programs' organizational structure. The mentor's initial approach largely determines if this trust is developed or not (see Sipe, 1996).

PEERS AS FRIENDS

As children enter and progress through adolescence, they spend increasing amounts of time with peers and place increasing value on these relationships. The peer group includes both friends of varying closeness and others in their age group with which they interact. Our FRIEND schema captures the many positive and negative ways other youth can influence adolescents' development. The peer group offers opportunities for FRIENDSHIP, risks for not RESISTING negative influences, chances for developing shared or new INTERESTS, EXAMPLES of different attitudes and behaviors (and their consequences), the influential power in NUMBERS, and the danger of associating with DEVIANT youth.

Friendship   Peer influences are commonly believed to powerfully shape adolescents' behavior, perhaps even more so than parents (Harris, 1998). Ample research has documented the role of peers in instigating engagement in such health-compromising behaviors as cigarette smoking (Botvin, Epstein, Schinke, & Diaz, 1994), substance use (Coombs, Paulson, & Richardson, 1991), early sexual activity and pregnancy (Bearman & Bruckner, 1999), and violence (Dishion, Andrews, & Crosby, 1995).* Friendships also promote moral development, coping strategies, increased self-esteem, and assistance in dealing with stressful situations (Hartup & Stevens, 1999; Piaget, 1932/1965). Peer relationships allow adolescents to recognize societal norms, practice defining and sharing leadership roles, and initiate and maintain social bonds (Gottman & Parker, 1987). Regardless of the direction, close and best friends have the greatest influence and are also the most important to adolescents (Berndt, 1996).

Peer influence does not operate as a single force in adolescents' worlds (Collins, Maccoby, Steinberg,

Hetherington, & Bornstein, 2000). Rather, the susceptibility of adolescents to peer influence is determined by several factors. Adolescents with poorer relationships are more influenced by peers (Hartup & Stevens, 1999). In particular, adolescents are influenced more by friends when they experience neglecting or rejecting parental relationships (Dishion, 1990). Adolescent research also suggests that youth who are alienated from conventional groups (e.g., school and family) often establish strong social bonds with antisocial peer groups in order to establish a sense of belonging (see Fuligni & Eccles, 1993). Finally, adolescents who engage in health-compromising behavior perceive, often inaccurately, that their friends' attitudes and behavior match their own. In a number of studies, adolescents assumed more similarity than actually existed between their friends' and their own attitudes toward sexuality (Alan Guttmacher Institute, 1994), use of cigarette smoking and alcohol (Graham, Marks, & Hansen, 1991), and use of illegal drugs (Ianotti & Bush, 1992).

Resistance   Consistent with popular perception, program developers focus on the negative effects of peer pressure. Many successful prevention programs teach youth how to resist peer pressure. For example, the Life Skills Training Program, a classroom-based multimodal cognitive-behavioral approach to alcohol and drug prevention, teaches resistance skills as part of the broader curriculum promoting personal and social competence. Designed for seventh graders, the main emphasis is the development of skills for coping with social influences to smoke, drink, or use drugs (Botvin, Baker, Dusenbury, Tortu, & Botvin, 1990).

Interest   As children move into the adolescent years, friendships become increasingly based on similarity of interests. Youth programs devoted to the pursuit of a particular skill or hobby, such as art or music, provide participants with the opportunity to meet other youth with similar interests and passions. Naturally, not all youth share similar interests. An assortment of activities, either housed within one program or throughout the community, offers participants new opportunities for both friendships and skill development. The goal of this menu of activities would be to foster both the emerging interests and friendships of youth.

In order to avoid falling into the same traps as before, adolescents who are attempting to take a new path may require assistance in establishing a new image among peers (Brown, Dolcini, & Leventhal, 1997). Programs may need to facilitate friendships among youth who would otherwise not interact. This

---

*Research on peer relationships is plagued by methodological shortcomings. Most research examines the amount of similarity among adolescents and their friends. Similarity, however, cannot be used to determine the influence of friends; adolescents frequently choose friends similar to themselves. Thus, we must be cautious about the influence of peers (Brown, 1990).

could be done by providing youth with new opportunities not associated with their prior behavior, such as the chance to do volunteer work.

Numbers   Risky behavior often occurs in clusters, as exemplified by the literature on the effects of neighborhoods on children's development. This research indicates the possibility of a contagion effect. For example, Crane (1991) suggests that tipping points might exist. That is, after a certain proportion of the population engages in a specified behavior, the incidence of the behavior accelerates. The number of professionals residing in a neighborhood can also affect youth. If this number is below a certain threshold, a higher proportion of teenage out-of-wedlock childbearing occurs (Brooks-Gunn, Duncan, Klebanov, & Sealand, 1993). Finally, Sampson and Morenoff (1997) note that when large numbers of youth engage in delinquency, it becomes much more difficult for the usual routes of neighborhood control through informal norm setting and monitoring to be efficacious, leading to an increase in youth delinquency.

Deviance   Parents are perhaps most alarmed by their adolescents' choice of friends when those friends display deviant behaviors. There is little discussion in the literature, however, about the role fellow program-going peers take in influencing other program participants' behavior. Deviant friendships within an intervention program can lead to an escalation in problem behavior (Dishion, McCord, & Paulin, 1999). Peer contact during an intervention offers an opportunity for active reinforcement, through laughter, attention, and interest, for deviant behavior, which is likely to increase such behavior. And, high-risk adolescents derive meaning and values from positive reactions to rule-breaking discussion (called deviancy training), which is more likely to occur within friendships among delinquent youth. These findings have implications for the composition of program participants, especially for programs that target high-risk youth. They suggest that including only high-risk youth may be counterproductive.

THE ABC'S OF SCHOOL

Adolescents consistently spend large periods of time in school, so it is not surprising that what occurs in school has an impact. Our review of the world of school highlights the ABC's of school–the importance of a developmentally APPROPRIATE environment for youth, particularly young adolescents; the influence of the BEHAVIOR of others in the school; and the powerful role of CONNECTION, to the institution of school as well as to teachers and other students.

Appropriate environment   One line of research brings together characteristics of the school environment and the developmental needs of adolescents to explain the decline in academic achievement and increase in social, emotional, and behavioral problems that begin to appear during early adolescence. Eccles and her colleagues (1993) document fewer such changes among students in K–8 schools compared to students attending K–6 schools. They ascribe the detrimental changes to the timing of the switch to a new middle or junior high school. At the same time as most adolescents are experiencing the physical, psychological, and social changes of puberty, they must also begin at a new school. This transition requires young adolescents to adjust to the different demands of a new peer group, new teachers, and new class structure.

Further compounding the problem, students' elementary schools are more aligned with their psychological needs then their new middle or junior high school environment (Eccles et al., 1993). Middle and junior high schools are characterized by increased school size, bureaucratic organization, departmentalization, and decreased individual attention and opportunities for close relationships with teachers compared to elementary schools. In the classroom, middle and junior high school teachers tend to place greater emphasis on teacher control and discipline, provide fewer opportunities for student decision-making, choice, and self-management, and employ more competitive standards for grading and judging competence than teachers in elementary school classes. They also feel less effective as teachers, especially for low-ability students. Thus, at a time when young adolescents need careful monitoring by caring adults and challenging, but safe, opportunities to explore different behaviors and identities, schools offer a less personal, more restrictive, and more competitive environment.

In *Turning Points*, the Carnegie Council on Adolescent Development (1989) called for curricular and structural changes in middle school education. Findings from the Project on High Performance Learning Communities, a network of almost 100 schools involved in restructuring following the Carnegie Council's recommendations, support the importance, and highlight the difficulties, of middle school reform (see Felner et al., 1997). Both the federal government and many foundations are investing heavily in improving schools for at-risk students in the ways discussed above, as well as building bridges between schools and other aspects of adolescents' lives (e.g., Schools of the 21st Century, Beacon Schools; see Dryfoos, 1998 for detailed discussion of recent efforts at "community schools"). Early evaluation results suggest the benefit of such changes for at-risk youth (Robinson, 1993).

Behavior   Faculty, like parents, can serve as role models for health behaviors. For example, Perry, Kelder, and Komro (1993) found lower adolescent smoking rates when faculty smoking in front of students is restricted. This suggests a very simple program, or school policy, that may influence youth behavior.

The behavior of other students sets the tone for the school culture. School safety offers a dramatic, and timely, example of this. When young people feel unsafe or victimized at school due to the behaviors of other students, they are more likely to suffer socially, emotionally, and academically (Scales & Leffert, 1999). How schools deal with both serious violations (possessing alcohol or weapons) as well as minor infractions (using profanity, disturbing the class) impact adolescents' feelings of safety in school (Anderman & Kimweli, 1997).

These findings on the behavior of adults and other students in school apply directly to youth programs. Foremost, how the staff behaves—how they treat participants as well as their health-related actions—shapes the message they send youth about appropriate and acceptable behavior. Feelings of safety are perhaps more salient in programs than in schools since attendance is voluntary. Urban youth particularly place security as the first requirement for a desirable youth program (McLaughlin, 2000). Security applies to the location of the program, transportation to and from the program or related activities, and the expectations for behavior from participants (i.e., no gang colors or weapons).

Connection As in families, the quality of student-teacher relationships also contributes to healthy adolescent behavior. In their longitudinal study of high-risk children, Werner and Smith (1992) found that disadvantaged youth who "beat the odds" found emotional support outside their own families, often in a favorite teacher who became a role model, friend, and confidant. Among participants in the Adolescent Health Study, youth who reported strong emotional attachments to their teachers were less likely to use drugs and alcohol, attempt suicide, engage in violence, or become sexually active at an early age (Resnick et al., 1997). In fact, positive relationships with teachers exerted a stronger influence on adolescents' health-related behaviors than the school structure variables (classroom size, attendance and dropout rates, school type, and amount of teacher training). As with parental relationships, the specifics of fostering a supportive teacher–student relationship may vary for different youth. DuBois, Felner, Meares, and Krier (1994) found an association between high levels of school support and student outcomes (better grades and lower alcohol use) only for youth with multiple disadvantages, such as living in poverty and experiencing family breakup, not for youth without disadvantages.

Adolescents' relationship to school also appears to influence their health-related behavior. Academic achievement and involvement in school-related activities are two ways of measuring adolescents' engagement with school. Research consistently finds that adolescents with poor academic skills and low grades are more likely to engage in health-compromising behaviors (e.g., Dryfoos, 1990). In a 16-year longitudinal study of school adaptation and social development, Cairns and Cairns (1994) found that engagement in extracurricular activities reduced health-compromising behaviors, particularly for students at greatest risk for dropping out. Using national data sets, Zill, Nord, and Loomis (1995) found that after controlling for race and poverty status, tenth graders who reported spending no time in school-sponsored activities were 57% more likely to drop out by senior year, 49% more likely to have used drugs, 37% more likely to become teen parents, 35% more likely to have smoked cigarettes, and 27% more likely to have been arrested compared to students spending one to four hours per week in extracurricular activities. However, involvement in activities did not lower the rates of binge drinking, and involvement in varsity sports actually increased such behavior (see also Eccles & Barber, 1999).

In addition to school reform, the evaluation literature suggests other ways programs can enhance healthy development—by encouraging a strong commitment and connection to school. This typically occurs indirectly through program staff expectations for adolescents' achievement, as well as directly through homework assistance or staff contact with participants' teachers and school personnel (Roth et al., 1998). Additionally, successful programs offer youth the opportunity to develop academic skills through active participation in structured activities that create challenges and provide fulfilling experiences (McLaughlin, 2000).

WORKING IN THE WORKPLACE

Today, almost all youth work at some point during their high school years. Over 70% of the participants in the Monitoring the Future study reported working for pay, and almost half the males and one-third of the females worked more than 20 hours per week (Bachman & Shulenberg, 1993). Despite the public's favorable attitudes towards employment during adolescence, the influence of the workplace on adolescent development remains controversial. The ideal adolescent workplace would offer youth the chance to WIDEN their horizons, particularly in terms of future careers, develop ORGANIZATIONAL skills, learn about RESPONSIBILITY, and gain valuable KNOWLEDGE. As the research summarized below suggests, however, the reality of youth employment presents risks as well as opportunities for adolescent development.

Recent efforts at bridging the school to work transition suggest increasing adolescent involvement in the workplace as a way to teach youth the practical tasks necessary for later success as adult workers and to expose them to a wide range of occupational options. Similarly, most parents approve of their adolescent's employment, believing it offers increasing autonomy and independence, opportunities for responsibility, and practice in time management (Finch, Mortimer, & Ryu, 1997). Empirical research shows some positive consequences from adolescent employment, including self-reported punctuality, dependability, and personal responsibility, and for girls' increased self-reliance (Greenberger & Steinberg, 1986), decreased high school dropout for employment of fewer than 20 hours per week (D' Amico, 1984), and increased employment and earnings in the years following high school (Steel, 1991). Ethnographic work with low-income youth finds that the adult monitoring and economic gains from employment can result in increased school engagement and decreased criminal and delinquent behavior (Newman, 1996).

Working during adolescence also carries risks. Health risks include increased exposure to dangerous machinery, noxious fumes, or excessive heat and cold, and chronic fatigue from long hours or working at night, which result in injury serious enough to require emergency room treatment for approximately 64,000 youth ages 14 to 17 per year (Finch et al., 1997). Psychological risks include stress from taking on adult responsibilities without adequate support or coping skills, disruptions in social relationships, and distress from the overload caused by school and work activities. Findings from prominent studies describe negative consequences of adolescent employment, such as emotional distress, increased cigarette, alcohol and illicit drug use, and higher rates of school tardiness and misconduct (e.g., Mortimer, Finch, Ryu, Shanahan, & Call, 1996).

The discrepancy in findings about the consequences of adolescent employment stem from the lack of distinction between informal work, such as babysitting or summer jobs, and formal part-time work, as well as the failure to consider the quality of the work environment. Long hours spent working in poor-quality formal jobs during the school year appear to be the most detrimental to adolescent's grades and health, particularly alcohol use and smoking (Finch et al., 1997). Restaurant work, the archetypal teenage job, characterizes a poor-quality job—it requires few skills, offers little adult supervision, is unconnected to anticipated future jobs, and is done only for money. Alternatively, the same research found many direct benefits of high-quality work experiences, including reduced substance use and better mental health.

There are parallels between program experiences and the qualities of high-quality work experiences. That is, adolescents who worked in jobs requiring the mastery of new skills and offered opportunities to help others showed more positive outcomes. Jobs, like programs, are the most beneficial when they challenge adolescents. One way programs have sought to involve participants in challenging experiences is through opportunities for community service or volunteer work. When youth volunteer in their community, they have the chance to broaden their knowledge and understanding of others, learn and practice important life skills in real settings, and make a valuable contribution to their community (Scales & Leffert, 1999).

NEIGHBORHOOD AS PLACE, SPACE, AND FACE

It is difficult to define an adolescent's neighborhood. School districts, census tracts, and town lines can often result in different neighborhood boundaries. Trying to identify one's community is further complicated when social relations are included, particularly with the increased use of technology. We see three ways to define neighborhoods, as Place, Space, and Face (Leventhal, Brooks-Gunn, & Kamerman, 1997).

Communities as place Geographical or bureaucratic lines—school districts, town or city boundaries—are the traditional way of defining neighborhoods. Where adolescents physically live influences their developmental risks and opportunities. For example, ease of access to health-compromising substances, such as the availability of cigarette vending machines and guns, or the enforcement of alcohol minimum age laws, varies from community to community.

Communities as space Neighborhoods can also be viewed as the collection of buildings and open spaces for living and working. Examples of community space more conducive to successful development include adequate school buildings and access to locations for constructive leisure-time activities, such as parks, libraries, and community centers. Wilson (1987) argues that the loss of neighborhood employment opportunities, due to deindustrialization in the inner cities, has led to increases in poverty, joblessness, and social isolation. He attributes inner-city residents' undesirable behaviors—out-of wedlock childbearing, crime, welfare dependency, and school dropout—with these changes.

Community as face Viewing community as shared relationships and social supports puts a human face on the traditional research approach to neighborhoods. Also referred to as social capital, these relationships can make a difference in the lives of youth. In a study of nearly 350 Chicago neighborhoods, the level of involvement of community residents, termed collective efficacy, significantly reduced both the perceived and actual levels of violence, even in the poorest neighborhoods (Sampson & Morenoff, 1997).

The lack of "face" within a community explains the concentration of adolescent problem behaviors in some communities. For example, the behavior of adults in the community can influence adolescent behavior through the presence of adult role models and monitoring (collective socialization) or by the concentration of problem behaviors influencing adolescents through peer influences (contagion; Leventhal & Brooks-Gunn, 2000). Still, family characteristics are more prominent than neighborhood characteristics in predicting youth outcomes (Brooks-Gunn, Duncan, & Aber, 1997).

Using the Search Institutes' 40 developmental assets, Benson, Leffert, Scales, and Blyth (1998) define healthy communities as places with a shared commitment to children and youth. They find more positive outcomes for vulnerable youth (defined as those with the fewest developmental assets) from the healthiest communities compared to those from the least healthy communities. These communities offer youth, particularly vulnerable youth, access to a caring school environment and connections to a religious organization and supportive adults.

A community's social capital, or relationships among people and organizations that facilitate cooperation and mutual support, is at the root of improving adolescents' lives. For example, the model driving the Public/Private Venture's Community Change for Youth Development (CCYD) initiative illustrates how the community dimensions (physical and demographic characteristics, economic opportunity structure, institutional capacities, and social exchange and symbolic processes) directly and indirectly affect adolescent outcomes, including adolescent health (Connell, Aber, & Walker, 1994). The CCYD initiative strives to increase resident and local governance participation in the design and delivery of youth development services. The model follows a systems-reform approach; it attempts to alter the ways community residents and institutions relate to one another. Optimally, such an initiative would seek to improve the "face" of distressed neighborhoods by improving knowledge, understanding, and trust between individuals and groups through communication and a shared vision, common goals, or a plan of action.

This type of reform is extremely difficult at best, as documented by the Annie E. Casey Foundation's report on their New Futures initiative (Nelson, 1996). The Casey Foundation learned the following six lessons from their efforts to restructure how midsize cities plan and deliver services to at-risk youth: more needs to be learned about the nuts and bolts of cross-system change; effecting change requires a long-term investment; such efforts are not for every community; political will must be present from the outset; frequent and substantive communication and flexibility are vital, as is determination in the face of discouragement; and real change often depends on increases in opportunity and social capital.

IS THERE A WAR ON TEENAGERS?

Public opinion towards adolescents is not favorable; most Americans look at today's teenagers with misgiving and trepidation. One recent survey showed that almost three-quarters of Americans think young people with poor education, poor job prospects, and problematic values pose a greater danger to the country than any threat from abroad (Princeton Survey Research Associates cited in Farkas & Johnson, 1997). The negative view of adolescents is not limited to disadvantaged youth. And, it has not changed in the last few years. Public Agenda pollsters again asked adults to describe today's teenagers. Adjectives such as disrespectful, irresponsible, and wild were used by 71% of the general public, and 74% of the parents. Only 15% of the general public, and 12% of parents, used positive descriptors, such as smart, curious, or helpful (Public Agenda, 1999). We offer four remedies for how youth programs can counter these very negative opinions about adolescents.

First, those of us who have studied, worked with, or raised teenagers know that the majority are not rude, irresponsible, or wild. We have not done a good job (or even an adequate one) of getting this message to the public. Media campaigns, legislative briefings, connections to journalists, and liaisons with groups such as the National Governors' Association are in order.

Second, the shift to promoting the positive, not just preventing problems, needs to be part of the message to these various constituencies. For example, indicator reports must include positive as well as negative behaviors. Publications like the Annie E. Casey Foundation's *Kids Count* could include data on the percentage of youth who are engaged in volunteer activities, after-school programs, and school clubs. Such a focus would also help communities (or states) estimate how many youth do not have access to these opportunities.

Third, more attention needs to be paid to the intersections among the many worlds of youth. The consistency or inconsistency of the norms and values regarding health-related behaviors among the different settings influence adolescents (Perry et al., 1993). Health-promoting behaviors are reinforced when the family, school, peer group, and media carry the same message. For example, school health campaigns of the 1980s increased their effectiveness by instituting home-based family participation programs aimed at increasing ties between the programs and the home environment (Perry et al., 1988). The program evaluation literature also shows that successful programs addressed more of the settings in which adolescents live (Catalano et al., 1999; Roth et al., 1998). Successful programs often included links to other settings, typically the school, or developed specific initiatives for strengthening relationships with others, either in the family or through mentors.

Fourth, we need to take seriously Benson's (1997) comments on the politicization of the African wisdom that "it takes a whole village to raise a child" (p. 103). There is a missed opportunity for constructive dialogue on what kind of village it really takes. The Search Institute, in their Healthy Communities–Healthy Youth initiative, extends the notion of developmental assets to the community to try to address this question (Benson et al., 1998). They outline a vision for what communities must do to raise caring and responsible children and adolescents that includes individuals and institutions in all of the contexts affecting youths' lives—from strengthening families to promoting cultural shifts in youth-serving systems such as schools, youth organizations, religious organizations, juvenile justice system, and gaining the involvement of local business and industry to promote the developmental assets for youth. This initiative, as well as other similar community mobilization efforts, such as the CCYD, the Social Development Research Group's Communities That Care, and the Kellogg Foundation's 20-year investment in 3 Michigan communities, rests on the belief that positive youth development can be promoted by all sectors of the community, particularly when they work together to provide a unified message of the value and potential of all youth.

We are hopeful that youth themselves can be seen as assets rather than liabilities to communities and our nation. And we believe that the public will for providing the necessary support for nurturing assets exists, albeit in nascent form. In the Public Agenda (1999) poll, 89% of the general public believed that given enough attention and the right kind of guidance, almost all teenagers can get back on track. Sixty percent of adults said that more programs and activities for adolescents after school, in places like community centers, would be a very effective way to help kids. And, 46% of the adolescents polled agreed.

REFERENCES

Alan Guttmacher Institute (1994). *Sex and America's teenagers.* New York: Author.

Anderman, E. M., & Kimweli, D. M. S. (1997). Victimization and safety in schools serving early adolescents. *Journal of Early Adolescence, 17,* 408–438.

Annie E. Casey Foundation, The. (1999). *Kids count data book: State profiles of child well-being.* Baltimore, MD: The Annie E. Casey Foundation.

Bachman, J. G., & Schulenberg, J. (1993). How part-time work intensity relates to drug use, problem behavior, time use, and satisfaction among high school seniors: Are there consequences or merely correlates? *Developmental Psychology, 29,* 220–235.

Baumrind, D. (1971). Current patterns of parental authority. *Developmental Psychology Monographs, 4* (1, Pt. 2).

Bearman, P., & Bruckner, H. (1999). *Peer effects on adolescent sexual debut and pregnancy.* Washington, DC: Paper for the National Campaign to Prevent Teen Pregnancy.

Benson, P. L. (1997). *All kids are our kids: What communities must do to raise caring and responsible children and adolescents.* San Francisco: Jossey-Bass Publishers.

Benson, P. L., Leffert, N., Scales, P. C., & Blyth, D. A. (1998). Beyond the "village" rhetoric: Creating healthy communities for children and adolescents. *Applied Developmental Science, 2,* 138–159.

Berndt, T. J. (1996). Transitions in friendship and friends' influence. In J. A. Graber, J. Brooks-Gunn, & A. C. Petersen (Eds.), *Transitions through adolescence: Interpersonal domains and context* (pp. 57–85). Mahwah, NJ: Lawrence Erlbaum Associates.

Botvin, G. J., Baker, E., Dusenbury, L., Tortu, S., & Botvin, E. M. (1990). Preventing adolescent drug abuse through a multimodal cognitive-behavioral approach: Results of a 3-year study. *Journal of Consulting and Clinical Psychology, 58,* 437–446.

Botvin, G. J., Epstein, J. A., Schinke, S. P., & Diaz, T. (1994). Predictors of cigarette smoking among inner-city minority youth. *Journal of Developmental and Behavioral Pediatrics, 15,* 67–73.

Bronfenbrenner, U., & Morris, P. A. (1998). The ecology of developmental process. In R. M. Lerner (Ed.), W. Damon (Series Ed.), *Handbook of child psychology: Vol. 1. Theoretical models of human development* (5th ed., pp. 993–1028). New York: Wiley.

Brooks-Gunn, J., Duncan, G., & Aber, J. L. (Eds.). (1997). *Neighborhood poverty: Context and consequences for children* (Volume 1). *Policy implications in studying neighborhoods* (Volume 2). New York: Russell Sage Foundation Press.

Brooks-Gunn, J., Duncan, G. J., Klebanov, P. K., & Sealand, N. (1993). Do neighborhoods influence adolescent development? *American Journal of Sociology, 99,* 353–395.

Brown, B. B. (1990). Peer groups and peer cultures. In S. Feldman & G. Elliott (Eds.), *At the threshold: The developing adolescent* (pp. 171–196). Cambridge, MA: Harvard University Press.

Brown, B. B., Dolcini, M. M., & Leventhal, A. (1997). Transformations in peer relationships at adolescence: Implications for health-related behavior. In J. Schulenberg, J. L. Maggs, & K. Hurrelmann (Eds.), *Health risks and developmental transitions during adolescence* (pp. 161–189). New York: Cambridge University Press.

Cairns, R. B., & Cairns, B. D. (1994). *Lifelines and risks: Pathways of youth in our time.* New York: Cambridge University Press.

Carnegie Council on Adolescent Development. (1989). *Turning points: Preparing American youth for the 21st century*. Washington, DC: Author.

Carnegie Council on Adolescent Development. (1994). *A matter of time: Risk and opportunity in the out-of-school hours*. Washington, DC: Author.

Carnegie Council on Adolescent Development. (1996). *Great transitions: Preparing adolescents for a new century*. Washington, DC: Author.

Catalano, R. F., Berglund, M. L., Ryan, J. A. M., Lonczak, H. S., & Hawkins, J. D. (1999). *Positive youth development in the United States: Research findings on evaluations of positive youth development programs*. Seattle, WA: University of Washington, School of Social Work, Social Development Research Group.

Collins, W. A. (1990). Parent-child relationships in the transition to adolescence: Continuity and change in interaction, affect, and cognition. In R. Montemayor, G. R. Adams, & T. P. Gullotta (Eds.), *From childhood to adolescence: A transitional period?* (pp. 85–106). Newbury Park, CA: Sage.

Collins, W. A., Maccoby, E. E., Steinberg, L., Hetherington, E. M., & Bornstein, M. H. (2000). Contemporary research on parenting: The case for nature *and* nurture. *American Psychologist, 55*, 218–232.

Connell, J. P., Aber, J. L., & Walker, G. (1994). *Using social science research to inform the design and evaluation of comprehensive community initiatives for children and families: A case study from the youth field*. Aspen, CO: The Aspen Institute.

Coombs, R. H., Paulson, M. J., & Richardson, M. A. (1991). Peer vs. parental influence in substance use among Hispanic and Anglo children and adolescents. *Journal of Youth and Adolescence, 20*, 73–88.

Council of Economic Advisors (2000). *Teens and their parents in the 21st century: An examination of trends in teen behavior and the role of parent involvement*. Washington, DC: Author.

Crane, J. (1991). The epidemic theory of ghettos and neighborhood effects on dropping out and teenage childbearing. *American Journal of Sociology, 96*, 1126–1159.

D'Amico, R. J. (1984). Does employment during high school impair academic progress? *Sociology of Education, 57*, 152–164.

Dishion, T. J. (1990). The family ecology of boys' peer relations in middle childhood. *Child Development, 61*, 874–892.

Dishion, T. J., Andrews, D. W., & Crosby, L. (1995). Antisocial boys and their friends in early adolescence: Relationship characteristics, quality, and interactional processes. *Child Development, 66,* 139–151.

Dishion, T. J., McCord, J., & Paulin, F. (1999). When interventions harm: Peer groups and problem behavior. *American Psychologist, 54*, 755–764.

Dryfoos, J. G. (1998). *Full-service schools: A revolution in health and social services for children, youth and families*. San Francisco: Jossey-Bass.

Dryfoos, J. G. (1990). *Adolescents at risk: Prevalence and prevention*. New York: Oxford University Press.

DuBois, D. L., Felner, R. D., Meares, H., & Krier, M. (1994). Prospective investigation of the effects of socioeconomic disadvantage, life stress, and social support on early adolescent adjustment. *Journal of Abnormal Psychology, 103*, 511–522.

Eccles, J. S., & Barber, B. L. (1999). Student council, volunteering, basketball, or marching band: What kind of extracurricular involvement matters? *Journal of Adolescent Research, 14*, 10–43.

Eccles, J. S., Midgley, C., Wigfield, A., Buchanan, C. M., Reuman, D., Flanagan, C., & MacIver, D. (1993). Development during adolescence: The impact of stage-environment fit on young adolescents' experiences in schools and in families. *American Psychologist, 48*, 90–101.

Farkas, S., & Johnson, J. (1997). *Kids these days: What Americans really think about the next generation*. New York: Public Agenda.

Feldman, S. S., & Elliot, G. R. (Eds.). (1990). *At the threshold: The developing adolescent*. Cambridge, MA: Harvard University Press.

Felner, R., Jackson, A. W., Kasak, D., Mulhall, P., Brand, S., & Flowers, N. (1997). The impact of school reform for the middle grades: A longitudinal study of a network engaged in Turning Points–based comprehensive school transformation. In R. Takanishi & Hamburg, D.A. (Eds.), *Preparing adolescents for the twenty-first century: Challenges facing Europe and the United States*. (pp. 38–69). New York: Cambridge University Press.

Finch, M. D., Mortimer, J. T., & Ryu, S. (1997). Transition into part-time work: Health risks and opportunities. In J. Schulenberg, J.L. Maggs, & K. Hurrelmann (Eds.), *Health risks and developmental transitions during adolescence* (pp. 139–160). New York: Cambridge University Press.

Fuligni, A., & Eccles, J. S. (1993). Perceived parent-child relationships and early adolescents' orientation toward peers. *Developmental Psychology, 29*, 622–632.

Galambos, N. L., & Ehrenberg, M. F. (1997). The family as health risk and opportunity: A focus on divorce and working families. In J. Schulenberg, J.L. Maggs, & K. Hurrelmann (Eds.), *Health risks and developmental transitions during adolescence* (pp. 139–160). New York: Cambridge University Press.

Galambos, N. L., & Maggs, J. L. (1991). Out-of-school care of young adolescents and self-reported behavior. *Developmental Psychology, 27*, 644–655.

Gottman, J. M., & Parker, J. G. (Eds.). (1987). *Conversations of friends*. New York: Cambridge University Press.

Graber, J. A., Brooks-Gunn, J., & Petersen, A. C. (Eds.). (1996). *Transitions through adolescence: Interpersonal domains and context*. Mahwah, NJ: Lawrence Erlbaum Associates, Inc.

Graham, J. W., Marks, G., & Hansen, W. B. (1991). Social influence processes affecting adolescent substance abuse. *Journal of Applied Psychology, 76*, 291–298.

Greenberger, E., & Steinberg, L. (1986). *Why teenagers work: The psychological and social costs of adolescent employment*. New York: Basic Books.

Grossman, J. B., & Rhodes, J. E. (2002). The test of time: Predictors and effects of duration in youth mentoring relationships. *American Journal of Community Psychology, 30,* 199–206.

Harris, J. R. (1998). *The nurture assumption: Why children turn out the way they do*. New York: The Free Press.

Hartup, W. W., & Stevens, N. (1999). Friendships and adaptation across the lifespan. *Current Directions in Psychological Science, 8*(3), 76–79.

Herman, M. R., Dornbusch, S. M., Herron, M. C., & Herting, J. R.(1997). The influence of family regulation, connection, and psychological autonomy on six measures of adolescent functioning. *Journal of Adolescent Research, 12*, 34–67.

Hofferth, S. L., & Sandberg, J. (1998, November 9). *Changes in American children's time, 1981–1997*. Bethesda, MD: National Institute of Child Health and Human Development.

Ianotti, R. J., & Bush, P. J. (1992). Perceived vs. actual friends' use of alcohol, cigarettes, marijuana, and cocaine: Which has the most influence? *Journal of Youth and Adolescence, 21*, 375–389.

James, D. W., & Jurich, W. S. (Eds.). (1999). *More things that do make a difference for youth: Vol 2. A compendium of evaluations of youth programs and practices*. Washington, DC: American Youth Policy Forum.

Jessor, R. (1993). Successful adolescent development among youth in high-risk settings. *American Psychologist, 48*, 117–126.

Jessor, R. (Ed.). (1998). *New perspectives on adolescent risk behavior*. New York: Cambridge University Press.

Kerr, M., & Stattin, H. (2000). What parents know, how they know it, and several forms of adolescent adjustment: Further support for a reinterpretation of monitoring. *Developmental Psychology, 36*, 366–380.

Larson, R., Richards, M. H., Moneta, G., Holmbeck, G., & Duckett, E. (1996). Changes in adolescents' daily interactions with their families from ages 10 to 18: Disengagement and transformation. *Developmental Psychology, 32*, 744–754.

Larson, R. W.(2000). Toward a psychology of positive youth development. *American Psychologist, 55*, 170–183.

Lerner, R. M., Fisher, C. B., & Weinberg, R. A. (2000). Toward a science for and of the people: Promoting civil society through the application of developmental science. *Child Development, 71*, 11–20.

Lerner, R. M., Lerner, J. V., von Eye, A., Ostrom, C. W., Nitz, K., Talwar-Soni, R., & Tubman, J. G. (1996). Continuity and discontinuity across the transition of early adolescence: A developmental contextual perspective. In J.A. Graber, J. Brooks-Gunn, & A. C. Petersen (Eds.), *Transitions through adolescence: Interpersonal domains and context* (pp. 3–22). Mahwah, NJ: Lawrence Erlbaum Associates, Inc.

Leventhal, T., & Brooks-Gunn, J. (2000). The neighborhoods they live in: The effects of neighborhood residence upon child and adolescent outcomes. *Psychological Bulletin, 126*, 309–337.

Leventhal, T., Brooks-Gunn, J., & Kamerman, S. B. (1997). Communities as place, face, and space: Provision of services to poor, urban children and their families. In J. Brooks-Gunn, G. J. Duncan, & J. L. Aber (Eds.), *Neighborhood poverty: Context and consequences for children: Vol. 2. Conceptual, methodological, and policy approaches to studying neighborhoods*. New York: Russell Sage Foundation Press.

Mason, C. A., Cauce, A. M., Gonzales, N., & Hiraga, Y. (1996). Neither too sweet nor too sour: Problem peers, maternal control, and problem behavior in African American adolescents. *Child Development, 67*, 2115–2130.

McLaughlin, M.W. (2000). *Community counts: How youth organizations matter for youth development*. Washington, DC: Public Education Network.

Millstein, S. G., Petersen, A. C., & Nightingale, E.O. (Eds.). (1993). *Promoting the health of adolescents: New directions for the twenty-first century*. New York: Oxford University Press.

Moore, K. A., Evans, J., Brooks-Gunn, J., & Roth, J. (2001). What are good child outcomes? In A. Thornton (Ed.), *The well-being of children and families: Research and data needs*, (59–84). Ann Arbor, MI: University of Michigan Press.

Moore, K. A., & Halle, T. G. (2000). *Preventing problems vs. promoting the positive: What do we want for our children?* Washington, DC: Child Trends.

Mortimer, J. T, Finch, M. D, Ryu, S., Shanahan, M. J., & Call, K. T. (1996). The effects of work intensity on adolescent mental health, achievement, and behavioral adjustment: New evidence from a prospective study. *Child Development, 67*, 1243–1261.

Nelson, D. (1996). The path of most resistance: Lessons learned from New Futures. In A. J. Kahn & S. B. Kamerman (Eds.), *Children and their families in big cities: Strategies for service reform* (pp. 163–184). New York: Cross-National Studies Program, Columbia University School of Social Work.

Newman, K. S. (1996). Working poor: Low-wage employment in the lives of Harlem youth. In J. A. Graber, J. Brooks-Gunn, & A. C. Petersen (Eds.), *Transitions through adolescence: Interpersonal domains and context* (pp. 323–344). Mahwah, NJ: Lawrence Erlbaum Associates, Inc.

Paikoff, R., & Brooks-Gunn, J. (1991). Do parent-child relationships change during puberty? *Psychological Bulletin, 110*, 47–66.

Perry, C. L., Kelder, S. H., & Komro, K. A. (1993). The social world of adolescents: Family, peers, schools, and the community. In S. G. Millstein, A. C. Petersen, & E. O. Nightingale (Eds.), *Promoting the health of adolescents: New directions for the twenty-first century* (pp. 73–96). New York: Oxford University Press.

Perry, C. L., Luepker, R. V., Murray, D. M., Kurth, C., Mullis, R., Crockett, S., & Jacobs, D. J. (1988). Parent involvement with children's health promotion: The Minnesota Home Team. *American Journal of Public Health, 78*, 1156–1160.

Piaget, J. (1932/1965). *The moral judgement of the child*. New York: The Free Press (Original work published in 1932).

Pittman, K. (1991). *Promoting youth development: Strengthening the role of youth serving and community organizations*. Washington, DC: Center for Youth Development and Policy Research, Academy for Educational Development.

Public Agenda. (1999). *Kids these days '99*. [On-Line]. Available: *www. publicagenda. org/specials/kids/kids.htm*.

Quinn, J. (1999). Where need meets opportunity: Youth development programs for early teens. *The Future of Children, 9*(2), 96–116.

Resnick, M. D., Bearman, P. S., Blum, R. W., Bauman, K. E, Harris, K. M., Jones, J., Tabor, J., Beuhring, T., Sieving, R. E, Shew, M., Ireland, M., Bearinger, L. H., & Udry, J. R. (1997). Protecting adolescents from harm: Findings from the National Longitudinal Study on Adolescent Health. *Journal of the American Medical Association, 278*, 823–832.

Robinson, E. (1993). *An interim evaluation report concerning a collaboration between the Children's Aid Society, New York City Board of Education, Community School District 6, and the I.S. 218 Salome Urena de Henriquez school.* New York: Fordham University, The Graduate School of Social Sciences.

Roth, J., Brooks-Gunn, J., Murray, L., & Foster, W. (1998). Promoting healthy adolescence: Synthesis of Youth Development program evaluations. *Journal of Research on Adolescence, 8,* 432–459.

Rutter, M. (1989). Pathways from childhood to adult life. *Journal of Child Psychology and Psychiatry and Applied Disciplines, 30,* 23–51.

Sampson, R. J., & Morenoff, J. (1997). Ecological perspectives on the neighborhood context of urban poverty: Past and present. In J. Brooks-Gunn, G. J. Duncan, & J. L. Aber (Eds.), *Neighborhood poverty: Vol. 2. Policy implications in studying neighborhoods* (pp. 1–22). New York: Russell Sage Foundation Press.

Scales, P. C., & Leffert, N. (1999). *Developmental assets: A synthesis of the scientific research on adolescent development.* Minneapolis, MN: Search Institute.

Schulenberg, J., Maggs, J. L., & Hurrelmann, K. (Eds.). (1997). *Health risks and developmental transitions during adolescence.* New York: Cambridge University Press.

Sickmund, M., Snyder, H., & Poe-Yamagata, E. (1997). *Juvenile offenders and victims: 1997 update on violence.* Washington, DC: US Department of Justice, Office of Juvenile Justice and Delinquency Prevention.

Sipe, C. L. (1996). *Mentoring: A synthesis of P/PV's research.* Philadelphia: Public/Private Ventures.

Steel, L. (1991). Early work experience among white and non-white youth. *Youth and Society, 22,* 419–447.

Tierney, J. P., Grossman, J. B., & Resch, N. L. (1995). *Making a difference: An impact study of Big Brothers/Big Sisters.* Philadelphia: Public/Private Ventures.

U.S. Department of Health and Human Services. (1991). *Healthy People 2000.* Washington, DC: United States Government Printing Office.

U.S. Department of Health and Human Services. (2000). *Healthy People 2010.* Washington, DC: United States Government Printing Office.

Werner, E. E., & Smith, R. S. (1992). *Overcoming the odds: High risk children from birth to adulthood.* Ithaca, NY: Cornell University Press.

Wilson, W. J. (1987). *The truly disadvantaged: The inner city, the underclass, and public policy.* Chicago: University of Chicago Press.

Zill, N., Nord, C. W., & Loomis, L. S. (1995). *Adolescent time use, risky behavior, and outcomes: An analysis of national data.* Rockville, MD: Westat, Inc.

QUESTIONS

1. Is it sufficient preparation for adulthood that adolescents simply be problem-free? Why or why not?
2. What are the "five C's" of healthy adolescent development?
3. According to this article, how does Benson describe positive youth development?
4. How do health-compromising behaviors and risky lifestyles create barriers to well-being in adolescence?
5. From a developmental perspective, why should youth programs be designed to promote positive development rather than to focus on preventing problem behavior?
6. What problems are common among adolescents who are overwhelmed by the challenges that occur during this period of development?
7. What is TLC, and why are these aspects of the family setting important during adolescence?
8. What roles can peers play in promoting positive youth development?
9. Is employment in adolescence a positive or negative influence on development? Explain.
10. Why is it important for psychologists and the media to stress the positive aspects of adolescent development? How do you think adolescents would respond if such a shift in the characterization of youth occurred in our society?